CONSUMER BEHAVIOR:
BASIC FINDINGS AND MANAGEMENT IMPLICATIONS

THEORIES IN MARKETING SERIES

CONSUMER BEHAVIOR: BASIC FINDINGS AND MANAGEMENT IMPLICATIONS

GERALD ZALTMAN
University of Pittsburgh

MELANIE WALLENDORF
University of Michigan

JOHN WILEY & SONS
New York   Chichester   Brisbane   Toronto

Library of Congress Cataloging in Publication Data:

Zaltman, Gerald.
  Consumer behavior.

  (The Wiley Series in Marketing)
  Includes index.
  1. Consumers. I. Wallendorf, Melanie, joint author.
II. Title.

HF5415.3.Z28   658.8'34   78−23335
ISBN 0−471−98126−5

Printed in the United States of America

10 9 8 7 6 5 4 3 2 1

THIS BOOK IS DEDICATED TO

Sidney J. Levy (G.Z.)

"A tout seigneur tout honneur"
(To the master, all honor.)

and

William R. Torbert (M.W.)

for helping me find out what education
and inquiry are and can be

ABOUT THE AUTHORS

Gerald Zaltman has a Ph.D. degree in sociology from the Johns Hopkins University and an M.B.A. degree in marketing from the University of Chicago. He is currently the Albert Wesley Frey Distinguished Professor of Marketing, University of Pittsburgh. He previously taught marketing at Northwestern University where he was the A. Montgomery Ward Professor of Marketing. Professor Zaltman is very active as a researcher and as a consultant to numerous firms and government agencies in the United States and abroad. His special interests focus on the responses of individual consumers and organizations to new products and services and the development of product management strategy. He is author, coauthor, or editor of numerous books and monographs, including *Readings in Consumer Behavior: Individuals, Groups, and Organizations; Industrial Buyer Behavior; Metatheory and Consumer Research; Marketing, Society, and Conflict; Marketing Research: Fundamentals and Dynamics; Cases in Marketing Research; Innovations and Organizations; Strategies for Planned Change; Dynamic Educational Change;* and *Marketing: Theoretical Perspectives on an Applied Social Science.* Professor Zaltman is a frequent contributor to professional journals and conferences, and is a past member of the Board of Directors of the Association for Consumer Research. He is on the editorial boards of numerous journals in the management and social science areas.

Melanie Wallendorf is an Assistant Professor of marketing at the University of Michigan. She received her M.A. degree in sociology in 1977 and her Ph.D. degree in marketing in 1979 from the University of Pittsburgh. Professor Wallendorf's interests center on the social aspects of consumer behavior and the social research methodologies that can be used for empirically exploring this area. Specifically, her interests include such topics as the diffusion of innovations, social roles, the structure of exchange transactions, consumer satisfaction/dissatisfaction and complaining behavior, and consumerism.

PREFACE

Consumption is a central element of much of human behavior. Substantial amounts of our time are spent acquiring the financial resources to be consumers, planning to make purchases, making purchases, and using with varying degrees of satisfaction the multitude of products and services we buy. In all of these activities consumers are the focus of considerable influence attempts by major social institutions such as businesses, government agencies, and consumer advocate groups. Through this book we hope the reader will develop insights into how people behave as consumers and how various attempts to influence consumers may be made both more and less effective. A central assumption of this book is that the same knowledge or findings about consumers may be used in beneficial or harmful ways by any social institution. In this book we suggest beneficial ways this knowledge may be used, especially by business. A special challenge to readers is to determine for themselves what the appropriate uses of this knowledge are for various social institutions.

There are at least three perspectives from which one can view consumer behavior. The first involves examining consumers on the basis of research conducted in nonconsumer settings. For example, from focusing on summer camps, kindergarten classes, and church groups, we can speculate about the impact that group membership has on consumer choices. Also, in experimenting with rats or monkeys—a more behavioristic approach—we can speculate about how human consumers learn from advertising.

Another perspective involves direct research about consumers themselves. This is valuable, of course, because theories developed in nonconsumer settings need to be tested—and either rejected or refined—by exploring their usefulness in actual consumer contexts.

The first perspective—research done in nonconsumer settings—is prevalent, and necessarily so, for it is essential to the opening of new vistas of theory and research. The second perspective—research in consumer contexts—is also prevalent and will continue to be an important feature of the consumer behavior field. We believe, however, that there is a third perspective that is the most noteworthy. This perspective involves the synthesis of knowledge about consumer behavior that is based on research—in both consumer and nonconsumer settings—resulting in new ideas for research and application. In the process of application and implementation (when the ideas developed in nonconsumer settings and tested in consumer contexts have been carried out in practice), the feasibility of some theories is eliminated, while other theories are substantiated with little or no modification, and new research based on earlier consumer studies begins. This third perspective is warranted because a background of consumer research exists on which to build an inventory or synthesis of knowledge on the subject.

That such a synthesis is warranted justifies our writing this book, a challenge that we have found intriguing. We present a better than general picture of what researchers in the field of consumer behavior believe is true about the behavior of consumers, and we present this inventory of knowledge in the form of propositions. Instead of asserting absolute laws or principles about consumer behavior, these propositions synthesize convincing, though not necessarily final, conclusions and theories.

We also discuss important studies that concern topics where little research has been done, and we expect that these recent studies will prove to be the cornerstone of future research in the area. These studies employ the second perspective toward consumer behavior—a direct examination of consumer contexts.

In addition, we present ideas not yet formally tested in consumer settings, but that are highly relevant because they offer insights (which would not be obtained otherwise) into consumer behavior. As such, these theories are derived from studies of nonconsumer settings and fall within the first perspective that we mentioned earlier.

Consumer Behavior: Basic Findings and Management Implications is different from other texts on consumer behavior in that we provide simple statements of basic findings (propositions), an explicit discussion of the implications that these findings have for marketers, an emphasis on the importance that sociology has for consumer studies, and a perspective on organizations as consumers. These differences give us a wider scope with which to deal with the topics integral to all consumer behavior texts.

Of course, in a field that is as broad and growing as rapidly as the study of consumer behavior, any text must emphasize some topics rather than others. Though some readers might find one topic or another treated more briefly than they would like, we urge them not to conclude that we believe those topics to be unimportant.

Although this book is intended primarily for the introductory course on consumer behavior, and was developed for and tested with undergraduates, it has also been successfully used at the graduate level. While the language is direct and accessible to all readers, the content has not been diluted in any way. We have been helped considerably in this task by undergraduates in classroom situations, teachers of undergraduates, and specialists in reading skills, and we believe the result is a readable and worthwhile book.

Gerald Zaltman
Melanie Wallendorf

ACKNOWLEDGMENTS

The preparation of a basic text is rarely—if *ever*—a product of only the authors' efforts; and this book is no exception. Many people have made many contributions to this book. As such, *Consumer Behavior: Basic Findings and Management Implications* has benefited from the very thoughtful scrutiny and insightful observation provided by people with unique expertise in one or more areas of importance. We invited and received advice from undergraduate and graduate classes in consumer behavior who used the book at different stages of its development, from teachers of consumer behavior known for their excellence in understanding student learning needs, and from researchers with widely acknowledged expertise in the substantive matter of one or more of the book's chapters. Our advisors worked us hard and were vigilant in reviewing the several drafts the manuscript underwent, and we thank them for their own hard work and the substantial value they added to the book.

Our deep appreciation is extended to those who collaborated with us in writing several chapters in this book, including Thomas V. Bonoma (University of Pittsburgh), Wesley J. Johnston (Ohio State University), Lakshmanan Krishnamurthy (Stanford University), Ronald Valle (University of Pittsburgh), and Valerie Valle (University of Pittsburgh).

We also appreciate the careful attention that our advisors gave to the manuscript. This group includes David A. Aaker (University of California at Berkeley), Helmut Becker (University of Portland), Richard J. Lutz (University of California at Los Angeles), and Steven E. Permut (Yale University).

In addition to formal reviewers, we requested and received comments on the manuscript from people with many interests and perspectives: Johan Arndt (Norwegian School of Economics), Michael A. Belch (San Diego State University), Joel Goldhar (Advanced Technology Management Associates, Inc.), Kjell Grønhaug (Norwegian School of Economics), Karen Lawther (University of Pittsburgh), Jacob Naor (University of Maine), Frederick Scherr (West Virginia University), Norman Smith (University of Oregon), Alladi Venkatesh (State University of New York at Binghamton), and Karl-Erik Warneryd (Stockholm School of Economics).

Recognizing that the book needed input from students, we "pilot tested" it in consumer behavior classes. We are grateful to Nora Ganim (Boston College) and Donald Hempel (University of Connecticut), and to their students in consumer behavior for using the manuscript and for sharing with us their own thoughts on consumer behavior and how it is described in the book. In addition, we express our appreciation to our own students in consumer behavior at the University of Pittsburgh who not only used the manuscript, but also pointed out ways to make the book more useful.

The Marketing Science Institute has provided support to one of the authors that facilitated the development of many of the ideas about organizations as consumers. We particularly thank Professor Stephen Greyser of the Harvard School of Business and the Executive Director of the Marketing Science Institute, and Alden Clayton, Director of Research Planning at the Marketing Science Institute.

We also thank Dean H. J. Zoffer, Dean David H. Blake, and Dean Andrew R. Blair for their administrative support and encouragement that greatly facilitated the work on this book. Mrs. Arlene Wycich performed superbly in the physical preparation of the manuscript over the course of many versions. Her good humor and skills are valued highly by us.

Much as we would like to share with others the responsibility for errors, we cannot. Responsibility for any significant omissions and factual and judgmental errors rests solely with us.

G.Z.
M.W.

CONTENTS

PART IV. SPECIAL TOPICS

INTRODUCTION

INTRODUCTION TO CONSUMER BEHAVIOR

INTRODUCTION   There are few areas of human behavior which are as diverse, complicated, socially significant, and intriguing to study as the area of consumer behavior. Indeed, studying consumer behavior involves an examination of everyday life. And everyday life involves both serious and minor social problems together with a variety of behaviors on the part of people and organizations. Consider several consumer-related phenomena:

— Each year approximately 20 million Americans are injured severely enough in product-related incidents to require medical treatment. Of these, 110,000 people are permanently disabled, and 30,000 die.

— Congressional investigators have recently concluded that illicit marketers are unsurpassed by legitimate marketers in their understanding of consumers. For instance, illegal dealers in drugs adeptly use free trial offers, quantity discounts, and complicated interpersonal advertising networks. Similarly, many professional thieves steal only upon demand (request), so that they are assured a market for their merchandise. Potential buyers simply indicate the year, color, and make of the auto or television they want to buy.

— A high price on an appliance might be associated in the consumer's mind with high quality when the product is distributed through a high prestige store. However, the same consumer will usually make no such association when the same brand appliance is distributed at the same price through a low prestige store.

— The brand name assigned to a new consumer product may account for over 40 per cent of its success or failure.

— Without any analysis of consumer needs, preferences, and behavior, an international agency recently shipped 16,000 gross (1 gross = 144 items) of brightly colored condoms to a Latin American country having a population of only slightly more than 3 million people. Unfortunately, the image held of the consumer in this country by the international agency was at odds with the actual sexual behavior and contraceptive methods of the country's residents.

— Although most beer drinkers have definite brand preferences, they find it difficult to distinguish their own brand from others when the identifying cues, such as labels or container size and shape, are removed.

— Over $4,000 per year per physician is spent by the pharmaceutical industry to influence the selection of prescription medicine by doctors; however, only about one-half of all physicians ever prescribe medication, and therefore much of this advertising is wasted.

Consumer Behavior Topics Being Researched

Researchers are concerned with all the questions implied in the phenomena described above. What is the impact on doctors of advertising by firms in the pharmaceutical industry? Why do beer drinkers insist that they can tell the difference between a preferred brand of beer and others when research suggests they cannot? Why didn't the international agency study the consumer market for condoms?

Perhaps a small sampling of the topics researched by actual firms will help inform the reader of what is being done in the consumer behavior field.

— Joseph Schlitz Brewing Company is studying how consumer buying behavior conforms to attitudes and how the motives for drinking different beers differ from brand to brand.

— Chrysler Corporation is studying how the ease with which the gas pedal is depressed affects feelings of acceleration and speed.

— Eastman Kodak Company is studying why people are taking fewer photographs compared to a decade ago.

— The Supermarket Institute is concerned with learning what consumers consider to be the most salient characteristic of a store's "atmosphere."

— The Grocery Manufacturers Association is studying the effect of including the nutrient content of food in all printed and broadcast advertising.

— The National Science Foundation is actively seeking and supporting research which describes and explains how consumers process information.

— *Business Week* is supporting work which will help advertisers better understand industrial buying.

— The Xerox Corporation is forecasting organizational change so that they may fulfill the office needs of the future.

— The Marketing Science Institute is sponsoring research about how various members of an organization interact to reach a buying decision.

— U.S. Steel is researching organizational buyer behavior.

— Many organizations and individuals are studying the major discrepancy which often exists between consumer attitudes and actual behavior.

Importance of the Study of Consumer Behavior

Thus, the field of consumer behavior is probably one of the most intriguing and important fields in the social sciences. Consistent with contemporary marketing thought, consumers are the focal point of any marketing activity.[1] Given the broadened concept of marketing, nearly all organizations and individuals are marketers in some respect, and hence all are concerned with consumers.[2] An adequate understanding of consumer behavior is essential for the prosperity of any marketing enterprise, whether it is selling soap, a political candidate, a document duplicating service, or holding a garage sale. Thus, working in an area which is so critical to almost every activity brings a high degree of excitement and a justifiable sense of importance.

Being a consumer is one of the basic attributes shared by individuals and organizations of all types and in all contexts. A substantial portion of social activity consists of behaviors directly and indirectly related to the consumer role. In consumption-oriented societies such as the United States, buying is a pervasive activity and a basic cultural tie. Improvements in our understanding of this area of social activity can lead to actions by public and private organizations, as well as by individual consumers, which will enhance the quality of consumption-related behavior. Thus, another source of importance and challenge stems from working in an area having such a strong impact on societal well-being and the general quality of life.

The study of consumer behavior is especially important as public and private agencies undertake programs in response to the question, "How *should* consumers buy?" Nearly all research and theory has asked, "How *do* consumers buy, and how will this change if the marketing program is changed?" Increasingly, however, federal and state legislation and regulations, and the programs of consumer interest groups, have taken on a prescriptive character, conforming to their respective notions of what consumers should do. For example, the idea that consumers should compare interest rates among lending institutions before signing a loan contract led to the passage of the truth-in-lending legislation. This legislation requires lending institutions to state their interest rates in a standardized format in order to make it easier for consumers to compare rates among companies. Knowledge about consumer behavior is essential as this prescriptive trend becomes

---

[1]Philip Kotler, *Marketing Management,* 3rd. ed., Englewood Cliffs, NJ: Prentice Hall, 1976.

[2]Sidney J. Levy and Gerald Zaltman, *Marketing, Conflict and Society.* Englewood Cliffs, NJ, Prentice-Hall, 1975; Sidney J. Levy and Philip Kotler, "Beyond Marketing: The Furthering Concept," *California Management Review,* Vol. XIII, No. 2 (Winter, 1969); Philip Kotler and Sidney J. Levy, "Broadening the Concept of Marketing," *Journal of Marketing,* Vol. 33 (January, 1969), pp. 10–15; Philip Kotler and Gerald Zaltman, "Social Marketing: An Approach to Planned Social Change," *Journal of Marketing,* Vol. 35 (July, 1971), pp. 3–12.

more pronounced. Such knowledge can lead to both consumer protection efforts and to a better understanding of the impact that these efforts have on consumers.

Consumer behavior is also important from an intellectual standpoint. For the most part, consumer behavior is a relatively unexplored field in the social sciences, but is an excellent context in which to develop and test theories from virtually every scientific area concerned with human behavior. It is a context which has been widely used for studying the diffusion of innovations after the introduction of new consumer products. Although there are notable exceptions, most of the past research in consumer behavior has been conducted by one particular professional group, namely marketers. While marketers have conducted some excellent research in consumer behavior and are devoting more time to this field, only the surface has been scratched. Other perspectives, including those of geographers, sociologists, political scientists, anthropologists, and psychologists, are greatly needed to augment the applied orientation of many marketers. There is a great potential for those in the marketing professions, and in other professions, to contribute to the general inventory of knowledge about human behavior.

What is Consumer Behavior?

Briefly, consumer behavior involves the purchasing, and other consumption-related activities of people engaging in the exchange process. This definition is consistent with the emergence in the past several years of a broadened concept of marketing and an increased focus on marketing as an exchange system.[3] A more specific definition is adapted from Bagozzi and Zaltman.

> Consumer behaviors are acts, processes, and social relationships exhibited by individuals, groups, and organizations in the obtainment, use of, and consequent experience with products, services and other resources.[4]

Consumer behavior is motivated or purposive, directed toward the goal

---

[3]Richard P. Bagozzi, "Marketing as Exchange," *Journal of Marketing*, Vol. 39 (October, 1975), pp. 32–39; Chester R. Wasson, *Consumer Behavior: A Managerial Viewpoint*, Austin, TX: Austin Press, 1975; Gerald Zaltman and Brian Sternthal (eds.), *Broadening the Concept of Consumer Behavior*, Association for Consumer Research, 1975; Philip Kotler, 1976, *op. cit.*; Kotler and Levy, 1969, *op. cit.*; Kotler and Zaltman, 1971, *op. cit.*; Levy and Zaltman, 1975, *op. cit.*

[4]Richard Bagozzi and Gerald Zaltman, "A Structural Analysis of the Sociology of Consumption," paper presented at The American Sociological Association Meetings, San Francisco, CA, 1975.

of obtaining products, services, or other resources for use in their own right or as a medium for future exchange. The "acts, processes, and social relationships" referred to above include such diverse consumer activities as experiencing a need, window shopping, comparison shopping among stores, simply thinking about the available information concerning a product's relative benefits and liabilities, or seeking a friend's advice about a new product. In the case of organizational buyer behavior, a purchasing agent may evaluate suppliers of raw materials, capital goods, or component parts, and seek the approval of the vice-president to sign a purchase agreement for a piece of equipment. A buying committee in an organization might engage in such consumer behaviors as establishing product requirements, and evaluating competitive bids by vendors who hope to sell the firm needed goods and services.

The activities just mentioned are oriented toward "obtainment" or "getting." Consumer behavior, however, also involves the experiences which are consequences of using products and services. Issues such as product satisfaction (whether or not the product performed as expected) and product safety are also relevant here and are of increasing concern to many government, private industry, and private groups in the consumerism movement. Buying a product involves such experiences as physical and mental stimulation, sedation from foods and drugs, and changes in social well-being, such as increased status and power.

Thus, our definition of consumer behavior sensitizes us to three related groups of phenomena:
1. Activities: acts, processes, and social relationships
2. People: individuals, groups, and organizations
3. Experiences: obtaining, using, and consequences
In acting out a certain role, such as that of a medical patient, an individual may be active in seeking word-of-mouth information (a communication process) from other people (which involves social relationships) about medical services (a product), which may lead to an appointment for medical consultation, involving a new relationship with a physician. During the consultation with the physician, the consumer obtains advice which is presumably used or followed, with a subsequent improvement, or conceivably a deterioration, in mental or physical health. Satisfaction or dissatisfaction with the medical services is the immediate consequence.

Alternatively, consumer behavior may be displayed by a buying committee in a business organization which meets to consider information related to a major purchase. The meeting is an act involving social relationships within the group, consisting of people from many parts of the organization. The buying committee processes purchase-related information and sometimes delegates to one member of the buying committee or to a purchasing agent the responsibility for implementing the decision. This person will go ahead and obtain the product, or at least identify suppliers and solicit bids, as part of the process of obtaining the desired product. In the case of capital equipment, the use of the product may decrease the unit cost of items produced, which may be the major desired consequence of the purchase.

There is one very important point about the nature of consumer behavior which deserves special emphasis: consumer behavior is basically social in nature. This means simply that consumers must be understood in terms of their relationships with others, because a person can only be a consumer by virtue of there being another person who is a seller.[5] This approach is in contrast to one which focuses on the individual as an isolated entity who can be understood apart from a social environment. Everett M. Rogers refers to this social approach as "relational analysis," in which relationships between two or more people become the main unit of study rather than the individual alone.[6] The relationships which are relevant may involve people from some past, present, or future situation. Direct contact with these people may be desired or undesired, and may not actually take place. The contexts in which purchases are made and products used often involve other people, and such consequences as satisfaction and safety may depend heavily upon how other people respond.

Major portions of this book are devoted to exploring the social nature of consumer behavior, and for this reason we will not elaborate further here on this important point. We must point out, however, that the single individual approach is the more common way of addressing consumer behavior. A content analysis of all major consumer behavior books reveals that nearly two-thirds of their topics were treated from the individual, rather than the social, perspective. Thus, traditional psychological issues—such as personality, learning, perception, and motivation—receive more attention than social psychological, sociological, anthropological, and political science issues. Even the individual psychological phenomena and issues, which are certainly very important, are usually treated without recognition of the impact of the wider social context.

The majority of consumer behavior texts focus exclusively on individual consumers, on private individuals who purchase products and services for

---

[5]Richard Bagozzi, Thomas V. Bonoma and Gerald Zaltman, "The Dyadic Paradigm in Marketing Thought," unpublished working paper, University of Pittsburgh, 1976; Matilda Frankel, "A Summary Report: What Do We Know About Consumer Behavior?" report prepared for RANN program of National Science Foundation, 1977.

[6]Everett M. Rogers, "Network Analysis of the Diffusion of Innovations," paper presented at the Mathematical Social Science Board's Research Symposium on Social Networks, Hanover, New Hampshire, September 18–21, 1975.

themselves, their families, or their friends. Formal organizations, which purchase products and services for use in organizational functions (such as production) or for resale, are often not discussed in textbooks, despite their greater importance to the economy and the fact that they are the main consumers served by many other organizations. In general, the field of organizational buyer behavior has been ignored, for there are few marketers active in the consumer behavior area who are either interested in, or have seen the relevance of, organizational buying behavior.[7]

In many ways, however, the same concepts can be used for understanding both individual consumer behavior and organizational buyer behavior. For example, both individuals and organizations are affected by the culture in which they exist, by the norms governing purchase behavior, and by the role expectations of others. Both types of consumers are the targets of promotional communications from sellers. In the process of making a purchase, each gathers information about alternatives, processes this information, learns about the available products, determines which alternative matches the perceived needs most closely, and carries through by making a purchase.

Some researchers have contended that individual consumers and organizational buyers are different in two ways: (1) organizations make decisions by having a group of people decide what will be purchased, while individual consumers do not engage in this type of group decision making, and (2) organizational buyers are more rational in their decisions, while individual buyers often make choices on more subjective bases. However, neither of these contentions is true. Organizations make group decisions concerning large or important purchases (e.g., the purchase of a computer or a major piece of production equipment); but similarly, private individuals often make large purchase decisions as a group within their families (e.g., the purchase of an automobile or a house). Also, organizations rely on individual purchasing agents to make less important purchase decisions (e.g., the purchase of paper clips by a large business firm); similarly, individuals also make less important purchase decisions on their own (e.g., the purchase of a package of breath mints).

With regard to the basis on which choices are made, organizations and individuals do not differ much as consumers. Both organizations and individuals make choices based on such objective criteria as price or unit price, gas mileage, or time efficiency. Both also make choices, however, based on more subjective factors (which are not necessarily irrational).

---

[7]Frederick Webster and Yoram Wind, *Organizational Buying Behavior,* Engelwood Cliffs, NJ,: Prentice-Hall, 1972.

Individuals may purchase a particular automobile because they believe it will enhance their status. Organizations have also been known to purchase certain kinds of automobiles for their employees (especially limousines for their executives) because they believe the cars will enhance the status of the organization.

Therefore, some types of organizational buyer behavior are more similar to certain individual consumer behaviors than they are to other organizational buyer behaviors. For example, organizational decisions concerning computer purchases may be more similar to family automobile purchases than they are to organizational paper clip purchases. For these reasons, in this book we have discussed family and organizational consumer behavior side by side, and concepts are illustrated using examples from both. Therefore, the organization of the book centers around general concepts rather than who does the purchasing.

Nature of this Book   Most consumer behavior is a complex process shaped by broad social or cultural forces, close interactions with other people and organizations, and highly individual dispositions. An accurate description of consumer behavior entails a holistic approach in which all of these factors are shown to be operating at once, both individually, and in interaction with one another. Thus, the purchase of a new product is shown to be determined simultaneously by how a consumer learns and processes information, how the consumer acquires information in interaction with other people, and how the content of information and who passes it along to the consumer are determined by cultural mores. Moreover, we see that learning and information processing are affected by cultural factors and vary from culture to culture; the way in which consumers learn about new products is affected by their social interactions, and the process of consumer learning in turn influences when, how, and with whom the consumer interacts.

Most models or theories of consumer behavior found in the marketing literature have a strong psychological approach, stressing the single individual as the basic unit of analysis. Prominence is given in these models to individual learning and perception, with relatively little attention given to the impact on behavior of many forces external to the single consumer. This approach is out-of-step with contemporary behavioral science thinking about human behavior, and is also inconsistent with current treatments of marketing as a social exchange process. Human behavior is irreducibly social in nature and must be studied this way.

Because most theories of consumer behavior are limited to individual consumers, they are incomplete. The proliferation of these single person theories was uppermost in the mind of one of the leading consumer behavior psychologists, Jacob Jacoby, when he delivered his presidential address at a meeting of the Association for Consumer Research:

> Several of our most respected colleagues seem to belong to a sort of "theory of the month" club which somehow requires that they burst forth with new theories periodically and rarely, if ever, bother to provide any original empirical data collected specially in an attempt to support the theory.[8]

Two other researchers offer a similar observation about the futility of pursuing comprehensive theories or models of consumer behavior:

> The literature dealing with the topic of consumer behavior is replete with theoretical constructions and models of varying degrees of complexity. *A careful review of this literature leads one to the inexorable conclusion that the search for a "grand theory" of consumer behavior would be quixotic.*[9]

This book does not present another formal model of consumer behavior, although several models are discussed in Chapter 20, but possesses a structure, which reflects the dynamic setting of consumer behavior.

Perhaps the drawing in Figure 1-1 is the simplest way to picture the

FIGURE 1-1.

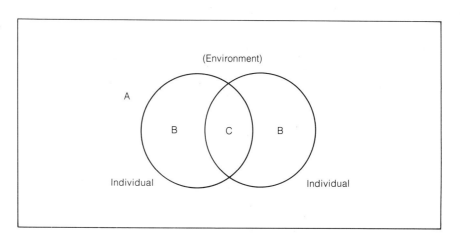

dynamics of consumer behavior, and we shall use this diagram to illustrate different points. The area denoted by "A" represents anthropologists', political scientists', economists', and sociologists' concern with large social systems. The

[8]Jacob Jacoby, "Consumer Research: Telling It Like It Is," in *Advances in Consumer Research,* Vol. III, Beverlee B. Anderson (ed.), Association for Consumer Research, 1976, pp. 1–11, p. 3.

[9]J. Paul Peter and Lawrence X. Tarpey, Sr., "A Comparative Analysis of Three Consumer Decision Strategies," *Journal of Consumer Research,* Vol. 2, June, 1975, p. 29.

two overlapping circles represent smaller social systems or, at a minimum, two interacting individuals. This area, here denoted by "C," is the concern of social psychologists and sociologists. The area in each circle denoted by "B" is often considered to be the domain of psychology, although many psychologists are actively involved in area "C" as well.

The interacting dynamic nature of this simple picture is shown in Figure 1-2. The double arrows indicate the flow of influence: the environment influences and is influenced by individuals in interaction with each other (arrow 1); individuals interacting with one another are also influenced by the unique personal characteristics they bring to the interaction (arrow 2); the unique individual properties of individuals are affected, too, by past, current, or even anticipated interactions with others, as well as by the larger environment (arrow 3). No two people are always affected the same way by the same stimuli.

The dynamic interactions shown by the arrows in Figure 1-2 indicate one of the major problems of consumer behavior models: interactions are usually presented in a linear flow chart following a specific sequence of steps, when the process of consumer behavior is, in fact, much more continuous, simultaneous, and dynamic. Consumer behavior is not adequately represented by

FIGURE 1-2.

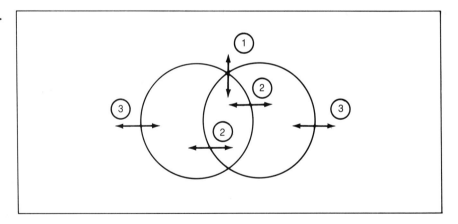

the logical sequences shown in the flow charts which serve as models for consumer behavior theories.

This book is deliberately structured to reflect a truer, more dynamic, and fluid picture of consumer behavior. Figure 1-3 shows the approximate concerns of various chapters in the book. We begin in Chapter 3 with a discussion of demographics, the study of the characteristics of a population. Then, in Chapter 4, we discuss the consumer behavior of large-scale social systems, such as national societies, or other large-scale social structures, such as social classes, industries, and public and private sectors. Chapter 5 focuses on smaller groups within the larger settings, and on norms, or the regulators of relationships within both larger and smaller settings. We cannot discuss any

FIGURE 1-3.
(Excludes special topics and introductory chapters)

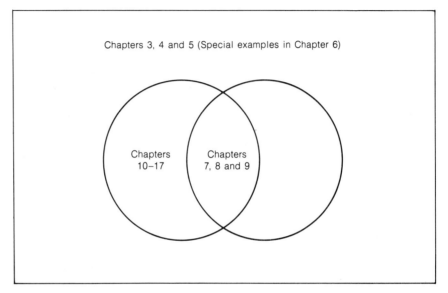

social entity without a discussion of the norms which regulate behaviors within those entities. Chapter 6 focuses on the formal organization and the family.

An examination of the influence of social roles on relationships between people is central in Chapter 7. The ways in which these relationships are defined and acted upon is the subject of Chapter 8. Chapter 9 is concerned with the means by which individuals, both alone and together in small and large social systems, influence one another through communication.

Part III (Chapters 11–17) discusses phenomena which are most easily conceptualized in terms of individual psychology. In this section we look at the important topics of learning, perception, information processing, personality, needs, motivation, attitudes, and attributions (a relatively new topic for consumer behavior researchers). Though these processes have received the greatest attention in consumer behavior literature, the full importance of their connection with the broader social forces (such as those discussed in Part II) has not yet been adequately examined. In addition, individual psychology is seldom discussed in regard to organizational consumers (who also learn and have needs).

To further clarify the structure of the book, an example is in order. Consider parents in a children's clothing department in late summer purchasing new clothes for the child's first day in school. First, the fact that formal education is even available is a cultural or social system phenomenon (Chapter 4) lacking in many parts of the world. This social system characteristic of the availability of educational institutions (whose attendance is often mandated by law) is partially responsible for the parents being in the department store at that time of year. The desire or perceived need (Chapter 14) to purchase new clothing is largely a social artifact, and not usually caused by an urgent physical need; for there is probably something else at home the child could wear to school. However, the preference for new rather than presently owned clothes is partially a function of social class (Chapter 4) and of the dynamics of small groups (Chapter 5). The parents want the child to look as good as, or better than, other children in the neighborhood who may share the same car pool because the child is likely to be seen by other parents and the teacher. Dressing the child well helps prevent other people from making attributions which the parents consider undesirable (Chapter 17). For instance, people may attribute the absence of new clothes on the child to low family income or a lack of parental caring. This attribution is especially likely if the child attends a private school. The selection of a private school over a public school is almost certainly a result of social pressures, especially those pressures associated with social roles (Chapter 7). Thus, the social roles of the parents account for their presence in the children's clothing department. The kind of clothing bought and the type of store frequented are, to a large measure, consequences of informal group influence (Chapter 5); for, importantly, group influence has a major impact on how consumers learn (Chapter 10), perceive (Chapter 11), and process information (Chapter 12). For example, some learning and information processing involves simply observing how others dress their children and select stores. This may involve accompanying esteemed persons on shopping trips, or reading advertisements (Chapter 9) in magazines. Information may also be obtained more directly by asking someone what he or she thinks of a particular store, thereby helping the parents form attitudes (Chapter 16) toward various types of outlets. Parents' attitudes, as partially determined by informal social groups, influence how they perceive (Chapter 12) and process information concerning clothing stores.

The interactions which take place among the members of the child's household (Chapters 5, 6 and 7) help determine whether one or both parents participate in the clothing choices. The child, too, may have a say in the matter. Thus, who is present at the time of purchase and whether veto power ("Take it back!") is exercised in the home by any person are the result of many factors, including how social roles are perceived (Chapter 7). This, in turn, is partially the result of interpersonal power and bargaining (Chapter 8), and social norms (Chapter 5).

The illustration in Figure 1-4 shows the interrelation of the chapters. A true picture of consumer behavior, shown schematically, is a multidimensional matrix showing the interconnectedness of a very large array of factors. In many of these cases, influence flows back and forth between these factors.

FIGURE 1-4.

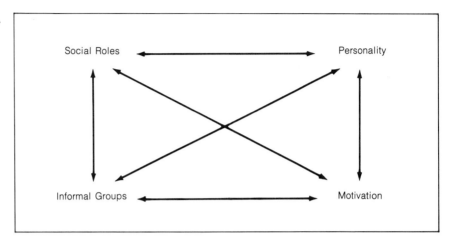

Unique Features of This Book

The reader will find four unique features in this book. First, while covering important psychological perspectives, the book also develops as an equally important emphasis a social perspective on the essentially interpersonal character of consumer behavior. The reader will find discussions in the early chapters concerning the social settings in which consumer behavior occurs.

Second, the text includes organizations as a category of consumers. Many readers have found or will find themselves in occupational situations where the consumer behavior of other organizations is important in helping the reader sell to organizations and in developing promotional material directed toward these organizations. Understanding how organizations behave as consumers will also help the reader in product planning and in developing strategic marketing plans in industrial settings.

Third, this book contains an inventory of statements or propositions about consumer behavior which are general in nature and express approximate answers to certain implied research questions. A very well-known statistician, J. S. Tukey, has observed: "Far better an approximate answer to the right question which is often vague than an exact answer to the wrong question which can always be made precise."[10] The propositions represent approximate answers to what might be vague questions. This approach,

---

[10]J. S. Tukey, "The Future of Data Analysis," *Annals of Mathematical Statistics,* Vol. 33 (1962) pp. 1–67.

however, reflects the basic state of knowledge in the consumer behavior field, and is echoed by several researchers, including Joe Kent Kirby:

> Because we are on the frontier in our understanding of consumer thought and behavior patterns, there are few thoroughly tested theories that we can confidently categorize as law. Consequently, the student in this area must be willing to live with uncertainty and recognize that there is little of a concrete nature to cling to. He must be willing to think and reason rather than trust and memorize. He must learn to be critical of the experts lest he be misled by them. He must be able to perhaps reorganize it, and then apply it to a particular situation... in this field there are no absolutes.[11]

More will be said about propositions shortly.

A fourth unique feature of this book is that most propositions are followed by corresponding action implications which serve as examples of how these and other propositions known to the reader can be applied in practical marketing settings. This, too, should be of importance to many readers who will be making important decisions on the basis of consumer behavior information. Seeing how consumer research can be translated into action will, we hope, encourage readers to remain open to research and theory when they leave the classroom for the office.

An Excursus on Propositions

In order to prepare the reader for the following chapters, a brief discussion about propositions may be useful. Chapter 2 shows that, directly or indirectly, we all think in terms of propositions. This is especially important for marketing managers concerned with decisions involving consumer behavior. The subsequent chapters contain more explicit and systematic treatments of propositions.

A proposition is a statement which proposes that two variables are related to one another in some way. Examples of consumer behavior propositions include the following: increases in income lead to increases in spending; repetition of advertising leads to increased awareness of a new product; larger shelf display space for a brand increases the likelihood that the brand will catch consumer attention. The nature of the connections may vary widely, as we see in the following consumer behavior propositions (all of which are intended to illustrate particular kinds of relationships rather than to reflect what is actually known about the relationships between the concepts used).

---

[11]Joe Kent Kirby, *Consumer Behavior: Conceptual Foundations,* NY: Dun-Donnelley Publishing Corp., 1975, pp. 13–14.

Each of these propositions is concerned with brand loyalty—the consistent preference for and choice of a particular brand by consumers. Brand loyalty will be discussed in more detail in Chapter 11.

1. *Brand loyalty is a function of innovativeness.* The simple connection here is "a function of," which implies little information about the character of the relationship between brand loyalty and innovativeness.

2. *Brand loyalty increases with innovativeness.* "Increases with" is the connective here and implies positive correlation between brand loyalty and innovativeness.

3. *Brand loyalty decreases with innovativeness.* "Decreases with" implies negative correlation between brand loyalty and innovativeness.

4. *Innovativeness causes low brand loyalty.* "Causes" is the critical element here, and is a significant departure from merely associational statements.

Proposition 4 could be further refined by specifying whether the causal variable is (a) a necessary and sufficient condition to affect the "caused" variable; (b) a necessary but not sufficient condition; or (c) a sufficient but not necessary condition.

The connectives in propositions 2 and 3 may also be merged with those in proposition 4. Thus:

5. *A decrease in brand loyalty is caused by an increase in innovativeness.* We might further specify that:

6. *An increase in innovativeness is sufficient but not necessary to cause a decrease in brand loyalty.* Note that this proposition gives us more information than any of the earlier propositions. Thus, the more refined a proposition is, the more information it will yield.

The propositions presented in this book will vary widely in their degree of specificity, for much more is known about some consumer phenomena than others. The propositions are presented in a way which maximizes the amount of information conveyed to the reader. This is not always consistent with the way a proposition should be stated to be readily tested, although the ease with which a proposition can be tested is often merely a function of the imagination and cleverness of the investigator.

There are several reasons for choosing a propositional approach:

1. Social scientists generally agree that all people think in propositional terms even though they may not be aware of it.[12]

---

[12]See Georg Henrik Von Wright, *Explanation and Understanding,* NY: Columbia University Press, 1971; Georg Henrik Von Wright, *Causality and Determinism,* NY: Columbia University Press, 1974; Charles A. Love and James G. March, *An Introduction to Models in the Social Sciences,* NY: Harper & Row, 1975; and Peter Abell, *Organizations as Bargaining and Influence Systems,* NY: Halsted Press, 1975.

2. Since propositions are implicit in how we think about events, it is desirable to express propositions formally so that the bases for actions are clearer.

3. If knowledge about consumer behavior is to be expanded, it is necessary to express current ideas in ways which can be tested in various contexts. This involves developing testable propositions, determining how widely they can be applied and, if necessary, how they must be modified to cover many contexts.[13]

4. By clearly labelling present knowledge in propositional form, the tentative nature of the knowledge is highlighted rather than overlooked. Most of the research in the consumer behavior area which is both conceptually and methodologically sound has been conducted in highly specific contexts with little replication. Moreover, there is an unfortunately small number of truly rigorous studies involving realistic samples of the consumer population in realistic settings.[14]

5. The reader should treat the propositions as sound ideas to be considered for testing in situations of interest, at either a conceptual or empirical level. Readers may treat their experiences as data and compare these data to a proposition, or they may prefer to conduct traditional research to test the propositions.

6. A propositional approach is particularly conducive to developing action implications. Most professional people interested in consumer research and most readers of this book have (or will have) a managerial concern. For these people, consumer behavior findings will have their primary value in suggesting marketing mix strategies. Thus, we express some of the implications that the various propositions have for a brand manager, new product manager, sales manager, advertising account executive, and other action-oriented marketing management roles. This is not to say, however, that the action implications mentioned are the only ones suggested by the propositions.

7. Stating ideas and findings in explicit propositional form permits greater experimentation with the basic variables involved in the proposition, for

---

[13]Thomas S. Robertson and Scott Ward, "Consumer Behavior Research: Promise and Prospects," in Scott Ward and Thomas Robertson (eds.), *Consumer Behavior: Theoretical Sources,* Englewood Cliffs, NJ: Prentice-Hall, 1973, pp. 43–44; Peter and Tarpey, 1975, *op. cit.;* Shloms I. Lampert, "Word-of-Mouth Activity During the Introduction of a New Food Product," in J. U. Farley, *et al.,* (eds.), *Consumer Behavior,* Boston: Allyn & Bacon, 1974

[14]Steven E. Permut, Allen J. Michel, and Monica Joseph, "The Researcher's Sample: A Review of the Choice of Respondents in Marketing Research," *Journal of Marketing Research,* Vol. 13 (August, 1976) pp. 278–283; Kirby, *op. cit.;* and Jacoby, *op. cit.*

developing alternative formulations of relationships between variables is easier when one type of relationship is already specified.

The propositions selected for presentation in this book all meet at least one of the following conditions:

1. Sound empirical data must exist supporting the proposition even if in a very specific context.
2. The proposition has plausibility in at least two different contexts.
3. Other good theories and propositions exist which suggest the particular proposition, i.e., when there is a sound conceptual undergirding to the proposition.
4. The proposition has expert validity, i.e., the proposition is suggested by experts in an area.

Additionally, nearly all propositions have action implications. The propositions are also presented with at least one reference to another work, so that the reader may pursue a particular proposition in greater depth. Each reference, in turn, has a large number of additional sources which can further direct the reader to the most relevant literature concerning the proposition.

The reader may find the action implications of the propositions particularly useful, and the propositions will be of substantially greater value if the reader is able to generate still more action implications from the propositions. A few guidelines for generating action implications from propositions follow. The simple proposition "Innovativeness causes decreases in brand loyalty" is a good illustration. The first question to be asked is, "In what *context* is this likely to be true?" This proposition applies more to a consumer products than to an industrial products setting. The context can be further refined in terms of the type of product (e.g., durable products versus convenience foods) and the type of consumer (e.g., teenagers versus adults). The second question to be asked concerns which variables are manipulable and which are accepted as given by the marketer. This is a *control* issue. Brand loyalty, although itself difficult to manipulate, is probably easier to manipulate than consumer innovativeness. Thus, the control issue involves a decision about which variable in the proposition can or cannot be changed through adjustments in the marketing mix. This brings us to the third question: "What changes are indicated in the marketing mix to make the product consistent with unalterable consumer or situational factors?" One strategy is to try to increase brand loyalty, which may be done by stressing product quality (a product attribute) and the low risk (a psychological attribute) involved in the purchase of a particular brand.

The challenge, then, is: What is the action implication you would draw? The process of translating propositions into actions is a very subjective process, yet a very important one. The ability to translate propositions into actions is a major factor which distinguishes successful marketers from less successful ones, and it is important for the reader to engage in this process.

Indeed, one of the major reasons for taking a propositional and action implication approach in this book is to encourage the reader to formulate propositional and action implications, and thus to improve his or her skills in this process which is so critical to managerial success.

SUMMARY   Consumer behavior is social in nature. This book emphasizes the relationships which consumers have with each other and with the environment. Both ultimate consumers and formal organizations as buyers are important units of study. A dynamic process view of consumer behavior is adopted, in contrast to traditional treatments of the subject in which linear, static models have been stressed. A propositional format is used throughout the book, with action implications suggested. Chapter 2 focuses on the development and use of propositions.

KEY CONCEPTS   Brand loyalty

Consumer behavior

Organizational consumer

Proposition

Relational analysis

Ultimate consumer

PROPOSITIONS IN PRACTICE

CHAPTER GOALS   The objective of this chapter is to help readers understand:
1. **the implicit and explicit use of propositions by managers;**
2. **how propositions are used as the basis for action (i.e., how they are translated into action implications);**
3. **the diverse range of behavioral phenomena that impinge on a single consumer setting.**

INTRODUCTION   Effective use of knowledge is the main ingredient of success in action-oriented fields such as marketing. Knowledge may be obtained in a variety of ways which divide into two basic types: (1) knowledge derived from formal research projects which gather data through surveys and laboratory experiments; and (2) knowledge derived from seeing the results of actions based on educated hunches, trial and error choices, etc. The two types of knowledge may have synergistic relationships: A piece of formal research may provoke a hunch in the mind of a practitioner, and the practitioner's experiences may provide the foundation for a formal proposition to be tested by a researcher. Typically, marketing practitioners (or people who engage in marketing primarily as a practice rather than as a field of study) fall into three categories:
1. Practitioners who rely heavily on the results of formal research as a basis for their strategy and rely relatively little on hunches.
2. Practitioners who actively use research to stimulate hunches or to make educated guesses, but do not depend greatly on formal research.
3. Practitioners who rely primarily on the results of past trial and error learning experiences and have little contact with formal research.
      As indicated in Chapter 1, all three types of practitioners rely on "if–then" statements, which are causal propositions that assume "doing this

may/could/will cause that."[1] A proposition may be simply that "displaying fruits in their original shipping crates will cause people to think the fruits are fresher than those displayed in transparent wrappers." This last statement fully qualifies for status as a formal proposition even though it is derived from the accumulated experiences of a produce manager in a food store rather than from the theory and research of behavioral scientists.

One basic type of "if–then" proposition about consumer behavior is often evident in the statements of marketing practitioners, particularly those who do not rely on formal research (type #3 above). This type of proposition compares the response of the practitioner with the expected responses of consumers (see Figure 2.1), for example:

(1) If I like it, then they'll like it.
(2) If I like it, then they won't like it.
(3) If I don't like it, then they won't like it.
(4) If I don't like it, then they'll like it.[2]

Notice that propositions 1 and 3 assume that the practitioner is an adequate indicator or sample of the preferences of the population of consumers, whereas propositions 2 and 4 assume that the practitioner's tastes are different from the general population.

These propositions are often used as criteria for selecting marketing strategies. One of the goals of this book is to provide practitioners with propositions which are more reliable and more refined than these four.

Virtually all experts in the fields of research and utilization emphatically agree that the researcher and practitioner must interact in order to develop sound bases for marketing strategy. This chapter presents a story involving all three types of practitioners and the researchers with whom some of the practitioners interact, the purpose of which is to illustrate: (1) the implicit and explicit use of propositions by management, and (2) the diverse range of behavioral phenomena that impinge on a single consumer setting. Creating an in-depth understanding of the marketing of new wines is *not* the primary purpose of this story. Rather, the story serves as a fictional, though realistic, illustration of the process of proposition development.

BENNE BROTHERS' VINEYARDS, INC.

In early August, 1978, Benne Brothers' Vineyards board of directors decided to add a new California wine to the several varieties they had been producing and marketing nationally for the past fourteen years. The new wine was a dry red burgundy which was one of a number of wines with which the firm had

---

[1]There is strong support for this statement in the behavioral science and philosophy of science literature.

[2]These were originally suggested by Professor Sidney Levy of Northwestern University.

FIGURE 2-1.
*Example of
practitioner-consumer
comparison.*

Source: Advertising Age, October 6, 1975

been periodically experimenting during the past nine years. Benne Brothers' engaged in modest advertising which was handled by a moderately small national advertising agency. This wine was the first addition to their line of wines in seven years. Marketing plans called for the new wine to be introduced in the spring of 1979.

Two issues of major concern to Benne Brothers' management were the market segmentation strategy to be used to introduce the wine and the content of promotional messages. Overall marketing considerations were assigned to Mr. Albert Gordon, a senior vice-president in the firm. Each person under Gordon had responsibility for marketing activities in particular regions of the United States.

Gordon and his staff associates met frequently during August and September to develop the marketing plan for the new wine (see Figure 2-2). The first problem was whether to go national at once or to choose only one or a few regions for initial distribution. The decision was made, however, to go national from the outset in order to be able to use national media in advertising the product. In addition, production facilities already existed for the wine so there was no problem in getting production started. In fact, wine was

FIGURE 2-2.
Partial Organization Chart for Benne Brothers' Vineyards, Inc.

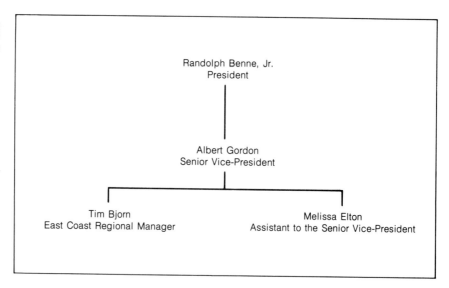

increasing in popularity to such an extent that the company believed the time was ripe for introducing new products. For example, in 1975 retail sales of wine amounted to $2,068,860. This figure was a 33.9 per cent increase over the 1971 sales figures.[3]

The second problem concerned the general strategy to be used in going national, and this issue sharply divided the marketing team. Gordon and three others believed a strategy of least resistance, of devoting promotional atten-

---

[3]"Consumer Spending in 1975," *Product Management*, September, 1976, pp. 46–47.

tion to the *most likely* people to try something new, should be pursued. The other group of four believed, on the other hand, in devoting promotional attention primarily to those persons who are *least likely* to try a new wine (a decision had already been made to appeal only to current wine drinkers). The issue then was whether to concentrate on the easier early adopters (early buyers of new products) or the more difficult later adopters. [Note here the basic proposition that earlier adopters are easier to influence than later adopters. This notion will be questioned later, partly on the basis of defining "early" adoption.]

Gordon wanted to follow a strategy of least resistance, partly because it could produce an early success. He and the other supporters of this position argued that the early adopters were important to reach because early adopters were believed to be influential with many people. [Here the proposition seems to be that early adopters exert more interpersonal influence than late adopters.] Tim Bjorn, East Coast regional manager, articulated this position best, but when pressed for formal evidence, he admitted he knew of none in the wine and spirits industry; he stated only that this was something he learned long ago when he was a proprietor of a liquor store. Bjorn had held various jobs in the food and beverage industry during the past twenty years. Gordon, on the other hand, indicated that this notion of early adopters being influential was demonstrated for a wide array of other food products and was probably true for wines as well. [Note the generalizing of a proposition from one context to another as well as drawing propositions based on past experiences.]

The group advocating a strategy of greatest resistance was skeptical of the notion of early adopters and their influence. They based their propositions, however, primarily on a research report which had been undertaken by their advertising agency four years earlier. This report indicated that those persons who were among the first to try a new wine were less likely to repeat the purchase than were late adopters. In effect, early adopters had little loyalty in contrast to late adopters. They also argued that early adopters would buy regardless and that promotional efforts would simply reinforce their inevitable behavior. Therefore, they saw success in getting late adopters to adopt earlier. Gordon and Bjorn disputed the notion that early users were less loyal and added that early adopters probably had greater volume potential, i.e., they not only bought wine frequently, but bought more on each occasion, probably serving it while entertaining.

Research Ideas and Suggestions The entire marketing group agreed that these issues were important and should be investigated carefully, although there were differences as to which ideas most needed research. The collective ideas of the group were summarized by one of the research-oriented members and presented to management in propositional form to serve as a guide to what had to be researched before a decision could be made. Financial support was requested to research these propositions. The propositions which were submitted were as follows:

1. Early first time users of new wines have more influence on other people with regard to product choices than late first time users.
2. Early users of new wines have contact with more people than do late users.
3. Early first time users are less likely to repeat a purchase than are late first time users.
4. Promotional efforts have relatively little impact on early first time users, i.e. they will tend to know of the wine and try it soon anyway.
5. Early first time users drink wine more often than late first time users.
6. Early first time users serve wine more to other people than do late first time users.

The opinion of Margaret Citrini, a consultant with Benne Brothers' Vineyards, was solicited. She suggested the group clarify what it meant by early users. Her basic question was, "Early relative to what? Early users relative to the time when a wine was first introduced in a market or relative to when a person first becomes aware of the wine?" Ms. Citrini emphasized that the research should be conducted using both reference points. She also suggested that the personalities of early and late users of new wines be explored, although she proposed neither a set of possible traits nor a particular personality test. Ms. Citrini urged Gordon to take into account possible differences in perceived price-quality relationships between early and late first time users. She admitted her intuition was that early first time users perceived a substantially lower and at best modest relationship between price and quality, whereas late first time users perceived a higher and important relationship between price and quality. [One proposition which is implicit in the consultant's comments about price-quality relationships is that the later the time of first use of a new wine, the stronger the perceived relationship between price and quality. Presumably the relationship is positive in nature.]

Gordon's initial reaction to this last idea was to agree, although it wasn't clear to him what he would do with the information on price-quality relationships. [Notice that Gordon is having trouble drawing action implications from this proposition.] He felt it would be necessary to determine such things as whether a low price for a good wine would be considered a more attractive bargain than a moderately high price for an excellent wine.

The president of Benne Brothers' Vineyards, Randolph Benne Jr., refused Gordon's request for research funds. Benne told Gordon that any research was to be done by their advertising agency. More significantly, however, Benne didn't see how information on the issues being proposed for further research would make much difference in how well the new wine succeeded. He argued that while advertising was important for creating awareness of a new wine, it was essentially the image of the producer, whose name was on the bottle, that determined the consumer response. Furthermore, he maintained that repeat purchase was largely a function of taste satisfaction. [Note the three propositions implied for wine here: Advertising primarily establishes awareness, but not initial or repeat purchases; consumers' images of the manufacturer are more important than product advertising in influencing first purchases; and product test satisfaction more than advertising and image of the manufacturer determines repeat purchase behavior.]

Gordon replied by pointing out certain studies of beer which indicated that people's perceptions of different brands of beer seemed to be influenced to a significant degree by brand advertising. This was dismissed by Benne, "Beer is beer and wine is wine." [Notice that implicit in this statement is the assumption that different kinds of alcoholic beverages differ in their meaning to consumers and, in effect, are not in the same generic class.] Although Benne and Gordon had worked together for a number of years on a more or less cordial basis, strain had begun to develop between them for the past several months. It was not unusual now for Benne to reject Gordon's requests.

Shortly after his meeting with Benne, Gordon met with the account executive who handled the Benne Brothers' Vineyard account for the Satchel Associates advertising agency (see Figure 2-3). The account executive, Mr. Edward Fallon, listened carefully to Gordon's research ideas and to Gordon's description of Benne's response. Fallon, who knew Benne relatively well, speculated privately that Benne would just as soon not see the advertising agency do the work Gordon had proposed either. Fallon's first comment was that the agency had already drawn up a research plan to guide them in their development of promotional material for the new wine, and that he was

FIGURE 2-3.
Other Organizational Affiliations in the Benne Brothers' Vineyards Case.

Franklin Caplow: University professor who is an authority on the introduction of new products and services.

Margaret Citrini: Consultant on retainer to Benne Brothers' Vineyards.

Edward Fallon: Account executive at Satchel Associates advertising agency, handles BBV account.

Fleming Gillespie: Advertising researcher at Satchel Associates advertising agency, in charge of planned research for BBV new wine introduction.

Anne Mandel: Specialist in research design at Satchel Associates advertising agency.

Seldon Vera: Head of creative department at Satchel Associates advertising agency.

rather doubtful that additional funds could be found within the existing budget included in the Satchel/Benne Brothers' contract.

Gordon became furious and told Fallon that he (Gordon) and his staff should have been consulted prior to the development of the research plan to enable them to have some input. Gordon pointed out, and Fallon reluctantly agreed, that this prior consultation was called for in the contract. Fallon somewhat lamely indicated that he had talked some with Benne about the research, although not in detail. He quickly offered to bring some of his staff to Gordon's office for a discussion of the research plan.

Reformulating Research Questions

Two weeks after the first meeting, Fallon and Gordon met again, this time with their respective staffs. Fallon made the basic presentation, stating that he was making two key assumptions. First, wine drinking is primarily a class-related phenomenon, with people in the higher social classes drinking more wine than people in lower social classes. Secondly, wine consumption occurs primarily in the context of entertaining guests at dinner parties. Fallon pointed out that earlier research performed by Satchel Associates strongly supported the first assumption, and that the second assumption would be tested in the proposed research, although it was "intuitively obvious."

Fallon continued by saying that as a result of their past research with the Benne Brothers' account, and thinking further about the problem, it was the consensus of his staff that the new wine ought to be targeted initially to upper social class groups as a proper wine to serve dinner guests. [Note that the basic propositions Fallon is espousing are: The higher the social class of an individual the more likely that person is to drink wine; wine is served more often with dinner guests than when dining alone; it is better (in some undefined way) to market to higher social class groups than lower social class groups; and it is preferable (again, in some undefined way) to promote the new wine as something to serve to guests rather than for consuming alone.] Fallon stated that the research they planned to undertake was intended to provide clues to help develop effective themes and advertising copy.

Once again Gordon grew angry. However, before he could speak, Ms. Melissa Elton, an assistant to Gordon, challenged Fallon: "Why are you ruling out promotional themes directed to other social class groups such as middle-class people, since the probable price of the new wine would be modest, approximately $2.99." Gordon broke in, "Also, it seems absurd to assume that people serve wine primarily in the context of entertaining guests at dinner, and even if that were true, why not try to get people to consume wine when dining alone?" [Note here the implicit proposition that people who consume wine only in the context of entertaining guests might also be induced to consume wine when dining alone. A still more basic proposition held by Gordon is that there is a reasonable likelihood that basic behavior patterns in wine consumption can be altered. Paralleling this is the implied proposition that promotional campaigns may be effective in altering behavior patterns involved in wine consumption.]

Seldon Vera, of Satchel Associates, who would be in charge of developing promotional themes for the new wine, and who was also a connoiseur of wines, responded to Gordon; "Wine is a festive drink; there is no way you can make drinking wine by yourself or with just your spouse a festive occasion. In fact…" At this point Bjorn cut Vera off in an impatient tone, "Certainly, any half-competent, creative advertising person could come up with an imaginative ad showing precisely that." Showing visible signs of self-restraint, Vera continued, "In fact, there seems to be something bad about drinking wine with no one else around, while it is acceptable to be by yourself and have some bourbon. No other alcoholic beverage has a counterpart to the stigma 'wino' and the downtrodden character or image of the person who receives that label. No, if you drink wine by yourself and you're caught at it, you're a 'wino' and that's uncouth."

[Note here the implicit propositions: The social acceptability of drinking wine varies with the presence of others at the time the drinking is initiated; the acceptability is further affected by whether or not these other persons are also drinking an alcoholic beverage. A number of things are unclear. Does the social acceptability of a particular person drinking wine depend on whether others are drinking an alcoholic beverage, and does their beverage also have to be wine? Does it make a difference, alone or in the presence of others, if wine is being consumed as part of a meal or simply as a drink by itself? The basic proposition implicit in Vera's statement is rooted in his various selective perceptions, exposures, and recalls. These propositions, apart from their accuracy, are firmly held by Vera and are the basis for his strong predisposition toward promoting wine as a proper ingredient in festive, interpersonal situations, rather than as appropriate for consumption in solitary settings. Dramatic formal consumer research would be necessary to convince Vera otherwise.]

The meeting continued with undercurrents of animosity, distrust, and open disagreement. Undoubtedly, however, there were many areas and issues on which agreement did exist. Neither group was new to the wine industry, although only Gordon and two members of Gordon's staff had ever been involved in introducing a new wine. The unsatisfactory first meeting between Gordon and Fallon probably accounted for the rocky start of the second meeting between the two staffs. Since the second meeting began with personal challenges (Gordon calling one of Fallon's cherished ideas absurd, Bjorn implying Vera was less than half-competent as a creative person, and the fact that the ad agency was stealing Gordon's thunder by doing the marketing research without any obvious inclination to consult Gordon), its ending on a strong, positive note would have been surprising.

There was, however, one promising note. Fleming Gillespie, with a Ph.D. in psychology, was an experienced advertising researcher at Satchel Associates, and was in charge of the research to be conducted for the new wine. Revising the truth, Gillespie presented his research ideas and plans as being tentative, asserting that he had never considered proceeding very far without consulting with Gordon's group. He provided some badly needed comic relief with the understatement of the day: "Of course, I don't think this meeting is the appropriate setting for brainstorming ideas." Apart from what he meant about the meeting being inappropriate to a free, nonevaluative discussion of ideas, he also meant that a smaller group consisting of himself and two aides and a few people from Gordon's staff should get together. He indicated that this would be the best procedure. This elicited a lot of positive head nodding, and Gordon responded, "Fine," in a way which clearly signaled the end of the meeting. As the meeting ended Gordon, Gillespie, and Fallon huddled and set a date two weeks hence for a subgroup of the two staffs to meet to discuss research needs and strategies.

This meeting took place at the Satchel Associates' offices. In addition to Gillespie and Gordon, those present included Seldon Vera and Anne Mandel from Satchel, and Tim Bjorn and Melissa Elton from Benne Brothers'. Vera initiated the discussion by indicating that while the two different groups had been "coming from different directions," their respective ideas were not incompatible. He went on to point out that while his staff believed it important to focus on upper-class entertainment settings, it was also appropriate to distinguish within the upper classes between early and late first users in social settings of a new wine. Vera indicated that he thought the differences between early and late first users with which Gordon and his staff were concerned may indeed exist and, if so, were important. "In any event," Vera concluded, "we should focus on upper social classes and see if there are significant differences between early and late first users which can be helpful in developing our copy." Mandel added that it was her hunch that the "great majority of upper social class wine drinkers are also early first time users." [Mandel seems to hold the proposition that early first use of a new wine is directly associated with social class: Higher social classes have proportionately more early first time users than do lower social classes.] Elton asserted that lower classes may also contain many early first time users. Gordon added that it would make him a lot more comfortable if he knew this question would be pursued.

At this point Gordon presented an analysis of the problem: "There seem to be two approaches we can take. Alternative #1 is that if social class is the most important variable to consider, then it may be appropriate to distinguish between early or late first time users. Alternative #2 says that we should focus primarily on time of first use and be concerned only secondarily with social class. I guess the alternative to follow depends upon what your research findings are. One thing I do know is that we can possibly change the time of first use but not social class, so I guess that's why I'm inclined toward alternative #2 in the absence of data." Considerable discussion ensued around the two alternatives. The group speculated about how the data might be distrib-

EXHIBIT 2-1
Fallon's Original Conception

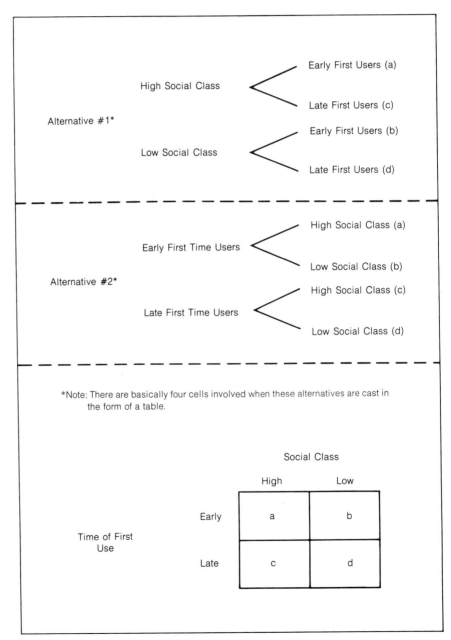

Alternative #1*

High Social Class
— Early First Users (a)
— Late First Users (c)

Low Social Class
— Early First Users (b)
— Late First Users (d)

Alternative #2*

Early First Time Users
— High Social Class (a)
— Low Social Class (b)

Late First Time Users
— High Social Class (c)
— Low Social Class (d)

*Note: There are basically four cells involved when these alternatives are cast in the form of a table.

	Social Class	
	High	Low
Early	a	b
Late	c	d

Time of First Use

uted among the four groups implied in Exhibit 2-1 and what the implications of the different distributions might be.

This discussion proved to be of value, for in the course of discussion (guided skillfully by Vera), understanding and rapport were established between the two staffs. There was agreement that the next step would be to conduct some focus group interviews. Fallon indicated that he or Vera would be in touch with Gordon as "things" developed, and Gordon left the meeting feeling his ideas would be taken into account in whatever research Satchel Associates conducted.

[Note: It is probably very evident to the reader that there was very little attention given to the nature of the concepts being discussed. No one raised the issue of what is meant by social class: What does it reflect or represent? What are its components? How is it measured? Similarly, no attention was given to the notion of first time use despite its being raised earlier by Margaret Citrini, the consultant. Was it early (or late) first time use relative to when a wine was first available to a consumer? The distinction between time of first use relative to awareness, versus time of first use relative to availability, is important. Consumers may be early adopters upon awareness but be late in finding out about a new wine and thus appear to be "laggards" in the diffusion process. Also, no mention was made about making operational the terms "early" and "late"—how soon after availability and/or awareness must someone purchase a wine to be considered an early first time user?]

Research Results Several weeks later, Gillespie presented the results of the focus group interviews to Gordon, Bjorn, Elton, Fallon, Vera, and Mandel. Believing (correctly) that the Benne Brothers' people were not current in their knowledge of marketing research methods, Gillespie outlined the basic purpose of focus group interviews. "What we do is get a group of about eight to ten people together, people who use the basic product—wine, in this case—at least occasionally. We get them to talk about why, when, and how they use the product and what they think about different product characteristics—for example, white and red wines, imported and domestic, and expensive and inexpensive. We don't try anything out on them, such as promotional copy or different packages. Instead, we just try to get a feel for what the actual consumers are like."

Gillespie had conducted two kinds of focus group interviews; the first consisted of interviews with wine consumers, and the second involved group interviews with salespersons from retail liquor stores. Two types of interviews were conducted because both Gillespie and Fallon believed that consumers were not always aware of the common patterns they followed while they were actually in the liquor stores. Thus, the interviews with consumers were used to provide information about their feelings about wine and the circumstances surrounding their actual wine consumption, and the interviews with wine salespersons were necessary to gain information about in-store purchase behavior patterns. [Note the implied proposition by Gillespie and Fallon that consumers are not necessarily aware of their own buying patterns.]

In discussing the results concerning the relationship between social class and wine consumption, Gillespie made it clear that the issue was much more complex than Fallon had originally speculated. Fallon had stated earlier that wine consumption increased the higher the social class. "However," said Gillespie cautiously, "my research shows that the relationship is curvilinear with high levels of wine consumption taking place in both the upper and in the lower social classes and very low levels of consumption taking place in the middle social classes." At this point, Gillespie pointed to a display board with the graphs shown in Figure 2-4 on it. Gillespie, remembering Fallon's displeasure two weeks earlier when the results were first shown to him, was quick to

FIGURE 2-4.

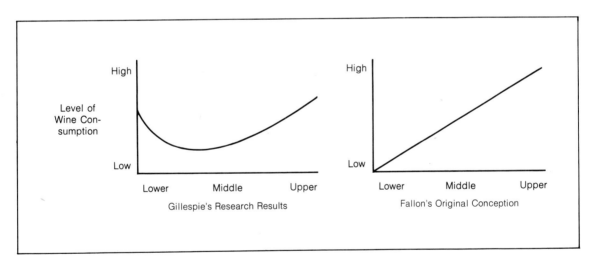

Gillespie's Research Results

Fallon's Original Conception

point out that "both graphs are correct depending on the conception of the problem. Although overall wine consumption is relatively high in the lower income classes, as in my conception, none of the wines consumed by this group are of the quality produced by Benne Brothers'. Thus, for Benne Brothers' wines (and wines of similar quality), Fallon's conception is probably correct."

At this point, Melissa Elton interrupted to note, "The real issue of interest to me is why the different classes consume different amounts of our type of quality-image wine. Why are they different? Can your research answer that?"

"Yes," said Gillespie, "we now have a good understanding of the reasons for these differences. Clearly, lower-class people are looking for a cheap alcoholic beverage and are relatively unconcerned about taste. Wine doesn't have the social and status connotations for them that it has for other people. To them, it is a substitute for liquor—their main concern is price.

[Note here the implied propositions that as social class increases, the importance of price decreases and the importance of taste increases; and that as social class increases, the status connotations of wine become more apparent and the significance of nontaste, physiological experiences decreases.]

"Middle-class people, however, are not that concerned about price. Benne Brothers' wine, unlike some imported wines, is in their price range. However, the problem seems to be that wine is not in their social knowledge. For example, they don't know what wines to serve with what foods. They don't know French and so they are often frightened by French terms such as 'gamay beaujolais' and 'cabernet sauvignon.' That may give you some clues about what kind of name you should give this wine if you want to expand the market," Gillespie said, looking at Gordon.

He continued, "There's also the problem of each middle-class person thinking that he or she is the only one in the world who doesn't know everything there is to know about wines. Rather than experimenting and trying different wines, many middle-class people just avoid buying wines. Those who do buy wine rely heavily on unsolicited information from advertisements or the recommendations of friends. They also rely on the brand names of certain vineyards, since these are easy to remember.

"Upper-class people provide a very different picture. There appear to be two kinds in this group—the real wine connoisseurs and those who enjoy trying different wines. The connoisseurs are much the way the middle-class people perceive all wine drinkers, except that the experts realize that not everyone is a wine connoisseur and therefore don't expect everyone to have their knowledge. Only when someone acts like a connoiseur (which is the way many middle-class people think they should act when purchasing wines) does the actual connoiseur expect them to have knowledge. Contrary to the conception of middle-class people, connoiseurs get their greatest joy in introducing wines to those who don't know much about wine, but who want to try different wines. They often hold wine-tasting parties for such friends.

"This brings us to the second group of upper class wine consumers—those who enjoy trying different wines. They also rely on advertisements and unsolicited recommendations (especially from connoiseurs), but they're also likely to solicit information from others." [The reader is challenged to write down all the propositions stated or implied in Gillespie's comments.]

At this point, Gillespie read some comments made by a wine salesperson in one of the interviews:

> You can tell what kind of person somebody is by the way they act in the store. Now the real connoisseurs, they're regulars—they either buy one bottle to sample, or a case of something they sampled and liked, or one bottle of a really fine

expensive imported wine. They usually have cellars or storage space set aside for wine. They don't look at prices so much because they're more interested in what's on the label and what other people have told them. But then they often ask us what we think or if anything new has come in—and the way to get them as regulars is to respect their knowledge.

Then there's "the triers." They usually come in and I let them look around and get the feel of the place if I don't recognize them. Then in a little while, I'll offer to help them. They often accept my offer, realizing that its my job to help people select wines. I think they get their kicks out of finding good wines for a medium price—a few dollars. They buy a lot of American wines, but also buy some imported wines. Occasionally, they'll buy several bottles of one wine, but usually they like to try one of this and one of that.

The last group I don't like. They act very nervous and also try to put on that they're better than us (the salespersons). A lot of the people in my chain say they just play the put-down game as viciously as the customer does. These are people who really should ask for some advice, but instead they won't. A lot of times, they end up buying something that's overpriced for its quality.

[Note that this commentary has given disconfirming evidence to the proposition that "those who know the least about wines are more likely to request or accept assistance from a salesperson." Instead, the proposition about promotional channel effectiveness which is implied is that "the less one knows about wine, the more important are unsolicited channels; those who have medium or high levels of interest in and information about wines are more likely to solicit information and accept offers of information and assistance." It appears that social class is a correlate of these different responses to different promotional channels.]

Gillespie then highlighted some conclusions and inferences he had drawn from the information on social class differences. He pointed out that some people (most notably the connoiseurs) sample a bottle of a new wine as a prelude to buying a case if they like it. This means they have ample and adequate storage space for wine. Another group which seemed to have at least some storage space (such as a twelve to sixteen bottle wine rack) are the "triers"—but they are more likely to have only one or two bottles of any particular wine. The last group, the middle-class, buys wine only for a particular occasion, and they don't usually store wine at home.

With respect to who could be considered early adopters, Gillespie implied that anyone could fit into this category. He said, "Wine connoiseurs might try a new wine soon after they've heard about it (which would probably be soon after its introduction, since they have contact with many sources of information about wines), but it is doubtful that they would become steady users since they usually stick to imported wines and classic vintages. The 'triers' are the most likely to be early adopters, but, because of their propensity to try many wines, they probably will never become heavy users of one wine. Instead, they will be light users of many wines.

"The middle-class people are less likely to hear about a new wine unless initial media promotion is intensive. If the name of a new wine, however, is repeated to them enough times, they'll think of it when they go to buy a bottle of wine."

[Notice the implicit proposition about middle-class wine consumers: If they are exposed to the name of the wine frequently, they will be favorably disposed toward buying the wine. Thus, according to this proposition, the marketer must create awareness rather than stressing the merits of the wine. This is a proposition which is often implicitly used by marketers without much success. With the plethora of products available to consumers, it is naive to believe that all the marketer must do is tell consumers the product name many times and they will buy the product. Perhaps Gillespie should have drawn a slightly different inference from the interviews with middle-class wine consumers: "Because of their self-consciousness about their knowledge of wines, getting this group to remember the name of a wine is an important element in the promotional strategy—convincing them of the merits of this wine over others is the second most important element."]

Gillespie continued his presentation by turning to the social aspects of wine consumption. He noted that people seldom drink wine when they are alone (as they do other alcoholic beverages), but this may be a consequence of the way wine is packaged (in bottles containing either four or eight servings). He mentioned the remarks of two consumers in the interviews. The first was from a twenty-five year old single woman who lived alone:

> I grew up in a family where we always had wine with dinner—I guess that comes from the way meals were served in the old country. When I fix a big dinner, I'd like to have a glass of wine with it—but I don't want to drink the whole bottle and you can't keep wine very long after it's been opened. Usually, I end up drinking iced tea and only having wine when I go out or have people over to my place.

The second example was from a fifty-five year old married business executive:

> When I come home in the evenings, I often feel like having a glass of wine with dinner. But Marie (the man's wife) doesn't drink and I usually have work to do in the evening, so I don't want to drink very much—you know, just a glass to unwind. It seems like I either end up drinking two glasses and letting the rest go to waste or not drinking anything. Either way, I feel a bit unhappy.

Gillespie was quick to add that these two people were exceptions—most of the consumers who were interviewed consumed wine with others and these others usually included people in addition to the person's spouse. Very frequently, wine was consumed at dinner parties or when dining out. Wine was connected in the consumers' minds with food to a greater extent than were other alcoholic beverages. Gillespie further indicated that wine also brought to mind romantic images, whereas other beverages did not.

EXHIBIT 2-2

Vintner's 'glass' is part of packaging

A WELL-PAID marketing manager may have planned a packaging concept introduced by Los Hermanos Vineyards, St. Helena, Calif.

Wine by the Glass is an individual 6.3 ounce bottle of wine with a plastic wine glass fitting over the top, held to the bottle and kept clean by the label, which is really a shrink wrap.

The drinker pulls a tab to release the wrap, lifts off the glass, unscrews the bottle cap (no corkscrew necessary), and pours.

Originally designed for use on airlines, the bottle-glass combinations are available for use in restaurants and for sale in stores. Retail price for chablis, chenin blanc, vin rose', or burgundy is 79¢.

At this point, however, Melissa Elton said that she had heard a rumor that one of Benne Brothers' competitors was testing the concept of single serving wine bottles on consumers (see Exhibit 2-2). She had also heard, however, that the company was finding that for certain situations consumers could see the merits of the new packaging approach, but in general they preferred standard size bottles (particularly full bottles, but also splits). Therefore, she believed that the major market for wines was for full bottles to be shared by several people.

Then Gillespie began to summarize the research results and their strategy implications. He again made use of a display board (see Table 2-1). Gillespie turned to Gordon, Bjorn, and Elton and concluded, "Now it's up to you to decide which segments to pursue. We've developed the basic themes, and the copy and creative people are working on specific executions. But before they can do those, you have to tell us which way or ways you want us to go."

Gordon expressed the sentiments of everyone when he complimented Gillespie on the impressive research. Although he would have to get final approval from Benne, he was most excited about targeting their efforts to the middle-class consumers, the upper class "triers," the restaurant consumers,

TABLE 2-1	USE SITUATION OR SEGMENT	PURCHASE PATTERNS	ACTION IMPLICATIONS
	(not mutually exclusive)		
	Lower-class consumers	Cheap wine as substitute for beer or liquor. A high level of consumption.	Not a market for Benne Brothers' wines.
	Middle-class consumers	Moderate wine consumption. Confused by French names. Self-conscious about lack of knowledge; often pretend to know more than they do. Rely on price as indicator of quality. Buy wine for specific occasions. Does not store wine at home.	Increase level of consumption through stressing name (especially name of vineyard rather than name of each wine), large point-of-purchase displays, information on bottle about what foods to serve the wine with, heavy introductory mass media promotion. Might get them to buy and use more if they had wine racks—a possible tie-in promotion. Theme: "The wine that's always right…"
	Upper class "triers"	High level of wine consumption spread over many different wines. Use wine salesperson and others for information. Look for good wines at moderate price. Early adopters.	Heavy promotion will lead them to try it. Will not be able to get loyalty from this group, although repeat purchases will occur. Encourage retail wine salespersons to suggest this wine. Theme: "Delightfully new."
	Upper-class wine connoiseurs	Often sample, then buy case. Mostly interested in imported wines. Often hold wine-tasting parties for "triers."	Probably will try the wine, but will not be major market segment. Important because of their influence on others. No specific media promotion—try to get writeups in gourmet magazines.
	Restaurant consumers (people who have a a bottle of wine with dinner in a restaurant).	Often limited by selections on wine list. A high level of consumption.	Might urge restaurants to promote or feature Benne Brothers' wines on wine list.

Lone consumption	Prevented by bottle size. Social norms against drinking alone.	Introduce single serving bottles. Theme: "Its so good, its a shame to wait for a party…"
Dinner and wine-tasting party consumption	One person decides and purchases for many others. Socially crucial for entertainer to have food and wine that go together.	Print serving suggestions on bottle (e.g. "perfect with beef, pasta, veal, or cheese). Have free booklet available describing which Benne Brothers' wine goes best with which dishes.

and the party consumers (in that order). He particularly liked the idea of cultivating the middle-class market because it would be easy to win (by creating high levels of awareness) and would be easy to reach (that is, it watches a lot of television). The meeting broke up with a generally positive feeling. Gordon promised to be in touch with Fallon in the next few days.

A Third Perspective   Although Gordon and his staff believed they knew the wine industry well, a feeling of discomfort crept in as they thought over and discussed the focus group findings (they had a copy of the display board, Table 2-1). Melissa Elton suggested they solicit a third perspective on the entire issue before committing themselves to any one strategy. Gordon agreed, although reluctantly, because he wanted to "get on with it" because of the press of other responsibilities.

It was decided to bring in someone who had little knowledge of the wine industry per se to see what an unbiased approach would be like (although it is questionable whether a lack of familiarity with a context produces less bias and more objectivity.) A decision was also made not to inform the people at Satchel that a consultant was to be hired. Three names were suggested with the first choice being a university professor. He was reached by a long-distance phone call and agreed to spend two days at Benne Brothers'. The consultant used earlier was felt to be too close to the market and was also perceived by the rest of the staff as a voice for Randolph Benne, Jr.'s ideas. Someone with more objectivity and creativity was desired. It might be mentioned that Benne was not informed of the second consultant's visit until after it had taken place. When he was told, he severely criticized Gordon for not informing him in advance and for not using the consultant who was already on a retainer with the firm. He also reminded Gordon in a harsh manner that he shouldn't be second-guessing the advertising agency.

The consultant who was brought in was Franklin Caplow, a well-known authority on the introduction of new products and services. Caplow had received a copy of Satchel's focus group report prior to his visit to Benne Brothers'. Bjorn met him at the airport, and, while enroute to the hotel, briefed Caplow on the background of ideas and activities with regard to the new wine.

Caplow presented a framework for thinking about the wine which was quite new to the Benne Brothers' marketing group. The framework involved considerations which the marketing group could see were relevant, but which they either hadn't encountered or hadn't articulated clearly in their own minds. Initially, Caplow kept away from the various ideas and concerns expressed by the different people from Satchel and Benne Brothers'. Instead, he stressed the importance of having an analytical framework to guide research itself, and the marketing actions based on research.

Caplow indicated at the outset that while he could present one or several analytical frameworks, it was ultimately up to the Benne Brothers' staff whether it would be helpful: "Only you can or should make the final judgment about whether the framework I present can be easily translated into relevancy in the wine market. I can answer questions that will help you reach that judgment and perhaps provide assistance in translating the framework into your context."

Caplow continued, "My approach is to think first in terms of the value of potential new product adopters and then to determine whether and how the most valued potential adopters are similar. Next, of course, one must consider whether these similarities provide a basis for developing marketing strategies." Caplow then presented a chart (see Exhibit 2-3) describing how the value of potential adopters can be determined. He presented a verbal formula which states that the:

Value of a Potential Adopter = Adoption Propensity × (Volume Propensity + Influence Propensity) − Cost of Effective Exposure.

[Note that volume propensity and influence propensity are added together and then multiplied by adoption propensity.]

Referring to his chart (Exhibit 2-3) Caplow pointed out that each of the components of the formula were derived in turn from other factors. For example, influence propensity is determined by such factors as how many people a potential adopter knows and how often he or she interacts with these individuals, how much influence a potential adopter has on people who wouldn't ordinarily try a product, and the average amount of use by the people who are influenced.

"Notice," Caplow continued, "the many different kinds of relationships here: (1) the greater the degree of social interaction, the greater the influence propensity (i.e. the greater the likelihood of there being someone who could be influenced); (2) the greater the influence over people who would not

EXHIBIT 2-3.
Formula for Determining the Net Value of a Potential Adoption of a New Idea

Net Value of Potential Adopter = Adoption Propensity × (Volume Propensity + Influence Propensity) − Cost of Effective Exposure

Adoption Propensity Determined By:
1. Potential of the Innovation to Satisfy a Key Need
2. Innovativeness of Potential Adopter
3. Ease With Which Innovation Can Be Adopted

Volume Propensity Determined By:
1. Degree of Initial Satisfaction with the Innovation
2. Frequency of Normal Use
3. Average Amount of Use

Influence Propensity Determined By:
1. Degree of Social Interaction (Number of people known plus frequency of interaction)
2. Influence Over People Who Would Not Otherwise Try the Innovation
3. Average Amount An Influenced Person Buys and Uses

Cost of Effective Exposure to the Innovation Determined By:
1. Probability of Message Exposure, Perception, Evaluation, etc.
2. Actual Delivery Cost

otherwise try the product, the greater the influence propensity [Note, however, that influence propensity is really a composite of social interaction and influence over nonusers, and thus it is illogical to argue that influence over nonusers, for example, increases influence propensity when influence over nonusers is used to compute influence propensity.]; (3) the greater the degree of social interaction, the greater the likelihood of influencing people who would not otherwise try the product (exposure to many people enhances the probability of at least encountering nonusers without intentions to try a product); and (4) the greater the influence propensity the greater the value of the potential adopter." Caplow illustrated his point on a chalk board:

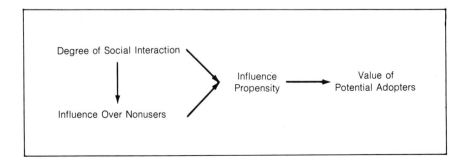

"You can see this may become very complicated when the possible interrelationships among all the concepts on the chart are taken into account, and also that the nature of the relationships may be highly varied. For instance, some may be additive and others multiplicative.

"I hope," said Bjorn with mock alarm, "that you're not going to lay all that on us along with formulas and stuff."

Caplow grinned, "I can if you want; there is a fantastic set of equations which can be very useful in portraying the model implicit among all the variables in this chart." Not wishing to appear intimidated Bjorn replied, "Well, if it's vital…" Gordon then cut in, "No, I'm sure it is not." Caplow, who had never intended to introduce a complex or even simple set of equations or diagrams, added, "Let's do that only if necessary; but it's unlikely we will need to. One can cover a lot of ground with this chart as it is now."

Caplow spent about one day working with the staff to develop many questions which could be asked of consumers by telephone to gain information about the variables involved in the net value of a potential adopter formula. Other questions were formulated to help determine whether potential adopters who had differing values also tended to differ in some systematic way, such as by social class or its components, time of adoption relative to availability and awareness, or the number of other consumers adopting earlier.

Gordon planned to approach Randolph Benne, Jr. again for financial support for the research plan developed with the consultant. As noted earlier, however, Benne's reaction to Gordon's news about the consultant discouraged Gordon from requesting the funds or even mentioning that a research plan had been developed to augment Satchel's plan. Following this rebuke, Gordon called Fallon and told him to proceed with their activities in whatever way they felt appropriate.

Developing and Using Propositions and Research Information

The reader should now have a sense of the following phenomena within the context of consumer behavior:

1. Practitioners in marketing use propositions either implicitly or explicitly, and generally in both ways.
2. The propositions vary widely in terms of their (a) complexity; (b) relative accuracy; and (c) clarity.
3. Propositions are often used by practitioners to guide marketing strategy without ever being tested in a formal way.
4. The number of alternative propositions about a given concrete phenomenon can be very large.
5. The concepts involved in propositions used by practitioners are often ill-defined.

6. The context in which a proposition may or may not be tenable is seldom specified.
7. Propositions as generally stated by practitioners vary in the ease with which they may be tested.
8. The action implications of a proposition may be interpreted very differently by different practitioners.

It is most important for the reader not to become unduly critical of practitioners on the basis of any or all of the points considered above. First, only one or at most a few of the points above are likely to characterize a good practitioner. Second, there are many practitioners who do meet the standards implied by some of the various points. Third, the implied standards are not always necessary or even possible to meet in all situations.

This last comment needs clarification. An eminent social scientist, James S. Coleman, has identified several principles governing policy research. These principles are very important to the marketing manager who must make policy decisions involving consumer-related information. Some of the implications of these principles will be noted here. First, "partial information available at the time an action must be taken is better than complete information after that time."[4] In the case of Benne Brothers', it would have been impossible to gather and interpret the kind of data either consultant felt necessary or to test in a rigorous way the propositions put forth in time for the planned introduction of the new wine. The type of marketing research which would have been helpful should have been considered at least a year in advance of the product launch date. Given this, insights provided by the focus group interviews and the personal experiences of the agency staff and the Benne Brothers' marketing group were better than no information at all, although this approach is inferior to a more rigorous research effort.

On the other hand, a highly sophisticated research effort might not have been worth the cost involved. It is more important for the marketing practitioner to have research procedures with a high probability of good results, especially good predictions, rather than procedures which give refined results if they are correct, but which depend upon a large number of assumptions being correct (e.g., no measurement error, no variables overlooked, no sampling bias). Coleman uses the example of firing projectiles through the air. Modern artillery has sophisticated computers which take into account a wide variety of factors such as the exit velocity of the shell, wind direction(s), weight of the shell, air pressure, and estimated distance to the target. "But even now, artillery units use 'forward observers' who report back to the gun battery

---

[4]James S. Coleman, *Policy Research in the Social Sciences*, Morristown, NJ: 1972, p. 4.

where the shot has ended relative to the target and indicate the direction of adjustment required. Many artillery units depend more on their forward observers than on calculations carried out by their control equipment."[5] The focus group interviews (the "forward observer"), if done correctly—which is not evident in the story—plus the much more detailed research the Benne Brothers' marketing staff and their consultants wanted (the "control equipment") would have been ideal. However, neither the second consultant nor Gordon believed that highly detailed and technically complex models were necessary.

It is important when using broad gauge, rather than highly refined, research to look for redundancy—do different sources of information yield the same conclusions? For example, do the different people involved in the story more or less agree on their hunches? Do they agree on what their experiences and the interpretations of those experiences tell them? Redundancy is more absent than present in the story. The marketing staff was not in total agreement with one another, nor was Benne in agreement with the marketing staff; Satchel Associates personnel were not in agreement with the Benne Brothers' marketing staff; and neither consultant particularly liked the situation and information presented to him or her. Although some effort was made by Gillespie to show that his group and Gordon's were not that far apart, and although Gordon appeared to have been reassured, this feeling was temporary. In fact, as Gordon thought more about it, the apparent redundancy disappeared, and he was moved to call in another consultant. Although this action was taken too late, given the launch date and the strong likelihood that Benne would have vetoed any suggestion or move to delay the introduction of the new wine, Gordon was correct in responding to the lack of redundancy by considering a more sophisticated field research effort. Such research could have provided much more reliable guidelines than the conflicting opinions of all the parties involved in the story. Given the fact that Gordon couldn't follow his most preferred course of action, however, he was probably correct in going with what the advertising agency had already done.

The ultimate objective of research in guiding the formulation of marketing policies is to produce policies which will have superior market results, compared to what would otherwise have occurred with a policy formulated without the benefit of research. The prime participants in this story were generally concerned with the action implications of their thinking. For example, Gordon questioned the practical value of the first consultant's concern with differences in the perceived relationship of price-quality between early and late first time consumers of a new wine. Benne flatly rejected the propositions developed by Gordon's staff as not being relevant to the success of the

---

[5]Coleman, *op. cit.,* pp. 4–5.

new wine. Perhaps a mistake was made here by not detailing in writing for Benne the action implications of different answers to each proposition.

In general, the propositions expressed by the story participants are formulated in a manner which suggests a policy orientation rather than an interest in the propositions' relevancy for people concerned primarily with extending knowledge. Recall how careful Caplow was to indicate that his analytical framework, culled in part from existing academic research, might not be appropriate. He shifted the responsibility to Gordon's staff for discovering significant action implications. In truth, Caplow did think his framework relevant, although the story does not clearly indicate this. Caplow may have been trying simply to engage Gordon's staff as early as possible in thinking about the model, rather than having them passively listening to him discuss the action implications of his model of the value of a potential adopter. Caplow did state that he was willing to help translate the conceptual model into the world of the practitioner-client.

It should be added that both consultants performed an important function in translating the marketing problem into problems related to scientific research and theory. For example, the first consultant, Margaret Citrini, raised an important definitional question—"Early (adoption) relative to what?" The answer to this question has important methodological, as well as theoretical, implications. The second consultant, Franklin Caplow, highlighted the concepts of influence propensity and volume propensity, and how they are determined and related in an overall model. In doing this, he had taken a problem presented by Gordon in their pre-visit communication, and translated Gordon's problem into a more scientific framework. Unlike the first consultant, Caplow was also of assistance in translating this model into a questionnaire which could provide data that would presumably be of applied value to Benne Brothers'. This met another important principle of Coleman's concerning the need to translate practical problems into academic questions so that the relevant concepts can be identified.

Benne's refusal to allow a second research effort independent of research planned by Satchel Associates, or even to approve of soliciting the opinion of a second consultant, violates another principle suggested by Coleman: "For policy research, the existence of competing or conflicting interests, together with the time-coupling of research to policy, require special self-corrective devices, such as the commissioning of more than one research group, under the auspices of different interested parties, and independent review of research results, using an adversary or dialectical process."[6] Conflicting interests were present, but there was no procedure for the constructive resolution of the conflict.

---

[6]Coleman, *op. cit.,* p. 10.

SUMMARY The following guidelines are offered for the practitioner formulating the strategy for introducing a new product: (1) The practitioner may not always have desirable information at the time it is needed or the financial or other resources to obtain ideal data even if adequate time is available. (2) The practitioner may find less specific information or a general proposition better for prediction than highly refined information or a very specific proposition. Highly refined information or a highly specified proposition may run a greater risk of having less predictive power for fewer consumer settings because of the larger number of potentially wrong assumptions. However, when the available evidence clearly supports tenable assumptions, the more specific propositions will, of course, be of greater value. (3) If more general propositions which are not very rigorous must be used, practitioners or policy makers should seek redundancy; they should try to determine whether other available indicators (e.g., experts) also point to the same proposition. (4) The practitioner should spend little time with propositions for which there are not direct clear-cut action implications or which do not clarify the action implications of other propositions. (5) The practitioner must be open to translating problems into questions of interest to academic researchers, and be willing to work with the researchers in translating their research into action implications. (6) The practitioner should not only allow, but should also encourage the expression of conflicting and competing positions in the definition of a problem in the research process, and in the interpretation of data. (7) Ideally, there should be a provision for evaluating the impact of a particular marketing policy.

SOCIOLOGICAL PERSPECTIVES

PART

2

DEMOGRAPHIC CHARACTERISTICS

3

CHAPTER GOALS The objective of this chapter is to help readers understand:
1. **how persons' demographic characteristics affect their consumer behavior;**
2. **which demographics are used by managers for segmenting the market.**

INTRODUCTION Demography is the study of population structure and processes, through an examination of different statistical measures of the characteristics of a group of people.[1] Demographers usually study one or more of the topics shown in Exhibit 3-1.

Consumer behavior research and marketing mix decisions rely immensely on demographic variables. In fact, the inclusion of demographic variables in consumer research studies is almost automatic. Demographic variables are probably the most commonly used variables in market segmentation and in readership/viewer profile studies in advertising media research. Market segmentation is the process of dividing a market into segments of people who are similar as consumers, and can therefore be appealed to using one set of marketing strategies. For example, all major magazines and newspapers which accept advertising provide potential advertisers with detailed

---

[1]For an interesting discussion of the impact of demographic changes on businesses and the economy, see "Americans Change," *Business Week,* Feb. 20, 1978, pp. 64–70.

EXHIBIT 3-1.
Topics Studied by
Demographers

1. The number and geographic distribution of a population.
2. The composition or characteristics of a population.
   (a) Age
   (b) Sex
   (c) Rural or urban residence
   (d) Ethnicity and national origin
   (e) Marital status and family life-cycle
   (f) Occupation
   (g) Educational status
3. The vital processes.
   (a) Birth rate
   (b) Mortality
4. Migration.
   (a) Immigration
   (b) Emigration
   (c) Internal migration

information about the demographic characteristics of their readers. The advertisement for *Black Enterprise* magazine (Figure 3-1) presents a sample of the demographic data this magazine collects and disseminates to prospective advertisers. Note that data on education, ethnicity, age, sex, domestic and foreign travel (migration), and residence are dominant in this advertisement. The full advertising brochure for this magazine contains even more detailed demographic data.

Other industries also depend on demographic variables. The food industry relies more on demographic than any other consumer variables in making market segmentation and product promotion decisions. The baby products industry also has a major concern with demographic data. The importance of carefully monitoring and interpreting these data is evidenced in the disposable diaper market. According to one observer of the baby products industry, alert diagnosis of some of the reasons behind the declining birth rate in the United States enabled Proctor and Gamble to be the first on the market with a disposable diaper.[2] One of their observations was that more women were entering the working force (a demographic factor) and remaining in the work force even after the birth of their children. This suggested that working

---

[2]Curt Schleier, "The Baby Business: Can You Succeed in a Failing Market," *Product Management*, April, 1977, pp. 29–34.

FIGURE 3-1.

OUR AVERAGE READER IS WAY ABOVE AVERAGE.

The primary circulation* of Black Enterprise Magazine is 230,000 of the most successful, most affluent, most influential black men and women in the United States.

They include nearly one-third of all blacks in the country who have household incomes of $25,000 and up.

Their total income adds up to over 5.3 billion dollars.

There are 230,000 reasons why your advertising works harder in Black Enterprise: our readers.

Their median income: $22,500
Median age: 39
90.4% attended college
73% graduated
38.3% hold Masters or Doctorate degrees
73% own their own home
53% use travel and entertainment cards
94% use bank charge cards
64% flew commercial airlines in the past 12 months
61.5% took a business trip in the last year
33% went outside the U.S. in the last 3 years
92% own a car
74% acquired it new
63% own 2 cars
More than 50% own a console and a portable color TV

Our readers are hard to duplicate:
11.6% read Business Week
5.5% read Nation's Business
6.8% read Fortune
4.4% read Forbes
29% read Newsweek
24.2% read Time
13.2% read U.S. News
45.6% subscribe to no other business magazine
63% are male
37% are female
All of them average 1.2 hours an issue reading the pages of Black Enterprise.

In fact, our average reader does just about everything your average customer does—only more so. We can prove it.** Call Robert A. Tate, Director of Advertising Black Enterprise Magazine today. He'll show you a lot of good reasons why advertising pages and advertising results are up in '77 in Black Enterprise.

BLACK ENTERPRISE MAGAZINE

295 Madison Avenue, New York, N.Y. 10017 (212) 889-8220
West Coast Representative: James K. Levitt Associates, Inc.,
13208 Saticoy Street, No. Hollywood, Cal. 91605. (213) 875-1517

* U.S. Rate Base, 10/77
  Total Readership, 1 million plus
** Erdos and Morgan CPM Survey, 1976

Source: *Advertising Age,* January 9, 1978, p. 50.

mothers of infants might be willing to pay a special price for convenience, and led to the extremely successful introduction of Pampers. According to this same source, the failure of Union Carbide to spot the demographic change cost them $7 million in their unsuccessful effort to launch Drydees. For the same reason, Scott Paper lost $11 million in their introduction of BabyScott. Neither Union Carbide nor Scott Paper could overcome Proctor and Gamble's competitive advantage of being first in the market because of their greater alertness to demographic variables.

In this chapter we shall highlight the importance of several of the topics in Exhibit 3-1 for understanding how and why consumers behave as they do.

THE NUMBER AND GEOGRAPHIC DISTRIBUTION OF A POPULATION

A "population" may be a trading area, a town or city, a county, or nearly any other kind of social group. The "density" of a population is the number of people in the city, state, region, or other geographical area. The more people there are in a city, the denser is the population of that city. In general, density influences the speed with which information moves through a geographical area—the greater the density of a geographical area, the more rapidly information will flow from consumer to consumer in that area.[3] The closer together people are, the more they come into contact and the easier it is to communicate verbally or even nonverbally. Thus, information about a new product is likely to reach people faster in a dense population than in a population that is less dense. This implies, too, that a given level of sales will be reached earlier in the dense population. In Chapter 18, a distinction is made between early knowers and early adopters of an innovation. A more rapid adoption rate for a new product in one community or region compared to another may be accounted for partly in terms of their relative population densities. People in the higher density group are more apt to learn of a new product earlier, and hence are more likely to be early purchasers (also called early adopters).

THE COMPOSITION OF A POPULATION

Many features, such as age and sex, distinguish one person from another. These features are sometimes obvious, but quite important nevertheless. The distinguishing features to be discussed here are among the most important variables affecting consumer behavior—variables which have direct as well as

---

[3]J. D. Kasarda, "The Structural Implications of Social System Size," *American Sociological Review,* Vol. 39, February, 1976, pp. 19–28; Bruce H. Mayhew and Roger L. Levinger, "Size and the Density of Interaction in Human Aggregates," *American Journal of Sociology,* Vol. 82, July, 1976, pp. 86–110.

indirect influences. Indirect influences are cases in which the demographic characteristic affects other variables which in turn influence consumer behavior.

Age If there is any one variable which is consistently important in influencing consumer behavior, it is age. Age groupings refer to various stages people pass through, such as childhood, adolescence, and young adulthood, and somewhat differing bundles of consumer goods and services are purchased at each stage. Medical services and products (such as sleeping and hearing aids) are in greater demand among older as compared to younger persons. Consumer concern with clothing style and fashion, and leisure time pursuits, also varies with age. This is not to say that these concerns exist only at certain ages. Rather, the concern is always there, though the person is interested in different fashions and recreations at different ages.[4] This is also evidenced in the cosmetics market. For example, Helena Rubinstein products are positioned to capture specific age groups. "Bio Clear is the line for teenagers to treat acne. Fresh Cover speaks to the woman in her mid-twenties with the line 'it let's your skin breathe.' Skin Dew is aimed at the woman in her early thirties who is looking for protection from aging. Ultra Feminine is for the middle-aged woman, providing moisturizing, and the latest, Madame Rubinstein, just out this fall, is positioned for the over-fifty woman, offering sebum replacement."[5] The Helena Rubenstein advertisement shown in Figure 3-2 indicates that these different age groups have different concerns. The advertisement indicates a changing concern among women over fifty for cosmetics that will make them look healthier rather than younger. Other purchases which vary with major age categories are type of housing, amount of travel, and type of food. Consumers' abilities to read and mentally process product label information or product use instructions also vary by major age category.[6]

Susceptibility to consumer fraud is positively correlated with age. For example, elderly consumers appear to be more susceptible to fraud than are younger consumers. However, it is not yet clear whether they are more susceptible because they are especially vulnerable or because they are simply

---

[4]Claude R. Martin, "A Transgenerational Comparison—The Elderly Fashion Consumer," *Advances in Consumer Research*, Vol. III, Beverlee B. Anderson (ed.). Proceedings of the Association for Consumer Research Sixth Annual Conference, 1976, pp. 453–456.

[5]*Product Marketing*, November, 1977, p. 32.

[6]Lynn W. Phillips and Brian Sternthal, "Age Differences in Information Processing: A Perspective on the Aged Consumer," *Journal of Marketing Research*, Vol. XIV, November, 1977, pp. 444–457.

FIGURE 3-2. *Product Management,* April, 1977.

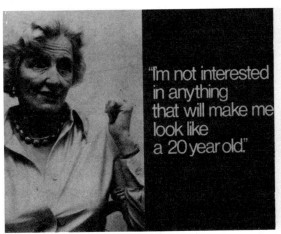 

Rubinstein hopes to get the "woman over 50" back in the fold with its Madame Rubinstein line.
The woman in this age bracket, a traditional user of the firm's products, is being offered
a moisturizer, cleanser and a night time cleanser.

more frequent targets of fraud by disreputable vendors, or whether both factors are present. Thus, because of a correlation between the experience of fraud and aging, one cannot conclude that simply aging increases one's susceptibility to fraud. For purposes of sales planning, marketers are often interested in changes among special age groups. An age group of major interest is the young adult category. Table 3-1 shows this group to be growing rapidly, moving to the suburbs, and acquiring certain household items. This suggests increased sales opportunities for products and services desired by young adults. These new sales opportunities will be disproportionately concentrated in suburban areas. One automobile maker, Cadillac, who used to label its market a "fifty-fifty" group (fifty years old making at least $50,000) is beginning to broaden the definition of its market. Cadillac has now begun a campaign to appeal to a different market segment: young couples in their early thirties who are career- and prestige-oriented and together earn $40,000 to $50,000. The theme of the campaign is "Haven't you promised yourself a Cadillac long enough?"[7]

Specific changes in consumption patterns are particularly associated with chronological age. The consumption of alcoholic beverages is one example. Forced retirement at a particular age will also directly alter consumption prac-

---

[7]Ralph Gray, "Cadillac Finds Youth Market: Couples Earning $40,000-plus," *Advertising Age,* January 2, 1978, p. 21.

TABLE 3-1. *Young Adults: A Dominant Market Influence*

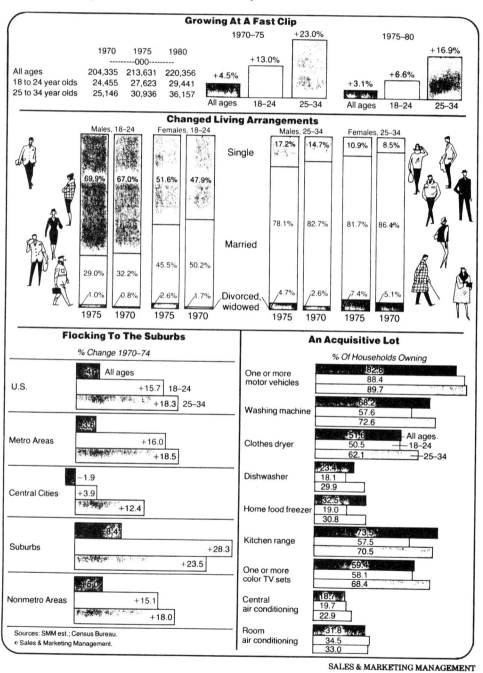

Growing At A Fast Clip

	1970	1975	1980
	---------000---------		
All ages	204,335	213,631	220,356
18 to 24 year olds	24,455	27,623	29,441
25 to 34 year olds	25,146	30,936	36,157

1970–75: All ages +4.5%, 18–24 +13.0%, 25–34 +23.0%
1975–80: All ages +3.1%, 18–24 +6.6%, 25–34 +16.9%

Changed Living Arrangements

Males, 18–24: Single 69.9% (1975), 67.0% (1970); Married 29.0% (1975), 32.2% (1970); Divorced, widowed 1.0% (1975), 0.8% (1970)

Females, 18–24: Single 51.6% (1975), 47.9% (1970); Married 45.5% (1975), 50.2% (1970); Divorced, widowed 2.6% (1975), 1.7% (1970)

Males, 25–34: Single 17.2% (1975), 14.7% (1970); Married 78.1% (1975), 82.7% (1970); Divorced, widowed 4.7% (1975), 2.6% (1970)

Females, 25–34: Single 10.9% (1975), 8.5% (1970); Married 81.7% (1975), 86.4% (1970); Divorced, widowed 7.4% (1975), 5.1% (1970)

Flocking To The Suburbs

% Change 1970–74

U.S.: All ages +4(?), 18–24 +15.7, 25–34 +18.3

Metro Areas: +3.6(?), +16.0, +18.5

Central Cities: −1.9, +3.9, +12.4

Suburbs: 8.4, +28.3, +23.5

Nonmetro Areas: 6.0(?), +15.1, +18.0

Sources: SMM est.; Census Bureau.
© Sales & Marketing Management.

An Acquisitive Lot

% Of Households Owning (All ages, 18–24, 25–34)

	All ages	18–24	25–34
One or more motor vehicles	82.8	88.4	89.7
Washing machine	68.2	57.6	72.6
Clothes dryer	51.6	50.5	62.1
Dishwasher	23.4	18.1	29.9
Home food freezer	32.5	19.0	30.8
Kitchen range	73.5	57.5	70.5
One or more color TV sets	59.4	58.1	68.4
Central air conditioning	18.7	19.7	22.9
Room air conditioning	31.8	34.5	33.0

tices. For other things, such as the purchase of sleeping pills, laxatives, digestive aids, magnifying glasses, and so forth, age is simply a surrogate measure of biological changes. Concerning the ownership of a home versus the rental of an apartment, age is a reflector of a social situation involving family size. Thus, one of the reasons age is so important is that it serves as a convenient, although imperfect, measure of other phenomena which cannot themselves be measured easily.

Another caution is in order in examining age-related phenomena. Many statistical analyses point to differences between people who are currently in the over sixty-five age bracket and those who are, for instance, in the thirty-five to forty age bracket. However, this type of data cannot be taken to mean that today's younger group will be, in twenty-five to thirty years, like today's older group. Those who are in the older group grew up in a time when attitudes, family relationships, and educational opportunities were different. So, differences between age groups (or "cohorts," as they are often called) may or may not be due to the process of aging.

Sex   Anyone reading this book does not need much said about the importance of sex from a demographic viewpoint (or from most other viewpoints for that matter). Social and biological differences between males and females are often dramatized through consumption patterns. There is no known culture in which sexual differences have no effect on consumer behavior.

In some instances, there are clear boundaries which are seldom crossed by either sex. With regard to tobacco products, few women smoke pipes or cigars and few men (in the United States) smoke Virginia Slims or use long cigarette holders. On the other hand, some boundaries may be crossed in one direction; for instance, it is now culturally acceptable in Western society for women to wear men's clothing, but not the reverse. (It is true that Joan of Arc got into trouble for transvestism, but only by pushing things too far.[8]) Women may wear men's clothes or clothing styles without much notice, whereas men cannot wear women's clothing without considerable social risk. However, as the advertisement in Figure 3-3 indicates, changes in cultural norms may also cause changes in product usage patterns associated with sex boundaries. The hair spray story shows that a market "defined as one sex may actually include both."[9]

---

[8]Vern L. Bullough, "Transvestites in the Middle Ages," *American Journal of Sociology,* Vol. 79, No. 6, May, 1974, pp. 1381–1394.

[9]*Business Week,* January 16, 1978, p. 48.

FIGURE 3-3.

What the hair spray story can teach us all.

Whether we sell cars, food, toiletries, (or magazines), we all can profit from the experience of the hair spray makers who once thought only women used their products.

It started with a quiet little *woosh*. Some husband somewhere gave his hair a quick once-over with his wife's hair spray.

From that moment on, the hair spray market developed a whole new dimension: *men*. Remember?

The Point

What the hair spray story teaches is that a market traditionally defined as one sex may actually include both. And that goes far beyond this particular case of a product designed for one sex also being used by the other.

It extends all the way to this: To get maximum sales of just about *every*thing today, you should advertise it to *both* men and women. Because both will influence the purchase.

Using the Point

There's a study* that tells by exactly how much husbands and wives influence the purchase of specific products. The study provides this marketing data in hard, usable numbers.

Left on the pages of the research report, however, these numbers inform, but don't really work for you. These numbers work only when you (or your agency) put them where they *can* work: into the computer that helps tell you where to advertise.

Bottom Line

When you factor in the relative influence of *both* sexes, you profit. Because that's what marketing stories such as this one, and also the Purchase Influence study tell us to do.

Get the husband/wife Purchase Influence numbers, and get them into your computer.

*Measures of Husband/Wife Influence on Buying Decisions, Haley, Overholser & Associates. Copies available from Jack Nephew, Reader's Digest, 200 Park Avenue, New York, N.Y. 10017

Reader's Digest

Source: *Business Week,* January 16, 1978, p. 48.

One of the interesting changes in the sex demographic factor concerns working women. Table 3-2 indicates clear upward trends in female employment, especially among the younger age groups. Moreover, Table 3-2 shows that married women's employment has a major effect on family income. In fact, a very substantial share of total family income in the United States is accounted for by families where the wife also is employed. In addition, it appears that two families with the same income, but with different sources of income (i.e., from the husband's salary only or from the combined salaries of employed husband and wife), are quite different in their attitudes and behaviors. More will be said later about the effects that a career has on the consumer behavior of women.

Chapter 15 on personality discusses the importance of masculinity and femininity as factors to be considered in designing products and promotional appeals; it will suffice to say here that sexuality is an extremely important force in consumer behavior.[10] Important changes are occurring in Western society, particularly in the United States, with regard to the concepts of masculinity, femininity, and sexual behaviors generally. These changes may cause marketers to make major changes in the way in which sex is used in product and promotional development.

Rural/Urban/ Suburban Residence

Many consumer phenomena are the result of where people live. People living in rural areas purchase more things through mail-order catalogues than do people living in urban areas. This is due to the fewer shopping areas available to persons in rural areas, the smaller selections those outlets have, and the inconvenience of visiting those shopping areas. Transportation needs and behaviors also differ between consumers living in rural and urban areas. Excluding farm equipment, consumers in rural areas use fewer transportation services, partly because there are less services available. Housing purchases also differ. As one would guess, apartment living is a more prevalent practice in urban areas. Entertainment consumption also varies according to rural/urban/suburban residence. It is important to keep in mind that when we use the term "rural residence" we are usually referring to a constellation of factors, such as income (often low), occupation (often farm-related), and population density (usually low).

Over the past few years, several trends in residence location have taken place. Previously, the major pattern of movement was from rural to urban

---

[10]For an excellent discussion of the consumer behavior of women, see Rosemary Scott, *The Female Consumer,* NY: Halsted Press, 1976.

TABLE 3-2 *Women: Coming Into Their Own in More Ways Than One*

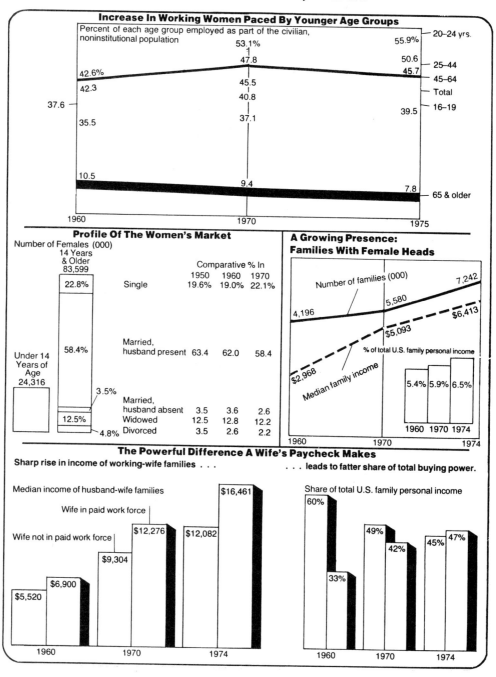

Increase In Working Women Paced By Younger Age Groups

Percent of each age group employed as part of the civilian, noninstitutional population

53.1%		55.9%	20–24 yrs.
	47.8	50.6	25–44
42.6%		45.7	45–64
42.3	45.5		Total
37.6	40.8		
35.5	37.1	39.5	16–19
10.5	9.4	7.8	65 & older

1960   1970   1975

Profile Of The Women's Market

Number of Females (000)

14 Years & Older 83,599

Under 14 Years of Age 24,316

		Comparative % In		
		1950	1960	1970
22.8%	Single	19.6%	19.0%	22.1%
58.4%	Married, husband present	63.4	62.0	58.4
3.5%	Married, husband absent	3.5	3.6	2.6
12.5%	Widowed	12.5	12.8	12.2
4.8%	Divorced	3.5	2.6	2.2

A Growing Presence: Families With Female Heads

Number of families (000)

7,242

5,580

4,196

Median family income

$2,968 $5,093 $6,413

% of total U.S. family personal income

5.4%	5.9%	6.5%
1960	1970	1974

1960   1970   1974

The Powerful Difference A Wife's Paycheck Makes

Sharp rise in income of working-wife families . . .   . . . leads to fatter share of total buying power.

Median income of husband-wife families

Wife in paid work force

Wife not in paid work force

$5,520	$6,900	$9,304	$12,276	$12,082	$16,461

1960   1970   1974

Share of total U.S. family personal income

60%	33%	49%	42%	45%	47%

1960   1970   1974

Source: SMM est., Census Bureau, Bureau of Labor Statistics
Sales & Marketing Management.

areas (cities). People left their farms and worked in the factories in the cities. Then, about fifteen years ago, the suburbs began to grow rapidly. Presently, more people live "in suburbia (more than 38 per cent) than in either the central cities (30 per cent) or in rural areas (32 per cent)."[11] Because of this sudden growth, the suburbs are becoming urbanized and self-contained. Therefore, present movement seems to be in two directions. First, many people who have lived their entire lives in suburbs, rather than in cities, are moving to suburbs which are divorced altogether from the nearby central cities. Thus, the movement is from suburb to suburb. The second developing pattern of movement is from suburb to exurb, or to rural areas.[12]

These patterns are very important for marketing and consumer behavior. As population shifts occur, so must there be shifts in the availability of retail stores and shopping centers in various areas. For example, consumers moving from suburbs to exurbs will still want many of the conveniences and product availabilities they experienced in the suburbs. Consumers living in suburbs asserting their independence from the central city may not patronize suburban branch stores of regional department stores. Persons moving from rural areas to urban areas are likely to be amazed at the services and specialties which are available. Thus, a person's previous as well as present residence will affect behaviors related to consumption.

Looking back to Table 3-1, we can see other implications of these trends. *Sales and Marketing Management* highlights the importance of looking at urban/rural population distributions in conjunction with other demographic variables: "What invests the suburbs with a special importance insofar as sales planning is concerned is that, as a rule, their population is younger, with a higher level of schooling, holding down a greater proportion of white collar and professional jobs, and commanding relatively greater spending power than their counterparts in the central cities and outside the metro areas."[13]

A study involving residential location and other demographic variables discussed in this chapter, and their impact on "outshopping," was conducted by William Darden and William Perreault. "Outshopping" refers to the phenomenon of consumers shopping outside their local trade area. Outshopping was defined in the Darden and Perreault study in terms of the dollars spent outside the trade area for each of a number of products within a one-year period. The data for the study were obtained by interviews with 278 middle-class housewives randomly selected from sixteen suburban locations

---

[11]Louis H. Masotti, in "Preface" to issue on "The Suburban Seventies," *The Annals of the American Academy of Political and Social Science,* Vol. 422, November, 1975, p. vii.

[12]Sylvia Fava, "Beyond Suburbia," *The Annals of the American Academy of Political and Social Science,* Vol. 422, November, 1975, pp. 10–24.

[13]*Sales and Marketing Management,* July 26, 1976, p. A-29.

in the Athens, Georgia area. Several findings were reported involving age, stage in life cycle, occupation, education, geographical mobility, and income. These findings reveal that:

1. Product-specific outshoppers are younger.
2. Neither occupation, household size, nor education of their spouse is related to the outshopping groups in this study. In prior studies education was found to relate to outbuying.
3. Distance residential moves over the last five years and expectations of moving in the coming year are related to the outshopping groups in the study. The authors find that big-ticket home product outbuyers are extremely mobile.

Darden and Perreault also present several management implications:

1. It is likely that some outshopper types find outshopping is a pleasant way to spend their time. Convincing these consumers to shop in the local trade area calls for an approach that is different from that used for outshoppers with economic motivations (selections, quality, and price). For example, improving the dining, entertainment, and recreational facilities, keeping in mind the sociological and cultural backgrounds of residents, might enhance the appeal of local trade areas.
2. Local trade areas characterized by a mobile population (residential movers) face stiff competition from surrounding trade areas for sales of big-ticket home products (e.g., major appliances, furniture). Because household turnover is a constant phenomenon in these communities, newcomer welcoming services offering genuine discounts on such products might be effective.[14]

Ethnicity and National Origin

Ethnic background is also an important factor in consumer behavior. In New York City, for example, Puerto Ricans are purported to use frozen T.V. dinners more often than Jews. Blacks are supposed to prefer well-known brand name scotch whiskeys disproportionately more than do whites. In general, food consumption is highly influenced by ethnic background. The more closely a person is tied to an ethnic community, the more his or her food consumption practices will be influenced by that community.

The consumer behavior of blacks has been widely researched. However, as with many demographic variables, researchers must be cautious in making

---

[14]William R. Darden and William D. Perreault, Jr., "Identifying Interurban Shoppers: Multiproduct Purchase Patterns and Segmentation Profiles," *Journal of Marketing Research,* Vol. 13, February, 1976, pp. 51–60.

statements about differences between various racial or ethnic groups, because race is closely associated with several other social characteristics such as income, education, family structure, and residence area. In fact, some of these other social characteristics (such as being poor or living in a ghetto) may be the result of a person's race. However, whatever the causes, it does appear that the consumer behavior of blacks is different from that of whites in some respects.

Several studies of differences between blacks and whites in the allocation of money to various product categories have found that with income controlled:

1. Blacks spend more on personal care items (cosmetics and toiletries).[15] In fact, an advertisement for a magazine appealing to black women states that black women use cosmetics and fragrances at a rate of two to one when compared to all other women. This amounts to 20 per cent of the national total spent for cosmetics and fragrances.[16]

2. Blacks spend less than whites for food consumed at home, housing, medical care, and automobile transportation (even though black households tend to be larger than white households).[17] The lower expenditure for food has been accounted for by greater preferences among blacks for lower-cost foods and by lower preferences for protein by blacks in lower-income brackets.[18]

3. Blacks spend more than whites for clothing and non-automobile transportation.[19]

4. Black women report less use of impersonal sources of information such as newspaper ads than do white women.[20]

5. Blacks frequently report that they prefer to rely on television and black-oriented radio, rather than newspapers, for news and entertainment.[21]

6. In many contexts, blacks are less likely than whites to adopt innovations or new products.[22]

---

[15]Raymond A. Bauer and Scott M. Cunningham, *Studies in the Negro Market,* Cambridge, MA: Marketing Science Institute, 1970.

[16]Advertisement for *Essence* Magazine in *Product Management,* September, 1976, p. 53.

[17]Marcus Alexis, "Some Negro-White Differences in Consumption," *American Journal of Economics and Sociology,* Vol. 21, January, 1962.

[18]Discussed in Alan R. Andreason, *The Disadvantaged Consumer,* NY: The Free Press, 1975.

[19]Alexis, *op. cit.*

[20]Bernard Portis, "Negroes and Fashion Interest," *Journal of Business,* Vol. 39, April, 1966, pp. 314–323.

[21]Bauer and Cunningham, *op. cit;* Raymond O. Oladipupo, *How Distinct is the Negro Market?,* NY: Ogilvy and Mather, Inc., 1970.

[22]Bauer and Cunningham, *op. cit.*

Obviously, most if not all of these differences are not caused by race, but result from the various racial subcultures. Since racial subcultures are rapidly changing, however, it is expected that racial differences in consumer behavior will also change. Therefore, changes should be closely and frequently monitored by the manager for whom an understanding of racial subcultures is essential.

Marital Status and Family Life Cycle

Consumption by married couples differs from that of individuals living alone or unmarried persons living together. The average per person expenditure of a married couple is generally greater than that of an unmarried person. For the most part, two cannot live as cheaply as one. Many purchase decisions are also engaged in differently by a person after he or she is married, compared to his or her premarriage behavior. After one is married, each of the person's purchases usually affects another person, the spouse, as well. This other person, therefore, has a psychologically "larger" presence as a spouse than as a friend or stranger.

That the singles market is undergoing interesting changes which have importance for the purchase of household durables is an observation that has been made by several researchers. We quote from one of them:

> Household durables become important both because of the increasing number of young singles who live in their own households and because of the changing nature of the singles' years. In essence, the single adult's household is metamorphosing from a place in which to "camp out" while waiting for marriage to a setting in which to express one's own individuality and one's own accomplishments. It is also becoming a place of comfortable retreat from the world and, increasingly, a place to entertain.
>
> Depth interviews conducted among young single adults (again, concentrating on college graduates) confirm this metamorphosis and indicate that it is most strongly apparent among career-committed women. A well-furnished, well-decorated apartment makes a strong statement about the owner's independence, her ability to support herself, and her career progress. It has, perhaps, been quite important for career-committed young women to make such non-verbal statements in order to be taken seriously. Increasing purchase of household durables, incidentally, appears to go beyond furniture and decorative accessories. Cooking, for example, may be in transition from a necessary to a recreational activity. If, and as this transition becomes accomplished, the singles' household will increase further its stock of cooking and food preparing accessories.

Such changes as just discussed can have some interesting consumer behavior ramifications. Purchase of many household durables has tended to concentrate in the period between engagement and the first few months of marriage. To the extent that durables purchases are made independently of marriage plans, the accumulation period is bound to be longer, and a new set of variables will be required to identify prospective purchasers. It is also worthwhile speculating as to the extent to which young adults will be bring household goods rather than bank accounts to their marriages.[23]

In addition, many products are being developed especially for single people. For example, Campbell Soup Company has introduced single serving cans of soup for use by single people as well as by members of larger households who are increasingly eating alone to meet the demands of individual schedules.[24]

Consumer behavior is also influenced by the stage of the family life cycle consumers are in. We can describe several stages which consumers go through in their family situation. Not all persons go through all stages, but together, these stages explain the family positions of many people.

(1) Childhood and adolescence: Live with parents, supported by parents, make some consumer choices individually.

(2) College stage: Do not live with parents, supported by parents, make some consumer choices individually.

(3) Singles stage: Do not live with parents, self-supporting.

(4) Cohabitation stage: Live with partner, but not married; self-supporting.

(5) Newly married stage: Young, no children.

(6) Young parent stage: Children not yet in school.

(7) Older parent stage: Children in childhood and teenage stage.

(8) Empty nest stage: Children have left home, but may still be dependent; adults are still employed.

(9) Retirement stage: Children have left home, but may still be dependent; adults are not employed.

(10) Survivor: Widowed spouse, may or may not be employed.

This set of stages has changed in the past few years. For instance, it is now quite common for there to be stages between the childhood and newly married stages. The most recent stage to be added to the list is the cohabitation stage. In March, 1977, there were 1.9 million cohabiting couples in the United States. This is 2 per cent of the 48 million "couple households," which is considerably less than the 12 per cent of Swedish unmarried couple households. The 1977 figures for the United States represent an 83 per cent increase over the 1970 figures, which themselves represented a 19 per cent

[23]Lawrence H. Wortzel, "Young Adults: Single People and Single Person Households," *Advances in Consumer Research*, Vol. IV, 1976 edited by William D. Perreault, Jr., Association for Consumer Research.
[24]"Modern Life Styles Lead to New Soup Entry," *Product Management*, December, 1976, pp. 52–53.

increase over the 1960 figures. This is obviously a growing life-style trend.[25] Cohabitation describes several types of relationships:

(a) casual dating;

(b) transitory: currently an exclusive relationship, but future plans are uncertain;

(c) trial marriage;

(d) permanent alternative to marriage.

The effect on consumption is that the less committed the partners are, the more likely they are to buy their own packaged products and nondurables. The more committed they are, the more likely the partners are to jointly purchase items.[26]

Movement through the family life cycle stages follows a somewhat sequential order. However, some cohabitation couples will be older than couples in the parent stages. Some cohabitating couples and some singles may decide never to move into the other stages. Thus, patterns of movement through these stages are becoming more individualistic. For instance, some people retire very early, while others decide never to retire.

Consumption does vary, however, according to the stage one is in. Therefore, although decisions to move into different stages may be individualistic and difficult to predict, we can make predictions about the types of purchases one will engage in if it is known what stage the person is in. For instance, the automobile purchased by parents after children have moved away from home is likely to be smaller than the auto purchased when all the children were in their childhood years. Food shopping is likely to vary greatly as the family moves through various stages. Similarly, housing needs vary as family size changes.

Occupation The behaviors required by various occupations may be reflected in consumption activities. For example, business executives, who may be required to entertain or do business over food and beverages, may frequent restaurants more often than people in the manual trades. A salesperson may need a company car due to the travel requirements of the sales job, and hence may not own a car or may own only one family car. People who work in one location, on the other hand, such as an office or hardware store, may own two

---

[25]Figures from report prepared for Population Reference Bureau by Paul Glick, Population Division, and Arthur Norton, Marriage and Family Statistics Branch, U.S. Census Bureau. See October, 1977 *Population Bulletin,* Population Reference Bureau.

[26]From speech by Lawrence H. Wortzel, reported in *Marketing News,* December 31, 1976.

family cars. In addition, many consumer behaviors with regard to clothes are largely determined by the person's occupation. The number of suits owned may be a direct consequence of occupation.

Occupation may also change shopping patterns. The upsurge in the number of working women is believed to be a major cause of the sales boom being experienced by mail-order businesses. Maxwell Sroge, president of a Chicago company in the mail-order business, claims that "women abandoned 11 billion hours shopping time when they went to work."[27] The estimated spending loss to retail shops in 1976 was placed at $55 billion.

As with other demographic variables, care must be exercised not to confuse the effects of occupation with the effects of other variables for which occupation may be a surrogate measure. Consumption differences associated with occupation may actually reflect differences in income and education. These three variables taken together are used as a measure of (that is, they are surrogates for) social class (see Chapter 4).

THE VITAL PROCESSES

Birth rates and death rates are useful in long-range planning. Enduring changes in these rates portend increased or decreased markets for various products and services. Forecasts for baby foods, insurance and medical services, and other products and services are based on present birth and death rates. As is shown in Tables 3-3 and 3-4, the composition of the population of the United States is changing. In the past decade, planned parenthood and improved birth control devices and techniques have considerably decreased the birth rate. Yet, improved medical technology has lengthened the life expectancy and has thus decreased the death rate. The result has been decreased demand for children's products and increased demand for products designed for older adults. Because of these rates, several baby food companies have had to diversify into other areas, such as selling baby foods as convenience snacks in vending machines.[28] However, at least one forecaster has suggested that a baby boom is looming on the horizon. "A baby boom seems inconceivable right now but demographers and social scientists say a fever of fertility will shortly be sweeping the nation and pregnancy will once again become chic."[29] Many social scientists believe that the present decreases in the birth rate are due to couples postponing having children rather than deciding not to have children at all.

---

[27]*Product Management,* September, 1976, p. 62.
[28]Curt Schleier, *op. cit.*
[29]Linda Wolfe, "The Coming Baby Boom," *New York,* January 10, 1977.

TABLE 3-3.
Population pyramids,
United States: 1870,
1900, 1940 and 1970

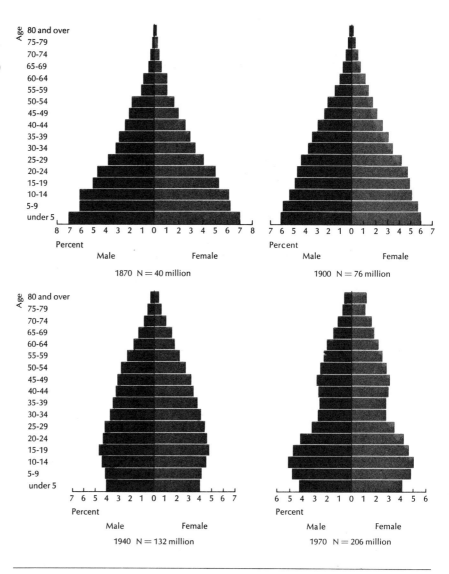

Source: *Sales and Marketing Management,* July 26, 1976.

MIGRATION   Changes in birth and death rates are not the only factors which account for increases or decreases in the size of populations. Populations also grow or shrink due to immigration and emigration. Of greater importance than these in explaining changes in consumer behavior within a given population is internal migration—movement from one location to another within a county,

TABLE 3-4.
Estimated crude birth and death rates for selected countries, 1969

Country	Rates per 1,000 of population	
	Births	Deaths
World	36	15
Australia	20	9
Canada	18	7
Ceylon (Sri Lanka)	32	8
China	43	21
France	17	11
West Germany	15	12
India	44	16
Ireland	22	12
Japan	19	7
Mexico	43	9
USSR	17	8
United Kingdom	17	12
United States	18	10

Source: AID, 1970: 172−178.

city, or some other unit. For example, the movement to the suburbs resulted in increased purchases of automobiles and increased the demand for single dwelling housing. The home maintenance and repair market increased considerably as many people moved into private homes for the first time. A recent shift from suburbs to the city has been noted and is of concern to marketers in the home construction industry. For example, there is an expected shift away from do-it-yourself home improvements as people move back into apartments.

Americans are very geographically mobile. The entire industry of moving companies and rental trucks is based on this mobility. The average American moves from one dwelling to another nine times during his or her life, and this figure is increasing. College professors and computer programmers move more often than the average, while lawyers, physicians, and persons who own their own businesses move less often (because their professions require that they develop a practice or a clientele). This mobility affects consumer behavior in several ways. In purchasing homes and home furnishings, people are likely to consider the effect of future moves even when these are not currently planned.

Projected migration patterns within a large market are important aspects of consumer behavior for marketers (paychecks follow people). Such data provide guidelines for planning work force needs, for deploying the field sales force, for establishing sales targets, and for shifting marketing emphasis to fast growing markets and away from slow growing or declining markets. Table 3-5 contains data concerning relative regional growth which indicates well above average increases in the population of the Rocky Mountain and the South-

TABLE 3-5.
SURVEY
HIGHLIGHT
Regional Growth's
Continuing
Imbalance

Region	Projected 1980 Total Pop. (Thous.)	% Change 1975–80	Projected 1980 Metro Pop. (Thous.)	% Change 1975–80	Projected 1980 EBI Per Hsld.	% Change 1975–80
New England	12,316.8	+0.8%	10,340.7	+0.2%	$20,092	+26.4%
Middle Atlantic	42,802.5	−0.1	37,467.6	−1.0	20,488	+26.9
Great Lakes	41,540.1	+1.1	32,882.0	+0.3	20,945	+32.1
Plains	17,267.6	+2.3	8,962.9	+0.7	19,913	+40.7
Southeast	51,652.5	+9.4	31,523.9	+8.1	17,919	+37.9
Southwest	20,274.5	+9.1	14,850.1	+9.8	18,027	+33.9
Rocky Mountain	6,303.3	+9.6	3,878.0	+8.5	19,826	+42.4
Far West	31,081.4	+7.2	26,984.2	+6.6	19,100	+25.6
U.S.	**223,238.7**	**+4.1%**	**166,889.4**	**+3.4%**	**$19,437**	**+31.4%**

New England—Conn., Me., Mass., N.H., R.I., Vt. **Middle Atlantic**—Del., D.C., Md., N.J., N.Y.,
Pa. **Great Lakes**—Ill., Ind., Mich., Ohio, Wis. **Plains**—Iowa, Kan., Minn., Mo., Neb., N.D., S.D.
Southeast—Ala., Ark., Fla., Ga., Ky., La., Miss., N.C., S.C., Tenn., Va., W. Va. **Southwest**—
Ariz., N.M., Okla., Texas. **Rocky Mountain**—Colo., Idaho, Mont., Utah, Wyo. **Far West**—
Alaska, Cal., Hawaii, Nev., Ore., Wash.

Source: *Sales & Marketing Management's 1976 Survey of Buying Power—Part II,* p. 8

west regions and a well above average increase in the effective buying power
of households in these regions. Table 3-6 shows the unequal regional growth
patterns more simply and dramatically. These regional changes have already
affected consumer purchases of several products. For example, the migration

TABLE 3-6.	No. of States Above Average Growth for 1975–80	No. of States Below Average Growth for 1975–80
Northwest	2	7
Midwest	2	11
South	13	3
West	12	0

Source: Sales and Marketing Management's 1976 Survey of Buying Power—Part II, p. 9.

to the Southwest has meant sharp increases in the sales of Mexican foods, sunscreen products, and salad dressings. It is also expected that cosmetics will be geared for the outdoor life characteristic of this area.[30]

SUMMARY Demographics are essential for a complete understanding of consumer behavior; however, by themselves they do not offer a complete explanation. For instance, demography tells us that there are shifts in the age composition of the population. But, we must turn to attitudes, social pressures, and role definitions to understand why young couples have decided to postpone having children, or to not have them at all.

KEY CONCEPTS
Cohort
Demography
Emigration
Immigration
Internal migration
Market segmentation
Media audience profiles
Outshopping

[30]"Sunbelt Growth to Determine Future New Product Development," *Product Management,* September, 1976, p. 60.

LARGE-SCALE SOCIAL STRUCTURES AND CONSUMER BEHAVIOR

CHAPTER GOALS   The objective of this chapter is to help readers understand:
1. **ways in which nations can be differentiated from each other in terms of climates for change;**
2. **the link between several social class concepts and their manifestations in consumer behavior;**
3. **how industries as social systems are distinguished from each other by many types and levels of consumer behavior.**

INTRODUCTION   One of the most fundamental and intriguing of all human phenomenan is the tendency in people to both differentiate themselves from one another and to group together on the basis of similarities. This phenomenon is the basis for one of the most central concepts in marketing: market segmentation. Market segmentation is based on the idea that actual or potential consumers, i.e., the market for a product or service, may be subdivided into homogenous subsets of consumers.[1] Consumers in one subset share important similarities which also differentiate them from other subsets.

Different market segments have different patterns of behavior. This is basically what sociologists refer to as social structure. That is, a group of

---

[1]Philip Kotler. *Marketing Management*, 3rd edition. Englewood Cliffs, N.J.: 1976.

people (a market) can be structured (subdivided into smaller groups) on the basis of differences in their patterns of social behavior. There are many ways in which groups of consumers may be structured. First, there may be differences in their demographic characteristics such as occupation, sex, geographical location, and marital status. These were covered in the preceding chapter. Second, consumers may differ from one another in the degree to which they possess scarce and valued things such as money, knowledge, or skills. The concept of social class has often been used to describe these differences. Third, one group of consumers may differ from another group on the basis of the customs they practice.

These and other differences are interrelated. For example, some consumers with unskilled blue-collar jobs may receive less money than white-collar professionals who are highly skilled. Because of the tendency for people who are similar in important ways to associate together, the unskilled, low-income, blue-collar workers will interact with one another as will the well-paid, highly skilled white-collar workers. Because of the differences in income, skills, and employment, each group will have different life-styles and norms of behavior.

Differences in life-styles and norms of behavior associated with different social structures will normally produce different consumption patterns. For this reason, it is necessary to study various kinds of social structures in order to better understand consumer behavior.[2] Sociologists often distinguish between different social structures on the basis of the number of subgroups found within them. (There are, of course, many other criteria for distinguishing among different social structures.) For convenience we shall distinguish between large-scale social structures which have many subgroups and small-

[2]Several strong arguments for studying the impact of social structure on consumer behavior can be found in Alan R. Andreasen, *The Disadvantaged Consumer,* NY: The Free Press, 1975; Fred Hirsch, *Social Limits to Growth,* Cambridge, MA: Harvard University Press, 1976; Robert Nathan Mayer, "Exploring Sociological Theories by Studying Consumers," *American Behavioral Scientist,* Vol. 21, March/April, 1978, pp. 600–613; Marcus Felson and Joe L. Spaeth, "Community Structure and Collaborative Consumption: A Routine Activity Approach," *American Behavioral Scientist,* Vol. 21, March/April, 1978, pp. 614–624; Frederick D. Sturdivant, "Subculture Theory: Poverty, Minorities, and Marketing," in Scott Ward and Thomas S. Robertson (eds.), *Consumer Behavior: Theoretical Sources,* Englewood Cliffs, NJ: Prentice-Hall, 1973, pp. 469–520; Luis V. Dominquez and Albert L. Page, "Stratification in Consumer Behavior Research: A Reexamination," unpublished working paper, Case Western Reserve University. 1978; and Goran Ahme, "Normative Order, Reification and Role Distance Applied to Consumer Behavior," *Acta,* Vol. 4, 1974, pp. 330–343.

scale social structures which have few, if any, subgroups. This chapter will focus upon selected large-scale social structures. Chapter 5 will examine smaller-scale social structures. Two important examples of smaller-scale social structures—the business firm and the family—are the topic of Chapter 6.

The literature on large-scale social structure is vast. It includes such topics as differences in the structure of various industries which lead to differences in technological innovativeness; differences between urban, suburban, and rural living; ethnic differences such as the purchase patterns of blacks and whites; demographic differences such as the age distribution of a population; and differences among various occupations that cause differences in communication patterns. These and many other large-scale social structures are important in trying to understand consumer behavior. Unfortunately, we cannot touch upon all of these. This chapter will present an approach to differentiating between the cultures of different nations. Social class, as an expression of social differences, will also be discussed, as will mobility, status, and several other related concepts. Industries as social systems will be discussed, including a differentiation of public sector from private sector industries.

DIFFERENCES AMONG NATIONS

A major basis for distinguishing one social structure from another is that of geopolitical boundaries. Consider the advertisement in Figure 4-1 by a firm specializing in the development of fragrances for use with a wide variety of products. This firm is active in a large number of countries and in virtually all parts of the world, thus indicating how universally pervasive the commercial use of fragrance is. A spokesperson for this firm pointed out two particular facets of this advertisement. First, by indicating the variety of countries in which they maintained offices and/or laboratories, they were saying to the product manager that each country has its own unique set of requirements concerning the use of fragrances. For example, while a lemon fragrance may indicate "freshness" in the United States, it may connote ill-health in the Philippines, so this would hardly be the kind of fragrance to have in a dishwashing detergent in that country. Most importantly, the advertisement suggests that the world is changing and product fragrances may also have to be changed from time to time. In most countries there apparently are fads and fashions concerning fragrances. So-called sweet smells are less popular now in Kuwait and parts of Latin America compared to a few years ago. This has suggested product modification in certain canned foods and household supplies being exported to these areas.

Let us turn now to a different and more extended example. The discussion to follow is based on an actual attempt by a commercial firm to differentiate between various developing countries, and the same procedure would apply to differentiating between various groups *within* any particular country.

FIGURE 4-1.

The idea of fine fragrances created in Brooklyn may seem foreign to you. But not to us.

We're Felton. From Brooklyn.

Our fragrances can and do compete successfully with anything produced by our competitors from across the river. And across the ocean.

The reason is simple.

Felton has a talented team of highly creative perfumers. Supported by the latest in fragrance technology. And backed by an international organization committed to quality and service.

When you think about it, that's all it takes to create exceptional fragrances. That, and a whole lot of hard work. Which is what you'll get from Felton.

After all, when you're from Brooklyn, you just have to work harder.

A pharmaceutical firm intending to introduce multiple-vitamin tablets in developing countries was faced with the task of selecting two countries in which to test market strategies and product acceptability. Their marketing program was partially supported by an agency of the United Nations. A team of social scientists from the United Nations worked with the marketing staff of the pharmaceutical firm.

The Basic Propositions Guiding the Marketing Research

The basic initial task was to determine which of the many developing countries in Africa, Asia, and Latin America had social structures most conducive to accepting new products. Several propositions were developed by the team. A few of these propositions are presented in Exhibit 4-1.* Figure 4-2 portrays the basic propositions in graphic form.

EXHIBIT 4-1.
Propositions Related to Climate for Change

PROPOSITION 4-1.
The larger the number and variety of mass media channels in a society, the greater the communication exposure of consumers.

PROPOSITION 4-2.
The greater the communication exposure, the more favorable is the climate for change.

PROPOSITION 4-3.
The greater the desire for excellence in order to accomplish personal goals (that is, the higher the need for achievement), the more favorable the climate for change in a society.

*The reader is reminded once again that these propositions are based on research findings. Since these statements are not natural laws, however, they could therefore conceivably change with future research. In addition, though they are drawn from research in specific contexts, they are often stated in such a way as to appear applicable regardless of the context. Hence, the reader is encouraged to consider the propositions as descriptive of current basic research findings. This must be done, however, with skepticism and openness, which are necessary to the understanding of any subject matter, and creativity, which is needed when adapting and applying the propositions.

FIGURE 4-2.
Selected Factors
Affecting Climate for
Change

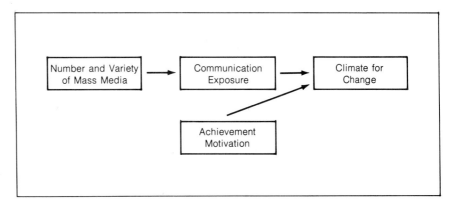

The culture of a society having the better developed communication system provides more opportunity for the marketer to disseminate information about a product to a large variety of people. In assessing the number and variety of communication channels in other countries, the marketer must be careful not to focus on only the mass media. In some Latin American countries where literacy is low, parades, the clergy, and cartoons carrying messages to movie audiences are important communication channels.[3] Thus, the adequacy of communication channels was an important consideration in the decision of which countries would be selected as possible markets for the firm's vitamin tablets.

The project team also relied on another proposition: The greater the desire for excellence in order to accomplish personal goals, the more favorable the climate for change in a society. This personal desire for excellence or need for achievement has been intensively studied with regard to developing nations.[4] Societies whose members have a high need for achievement are more likely to have and to use institutions which improve well-being, such as medical centers and adult education centers. This, in turn, reinforces the original achievement motivation. As a by-product of this desire and the available institutional structures for satisfying it, there will be a general openness to products and services which promise to enhance aspects of well-being such as health. The implication is that new products will be more easily introduced in

[3]Everett M. Rogers, "Social Structure and Social Change," in G. Zaltman (ed.), *Processes and Phenomena of Social Change,* NY: Wiley-Interscience, 1973, pp. 75–87.

[4]J. W. Atkinson (ed.), *Motives in Fantasy, Action, and Society,* Princeton, NJ: Van Nostrand, 1958; and David C. McClelland, *The Achieving Society,* NY: The Free Press, 1961.

systems where achievement motivation is high and where the product or service being offered can be related explicitly to a particular desire for well-being such as the concern for health.

The project team consisting of both United Nations personnel and personnel from the pharmaceutical firm constructed a large matrix for evaluating the countries, using the ten factors in Table 4-1. Each factor is a variable which can be used for noting differences among nations. A small version of this matrix shown on the next page. Several countries were eliminated on the basis of essentially political considerations.

TABLE 4-1.
Individual Factors Associated with Societal Change

Literacy	The degree to which an individual possesses mastery over symbols in their written form.
Mass media exposure	Exposure to such communication channels as newspapers, radio, films, and so forth.
Cosmopoliteness	The degree to which an individual is oriented outside his social system.
Empathy	The individual's ability to identify with others' roles, especially with those who are different from oneself.
Achievement motivation	A social value that emphasizes a desire for excellence in order for an individual to attain a sense of personal accomplishment.
Aspiration	Desired future state of being.
Fatalism	The degree to which an individual perceives a lack of ability to control his future.
Innovativeness	The degree to which an individual is earlier than others in his social system to adopt new ideas.
Political knowledge	The degree to which an individual comprehends facts essential to his functioning as an active and effective citizen.
Opinion leadership	The ability to influence informally other individuals' attitudes in a desired way and with relatively high frequency.

Source: Everett M. Rogers, *Modernization Among Peasants,* NY: Holt, Rinehart & Winston, 1969.

	Country 1	Country 2	Country 3
Structure of Mass Media	Favorable	Favorable	Unfavorable
Structure of Achievement Motivation	Favorable	Unfavorable	Unfavorable

(Partial Matrix Based on Table 4-1)

Thus, in the simplified matrix, countries 1, 2, and 3 are different from one another on the basis of two factors: mass media and achievement motivation. This evaluation indicates that country 1 is the most preferred country for the initial distribution of the special vitamin tablets.

The reader should realize that although this example involved different countries, one could easily substitute subgroups within a given country. These subgroups may be characterized by ethnic, geographical, social class, or numerous other differentiating criteria.

Climate for Change   The project team then tried to clarify their concept of "climate for change." This concept was divided into five factors: perceived need for change; openness to change; potential for change; perceived control over the change process; and commitment to change. Table 4-2 defines each of these components of the climate for change. The potential for change, for example, refers to existing capabilities such as financial resources, material resources, and human resources, which can be used in accepting and implementing the change.

Marketers must determine what kinds of resources are necessary to consumers in order for them to implement change. In the vitamin case, the pharmaceutical firm had to identify the resources consumers needed in order to accept and use vitamins. Since the price was subsidized in this case, financial resources were of lesser importance than the level of knowledge among consumers about vitamin needs and their relevance to physical well-being. A favorable attitude toward taking pills was also necessary. Consumers in different cultures differ with respect to whether they believe taking pills is an

TABLE 4-2.	Perceived need for change	The extent to which an individual or group experiences a problem.
Factors Involved in the	Openness to change	The readiness to accept change.
Climate for Change	Potential for change	The capacity to accept and implement change.
	Perceived control over the change process	The extent to which the individual or group feels it can influence the selection and implementation of the change.
	Commitment to change	The recognition of the importance of undertaking remedial action (social change) in response to a problem.

effective medical treatment. The availability of effective channels of distribution is another important resource.

Effect of Individual Change Factors on Climate for Change

Each of the factors associated with change (Table 4-1) is related to one or more factors associated with the general climate for change (Table 4-2). Here we shall discuss only the most prominent associations between the two sets of factors (see cells with an "X" in Table 4-3).

Literacy. Literacy appears to have its strongest association and causal impact on openness to change and on potential for change.[5] Becoming literate appears to unlock creative abilities which enable consumers to mentally picture themselves using the product being sold. This suggests Propositions 4-4 and 4-5 in Exhibit 4-2 (Note Figure 4-3). The higher the literacy skills of consumers and the more accustomed they are to reading, the greater their flexibility in thinking; and greater flexibility in thinking increases the readiness

[5]For an excellent discussion of the profound impacts of literacy on culture, see Jack Goody and Ian Watt, "The Consequences of Literacy," *Comparative Studies in Society and History,* Vol. 5, 1963.

TABLE 4-3.	Components of Climate for Change				
Effect of Individual Change Factors on Components of Climate for Change					
Individual Change Factors	*Perceived need for change*	*Openness to change*	*Potential for change*	*Commitment to change*	*Perceived control over the change process*
Literacy		X	X		
Mass media	X			X	
Cosmopoliteness	X				
Empathy			X		
Achievement motivation		X			
Aspirations	X				
Fatalism				X	X
Innovativeness		X			
Political knowledge					X
Opinion leadership					X

to accept new products. Literacy enhances the potential for change by satisfying the first criterion—being able to read—for reaching people through the printed media. The addition of this channel of communication increases the ability of the individual to comprehend new ideas. The greater the consumers' reading abilities and the more materials they read, the more likely it is that they will possess the knowledge or skills necessary to accept and use new products in an effective manner.

Mass Media. Mass media exposure is especially important for establishing a perceived need for change. To the extent that exposure to a variety of media makes individuals aware of more desirable alternatives for satisfying current needs, these communication media can create or enhance a perceived need for change.

EXHIBIT 4-2.
*Propositions
Involving Literacy
(Reading Skills),
Flexibility in
Thinking, and
Empathy*

PROPOSITION 4-4.
The better the reading skills of consumers and the more accustomed they are to reading, the greater their flexibility in thinking.

PROPOSITION 4-5.
The greater the flexibility in thinking among consumers, the greater their readiness to accept new products.

PROPOSITION 4-6.
The more consumers can empathize with a salesperson, the more readily they will buy products and services advocated by the salesperson.

Cosmopoliteness. Cosmopoliteness appears to function in a manner similar to mass media exposure. By having ties to others outside the immediate area, cosmopolite consumers have broadened exposure to and experience with products and services which may solve current problems. The advertisement shown in Figure 4-4 is an attempt to create a cosmopolite worldly image for a firm which had an image of being "local" and unexciting in its product offerings. According to the firm's management, this and other promotional themes stressing a more cosmopolite image had a very favorable impact on product managers who buy fragrances and for whom a cosmopolitan image is important.

Empathy. Empathy is probably most closely associated with potential for change. The greater the degree to which consumers can identify with a salesperson and view their situation from the vantage point of the salesperson, the easier it will be for consumers to accept and implement change (this is reflected in Proposition 4-6 and in Figure 4-3). Empathy also affects potential for change in another related way. It permits the customer with empathetic abilities to experience vicariously (through an existing user of a product) the consequences of adopting the product. It is important, of course, to choose as models persons with whom consumers may easily identify. For example, ten years ago, the diamond conglomerate De Beers made a major attempt to increase the sale of diamonds in Japan. Their advertisements used European models and copy themes which had worked successfully in Europe. The campaign failed miserably. They quickly switched to Japanese models and

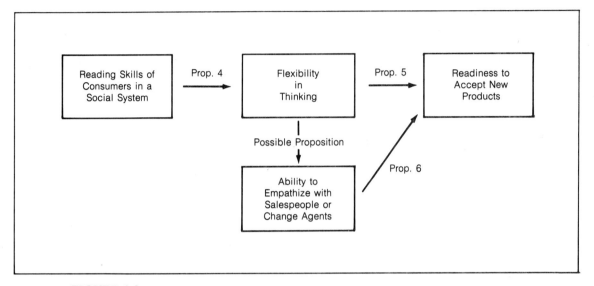

FIGURE 4-3.
Relationships Among Factors Affecting Readiness to Accept New Products in a Given Social System

appeals. For example, a fawn is a strong image for a lovely, virginal girl in Japan. The romantic copy accompanying one very successful diamond advertisement read: "Who whispered the words of love to a fawn astray in the forest of dreams and yearnings? Who lovingly kissed her hand?" Needless to say, the picture in the advertisement was a lovely and presumably virginal young Japanese woman whose hand had been "lovingly kissed" with a diamond ring.

Achievement Motivation.   Achievement motivation enhances openness to change by sensitizing consumers to products and services which could be helpful in achieving their desired goals. Many educational products, especially for children, are sold because parents desire to improve a child's intellectual skills.

Aspiration.   The more a desired future state of being differs from a present state of being, the greater the perceived need for change will be. Marketers are often concerned with stressing the feasibility of having a different and presumably better future state of being.

Fatalism.   Fatalism is relevant to perceived control over the purchase and use of the product. Strong fatalistic attitudes are reflected in *action apathy*: "Since-there-is-nothing-I-can-do-about-it-why-bother?" Fatalistic consumers

FIGURE 4-4.

deny that any purchase can help them or that the consumer has any control over what manufacturers produce. There is an element of self-fulfilling prophecy here. If consumers believe they have no control over the manufacturing and quality of a product, then they will not be selective in their purchases. As a result, the manufacturers will not have the adequate consumer feedback necessary to know what consumers actually need and prefer. Also, it has been found that people with a fatalistic attitude complain less than others to retail stores and manufacturers if they are unhappy with a product.

Innovativeness. Openness to change, or innovativeness, results in a readiness to accept new products. In other words, readiness to accept change leads to the adoption, or acceptance, and use of the change (in this case, the product). This topic is discussed at length in Chapter 18.

Political Knowledge. Political knowledge is the degree to which individuals comprehend facts essential to their being active and effective citizens. Apart from an awareness of public affairs, political knowledge may be a good indicator of other less readily measured factors such as how well people are integrated into society.[6] Political knowledge is closely associated with perceived control over the change process.

Opinion Leadership. Opinion leadership is the ability to informally influence others' attitudes in a desired way with relatively high frequency. The greater a consumer's awareness of this influence, the greater his or her perceived control over the change process. As a result a consumer's awareness of his or her ability to informally influence other people may lead to frequent, deliberate attempts to exercise this influence. This topic is discussed again in Chapters 9 and 18.

An important caution is in order here, the *caution of transferability*. Many concepts such as empathy, achievement motivation, and climate for change have been mentioned. The marketer must examine very carefully (1) whether these concepts are relevant for a particular culture, and if so, (2) how these concepts are expressed in the culture. Empathy may be a relevant concept for a product or service in many cultures but the answer to the question, "Empathy with whom?" may vary as the marketer goes from one culture to another. Thus, in promoting cigarettes in the United States, a ranch hand may

[6]Emile Durkheim, *The Division of Labor in Society,* George Simpson (trans.), NY: The Free Press, 1964.

be someone with whom diverse consumers may identify, while in Venezuela such a person would be inappropriate.

Let us shift our attention now from global social structures involving differences among nations to structures, such as social class, which involve differences within a given nation. As mentioned earlier, every factor differentiating one country from another could be used to differentiate groups within countries.

SOCIAL CLASS

A social class is a group of people with similar levels of prestige and esteem who also share a set of related beliefs, attitudes, and values which they express in their thinking and behavior. A person's social class is the group with which the person is similar in these respects. The concept of social class has long been considered a major factor for explaining consumer behavior.[7] Until recently, one of the most frequent measures of social class was a combination of source of income, level of education and occupation. Some measures have since deleted income, replacing it with property value, while others use just education and occupation. These factors divide consumers into six social class categories: lower-lower, upper-lower, lower-middle, upper-middle, lower-upper, and upper-upper.

Major social changes in the United States have made conventional social class measures less reliable predictors and explainers of market behavior. Possibly, the concept of social class, as conventionally used in the consumer behavior literature, is no longer helpful.[8] This is *not* to say that social classes do not exist, for they most certainly do. Rather, traditional measures of social class appear to be unreliable in explaining and predicting many consumer behavior patterns. Certainly there are differences in consumers' behaviors associated with differences in their income, education, and occupation. Each of these variables, however, might best be employed independently of the others and their relevance reassessed for particular groups of products and

[7]Pierre Martineau, "Social Classes and Spending Behavior," *Journal of Marketing,* Vol. 23, October, 1975, pp. 121–141; and Richard P. Coleman, "The Significance of Social Stratification in Selling," in *Marketing: A Maturing Discipline,* Martin L. Bell (ed.), Chicago: American Marketing Association, 1961, pp. 171–184.
[8]Dominguez and Page, *op. cit.*

services; but they probably should not continue to be utilized to construct a social class index which is then used to predict and explain consumer behavior. In this section we will first discuss how social class has traditionally been measured and some problems with this approach. Some suggestions for change are made. We then review several studies of social class and its effect on consumer behavior.

Problems With Marketers' Approach To The Concept Of Social Class

Marketers are quite interested in the relationship between a consumer's social status and his or her purchasing patterns. Social classes are status groups which are differentiated by various factors such as the member's education, occupation, income, possessions, family background, performance in occupation, community service, friends and acquaintances, club and organizational memberships, and residence area. The relative importance of these factors varies from situation to situation. In general, the better off a consumer is on any one factor, the more social status he or she has.

There are correlations between some of these factors. For instance, people from wealthy families usually have better opportunities for entering prestigious occupations and reaching high income levels.

Marketers, who are very interested in the concept of social class, believe there is a high correlation between a consumer's social class and his or her purchasing patterns. This includes what is purchased, where it is purchased, the frequency of the purchases, the means of payment, the reasons for the purchase, and the cognitive processes involved in coming to a decision. Without denying the possibility that the concept of social class is both analytically useful and relevant for marketers, it is necessary, as stated earlier, to closely examine the ways marketers have used the concept.

There have been many problems with the way marketers have measured social class. The most widely used measurement technique has been an index developed by W. Lloyd Warner.[9] This index combines four variables with the following weights:

---

[9]W. Lloyd Warner, Marcia Meeker, and Kenneth Eels, *Social Class in America: A Manual of Procedure for the Measurement of Social Status,* Chicago: Science Research Associates, 1949.

Occupation rating	× 4
Sources of income rating	× 3
(wages, salary, investment)	
House type rating	× 3
Dwelling area rating	× 2

At least one sociologist, Marcus Felson, criticized marketing's reliance on this measurement technique:

> What most market researchers call "social class" is a 20-year-out-of-date concept popularized by W. Lloyd Warner. The Warnerian model of social class is characterized by (1) reasonably clear-cut class boundaries, (2) a single dimension summarizing social inequality, and (3) a single type of relationship between social class and other variables.
>
> Warner's model simply cannot stand up to the evidence collected in modern America for several reasons. First, the correlations among stratification variables taking individuals or households as units of analysis are not so high that one can reasonably treat social class as a single dimension....Second, stratification variables have causal relationships to one another which Warner ignored. ... Third, education, occupation, race, and other stratification variables often have *different* sorts of consequences for social life....Fourth, Warner failed to consider how various rewards come at various stages of the life cycle or even change in the period of a few years....Fifth, Warner did not realize that clear boundaries between social strata simply do not exist with respect to most stratification variables.[10]

Instead of the Warnerian approach, Felson suggests that marketers consider the availability of various opportunities to consumers. Such opportunities would include the availability of material resources (including money, often measured by income), time, knowledge, ability (which varies by age), and stage in the life cycle.

Inclusion of opportunity availability as well as other social class concepts should make social class a more useful concept for marketers. However, before these other concepts are introduced and related to consumer behavior, the deficiencies of marketers' current approach to the concept of social class must be enumerated.

Marketing's treatment of social class suffers from its:

(1) Neglect of the process whereby social strata or levels develop (how and why certain positions become associated with certain levels of prestige).

(2) Assumption that a person's social class is an average of his or her positions on several prestige hierarchies, thus ignoring the effects of various

[10]Marcus Felson, "A Modern Sociological Approach to the Stratification of Material Lifestyles," in *Advances in Consumer Research*, Vol. 2, Chicago, 1975, pp. 33–34.

kinds of *status inconsistency*,[11] whereby people might rank high on one dimension (e.g., income) but low on another dimension (e.g., education).

(3) Assumption that a person's present social class is and has always been stable, thus ignoring the effects of *intergenerational mobility, career mobility,* and *status persistence* (class of origin characteristics which stayed with the mobile person).[12]

(4) Assumption that a person identifies with the social class with which he or she objectively is measured, thus ignoring the effects of reference groups other than one's own social class (*subjective social class* and *class consciousness*).

(5) Neglect of the effect of a person's aspirations and plans for the future (*mobility aspirations*).

(6) Occasional confusion of the variables which are indices of social class with social class itself (i.e., education, income, occupation, and possessions are each highly correlated with social class, but are not actual measures of social class—they are proxy variables used to make estimations of a person's social class).

(7) Measurement of status by examining consumers' positions in the social system while ignoring their performance in that position as another element of social status.[13]

(8) Measurement of the social class of an entire family by examining only the characteristics of the adult male wage earner, thus ignoring the effects of family size, and the employment and education of the adult female in the family.

(9) Inattention to the effect of marketing efforts on the stratification system.

Propositions about the effects of some of these variables (e.g., status inconsistency, mobility, and stratification system development) will be discussed later in this chapter. Although their inclusion makes the study of the relationship between social class and consumer behavior more complex, it also produces richer discoveries and more useful action implications.

---

[11]Elton Jackson, "Status Inconsistency and Symptoms of Stress," *American Sociological Review,* Vol. 27, August, 1972, pp. 469–480.

[12]Leo Goodman, "On the Measurement of Social Mobility: An Index of Status Persistence," *American Sociological Review,* Vol. 34, December, 1969, pp. 831–850.

[13]James Kimberly, "A Theory of Status Equilibration," in J. Berger, *et al.* (eds.), *Sociological Theories in Progress,* Vol. 1, Boston: Houghton-Mifflin Co., 1966, pp. 213–226.

Studies of Social Class and Consumer Behavior

Certainly, there have been problems with the way social class has been used to explain consumer behavior. Changes are needed in the dimensions used, their weightings, and the ways in which they are combined. In spite of these problems, however, there have been several studies of the relationship between social class and consumer behavior which provide useful insights.

Shopping Behaviors. The authors of one study indicate that social class and life-style may be of limited value or at least of less value than in earlier years in predicting certain shopping behaviors.[14] They argue that such changes as increases in discretionary income, increased educational opportunities, and movement to suburbia have had a homogenizing effect on certain consumption behaviors. For instance, this study found that women in all social classes and life cycle stages did not differ with regard to:

(1) Interest in fashion (all classes were equally interested).
(2) Use and perceived value of newspapers as a source of information about fashion (all thought newspapers were important).
(3) The influence of friends on shopping.

Life cycle and social class did not differentiate among women in their enjoyment of shopping; however, some differences associated with social class were found in the reasons for enjoying shopping. Lower-class persons seemed to enjoy the acquisition of products more, whereas a pleasant store atmosphere, display, and excitement were specified as reasons for enjoying shopping by a greater proportion of the women in the upper-middle, lower-upper and upper-upper classes.[15]

Social class was found to be related to the choice of downtown or suburban shopping centers. The lower the social class, the greater the proportion of shopping done in downtown areas, a phenomenon explained by the concentration of persons of lower-class status in urban areas.

This study also suggests that the higher a woman's social status, the greater the preference for shopping in regular department stores. This is consistent with the findings of research on discount store shoppers in small cities, which found a significant inverse relationship between a shopper's social class and the volume of purchases of clothing and household textiles at discount stores.[16]

[14]Stuart A. Rich and Subhash C. Jain, "Social Class and Life Cycle as Predictors of Shopping Behavior," *Journal of Marketing Research,* Vol. 5, February, 1968, pp. 41–49.
[15]*Ibid.,* p. 44.
[16]Rachael Dardis and Marie Sandler, "Shopping Behavior of Discount Store Customers in a Small City," *Journal of Retailing,* Vol. 47, 1971, pp. 60–72.

Credit Usage   The relative importance of social class and income as segmentation variables with respect to credit has been examined.[17] Investigators in one study hypothesized "that installment and convenience use of credit cards would vary among social classes within an economic level."[18] The measure of social class was based on occupational and educational variables. The researcher found that use of commercial bank credit cards varied by social class alone and by income alone. The researchers "were not able to conclude that social class within a given income class is a good indicator of credit card behavior . . . Social class does not significantly differentiate credit behavior within all income categories."[19]

It was found, however, that "Within different social classes income levels demonstrate an effect upon attitudes toward charging goods."[20] This was true primarily in the case of the middle social class, where the higher income groups were more favorably disposed to the use of credit than were lower income groups. In the lower-middle income category ($7,000–$9,000) persons with higher social class had more favorable attitudes toward charging goods. The researchers conclude that social class may not be as good an indicator of buying behavior, and hence not of as much value as a segmentation variable, as earlier writers have claimed. With respect to credit card use, income may be at least as good an indicator as social class. Thus, the relevance of social class may very well vary according to product and situation.

Decision Making.   Fry and Siller compared working-class and middle-class homemakers in their purchase decision making.[21] Using a simulated shopping experience they compared behavior in the scope and duration of product search, and price sensitivity. In general, they found the two groups to be quite similar along these dimensions. The researcher did make certain inferences about their data, however, which, when coupled with other plausible inferences, lead to the following idea: Working-class women are more likely than middle-class women to attribute shopping difficulties to characteristics unique to their own personal and social situation rather than to charac-

---

[17]John W. Slocum and H. Lee Mathews, "Social Class and Income as Indicators of Consumer Behavior," *Journal of Marketing,* Vol. 34, No. 2, April, 1970, pp. 69–74.

[18]*Ibid.,* p. 70.

[19]*Ibid,* p. 71.

[20]*Ibid.,* p. 73.

[21]Joseph N. Fry and Frederick H. Siller, "A Comparison of Housewife Decision Making in Two Social Classes," *Journal of Marketing Research,* Vol. 7, August, 1970, pp. 333–337.

EXHIBIT 4-3.
*Propositions About
Social Class*

PROPOSITION 4-7.
Level of income has a stronger impact than education, property value, and occupation combined on the decision to purchase products for in-home use which are of a staple and inconspicuous nature.

PROPOSITION 4-8.
Regardless of the level of economic risk, the greater the social risk of a product, the greater are the differences between consumers of different social classes in their patronage attitudes toward discount stores. In the case of products with high social risk, higher social classes will have less favorable attitudes toward discount stores than will lower social classes.

PROPOSITION 4-9.
The less the social risk of a product, the less the difference between consumers of different social classes in their patronage attitudes toward discount stores. This holds for products of all levels of economic risk.

PROPOSITION 4-10.
The buying behavior of the overprivileged blue-collar workers is much closer to the behavior of the overprivileged professional and white-collar workers than it is to the behavior of the (lower income) blue-collar workers.

teristics unique to the product or service (Chapter 17 will deal more extensively with attribution processes).

One implication of this idea is that working-class women may be more reluctant than middle-class women to try new products and services because they believe they lack the personal knowledge and skills necessary to assess the quality of the new product. This causes working-class women to rely more upon price as an indicator of quality than would middle-class women. Thus, in an instance where price does not reflect quality, the marketer might reassure the working-class woman that she *is* capable of discerning differences among products. This may involve providing guidelines for making comparisons and judgments. Thus, advertising which compares competing brands might be particularly appropriate. Price deals may be most effective when used to attract older working-class women. On the other hand, price deals may be least effective when used to attract high-volume consumers among middle-class women.

Social Class and Level of Income. Myers, Stanton, and Haug compared social class and level of income to determine which is the superior correlate of buyer behavior for selected consumer goods.[22] They used three items to measure social class: education, property value (or amount of rent paid), and occupation. The types of products studied were household toiletries, drugs, cosmetics, soaps, paper, various household plastic items, soft drinks and liquor, frozen and nonfrozen foods, and pet foods. The researchers observed the presence ("having on hand") of these products in the home rather than the volume consumed. The particular brands on hand were not studied, and for the most part the items were staple products rather than "expensive" items which might have more social significance.

Taking into account some of the limitations of this study, a general finding can be presented as Proposition 4-7: Level of income has a stronger impact than social class on the decision to purchase products for in-home use which are of a staple and inconspicuous nature. Again, social class here means a particular combination of education, property value or rent paid, and occupation. The impact of social class considered alone is usually greater for convenience-type products as opposed to other types of products.

An action implication of Proposition 4-7 is that the promotion of staple food products should be based on income rather than social class differences. This suggests the use of deals such as "cents-off" coupons and introductory offers which manipulate the price of the good or service being sold.

However, other researchers in a different context went beyond this comparison of income and social class as predictors of purchase.[23] They also examined the relationship between income and social class on the one hand and *frequency* of involvement in various recreational activities. They found that income was a better predictor than social class of whether the person had participated in the activity during the past year. Social class was a better

---

[22]James H. Myers, Roger R. Stanton, and Arne F. Haug, "Correlates of Buying Behavior: Social Class *vs.* Income," *Journal of Marketing,* Vol. 35, No. 4, October, 1971, pp. 8–15.
[23]Robert D. Hirsch and Michael P. Peters, "Selecting the Superior Segmentation Correlate," *Journal of Marketing,* 38 (July 1974), 60–63.

predictor, however, of *how frequently* the person had participated in the activity during that time period. For example, lower-class people participated in bowling more frequently than did upper-class people. This implies that social class affects the frequency of the use of a product or service more strongly than it affects whether the person will make at least one purchase.

Patronage Preferences and Product Risk. Prasad has investigated the relationship between social class and patronage attitudes toward discount stores.[24] Two propositions were suggested, both of which received strong support. The first proposition was: "For the purchase of products of high social risk (i.e., the risk that other people will disapprove) consumers in different social classes differ significantly in their patronage attitudes toward discount stores. This pattern is believed to remain regardless of the level of economic risk generally associated with products."[25] The second proposition was: "For the purchase of products of low social risk, consumers in different social classes do not differ significantly in their patronage attitudes toward discount stores. This pattern is hypothesized to hold regardless of the level of the economic risk generally associated with the products."[26]

The two propositions above were based on earlier research.[27] These and other research studies indicated the importance of distinguishing social risk from economic risk, and understanding the role of personal influence within a social class for products involving social risk.

Four product risk categories involving twenty-four products were used in Prasad's study. These are shown in Figure 4-5. An index of social class was constructed using the education and occupation of the male heads of households, with female shoppers as the respondents in the study. Both of the above propositions were supported. "In the case of the products with low social (risk) – low economic risk and those with low social (risk) – high economic risk, there were no statistically significant differences in patronage attitudes toward discount stores among consumers of different social classes. On the other hand, for products of high social (risk) – low economic risk, consumers in different social classes differed significantly in their patronage

---

[24]V. Kanti Prasad, "Socio-economic Product Risk and Patronage Preferences of Retail Shoppers," *Journal of Marketing,* Vol. 39, July, 1975.

[25]*Ibid.,* p. 43.

[26]*Ibid.*

[27]Robert Hisrich, Ronald Dornoff, and Jerome Kerman, "Perceived in Store Selection," *Journal of Marketing Research,* Vol. 9, November, 1972, pp. 453–459; and Michael Perry and B. C. Hamm, "Canonical Analysis of Relations Between Socio-Economic Risk and Personal Influence

FIGURE 4-5.
*Product Risk
Categorization*

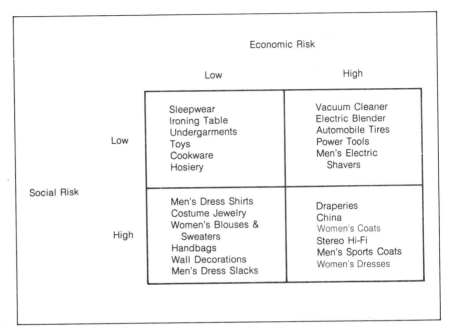

	Economic Risk	
	Low	**High**
Low	Sleepwear Ironing Table Undergarments Toys Cookware Hosiery	Vacuum Cleaner Electric Blender Automobile Tires Power Tools Men's Electric Shavers
High	Men's Dress Shirts Costume Jewelry Women's Blouses & Sweaters Handbags Wall Decorations Men's Dress Slacks	Draperies China Women's Coats Stereo Hi-Fi Men's Sports Coats Women's Dresses

Social Risk (row label)

attitudes toward discount stores."[28] The higher social classes, as compared to lower social classes, displayed less favorable attitudes toward discount stores for high social risk products. Interestingly, level of income was found to be as good as this index of social class as a predictor of patronage attitudes toward discount stores for the four groups of products in Figure 4-5. Both level of income alone and social class alone as predictors yielded the same pattern of responses.

Both propositions have important implications for retailers. First, retailers must realize that the product category may be a significant determinant of a shopper's patronage—stores will be perceived differently by different social classes depending upon the social risk involved in the purchase of a particular product. Second, marketers may find it effective to differentiate their operations by product categories. For example, a manufacturer or large retailer might use a discount store operation for distributing products of low social risk; and, on the other hand, an attractive store with many services might be more appealing to higher social class customers for products involving high social risk. Filenes of Boston and H. C. Prange Company of Wisconsin have

---

[28]Prasad, *op. cit.,* p. 45.

used this technique successfully. Third, retailers may want to use promotional themes stressing the particular appropriateness of their store for products involving social risk. This could be done through testimonials describing a store as the place at which wise buyers shop.

Relative Income.   The concept of "relative occupational class income" is interesting and important.[29] This concept refers to the relationship between a family's total income and the median income for the same occupational class. Families whose total gross income is above the median range are over-privileged," and those below the median range are "underprivileged." Those in the median range are "average." One researcher has raised the following questions: Is the buying behavior of overprivileged blue-collar workers, white-collar workers, and professionals similar? Or, do all blue-collar workers have similar buying behavior? Is relative occupational class income a better tool for market segmentation than either absolute income level or occupation use alone?

The data from this study suggest and support the following proposition: "The buying behavior of the overprivileged blue-collar workers (is) much closer to the behavior of the overprivileged professional and white-collar workers than it (is) to the behavior of the less fortunate blue-collar workers."[30] This proposition was tested in automobile markets. The "average" income class in all occupational groupings was found to own more foreign, economy, intermediate-sized, and compact cars than would be expected. The over-privileged group, regardless of occupation, clearly owned more medium-sized and large cars than would be expected. Implicit in this work is the idea that consumers' behavior changes in response to their deviation from the median income for their occupational grouping, and that occupational grouping per se is relevant only for determining this deviation. Thus, occupation alone is not a good predictor of market behavior. If this is true, it is very important, for it suggests that occupation is less meaningful as a predictor of consumer be-havior than has been believed in the past. This weakens positions which call for the inclusion of occupation as a component of social class. It must be stressed, however, that Peters studied only the automobile market. His ap-proach should be tested in other contexts.

---

[29]William Peters, "Relative Occupational Class Income: A Significant Variable in the Market-ing of Automobiles," *Journal of Marketing,* Vol. 34, No. 2, April, 1970, pp. 74–77; see also an earlier work by Richard P. Coleman, "The Significance of Social Stratification in Selling," in Martin Bell (ed.), *Marketing: A Maturing Discipline, Proceedings of Winter Conference of American Marketing Association,* 1960, pp. 171–184.
[30]Peters, *op cit.,* p. 75.

The implication of the concept of relative occupational class income is clear. Rather than relying simply upon level of income as an indication of ability to buy, the marketer should also consider income relative to the median occupational class income. Median occupational income may serve as a more important frame of reference than occupational category.

In other research, the styles of consumers' living rooms have been found to reflect social status. Such differences are now much less related to income than they were several years ago.[31] Observations made in the home by salespersons or interviewers should no longer be used as readily to estimate a client's social class, intentions, and ability to buy. Rather, furniture and other objects in living rooms often reflect the consumer's education and occupation. For products associated with education and occupation, the use and style of a living room in an advertisement should reflect a particular occupation or education level. For example, an advertisement selling low-cost life insurance involved an interview with a husband and wife who evidently had little education and a low occupational status. A sizable library was in the background and two large art books were on the coffee table. This display of books was very inconsistent with the reading habits of persons buying low-cost life insurance and with the implied educational and occupational background of the persons interviewed. This particular advertisement carried little credibility and was discontinued after ten days.

Social Mobility

Just as people experience geographic mobility (as discussed in the previous chapter), they also experience social mobility, which is a movement from one social status to another. The social mobility of consumers may be a central basis for marketing strategy. For example, Estee Lauder, a producer of cosmetics and toiletries, has designed many of its new men's fragrances and toiletries for men who are upwardly mobile socially. Promotional imagery for these products is designed to be consistent with the customers' "good taste and fantasies of upward mobility."[32]

Two consumers of the same status position may have very different purchasing patterns because of past mobility, present mobility, or anticipated mobility.[33] Traditional measures of social class analyze only a consumer's

---

[31]Marcus Felson, "Social Stratification in Household Attributes: Changes Since the Great Depression," paper presented at the American Sociological Association, August, 1975.

[32]Peters, *op. cit.,* p. 76.

[33]Melvin M. Turmin, *Social Stratification: The Forms and Functions of Inequality,* Englewood Cliffs, NJ: Prentice-Hall, 1967.

present social class position, and do not take into account the past social class, the mobility processes currently being experienced of which present social class is merely a phase, or one's expectations about the future. Social mobility, however, can have a profound effect on one's purchasing patterns. A consumer who is upwardly mobile with respect to income, education, or some other indicator of status is likely to engage in the consumption patterns characteristic of the status grouping toward which he or she is striving. The upwardly mobile consumer, relative to the "stationary consumer" at the same status level, might buy many more things, or purchase higher quality commodities, or both. Figure 4-6 shows an advertisement intended for upwardly mobile consumers. Such a consumer is likely to be more sensitive to brand names and prices. This price sensitivity, however, is not for economic reasons, but for social reasons, for this consumer may seek expensive brands rather than avoid them. Unfortunately, there has been little sound research into the effects of upward and downward mobility on consumption patterns. Also, little is known about the differential effects on consumption caused by the *anticipations* of upward or downward mobility.

In probing the mobility patterns of consumers it may be useful to refer to the definitional description in Table 4-4 of the components of social mobility.

In one hypothesis about social mobility (referred to as the "disassociative hypothesis"), the consumer who is upwardly mobile is believed to participate less in the norms, beliefs, values, and pressures for conformity of both the status level left behind (the status of origination) and the status level sought (the status of destination). This usually produces anxiety, alienation, and insecurity.[34] Thus, we have Proposition 4-11: If consumers, when shifting from one status level to another, do not participate in any substantial way in the values, attitudes, and beliefs of either the status of origination or that of the destination, a feeling of insecurity is likely. This is not necessarily true for all consumers. It is, however, a likely event.

There are at least two important implications of Proposition 4-11. First, since mobile consumers may feel insecure or anxious, care should be exercised to show the compatibility of a product or service with the status of destination. Secondly, promotional appeals may be used to show that others may also feel the same way, that uncertainty is not uncommon or even bad, and that the product or service is a way of reducing anxiety. This may be done, for instance, by demonstrating the acceptability of the product by both

---

[34]For example, cf. Pitirim Sorokin, *Social and Cultural Mobility*, NY: The Free Press, 1959; and Robert Stuckert, "Occupational Mobility and Family Relationships," *Social Forces*, March, 1963, pp. 301–307.

FIGURE 4-6.

UPWARD MOBILITY FOR THE WHOLE FAMILY...THE LIVELY DATSUN 710.

Would your family like to move up in the world?

We say more power to you—the power of a responsive 2000cc overhead cam engine that's made this family-size Datsun 710 National SCCA racing champ 2 years in a row.

But upward mobility requires more than power. You need social graces, like this Datsun's wall-to-wall nylon carpeting, its contoured bucket seats and custom instrumentation. How about a pedigree? Datsun has a background of more than 40 years building today's size cars.

Of course a family's future is important, too, and Datsun takes care of that with a solid, unibody construction that's put together to stay together for years to come. Down the road, you can count on nearly 4,000 factory-trained service technicians coast-to-coast to service your car wherever and whenever necessary.

Maybe some *saving graces* are in order. How about these: 33 MPG on the highway and 23 in the city. (Those are EPA mileage estimates with manual transmission. Your MPG may be more or less depending on the condition of your car and how you drive. California figures may vary slightly.)

Why not take the whole family out to visit a Datsun dealer now? Size up all the 710 models — 2- and 4-Door Sedans, the 5-Door Wagon and the sporty Hardtop. You'll find yourself moving up in the world—fast.

Datsun Saves
America's #1 Selling Import.

Source: *Time,* March 15, 1976.

TABLE 4-4.
Components of
Social Mobility

Social Mobility has:

(1) *Direction*—vertical (upward or downward), horizontal
(2) *Time*—intragenerational (career) or intergenerational (parent to child)
(3) *Context*—occupational, educational, material resources, power
(4) *Mechanisms*—ascription, achievement, maturation, validation
(5) *Unit*—person, family, group, strata, society
(6) *Point of View*—objective, subjective

the group of origination and the group of destination (assuming, of course, that it is acceptable).

INDUSTRIES AS SOCIAL SYSTEMS

Thus far, we have looked at societies as social systems which have social structures differentiating groups of people. We can also view industries, however, as social systems which have social structures differentiating groups of firms which are also consumers. The structure of an industry may have an important impact on the consumption patterns of firms within that industry.[35]

Industries as social systems are important to firms that are looking for new market opportunities for existing products, newly developed products, or for a general expansion of the firm's activities. Researchers must determine which industries have the greatest consumption potential and the greatest likelihood of reaching this potential.

EXHIBIT 4-4.
Proposition About Social
Mobility

PROPOSITION 4-11:
If consumers, when shifting from one status level to another, do not participate in any substantial way in the values, attitudes, and beliefs of either the status of origination or that of the destination, a feeling of insecurity is likely.

[35]Kotler, *op. cit.*

The Industry
System

Entire industries can be conceptualized as large-scale social systems of consumption. Paul M. Hirsch refers to this perspective as the industry system model.[36]

The industry system has several components as noted below:

Technical Subsystem
(i.e., singers)

Managerial Subsystem
(i.e., recording companies and their contact people)

Institutional Subsystem
(i.e., radio stations and their disc jockeys)

Societal Subsystem
(i.e., listeners)

Hirsch describes his model by using the example of the industry system of popular culture.[37] Within this system, creative people such as musicians and artists represent the technical subsystem; and the managerial subsystem is represented by "talent scouts" from various organizations who identify potentially profitable opportunities. Examples of such organizations would be record companies, baseball franchises, and art galleries.

The institutional subsystem is represented by the mass media. Consumers make up the societal subsystem which, through box office sales, feeds back cues to producers and distributors about the desirability of a particular cultural product. In effect, consumers can buy only those products of popular culture which the other systems collectively choose to make available. The consumer is partially limited by the fact that the institutional subsystem of the popular culture industry largely determines what is passed on to consumers: "The diffusion of particular fads and fashions is either blocked or facilitated at this strategic checkpoint."[38] That is, consumers can only rank or choose those songs or records which disc jockeys play and which are available in record stores. This function, called gatekeeping, is prevalent in many industries.

---

[36]Paul M. Hirsch, "Processing Fads and Fashions: An Organization-Set Analysis of Cultural Industry Systems," *American Journal of Sociology,* Vol. 77, January, 1972, pp. 639–659.

[37]The reader with a special interest in the liquor industry should read Norman K. Denzin, "Notes on the Criminogenic Hypothesis: A Case Study of the American Liquor Industry," *American Sociological Review,* Vol. 42, No. 6, December, 1977, pp. 905–920.

[38]See, for example, Lewis A. Coser, "Publishers as Gatekeepers of Ideas," the *ANNALS,* September, 1975, Vol. 421, p. 15.

Subsystems
Each subsystem has its own unique structure. Thus, one could study the managerial subsystem, i.e., the collection of different manufacturers producing competing substitute products. In addition to the constraints that the institutional gatekeepers place on the managerial subsystem, the managerial subsystem is also constrained by its ability to obtain "raw materials" such as singers or other performers. In the popular culture industry system, the managerial subsystem tries to reduce these two kinds of constraints through at least three strategies. One is to increase the number of boundary-spanning roles. These are roles, usually performed by representatives or salespeople, which serve to maintain contact with members of the institutional subsystem or with talent scouts who search for new material. Other examples are salespeople in the drug and chemical industry.

The processes involving boundary spanning roles in the textbook industry are particularly interesting. Boundary-spanning roles are social positions which overlap two or more social systems. Booksellers from publishing firms serve as the interface between the technical subsystem (authors) and the firm as well as between the institutional subsystem (instructors) and the firm. Moreover, the technical subsystem and institutional subsystem may involve the same people, although in different capacities. For example, a bookseller from John Wiley and Sons may find faculty members who are writing or planning to write a textbook. The author, like the singer, is a technical resource. An editor from the publisher then tries to sign a contract with the author if the potential book is judged to be a good product. The same faculty member, however, represents an institutional gatekeeper for particular texts relevant to courses he or she teaches. In most cases it is the faculty member who determines which book(s) the students must read for the course.

In the example just cited, teachers (or members of institutional systems) make the decisions about which books will be ordered, but do not actually purchase these books. They decide which book(s) other people (the students) must purchase. Because of the instructor's power to make a decision which will produce many purchases (by students), the publisher often gives a free copy of the book to the instructor. In such situations, the manufacturer must have a large number of contact people, provide them with considerable autonomy, and increase their skills in exerting personal influence. This tends to be "a structural feature of any industry system in which: (a) goods are marginally differentiated: (b) producer's access to consumer markets is regulated by independent gatekeepers; and (c) large-scale, direct advertising campaigns are uneconomical or prohibited by law . . . ." Where independent gatekeepers neither filter information nor mediate between producer and consumer, the importance of contact men at the organization's boundary is correspondingly diminished. In industry systems where products are advertised more directly to consumers, the contact man is superseded by full-page advertisements and sponsored commercials, purchased outright by the producer's organizations and directed at the lay consumer.''[39]

A second strategy for reducing the degree of dependence a firm has on the technical and institutional subsystems is to overproduce and differentially promote new products. This is particularly relevant when there is a relatively small capital investment required for each product. Over production is a way of hedging bets when the market is as uncertain as it often is in the popular culture industry system. It is apparently ''more efficient to produce many 'failures' for each success (in the cultural system) than to sponsor fewer items and pretest each on a massive scale to increase media coverage and consumer sales.''[40] Only 10 per cent of the over fifteen thousand books published each year are likely to appear in a given bookstore and no more than 20 per cent of over six thousand (45 rpm) singles are likely to be found in a retail record outlet. In the record, movie, and book industries, among others, most new products receive no advance publicity and little introductory fanfare. A few items, however, are given large-scale advance promotion.

A third strategy is to convince gatekeepers that a particular product will be a success so that they, through their response to this conviction (by playing records or selecting textbooks), help make the company's claim come true. This is, of course, a circular process. By convincing the gatekeepers that the product will be a success, the company gets them to act in such a way as to bring about its success.

THE PUBLIC SOCIAL SYSTEM

Traditionally, marketing has dealt with private industries. Contemporary marketing size is also used in the social system called the "public sector"—government agencies and government funded programs.[41] Public sector organizations at federal, state, or local levels often differ from private sector organizations as consumers and warrant special treatment as a social system. These are some of the factors that differentiate this social system from the private social system. (1) Public sector organizations might be more responsive to changes in federal funding than the private sector organizations. (2) Adoption of a new product is more a function of the physical depreciation of

---

[39]*Ibid.*, pp. 651–652.

[40]*Ibid.*, p. 652.

[41]Christopher Lovelock and Charles B. Weinberg, "Contrasting Private and Public Sector Marketing," *Proceedings of the American Marketing Association Fall Conference,* 1974, pp. 242–247.

the product being replaced in a public sector organization than in a private sector organization. (3) The impact of a purchase on organization goals is more difficult to evaluate in a public sector organization than in a private sector organization. (4) There might be differences in the kind of people working in the two different areas.[42]

SUMMARY   The degree of differentiation within a social system is a very important consideration for marketers attempting to understand consumer behavior. This chapter has focused on selected large-scale social structures.

Nation differentiation is the procedure of differentiating among various developing countries, or among various groups within a particular country. The marketer attempts to determine which countries have social structures most conducive to change (e.g., most likely to accept new products). A favorable climate for change is created when a large number and variety of mass media channels exist in a society, increasing the consumer's communication exposure. The climate for change is also enhanced in societies whose members have a desire for excellence. Important components in the climate for change include the following: perceived need for change; openness to change; potential for change; perceived control over the change process; and commitment to change. These combine with individual factors to differentiate one country from another.

Social class has long been considered a major factor for explaining consumer behavior. Major changes in American society have tended to make traditional social class measures less reliable predictors of market behavior. Several studies are cited to illustrate why a social class index of income, education, and occupation might be unreliable in explaining behavior. These conventional measurements have ignored many important variables, such as status inconsistency, mobility, and stratification system development. Two consumers of the same status position may have very different purchasing patterns because of past mobility, present mobility, or anticipated mobility.

Industries as social systems are important to firms looking for new market opportunities. The industry system model consists of various subsystems, each with its own unique structure. These structures influence the consumption behavior of firms. Both private and public sectors are important to the marketer.

---

[42]Irwin Feller and Donald C. Menzel, "Diffusion Milieux as a Focus of Research on Innovation in the Public Sector," paper presented at the American Political Science Association, San Francisco, California, September, 1975.

KEY CONCEPTS Boundary-spanning roles

Career mobility

Disassociation

Gatekeeper

Innovativeness

Intergenerational mobility

Social class

Social mobility

Social status

Social structure

Social system

Socialization process

Status inconsistency

Status of destination

Status persistence

SMALL-SCALE SOCIAL STRUCTURE AND CONSUMER BEHAVIOR:

GROUPS AND NORMS

CHAPTER GOALS   The objective of this chapter is to help readers understand:
1. **the characteristics of various types of groups and how they influence consumer behavior;**
2. **the dimensions on which norms can vary;**
3. **the ways in which social norms affect consumer behavior.**

SOCIAL GROUPS   Social groups have an enormous effect on our lives and choices, for between infancy and death much of our behavior is devoted to becoming identified with or belonging to various groups. For example, a person might choose a particular college or style of dress because he or she would like to become or be considered a member of a certain occupational group (e.g., East Coast investment bankers).

Both this and the subsequent chapter discuss smaller-scale social structures and how they affect consumer behavior. In this chapter we examine several selected studies of the impact of groups on consumer behavior, and in Chapter 6 we will explore the impact of families and organizations.

One of the ways in which groups affect consumer behavior is through the development and enforcement of norms. In other words, groups are the mechanisms through which norms are developed and enforced. Of particular interest are small groups, such as friendship cliques or one's immediate colleagues at work, which have a strong influence on consumer behavior. Small groups influence:
1. whether or not a consumer ever becomes aware of a product;
2. what a consumer learns and believes about a product;
3. whether a consumer ever tries a product (independently of what that consumer knows and feels about the product);

4.   how a product is used; and

5.   how satisfied a consumer is with a product's performance.

For example, a recent study, sponsored by the United States Department of Health, Education, and Welfare, on product satisfaction and dissatisfaction among elderly consumers found that elderly people's close friends had a profound influence on their purchase and use of a wide variety of products and services. Most elderly consumers learned of service stations to repair their cars primarily from their friends and family. Again, friends and relatives were the primary sources of information about the advantages and disadvantages of over-the-counter medications, and were the major influence in the decision of whether to try particular brands of such medications. Moreover, this study found that the misuse of various products often resulted from the acceptance of a family member's advice which was contrary to instructions for use accompanying the product.

A senior marketing researcher at Joseph Schlitz Brewing Company stated recently that a major focus of their research is on the impact of small groups on the purchasing and drinking of beer. Beer is often consumed in small group settings, and the social norms of these groups greatly influence the selection of brands of beer. This same researcher described the experience of a competitor in the Northwestern United States who attempted to introduce a new low calorie beer without any research into the ways in which small groups influence the selection of this type of beer. This brewery lost nearly $2 million before they rectified this mistake by conducting the appropriate research and modifying its marketing strategies accordingly. Thus, marketers are interested in groups because they help managers understand how consumer behavior develops, and this understanding is necessary for developing effective marketing strategies.

The reader should become familiar with some of the basic terminology regarding groups. These terms are likely to be encountered when studying groups in connection with a marketing research project or the development of marketing strategy. First, there are *primary groups* such as the family, friendship groups, and work groups where interaction is usually on a face-to-face basis. *Secondary groups* such as the American Marketing Association, the Association for Consumer Research, and alumni groups maintain communication among much larger numbers of people, who are often geographically dispersed, and use mainly impersonal channels of communication to maintain identification and interaction. Both types of groups may serve as consumer *reference groups,* which are those groups consumers keep in mind when forming an attitude or expressing a behavior. Reference groups to which consumers actually belong are referred to as *affiliative groups*. However, when a person wants to belong to a reference group but does not, the group is referred to as an *aspiration group.* For example, a young musician may want to belong to a well-known rock band, and therefore this will be an aspiration group for the young musician. Finally, there are groups to which the consumer does or does not actually belong but which the consumer uses as a negative point of reference in the development of attitudes and the expression of behavior. Consumers will avoid any activity which would associate them with such groups, which are often referred to as *dissociative groups*. For example, the parents of a young musician may have very negative attitudes toward rock music, and therefore rock bands are a dissociative group for the parents.

SELECTED STUDIES OF GROUP INFLUENCES

Because group influences on consumer behavior are so pervasive, researchers have tried to determine how and when these influences operate. We now review the results of several studies on the impact of groups on individual behavior.

Reactance

Group pressures may be exerted in direct or indirect ways. When pressure is overt and direct, a phenomenon known as *reactance* might occur, which is when the individual attempts to establish his or her own freedom by reacting against pressure to conform. Thus, consumers do not always behave in accordance with what the group is advocating.[1]

Two basic conclusions about when a person will or will not comply with group pressure are summarized in Propositions 5-1 and 5-2 in Exhibit 5-1. These propositions were tested using college juniors and seniors. Students were tested partially because they are an affiliative reference group for each other. The students were asked to evaluate and choose the *best* suit among three identical men's suits labeled A, B, and C. The three suits were of the same style, color, and size. The students were told that the suits were from different manufacturers, that they differed in quality, that clothiers and tailors were able to select the best suit, and that the study was to determine whether consumers could pick the best suits. Confederates or stooges were planted as the face-to-face informal group which tried to influence the subjects' choices. The confederates varied their behavior. With the first test group they were unanimous and firm in their suit selection, and with the second test group they were unanimous but quite uncertain about their selection. We will call the first group the compliance group and the second the reactance group.

---

[1]M. Venkatesan, "Consumer Behavior: Conformity and Independence," *Journal of Marketing Research,* Vol. 3, November, 1966.
[2]*Ibid*

EXHIBIT 5-1.
*Propositions About
Conformity and
Reactance*

PROPOSITION 5-1.
"In a consumer decision-making situation where no objective standards are present, individuals who are exposed to a group norm will
tend to conform to that group norm."

PROPOSITION 5-2.
"In a consumer decision making situation where no objective standards are present, individuals who are exposed to a group, and are
induced to comply, will show less tendency to conform to the group
judgment."[3]

The results of the study showed that in a control group where group
influence was absent each suit was equally likely to be chosen as the best suit.
On the other hand, Proposition 5-1 was supported by the compliance group
test, when subjects chose the suit recommended by the confederates well in
excess of what would be expected by chance. Thus, individuals were influenced by group pressure and conformed to the group's consensus concerning
the best suit. Proposition 5-2 received limited support; the subjects tended
either to be indifferent or to deliberately make a choice that would negate the
effect of group pressure.

The action implications of this study are that marketers should be particularly concerned with social group pressure and the manner in which information is provided by social groups when the product is difficult to evaluate
objectively. Since consumers might, under certain conditions, resist clear efforts to get them to conform, it is important to offer such consumers an
acceptable alternative to the product or brand selected and stressed by the
group. Thus, the group may be important in influencing the decision to
purchase a given product type, but the individual may wish to differ from
other group members with regard to brand or make.

**Socially Distant
Reference Groups**

Cocanougher and Bruce have investigated the significance of reference
groups with which the consumer does not interact regularly.[4] This study of
socially distant reference groups suggests Proposition 5-3 and 5-4 in Exhibit

[3]*Ibid.*
[4]A. Benton Cocanougher and Grady D. Bruce, "Socially Distant Reference Groups and
Consumer Aspiration," *Journal of Marketing Research*, Vol. 8, August, 1971, pp. 379–38.

5-2. These propositions closely parallel the more specific formulations expressed by the researchers in their study involving students as consumers and established business people as the reference group. In fact, the researchers advise using both propositions together, i.e., using attitudes toward *members* of a reference group and attitudes toward the *activities* of the members of the reference group to explain consumer behavior.

EXHIBIT 5-2.
*Propositions About
Socially Distant
Reference Groups*

PROPOSITION 5-3.
The more favorable consumers' attitudes are toward the *activities* of a socially distant reference group, the more influenced consumers will be by that group.

PROPOSITION 5-4.
The more favorable consumers' attitudes are toward the *members* of a socially distant reference group, the more influenced consumers will be by that group.

This study suggests two action implications. First, it is useful to identify various market segments by finding individuals who find the same distant reference groups attractive. Promotional appeals could then be developed for each market segment. For example, in promoting shampoo it may be appropriate to stress athletes' use of the product in order to appeal to the younger market segment, while stressing movie stars' use will appeal to the older market segment. A second implication is that consumers probably have negative distant reference groups. When selecting a reference group for one market segment, care must be exercised not to select a group which may alienate other significant market segments. For instance, perhaps younger users of a particular hair shampoo would be turned off by advertising involving movie stars.

**Social Involvement
Associated With
Products**

Other research indicates that the strength of group influence varies according to the social involvement associated with different products (this is reflected in Proposition 5-5).[5] Products high in social involvement are those which are

[5]Robert E. Witt and Grady D. Bruce, "Purchase Decisions and Group Influence," *Journal of Marketing Research*, Vol. 7, November, 1970, pp. 533–535.

frequently used in the presence of other people and which have certain images which are transferred to the user. For example, cigarettes and beer are high in social involvement. Similarity of brand choice within a group can also be explained "in terms of group structure and the [significance] of products in the interpersonal situation in which they are purchased and sold."[6] However, this is not necessarily the case for all products, for each product should be considered separately. There are many implications for promotion managers:

> The promotional manager who attempts to take social influence into account in designing promotional messages must know what aspects of the social influence process are the primary determinants of the nature and amount of social influence in a given purchase decision context. One or more of the following aspects of the social influence process might be involved in a given purchase decision: (1) the perceived conspicuousness of the product or service involved; (2) the level of perceived risk associated with the purchase decision; (3) the nature and extent of the product or service's symbolic involvement in the purchaser's social interaction framework; (4) the attractiveness of the purchaser's reference group, social class, etc.; (5) the perceived purchase decision expertise of the referent involved; (6) the purchaser's need for social approval or reinforcement; and (7) the extent to which the anticipated satisfaction associated with a given purchase is derived from the purchaser's social environment.
>
> The findings of this study suggest that it may be possible for the promotion manager to identify the primary determinants of a given purchase decision — social influence relationship. For example, the expertise of the referent appears to be critical in instant coffee purchase decisions, where for cook-in-bag frozen vegetables it would appear that a critical factor in the referent influence process is the potential consumer's perception of the likelihood that relevant referents will be aware of her purchasing behavior.[7]

EXHIBIT 5-3.
Proposition About the Influence of Reference Groups for Different Types of Products

PROPOSITION 5-5.
The greater the degree of social involvement a product entails, the greater the importance of group cohesiveness.

[6]Robert E. Witt and Grady D. Bruce, "Group Influence and Brand Choice Congruence," *Journal of Marketing Research,* Vol. 9, November, 1972, pp. 440–443.
[7]*Ibid.*

Group Innovativeness

An interesting study of a middle-class neighborhood in a Los Angeles suburb tested several hypotheses about group effects on purchase behavior.[8] The general conclusions drawn were that friends did indeed exert considerable influence on each other, but the degree of influence varied greatly according to the product category. Also, groups were found to be more innovative when there was a norm favoring innovation, when the groups were cosmopolitan, and when perceived risk was low. These findings, however, did not apply equally to all of the product contexts studied.

Once again, the action implication is for the marketer to consider the relevance of various group phenomena for the product category and not to generalize from the effects of groups on purchasing behavior in other contexts. But, in considering the relevance of groups, the important variables to include when segmenting groups or developing appeals are: (1) group norms or rules about trying new things, (2) the cosmopolitan orientations of the group, (3) the level of perceived risk, and (4) group cohesion.

Susceptibility to Group Influence

One study, by George P. Moschis, attempted to explain consumer susceptibility to group influence.[9] The researcher used social comparison theory, which says that people compare themselves on various attributes with other people (reference groups) in order to assess the consequences of their behavior when physical evidence about these consequences is unavailable.

The researcher employed the work of Jones and Gerard to distinguish between two different processes of reference group comparisons.[10] One process consists of a consumer assessing the likelihood that a reference group would approve of a value or attitude he or she has by asking a member of that group what he or she thinks of a product such as a new style of men's suits. The consumer does not ask outright, "Do you agree with my attitude toward that style?" but simply, "Do you like that style?" This is referred to as *reflected appraisal,* and involves direct, verbal interaction.

Comparative appraisal involves simply observing whether members of a reference group behave in ways which are consistent with one's own thinking. For instance, this would involve observing the style of clothing worn by

[8]Thomas S. Robertson, "Group Characteristics and Aggregate Innovative Behavior: Preliminary Report," in J. Sheth (ed.), *Models of Buyer Behavior,* NY: Harper & Row, 1974, pp. 310–326.

[9]George P. Moschis, "Social Comparison and Informal Group Influence," *Journal of Marketing Research,* Vol. 13, August, 1976, pp. 237–244.

[10]Edward E. Jones and Harold B. Gerard, *Social Psychology,* NY: John Wiley and Sons, Inc., 1967.

members of the reference group. The persons or groups that are selected as references are typically those who are similar to the consumer in ways which are presently important. For example, similarity in occupation may be an important attribute when asking about the appropriateness of clothing being selected for employment situations.

This research was concerned with the prediction of informal group influence, information seeking, the credibility attached to information from informal group members, and the reason for purchasing products recommended by informal group members. Data were collected concerning perfume, face makeup base, hand cream or lotion, lipstick, and at least one eye makeup product. It was found that reflected appraisal tended to be more prevalent than comparative appraisal when consumers were seeking information about a product and later when they actually were making a product selection. The data suggest that it is most desirable to use both types of appraisals to explain variations in an individual consumer's susceptibility to informal group influences at all stages of a decision-making process. These stages include becoming interested in a product, seeking more information, evaluating the product, and making a final product selection.

Group Decisions Since there are relatively few studies in the consumer behavior area concerning groups, it is especially desirable to go beyond the consumer literature in order to find propositions which may be relevant to consumer behavior. There is much literature on group dynamics. One researcher has developed a set of plausible propositions based on an extensive review of the empirical and theoretical literature.[11] A few of these propositions and their relevance to the study of consumer behavior and marketing are presented in Exhibits 5-4 and 5-5.

Proposition 5-6 in Exhibit 5-4 concerns the inefficiency of group decision making with respect to the dimension of time. This proposition tends to be true both in terms of the hours expended per person and in length of time elapsed. The greater the number of people involved in making a decision, the longer it takes. Length of time, however, says nothing about the quality of the decisions made in a group. An action implication of this hypothesis pertains to industrial selling situations. When there is a buying committee which makes purchase decisions, the salesperson must coordinate his or her efforts with a more protracted decision process than might normally take place when only

---

[11]Marvin E. Shaw, *Group Dynamics: The Psychology of Small Group Behavior,* NY: McGraw-Hill, 1971.

EXHIBIT 5-4.
*Propositions About
Group Dynamics*

> PROPOSITION 5-6.
> "Groups usually require more time to complete a test than do individuals working alone."
>
> PROPOSITION 5-7.
> "Decisions made after group discussion are more risky than decisions made by the average individual prior to group discussion."[12]

one individual, a lone purchasing agent, for example, makes the decision. The salesperson must be wary about trying to "close" the sale too early when dealing with a buying committee.

Proposition 5-7 in Exhibit 5-4 suggests that sometimes in a group setting the responsibility for a decision which might have some bad consequences does not fall entirely on one person's shoulders, but is spread among members. Thus, a group might make a decision which involves more risk than the members would accept individually. An action implication of this idea is simply that when a purchasing agent perceives an equipment purchase as risky, the salesperson might encourage the formation of a group within the firm to participate in the purchase decision. Also, by finding a reference group that chose this product previously, the agent can, if the product fails, point out that other similar firms in the industry had made the same decision. This makes the purchasing agent's initial decision seem plausible, for the agent cannot be blamed as much if significant other firms had arrived at the same decision. Similarly, ultimate consumers might be encouraged to make important decisions together with their families.

Impact of Cohesiveness

Group cohesiveness is an important consideration in understanding the impact of social groups on consumers. The degree of cohesiveness is determined by group members' attraction to each other and their motivation to stay in the group. A number of propositions about group cohesion exist and are adapted from Shaw's work.[13] These are shown in Exhibit 5-5.

---

[12]*Ibid.*, p. 81.
[13]Shaw, *op. cit.*

EXHIBIT 5-5.
*Propositions About
Cohesiveness*

PROPOSITION 5-8.
The greater the cohesiveness of a group of consumers, the greater the amount of communication among those consumers.

PROPOSITION 5-9.
The greater the cohesiveness of a group of consumers, the more positive will be the interactions among group members.

PROPOSITION 5-10.
The greater the cohesiveness of a group of consumers, the greater the degree of influence the group will have over consumers' choices.

The main action implication of these propositions is that highly cohesive groups are more desirable advertising targets than less cohesive groups. Product information will diffuse faster within highly cohesive groups and thus reach target consumers earlier than within less cohesive groups. Because of the more positive orientation of highly cohesive groups, there is a better chance that communications will stress the positive aspects of the product or service. Also, the greater the influence exerted over individual consumers by highly cohesive groups, the stronger will be the impact of this positive information.

For example, a person recently running for election to the United States Senate in a Midwestern state decided that prior to actually filing for office, he would personally interact with as many people as possible. One of his aides suggested a series of teas, and wine and cheese parties. The strategy they worked out was as follows: They drew up a list of ten people whom they knew and who lived in different parts of the district and who did not know each other (i.e., they did not choose people who were very active in the state's Democratic party and who might therefore know each other). Then they set aside one weekend and asked each of these ten people if they would be willing to have an informal party in their home so that their friends could meet the candidate. They requested that the host or hostess invite a diverse group of people to the party. In other words, hosts and hostesses were requested to invite a few business associates, a few neighbors, a few bridge club friends, and a few friends from other groups they might belong to. At the parties the candidate spoke informally and answered questions. Aides circulated a guest book so they could get the names and addresses of guests for future direct mail solicitations of contributions as well as solicitations of votes. It was hoped that at each party one or two people who seemed particularly interested in the candidate could be persuaded to have parties in their homes.

The idea behind inviting a diverse group was to give the candidate exposure to as many types of people as possible. This strategy backfired. Since the group of guests was not very cohesive, not many of the guests spoke with the other guests about politics before the arrival of the candidate. More importantly, even after the candidate spoke and answered questions, the guests did not have much influence over each other's choice about whether to support the candidate. The candidate would have been wiser to request that the hosts and hostesses put together a guest list that was fairly cohesive.

SOCIAL NORMS Consumer behavior is essentially a social phenomenon. That is, the behavior of consumers is heavily influenced by the relations they have with other people. These important relationships are regulated by social norms, which influence such fundamental consumer processes as: (1) the seeking of information prior to a purchase, (2) what product and brand choices are made, (3) where a product is purchased, (4) the way a purchase is made, (5) the purpose of the purchase, and (6) how the product is used and even where it is used. Because of these and the other influences that social norms have on consumers, one consumer researcher specializing in new product marketing has suggested it is unthinkable for him to advise a client about introducing a new product or service without a thorough understanding of the various norms held by the intended consumers.[14] For example, credit card companies in both the United States and Europe have found that consumer norms about borrowing are one of the major variables which distinguish among heavy users, light users, and nonusers of credit cards. These norms are derived largely from immediate family and friendship groups.

Norms are defined as: "1) A collective evaluation of behavior in terms of what it *ought* to be; 2) A collective expectation as to what behavior *will be*; and/or 3) particular reactions to behavior, including attempts to apply sanctions or otherwise induce a particular kind of behavior."[15] Thus norms are guides to behavior which have several key attributes:

* norms are collective—that is, they are held by many members of a social system or group;

---

[14]*Advertising Age,* January 9, 1978, pp. 57ff.

[15]Jack P. Gibbs, "Norms: The Problem of Definition and Classification," *American Journal of Sociology,* Vol. 70, March, 1965, pp. 586–594, at p. 589.

* norms are only guides or expectations about what behavior should be—
they are not necessarily followed; however,
* norms are enforced—people are either positively rewarded for complying or negatively rewarded (punished) for not complying; and
* norms usually reflect the values of the social system or group.

Each of these will be discussed in the next section along with other dimensions of norms, but first some brief examples will be given of some behaviors
which are or are not norms. The first example is a person who shoplifts a
candy bar in a supermarket. This violates a norm (as well as a law) which is
based on values about private property and private ownership. The law,
however, is not the norm; the law is the means used to enforce the norm.
Whether or not the shoplifter is arrested, prosecuted, and punished, the norm
has been violated.

A second example is provided by a family purchasing a pair of shoes for
the youngest child, a seven-year-old. They pick out a pair of shoes and tell the
salesclerk they wish to buy the shoes. The salesclerk suggests (and practically
insists) that the child first "try on" the shoes. Is there a norm existing here?
There is no law which says one must try on shoes before purchasing them.
But the positive or negative rewards for complying or deviating from a norm
can be formal (as in a law) or informal, as in the salesclerk's "suggestion." But
what value is reflected? This is less obvious than in the first example. The
valued characteristic here is rationality, exemplified by careful and thorough
decision making.

Consider, now, a third and final example. In grocery stores (especially in
refrigerated cases of dairy products), consumers have a tendency to select
items which are not in the very front of the case. For instance, they take
cartons of milk which are not in the very front. Is there a norm operating here?
No, this is merely a pattern of behavior (which is possibly related to a preference for products that haven't been touched by all of the other dairy product
purchasers or haven't gotten warm in the front of the case). If a person selects
an item from the front of the case, it is unlikely that observers will frown on or
attempt to discourage this behavior, for there is no cultural value attached to
the behavior. Just because many consumers behave a certain way does not
mean there is a norm operating. Instead, they may be responding similarly to
particular life situations, or their behavior may be satisfying to them.

**Dimensions of
Norms**

While the discussion above serves as a brief introduction to norms, a more
complete examination of the dimensions of norms is necessary before propositions about their impact on consumer behavior can be derived. Three basic
strategies are available to the marketer with respect to norms: (1) the marketer
can try to conform to the norms; (2) the marketer can deviate from the norms;

or (3) the marketer can attempt to change the norms. Where the norm fits in the dimensions in Table 5-1 will, in part, determine which strategy should be followed.

Content.   It is useful to think of norms in terms of *when* they become important in the decision-making process. Some norms are most relevant prior to a purchase, while others become important at the time of purchase, and still others become important after the purchase. It is generally accepted that, prior to a purchase, all relevant information about the product should be disclosed to consumers, especially upon request. This norm is sufficiently important so that laws exist to require compliance with the norm. There are various information disclosure laws requiring that certain information be placed on labels and that other sources of information, such as contracts and warranties, be available to consumers prior to making a purchase. An example is the truth-in-lending law requiring pre-purchase disclosure of the true annual interest rate involved in a credit transaction.

Some norms govern what degree of bargaining, if any, is permitted prior to a purchase. Some norms say, in effect, that bargaining is appropriate with both new and used products, as in the case of automobiles. On the other hand, much less bargaining is expected or permitted with new homes relative to older homes. Bargaining doesn't occur in supermarkets except when management permits and even then it is restricted to a given special sale price for a limited time.

Certain norms govern the actual purchase transaction. It is generally accepted that commissions for real estate transactions be paid by the seller and not the buyer. In most states no laws exist governing this although the norm is usually made explicit and has legal force in a signed contract. A somewhat different norm exists about tipping. It is tacitly understood by all parties involved that a restaurant pays only a modest portion of a waiter's or waitress's salary and that the restaurant diner pays another portion. It is further understood that the portions paid by the customer will generally be based on the total dollar amount of the dinner bill. The content, then, of these norms concerns responsibility for purchase payments.

The content of some norms applies to post-purchase situations. Seller obligations exist describing what a seller should do for the consumer after the product has been purchased and put into use. Post-purchase obligations are often expressed by warranties and may apply to both buyer and seller. For example, the automobile manufacturer or dealer is obligated to do certain repairs only if the consumer has complied with the necessary servicing of the car as described in the warranty. Post-purchase norms are often maintained by sellers not to make a given sale likely, but to increase the likelihood of future sales to the same and other customers. If a store refuses to allow the return of a product, even for some valid reason, the customer may initiate unfavorable word-of-mouth communication about the store.

We do not suggest a specific proposition here. The critical idea is simply that different norms are relevant to different stages in the consumer decision process. This idea is expressed in Table 5-2. Exactly what norms are relevant will be largely determined by the specific buying situation.

The content of some norms may apply to the strategy or means by which consumers purchase their products and services. The norm of reciprocity in the industrial setting, while illegal if explicitly required by a buyer, is an example. This norm simply says, "if you buy our products, we'll buy yours." A

TABLE 5-1.
Dimensions of Norms[a]

I. Content
  A. Pre-purchase
  B. Purchase
  C. Post-purchase

II. Mode of transportation
  A. Primary socialization (through the family)
  B. Secondary socialization (through formal institutions such as the school or the church)

III. Source of authority for the origination of the norm (rationalization for its existence)
  A. Supernatural
  B. Tradition
  C Law
  D. Society
  E. Public Opinion
  F. Religion
  G. Reference Group
  H. Family

IV. Acceptance (cognitive) of the norm
  A. Extent to which norm is known
  B. Extent to which knowledge is recognized
    1. Conscious
    2. Unconscious
  C. Extent of acceptance of evaluation of behavior as acceptable or unacceptable (by what percentage of the population)
  D. Degree of acceptance of evaluation (mild or strong)
  E. Relative importance compared with other norms (which wins if two conflict)—will depend on centrality of the value it is associated with
  F. Degree of individual interpretation allowed (rigidity or flexibility)

V. Extent of application of the norm
  A. Situational range of application (all situations or some; conditions under which the norm is relaxed)
  B. Status range of application
    1. All people
    2. Only persons in certain statuses (possibly a role expectation or prescription)

VI.   Formal properties of the statement of the norm
      A.   Prescriptive (should) or prohibitive (should not)
      B.   Specificity (clear or vague)

VII.   Sanctioning
      A.   Presence or absence of positive sanctions
      B.   Presence or absence of negative sanctions
      C.   Intensity or severity of sanctions (i.e., force used or not used)
      D.   Repressive or restitutive negative sanctions
      E.   Enforcement authority
          1. Fate
          2. Deity
          3. Law enforcement and judicial authorities }   formal
          4. Religious leaders
          5. Reference group members }
          6. Family members   informal
          7. Anyone
      F.   Universality of enforcement
          (percentage of nonconforming behaviors in which enforcement attempts are made; all deviants or only a few examples)
      G.   Success of enforcement attempts in gaining punishment
          (percentage of "prosecuted" cases which are "convicted")
      H.   Success of enforcement attempts in gaining compliance
          (percentage of "rehabilitated" violators)

VIII.   Compliance (Behavioral) or Deviance
      A.   Effectiveness (amount of compliance; extent to which norm is followed)
      B.   Reason for consistency of behavior and norm
          1. Internalization
          2. Threat of punishment
          3. Sanctioned rewards from compliance
          4. Inherent rewards of behavior (gratification that is connected to the behavior, not to the norm).
      C.   Perceptions about extent of compliance (collective belief about whether or not others follow or comply with the norm); behavioral norms[b]

---

[a]This table has been compiled by combining the typologies, listings, and discussions of norms in the following articles: Judith Blake and Kingsley Davis, "Norms, Values, and Sanctions" in Robert E. L. Farris (ed.), *Handbook of Modern Sociology,* New York: Rand McNally and Co., 1964; Leonard Broom and Philip Selznick, *Sociology* (fifth ed.). New York: Harper and Row, 1973.

[b]Term "behavioral norm" used by M. D. Buffalo and Joseph W. Rodgers, "Behavioral Norms, Moral Norms, and Attachment: Problems of Deviance and Conformity," *Social Problems,* Vol. 19 (Summer, 1971), 101—113.

buying firm will sometimes exercise this norm as a means of increasing its own sales, though the exercise of this norm will be subtle.

    Among some especially frugal families there will be family rules such as avoiding the use of credit or buying certain foods only when they are on sale.

	Pre-purchase Stage	Purchase Stage	Post-purchase Stage
TABLE 5-2. *Examples of Norms Applicable to Particular Purchase Stages*	Reciprocity.	Commissions, tipping, kickbacks.	Warranty.
	Frugality as an ethic rather than as a necessity.	Patronizing a prestige outlet such as Tiffany's.	Deliberate display of selected purchases.

Frugality may sometimes reflect simply a lack of resources. Often, however, it also reflects a particular value of the type, "a penny saved is a penny earned."

It is important to know whether the content of a norm is more relevant in influencing the way a purchase is made or in influencing what product and/or brand is purchased. Consider the example just given. If frugality were a goal in itself, then a salesperson might directly stress the idea of *money saved* through the purchase of a particular life insurance policy as compared to another. If frugality were related more to some absolute economic need to save, then a salesperson selling the same policy would stress the *low cost* of the policy relative to a competing policy. The idea of money saved is not the same as the idea of low cost, and hence it may not be possible to express both with the same sales talk or advertisement.

Mode of Transmission and Source of Authority.   The mode of transmission of norms is important. Norms are sometimes transmitted to individuals through their families or through immediate peer groups. Other norms are transmitted via groups such as schools or other institutions. A product or service which is compatible with a particular norm is probably best promoted with reference to the type of group which transmits the norm, since the product might be accepted if it is shown to be appropriate in the setting of the transmitting group. The group transmitting a given norm is relevant to a consumer whether that norm is relevant to a consumer's pre-purchase, purchase, or post-purchase behavior. Norms from primary or most important groups influence behavior more than those transmitted from less important or peripheral groups. This idea has already been discussed somewhat and is expressed as Proposition 5-11. For example, for teenagers, nutrition-related norms stemming from peer groups are more influential than those stemming from teachers and other authorities. Moreover, the sources of norms transmit norms somewhat differently: peer group and family norms about nutrition are likely to be transmitted informally and by casual demonstration; while formal authorities are likely to transmit norms more explicitly.

Sometimes consumers will actively seek information about norms from authorities. In the area of fashion, clothing sales personnel may be asked to show the customer what is chic or what is appropriate for a particular occasion. In the selection of foods and beverages, advice may be sought about

EXHIBIT 5-6.
*Propositions About
Transmission and
Authority*

PROPOSITION 5-11.
Norms from primary groups are more influential than norms from peripheral groups.

PROPOSITION 5-12.
The greater the degree of uncertainty about behavior in a situation, the more likely it is that consumers will seek advice from sales personnel.

what combinations are proper to serve, as was stated by wine salesclerks in The Benne Brothers' case in Chapter 2. The greater the degree of uncertainty about appropriate behavior in a situation, the more likely it is that consumers will seek advice from sales personnel. If the consumer perceives, however, that there will be negative consequences from seeking this advice (e.g., embarrassment or being chastised by the salesperson), then it is less likely that the consumer will ask for the salesperson's advice.

It is only common sense that norms arising from highly authoritative primary groups will be more influential in guiding buying behavior than those norms which do not. But there is a practical problem here. Consider the figure below:

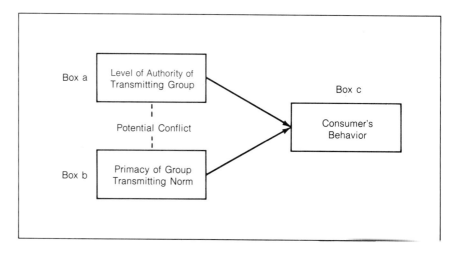

The connection between level of authority of the transmitting group and consumer behavior is plausible and clear, and so is the connection between primacy of the norm-transmitting group and consumer behavior. The catch is that the norm transmitted by a group which is primary sometimes conflicts with or differs from the norm being transmitted by a high authority group. A medical society (box a) may try to create or reinforce a norm against the use of certain drugs, while a primary group (box b) of friends may stress that such use of drugs is harmless or even desirable. If norms conflict, consumer behavior (box c) may be erratic. This is seen in conventional settings where a person is always alternating between smoking and concentrated efforts to stop smoking. The absence of primary group norms prohibiting smoking makes the anti-smoking efforts of medical personnel and others much less effective than would be the case if primary group norms against smoking were present.

Acceptance of Norms. The acceptance of norms has two main dimensions. First, acceptance of a norm can occur because the norm is genuinely believed to be intrinsically valuable or rewarding. Second, a norm may be accepted in order to gain favor or avoid punishment from a person or group. In a sense, the most useful question to ask is not what norm is active in a situation, although that is obviously important, but rather, why do consumers accept the norm? Knowing *why* consumers follow certain norms in their overall buying behavior enables the marketer to develop a more effective marketing mix than would be possible on the basis of knowing only what the key norms are.

Many factors influence the degree of acceptance of a norm. The more widely accepted a norm is (box a in Figure 5-2) among a relevant population, the more likely it is that someone entering that group will accept the norm. This is partly so because a widely accepted norm is probably important enough to warrant punishment for any failure to behave accordingly. Also, norms integral to a group are communicated more effectively (box c) both explicitly and implicitly. A number of ideas about norms are expressed schematically in the drawing below. Thus, the more strongly held a norm is (box d), the more likely it is that there will be conformity (box e). The widely held norms also influence conformity less directly by limiting flexibility in the application of the norm (box b), which in turn increases the likelihood of conformity. When a family norm against the use of credit is very strong, the family is unlikely to make any credit purchases. This is especially true if this norm permits no exception. The more one spouse demands that the other spouse not use credit cards, the more difficult it is for the demanding spouse to justify his or her own use of a credit card. While these statements could be translated into formal propositions because they have theoretical support, they have not been stated as propositions because they have not been tested directly in a consumer context.

FIGURE 5-2.

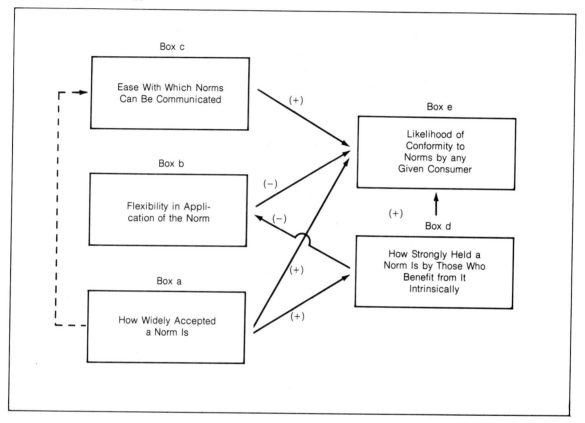

Application of Norms.   There are two dimensions to the application of norms. One dimension concerns the range of *situations* in which the norm is applied. As noted earlier, there are purchase occasions when norms permit bargaining and other occasions when they do not. There has been little research into the conditions which cause norms to be applied in varying degrees in different situations. It does appear, however, that conformity to norms is greater in any one instance when the same norm operates in many situations. For instance, when many manufacturers of different appliances provide written warranties on their products, it is likely that a manufacturer introducing a new appliance will do the same. Consumers expect this feature because it is a common standard of behavior for appliance manufacturers. Thus, as stated in Proposition 5-13 in Exhibit 5-7, the wider the situational applicability of a norm, the more likely conformity is in any one situation. For instance, when a family norm establishes a pattern of influence among hus-

EXHIBIT 5-7.
Propositions
Concerning
Applicability of
Norms

PROPOSITION 5-13.
Consumers are more likely to conform to a norm in any given situation when that norm applies to a wide array of situations.

PROPOSITION 5-14.
Norms apply differentially to people of different statuses.

PROPOSITION 5-15.
The larger the number of consumers in any one status group who conform to a norm, the greater the likelihood that any given consumer entering that group will conform.

band, wife, and children in one product context, that pattern of influence is likely to hold for the purchase of all products in that context.

A second dimension of the applicability of norms concerns the range of *social statuses* a norm may cover. Does a norm apply to all people in a given situation? Who in a family has to justify an expenditure to others in the family? Although it may vary across families, certain persons have more freedom in spending than others, at least in given product contexts. Thus some behaviors that need not be explained or justified by one spouse, might require considerable justification by the other. Not all standards of behavior apply equally to everyone in a social system. Norms are generally followed only by persons in the status category covered by the norm or when the norm applies to a large number of people. Propositions 5-14 and 5-15 embody this idea.

Statement of Norms.   Norms may be expressed clearly and directly or they may never be mentioned openly. It would seem that the more explicit a norm is, the more likely it is that conformity will occur, but here, too, little attention has been given by researchers to the relative impact on conformity of the explicitness of a norm. We can surmise, however, that people's behavior with regard to a norm does depend on how explicitly it is stated and whether it is stated positively ("you should…") or negatively ("you should not…"). When a norm is expressed in a positive fashion the marketer should stress the approval consumers will obtain through a purchase; and when a norm is negatively stated, emphasis should be placed on the avoidance of punishment.

An example of a norm which is stated only informally and implicitly was mentioned in Chapter 2. Recall the discussion about the social appropriateness of drinking wine, and the debate as to the different occasions when serving wine is most proper. Has the reader ever explicitly heard or read a prohibition about drinking wine alone? Contrast this to dress codes. It is not uncommon to encounter explicit statements enforcing dress codes. Examples would be restaurants which display signs stating that jackets and ties are required after 6:00 p.m. or supermarkets that prohibit shoppers who are not wearing shoes and/or shirts.

Sanctioning of Norms.   The way norms are enforced influences the degree to which people conform to them. Norms are more likely to be effective when they are enforced both formally through laws, regulations and procedures, as well as informally. Also, the more intense or severe the punishment for not conforming, the more likely it is that conformity will occur. As mentioned earlier, however, reactance can occur.

Certain groups exist to impose negative sanctions on persons who deviate from a norm; in fact, members join these groups to benefit from negative (as well as positive) sanctions. Examples are Weight Watchers and Alcoholics Anonymous. Consider Weight Watchers, where progress in losing weight is a public matter with public weigh-ins at each meeting. This imposes considerable social pressure on the dieter to lose weight and to practice the behavior necessary to do so. Weight Watchers, as do other similar kinds of groups, provides assistance in positive ways as well.

Compliance by others affects an individual's own compliance. Thus, consumers will be more likely to conform when the norm is perceived to be followed by almost everyone. A marketer should try to associate the product or service with a widely held norm and indicate the appropriateness of the product as an expression of complying to that norm. The more internalized a norm is in the consumer's mind, the greater the consumer's responsiveness to this approach.

Compliance or Deviance.   Complete conformity to norms does not always occur. Deviance from norms is simply the discrepancy between what behavior a norm calls for and what behavior actually is.[16] Thus:

Deviance = Norm minus Actual Behavior

Deviance may be expressed by over-conforming or under-conforming. Deviance results in a change in behavior away from an existing norm or from a norm changing while an individual's behavior remains the same. A person who decides not to adopt a new product when it first becomes available is not

[16]Robert K. Hawkes, "Norms, Deviance, and Social Control: A Mathematical Elaboration of Concepts," *American Journal of Sociology,* Vol. 80, (January 1975) pp. 886–908.

usually considered a deviant. As norms change or develop, however, and ownership or use of the product becomes an expected behavior and the consumer still refrains from getting involved with the product, that person becomes labeled as a "laggard," a term expressing deviation from a norm. Deviance from norms may be more or less legitimate or accepted, or it may be illegal. Deviance is likely to become illegal the more dangerous to a group deviation is. We now turn to the subject of legal and illegal deviations.

AN EXCURSUS ON NORMS AND THE LAW

Norms Not Enforced by Law

There are many examples of over- and under-consumption which constitute deviance. Excessive eating and the consequent weight gain is considered deviant (although very prevalent). As indicated earlier, groups exist solely for the purpose of helping people who are excessive in their food consumption conform to norms. It is not illegal to be overweight or to be an alcoholic.

Some people are valued for their deviance. In a later chapter (Chapter 7) we shall discuss persons who accumulate many different social roles. These persons deviate more from the norms of each group they belong to than do other members of these groups. As we shall see, the nature of their deviance results in group members being better informed about new products and services. (However, any one group does not tolerate such deviance among most of its members.) The group allows the deviance in exchange for the information the deviant supplies.

Norms also exist concerning what kinds of products particular retail outlets stock. These norms express expectations about organizational behavior. Consumers expect to find greeting cards in a pharmacy, hosiery in a supermarket, and kitchen appliances in a hardware store. Dissatisfaction will be expressed by consumers when organizations deviate from expectations about what products should be made available by the organization.[17] It is interesting to speculate on consumer responses to the introduction of durable goods and high ticket items such as televisions in supermarkets.[18]

Similarly, norms exist for product performance. When a product deviates from its expected performance level, it may be returned by the consumer who did not experience or obtain the expected level of satisfaction. This will be discussed further in Chapter 17 on consumer attributions.

---

[17]For a good discussion of this issue, see Earl W. Morris, "A Normative Deficit Approach to Consumer Satisfaction," in H. Keith Hunt (ed.), *Conceptualization and Measurement of Consumer Satisfaction and Dissatisfaction,* Cambridge, MA: Marketing Science Institute, 1977, pp. 340–374.

[18]"Safeway: Selling Nongrocery Items to Cure the Supermarket Blahs," *Business Week,* March 7, 1977, pp. 52–58.

Norms Enforced by Law

Almost all studies of consumer behavior have focused on how consumers or firms purchase and use products and services which are legally produced, sold, and used. Sociological studies of deviance and crime, however, focus on another aspect of consumer behavior: marketing exchanges which violate a societal norm which is enforced by laws—deviant marketing transactions. A few examples include:

> Selling stolen goods (fencing)
> Selling illegal drugs
> Shoplifting
> Prostitution
> Gambling (i.e., illegal numbers games)
> Hiring someone to kill someone else
> Illegal abortions (prior to 1973 Supreme Court ruling)
> Selling liquor during the Prohibition
> Sales of certain products (cigarettes, liquor) to minors
> Political bribery (the selling of ''favors'')

Why should the study of illegal exchanges be a part of the study of consumer behavior? Why not leave it to sociologists interested in deviance? The first reason is that illegal exchanges constitute a large sector of the economy. It has been estimated that in 1973 the resale of stolen goods amounted to $16 billion.[19] Legal gambling at race tracks has been estimated to amount to about $5 billion annually. Compare this with the estimates of annual illegal gambling which range from $7 billion to $50 billion. Most law enforcement officials agree that the figure totals at least $20 billion a year—four times the amount spent on legal gambling. Compare this also with the $30 billion spent by the United States on the Vietnam war, and with the American foreign aid expenditures of about $2 billion annually.[20] Not only do the illegal exchanges themselves constitute a large segment of the economy, but large expenditures are also made on efforts to enforce the laws associated with these practices.

Secondly, and perhaps more importantly for students of consumer behavior, the study of illegal exchanges can provide a way to study the isolated effects of interpersonal communication. Since media promotion is not used to advertise illegal drugs, prostitution, or hit men, consumers must rely on information they receive from other people. Thus, this is an area for studying interpersonal communication about products without the help of media ad-

---

[19]United States Congress, Senate Hearings before the Selected Committee on Small Business. *Criminal Redistribution (Fencing) Systems,* 93rd Congress, 1st Session, Part 1, p. 1.

[20]Donald R. Cressey, *Theft of the Nation: The Structure and Operations of Organized Crime in America,* NY: Harper and Row, 1969.

vertising. What one learns about the communication process can be used for drawing up propositions about behavior related to legal products which rely heavily on interpersonal communication or which are prohibited from using media advertising.

A third reason for studying illegal exchanges is that it provides a mechanism for studying the isolated effects of an extended search for information and for the product, for this is one area in which consumers must actively search for the product as well as information about it. For instance, how does one go about finding a hit man? Although one knows that in our society hiring a hit man violates a norm and a law, how does one go about finding out the norms of the subculture in which this type of exchange exists? How does one find out how to buy heroin, let alone, where to buy it?

A fourth reason for examining illegal exchanges is that it gives clues about what needs or preferences are not met within the legal marketing system. For instance, the fact that some consumers will buy stolen television sets is evidence that they are sensitive enough to price deals (price is usually lower when consumers knowingly purchase stolen goods) to take the risk.

Finally, studying illegal exchanges and comparing them with legal marketing exchanges can help one identify the effects of norms which are strong enough to be enforced by laws. For instance, comparing the sale of legal goods with that of fencing stolen goods, or the sale of legal prescription drugs with illegal drugs, provides insights into the effects of legality.

Therefore, given the reasons for studying illegal marketing transactions, we must determine the extent to which these activities are accepted (cognitively) by the society as deviant from or contrary to the norms. (This is included in dimensions IV-C and D in Table 5-1 on page 117.) Peter H. Rossi, *et al.* conducted a study in which two-hundred respondents were asked to rank 140 criminal acts on a nine-point scale of seriousness.[21] (A score of one reflected low seriousness; a score of nine reflected high seriousness.) Many of these acts were marketing transactions. Those which involve illegal exchanges are listed in Table 5-3 along with their mean ranking on the nine-point scale, the variance, and a label as to whether the act is a selling behavior or a buying behavior.

There are several points to make concerning these findings. The first is a cautionary note. Many crimes which are adjacent or close in rank have very close means. Thus, the reader must not assume that differences in rank are statistically significant. We can only use the rankings and means as rough approximations of the perceived seriousness of the crimes.

---

[21]Peter H. Rossi, *et al.,* ''The Seriousness of Crimes: Normative Structure and Individual Differences,'' *American Sociological Review,* Vol. 39, April, 1974, pp. 224–237.

TABLE 5-3.
Seriousness of Illegal Exchange Activities

Rank	Crime	Mean	Variance	Buyer or Seller
1	Planned killing of a policeman	8.474	2.002	Seller
2	Planned killing of a person for a fee	8.406	2.749	Seller
3	Selling heroin	8.293	2.658	Seller
10	Selling LSD	7.949	3.048	Seller
25	Manufacturing and selling drugs known to be harmful to users	7.653	3.280	Seller
26	Knowingly selling contaminated food which results in death	7.596	5.202	Seller
28	Using heroin	7.520	4.871	Buyer
34	Selling secret documents to foreign governments	7.423	5.772	Seller
49	Selling marijuana	6.969	7.216	Seller
54	Selling pep pills	6.867	5.683	Seller
63	Manufacturing and selling autos known to be dangerously defective	6.604	5.968	Seller
71	Performing illegal abortions	6.330	5.723	Seller
73	A public official accepting bribes in return for favors	6.240	6.467	Seller
75	Knowingly selling stolen stocks and bonds	6.138	4.960	Seller
78	Theft of a car for purpose of resale	6.093	5.085	Seller
79	Knowingly selling defective used cars as completely safe	6.093	5.023	Seller
82	Knowingly selling stolen goods	6.021	4.463	Seller
85	Shoplifting a diamond ring from a jewelry store	5.939	5.466	Buyer
90	Knowingly selling worthless stocks as valuable investments	5.821	5.021	Seller
92	Selling liquor to minors	5.789	7.572	Seller
94	Using stolen credit cards	5.570	5.832	Buyer
97	Lending money at illegal interest rates	5.653	5.775	Seller
98	Knowingly buying stolen goods	5.596	5.794	Buyer
102	Using false identification to obtain goods from a store	5.438	6.628	Buyer
103	Bribing a public official to obtain favors	5.394	6.198	Buyer
108	Soliciting for prostitution	5.144	7.687	Seller
110	Overcharging on repairs to automobiles	5.135	6.455	Seller
111	Shoplifting a dress from a department store	5.070	6.308	Buyer
115	Shoplifting a pair of shoes from a shoe store	4.990	6.781	Buyer
116	Overcharging for credit in selling goods	4.970	6.213	Seller
117	Shoplifting a carton of cigarettes	4.969	6.793	Buyer

118	Smuggling goods to avoid paying import duties	4.918	5.618	Buyer
121	Knowingly using inaccurate scales in weighing meat for sale	4.786	5.902	Seller
126	Fixing prices on a consumer product like gasoline	4.629	6.069	Seller
127	Fixing prices on machines sold to businesses	4.619	6.218	Seller
128	Selling pornographic magazines	4.526	7.826	Seller
129	Shoplifting a book in a bookstore	4.424	6.551	Buyer
132	False advertising of a headache remedy	4.083	7.972	Seller

Source: Rossi, *op. cit.*

One striking consistency in the table is in the right-hand column. Of the thirty-eight crimes concerned with illegal exchanges, twenty-seven deal with illegality on the seller's part in the exchange, and only eleven deal with illegality on the buyer's part, a curious double standard. Of the eleven concerned with buyers' activities, five deal with shoplifting. Another way of approaching the table is to compare the seriousness with which sellers' illegal activities are regarded to the seriousness of buyers' participation in the same activities. Compare the rankings of:

(a) selling heroin (#3) with buying heroin (#28);

(b) accepting bribes for favors (#73) with offering bribes for favors (#103);

(c) knowingly selling stolen stocks and bonds (#75), selling stolen automobiles (#78), and selling stolen goods (#82) with knowingly buying stolen goods (#98).

In all cases, the seller's participation is ranked as more serious than the buyer's. A final way of viewing this differential application of the norms to different groups of people (buyers and sellers in this case—see dimension V-B-2 in Table 5-1) is to see which seller practices are listed in Table 5-3 for which the buyer participation (which is also illegal) is not listed. These include (by rank) Numbers 1, 2, 10, 49, 54, 92, 108, and 128. Thus, we arrive at a typology of exchanges.

Type I: Both the seller's participation and the buyer's participation are illegal (e.g., selling and using heroin).

Type II: Only the seller's participation is illegal (e.g., overcharging for credit or using inaccurate scales; commonly referred to as deception or fraud).

Type III: Only the buyer's participation is illegal (e.g., shoplifting).

Type IV: Neither the buyer's nor the seller's participation is illegal (e.g., buying nails in a hardware store).

Comparisons Between Legal and Illegal Exchanges

Earlier, we stated that one of the advantages of studying illegal exchanges is that it can help us understand the distinct differences in exchanges which result from their legal status. In what ways does deviance differ from conformity?

First, we must note that there are many similarities. In both legal and illegal exchanges, sellers must respond to identified buyer needs and preferences. For instance, some professional thieves steal to order; that is, they are asked by potential buyers to obtain certain products.[22] This sensitivity to the needs of different consumers is tied to another similarity between legal and illegal exchanges, specifically, segmenting the market and providing different products and services for each group. For instance, different kinds of prostitutes exist (i.e., streetwalkers and call girls) for different market segments.

One difference between legal and illegal exchanges is the difficulty for the first-time potential buyer of learning the subcultural norms. Given that the potential buyer knows that the exchange is in violation of the norms which are legally enforced, and that the buyer has still decided to engage in such an exchange, he or she must find a supplier and learn the norms of the subculture in which the exchange takes place. Unlike most other products, the consumer searching for a stolen television set or heroin cannot look in the Yellow Pages. The supplier of illegal products and services therefore has a more difficult time getting information to the potential first-time consumer. Much of the information comes through friends and acquaintances who are also part of the subculture. For instance, one's friends are usually the first source of supply for illegal drugs.[23]

Thus, we see that there is a beginner segment and a user segment (as with legal exchanges) which have different information needs. Beginning consumers of illegal products and services will be more sensitive to information focusing on encouraging trial and providing information about supply sources than that which emphasizes "brand" attributes and price. Consumers who are already users will be most sensitive to information on supply sources, price, and "brand" attributes.

Once the buyer and seller have found each other, what is the negotiation pattern? Since they are both violating a norm (although the seller's violation is considered more serious as discussed earlier), how do they come to trust each other? In illegal transactions, the buyer must ascertain whether the other person is actually a seller. Also, the seller must ascertain whether the other

---

[22]James A. Inciardi, *Careers in Crime,* Chicago: Rand McNally College Publishing Co., 1975.

[23]Howard S. Becker, "Becoming a Marijuana User," in *Outsiders: Studies in the Sociology of Deviance,* NY: The Free Press, 1963.

person is a potential buyer or a potential enforcer of the societal norm (for instance, an undercover police officer). Thus, there is a norm of mutual evaluation which is not usually present in legal transactions.[24]

These efforts by the seller to assess who the buyer is will vary, depending on the intensity or severity of the negative sanctions which could be invoked by authorities if the seller were discovered. Of course, the same variable will affect buyers, but to a lesser extent since their violation of the norms is viewed less seriously and, thus, is punished less severely. One thing the seller must do as the intensity of the negative sanctions increases is to selectively market the illegal products or services. The seller wants potential buyers to know about him or her as a supply source; however, the seller does not want enforcement authorities to know of the illegal exchanges. Controls on information will increase relative to the negative sanctions for violating the crime. The severity of negative sanctions will also affect the efficiency of distribution channels in getting illegal products to consumers without being visible to enforcement authorities (these ideas are summarized in Propositions 5-16 and 5-17).

Finally, we can compare situations where the possibility of either an illegal or legal exchange exists. For instance, one can purchase a television from thieves rather than from legal retailers, or one can buy amphetamines for pleasure rather than for medical reasons. If consumers decide to partici-pate in the illegal exchange (i.e., buying a television from thieves), they will

EXHIBIT 5-8.
Propositions About Negative Sanctions

PROPOSITION 5-16.
The greater the negative sanctions which could be invoked by au-thorities against those engaged in an illegal exchange, the more efforts will be made by the seller to segment the market and make certain his or her presence is not known to the segment which could enforce the norm.

PROPOSITION 5-17.
The greater the negative sanctions which could be invoked by au-thorities against those engaged in an illegal exchange, the greater will be the pressures for efficiency in the channels of distribution.

[24]Melanie Wallendorf, "A Comparative Analysis of the Structure of Illegal Exchanges: Abortion, Drugs, Fencing, Gambling, and Prostitution," unpublished M.A. thesis, Depart-ment of Sociology, University of Pittsburgh, May, 1977.

only do so if the price of the illegal purchase is cheaper. In other words, a lower price is expected by buyers in order to compensate for the risks of being arrested or of product failure (since an illegal purchase is not protected by warranties or consumer bureaus). Of course, if an illegal activity is legalized, or the penalty lessened due to a change in norms or beliefs, then the price for the items will decrease because of the removal or lessening of risk. Also, the quality may increase as new technological skills are brought into the marketing system for that product or service. This suggests that the price of illegal products and services is less sensitive to quality fluctuations, but is more sensitive to fluctuations which decrease supply.[25]

SUMMARY In this chapter, we examined how norms develop and are enforced through the mechanism of the group. Reference groups tend to have the most influence on individual purchases of unique, socially visible products. Groups having norms favoring innovation, and members who are cosmopolitan in outlook, will be more innovative than groups not possessing these characteristics. Likewise, a highly cohesive group will exert more influence over consumers' choices than one that is weakly held together.

Norms differ with respect to the stage in the decision-making process during which they become relevant. During the pre-purchase process, a norm specifying the disclosure of information to the consumer is operating. A norm determines, for instance, which party pays the commission in a real estate transfer. And, in the post-purchase phase, norms specify the obligations of the seller and the buyer, often expressed in warranties. How norms are transmitted is also important. The norms of primary groups are more influential than those of peripheral groups.

Norms are distinguished further according to their acceptance, application, degree of explicitness, methods of enforcement, and level of conformity. Traditionally, studies of consumer behavior have excluded illegal marketing exchanges; however, the study of illegal transactions enables us to analyze interpersonal communication processes completely isolated from mass media effects, and to identify the effects of norms enforced by laws. Further research in this area, as well as in the area of group influence in general, is needed to arrive at a better understanding of how consumer behavior develops.

---

[25]See Lawrence J. Redlinger, "Dealing in Dope: Market Mechanisms and Distribution Patterns of Illicit Narcotics," unpublished doctoral dissertation, Northwestern University, Department of Sociology, 1969.

KEY CONCEPTS
Affiliative group
Aspiration group
Behavioral norms
Cohesiveness
Deviance
Dissociative group
Expressive norms
Instrumental norms
Moral norms
Norm of reciprocity
Norms
Primary group
Reactance
Reference group
Sanction
Secondary group
Socially distant reference groups
Word-of-mouth communication

SMALL-SCALE SOCIAL STRUCTURE AND CONSUMER BEHAVIOR:

FAMILIES AND ORGANIZATIONS

CHAPTER GOALS   The objective of this chapter is to help readers understand:
1. **the decision-making structures which are used by husbands and wives;**
2. **how several types of decision-making strategies are implemented by families;**
3. **some of the issues and problems which characterize family consumer research;**
4. **the effects of some parental strategies for influencing children's purchase choices;**
5. **the sources of influence on organizational buyer behavior.**

INTRODUCTION   In this chapter we consider two types of small-scale social structures: the consumer behavior of families and of organizations. Both families and organizations are involved in consumer decisions which involve more than one person. The decisions which are made are ones which the participants believe will maximize the welfare of the group (either the family, the organization, or the organizational subunit) in the long run. For example, a family might decide to purchase a bicycle for the oldest child because the happiness which the bicycle will bring the child and the family outweighs the dollar cost of the bicycle. Again, the group tries to maximize long-run group welfare rather than short-term benefits to an individual or to the group.

Families and organizations are also similar as consumers because the purchase and use activities of one individual or subunit affect the other members of the group. For example, the purchase of a consultant's services by the finance division of a corporation may lead to the identification of a new source of funds which can be used to purchase the additional machinery which the production division has wanted for a long time.

Both families and organizations pool their financial resources, although some members might have special allocations or more power over how the pooled resources are used. Within each group, the members are aware of who has what power over the resources. For example, in a family, older children sometimes have their own copies of their parents' gasoline credit cards. There might be a family understanding, however, that the cards will only be used in an emergency. Similarly, in a corporation, some employees might have gasoline credit cards in the company's name. Of course, there are usually guidelines which govern the use of such cards (e.g., "Only use the card for gas when traveling to a different city on company business.").

Finally, both families and organizations are formalized. Families are governed by legal contracts, marriage contracts, birth certificates stating who the child's parents are, or divorce agreements which include specifications of who has what rights and responsibilities for the children involved. Organizations are governed by legal contracts, articles of incorporation, debt agreements, and contracts with buyers and sellers.

So, families and organizations are similar in many ways. In this chapter we will discuss them separately so that their unique features as well as their similarities can be highlighted. They are both, however, examples of small-scale social structures which have a profound impact on the consumer behavior of the persons involved.

FAMILY STRUCTURE AND DECISION MAKING

Families are important social systems for at least two consumer-related reasons. First, a large array of food, shelter, transportation, medical, recreational, and other products and services are consumed jointly by the family. Secondly, the purchase and use of many products and services which we ordinarily think of as individually consumed, such as clothing, are usually influenced by the family. In fact, it can be convincingly argued that the family should be the main focus for studying consumer behavior.[1] Increasingly, consumer research firms are urging their clients to focus on family (and other group) influences on what appear to be ostensibly individual consumer decisions. For example, a senior executive from Burke Marketing Research, Inc., a major consumer

[1]A recent statement to this effect may be found in Harry L. Davis, "Decision Making Within the Household," in *Selected Aspects of Consumer Behavior: A Summary from the Perspective of Different Disciplines,* a report of the National Science Foundation, Washington, D.C., 1977, pp. 73–97.

research agency, said recently that nearly all of their consumer research projects give very careful attention to family influences on consumer behavior.

Families are small-scale social systems which have structures developed by their members, usually according to prevailing cultural mores. Family social structures typically specify the power, influence, responsibilities, activities, and role expectations of each member. There is a trend in the United States, however, toward individuals consciously negotiating and formalizing these structures to meet personal needs (through pre-marital counseling, marriage contracts, family planning, parenthood training, reliance on child-rearing manuals, and marriage counseling and therapy). This trend is replacing the traditional pattern of relying solely on unconsciously generated structures which are usually very close to the culturally prescribed structures.[2] In addition, families are relying more on outside institutions to take over functions that were previously performed by either the nuclear or extended family. The most recent change is the reliance on schools and day-care centers to perform routine child watching and caring. With such changes occurring, marketers must become even more sensitive to the ways family structures emerge and how they influence purchase decisions and consumption activities. In addition, marketers must keep in mind that the proportion of the population which is single, separated, divorced, or widowed is growing (see Chapter 3 on demographic patterns). Thus, marketers must not assume that the family decision-making structure refers only to traditional nuclear families (husband, wife, and child or children).

Nearly every chapter of this book relates in one way or another to family consumption behavior. In this section, however, research on family decision making is the primary focus. First, we describe family decision-making structure as it has traditionally been treated by marketers. This description offers an insight into the cultural prescriptions placed on family structures. Next, some of the problems (both methodological and conceptual) with many studies of family decision making will be explained. This discussion has two advantageous outcomes: (1) it offers a guide for marketers and students trying to evaluate the studies of family decision-making structures, and (2) it offers guidelines for future research on family decision-making structures. Finally, we offer propositions about family decision-making structures, along with the action implications drawn from them. Because of the problems inherent in present studies, however, these propositions are less definitive than others in this book.

---

[2]John Scanzoni, "Changing Sex Roles and Emerging Directions in Family Decision Making," *Journal of Consumer Research*, Vol. 4, December, 1977, pp. 185–188.

Traditional Approaches

Traditional studies of family decision making have focused on who is "dominant" in a particular decision, but what is meant by "dominance" is often not specified. Generally, dominance refers to high relative influence (that is, having more influence on decision making than other members of the family). Using this concept of dominance, four types of decision-making structures are specified:[3]

(1) autonomic—approximately an equal number of decisions are made by each spouse, but these decisions are made separately.

(2) husband-dominant.

(3) wife-dominant.

(4) joint—equal influence by each spouse in each decision.

Using this typology, studies have tried to determine when the different decision-making structures exist. For instance, one study concludes that:[4]

(1) husband-dominance is more likely when the product is used manually outside the home (e.g., lawnmowers, gardening supplies).

(2) husband-dominance is more likely when the product is mechanically complex and expensive (e.g., automobiles).

(3) wife-dominance is more likely when the product is used inside the house, especially if it relates to decor (e.g., rugs).

(4) wife-dominance is more likely when the product is a cleaning supply or appliance (e.g., detergents, washing machines).

Obviously, these decision-making structures conform to traditional cultural definitions of the husband and wife roles.

Decision-Making Strategies

One researcher on family consumer behavior has suggested an interesting summary of various family decision-making strategies.[5] Two types of decision making are suggested. *Consensual* decision making means an agreement among family members about what the goals or desired outcomes of a decision should be. For example, for whatever car is purchased there is complete agreement that it should be a compact station wagon. The second type of decision making is *accommodative*. For instance, one family member may want a compact station wagon, while another may want a larger luxury car or perhaps a different type of product altogether. The decision that is reached

[3]P. G. Herbst, "Conceptual Framework for Studying the Family," in O. A. Aeser and S. B. Hammond (eds.), *Social Structure and Personality in a City*, London: Routledge, 1954.

[4]Arch Woodside, "Dominance and Conflict in Family Purchasing Decisions," in M. Venkatesan (ed.), *Proceedings of the Third Annual Association for Consumer Research Conference*, 1972, pp. 650–659.

[5]Davis, *op. cit.*, 1977.

involves accommodations or compromise by at least one person and quite possibly by everyone in the family. Of course, family decisions are seldom either totally consensual or totally accommodative; but these two descriptions of decisions, though simplifications, are useful for discussing decision-making strategies and ways of implementing them. Alternative decision-making strategies will be discussed in terms of a perspective expressed by Davis which is shown in Table 6-1.[6]

Role Structure Strategy. In the role structure strategy, one person assumes the role of expert or specialist in a particular product or service area, and this person assumes primary responsibility for making decisions in that area. Others in the family generally accept that person's decisions concerning which automobile to purchase or where to have it serviced. Others in the family will have little concern or interest in the final decision about where to bring the car for a tune-up. This strategy will then result in some decisions being husband-dominant in their structure and others being wife-dominant.

The Budget Strategy. Under a budget strategy, certain rules are established which control the decision making. For example, the purchase of an inexpensive appliance brand rather than a more expensive alternative may be dictated by the amount of funds allocated in advance to that purchase. Once the rule or budget is set—"Spend no more than forty-five dollars"—there can be no disagreement about which brand to purchase if one brand is above the budgeted amount and one below. There may be disagreement about what the rule or budget should be; however, once the decision rule is established, decisions are made as if total consensus exists.

Problem-Solving Strategy. Sometimes group discussion is necessary for creating consensus when a problem is encountered. Expert advice may be sought to enlighten the family's discussion (e.g., "Why don't we ask Emily? I believe she just bought one."). In discussing the problem a solution may emerge which is for everyone superior to those solutions suggested initially by individual family members, and this solution may involve doing what everyone wants. For example, a vacation spot or restaurant might be located which has features which appeal to everyone, or a national park which offers fine boating facilities for the boating enthusiasts in the family as well as excellent hiking trails for the hiking enthusiasts may be found.

---

[6]*Ibid.*

TABLE 6-1.
Alternative
Decision-Making
Strategies

Goals	Strategy	Ways of implementing
	Role structure	"The Specialist"
	Budgets	"The Controller"
"Consensus" (Family members agree about goals)	Problem solving	"The Expert" "The Better Solution" "The Multiple Purchase"
"Accommodation" (Family members disagree about goals)	Persuasion	"The Irresponsible Critic" "Feminine Intuition" "Shopping Together" "Coercion" "Coalitions"
	Bargaining	"The Next Purchase" "The Impulse Purchase" "The Procrastinator"

Source: Davis, *op. cit.*, 1977.

Persuasion Strategy. A persuasion strategy involves one person attempting to convince another to accept an action which the second person considers unacceptable.[7] Persuasion can be very subtle. A child might threaten, through a facial expression, to throw a tantrum in a public place if a box of cookies is not purchased. An icy "I told you so" may cause a spouse to serve a more conventional dinner in lieu of a gourmet treat. The formation of a coalition may also be used, e.g., "Everyone else wants this, why should you get your own way?!" The counter to this may simply be, "Because I know better" or "I'm your parent." This is a coercive exercise of authority.

Bargaining Strategy. A bargaining strategy involves mutual give and take, and can be expressed in a variety of ways. Some family members may "get their way" on one purchase with the understanding that others will get their way on other purchases. Or, through mutual agreement one spouse may select the make of an automobile to be purchased, while the other spouse gets to select the color and accessories.

[7]Gerald Zaltman and Robert Duncan, *Strategies for Planned Change*, NY: Wiley-Interscience, 1977.

It is unlikely that one decision-making strategy will dominate all or even most family consumption decisions, for the relative involvement of family members and the type of strategy used will vary by product category. Moreover, for any given product different strategies are used during different stages of the larger decision. For example, role structure strategy may dominate the selection of a product, but a persuasion or a bargaining strategy may prevail in the selection of a retail outlet in which to buy the product.

Problems with Family Consumer Research

When examining studies of family decision-making structure and evaluating their results, one must keep in mind the problems inherent in many of them. The relative influence of each spouse in decision making varies by product class.[8] There has been a tendency, however, to study one type of purchase (such as durables or a new home) and then apply its structure to a broader range of purchases. Unfortunately for marketers, family decision making is not that simple.

Not only does the relative influence of the husband and the wife in the decision process vary by product class, it also varies by stage in the decision process.[9] In other words, one spouse may be the first one to suggest a purchase; the other spouse may go to different stores to get information on price, product features, delivery, and service; they may jointly evaluate the alternatives and decide which product to buy and from what dealer; and only one of the spouses may go to the selected dealer and complete the transaction. So who is dominant? Depending on what stage is studied, either spouse could be called dominant or the process could be termed joint. What is important for the marketer is to understand the relative influence of each person in each stage and how the family implements that influence.

Decision-making structures for any particular family also change over the life cycle. There is usually more joint decision making in the early years of a marriage. But, as the years pass, the spouses' familiarity with products and with each other's preferences, and with each other's competencies to

---

[8]Richard C. Becherer, Jon F. Bibb, and Edward A. Riordan, "Spousal Perceptions of Household Purchasing Influence: A Multiperson-Multiscale Validation," in Thomas V. Greer (ed.), *Combined Proceedings of 1973 American Marketing Association Spring and Fall Conference,* pp. 289–292; Harry L. Davis, "Dimensions of Marital Roles in Consumer Decision Making," *Journal of Marketing Research,* Vol. 7 (May, 1970), pp. 168–177; Gilbert A. Churchill, Jr., and Robert A. Hansen, "An Empirical Examination of Some Husband-Wife Decision Making Propositions," in Ronald C. Curhan (ed.), *Combined Proceedings of 1974 American Marketing Association Spring and Fall Conferences,* pp. 67–70.

[9]Woodside, 1972, *op. cit.;* Churchill and Hansen, 1974, *op. cit.;* and Davis, 1970, *op. cit.*

evaluate products increases. Thus, there is more specialization in (or division of) purchase tasks.[10] Therefore, studies should not aggregate the patterns of families but should isolate the decision-making patterns characteristic of families in different stages of the life cycle (see Chapter 3 for a discussion of the family life cycle).

As was mentioned earlier, traditional family roles are changing. On the basis of traditional role patterns, one would expect that women would be more likely to do things to help keep the decision-making process going smoothly (social-emotional acts), while men would be more likely to perform tasks more closely related to the actual decision, such as asking for or giving ideas (task-oriented acts). As can be seen in Table 6-2, however, one research study found that overall there is a high level of equality.[11]

TABLE 6-2. Husband-Wife Decision Patterns		Task-Oriented Acts	Social-Emotional Acts	Total Acts
	Husband	54%	49%	53%
	Wife	46%	51%	47%
		100%	100%	100%

Thus, while in the past marketers may have been able to predict with reasonable accuracy which decision-making structure applied to many families (that being the culturally prescribed pattern), there is now a substantial deviation from the traditional family structural pattern, thereby making consumer research for each product even more important. For instance, in a study of decision making in two product categories (automobiles and furniture), respondents were questioned about who had greater relative influence with respect to six smaller or component decisions included in each of the two purchase decisions. The six component decisions included in the decision to purchase an automobile were when to purchase, how much money to spend, the make, the model, the color, and where to purchase the automobile. Four basic findings highlight the complexity of relative influence in decision making:

---

[10]Donald J. Hempel, "A Cross-Cultural Analysis of Husband Wife Roles in House Purchase Decisions," in M. Vankatesan (ed.), *Proceedings of the 3rd Annual Association for Consumer Research Conference,* 1972, pp. 816–829; Donald J. Hempel, "Family Role Structure and Housing Decisions," in Mary Jane Schlinger (ed.), Advances in Consumer Research, Vol. 2, *Proceedings of the 1974 Association for Consumer Research Conference,* pp. 71–79.

[11]Johan Arndt and Edgar Crane, "Marital Roles in Intrafamilial Decision Making on Spending Matters," in Ronald C. Curhan (ed.), *Combined Proceedings of 1974 American Marketing Association Spring and Fall Conferences,* pp. 63–66.

1. There was little relation in the relative influence patterns for the different product categories (e.g., automobile and furniture patterns were different).

2. There were marked differences in the relative influence of husband and wife on the six component decisions for a particular product category (e.g., automobile make and automobile color decision patterns were different).

3. There was a wide variation among families on the relative influence of husband and wife for any particular component decision within a particular product category (e.g., different families had different decision patterns in choosing automobile color—this may be partially due to life cycle stage differences).

4. There were not family "types" in the configuration of relative influences on the six component decisions for a particular product category (e.g., the three most prevalent patterns on the six component decisions accounted for only 32 per cent of the husbands' responses and only 45 per cent of the wives' responses for the automobile purchase).[12]

Finally, studies of family decision-making structure suffer from methodological differences which make their results difficult to compare. For instance, some studies include only wives as respondents, some include both husband and wife, others include only children, and some include all members of the family as respondents. The latter, although the most desirable from a theoretical standpoint, is the least often used. One study found that less than 65 per cent of the husband-wife pairs were in complete agreement about the relative influence of each spouse in several aspects of two different product purchases.[13]

It was also found that the more specific the question, the greater the convergence of responses.[14] There is a problem as to whether a true, objective assessment of the relative influence of each spouse has any meaning for the person trying to understand consumer behavior. In fact, what may be important is to know how each spouse perceives the relative influences and how the agreement or disagreement between the two sets of perceptions affects the decision process itself.

Some studies ask respondents about actual decision making, others observe simulated decision making ("Decide what you would do if you received a cash prize of one thousand dollars"), and only a few observe *actual* decision

---

[12]Davis, 1970, *op. cit.*

[13]*Ibid.*

[14]Harry L. Davis, "Measurement of Husband-Wife Influence in Consumer Purchase Decisions," *Journal of Marketing Research,* Vol. 8, August, 1971, pp. 305–312.

making. Those which only observe decision making, however, neglect the impact of covert influence, which the respondents understand, but which the researcher is not aware of.[15] This oversight is avoided when observations are combined with studying the perceptions of the respondents. Some studies ask only about overall dominance in the decision, while some ask about relative influence in the different stages in the decision-making process and about relative influence concerning different product attributes (e.g., color and size). Again, the more complete investigation is rarer.

Yet, even if one is able to determine the relative influences of the husband and wife on the decision processes for a family at a certain stage in the life cycle, and for each of the component decisions in that purchase decision, one is still missing crucial elements which are essential to understanding family decision making and family structure. First of all, despite knowing that one spouse has much greater influence in a particular decision, it is still not clear why or how this person has more influence. For instance, consider a decision which is usually made by a wife. She may make this decision because the husband is not interested in it, or because she won an argument about what the decision would be. Or she might also make the decision after consulting all family members about their preferences. Although in each case the wife plays the role of decision maker, different family authority structures are implied by the different cases. Thus, in addition to knowing who makes what decisions, it is crucial to know the structure and process underlying this pattern.

Although marketers often focus on the purchase process, they should not, for obvious reasons, ignore the consumption process. One must ask how the spouses' relative influences on the consumption process affect relative influences on the decision-making and purchase process. At first one might suggest the proposition: "The more involved a consumer is in the consumption process, the more influence he or she will have in the decision-making and purchase process."[16] But, by considering products purchased as gifts (when the giver makes a selection based on his or her tastes as well as the tastes of the recipient) as well as many products purchased for children, we see that this proposition is not always true. In one study it was hypothesized that a child would have higher relative influence on the mother's selection of brands of cereal if the mother were very child-centered (measured by involvement in many activities which benefit the child). The results, however, were in the opposite direction: mothers who were not child-centered were

[15]Marilyn Dunsing and Jeanne L. Hafstrom, "Methodological Considerations in Family Decision Making Studies," in Mary Jane Schlinger (ed.), *Advances in Consumer Research,* Vol. 2, Proceedings of 1974 Association for Consumer Research Conference, pp. 103–111.

[16]Lewis A. Berey and Richard W. Pollay, "The Influencing Role of the Child in Family Decision Making," *Journal of Marketing Research,* Vol. 5, February, 1968, pp. 70–72.

those who made choices according to the child's wishes, and did so in order to placate the child (see Figure 6-1). On the other hand, mothers who were child-centered were more likely to discount the child's preferences and make selections based on what they thought was best for the child. Thus, even though the purchase was one in which the child would have high relative influence and participation in the consumption process, the child did not always have high relative influence in the decision-making process.

FIGURE 6-1.
Child vs. Mother

Berry's World

"And remember, if Mommy doesn't want to buy what Uncle Dudley recommends, throw a fit!"

Some Propositions Keeping in mind the difficulties of many existing studies, there are a number of propositions which are compatible with present theories about decision making. They are, however, still in need of testing. First, we propose that joint participation in decision making is more likely as the importance of the purchase increases.[17] Thus, to a certain extent, one could expect that lower income households would be more likely to have a higher level of joint decision making since many purchases will seem more important because of their income level.[18] One possible implication is that marketers of products which are considered high importance items (either socially, financially, or physically) should develop products which meet the desires of all family members and should aim their communications at all of them. Such communications could even be designed to encourage family discussion of the product. Marketers of other products should determine to which family members the product is important and design their messages for these persons.

Also, decision making is more likely to be either joint or autonomic (that is, it is less likely to be either husband or wife dominant) when the relative positions of the husband and wife (on occupation, education, and dollar contribution to family income) are approximately equal. Major decision making is more likely to be husband dominant when his status on these variables is higher than the wife's. Major decision making is more likely to be wife dominant when her status on these variables is higher than the husband's.

Support for this proposition is mixed. A positive association between education and participation in decision making has been found by Arndt and Crane,[19] by Hempel,[20] and in the proposed direction but at a statistically nonsignificant level by Churchill and Hansen.[21] In examining the wife's contribution to family income, her commitment to her occupation, the number of years she has worked, and the number of hours per week she is employed, Hempel found that all of these variables had a positive association with the wife's participation in decision making. In a simpler analysis, however, Arndt and Crane found that there was not a statistically significant difference (although the small difference was in the proposed direction) between the influence levels of employed and nonemployed women. Unlike the Hempel research, Arndt and Crane's analysis does not take into account the wife's position relative to her husband's. The only conclusion one can make from their research is that whether a woman is employed does not seem to explain differences in family decision-making structures. Thus, their research does not disconfirm the relative contributions proposition.

---

[17]Richard Hansen, Gary M. Munsinger, and Jean Draper, "A Dyadic Analysis of Power Roles in the Housing Decision Process," in Fred C. Allvine (ed.), *Combined Proceedings of 1971 American Marketing Association Spring and Fall Conferences,* pp. 397–401.

[18]Partial support is given to this expectation in spite of the limited data in the Churchill research.

[19]Arndt and Crane, *op. cit.*

[20]Hempel, 1972, 1974, *op. cit.*

[21]Churchill and Hansen, *op. cit.* page 146

EXHIBIT 6-1.
Propositions About Family Structure and Decision Making

PROPOSITION 6-1.
Joint participation in decision making is more likely as the importance of the purchase increases.

PROPOSITION 6-2.
Decision making is more likely to be either joint or autonomic (that is, it is less likely to be either husband or wife dominant) when the relative positions of the husband and wife (on occupation, education, and dollar contribution to family income) are approximately equal. Decision making is more likely to be husband dominant when his status on these variables is higher than his wife's. Decision making is more likely to be wife dominant when her status on these variables is higher than her husband's.

The research mentioned above has several implications. Marketers must be careful not to aggregate data on consumer decision processes without regard to the relative positions of husbands and wives. Instead, segments of consumers which are homogeneous with respect to relative husband-wife status should be defined, and then the decision processes of each segment should be studied. Where there are differences, separate marketing strategies which take these decision process differences into account should be developed. Where there are similarities (implying that relative positions of husband and wife are not relevant for decision processes for that product), segments can be combined and appealed to with one set of marketing strategies. The untested nature of the proposition makes it difficult to predict when the relative positions of husband and wife will be a crucial factor in the decision process. But, the proposition does have enough support that it should be taken into account when segmenting markets and doing research on family decision processes.

Other research has focused on children's decision making and how that is influenced by parents and advertising. One study investigated what decisions children make when their parents (mothers, in this case) disagree with a television advertisement.[22] After seeing a television program containing an advertisement for a new toy, the children received one of three types of communication from their mothers: (1) power-assertive, in which the parent

---

[22]V. Kanti Prasad, T. R. Rao, and Anees A. Sheikh, "Mother vs. Commercial," *Journal of Communication,* Vol. 28, Winter, 1978, pp. 91–96.

used power and authority; (2) reasoning, in which the parent warmly explained why the toy product was not considered a good one; and (3) no information. Then the children played a game and as a prize were asked to select a toy, one of which was the advertised toy. There were three basic findings from this research. First, the child took longer to make a choice when there had been no information from the parent than when the parent had used either a power-assertive or a reasoning strategy for communicating with the child about the product (Proposition 6-3 in Exhibit 6-2). Second, when the advertisement was highly attractive, the children chose the advertised product over an unadvertised product in the same proportions *regardless* of the mother's strategy. In other words, highly attractive ads are more effective than mother's opinion in influencing the child's choice. Finally, when the advertisement was moderately attractive, the children were likely to follow the mother's reasoning strategy and not choose the advertised product. Under this same condition, however, they were likely to react against the mother's power assertive strategy and choose the advertised product. These two findings are Propositions 6-4 and 6-5 in Exhibit 6-2.

This implies that, in situations where the child makes the product choice and actually purchases the product himself or herself, the advertiser will want to develop very attractive and convincing advertisements. But, if only moderately attractive ads can be developed, or if the parents actually make the purchase, it will be important to see that the product is also acceptable to the parents. The implication for the consumer educator is that it may be necessary

EXHIBIT 6-2.
Propositions About Parental Influence on Children's Purchase Decisions

PROPOSITION 6-3.
When children have only information from an advertisement about a product, their decision-making time will be greater than when they can combine advertisement information with information about how their parents regard the product.

PROPOSITION 6-4.
When an advertisement is highly attractive, children will choose their preferred product regardless of their parents' strategy.

PROPOSITION 6-5.
When an advertisement is moderately attractive, children will follow the suggestions of their parents if the parents use a reasoning strategy, but will react against their parents' suggestions if the parents use a power-assertive strategy.

to train parents in the use of reasoning strategies and to discourage the use of power-assertive strategies since the parent will want to have a positive influence on the child's product choices.

SOURCES OF INFLUENCE ON ORGANIZATIONAL BUYER BEHAVIOR

One of the major developments in the consumer behavior field has been the acknowledgement that the formal organization is an appropriate group for consumer researchers to study.[23] The published literature on organizational buying behavior has grown considerably in recent years.[24] The Association for Consumer Research and the American Marketing Association, through the sponsorship of various publications, symposiums, and workshops, have helped stimulate the study of organizations as consumers. The purpose of this section is not so much to introduce the reader to the research on organizational buyer behavior, but to identify a sample of the topics commonly discussed in this area. A framework which has been found useful for viewing organizational buyer behavior topics has emerged from a workshop sponsored by the American Marketing Association.[25] This framework is discussed below, and nearly all discussion in subsequent chapters about organizations as consumers is related to one of the elements in this framework.

Figure 6-2 presents a framework for viewing various factors which may influence an organization's buying decision. Cell 1 of Figure 6-2 concerns factors relating primarily to the purchasing agent. A substantial portion of the literature on organizational buying processes pertains to the purchasing agent.

Cell 2 pertains mostly to the buying center. The "buying center" refers to a group of individuals within a firm who participate in a particular purchase

[23]This is discussed most recently in Yoram Wind, "Organizational Buying Behavior," *Review of Marketing, 1978,* Gerald Zaltman and Thomas V. Bonoma (eds.), Chicago: The American Marketing Association, 1978. Further discussion of this development may be found in Yoram Wind, "On the Interface Between Organizational and Consumer Buying Behavior," *Advances in Consumer Research,* Vol. 5, H. Keith Hunt (ed.), Chicago: Association for Consumer Research, 1978; Arch Woodside, *et al.* (eds.), *Consumer and Industrial Buying Behavior,* N.Y.: North-Holland, 1977; and in Kjell Grønhaug, "Organizational Buying Behavior: A Research Area for the Social Scientist" *American Behavioral Scientist,* March, 1978.

[24]For reviews of this literature see Yoram Wind, "Organizational Buyer Behavior," *op. cit.;* Kjell Grønhaug, *op cit.:* Thomas V. Bonoma, Gerald Zaltman and Wesley Johnston, *Industrial Buying Behavior,* Cambridge, MA: Marketing Science Institute, 1978; Jagdish N. Sheth, "Recent Developments in Organizational Buying Behavior," in Woodside, *et al.* (eds.), *op. cit.;* and Francesco M. Nicosia and Yoram Wind, "Emerging Models of Organizational Buying Processes," *Industrial Marketing Management,* Vol. 6, No. 5, 1977, pp. 353–369.

[25]Thomas V. Bonoma and Gerald Zaltman (eds.), *Organizational Behavior,* Chicago: American Marketing Association, 1978.

FIGURE 6-2.
The Organizational Buying Locus of Influence Grid

ORGANIZATIONAL LOCUS

	Intrafirm Influences	Interfirm Influences
DEPARTMENTAL LOCUS	Cell 1. Intradepartmental, Intra-organizational Influences	Cell 3. Intradepartmental, Inter-organizational Influences
Within Purchasing Department	*The Purchasing Agent* Social Factors Price, Cost Factors Supply Continuity and Shortage Risk Avoidance	*Professionalism Among Purchasers* Word-Of-Mouth Communication Trade Shows and Press Supplier-Purchaser Reciprocity
	Cell 2. Interdepartmental, Intra-organizational Influences	Cell 4. Interdepartmental, Inter-organizational Influences
Between Departments	*The Buying Center* Organizational Structure Power and Conflict Processes Gatekeeper Role	*Organizations And Environment* Technological Changes Nature of Suppliers Cooperative Buying

decision process.[26] Relevant considerations here involve the relative influence of various persons or groups in a corporation and how these influence patterns may vary according to various aspects of the decision. Who, for example, is influential when the product is a component part rather than new capital equipment?

Cell 3 involves environmental factors affecting the purchasing agent or purchasing department. This cell suggests issues involving the impact of professional and trade associations on purchasing agents. Is there a sense of community or identity among purchasing agents, and if so, does this influence their behavior as purchasing agents? How does a purchasing agent receive general information about job-related tasks? How important are journals and

---

[26]Frederick E. Webster and Yoram Wind, *Organizational Buying Behavior,* Englewood Cliffs, NJ: Prentice-Hall, 1972.

magazines, trade shows, and personal contacts with purchasing agents in other firms in helping the purchasing agent make decisions?

Finally, Cell 4 focuses attention on interdepartmental and interfirm influences. This cell contains environmental opportunities and constraints posed by other firms (both consumers and competitors) and government agencies. Relatively little information exists about the impact of environmental factors on relationships among groups within a firm with respect to a purchasing decision.

The Purchasing Agent (Cell 1)

Social Factors. One researcher has stated that the friendships maintained by purchasing agents are very important, though they are often downplayed or even denied by many agents.[27] Purchasing agents buy from friends or individuals with whom they get along well. Although this does not mean that decisions by purchasing managers are not based on competitive bidding, it does imply that the purchasing agent may work diligently with a friend to make certain that the friend's bid is competitive. Such practices may involve writing specifications in the request for bids which uniquely favor the friend's organization. For example, a set of specifications for the purchase of roofing materials may state that slate will be used. If the friend's organization specializes in slate roofs, then it is more likely that the friend's firm will get the contract.

Tailoring specifications to fit the specialties of certain suppliers might be done for professional reasons as well, such as when the reputations of various selling firms is important. It may be believed that a particular firm, because of its size or reputation, would be particularly well-suited to provide a product or service. This often occurs in the purchase of computers. Also, purchasing agents prefer to buy from firms they know will be around in the future, especially if a large capital outlay is involved. These factors are included in Proposition 6-6 in Exhibit 6-3. For example, when capital equipment is expected to last for a number of years, there is a strong preference for a reliable, stable, and financially sound supplier who will be readily available when replacement parts are needed. This factor works against any supplying firm which is small, new, or new in the particular product line.

Purchasing managers' relationships with others in their organizations are another central factor which is influential in the buying process. A strong-

---

[27]George Hayward, "The Adoption of New Industrial Products," *Marketing,* November, 1977, pp. 44ff; and Lance P. Jarvis and James B. Wilcox, "True Vendor Loyalty or Simply Repeat Purchase Behavior," *Industrial Marketing Management,* Vol. 6, No. 1, 1977, pp. 9–14.

EXHIBIT 6-3.
*Propositions About
Organizational Buyer
Behavior*

PROPOSITION 6-6.
The larger the capital outlay for a purchase, the more concerned the purchasing agent will be with such factors as the selling organization's size, reputation, stability, and reliability.

PROPOSITION 6-7.
The greater the number of alternative suppliers, the lower the general concern with continuity of supply in any purchase decision.

PROPOSITION 6-8.
The more a purchasing agent sees himself or herself as a professional and participates in professional activities, the more contact the purchasing agent will have with other purchasing agents, and the more he or she will use these contacts as sources of information about available products and services.

PROPOSITION 6-9.
As the rapidity of technological change increases, the importance of the purchasing manager decreases, and the importance of technical and engineering individuals in the buying center increases.

PROPOSITION 6-10.
As price increases, the less importantly or the less directly involved is the purchasing manager in the purchase decision.

willed purchasing manager, for example, may exert a disproportionate influence on the opinions of others regarding a potential purchase. Weak or ineffectual purchasing managers may be unable to negotiate well, and, therefore, will not get favorable terms for their organization.

Price and Cost Factors. The influence of price and cost factors in the purchasing agent's decisions is a recurrent theme in the organizational buying behavior literature. Three viewpoints are common: (1) price and cost factors are less important than are social factors in the purchasing agent's decision; (2) price and cost factors in the organizational purchasing decision are very important; and (3) the significance of price and cost factors varies according to several factors such as the type of product or service and the nature of the purchasing agent.

Regarding the first viewpoint, empirical data exist which are extremely supportive of the position that price and cost factors are not the central mechanisms in purchasing. One study shows that the successful bidder in a competitive bidding situation was the low bidder in only 40 per cent of the cases, which suggests that low prices are not sufficient or even necessary for winning a contract. This implies that the industrial salesperson must analyze the situation in order to determine on what basis the contract will be awarded and then put the necessary efforts into seeing that his or her organization meets these criteria.[28]

The second position suggests that price and cost factors are the central (or at least a central) predictor of organizational purchasing behavior; however, for social or interpersonal reasons, purchasing agents will not admit their importance. It is seen as "bad taste" to admit that price is a central factor in supplier choice.[29]

The third position suggests that the importance of price and cost factors depends upon what is being purchased, the type of organization doing the purchasing, and the purchasing agent. For example, one researcher has indicated that when people with strong technical backgrounds in electrical engineering are elevated to positions as purchasing agents, cost may become of secondary importance to the technical aspect of the product. For a person trained in accounting, the reverse may be true.[30] Again, the type of product being purchased (for example, first-time purchase of capital equipment versus a rebuy of office supplies, or a commodity versus a specialty product) will have a strong effect on the importance of price for the purchasing agent. Of the three positions, this is the most tenable.

Supply Continuity and Shortages.   In addition to quality, price, and risk levels, supply continuity in a time of shortage, or even in a time of plenty when shortages are anticipated, can be a central factor in the buying decision. The greater the number of alternative suppliers, the lower the general concern with continuity of supply in any purchase decision (Proposition 6-7 in Exhibit 6-3). A familiar example of the concern over supply continuity occurred during the coal strike in the winter of 1978. Since union-mined coal was unavailable for a long period of time, public utilities in the Northeast had to

[28]J. Patrick Kelly and James W. Coaker, "Can We Generalize About Choice Criteria for Industrial Purchasing Decisions," paper presented at the AMA Workshop on Organizational Buyer Behavior, University of Pittsburgh, April 23–24, 1976.

[29]Robert Parket, "The Industrial Buyer—Human But Rational," *Journal of Purchasing,* Vol. 7, No. 4, November, 1971, pp. 63–74.

[30]S. Swallow, "The Attitudes and Behavior of Industrial Buyers Toward Price," *Management Decision,* Vol. 9, No. 1, Spring, 1971.

rely on coal shipped from other parts of the country or from nonunion mines. Therefore, since the number of suppliers was drastically reduced, public utility decisions about purchases of coal during this period were made very differently from the way coal purchase decisions were usually made.

Risk and Risk Avoidance.   One of the most frequently cited factors in the individual purchase decision is that of risk, or more appropriately, risk avoidance. It is generally assumed that purchasing agents and purchasing managers strive to minimize the social and financial risks associated with the acquisition of a new product or service. Secondary data sources (e.g., Dunn and Bradstreet) are often used to help reduce risk. Such factors as the unionization of factories, who the stockholders of the selling firm are, and other factors ostensibly unrelated to the purchase decision may be included in an evaluation of the risk involved in purchasing from that supplier.

Social factors such as knowing, trusting, or having favorable reports about the seller all act to reduce risk. Experience and expertise, another social factor, are also very important when risk is high. Not surprisingly, reliability, which often translates into size of the potential supplying firm, is used as an indicator of the degree of risk associated with the purchase.

The Buying Center (Cell 2)   Considerable research is needed to evaluate a number of key issues involved in the idea of a buying center. First of all, what individuals representing what departments usually comprise a buying center? Is such a question even meaningful? Is there a general pattern in the membership of organizational buying centers? Why and how do various members of a buying center make different judgments regarding a product or service acquisition? How are these judgments integrated?

For example, an accountant, a financial officer, an engineer, a metallurgical scientist, and a production vice-president might evaluate the qualities of a single piece of equipment quite differently. Depending upon the kind of organization, some of these individuals would not even be included in the buying decision.

Issues of Organizational Structure.   Some companies are designed so that the purchasing group's responsibility is only to implement buying decisions by doing the paper work, while other groups in the firm make the critical buying decisions. Other companies want an effective purchasing department made up of technically trained people who can combat fixed or rigid ideas held elsewhere in the firm, and who can contribute to the technical as well as to the marketing and business aspects of purchasing.

Power in the Buying Center.   Hospital decision making is an especially good example of the buying center concept at work, and also of power bases in the organization. The buying decision in hospital acquisitions often involves a hospital administrator, physicians, and nurses. The nurses are often the final purchasing authority with regard to office equipment, supplies, and other items such as the purchase of an important medical treatment apparatus. The administrator, charged with formal purchasing authority in the hospital organization, may primarily serve the role of an informant who keeps others in the organization aware of new purchase possibilities.

The Gatekeeper Role in the Buying Center.   Gatekeepers are persons who filter information as it flows from its source to its ultimate destination. Gatekeepers may be informal or unofficial decision makers. Intentionally or unintentionally, they sometimes allow more favorable information about a preferred bidder to reach the formal decision makers; and, at the same time, they may not allow favorable information about less preferred bidders to reach the decision makers.

Professionalism Among Purchasers (Cell 3)

The concept of interfirm or environmental factors as they affect the purchasing group is novel to the organizational buying behavior literature. One such environmental factor is professionalism. Increasingly, purchasing agents are seeing themselves as professionals who have specialized knowledge.[31] One consequence of increasing professionalism is increased interaction of purchasing agents with their colleagues in other firms. This contact might have a very influential effect on the organizational purchasing process. This is expressed in Proposition 6-8 in Exhibit 6-3.

Word-of-Mouth Communications.   One large-scale study has indicated that word-of-mouth communication among buying firms is very important in purchase decisions.[32] Such communication may be established by telephone, at trade shows and various professional meetings, or through other sources. For example, the purchasing agent of a smaller firm may ask the purchasing

---

[31]Robert Barath and Paul S. Hugstad, "To What Extent Does Increased Professional Status Affect the Buying Behavior of Purchasing Agents," *Industrial Marketing Management*, Vol. 6, No. 4, 1977, pp. 297–306.

[32]John A. Czepiel, "Communication Networks and Innovation in Industrial Communities," paper presented at the International Symposium on Industrial Innovation, University of Strathclyde, Glasgow, Scotland, September, 1977.

agent in a larger firm for advice about conveyor belts. Newly hired purchasing managers or other executives may also be excellent sources of information about new products or services. Thus, the major communication network for purchasing agents consists of other purchasing agents in the same industry. As one purchasing agent has remarked, "You know who is interested in the same petro-chemical or the same kind of equipment as you. You don't hesitate to get their experience with vendor companies or their opinions about price market trends."[33]

A second major source of information for purchasing managers is the marketing or sales staff of various vendors. Purchasing agents may talk with industrial salespeople even though they never order from them. By talking with the salesperson, they get information from the other side of the fence about available products and services. This information is combined with information from other purchasing agents.[34]

Trade Shows and Journals. Trade shows are important as a gathering place in which face-to-face communication between purchasers can occur, but they also provide a forum for directing promotional communications at prospective purchasers. What little literature there is that evaluates industrial advertising, whether occurring at a trade show or in the trade press, suggests that a considerable amount of industrial advertising is misdirected. In other words, it is not necessarily directed to the individual having the greatest influence in the buying process or it tends to stress the wrong (or at least the irrelevant) product attributes for that individual.

For instance, in the case of advertising directed at a purchasing manager, one analysis indicates that the technical or R&D elements of the product are too often stressed, rather than the cost savings or delivery capacity. These latter factors, however, are probably more in line with current surveys of what the purchasing manager uses in the overall evaluation of a potential product or service. Further support for this conclusion was provided by a content analysis of approximately one hundred products advertised in purchasing journals directed toward chemists and R&D people in firms. Approximately 80 per cent of the ads analyzed were found to be identical whether they were directed toward chemists or toward R&D people. The obvious conclusion is that many industrial marketers simply develop one ad and include it in several magazines without any concern for the fact that there might be completely different buying concerns for the two subgroups.

---

[33]Bonoma and Zaltman, *op. cit.*
[34]*Ibid.*

Supplier-Purchaser Reciprocity. The issues of formal and informal reciprocity ("You buy from us and we'll buy from you") at the supplier-purchaser level have been commented on at some length in the consumer behavior literature.[35] Much of the commentary, however, is speculative, for reciprocity has received little empirical study because of its sensitive nature. There is, though, little question among those who are involved in purchasing that reciprocity is a fact of life, whether it is the formal "You buy from me and I will buy from you," or the more informal activities such as luncheon dates, gifts, and other "sales promotions."

Organizations and Environments (Cell 4)

Cell 4 focuses on intradepartmental, interorganizational influences. This cell concerns itself with the environmental opportunities and constraints on the buying center posed by other firms (both customers and competitors) and government agencies.

Buying in an Era of Technological Change. Available evidence from one study indicates that as the rapidity of technological change increases, the importance of the purchasing manager decreases.[36] At the same time, the importance of technical and engineering individuals comprising the buying center increases. This is Proposition 6-9 in Exhibit 6-3. As the pace of technological change slows down, or in industries where the rate of change is not a problem, the importance of the purchasing manager may increase in the final purchase decision. This finding has implications for the marketing of highly technological or scientific devices and services, and for marketing in times of change. Thus, technological change functions much as price does in predicting the purchasing manager's relative influence on the buying act. As price or technological change increases, the less important or less directly involved is the purchasing manager in the purchase decision. This is Proposition 6-10 in Exhibit 6-3.

The Nature of Suppliers. The nature of suppliers has an important effect on organizational buying behavior, for both the size of potential suppliers and the number of alternative suppliers appear to be critical factors. Large

[35]F. Robert Finney, "Reciprocity: Gone But Not Forgotten," *Journal of Marketing,* Vol. 42, No. 1, January, 1978, pp. 54–59; and Monroe M. Bird and Wayne C. Sheppard, "Reciprocity in Industrial Buying and Selling: A Study of Attitudes," *Journal of Purchasing,* Vol. 9, No. 4, November, 1973, pp. 26–35.

[36]Mary Ellen Mogee and Alden S. Bean, "The Role of the Purchasing Agent in Industrial Innovation," in Bonoma and Zaltman, *op. cit.*

suppliers are evaluated on clearly different criteria than are smaller firms, since the former do not pose as many risks. Financial analyses of smaller suppliers might be made, whereas they are not usually performed on firms of larger size. Similarly, the larger the number of alternative suppliers of a given product or service, the more probable it is that the larger orders will be spread around among a number of different suppliers. This is done to assure supply continuity in case of crisis, changing environment, business failure, or other catastrophe. Firms might encourage supplier competition by providing the poorer suppliers with capital equipment (paid for by the buyer), technical assistance, and research collaboration. All of these investments are viewed as sound purchasing management strategies of maintaining competition in the supplier marketplace in order to avoid being dictated to by one or a few vendors.

Cooperative Buying Practices.   There is a growing practice among firms within the same industry or geographical area of pooling purchases under the label of "cooperative buying." This is most prevalent perhaps in the hospital supply and agri-business industries. Buying cooperatives have greatly increased the bargaining power of their member firms in negotiating price and delivery arrangements.

SUMMARY   This chapter focused on two examples of small social structures: the family and organizations. The two are similar as consumers because they both rely on group decision making of various types and have similar arrangements in making and carrying out consumption choices.

The current trend toward consciously-generated family structures should alert marketers to the importance and need for high-quality research information in this area. Market segmentation should take into account the relative positions of the husband and wife in the decision process. For instance, joint decision making is more likely when the spouse's relative positions (as determined by occupation, education, and contribution to family income) are fairly equal, and when the purchase is an important one. Children's purchase decisions differ depending on the attractiveness of advertisements and the strategies used by their parents. Additional research, including the testing of these propositions, is needed, but such research should be carefully designed so as to avoid some of the problems with family consumer research which were discussed in this chapter.

The suggested framework for viewing organizational buyer behavior highlights the importance of such factors as social situation, price and cost, supply continuity, and risk in influencing the consumer behavior of purchasing agents. In addition, the importance of such factors as organizational structure, power, and gatekeepers is best understood in terms of the effect these factors have on the consumer behavior of the buying center.

KEY CONCEPTS

Autonomic decision making

Buying center

Family

Gatekeeper

Purchasing agent

ROLE RELATIONSHIPS AND CONSUMER BEHAVIOR

CHAPTER GOALS   The objective of this chapter is to help the reader understand:
1. **the process people go through in acquiring roles, and how consumer behavior differs during this process;**
2. **the impact of role accumulation on word-of-mouth communication processes, consumer decision processes, and on role strain;**
3. **a typology of role relationships which has implications for the marketing manager;**
4. **the changes that occur in a consumer's behavior as he or she moves from one role to another;**
5. **the effects of interrole communication on consumer behavior.**

INTRODUCTION   Though the social role is one of the most fundamental concepts in the social sciences it is perhaps the least studied in the area of consumer behavior. A role is a set of behaviors which are expected of individuals in interaction with other people. As such, the performance of a role is a reciprocal process involving a relationship between two or more people. For example, a person is a buyer by virtue of there being a seller, and the buyer's behavior or role is largely determined by the expectations which comprise the buyer-seller relationship. Although roles involve a relationship between two people, one of the two persons might behave according to the role expectations even when the other person is not present. This is the case because individuals' self-perceptions about how they should behave in a role are, of course, important determinants of role behavior.

Table 7-1 provides a sample listing of one-hundred role relationships. Note that some of these role relationships have very explicit guidelines gov-

TABLE 7-1.
Role Relationships

1. barber—customer
2. judge—defense lawyer
3. abortionist—client
4. dean—college president
5. bridegroom—bride
6. bishop—priest
7. host—dinner guest
8. dancer—conductor
9. company president—private secretary
10. police chief—district attorney
11. social worker—supervisor
12. father—son (age 12)
13. screen star—autograph seeker
14. newspaper vendor—buyer
15. guard—convict
16. surgeon—head nurse
17. school superintendent—member/Bd. of Ed.
18. grandfather—grandson (age 12)
19. football coach—player
20. writer—editor
21. company president—union president
22. ward leader—voter
23. hospital administrator—benefactor
24. boyfriend (age 16)—girlfriend (age 15)
25. rabbi—minister
26. stripper—customer
27. assembly worker—foreman
28. policeman—speeder
29. psychiatrist—patient
30. elementary school teacher—student
31. aunt—nephew
32. kibitzer—card player
33. artist—model
34. typist—typist (same office)
35. social worker—unwed mother
36. husband—wife
37. best friend—best friend (same sex)
38. company president—member/Bd. of Dir.
39. combat soldier—enemy soldier
40. dentist—patient
41. professor—undergraduate student
42. father—son (age 22)
43. confessor—penitent
44. movie customer—usher
45. conductor—musician
46. office boy—typist
47. general practitioner—surgeon
48. boxer—manager
49. real estate salesman—buyer
50. policeman—reporter

51. social worker—slum teenage boy
52. chemist—laboratory technician
53. boyfriend (age 23)—girlfriend (age 22)
54. bridge player—partner
55. farmer—farmhand
56. company president—pool typist
57. army private—army private
58. surgeon—X-ray technician
59. professor—graduate student
60. uncle—nephew
61. minister—member of congregation
62. caddy—golfer
63. actor—director
64. company president—vice-president
65. mayor—local industrialist
66. social worker—prospective adoptive parents
67. prostitute—customer
68. bookie—customer
69. supermarket cashier—customer
70. politician—newspaper interviewer
71. general practitioner—drug salesman
72. housemother—student
73. brother (age 16)—brother (age 12)
74. priest—altar boy
75. boy scout—scout master
76. performer—accompanist
77. company president—bank president
78. judge—district attorney
79. resident surgeon—dietitian
80. school superintendent—high sch. prin.
81. mother—son (age 12)
82. star—supporting actor
83. sculptor—gallery owner
84. landlord—tenant
85. interrogator—captive
86. nurse—nurse's aide
87. dean—professor
88. prostitute—procurer
89. minister—church elder
90. quarterback—center
91. jazzman—audience member
92. assembly line worker—shop steward
93. head of state—head of state
94. surgeon—surgeon
95. high school teacher—high sch. teacher
96. sister (age 16)—brother (age 12)
97. bartender—customer
98. actor—agent
99. drug store mgr.—mfgrs.' representative
100. acquaintance—acquaintance

Source: Gerald Marwell and Jerald Hage, "The Organization of Role Relationships: A Systematic Description," *American Sociological Review,* Vol. 35, No. 5 (October, 1970), p. 900.

erning the relationship, as in the case of judge–defense lawyer, while others have few formal guidelines, as in the case of aunt–nephew. Some relationships are extremely transient, such as screen star–autograph seeker, while some could be long term, as in the case of guard–convict. Other important dimensions include the sex of the role participants, the degree to which a role is automatically bestowed on a person (ascribed) rather than being achieved by something that the person does, the location of the interaction, the openness or publicness of the relationship, and the importance of the role to the well-being of the people involved.

Role relationships are central to marketing. In fact, many role relationships *are* marketing phenomena, since the relationships are essentially transactional in nature and marketing is defined as an exchange or transaction process.[1] Some researchers argue that role relationships, rather than individuals alone, are the basic unit of analysis for marketing.[2] Accordingly, many products and services are purchased because consumption is *required by the role relationship*. In other cases, products and services such as engagement rings are purchased in order to *symbolize the existence of a role relationship*, although they are not necessary for the maintenance of the relationship despite their great psychological importance. Still other products and services are consumed because they *improve the quality of a role relationship*. Thus, a professor and student each acquire (and presumably read) books to enhance what they can contribute to and obtain from the relationship.

A person's various role relationships often affect one another. One implication of this is that people occupying the same kind of role may not always behave the same way. For example, purchasing agents in sheet metal factories may behave differently from one another due to differences in other role relationships maintained within the firm. In one firm, the plant manager may place little trust or confidence in the purchasing agent's technical knowledge. In this case the salesperson–purchasing agent relationship will be less important to the salesperson since the purchasing agent is less influential than is usually the case. Thus, the salesperson will interact less frequently with the purchasing agent and more frequently with the plant manager. Contrast this with another firm, however, where the purchasing agent has considerable authority because the plant manager has high confidence in the purchasing

[1]Sidney Levy and Gerald Zaltman, *Marketing, Society and Conflict,* Englewood Cliffs, NJ: Prentice-Hall, 1975.
[2]Thomas V. Bonoma, Richard Bagozzi and Gerald Zaltman, "The Dyadic Paradigm With Specific Application to Industrial Marketing," Working Paper No. 138, Graduate School of Business, University of Pittsburgh, 1976; Richard Bagozzi, "Marketing as Exchange: A Theory of Transactions in the Marketplace," *American Behavioral Scientist,* Vol. 21, April, 1978, pp. 535–556.

agent's technical competence. In this instance, the plant manager would probably not want to interact frequently with salespeople. In the former case, where the plant manager did not believe the purchasing agent had the requisite technical knowledge, the manager would want to have considerable interaction with a salesperson. This example is illustrated in Figure 7-1. Thus we have the plant manager–purchasing agent role relationship and the salesperson–plant manager role relationship. Note that in this illustration it would be a mistake for the salesperson to allow the social dynamics within Firm A, and the subsequent involvement with Firm A, to have too much influence on the expectations and initial behaviors with respect to Firm B. The salesperson should understand that the way plant managers relate to purchasing agents affects how the salesperson should relate to both people.

So, roles obviously have an effect on consumer behavior, and we will see how and why they have this effect as we examine role aspirations, acquisition, transition, and the other aspects of roles.

Hence, in this chapter we cover several aspects of roles and how they relate to consumer behavior. Given the definition of roles along with the one hundred examples of role relationships, a typology of six general consump-

FIGURE 7-1.   *Two Examples of Role Relationships Affecting other Role Relationships*

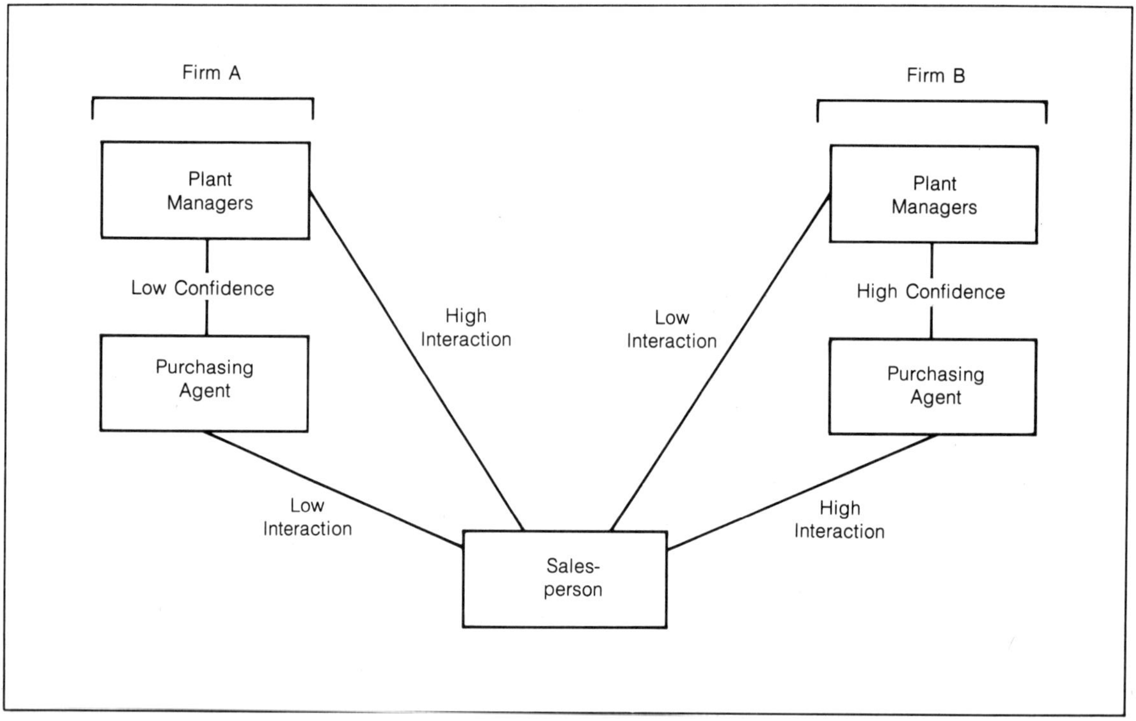

tion-related roles will be discussed. In the following section on role acquisition, we highlight the process through which consumers take on a new role. Next, we discuss how role strain can develop when many people and organizations accumulate many roles. The impact of role accumulation on consumer behavior is then discussed. Role relationships can be characterized by using three main dimensions: intimacy, visibility, and regulation. Each type of role relationship has different implications for consumer behavior. Since roles and their occupants do change, in the next section we examine role transitions and aspirations. We then turn our attention to central roles which are resistant to change. The chapter concludes with a discussion of the effect of other persons (both role partners and outsiders) on role behavior.

MAJOR ROLES RELATED TO CONSUMPTION

Generally, people do not view themselves as consumers per se, but as individuals behaving in ways which happen to involve the purchase of products and services. Much promotional activity is intended to make people (or groups) more aware of their roles as consumers and as persons who influence the overall buying process. There are basically six roles which are important to consumer behavior—roles which apply to both individuals and groups. The *gatekeeper* determines whether others hear about or encounter a product or service. A professor is often a gatekeeper with regard to students' exposure to particular textbooks and professional or scholarly information. An *influencer* helps shape another person's evaluation of a product and the ultimate decision to purchase a product. An interior decorator has such a role. A third role is the *decision maker*—a person or group who decides whether to purchase a product. For example, consider a hospital in which the Board of Trustees is the decision-making body that must decide whether to install a new and expensive lighting system. A fourth important role is that of the *implementor* or *buyer,* who carries out a decision and makes the actual purchase. A patient having a prescription filled is a buyer. In some cases, when pharmacists are allowed to choose the brand of medication for a prescription, they, too, are implementors; but, they are not buyers in this particular transaction. In many industrial situations implementors and buyers do not always overlap. For example, the firm as a whole may be the buyer of equipment while only a single person, the purchasing agent, actually implements the purchase decision. The role of *user* is assumed when one eats, wears, operates, views, or does whatever is involved in the consumption of a particular product or service. A sixth role is that of the *affectee,* a person who experiences the consequences of another person's use of a product but does not participate directly in the consumption of the product. For example, a parent is pleased when a child eats properly. A nonsmoker is annoyed and uncomfortable sitting next to someone who is smoking a cigar. A salesperson working on a commission basis feels gratified when a customer makes a large purchase. In an industrial setting, maintenance and repair personnel may be dissatisfied with a decision to purchase a brand of equipment which is difficult to keep in good running order.

To be effective, communication must take into account the differences among these roles. For example, persuasive communications must be aimed at reaching the person in the gatekeeper role (whether the intended communication flow is direct, as from the marketer to the gatekeeper, or indirect, as from the marketer to an influencer to the gatekeeper).[3] Information and materials must get past the gatekeeper in order to reach persons occupying the other role positions. Gatekeepers can be internal to the relevant group or organization (as with the purchasing agent in industrial buying situations) or external (as with a doctor in purchases of prescription medications for a family).[4] Thus, for each purchase context, the marketer must determine who performs each of the role functions and then develop persuasive communications aimed at the person performing the gatekeeper role.

The important considerations with respect to the above six roles are the following: (1) each role, by definition, involves a relationship between at least two people; (2) these roles apply to all consumption settings; (3) people are often not explicitly aware that they are performing these roles; and (4) in many situations one person may perform two or more roles. Research indicates that there is a multiplicity of sources outside the buying firm which affect its decisions. For example, the influences on a purchasing agent's decision to buy flat glass for a commercial building may involve the "architect of the building, the ultimate client, the heating and air conditioning consulting engineer, the prime contractor for construction, and the actual contractor who will install the windows."[5]

In the discussion to follow, several propositions are presented which are relevant to consumer behavior. Emphasis will be placed on the buyer role—including both ultimate buyers and those in industrial and organizational settings. We shall turn first to the process of acquiring a role, a process that has an important influence on consumer behavior.

---

[3]Gerald Zaltman, *Marketing: Contributions from the Behavioral Sciences,* NY: Harcourt, Brace & World, Inc., 1965, Chapter 5: "Group Influence in Marketing: Roles, Statuses, and Norms," pp. 75–102.

[4]See Chester R. Wasson, *Consumer Behavior: A Managerial Viewpoint,* Austin, TX: Lone Star Publishers, 1975, Chapter 7: "The Consumer as a Complex of Social Roles," pp. 147–171.

[5]P. T. FitzRoy and G. D. Mandry, "The New Role for Salesman-Manager," *Industrial Marketing Management,* Vol. 4, No. 1, March, 1975, p. 38.

ROLE ACQUISITION   Role acquisition is simply the "taking on" of a role. Traditionally, role acquisition has been viewed as a single step whereby people assume a new role and almost immediately conform to the requirements of that role. More recently, sociologists have stated that there is an interaction of the individual with the role in a give-and-take manner. Moreover, role acquisition is being viewed as a temporal process of four different stages. First there is the *anticipatory stage* in which people are exposed to what is the expected behavior associated with a role relationship. This occurs prior to the actual occupancy of the role. At the *formal stage* the individual assumes the role and begins to view it as an incumbent rather than as an outsider. At the *informal stage* the individual encounters informal and unofficial role expectations. The fourth and final stage is the *personal stage* in which the individual attempts to impose on others his or her own expectations and thoughts about appropriate role behavior.

The four stages differ in many ways. For example, the source of information about a role may differ at different stages. The various ways the stages differ are described in Table 7-2. The cells in Table 7-2 have important implications for consumer behavior which we shall address after considering two action implications of the notion that there are stages in the process of acquiring roles.

One implication is simply that the marketer should consider segmenting consumers in terms of role acquisition stages relevant to the product or service being marketed. Magazines sell themselves and sell advertising space on the basis of this consideration. For example, *Modern Bride* stresses the importance of reaching the bride-to-be as a buyer of a large array of products and services. An illustration of such advertising is presented in Figure 7-2. Note that the critical purchasing date with respect to assuming the bridal/wife role is the point at which the engaged couple sets a wedding date. This is the time a woman is most likely to start purchasing *Modern Bride* as well as wedding-related items and new home-related products. *Modern Bride* magazine seeks advertising by stressing the magnitude of this market and offering research data to potential advertisers. The data they present are impressive: between 1975 and 1985 there will be 26 million first-time marriages representing one-third of all United States households and spending 8 billion dollars annually.[6]

The marketer must also take into account factors which differentiate each stage from another, such as the information source and the degree of consensus. At the anticipatory stage product promotion should emphasize how a product would help the consumer adjust to a particular role. Evidence should

---

[6]Advertisement in *Advertising Age,* December 1, 1975, p. 47.

TABLE 7-2.
*Stages of Role
Acquisition*

Differentiating Factors	Anticipatory	Formal	Informal	Personal
Source of information	1 Direct contact with others in the role; mass media	6 Members of the role set; i.e., others with whom interaction is required	11 Informal interactions e.g., car pools, coffee breaks	16 An individual's abilities and skills
Content of information	2 Stereotyped conceptual-izations	7 Codes, as in formal job descriptions (the musts)	12 Tends to emphasize "ways" rather than "musts"	17 Individual's concept of what "should" be
Type of expectation	3 Idealized or normative	8 Journalized expectation, e.g., cus-tomer is always right	13 Implicit or explicit with regard to attitudes or behavior	18 Individual's expectations are expressed to others
Degree of consensus	4 High consen-sus about ideal	9 High consen-sus	14 Possibly less con-sensus	19 High con-sensus appears
Individual's reactions	5 Anticipate congruency between own and ideal-ized concep-tions of the role	10 Conformity of self to role expectations	15 Individual begins to adjust the relation-ships be-tween formal requirements and own preferences	20 Impose own style on the role and obtain ac-ceptance of it by others (adjust role to fit self)

be presented showing how the product brings together consumers' perceptions of themselves in a role and their idealized conceptions of that role (see
cell 5, Table 7-2). The use of stereotypes would be appropriate in advertising
(see cells 2 and 4, Table 7-2) when there is a high degree of public agreement
or consensus about ideal behavior for a particular role. For example, the
marketing of special cookbooks (e.g., *Dining for Two*) and magazines (e.g.,

FIGURE 7-2.
*Advertisement
Concerning Role
Transition*

"**My daughter has never been afraid to spend money on good things. But now she's getting married, and what she and Steven have spent in the past three months is remarkable! And their honeymoon is still to come.**" *"I'd simply forgotten how much young people need to buy when they're starting a new life together. And knowing my daughter, they'll buy the best."*

Her mother may think so, but this girl's not the exception. She's the rule—whenever young women decide to marry. They all want the best of everything. Now.

While most people can put off major purchases, girls getting married can't. Once the date is set, the spending *must* begin. On the wedding, the bridal gown, the reception. For the plane tickets, the hotel reservation, the honeymoon trousseau. For the floor coverings, television, appliances, and furniture to fill that empty first home.

There's no other way. That's why every study done on the bridal market shows the bride-to-be *spends more money, in a shorter period of time, than ever again in her life.*

Every year, over 1,650,000 girls go on that once-in-a-lifetime buying spree. And when they do, eight out of ten take Modern Bride along. All the way.

Modern Bride
...where eight out of ten new households get their start

Ziff-Davis Publishing Company, One Park Avenue, New York 10016

"Reprinted from SEPTEMBER MEDIA DECISIONS"

Gourmet) follow this strategy with regard to women about to be married. Also, such items are also purchased as gifts for engaged couples. This reflects the stereotype that a good wife should be able to cook well. *Gourmet* magazine is promoted differently to persons at the personal stage of role involvement. The magazine is presented as a source of information and ideas which could help the cook express his or her personality to others (cell 18, Table 7-2). The magazine also helps cooks gain acceptance for a more personalized definition of how someone should behave in a role involving food preparation (cell 20, Table 7-2).

A corollary may be derived from the discussion above: As time elapses after consumers begin the role acquisition process, they will be more likely to personalize the role by shaping it to suit their own needs and desires, and consumption behavior will reflect this personalization. Role personalization is more likely to occur if the role is vaguely defined, when the setting is informal, and when there is little agreement among people as to what is appropriate for that role. A good illustration is the popular advertisement, "Should a Gentleman Offer a Lady a Tipparillo?" While the main intent of the ad was not necessarily to promote Tipparillo sales among women, it did reflect the feminist movement by suggesting that the new role of the feminist woman could conceivably include cigar smoking. The role was not so well defined as to preclude this possibility.

Most other cells in Table 7-2 provide similar guidelines for a marketer sensitive to the different aspects of role acquisition. Although the above example involved ultimate consumers, the ideas stated in the action implication above and in Table 7-2 apply equally well to industrial and institutional settings. Thus salespeople could adjust their relationships with purchasing agents, depending upon the stage of role acquisition that person is in. Initially, agents conform closely to company policy and their own stereotypes about the job. Then, gradually, purchasing agents personalize their ways of carrying out the job's functions and seek acceptance for this style from others in the company. Since a salesperson can expect a new purchasing agent to conform to formal job guidelines, the salesperson must become familiar with these in order to understand the agent's behavior. Also, the new purchasing agent might presently exert less influence on the purchase decision than he or she would at a later personal stage. So, the salesperson should be especially concerned with identifying other influential people within the firm when the purchasing agent is in the formal stage.

One concluding observation should be made here. A progression from anticipatory to personal stages for a given role is not certain or inevitable. Consumers could remain permanently at one particular stage, especially if they are tightly rule-bound (and therefore ensconced in the formal stage) or very reliant on their peer groups' evaluations of them (and so remain in the informal stage).

ROLE STRAIN   Role strain, sometimes referred to as role conflict, is the experience of stress due to the competing demands made by different roles. Having voluntarily or involuntarily acquired several roles, the possibility of role strain arises. The larger the number of roles a consumer has, the greater the opportunity for role strain.[7]

EXHIBIT 7-1.
A Proposition on
Role Strain

> PROPOSITION 7-1.
> The larger the number of roles a consumer has, the greater the opportunity for role strain.

Role strain may develop as a result of limited resources. For example, limited time may prevent a person from giving adequate attention to any one set of role requirements. The role of employee, which could require considerable travel, may conflict with the role of parent, which requires being at home. Being both an employee and a parent might not permit much comparative shopping, resulting in a conflict with the person's role as a conscientious consumer. In an organizational setting, persons in the role of purchasing agent may experience strain if a large number of other demanding roles are required of them by the firm.

Role strain may also result from the conflicting demands made by the different requirements of the same role. A chief financial officer who also has the major responsibility for implementing buying decisions is concerned about price (consistent with the role of financial officer), but is also expected to be concerned with production and engineering considerations. When production requirements must be sacrificed to meet favorable price requirements (i.e., inexpensive machinery may have a high breakdown potential), the financial officer/purchasing agent may experience a role conflict.

When role strain exists among potential consumers, products should be developed and presented as a means of reducing the role strain. The popularity of frozen foods, including television dinners and the rapid increase in the number of people frequenting take-out and quick service restaurants, are examples of consumer activities which attempt to reduce the role strain resulting from the demands for time made by career and parental roles. Thus, products and services should be presented as freeing resources which are otherwise dominated by the various roles of the consumer.

---

[7]William J. Goode, "A Theory of Role Strain," *American Sociological Review,* Vol. 25, August, 1960, pp. 483–496.

Similarly, a product should be advertised as reducing the strain resulting from a conflict between the different demands of a particular role. Eating out or taking prepared foods home might be presented as a venturesome and enjoyable family experience rather than merely as a time-saver. In an organizational setting, the long-range cost of buying less expensive competitive equipment which has a higher maintenance and repair cost should be stressed to the purchasing agent who is concerned about sale price.

Despite role strain, individuals and organizations are still motivated to acquire or accumulate new roles.

ROLE ACCUMULATION: INDIVIDUALS

People may deliberately acquire roles despite the resulting role strain if there are net rewards from the additional roles. The larger the number of roles which a buyer voluntarily assumes, the greater the net satisfaction derived from all roles performed.[8] This satisfaction may produce extra energy for a person, thereby making role strain even less likely.[9]

Thus, Proposition 7-2 suggests that consumers may deliberately seek additional roles since having a larger number of roles is more gratifying. There can be several benefits derived from role accumulation. First, in addition to the obligations associated with a role, there are additional rights or privileges gained by acquiring new roles. Second, a greater sense of security might result from possessing a larger number of roles. If activities or events associated with one role are unpleasant, a person can usually fall back on one or more of his or her other roles. Third, most roles involve informal benefits which are not part of the formal rights and privileges. Examples would be the use of company tools or stationery, inside tips on contracts and investments, and invitations to social gatherings. Finally, acquisition of roles "may enrich the personality and enhance one's self-conception."[10] The larger number of roles provides more contact with varied people and more opportunities to develop particular interests and self-expression.

The notion of role accumulation has many implications for managers. For example, new products or services might be directed toward buyers who tend to voluntarily accumulate roles. The larger number of roles provides a better opportunity to associate a given product with a relevant role. Furthermore, each additional role carries with it the potential sources of gratification

[8]Sam Sieber, "Toward a Theory of Role Accumulation," *American Sociological Review*, Vol. 39, No. 4, August, 1974, pp. 567–578.

[9]Stephen R. Marks, "Multiple Roles and Role Strain: Some Notes on Human Energy, Time and Commitment," *American Sociological Review*, Vol. 42, December, 1977, pp. 921–936.

[10]Sieber, *op. cit.,* p. 576.

EXHIBIT 7-2.
Propositions About Role Accumulation

PROPOSITION 7-2.
The larger the number of roles which a buyer voluntarily accepts, the greater the net satisfaction derived from all roles performed.

PROPOSITION 7-3.
The higher the degree of role accumulation among consumers, the more their participation in word-of-mouth communication.

PROPOSITION 7-4.
The higher the degree of role accumulation among consumers, the earlier their adoption of innovations.

(mentioned above) to which the product or service could be connected. Also, the person who tends to accumulate roles will, by definition, have a large number of varied interpersonal contacts. Thus, not only does this type of buyer have a high *potential* for stimulating word-of-mouth communication, but also for doing so within groups which may have little overlap. This is reflected in Proposition 7-3. Because of their larger number of communication contacts, role accumulators are likely to be early knowers about a new product and hence might also have a higher tendency to be adopters of new products and services (see Proposition 7-4). In a study of the early adopters of a credit card innovation (the use of bank credit cards such as Visa and Master Charge in department stores), it was found that role accumulation was related to the early adoption of innovations.[11] Higher levels of social activity and group membership were associated with the adoption of the bank cards. That is, adopters of the credit cards belonged to more groups and were involved in more social activities in which they would interact with a wide set of people and receive or pass on new information (e.g., golf, tennis, camping, home entertainment, concerts, movies, sporting events). Hence, it is particularly important to study the behavior of consumers who are role accumulators and to develop feasible ways of determining who they are, where they live, and how to reach them. Additional empirical testing is needed to determine whether role accumulators tend to be (a) word-of-mouth communication stimulators, (b) early knowers about new products and services, (c) early adopters of new products or services, and (d) sought out by others for information.

[11]Elizabeth C. Hirschman and Melanie Wallendorf, "Role Accumulation and Early Adoption," Graduate School of Business, University of Pittsburgh, Working Paper, 1978.

ROLE ACCUMULATION: ORGANIZATIONS

Organizations also accumulate roles. They do this internally by adding new types of positions and externally by increasing the number of agencies with which they deal. The larger the number of different roles within an organization (i.e., the greater its complexity), the easier it is to initiate decision making about purchasing new products or services, but the more difficult it is to implement a purchase decision.[12] This idea is included here as Proposition 7-5 in Exhibit 7-3.

The reasoning behind this proposition is that the larger the number of different roles within the organization, the greater the contact between the organization and (a) sources of innovations generally, and (b) sources of information specifically about innovations. This enhanced contact increases the likelihood of a person or department encountering an innovation and bringing it to the attention of relevant people within the organization. However, innovations often affect many people or role positions. Thus, the larger the number of different roles affected by the innovation, the greater will be the amount of time which has to be spent preparing the people involved or adapting the innovation to make it compatible with diverse roles. This renders the implementation of a decision more difficult and time consuming.

One implication of the preceding discussion is that a salesperson should be available to facilitate the implementation of a purchase decision, particularly when the organization (or some subpart) is characterized by high role complexity. The number of different roles in an organization can be determined readily from a roster of company personnel. By following up on a complex firm's decision to innovate, the salesperson increases the chances that the product or service will be used effectively. This also increases the opportunity to make repeat sales or other first-time purchases by that company for other products.

Accumulated social roles can be organized into meaningful clusters or "role relationships." This topic is dicussed next.

TYPES OF ROLE RELATIONSHIPS

Marwell and Hage analyzed one-hundred role relationships.[13] Their analysis produced eight basic types of role relationships. Three core variables which emerged were *intimacy, visibility,* and *regulation. Intimacy* refers to expressive

---

[12]Gerald Zaltman, Robert Duncan, and Jonny Holbek, *Innovations and Organizations,* NY: Wiley-Interscience, 1973.

[13]Gerald Marwell and Jerald Hage, "The Organization of Role Relationships: A Systematic Description," *American Sociological Review,* Vol. 35, No. 5, October, pp. 884–900.

EXHIBIT 7-3.
A Proposition
About
Organizational Role
Accumulation

PROPOSITION 7-5.
The larger the number of different roles within an organization (i.e., the greater its complexity), the easier it is to initiate decision making about adopting new products or services, but the more difficult it is to implement an adoption decision.

social relationships which range from husband – wife (high intimacy) to movie customer--usher (low intimacy). *Visibility* concerns the susceptibility to intrusion or publicness of the role relationship. A high visibility relationship would be supermarket cashier--customer, while a low visibility role relationship would be abortionist--client or psychiatrist--patient. Regulation refers to the degree to which the persons involved in a role relationship can control or influence what happens in the relationship. A role relationship of high regulation would be company president--union president or dancer--conductor. Low regulation characterizes such relationships as newspaper vendor--customer or drugstore proprietor--customer.

By simplifying aspects of Marwell and Hage's work, the typology shown in Table 7-3 emerges. Table 7-3 has many action implications for marketing management. For instance, the marketing manager might classify consumers according to Table 7-3. Each of eight basic role relationships consumers could have with one another may have different marketing strategies. We shall examine two types. Type A role relationships are those which are characterized by basic interpersonal commitment in public contexts. Included in this type are coach--player relationships. Thus, the promotion of selected foods such as Gatorade or high protein snack foods would benefit from the use of coaches in testimonial advertisements. This would also apply to athletic equipment. In effect, promotional efforts would be using the strong interpersonal commitment that a young athlete typically has to a coach as leverage for increasing the appeal of the food item.

Type C refers to those relationships which are regulated and intimate, but low in visibility. Such role relationships are often occupational in nature. An example is a dean and college president or a company president and a vice-president. In industrial or institutional settings it becomes important to identify who is influential in a buying decision, who they have close ties with, and how people involved in these ties regulate or control the interaction. The product or service to be sold may be presented as being particularly relevant to the relationship and as a means of helping to shape that relationship. It is an interesting sidelight to note that most buyer--seller role relationships are either

TABLE 7-3.

*Classification of Role
Relationships*

	Dimensions		Examples
Intimacy	Visibility	Regulation	
A. High	High	High	Football coach–player Actor–director
B. High	High	Low	No examples were found in the research.
C. High	Low	High	Dean–college president Bridegroom–bride Company president— vice-president
D. High	Low	Low	Best friend–best friend Boyfriend–girlfriend Father–son (age 22) Prostitute–procurer
E. Low	High	High	Conductor–musician
F. Low	High	Low	Ward leader–voter Movie customer–usher Bartender–customer Newspaper vendor–buyer Stripper–customer
G. Low	Low	High	Social worker–unwed mother
H. Low	Low	Low	Prostitute–customer Bookie–customer

Type F or Type H. That is, buyer–seller relationships are characterized by low intimacy and low regulation, but vary in the degree of visibility of the relationship.

In general, a marketer must consider how intimate a role relationship is, how visible it is, and how much control over the relationship the people involved can exert.[14] The more intimate the relevant role relationship, the

[14]Robert E. Spekman and Gary T. Ford, "Perceptions of Uncertainty Within a Buying Group," *Industrial Marketing Management*, Vol. 6, No. 6, 1977, pp. 395–403.

more important it is to relate the product or service to that relationship. The more visible the relationship, the easier it is to promote a product as relevant to the relationship. Thus, of two role relationships equally relevant to a product and of equal intimacy, the most visible relationship should be selected as the target for promotional effort.

It is desirable to present a product as influencing or enhancing the degree of control one or both partners have in defining the activities, duration, time, and location of the relationship. For example, Illinois Bell Telephone conducted a campaign stressing the use of long-distance telephone calls as a means of overcoming location barriers between friends and relatives. One particular advertisement stressed the satisfaction that older long-time friends derived from making frequent long-distance telephone calls to one another.

As more and more individuals in the buying organization become involved in buying decisions, the buyer-seller situation is characterized more by a many-to-many role relationship. The role of sales person under these circumstances increasingly involves the task of managing several role relationships between the supplier and buyer groups. This expanded role of the salesperson is shown in Figure 7-3. In this expanded role, the salesperson's tasks are:

1. "To isolate and appraise the influence structure in the customer firm;"

2. "To identify the problems that customers face in the development of their business;"

3. "To identify criteria various influential persons within the firm will use to evaluate alternative goods and services;" and

4. "To organize and manage the resources within his company," to identify who should interact with specific people in the customer firm and to manage this interaction.[15]

Hence, the salesperson becomes a creator and manager of role relationships between the buyer and supplier firms. Under these circumstances the salesperson's role, as perceived by the buyer, changes from that of a representative of the firm to that of a role broker. The buyer firm sees the salesperson less as the outward manifestation of a firm and an expert on the seller firm's commodities and more as a go-between who connects related persons in the two firms. The buyer will place less emphasis on the salesperson per se in the decision process. The decision process may also be more protracted.

---

[15]FitzRoy and Mandry, *op. cit.,* p. 40.

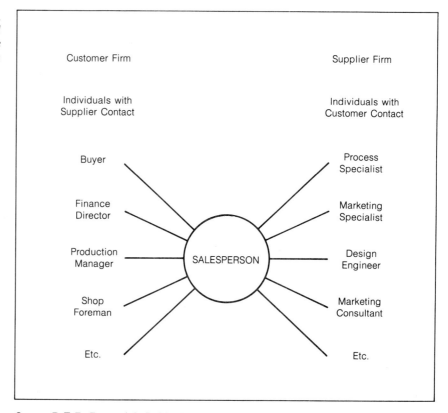

Source: P. T. FitzRoy and G. D. Mandry, *Industrial Marketing Management,* March, 1975, p. 41.

**ROLE
TRANSITIONS
AND
ASPIRATIONS**

Many material symbols of a role are purchased in the hope of obtaining the role associated with the product.[16] This is *aspirational overbuying.* The following are necessary conditions for the occurrence of aspirational overbuying:

1. The purchaser wants the user to acquire the role (purchaser and user may or may not be the same person).
2. The purchaser knows what many of the formal role expectations are and that some of these expectations entail purchasing, owning, or using certain material objects.

[16]Wasson, 1975, *op. cit.*

Aspirational overbuying is more than purchasing those items *necessary* for assuming a new role. Obviously, new parents must somehow acquire diapers; they are a necessary item. Aspirational overbuying also involves purchasing many material symbols which are not absolutely necessary. People acquiring a new role (or wanting others to acquire a new role) apparently spend a considerable amount of time thinking about and searching for products and services which are associated with the new role.[17] Usually, the use of the product is conspicuous enough that others will infer that the user has achieved the role in question. For instance, the common practice of displaying wedding gifts in a bride's home or at a wedding reception serves the purpose of displaying the new roles of the married couple.

Aspirational overbuying is more likely to occur when the purchaser is uncertain about the user's ability to fulfill the role expectations. This is particularly the case when the purchaser and user roles are performed by the same person. Also, aspirational overbuying is likely when the user does not look like a person who would be in that role. When the role transition process is formalized (that is, when there is a specified point in time when the person takes on the role and when rites of passage exist), aspirational overbuying is likely. Gifts given or items purchased on the occasion of becoming a parent, spouse, college graduate, or certified accountant are examples of this kind of overbuying. These ideas are expressed as Propositions 7-6, 7-7, and 7-8 in Exhibit 7-4.

Some examples will help clarify the idea of aspirational overbuying. Consider several role transitions that occur in people's lifetimes: high school student to college student, student to employee (first job), single to married, nonparent to parent, middle-aged to elderly. Some predictions about aspirational overbuying in these role transitions can be made.

Consider the transition from high school to college student. There are widely known role expectations associated with products (e.g., blue jeans, stereo, records, dormitory room knickknacks). Also, there are media vehicles which specifically inform high school students about this role transition (e.g., *Seventeen* magazine). The transition process is formalized to a small degree by high school graduation and freshman orientation programs. The context (living away from home) is often new. The following prediction can be made: Aspirational overbuying will occur to a moderate degree, and it will be intensified if the student is young looking, is uncertain about his or her ability to

---

[17]*Ibid.*

EXHIBIT 7-4.
*Propositions About
Role Transitions
and Aspirational
Overbuying*

PROPOSITION 7-6.
The greater the concern of consumers about their ability to satisfy role expectations, the greater the likelihood of aspirational overbuying.

PROPOSITION 7-7.
The less obvious it is under normal circumstances that a consumer occupies a given role, the greater the likelihood of aspirational overbuying.

PROPOSITION 7-8.
The more formal the transition process to a new role, the greater the likelihood of aspirational overbuying.

undergo the role transition, or if there is a parent who has these uncertainties.

Another transition is that from student to employee (first job). Role expectations are known (often stressed in classrooms by such statements as "when you get out into the business world, . . .") and purchases of new clothing often occur. Thus the following prediction: Aspirational overbuying will occur in moderate degree, and it will be intensified if the company is known for its rigorous and difficult program for new employees and if the employee does not look like the company's typical manager (that is, if the person is a very young-looking man or a pregnant woman).

An example of advertising appealing to aspirational overbuying is shown in Figure 7-4. This advertisement for the *Wall Street Journal* stresses upward aspirations and strongly associates such aspirations and their outcomes with the reading of the *Journal*. Note several things in the advertisement. There is the strong upward thrust of the building created by the camera angle. The office lit up is neither very high nor very low in the building, therefore suggesting a middle management situation where upward movement is conceivable. All other lights but those of the aspiring individual are off—he or she, however, is working late (or maybe in the hours before dawn).

Thus, where a product is strongly associated with a particular role, the role transition process should be examined for evidence of aspirational overbuying. Gift-Pax, Inc. in its advertising (see Figure 7-5) urges manufacturers to take advantage of the role transitions and purchases related to them. Note its strategy of using as a distributor the institution most closely associated with the transitional stage (e.g., schools, hospitals, marriage bureaus).

FIGURE 7-4.
*Wall Street Journal
Advertisement*

Everywhere, people
who get ahead in business read
The Wall Street Journal.

It's a fact. And a study by Opinion Research Corporation proves it. 74% of the executives and managers in top U.S. corporations, regularly read The Wall Street Journal.

No other publication even comes close.

When you advertise in The Journal expect results.

Because this is where business-men dig for facts every business day. Facts that solve problems. Facts that suggest opportunities. Facts that are used in making decisions. Big and small.

Advertise in The Wall Street Journal. You'll be read by people on the way up. And those who have arrived.

**THE WALL STREET JOURNAL.
IT WORKS.**

Sources: ORC Executive Caravan, 1/74-1/75;
W. R. Simmons 1974/1975.

4,559,000 readers every business day.

FIGURE 7-5.
Gift-Pax Advertisement

Role transition is sometimes associated with considerable anxiety due to a negative perception of a role, such as with divorce. Figure 7-6 is an advertisement by a firm which recognized this problem and has developed a service to aid men and women who are considering divorce. Note the very direct attack on the traditional notion of divorce as a bad experience or state.

FIGURE 7-6.
Reality Seminars

Divorce doesn't have to be a disaster.

Contrary to popular opinion, divorce doesn't have to wreak emotional, financial and legal havoc. Divorce can be a creative new beginning. The start of better, more rewarding individual lives for husband, wife and children.

If you're considering a divorce, a team of experts can give you the facts you need at a four-day Seminar on Successful Divorce. You'll get practical, jargon-free legal, financial and human relations help. Geared toward sane,

solvent, successful divorce. Seminars for men and women are held in get-away-from-it-all locations.

Before you finalize a major decision of a lifetime, get the experts behind you.

For confidential information about Seminars on Successful Divorce, write:

Reality Seminars
Division of Marshall Smith & Associates, Inc.; 5721 Odana Road, Madison, Wis. 53719.

ROLE SALIENCE AND CENTRALITY

Role salience is a factor affecting how quickly social change can alter various roles. The more salient and central a particular role is to a consumer, the more strongly held will be the attitudes toward products and consumption behavior patterns associated with that role. Also, the more central and salient a role, the more difficult it will be for the marketer to change these attitudes. These ideas are expressed as Propositions 7-9 and 7-10.

Roles vary in their degree of importance to the individual. Some roles (such as those of doctor, priest, well-known celebrity, parent, charity volunteer) are very important to some people, and in many cases, people form their self-concept based on these role positions. Other roles (such as those of grandchild, member of a movie audience, occasional team bowler) are much less important; that is, these roles do not serve as significant points of reference in the construction of the individual's self-concept. People are more

EXHIBIT 7-5.
Propositions About Role Salience and Centrality

PROPOSITION 7-9.
The more salient and central a role is, the greater the strength of attitudes toward products and behaviors associated with the role.

PROPOSITION 7-10.
The more salient and central a role is, the more difficult it is to alter attitudes toward products and behaviors associated with the role.

willing to change attitudes associated with roles that are less important or less central to them.

When a product or consumption behavior pattern is associated with a role that is very central to the consumer's self-concept, it is very difficult for a marketer to persuade the consumer to change or for a government agency to legislate and enforce such a change. In such cases, a more effective strategy is to find a way of bringing about the desired change while still conforming to the role expectations. Efforts should be made to learn what products and behaviors consumers perceive to be salient and central. Product design and promotional strategies should be altered to conform to consumers' role expectations and behaviors.

ROLE PARTNER PERCEPTIONS

Since a role automatically implies a relationship to one or more other people, the perceptions of those other people (role partners) are very important. They may, for example, influence how salient a role is. Persons who are very concerned about a particular decision are more likely to exert influence in that area on another consumer than are other persons in the role relationship who are less concerned about the area. So, when studying a decision area, it is necessary to identify the role partners having the greatest interest in that area and to allocate promotional effort accordingly. For example, Ferber and Lee found that the relative influence of husband and wife differed as a result of the per cent of income saved: "Other variables held constant, the higher the proportion of income saved, the more likely is the husband to be the family financial officer."[18] The family financial officer (FFO) is the person in a family

---

[18]Robert Ferber and Lucie Chan Lee, "Husband-Wife Influence in Family Purchasing Behavior," *Journal of Consumer Research,* Vol. 1, June, 1974, p. 47.

who pays the bills and handles the savings and investments. When the husband performs the role of FFO, the family is also likely to be more venturesome in its expenditures.

It is also important to consider whether different role partners have different degrees of influence at different stages of the decision making process. Davis and Rigaux found evidence that husband-wife role relationships varied in terms of who was most active in the problem recognition, information search, and final decision stage.[19] Moreover, the marketer must take into account the overall relative influence of each role partner. For example, when a husband has more influence in a particular purchase decision, messages have to be designed to appeal to that role. If role partners have equal influence at the decision stage for a particular product, a message may have to be tailored to the role partnership by showing a group decision or activity. If, on the other hand, a product is one for which one role partner is likely to be more influential at the decision stage, but there is no clear pattern of one particular role partner being consistently more influential, then a different approach is warranted. It might be, for example, that for 50 per cent of a product market it is the wife who makes the decision, for 35 per cent of the market it is the husband who decides, while the remaining 15 per cent of the purchase decisions are made more or less equally. The marketer in this instance may want to develop at least two communication strategies, one stressing appeals to the wife and another stressing appeals to the husband. If resources permit, a third appeal stressing joint decision making may be developed to appeal to the other 15 per cent of the market.

Changes in Perceptions of a Role

Not all persons occupying the same role will view it the same way, independently of whether they are at a formal, informal, or personal stage of role acquisition. Social change alters the perception of roles by role occupants as well as by members of the role set. Social change, however, does not take place evenly among all people, and hence, people's perceptions will vary. For example, perceptions of women's roles as spouses, parents, and employees have, in the past decade, changed considerably for some people but not for others. Thus, we can expect differences in the purchase patterns of people with varying perceptions of their roles as husbands and wives.

One study revealed many interesting differences in purchasing roles between wives who viewed themselves as conservatives, moderates, or liberals

[19]Harry Davis and Benny P. Rigaux, "Perception of Marital Roles in Decision Processes," *Journal of Consumer Research*, Vol. 1, June, 1974, pp. 51–62.

with regard to women's roles.[20] The husbands of liberal wives tended to make fewer purchase decisions than husbands of conservative and moderate women. This was especially true for decisions about major appliances, automobiles, and vacations. The data on decisions about how much to spend are shown in Table 7-4. It is concluded that "liberals are characterized by less husband and more wife decisions than are moderates and conservatives."[21] This is particularly true with regard to furniture, automobile, housing, and decisions about the amount to save.

TABLE 7-4.
Percent of "How Much to Spend" Decisions by Conservatives, Moderates, Liberals

	Conservatives	Moderates	Liberals
Husband	38.7%	31.1%	25.1%
Both	46.5	53.4	51.4
Wife	14.8	15.5	23.4
(number of cases)	(256)	(1266)	(525)

$x^2 = 27.27$, d.f. $= 4, p < .0001$.

Source: Green and Cunningham, *Journal of Marketing Research,* Vol. 12, August, 1975, p. 329.

The findings differed depending on the income of the couple. No significant differences in decision making were found among the lower income groups with respect to the three types of role perceptions. In upper income families, however, husbands of liberal wives made significantly fewer decisions than husbands of conservative wives. In the middle income group, liberal wives made more decisions on the average than did conservative or moderate wives. These data are presented in Table 7-5. In general, the findings imply that the changes in purchase decision making associated with the changes in the female role are more pervasive among liberals in the upper income groups and in the younger age groups.

One action implication of this discussion is simply that marketers should not conclude that social change affects everyone equally. Indeed, the different degree of impact a social change (e.g., a change in attitude toward women's roles) has upon people (e.g., women and their husbands) may be a basis for market segmentation. This study suggests that three meaningful segments might be conservative, moderate, and liberal women. The impact of their

[20]Robert T. Green and Isabella C. M. Cunningham, "Feminine Role Perception and Family Purchasing Decisions," *Journal of Marketing Research,* Vol. 12, August, 1975, pp. 325-332.
[21]*Ibid.*, p. 329.

attitudes on purchase behavior may be moderated, however, by income and age. Also, the impact may be greater for some products and services than for others.

Relative Importance and Interdependence of Different Roles in Organizational Decision Making

As with husband-wife decision making, in industrial settings the relative influence of members of the buying center varies by decision, by particular stages of the decision-making process, and by product category. *Business Week* magazine has conducted many case studies of organizational buying behavior to assist the magazine in obtaining more advertising. Two of these cases illustrate how the relative influences of different roles in an organization vary in purchase decisions. Managerial participants ranged from two in a brickwork repair purchase to twenty-eight in the purchase of a computer. The overall decision periods ranged from two months (concerning the purchase of fleet vehicles) to three years (in the case of a purchase of a conveyor system). Two of the actual cases are presented here. The first case history is of the purchase of fifty insulated freight cars. The reader will note that twenty-seven management people plus ten inspectors were needed to culminate the decision. The actual choice of supplier was made by the vice-president of purchases and stores in consultation with the purchasing agent. Note that different roles were differentially involved in different stages and for different amounts of time.

TABLE 7-5.
Mean Number of Purchase Decisions Within Income Groups for Conservatives, Moderates, and Liberals

	Conservatives	Moderates	Liberals	F-ratio
Lower income (Less than $10,000)				
Husband	9.20	7.80	10.11	.36
Both	22.40	21.10	16.44	1.11
Wife	6.20	9.00	10.56	.99
(n)	(5)	(20)	(9)	
Middle income ($10,000 to $19,999)				
Husband	11.15	8.99	8.00	1.21
Both	20.15	20.33	19.03	.38
Wife	6.69	8.58	10.97	4.08[a]
(n)	(13)	(86)	(30)	
Upper income ($20,000 and above)				
Husband	13.58	11.79	7.23	6.24[b]
Both	14.67	17.35	19.92	2.19
Wife	8.83	15.69	10.73	.27
(n)	(12)	(48)	(26)	

[a]$p \leq .05.$
[b]$p \leq .01.$

Source: Green and Cunningham, *Journal of Marketing Research*, Vol. 12, August, 1975, p. 329.

A large eastern railroad system purchased fifty insulated freight cars at a cost of $1,100,000. The need for these additional freight cars grew out of an agreement with a large package food manufacturer. This railroad company had been selected because its railroad network was compatible with the food manufacturer's distribution system, and because it could provide suitable vehicles. The vice-president of freight sales for the railroad company drew up the agreement and, based on the volume of goods the food company planned to transport via the railroad, estimated that fifty insulated freight cars would suffice.

Soon thereafter, the vice-president of freight sales called the director of equipment planning to discuss the agreement. After noting the volume of daily freight that the food company was going to transport and the long period of time involved, the director of equipment planning decided that it would be more practical to purchase fifty new insulated freight cars. This decision took three weeks.

The railroad's chief mechanical engineer now contacted and worked closely with the company's chief mechanical engineer to establish specifications for the freight cars. Both men agreed that seven-ton, fifty-foot freight cars would be adequate.

These specifications were sent to the purchasing agent, who estimated the preliminary cost. Relying on past experience, the purchasing agent drew up a list of five freight car builders, one of which was a wholly-owned corporation of the railroad company. The purchasing agent inquired if they could build fifty of these cars and deliver them by a certain date. Three of the builders said they could not, while the railroad's own building company and one other submitted their bids. After comparing these bids for two weeks, the purchasing agent sent a copy to the chief mechanical engineer.

After a week of deliberation, the vice-president of purchases and the purchasing agent selected their wholly-owned car building company, because it presented the lowest bid. Authorization of this expense took place at a budget meeting that was attended by the president of the company and the board of directors.

The purchasing agent then placed the order and when the cars were delivered they were assigned to the food company by the director of equipment planning. They were inspected by the director and the chief mechanical engineer to see that they met the specifications, and they will be subject to continuous inspection by the mechanical department for the rest of their time of use.

In another case involving the purchase of containers, a purchase was initiated by the complaints of over 250 salespeople. In this case, the vice-president of marketing authorized the purchase and gave final approval of the selection of a supplier. Thus, the purchase director was less influential than the role title might suggest. In this case, it would be very important for a salesperson or vending firm to contact the vice-president of marketing. The salesperson would have to interact with the largest number of persons in the buying center at the carton specifications stage and later at the market test and evaluation stage. This is shown in Figure 7-7. A brief description of the purchase history is presented below.

CASE 2.
A Purchase of Corrugated Containers

A large southwestern food manufacturer was prompted by complaints from the field to study the feasibility of adopting a new type of packaging container. Each of their approximately 250 salespersons expressed concern over the use of the present metal containers which were bulky, difficult to store, and easily dented. In addition, customers were required to leave a deposit to ensure the return of the metal containers. Consequently, the use of a disposable container, similar to one recently adopted by a competitor, warranted investigation.

The sales manager brought the problem to the attention of the vice-president of marketing. After reviewing their present packaging materials, the vice-president of marketing authorized a market study to test the feasibility of using a disposable corrugated container.

Prior to the test, the development of specifications to determine size, strength, crush resistance, deterioration, weight, cost, and availability was the joint effort of the vice-presidents of marketing, manufacturing, and transportation, in addition to the purchase director, the quality control director and a cost accountant. When the specifications were established, the purchase director was charged with finding a supplier who could meet the required standards.

The supplier who was finally recommended had, in the past, provided the company with other materials of proven quality. In addition, this supplier quoted the lowest cost. Another advantage was the fact that the cartons could be picked up directly from the supplier's warehouse, thereby saving substantial freight costs.

With the approval of the vice-president of marketing, the purchase director placed the order for the cartons to be used in the market study. The market test was conducted over a six-week period and the corrugated containers were found satisfactory. The vice-president of marketing authorized the adoption and continued use of the new method of packaging.

The purchase director, who had placed the order for the containers that were used during the test period, placed the subsequent order with the initial distributor.

CASE HISTORY OF A PURCHASE
Corrugated Containers

COMPANY: A Food Manufacturer
LOCATION: Southwest
ITEM PURCHASED: Corrugated Cartons
COST: $15,000

PERSONNEL

INVOLVEMENTS:	Need Initiated	Need Discussed	Preliminary Authorization to Conduct a Market Test	Carton Specifications Established	Supplier Recommended and Approved	Market Test & Evaluation of Results	Final Purchase Authorization	Placement of Order	Total Number of Stages Participated in
Vice-President of Marketing		O	O	O	O	O	O		6
Vice-President of Manufacturing				O					1
Vice-President of Transportation				O		O			2
Purchase Director				O	O	O		O	4
Quality Control Director				O		O			2
Sales Manager	O	O				O			3
Cost Accountant				O					1
Field Men* (Approx. 250)	O								1
Number of Participants	2+	2	1	6	2	5+	1	1	
Time for Stages	—	1 Year	1 Day	1 Month	10 Days	6 Weeks	1 Week	1 Day	Total Time 15 Months 5 Days

Note: • indicates participation in a particular stage of the purchasing process.
*Due to the large number of salesmen involved, it was decided not to include this total figure in the count of participating personnel, but rather to count the salesmen as a single unit.

FIGURE 7-7

INTERROLE COMMUNICATION

Not only are the perceptions of direct role partners important in determining role behavior, but the expressed perceptions of others not in a direct role partnership are also influential. Communication between two persons not in a direct role relationship is referred to as *interrole communication*. When two shoppers who are unfamiliar with each other engage in a casual conversation about clothes or foods for their families (with whom they have direct role partnerships) this is a case of interrole communication. Other examples are two physicians discussing a new drug at a medical conference where they have met for the first time, or a discussion between a company's legal counsel and its purchasing agent who don't normally interact but are doing so because of an unusual contract situation with a supplier. In general, when gathering product information, a purchasing agent will rely less upon other purchasing agents in other organizations and more on people in other roles in the same organization such as salespeople, production people, and other personnel within the firm. The more professionally-oriented a purchasing agent is, however, the more he or she will rely upon others in the same role in different organizations. Additionally, the less innovative a purchasing agent perceives the company to be relative to other companies, the more he or she will rely upon purchasing agents in other organizations for information.[22] Propositions 7-11 to 7-13 summarize these ideas.

Professionally-oriented purchasing agents participate more in communication systems such as newsletters and conferences which enhance the likelihood of direct or indirect contact with other purchasing agents. This in turn increases the opportunity for information exchange about industrial or institutional products and services. Perhaps because of this greater contact between professionally-oriented purchasing agents, which affords more information relevant to a purchase decision, the professionally-oriented purchasing agents may have a greater influence on the organizational buying process. This is reflected in Proposition 7-14 in Exhibit 7-6.

This last proposition also suggests that the salesperson can estimate the relative importance of a purchasing agent in a decision by determining how professionally-oriented that person is. Indicators of a professional orientation include memberships in professional societies, conferences/workshops attended, and subscriptions to journals and newsletters. Such information can be gathered quite easily and in a relatively unobtrusive or casual way.

It is relevant to note in this regard that persons occupying the role of the drug company salespeople are especially important as sources of information

---

[22]Leon G. Schiffman, Leon Winer, and Vincent Caccione, "The Role of Mass Communication, Salesmen, and Peers in Institutional Buying Decisions," in Ronald C. Curhan (ed.), *1974 Combined Proceedings of the American Marketing Association*, Spring and Fall Conferences, pp. 487–492.

EXHIBIT 7-6.
*Propositions About
Interrole Communication*

PROPOSITION 7-11.
The greater the professional orientation of purchasing agents (e.g., the more they identify with their professional counterparts in other firms), the greater will be their reliance on purchasing agents in other firms for product-related information.

PROPOSITION 7-12.
The greater the professional orientation of purchasing agents, the less reliant they will be on within-firm sources of product-related information.

PROPOSITION 7-13.
The less innovative purchasing agents perceive their own firm to be, the more reliant they will be on purchasing agents in other organizations for product-related information.

PROPOSITION 7-14.
The more professionally oriented purchasing agents are, the greater the influence they exert in the organizational buying process.

PROPOSITION 7-15.
The greater the complexity of a product, the greater the interrole communication (a) within the customer firm, and (b) between buyer and seller representatives.

and influence for physicians when the individual occupying the physician role is relatively isolated within the medical community. This is particularly interesting since this involves a relationship between a gatekeeper and decision maker rather than a direct relationship between a seller and a buyer or user.

Interrole communication changes as the complexity of the product or service being sold varies. In propositional form, this leads to the following statement: The greater the complexity of the product or service, the more interrole communication will take place (a) among persons in the organization who might not be very concerned with the purchase, and (b) between buyer and seller representatives.[23]

---

[23]Derived in part from Hikan Hikanson and Cales Ostberg, "Industrial Marketing: An Organizational Problem?" *Industrial Marketing Management,* Vol. 4, Nos. 2 and 3, June, 1975, pp. 113–123.

The two cases cited earlier involving insulated freight cars and corrugated containers illustrate this proposition from the buyers' standpoint. Both purchases involved not only different roles within the same department working together at certain stages, but also people from different departments interacting. The evaluation of complex products generally requires more than one skill, and it is unlikely that one person will possess all of these skills. We have already commented on interrole communication between organizations, particularly where the salesperson assumes a managerial role in establishing and facilitating interrole communication between organizations. A similar activity occurs within the seller organization. If a product is complex, its production may be lengthy, and hence a salesperson will need to interact with someone from the production department before promising a delivery date. Also, if the product needs to be made to specifications, the salesperson, the design engineer, and the production manager may need to interact. Moreover, the design engineer from the selling firm will probably meet with appropriate personnel in the buying firm. Figure 7-8 summarizes these possibilities.

SUMMARY   Role relationships are central to the study of consumer behavior and form a basic unit of analysis for marketing. Although consumers may not be aware of their roles as consumers, they actually perform in one or more important ways as gatekeepers, influencers, decision makers, buyers, users, and affectees. Persuasive communications must reflect differences among these roles in order to be effective. The roles are generic, applying to all consumption settings.

Role acquisition is viewed as a four-stage process which is useful as one basis of market segmentation. Marketers can adjust the components of their marketing mix according to the stage of acquisition currently prevalent.

Consumers who accumulate a large number of roles derive net benefits from their role accumulation. They participate heavily in word-of-mouth communication and adopt new products earlier than people with fewer roles. Organizations also accumulate roles, both within the firm and outside. Initiating decision making about the adoption of new products is easier in a firm with a large number of roles; however, the complexity of such an organization makes implementation more difficult. Identification of role accumulators is therefore desirable in both consumer and industrial marketing.

Role transition is another area of interest to marketers. Aspirational overbuying tends to occur during a transition when the consumer is unsure of his or her ability to meet the new role expectations, when the consumer's occupation of the role is not obvious, and/or when the transition process is highly formalized.

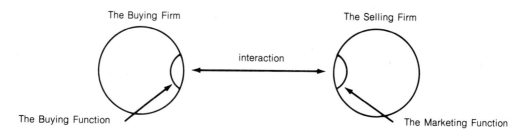

The N-organization — the exchange concerns a completely standardized product

The Buying Firm

The Selling Firm

interaction

The Buying Function

The Marketing Function

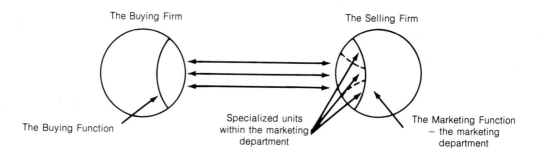

The A-organization — the exchange concerns a product of moderate complexity

The Buying Firm

The Selling Firm

The Buying Function

Specialized units within the marketing department

The Marketing Function – the marketing department

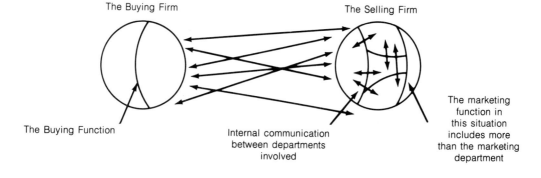

The C-organization — the exchange concerns a highly complicated product

The Buying Firm

The Selling Firm

The Buying Function

Internal communication between departments involved

The marketing function in this situation includes more than the marketing department

FIGURE 7-8.
A Subsystem Including One Buyer and One Seller in Three Situations

Source: Hakansson and Ostberg, *Industrial Marketing Management*, Vol. 4, June, 1975, p. 120.

Much interrole communication takes place in purchase decisions involving complex products and services. This increases the number of contacts made in the course of the transaction.

The concept of social roles is obviously of primary importance in consumer behavior. Extension of knowledge in this area and concentrated research efforts could produce significant benefits for marketers.

KEY CONCEPTS

Affectee

Aspirational overbuying

Decision maker

Gatekeeper

Implementor (buyer)

Influencer

Interrole communication

Role

Role accumulation

Role acquisition

Role salience

Role strain

User

SOCIAL INFLUENCE AND POWER CONTEXTS*

CHAPTER GOALS The objective of this chapter is to help the reader understand:
1. **the ways in which buyers and sellers are interdependent in the exchange process;**
2. **the various modes of social influence;**
3. **how consumer behavior differs in three different power/consumption systems.**

INTRODUCTION We often overlook how very social or interpersonal consumer behavior is. Because consumer behavior is social in nature, it might best be considered as a *transaction* rather than as a consumer *action* process, for a transaction is interactive and social, while the term action imposes an artificial separation between what consumers do and what marketers do. By definition, there cannot be a buyer unless there is a seller; a consumer must interact, directly or indirectly, with a seller. This social bedrock of consumer behavior is the basis of this chapter, and a view which is consistent with contemporary definitions of marketing as an exchange process.[1]

In this chapter, we first describe some basic elements of interaction, such as interdependence, conflict, and influence. Then, we demonstrate that power relations between consumers and sellers are of great importance in understanding shopping behavior. Next, we outline three different ways to

*Professor Thomas V. Bonoma, University of Pittsburgh, is a coauthor of this chapter.
[1]Richard P. Bagozzi, "Marketing as Exchange," *Journal of Marketing,* Vol. 39, October, 1975, pp. 32–39.

relate sellers and buyers in order to distinguish major patterns of consumption behavior. This chapter, then, describes the various interpersonal phenomena which characterize consumer behavior within the large- and small-scale social systems discussed earlier (see Chapters 4, 5, and 6). In this chapter we also give a more specific analysis of how relationships, as implied by social roles (discussed in Chapter 7), are carried out.

SOCIAL BUILDING BLOCKS: INTER- DEPENDENCE, CONFLICT, AND INFLUENCE

Interdependence

There is one fact about human existence which most stands out when a social perspective on behavior is adopted: all behavior involves *interdependence* with other people. Interdependence means that the satisfactions received from any purchase or other consumption-related activity are partly dependent on the choices others make. Consumers do not ordinarily gain satisfaction independent of others' involvement. Instead, consumer choices involve relationships with many other people—the marketer, the sales clerk, family, friends, and acquaintances. This is shown in Figure 8-1. Consumer behavior is

FIGURE 8-1.
The Social Nature of Consumption

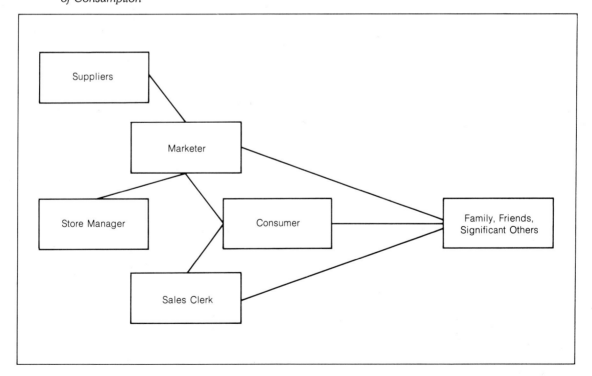

a social rather than an isolated individual process, and in this process the consumer actively negotiates exchanges.

The choice made in the grocery store between various brands of peas, for example, is probably designed to bring the buyer and other users future satisfaction and enjoyment when the peas are eaten. However, the outcome of buying one or another brand of peas is also dependent upon:

(a) the choices made by the supermarket purchasing agents about which brands to stock (which in turn is influenced by what other consumers have indicated they like or dislike), what price to charge, and where to display the peas;

(b) a similar set of choices made by the store's wholesaler;

(c) the choices made by each of the brand manufacturers about what varieties or types of peas it will can and the methods of canning (in water, or butter-base);

(d) the choices made by a farmers' cooperative somewhere about what varieties of peas it will grow, when to harvest them, and how to store and ship them to market; and

(e) a number of other choices, such as whether the government is giving subsidies to pea growers this year.

There is another, more personal way in which product and brand satisfaction is dependent on the behavior of others. The expressed wishes of those in the family who may eat the peas and their anticipated dissatisfaction if the "wrong" brand is purchased will certainly affect purchase outcomes. The influence of friends' brand choices and other recommendations also have an effect. And, even knowing that other shoppers may be observing which brands are in one's own shopping cart may affect choices, since one may be concerned about others drawing unfavorable inferences about him or her because of the purchase of "seconds," dented cans, or other unpopular canned goods.

Therefore, in this chapter the relational links of consumption systems (such as those in Figure 8-1) are explored. Particular emphasis is placed on the negotiated exchange relationships between the consumer and the marketer. Since this approach has not been used extensively in the study of consumer behavior, much of the empirical support for the propositions comes from literature on conflict and bargaining. The transferability of these findings to a consumer setting often has not been tested. Thus, the tentative nature of these propositions stems from questions about their transferability, rather than from their truth in the contexts in which they were originally generated. This, we might note, is one of the frustrations of studying consumer behavior—that in order to be sufficiently eclectic for the sake of substantive advances, one must be constantly aware of the limitations of generalizability.

Types of Interdependence

It is possible to identify three basic types of social interdependence which characterize people's satisfaction as a result of joint choices made during personal interaction. The basic types of social interdependence include: (1) cooperative, (2) competitive, and (3) mixed interdependencies. *Cooperative interdependency* is a situation in which the major problem confronting the interacting people is "getting it together." One writer gives as an example of cooperative interdependence two people talking on the phone who are suddenly disconnected.[2] If both call back immediately, they will, no doubt, get busy signals and not achieve recontact; if neither calls back, they also will not achieve a reconnection; but if one calls back and the other waits, the problem is solved and both achieve the satisfactions accruing from finishing their conversation. The problem, of course, is who calls back?

An example of cooperation in a consumer setting is the well-known marketing concept of exchange transactions. If a marketer offers a consumer a product which is compatible with the consumer's needs and desires, the consumer is more likely to buy the product and the purchase will bring profits to the marketer. If, after purchasing the product, the consumer is satisfied, there is a greater likelihood of repeat purchase, and therefore additional profits. Similarly, there is a greater probability of the satisfied buyer telling others about the product (see Figure 8-2).

Competitive interdependencies occur when the gains available to one person from an activity result in opposite and often equal losses to another person. That is, whatever A wins, B loses. Examples of pure competitive interdependencies include most parlor games, like chess, checkers, and tic-tac-toe, where a win for one player necessarily means a loss for the other (excepting draws). In a consumer setting where prices are negotiated, a shift in price favorable to the buyer involves a comparable loss to the seller. In times of shortages, such as shortages of fiberglass insulation for homes, the purchase of insulation by one consumer is a loss to another consumer because the purchase represents a lowered availability of insulation for the second consumer.

Situations that are exclusively cooperative or competitive don't usually occur in either social life or in consumer behavior, though they may form the basis for a particular consumption system. Rather, the situations we normally face are characterized by elements of both cooperation and competition, a *mixed interdependency.*

---

[2]T. C. Schelling, *The Strategy of Conflict,* NY: Oxford University Press, 1960.

FIGURE 8-2.
*Cooperation in
Exchange*

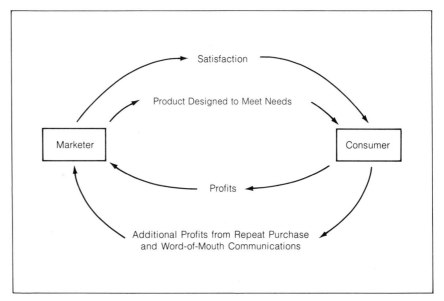

An example of combined cooperation and competition is that of credit users and credit agencies.[3] If a consumer misses an installment payment, the credit agency may repossess the product or take ownership of the collateral, if any. To do so, however, is not without cost. The repossessed item may be of little value secondhand, regaining the item may be difficult, and the use of collection agencies is expensive. Of course, the missed payment, even with a late payment penalty, is costly to the credit agency in terms of not having the funds on hand for other investments. Thus, the credit agency must carefully consider whether the missing of payments is likely to reoccur. Will the expected cost of missed or late payments exceed the expected costs of repossession? The choice between strategies is almost entirely interdependent with the anticipated behavior of the credit user.

The credit user's behavior is similarly contingent upon his or her anticipation of the credit agency's behavior. Given an unanticipated shortage of funds due perhaps to an expensive illness or to unemployment, the consumer must decide whether to "economize" by skipping one or more monthly payments on a loan or purchase, or to eliminate an expenditure in some other area. The decision is influenced partly by the consumer's concern for his or her credit

---

[3]Gerald Zaltman, "Simulations for Learning: A Case in Consumer Economics," in Michael Inbar and Clarice Stoll (eds.), *Simulation and Gaming in Social Science*, NY: The Free Press, 1972, pp. 125–145.

rating, so the credit agency can use this threat to influence the consumer's behavior. Additionally, the consumer will consider the probability of losing the item(s) purchased or established as collateral if a default occurs. Legal fees and late payment penalties are also part of the costs the credit agency could inflict on the consumer. Hence, the separate decisions by the credit agency and credit user in anticipation of one or several missed payments are greatly influenced by each party's beliefs about the other party's decision and corresponding behavior. So, there is an incentive for cooperation since late payments and repossession are costly to both credit agency and consumer. There is also competition in trying to outmaneuver the other party: the credit agency wants the threat of repossession to be taken seriously by the consumer, while the consumer wants the credit agency to believe there won't be any (more) missed payments. This is a situation of mixed interdependency.

In fact, in a situation of mixed interdependency, the nature of the payoffs from the situation may promote elements of cooperation and/or competition for the interacting persons regardless of their personal preferences about competing or cooperating. In the consumer credit illustration, the consumer could miss a payment despite having a strong ethic about meeting his or her obligations. The credit agency may repossess or call a default despite a general policy of doing this only as a last and unusual resort, and only after working very closely with the consumer to find agreeable ways of handling his or her financial difficulties. Perhaps the situation is hopeless from the credit agency's standpoint, or the agency might believe that an example must be made in order to make repossession a viable threat to other customers.

Social Conflict in Consumer Contexts

As long as there is any element of competition in a relationship, the people involved experience varying degrees of *social conflict*.[4] Conflict arises when (a) two or more persons in a relationship each desire a resource which is too short in supply to satisfy everyone, or (b) when the accomplishment of the preferences of one party in an interaction prohibits the accomplishment of the other party's preferences. The *intensity* or *level* of conflict in a consumption setting can vary from nearly zero (in which case the buyer and seller are in coordination and the only problem is to find a distribution point at which they can get together for an exchange) to an interaction almost totally characterized by one of the two social conflict conditions just mentioned. If, for example, the buyer prefers to purchase maximum quality products at minimum prices, and the producer or seller prefers to supply somewhat lesser

---

[4]See M. Deutsch, *The Resolution of Conflict,* New Haven: Yale University Press, 1973.

quality products (to keep costs down and insure obsolescence) at maximum prices (to keep profits up), the conflict level in the interaction will be relatively intense. Alternatively, the buyer and seller often desire the same resource, such as free use of "public domain" resources like air and water, but wish to employ these resources in such a way that if one wins (e.g., laws protecting the environment), the other must lose (e.g., excessive costs for the manufacturer or possibly a prohibition of industry altogether). Table 8-1 presents some hypothetical examples of buyer-seller conflict at different levels of intensity.

Social Influence   Marketing could be defined as the study and employment of social influence processes by the marketer in order to satisfy the consumer's needs at a profit to the firm. But this is only half of the picture, for consumers also use influence processes in encounters with marketers. The exercise of social influence results from conflict between two or more interacting persons or groups. Wells and LoSciuto, for example, directly observed both urban and suburban adults as they were influenced by their children with regard to three product classes: cereal, candy, and detergent.[5] When cereal was the product in question, 59 per cent of all (339 episodes observed) children attempted to influence their parents' decision, and 36 per cent were successful in getting the parent to adopt the child's preferred alternative. When candy was the purchase focus, 55 per cent of the children attempted influence, and almost 30 per cent were successful. And, almost unbelievable, 24 per cent of the children attempted to influence their parents' purchase of detergent, and 20 per cent of these were successful!

One of the problems with this study is that the kinds of social influence attempted by the children are not mentioned. It is customary to classify the different kinds of social influence attempts in a three-fold manner: overt influence, manipulation influence, and influence-related gestures.[6]

Overt Influence: Threats and Promises.   *Overt influence* occurs when a very explicit message goes from one person or group to another and offers or predicts rewards and/or punishments, depending on how the recipient of the message behaves in the future. There are two subclasses of overt influence.

---

[5]W. D. Wells and L. A. LoSciuto, "Direct Observation of Purchasing Behavior," *Journal of Marketing Research,* Vol. 3, August, 1966, pp. 227–233.

[6]T. V. Bonoma and H. Rosenberg, "Theory-Based Content Analysis: A Social Influence Perspective for Evaluating Group Process," University of Pittsburgh Graduate School of Business Working Paper No. 143, 1975; and J. T. Tedeschi, B. R. Schlenker, and T. V. Bonoma, *Conflict, Power, and Games: The Experimental Study of Interpersonal Relations,* Chicago: Aldine, 1973.

TABLE 8-1. *Some Hypothetical Conflicts Which Might Occur Between Consumers and Sellers or Producers*

Type of Conflict / Conflict Intensity	Preference Conflict	Resource Conflict
Low	Consumer Prefers Widest Possible Distribution Outlets. Seller-Producer Wishes to Limit Distribution Costs.	Consumer Wishes to Retain Disposable Income. Seller Wishes to Obtain Disposable Income.
Medium	Consumer Prefers Maximum Quality/ Minimum Price Mix. Seller-Producer Prefers "Satisfactory" Quality/Maximum Profit (Price) Mix.	Consumer Needs Durable Products To Minimize Replacement. Seller-Producer Needs Obsolescent Goods to Maintain Capacity and Growth.
High	Consumer Prefers Need Satisfying Products. Seller Prefers Promoting Existing Merchandise to Maximum Number of Consumers/Regardless of Need-Satisfaction.	Consumer "Needs" Air, Water Without Pollutants. Seller-Producer Needs Pollutable Resources for Manufacturing.

The first subclass includes both threats and promises. *Threats* are communications in which the source offers to *personally* provide the communication receiver with something unpleasant if the receiver behaves contrary to the source's wishes ("If you don't eat your vegetables, you'll not get dessert."). *Promises* are the logical complements of threats, with which the source offers to *directly* and *personally* reward the receiver for performing the desired behavior. An example of a promise made by marketers to the consumer is that of cash rebates given to consumers if they purchase the product.

Collectively, threats and promises are called the *hard modes* of overt influence. In other words, with threats or promises the source says that he or she will do or give something to the receiver if the receiver takes a certain course of action. Two general propositions about the effectiveness of threats and promises are contained in Exhibit 8-1. Buyers may have considerable influence in situations where a particular sale (which is the reward offered to the

PROPOSITION 8-1.
The effectiveness of threats and promises increases with: (a) the magnitude of the reward (punishment) offered, and (b) the credibility of the source.

PROPOSITION 8-2.
Threats are generally more effective than promises in obtaining compliance from a person.

PROPOSITION 8-3.
Warnings and recommendations increase in effectiveness with the magnitude of the consequences predicted and the predictive accuracy of the source.

PROPOSITION 8-4.
The efficacy of manipulational rewards and punishments depends on: (1) the magnitude of the reinforcer provided, and (2) the consistency with which it is used to affect the probabilities of a given consumer behavior.

PROPOSITION 8-5.
The more sellers there are, other things being equal, the more power consumers have.

seller) is very significant to the seller because there are many readily available alternative sales outlets offering essentially the same product. The ready availability of other distributors or manufacturers makes the seller attentive to the implicit or explicit threat of the consumer to go elsewhere. Note that here the buyer is the communication source and the seller is the receiver. The buyer is threatening to deprive the seller of potential profits (from the sale) if the seller fails to give the buyer the desired "deal." In such situations, sellers should try to maximize the positive differences between their products and those of other sellers so that buyers will be less inclined to go elsewhere. In personal selling situations, buyers, regardless of how impressed they may actually be with the product or service, can appear unimpressed so as to keep the seller on the defensive.

Overt Influence: Warnings and Recommendations. A second subcategory of overt influency modes is called the *soft* or *persuasion modes* which include *warnings* and *recommendations*. With warnings (as with threats), the source of influence offers something unpleasant to the receiver; with recommendations (as with promises), the carrot rather than the stick is employed. The difference between the hard and the soft modes is that in the soft modes, the influencer only *predicts* some environmental or social consequence which he or she does not directly control. Thus, when the Surgeon General warns that smoking cigarettes may lead to lung cancer, the Surgeon General is *not* threatening to inject consumers with virulent cancer cells if they continue to smoke. Rather, he or she is predicting something negative which scientific research has associated with cigarette smoking. Whether the event occurs is not under the Surgeon General's control. Similarly, when consumers are exhorted to buy "Trouble" aftershave lotion and are shown a picture of an ordinary-looking man having to fend off scores of pretty women, the advertisement is not promising that pretty women will be directly provided by the manufacturers of "Trouble." Rather, the message is that there is an association between the use of this product and one's potency as a sexual stimulus.

Historically, the "soft" overt influence modes have been those associated with marketing, and especially with the promotion aspects of marketing. In virtually all selling situations, recommendations are made about product performance and satisfaction, but the use of warnings is less frequent. Warnings, when used, sometimes describe negative consequences of buying a competing product. (This is a warning rather than a threat because the marketer, who is the communicator, cannot control what results from purchasing the competing product.) Such consequences might be the competing product's failure to provide the expected satisfactions, or failure to provide as much satisfaction as the product being promoted. The reader is probably very familiar with ads showing alternative products which fail to perform satisfactorily. Some of these involve dead batteries in winter, a presumably helpless wife standing next to a flat tire at night in pouring rain on a deserted highway, a trash bag whose bottom always rips with a predictable and unpleasant aftermath, and the loss of friends due to bad breath. The reader might find it instructive to list the threats, promises, warnings, and recommendations made by advertisers in a popular magazine or during an evening of television.

This leads to another proposition regarding the efficacy of warnings and recommendations: Warnings and recommendations increase in effectiveness respective to the magnitude of the consequences predicted and the predictive accuracy of the source. There is some evidence, however, that warnings of extreme punishment backfire and result in a decrease in persuasive efficacy due to a defensive fear reaction on the part of the receiver.[7] (See Chapter 9

[7]K. L. Higbee, "Fifteen Years of Fear Arousal: Research on Threat Appeals," *Psychological Bulletin,* Vol. 72, 1969, pp. 426–444.

for a more detailed discussion of fear appeals.) Unfortunately, there is currently no definitive direct or indirect evidence regarding the relative effectiveness of warnings compared to recommendations.

Many promotional appeals use both warnings and recommendations. For example, a television advertisement for automobile oil shows a service station owner or manager standing next to a car with an open hood. In one hand the man holds a can of the advocated oil and nods toward the car saying "You can pay me now…" and then points with the other hand to a burned out, yet still smoldering, engine and says "…or you can pay me later." This is a clear recommendation that the motorist should check his or her car oil frequently.

Manipulational Influence.   This is a type of social influence which often occurs in personal selling situations such as face-to-face bargaining for a car where there is direct personal contact between interacting people. In manipulational influence, the source rewards (or punishes) the receiver after the latter has behaved in a certain way. The purpose of this is to increase (in the case of rewards) or decrease (in the case of punishments) the probability of that behavior occurring again in the future. Manipulational influence is usually encountered in the form of praise or blame, that is, as verbal rewards or punishment given by one person to another during a conflict situation. The effectiveness of manipulation rewards and punishments depends on: (1) the magnitude of the reinforcer provided, and (2) the consistency with which it is used to affect the probabilities of a given consumer behavior. Generally, social (verbal) reinforcers have relatively weak effects on behavior when compared to economic reinforcers.

Examples of manipulation influence might be coupon promotions, where the buyer of a particular brand is given "cents off" on a future purchase or a partial refund of the original purchase price, or direct praise of existing owners of a product ("discriminating buyers own Cadillacs").

Two writers in their discussion of marketing as an exchange system, give a relevant example of the interpersonal interaction between a travel agent and a client: "If the travel agent expects a two-week vacation request and the client expresses an interest in a three-week vacation, a favorable discrepancy exists (a more expensive vacation implies more money or approval for the agent). The agent will, in all likelihood, express approving behavior for such actions to encourage the financially more attractive (to the travel agent) three-week plan. Approving behavior may take the form of indicating that the three weeks the buyer had in mind is indeed a more optimal period of time to spend on the type of vacation the client desires."[8] The client's returning again

---

[8]Sidney J. Levy and Gerald Zaltman, *Marketing, Society, and Conflict,* Englewood Cliffs, NJ: Prentice-Hall, 1975, p. 32.

to the same travel agent is an expression of approval which may motivate the agent to try even harder to plan an attractive vacation for the client. Of course, the travel agent may, in the interest of generating future business with this client, suggest that the two-week vacation is really a long enough time to see and do everything of interest. The travel agent might also point out his or her desire to help the client save money whenever possible. Trust and a rapport will develop if the client sees that the agent is more interested in the client than in trying to get a bigger commission (see Chapter 9 on source credibility).

Punishments and rewards have their social side effects. The threat of punishment often causes consumers to hide evidence of noncompliance, dislike, and general avoidance. Rewards encourage consumers to demonstrate compliance, and positive evaluations of both the source and the product.[9]

The most effective use of manipulational influence to affect consumer behavior is a combination of rewards (for the desired actions) and punishments (to discourage undesired behavior). For example, in some industrial settings reciprocity exists despite legal sanctions against it. Reciprocity, as we noted in Chapter 6, involves a seller purchasing the products or services of a client in return for that client purchasing the seller's products. Hence, the original seller offers rewards to a potential buyer by offering products and also threatens punishment if the potential buyer does not purchase from the original seller. The punishment involves the original seller not buying the products being sold by the potential customer.

Influence-Related Gestures. These are not influence gestures in themselves, but are strategic preparations for future influence exertions. Influence-related gestures include: (a) *strategic probes,* (b) *reinterpretations,* and (c) *self-disclosures.*[10] *Strategic probes* are attempts by the seller to find out more about the buyer's order of preferences in order to satisfy them more effectively. Two researchers, for example, analyzed the encounters between fourteen sales people who each dealt with fifteen customers (210 interactions) regarding the purchase of a major appliance.[11] Successful transactions, those in which a purchase was actually completed, involved significantly greater participation by the salesperson in "asking for information, asking for opinions, and asking for suggestions"—essentially, in probing the potential customer regarding his or her preferences.

---

[9]*Ibid.*

[10]Bonoma and Rosenberg, *op. cit.*

[11]R. P. Willett and A. L. Pennington, "Customer and Salesman: The Anatomy of Choice and Influence in a Retail Setting," in Raymond M. Haas (ed.) *Science, Technology, and Marketing,* Chicago: American Marketing Association, 1966, pp. 598–616.

Reinterpretations and self-disclosures, in contrast, have received no study to date in the consumer behavior area. A *reinterpretation* (or *reflection*) is essentially a clinically-derived technique in which a therapist (or other influencer[12]) attempts to "feed back" to the client in a slightly different form the same information the client has just given the source. This tactic has two general effects: first, since we are fond of our own opinions and words, it is usually reinforcing to hear them reiterated; and secondly, since conversations follow a culturally-prescribed pattern of "you talk—then I talk," by using information the consumer just gave, the salesperson "takes a turn" in interaction without actually adding anything to the conversation, thus putting the burden on the consumer or buyer to disclose more on the next turn. *Self-disclosures,* or statements by the influencer of a personal and intimate nature, encourage reciprocal disclosures from the recipient.[13] Hence, one way for a salesperson to get a potential buyer to disclose information about preferences is for the salesperson to disclose something first.

Relative Power The actual influence mode (overt, manipulational, or influence-related gestures) used by a buyer and seller depends on their relative power. The more sellers there are, other things being equal, the more power consumers have. This is Proposition 8-5 in Exhibit 8-1. Conversely, the more consumers there are, other things being equal, the more power sellers have since they presumably can sell to another consumer if any one consumer is dissatisfied.[14] Of course, it is necessary to take into account both the number of sellers and buyers and the relative importance or value to each party of the purchase or sale. The most common case is probably when the consumer is somewhat weaker (i.e., has fewer "bargaining chips") than the seller.

Power relations, however, need not always tilt in one direction or another. There are at least two other possible power relations between buyer and seller. The first is the kind of interaction in which the buyer and seller are better characterized as nearly equal in resource-control. These conditions occur quite frequently and produce radically different consumption transactions from the customary ones considered by students of consumer behavior. A second possibility occurs when consumers form what is known as unit-bonds.[15] In unit-bonds the welfare of the unit is put above the utility-

---

[12]Bonoma and Rosenberg, *op. cit.*

[13]Sidney Jourard, *Self-Disclosure: An Experimental Analysis of the Transparent Self,* NY: Wiley-Interscience, 1971.

[14]Gerald Zaltman and Pol Jacobs, "A Consumer Based Theory of Marketing Practice," paper presented at the *Symposium on Consumer and Buyer Behavior,* University of South Carolina, March, 1976.

[15]Fritz Heider, *The Psychology of Interpersonal Relations,* NY: John Wiley, 1958.

optimization of any one participant. As will be seen later, there are three subvariants of this system: the consumer welfare system in which consumers form units to maximize their group welfare, the seller's welfare subsystem in which sellers band together, and the more unusual third variety in which both a consumer (or consumers) and seller (or sellers) form a welfare system.

Thus, because of the nature of the power disparities possible between buyer and seller, we can isolate specific "systems" of consumer-seller behavior. Power disparity is a continuum (as is shown at the top of Table 8-2 in "the relative power continuum") which can vary from complete dominance of seller over buyer (on the left in the table) to relative (issue-specific) equivalence (in the middle) or power-irrelevance (on the right). These are the three major "ideal type" systems of consumer behavior. Actual consumer-seller systems vary all along the power disparity continuum. A given system may show characteristics of more than one of the ideal type systems. The next section of this chapter is devoted to articulating each system.

Three Power/ Consumption Systems and Their Behavioral Correlates[16]

Table 8-2 describes the character of three different social consumption systems occurring under various power disparity conditions between interacting buyers and sellers. The left side of the table lists some system characteristics differing across the three types, including the basic structure, the interdependence with the choice criteria employed by parties within it to make decisions, usable influence processes, ratification processes by which agreement is formalized, and legitimization mechanisms by which it is enforced. The bottom two rows of the table identify the major decision class occurring within each power/consumption system and also some marketing subareas commonly devoted to studying the system's operation or characterizing its functioning.

The Disparity System

The disparity system is by far the most common to consumer behavior. The major characteristic of this system is that the seller is in some way stronger than the buyer (or buyers).

Consider the usual retail buying situation. Ordinarily, for the actual purchase to take place, the seller does *not* go to the customer, the customer comes to the seller. (Of course, there are exceptions such as mail-catalogue purchasing and door-to-door selling.) The buyer cannot buy whenever he or she wants to ("blue laws," store hours), but only when the seller makes

[16]The basic trichotomy is adapted from Thomas V. Bonoma, "Conflict, Cooperation, and Trust in Three Power Systems," *Behavioral Science,* Vol. 21, 1976, pp. 495–514.

TABLE 8-2. *A Social Schematic of Three Power/Consumption Systems*

		The Disparity System	Functional Equivalence System	Group Welfare System
		S > B B = S B = S or Irrelevant		
		THE RELATIVE POWER CONTINUUM		
1.	Structure	Seller ⟶ Buyer	Seller ⟶ Utility Realignment ⟵ Buyer Or Exchange	Seller ⟷ Buyer ⟶ Group ⟵
2.	Interdependence Type	S: Production Orientation B: Competition Orientation	S: Marketing Orientation B: Bargaining Orientation	S: Problem-Solving Orientation B: Problem-Solving Orientation
3.	Seller's & Buyer's	Primarily Competitive	Primarily Mixed (Both Competitive and Cooperative)	Primarily Cooperative
4.	Seller's Choice Criteria	Profit/R.O.I.	Personally Favorable Exchange Ratio	Group Welfare
5.	Buyer's Choice Criteria	Price, Quality, Need Fulfillment	Personally Favorable Exchange Ratio	Group Welfare
6.	Acceptable Influence Moves	1. Persuasion (Promotion) 2. Bribes & Coercion	1. Threats & Promises 2. Influence-Related Moves	All
7.	Ratification Process	Physical Exchange	Contract: Norm & Rule-Maintenance	Consensus
8.	Legitimation/ Appeal Process	Force: Legal System "Caveat Emptor"	Norms & Rule-Structures Extrasystemic Force	Termination of Relationship
9.	Typical Decision Class	1. Low Importance Items 2. Rebuys; Staples; Recurrent Purchases 3. Emergency Items & Specialty Items	Major or Unique Purchases	Rebuys and Major or Unique Purchases
10.	Marketing Examples	1. Retail Selling 2. "Direct Marketing" & Promotions 3. Traditional Accounts of "Consumer Behavior"	1. Industrial, Reseller Sales 2. Personal Selling	1. Consumer's or Buyer's Assns. 2. Organizational Sales

products available for sale. The seller often sets a fixed price. Exactly where products can be purchased is determined by some coalition between manufacturer, supplier, and retailer (or sometimes by governments in the case of state-owned liquor stores). Even what colors, styles, and brands of merchandise are stocked in the store are decisions made by the same coalition. What is important to recognize is that in many respects, the power disparity system has been the traditional one in which consumer behavior analyses have been conducted. Indeed, it may be the major (i.e., most frequently entered) system in which individual consumers interact with sellers and suppliers.[17] Thus, in the disparity power/consumption system, the major flow of influence is from seller to buyer; the former is relatively strong, the latter relatively weak.

The second row of the first column in Table 8-2 illustrates that the power disparity system is generated from a competitive interdependence picture of the consumption process. The seller's or producer's major orientation toward the consumption transaction is what McCarthy has called the "production orientation," and is characterized by the seller trying to "push" what he or she has at minimum cost and maximum profit, setting inventory levels according to cost minimization factors, and treating customer credit as a necessary evil.[18] What McCarthy does not point out is that this viewpoint has its complement in the consumer's behavior within the transaction environment, and causes such consequences as a generally negative view of corporations and sellers.

Rows 4 and 5 show, not very surprisingly, that the seller's predominant choice criterion is the return on investment, while the buyer's is obtaining the "best" product quality for a given price. Row 6 shows that the most frequently employed influence modes imposed by the seller on the buyer are those relating to promotion of products available for sale. These are primarily the persuasive modes of warnings and recommendations. Thus, media promotions warn that not replacing a detergent with the preferred brand will cause "ring around the collar" and much social embarrassment, or they recommend that if the correct toothpaste is used sexual gratification is more likely.

One action implication of the preceding discussion is that ads promoting "specials," sales, and other price-reduction moves by the marketer are especially eye-catching to consumers with a competition orientation, and these promises of rewards increase purchase probabilities. The "credibility" of the source, as well as the size of the price reduction, also affect consumer re-

---

[17]Philip Kotler, *Marketing Management: Analysis, Planning, and Control,* 3rd Ed., Englewood Cliffs, NJ: Prentice-Hall, 1975.

[18]E. Jerome McCarthy, *Basic Marketing,* 5th Ed., Homewood, IL: Richard D. Irwin Co., 1975, especially Chapter 2.

sponse. Special sales and coupons represent to consumers a way of establishing equity, however temporary, in an otherwise unbalanced power situation.

Rows 7 and 8 of the disparity system column in Table 8-2 summarize the sorts of agreement ratification and legitimization mechanisms available for solidifying transactions. Interestingly, there is no good ratification process available apart from the physical exchange of money for a product or service; perhaps this is because the weaker party might very well choose to "get out" of a contract or agreement if the transaction were not finalized as soon as possible. The currently changing legal picture, with the federal government stepping in to provide consumers with a recourse they would not otherwise have in the disparity system, is an indication that the only effective influence on sellers comes from an even more powerful "source" (the government), and a comment that both government and business are well aware that sellers are stronger than consumers.[19]

The "typical decision classes" occurring within the disparity system, as well as some examples of disparity marketing, are instanced in the last two rows (9 and 10) of the disparity column. The disparity system operates best when the purchases being contemplated are either low importance items, emergency items, specialty items, or staples or other recurrent purchases which many consumers repeatedly need. The disparity system exists in these situations, however, for different reasons. With low importance "impulse" items and recurrent purchases, there is ordinarily an excess of consumers to products. With luxury, specialty, and emergency items, there is ordinarily a demand inelasticity (people want it despite what it costs) that again allows the disparity system free operation.

The Functional Equivalence System

There are other prominent power/consumption systems encountered in everyday life in addition to the power disparity system. Perhaps next in order of importance is the functional equivalence system, the defining processes of which are bargaining and negotiation. The essence of the functional equivalence system, as with the power disparity system, lies in the relative strengths of the consumer and the seller. In the functional equivalence system the buyer and seller are more equal in resource control. The seller does not view the

[19]For an interesting discussion of this, see Lawrence P. Feldman, *Consumer Protection: Problems and Projects,* St. Paul, MN: West Publishing Co., 1976.

buyer as trivial or easily replaced, nor is the buyer just a passive recipient of the seller's offers and influence attempts.

The major processes occurring in the functional equivalence system are *bargaining* or *negotiation* between buyer and seller. The essential preconditions are: (1) that there are at least *two* commodities, one each in the possession of buyer and seller, which are *exchangeable* from one to the other via some function or formula; and (2) that the buyer subjectively values the seller's commodity more than the seller, and that the seller subjectively values the buyer's commodity more than does the buyer. The first row in the functional equivalence system column summarizes the nature of this system. In consumer contexts, functional equivalence means that in a given situation neither party is so weak that one of them can overtly influence the other through force or manipulational punishments without the other retaliating.

An example of functional equivalence is the new car purchase in which each potential buyer is important because: (a) not that many prospects come around, and (b) each sale represents a relatively large proportion of total dollar volume. Thus, the consumer is not quite as replaceable as in the disparity system, and additionally, the consumer is trading a substantial number of dollars for the item to be sold. This radically changes the character of the consumption transaction. It is important to note that this equivalence between buyer and seller is "functional"—that is, it is issue-specific and may not extend to all areas of the interaction, or indeed, to any area except the contemplated exchange itself. But, for that one exchange, the consumer has a "bargaining chip" of such magnitude that it is no longer a "seller's market," but a functionally equivalent market as regards the parties' resource bases. Thus, as shown in the second row of the "functional equivalence" column in Table 8-2, the primary interdependence type is a mixed one of both cooperative and competitive elements.

The potential buyer usually goes to where the seller displays the product, but occasionally a seller will "drive over" a new car, or deliver it if bought. The seller offers the buyer amenities such as coffee in the showroom, or alcoholic beverages for men who are viewing a fashion show in order to purchase clothes for wives at Christmas. Also, in some casinos free alcohol is provided for people as they gamble. Real estate agents provide many "extra" services to show that they need the potential buyer. In functional equivalence situations, the asking price is an initial starting point for negotiation, not a fixed price which a buyer must either take or leave. Industrial buying and selling often involve functional equivalence, for bargaining and negotiation are more common in that setting than in ultimate consumer settings.

Because of the lesser replaceability of the consumer, he or she is usually reached through the most effortful of marketing moves, personal selling. In bargaining, which is a face-to-face endeavor, the dominant influence moves available are: (1) threats and promises, and (2) influence-related moves.[20] The sixth row of the second column in Table 8-2 reflects this fact. Bargaining is a system in which first one side makes an offer (traditionally the seller, via the "asking" price), and then the other reciprocates with a counteroffer until agreement is reached or a deadlock results. Here, each offer is both a threat and a promise—it is a threat that no further concessions will be forthcoming and the bargaining will be terminated if the other does not accept it, and a promise that further concessions *might* be forthcoming if the other just rejects it and "holds out." Since details of the bargaining process cannot be presented here, the interested reader should refer to other sources.[21]

An important implication of this discussion is that for products and services which are bargained for in a functional equivalence system, marketing strategies should emphasize that the consumer is an equal partner in the product design, as well as in the transactional process. Strategies should also transmit messages designed to heighten consumers' perceptions of the value and uniqueness of the product or service.

The Group Welfare System

Finally, there is the group welfare system which also occurs (but with lesser frequency) in the everyday world of consumers. The basic notion of the group welfare system is that the parties to consumption *consider themselves a functional unit and place maximal utility on the welfare of the unit above the satisfactions of any one member.* There are three basic subtypes of the group welfare system which need to be considered: the consumer-consumer welfare system, which arises when consumers form unions or co-ops; the seller-seller subsystem, which results when sellers form trade associations; and the consumer-seller subsystem, which consists of the rare instances when buyer and seller both subsume their personal preferences because of their loyalty to a larger unit (e.g., intradivisional buying and selling within a large firm; multinational bargaining).

The group welfare system has as its structure a triad, with two of the participants forming a coalition or ingroup, and acting to maximize their joint welfare in transaction with a third party (see column 3, rows 1 to 3, of Table 8-2). For example, the family is (under ideal conditions) a group welfare

---

[20]See Thomas V. Bonoma, "Some Determinants and Consequences of a Negotiations Construal of Social Behavior," presented at a Conference on Negotiation, Greensboro, S.C., James Wall, Chair., July, 1975.

[21]Levy and Zaltman, *op. cit.*

system in which a number of consumers make joint decisions according to some rules about their purchases.[22]

The major orientation of group members in the welfare system is one of problem-solving; that is, they are concerned with how to discern the preferences of the individuals (e.g., husband and wife) comprising the system so as to reach a joint decision for presentation to the outgroup (i.e., suppliers and sellers in the case of the family). Of course, that the interdependence type is cooperative and the orientation problem-solving does not mean that group deliberations and consensus achievement are a calm, peaceful process. In welfare systems, to be cooperative is to rigorously pursue what one individually thinks would be best for the unit, regardless of how one has to threaten, cajole, or bribe to achieve the desired end. The point here is that although all members of a family may want to buy the car or house which best satisfies and maintains the group welfare more than they desire their individual preferences, there will be just as much debate about what characterizes group welfare as there is debate in other systems about what would bring individual satisfaction. This suggests that promotional efforts directed toward group welfare units should be diversified, emphasizing the various individual ways group welfare will be maximized by product acquisition.

SUMMARY   In discussing consumer behavior as a transaction process, we have seen that the consumption act is built upon interdependence, conflict, and influence. The situation typically faced by the consumer is one of mixed interdependency, which is characterized by elements of both cooperation and competition. The relationship between consumers and credit agencies is a good illustration of this type of interdependence.

Because of the social conflict existing between buyer and seller, each uses various social influence processes to achieve satisfaction. Threats, promises, warnings, and recommendations are employed with different degrees of effectiveness. Manipulation influence is prevalent in personal sales situations, as are influence-related gestures.

The manner and effectiveness of buyer and seller influence are contingent upon their relative power. In a system of consumption disparity, the seller is in some way stronger than the buyer. In the functional equivalence system the buyer and seller are more equal in resource control. Group rather than

---

[22]Jagdish N. Sheth, "A Theory of Family Buying Decisions," in J. N. Sheth (ed.), *Models of Buyer Behavior,* NY: Harper & Row, 1974.

individual satisfaction is the priority of the group welfare system, where buyer, seller, or buyer-seller coalitions are formed. Traditional marketing literature has concentrated on the disparity system, though research is needed in both the functional equivalence and group welfare systems.

KEY CONCEPTS

Competitive interdependence

Cooperative interdependence

Disparity system

Functional equivalence

Group welfare system

Hard modes

Interdependence

Manipulative influence

Mixed interdependency

Overt influence

Promises

Recommendations

Reinterpretation

Self-disclosures

Social conflict

Soft modes

Strategic probes

Threats

Transaction process

Warnings

COMMUNICATION AND CONSUMER BEHAVIOR

CHAPTER GOALS   The objective of this chapter is to help the reader understand:
1. **how the source, message, communication channels, and the receiver affect communication processes in consumption contexts;**
2. **how organizations communicate with their external environment as well as how communication relevant to purchase decisions takes place within the organization.**

INTRODUCTION   Communication is the "glue" of social interaction, the bond between people involved in the role relationships and interactions discussed earlier. Consumer behavior as we know and study it today would barely exist in the absence of communication.

       This chapter has two basic thrusts. The first is a discussion of the effect of persuasive communication on individual consumers. This treatment emphasizes several communication factors such as source, message, and channel and their relation to one or more steps in the persuasive communication process. The second major thrust concerns communication and organizations. The initial discussion of this topic is largely in terms of communication between the organization and persons or agencies outside the organization. The discussion then switches to communication processes within the organization. Before proceeding, however, we want to introduce several terms which may be encountered in other discussions of communication issues. These terms are source, channel, receiver, and feedback.

       Communication is the process of establishing a commonality of thought between two or more people. There are many variations to this basic definition, but they all contain the idea of a sharing of meaning or thought between persons. A sender or *source* of a communication puts a thought together in symbolic form. This symbol of a thought travels through some path or *channel* to a *receiver* who translates the symbol of a thought into its intended meaning. The *channel* links the source and receiver. It may be simply the air which conducts and makes possible vocal sounds or light waves which permit vision. It may be much more complex involving sophisticated electronic equipment.

Figure 9-1 summarizes in visual form the most basic features of the communication process. However, a few additional comments are necessary about the notion of feedback. *Feedback* is a process whereby a receiver becomes a source who puts thoughts into symbolic form and displays or dispatches them through some channel to the original source who then translates them into understandable meanings. For example, the manufacturer is a source who develops an advertisement (a symbol), has it conveyed through television (a channel) to a consumer (receiver) who interprets the advertisement as a description of a product which will satisfy a need. The receiver now becomes a sender of information. The feedback may consist of the decision to try the product, which, through accounting channels such as sales reports and inventory turnover reports, is conveyed to the firm and the firm then inter-

FIGURE 9-1.   *Basic Features of the Communication Process*

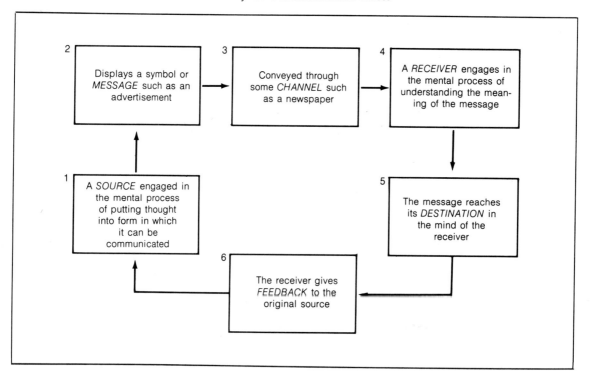

prets this message. This interpretation includes the conclusion that the original advertisement was effective. If the consumer fails to repeat the purchase, which is another communication process which is conveyed through accounting channels, the manufacturer might conclude that there is something wrong in the marketing mix. This interpretation may lead the manufacturer to improve the product. The improved product is a new symbol, and the process continues. Consumers can also give feedback to firms by writing complaint letters, telling other people about their experiences with the product, shoplifting, supporting product safety legislation, or responding to the firm's marketing research efforts.

PERSUASIVE COMMUNICATION AND THE CONSUMER

Seldom will a day pass when the reader is not the object of communications intended to change his or her attitudes and behavior. Efforts to change attitudes and behaviors are attempts at persuasive communication. Persuasive communication is present in nearly all social situations, and especially advertising.

Frequently, persuasive communications fail to have their intended effect, and may, as the cartoon in Figure 9-2 indicates, even have an opposite effect. Often, of course, advertising does have the desired effect on consumer attitudes and behaviors when used under the proper circumstances. Figure 9-3 from *Product Marketing* presents the comments of a leading advertising executive about the effects advertising can and cannot achieve.

FIGURE 9-2.
*Cartoon Suggesting
Reversal of Effects*

"These probably taste pretty good.
Too bad their commercials have made me hate
the very thought of them."

FIGURE 9-3.
The Power of Advertising

Inside a meat pie is a lesson in the power of advertising

A few years ago a prominent meat packer came to Needham, Harper & Steers with a great new product—a delicious meat pie inside a steel container that simply had to be popped into an oven to prepare. The agency created advertising that was tested and found effective. But so enthusiastic was the meat packer, he didn't test the product in home use. The product got strong trade support in a three state area, and advertising brought in the initial sales. Then the bottom fell out of the pie—the product was returned by the thousands because no homemaker had the tools to open an all-metal container.

Paul Harper cites this story to point out what advertising cannot do—sell a product that can't meet a need. To counter the sad episode related to the Conference Board recently, Harper then provided examples of what advertising can do: Advertising can induce trial; Crest toothpaste did this with its American Dental Assn. endorsement. Advertising can intensify usage; V-8 vegetable juice did this by repositioning as a enjoyable rather than healthy drink. Advertising can sustain preference; Parkay has been assaulted by margarine competitors for 30 years but still holds top spot. Advertising confirms imagery; Chivas Regal backs its premier scotch image with premier advertising. Advertising can build line acceptance; Kraft exudes a feeling of wholesomeness that benefits everything from cheese to mayonnaise. Advertising opens doors for salespersons; Avon ladies are welcome because of the lilting "Avon calling" theme. Advertising creates ambience; McDonald's is no longer millions of factory hamburgers but a "friendly" place for the family.

Source: *Product Marketing,* February, 1977, p. 10.

It is useful to divide the persuasion process into six steps, as shown in Figure 9-4.[1] As we shall see later, the mode of *presentation* as well as the message content is very important and is the beginning point of the persuasion process. The presentation of a message, however, does not guarantee that consumers will pay *attention.* There may be systematic avoidance of

[1]William J. McGuire, "Persuasion Resistance and Attitude Change," in Ithiel de Sola Pool and Wilbur Schramm (eds.), *Handbook of Communication,* Chicago: Rand McNally, 1973, pp. 216–252.

FIGURE 9-4.
*Six Steps in the
Persuasion Process*

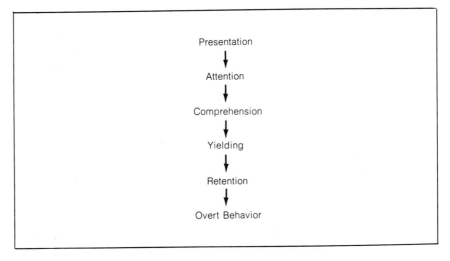

certain information and of the media through which this information may be found (of course, there may be systematic information seeking as well). Even if a consumer's attention is obtained, persuasion is unlikely if consumers do not *comprehend* the message, or if they comprehend it in a way which is not desired by the marketer. *Yielding* occurs when the consumer begins to accept the advocated change. Some researchers think of this as persuasion, but this view is restrictive. An effectively presented message designed to gain attention, comprehension, and yielding may not be ultimately effective unless the message and inclination to follow its suggestions are *retained.* Thus, an important element in the persuasion process is how long the yielding lasts. Will the effect of an advertisement last until the next day, week, month, or season when the consumer is in a position to actually buy the product? This brings us to the last component in the persuasion process, *overt behavior.* Securing the desired overt behavior of consumers is the payoff for the marketer. (Chapter 16 discusses the relationship between attitudes and actual behavior.)

Each of the six steps of the persuasive communication process can be pictured in conjunction with five communication factors. These actors are: source, message, channel, receiver, and destination. Each cell in Figure 9-5 represents a potential relationship between these communication factors and the steps of the persuasion process. Each cell therefore represents a basic communication consideration for the marketing manager. For example, the cell designated #1 prompts the question, what is the best way to present or to organize and structure a message? Cell #2 prompts us to ask which channel of communication should be used to gain the consumer's attention. Cell #3 causes us to ask whether the particular audience or target market is able to understand our messages. Cell #4 suggests the questions, what source of information is likely to be most believable and thus help get consumers to yield to the advocated change? Cell #5 asks how long a message will be remembered, and cell #6 asks how long the behavior will remain changed before consumers revert to their original brand preferences and purchases. Similar questions could be asked of each cell. The five basic communication factors in Figure 9-5 will serve as the organizing framework for this section of this chapter.

Source

Extensive research has been conducted on most factors and steps in Figure 9-5. One major research finding is that highly trustworthy and expert sources of information have a strong and immediate impact on attitude change. This is why most newscasters, and particularly Walter Cronkite (who is repeatedly found to be the most credible American public figure), take many steps to see that their reporting does not contain any attempt to change attitudes in a particular direction. Recent evidence, however, causes us to be a little more cautious in accepting findings about highly credible sources.[2] Dholakia and Sternthal have determined that highly credible sources, such as well-known experts, may be liabilities as well as assets in persuasive communication.[3] The more consumers rely on their own past behavior, the more likely it is that low credibility sources will have a greater influence on behavior than high credibility sources. High credibility sources may be more persuasive when consumers do not have past experiences on which to rely. This leads to Proposition 9-1 in Exhibit 9-1. The marketer must assess the past and present behavior of the consumer. If consumers have had little or no product experience, the use of highly credible sources might be appropriate. This would be the case with new products. On the other hand, low credibility sources, which would be far less expensive, might be more appropriate if consumers have had substantial experience with the product. Of course, which people are seen as highly credible will vary depending upon which group the message is supposed to appeal to. For example, Danny Thomas may be seen as highly credible by persons over fifty, whereas Billie Jean King might be a highly credible source for professionally-oriented or sports-oriented women.

In general, the believability of a message is greater when the source of the information is felt to be objective. The audience must believe that the source knows the truth and is "telling it like it is." Sometimes, however, an obvious attempt to bias consumers' attitudes might also be effective in per-

---

[2] A. Eagly and S. Chaiken, "An Attribution Analysis of the Effect of Communication Attractiveness," *Journal of Personality and Social Psychology,* Vol. 32, No. 1, July, 1975, pp. 136–144.

[3] Ruby Roy Dholakia and Brian Sternthal, "Highly Credible Sources: Persuasion Facilitators or Persuasive Liabilities?" *Journal of Consumer Research,* Vol. 3, March, 1977, pp. 223–232.

FIGURE 9-5.
*Persuasive
Communication Steps
and Basic
Communication Factors*

Persuasive Communication Steps	Communication Factors				
	Source	Message	Channel	Receiver	Destination
Presentation		1			
Attention			2		
Comprehension				3	
Yielding	4				
Retention					5
Overt Behavior					6

suading them to behave as desired by the marketer. Some researchers believe that an explicit attempt to persuade consumers sensitizes their thinking so that they comprehend the message better.[4]

Another important issue is how expert a source is perceived to be. A communication from a perceived expert will be more persuasive than one by a perceived nonexpert. There is, however, such a thing as too much expertise. The most persuasive source of information is one who is perceived by consumers to be a little more expert than they are. A perceived nonexpert or a person perceived to be greatly superior in expertise is relatively less persuasive. The person greatly superior in expertise may be seen as socially and psychologically "distant" and too unlike the consumer (see Proposition 9-6).

There are many other considerations which are usually taken into account when examining how source traits affect persuasion. These considerations include the effect of a source on opinion change over time, the effect on source credibility of presenting the audience initially with information with which they already agree, and the effect of the message on the source's credibility. An extensive discussion of these factors is not feasible here. Fortunately, consensus exists about how many of these factors work. Delozier has summarized this consensus in a list of principles which are presented (in propositional form) in Exhibit 9-1. Proposition 9-2 is straightforward. High credibility sources are generally more persuasive than low credibility sources,

[4]William J. McGuire, "Suspiciousness of Experimenter's Intent as an Artifact in Social Research," in R. Rosenthal and R. L. Rosnow (eds.), *Artifacts in Behavioral Research,* NY: Academic Press, 1969, pp. 13–57.

EXHIBIT 9-1.
Propositions Concerning Source Effects in Persuasive Communications [5]

PROPOSITION 9-1.
The more consumers can rely on their own past or present behavior (in addition to information about the source and message in a communication) as a guide for making a judgment, the more effective low credibility sources of information will be.

PROPOSITION 9-2.
In general, a source is more persuasive when the audience perceives the source as high, rather than low, in credibility.

PROPOSITION 9-3.
The more powerful and attractive a source is perceived to be, the more influence he or she has on a receiver's behavior.

PROPOSITION 9-4.
A source's credibility, and thus his or her persuasiveness, is reduced when the audience perceives that the source has something to gain from the persuasive attempts (intention to manipulate).

PROPOSITION 9-5.
Over time, the opinion change attributed to a high credibility source decreases, whereas the opinion change induced by a low credibility source increases, resulting in about the same level of retained opinion change for both low and high credibility sources.

PROPOSITION 9-6.
The more the members of an audience perceive the source to be similar to themselves, the more persuasive the source will be.

PROPOSITION 9-7.
A source increases his or her influence if at first he or she expresses some views already held by the audience, followed by the intended persuasive communication.

PROPOSITION 9-8.
A source who holds a positive attitude toward himself or herself, the message, and the receiver will be more persuasive than a source who holds negative attitudes.

[5]Source for Propositions 9-2 to 9-8: Wayne M. DeLozier, *The Marketing Communications Process*, NY: McGraw-Hill Book Company, 1976, pp. 84–85.

except in the case described by Proposition 9-1. Even if not seen as highly credible, nonexperts in an advertisement might be persuasive if they are perceived as powerful and attractive. For example, Proposition 9-3 suggests that in addition to credibility, the more charismatic a source is, the more influence that source will have with the audience. When the credible source, however, is perceived as gaining something from the testimony and as giving the testimony primarily for that gain, the source may not be very effective (Proposition 9-4). In this case, consumers will discount what the credible source has to say. If the marketing manager is concerned primarily with securing long-term change rather than an immediate change, the use of very expensive experts and other highly credible public figures may not be any more effective than low credibility sources. This is the implication of Proposition 9-5. In fact, sometimes the more consumers perceive the main figure in an advertisement to be similar to themselves (such as an ordinary citizen), the more effective that advertisement will be. This is implied by Proposition 9-6. Proposition 9-7 states that an effective way of establishing similarity is for the source to indicate at the outset that he or she also possesses some of the same views held by the audience. Proposition 9-8 recommends that a person giving testimony in an advertisement should display self-confidence, conviction about the message being delivered, and a favorable attitude toward and concern for the well-being of the audience.

Of course, consumers as well as marketers can be the source of communications. For example, a consumer with a product complaint is the source of a communication which may be written or verbal. In trying to persuade a company representative that the product is faulty (and that the consumer is not at fault), the consumer may unknowingly put some of these propositions into practice. Dissatisfied consumers may try to present themselves as credible, powerful ("I won't buy any of your products unless you replace this one," or "My best friend is a well-known consumer protection lawyer"), and attractive. To the extent that consumers are able to make credible complaints, they will be more likely to have their complaints satisfactorily resolved.

Content or Message   In addition to source considerations, the marketer must also take into account the content of information delivered by a source. One major content issue is what type of appeal to use in a persuasive communication. One appeal which has been popular with marketers is fear.[6] Fear appeals either facilitate or inhibit response to an advertisement. Fear appeals cause some consumers to follow the recommendations contained in an advertisement in order to avoid

[6]Michael L. Ray and William L. Wilkie, "Fear: The Potential of an Appeal Neglected by Marketing," *Journal of Marketing,* Vol. 34, January, 1970, pp. 54–62.

FIGURE 9-6.
Fear Appeals

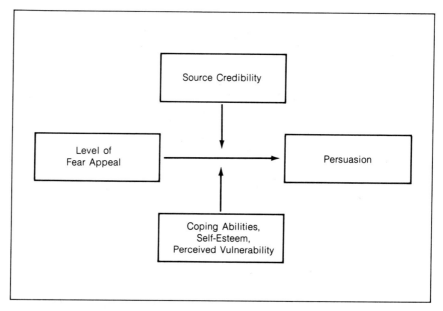

such things as bad breath or a flat tire on a rainy night on a deserted highway. On the other hand, fear appeals cause some people to act defensively and to avoid such advertisements, or to psychologically repress the content of the ads. Much attention is given to discerning the most effective level of fear. Ray and Wilkie suggest, for example, that "the greater the relevance of the topic for the audience, the lower the optimal level of fear appeal."[7] Another researcher reports that fear appeals are more effective in favorably changing the attitudes of nonowners of a product than in changing the attitudes of owners.[8]

Several propositions can be posited about fear appeals and persuasion.[9] Under conditions of high source credibility, threats involving physical harm may increase persuasion. Fear appeals are not likely to work when the source of information is not considered trustworthy or is not considered to have expertise. Thus, we have a situation such as that shown in Figure 9-6. As indicated above, audience characteristics also moderate the impact of fear on persuasion. Fear appeals are more successful in persuading those consumers who are able to cope well with threatening situations, who are high in self-

---

[7]*Ibid.,* p. 59.

[8]John J. Wheatley, "Marketing and the Use of Fear-Anxiety-Arousing Appeals," *Journal of Marketing,* Vol. 35, April, 1971, pp. 62–64.

[9]See, for example, Brian Sternthal and C. Samuel Craig, "Fear Appeals: Revisited and Revised," *Journal of Consumer Research,* Vol. 1, December, 1974, pp. 22–34.

esteem or, interestingly, who do not see themselves as vulnerable to the threat. These ideas are expressed as Propositions 9-9 to 9-12 in Exhibit 9-2. These propositions involve the impact of threat or fear on persuasion. They do not address the issues of commitment to change and actual behavior. Though threats may persuade consumers who do not see themselves as being vulnerable to an accident that it is bad to drive fast, their actual driving behavior may be unaffected by the convincing advertisement. Considerable research is needed in this area to determine how fear appeals work generally, how they work during specific stages of the communication process, with whom fear appeals are effective, and with what products.

An example of the use of fear in a social marketing advertising campaign conducted through television is shown in Figure 9-7. A teenaged girl, sitting in a rocking chair looking out a window, says, "I'm not sick or anything. I could go out more, but since the car crash, I just don't know...The crash wasn't Dad's fault. I go for walks after dark...that way I don't get, you know, stared at." She turns enough to reveal a large scar on what was the hidden side of her face. She continues, "It doesn't hurt anymore." An announcer says off-camera, "Car crashes kill two ways: right away and little by little. Wear your safety belts and live."

In a carefully designed study, this advertisement and similar others were found to be ineffective. That is, the ads did not increase the actual usage of seat belts. This was due to the desire of viewers to forget the unpleasant

EXHIBIT 9-2.
Propositions Concerning Fear Appeals

PROPOSITION 9-9.
Under conditions of high source credibility, as fear about physical harm increases, persuasion increases.

PROPOSITION 9-10.
The greater the ability of consumers to cope with a threat, the more likely they are to be persuaded by a threatening appeal.

PROPOSITION 9-11.
The greater the level of self-esteem of consumers, the more likely they are to be persuaded by a threatening appeal.

PROPOSITION 9-12.
The less vulnerable consumers perceive themselves to be to a threatening situation, the more likely they are to be persuaded by a threatening appeal.

FIGURE 9-7.
*Girl at the Window
Advertising Message.*

Source: Leon Robertson and others, "A Controlled Study of the Effect of Television Messages on Safety Belt Use," *American Journal of Public Health,* Vol. 64, No. 11, November, 1974, p. 1074.

suggestion that the girl in the advertisement might easily be themselves or close relatives.

There are numerous other appeals used in marketing communications. Nearly all consumers' desires and preferences are bases for building communication appeals. Appeals may be based on social consciousness, which is a frequent theme in communications concerning environmental matters. Appeals may be based on aspirations to improve social status, income, or education. Life insurance communications base their appeals in part on the need of individuals to continue to provide for their families after death. Many appeals, such as those in mouthwash ads, are based on the desire for social acceptance.

Humor is also used extensively in persuasive communications such as advertising, and contrasts sharply with fear appeals. Two communications behavior researchers examined whether humor is an effective tool for persuasion.[10] In an extensive review of the relevant communications literature they tentatively concluded that:

1. Humorous messages attract attention.
2. Humorous messages may detrimentally affect comprehension.
3. Humor may distract the audience, producing reduction in counter-argumentation (arguments against the main points of the message) and an increase in persuasion.
4. Humorous appeals appear to be persuasive but the persuasive effect is at best no greater than that of serious appeals.
5. Humor tends to enhance source credibility.
6. Audience characteristics may confound the effect of humor.
7. A humorous context may increase liking for the source and create a positive mood. This may increase the persuasive effect of the message.
8. To the extent that a humorous context functions as a positive reinforcer, a persuasive communication placed in such a context may be more effective.

Several conclusions can be drawn from existing research about what to include and what not to include in messages. Consumer comprehension tends to be greater if the source clearly states the conclusions. On the other hand, yielding may be better facilitated by allowing the consumer to draw his or her own conclusions. This last point is in need of more research. Overall, it seems preferable in persuasive communications to explicitly state conclusions. Another question concerns the frequency with which a conclusion or other points should be repeated through advertising. The answer seems to be that

---

[10]Brian Sternthal and C. Samuel Craig, "Humor in Advertising," *Journal of Marketing,* Vol. 37, October, 1973, pp. 12–18.

for any given consumer, some repetition is important in securing behavioral change. Substantial repetition, however, has little extra impact on consumers.[11]

An interesting dilemma faced by sales promotion managers is whether to present just the advantages of a product or service, or to present the disadvantages as well. It appears that the "one-sided" or "advantages only" approach is best when consumers initially agree with the marketer's position, when consumers possess little information, and when it is unlikely that consumers will be exposed to counteradvertising and sales presentations by competitors. It is best to present both the advantages and disadvantages when consumers initially disagree with the marketer's position, when consumers are well informed, and when consumers are likely to be exposed to counterarguments by competitors. (The reader may wish to note Figure 9-8.)

Table 9-1 contains three groups of ideas concerning comparison advertising, where competitors make direct comparisons of each other's products. In general, these ideas indicate that comparison advertising may enhance consumer attention, comprehension, and message acceptance.

Channels   There are basically two types of communication channels: interpersonal channels and mass media channels. Table 9-2 identifies the basic characteristics of these channels along six dimensions. Each channel has different, yet possibly complementary, functions. The mass media are usually more effective than interpersonal channels in increasing knowledge. On the other hand, interpersonal channels are more effective in changing attitudes. Both channels used together creatively can be very powerful in changing behavior. Evidence of this is contained in the research on the two-step flow theory of communication.

Models of Communication Flow.   The complementarity of mass media and interpersonal channels has been conceptualized in terms of the two-step flow model of communication. The two-step flow model is a model or theory which states "...that ideas often flow from radio and print to opinion leaders and from these to the less active sections of the population."[12] This is shown diagrammatically in Figure 9-9.

---

[11]McGuire, 1973, *op. cit.,* p. 235; See also, Leo Bogart, "Consumer Behavior and Advertising Research," in Ithiel de Sola Pool and Wilbur Schramm (eds.), *Handbook of Communication,* Chicago: Rand McNally, 1973, pp. 706–721.

[12]Paul F. Lazarsfeld, *et al., The People's Choice,* NY: Duell, Sloan, and Pearce, 1944.

FIGURE 9-8.
*Sequencing Pros and
Cons*

Dennis The Menace

"Which is smarter . . . the good news first, or the
bad news first?"

In step 1, information is transferred from the mass media to opinion leaders.
In step 2, influence and information are transferred from opinion leaders to
followers. The two-step model was developed in response to evidence that
the hypodermic needle model was inadequate. This model claimed that the
mass media has a powerful, direct impact on its audience, implying that there
is no interpersonal mediation. This model is shown diagrammatically in Figure
9-10. The audience is perceived to be atomistic. That is, members of the
target audience are not considered in terms of their possible relationships to
one another. The impact on the mass communication process of relationships, such as those between leader and follower, are ignored.

Probably the most accurate conceptualization of channels is a multi step

<table>
<tr><td>

TABLE 9-1.

*Hypotheses Regarding
Effects of Comparison
Advertising*

</td><td>

1. Attention

  *The novelty of a comparison ad will cause it to receive more attention than a standard ad.

  *Comparison ads will receive more attention from users of competing brands mentioned than from users of brands not mentioned.

  *Increasing the prominence of competing brands will increase attention from their users, but will also increase aggregate misidentifications of the sponsoring brand.

  *Aggregate recall levels of comparison ads will be higher than those for standard appeals.

2. Comprehension

  *Exposure to a comparison ad will lead to a "clearer brand image" than exposure to a standard ad.

  *Consumers will rate comparison ads as more "informative" and more "interesting" than most standard ads.

  *Users of a named *competing* brand are more likely to admit the sponsor brand into their evoked set than are users of brands not mentioned.

  *Users of the *sponsored* brand are more likely to *reduce* the size of their evoked set when exposed to a comparison ad than when exposed to a standard ad.

3. Message Acceptance

  *Claims made in a comparison ad are more likely to be accepted as "correct" than those in a standard ad.

  *Naming a competing brand will tend to increase support arguments by users of the sponsoring brand and counterarguments by users of the competing brand.

  *The level and duration of counterarguing will be negatively related to changes in brand preference.

  *Comparison ads will yield higher variance (i.e., increased polarity) in postexposure brand preferences than will standard advertisements.

  *On the average, comparison ads are *more effective* in improving consumer preferences for the sponsored brand than are standard advertisements.

</td></tr>
</table>

Source: William Wilkie and Paul W. Farris, "Comparison Advertising: Problems and Potential," *Journal of Marketing,* Vol. 39, October, 1975, pp. 7–15, at p. 14.

flow model, which combines and goes beyond the two-step flow and hypodermic needle models. The multi step flow model simply says that: (1) the mass media often do reach large numbers of persons in a social system; (2) some of the persons in the social system have unique relationships with one another; and (3) these relationships influence how information from the mass media is processed by members of the social system. Consider the diagram in Figure 9-11.

TABLE 9-2.
Characteristics of Communication Channels

Characteristics	Interpersonal Channels	Mass Media Channels
1. Message flow	Tends to be two-way	Tends to be one-way
2. Communication contact	Face-to-face	Interposed
3. Amount of feedback readily available	High	Low
4. Ability to overcome biases or tendencies to avoid undesired information	High	Low
5. Speed to large audiences	Relatively slow	Relatively rapid
6. Stage where it is most effective	Attitude formation and change	Knowledge change

Source: Adapted from Everett M. Rogers, ''Mass Media and Interpersonal Communication,'' in de Sola Pool, *et al., op cit.,* p. 291.

Information may flow directly from the mass media to a person who controls enough of a channel of communication to determine what information does or does not get relayed to others. This person is called a gatekeeper. In step 2, the gatekeeper relays the information to others. Among these ''others'' are some persons who are influentials or ''opinion leaders.'' In yet another step, these opinion leaders reinforce or contradict the original message. Section ''a'' highlights this process. Additionally, in yet another step, highlighted in ''b'', the followers discuss the information among themselves. This discussion also influences how each person interprets the information. The relationship between opinion leader and follower may be one in which the opinion leader

FIGURE 9-9.
The Two-Step Model of Communication

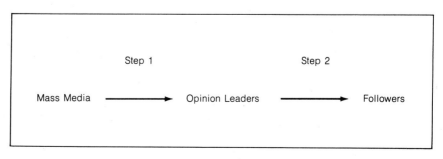

FIGURE 9-10.
*Hypodermic Needle
Model of
Communication*

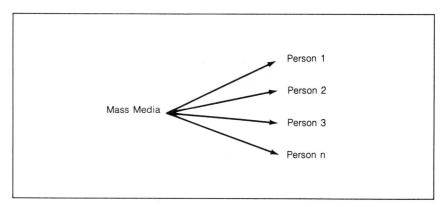

does not initiate discussion as implied in "a" and "b" in Figure 9-11, but the follower initiates discussion which is a step highlighted in "c". Thus, this might result in the situation shown in Figure 9-12. This can be easily complicated with the opinion leader seeking additional information from a gatekeeper who in turn may have to consult the mass media again.

Comparison of Information Channels.   It is useful to distinguish among three channels of information consumers may use. First, there are marketer-dominated channels, such as television advertising. Second, there are consumer-dominated channels, such as friends and neighbors. Finally, there are neutral channels, such as *Consumer Reports*. Woodruff investigated the effect of these different sources of information on consumer opinion change and on consumer uncertainty about color television brands.[13] Woodruff's study found that the neutral source was most likely to reduce uncertainty, but the reduction was likely to be small. On the other hand, consumer-dominated sources of information were the most influential sources in changing uncertainty when an opinion change also occurred. The probability of opinion changing, however, was less than for neutral sources. Thus, there is an important distinction between *whether* opinions will change and *how much* they will change. A source of information may not always change opinions or lower uncertainty about a brand; but when the source does cause opinions to change, the change may be substantial.

A marketer may want to use consumer-dominated sources to bring about a new perception of the quality of a home appliance. This source might

[13]Robert B. Woodruff, "Brand Information Sources, Opinion Change, and Uncertainty," *Journal of Marketing Research,* Vol. 9, November, 1972, pp. 414–418.

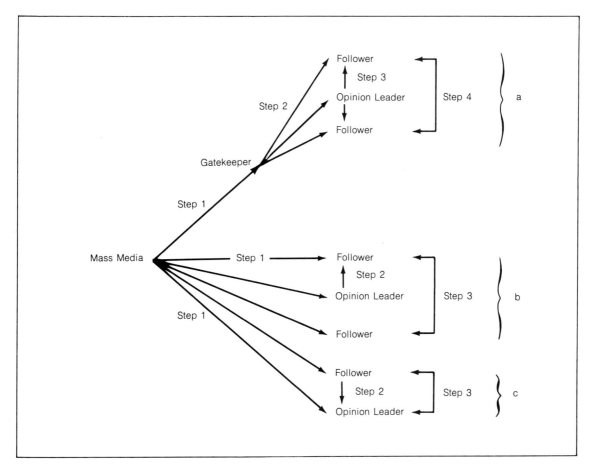

FIGURE 9-11.
Variations of the
Multi-step Model of
Communication

be used because market research indicated that for product quality (a brand attribute), consumer-dominated sources: (1) had a high probability of changing opinions favorably, (2) were likely to decrease uncertainty surrounding a new product, and (3) could substantially improve opinions. More realistically, however, the marketer may have to make trade-offs. That is, consumer-dominated sources of information might have a high likelihood of altering an opinion in a favorable way, but the magnitude of the change could be relatively small. At the same time, marketer-dominated communications might have a low likelihood of improving an opinion or lowering uncertainty, but be highly influential with those consumers whose opinions are altered.

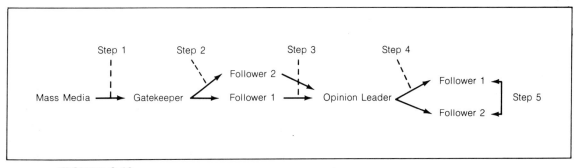

FIGURE 9-12.
A Possible Multistep Communication Flow

Classification of Interpersonal Communication. The most frequent type of communication is face-to-face. This communication is both verbal and nonverbal. A substantial portion of our verbal or oral communication is informal and not undertaken to advance the commercial interests of one of the parties.

It is possible to classify interpersonal communication in terms of the source's output and the receiver's input. This classification is shown in Table 9-3. The receiver has visual, auditory, tactile (touching) and olfactory (smelling) channels for input. The source has four basic sets of stimuli. One set consists of factors, such as race and sex, which cannot be changed even over a long period of time. A second set of stimuli are those which typically cannot be changed during any given episode of communication. For instance, hair style or clothing can't be altered during the course of most conversations. Next are factors which do change within a given communication episode but are not likely to change very much. For example, two persons in conversation will not normally alter the distance between each other very much or very often in the course of their discussion. On the other hand, some stimuli may change quite often in a given conversation. For example, people often pause with "uh's" or gesture with their hands during the conversation.

Oral communication which is informal and not intended to enhance one of the communicator's commercial interests is referred to as word-of-mouth communication. If it is favorable toward a product or service, it can be a very powerful and inexpensive form of promotion. It is no wonder, then, that marketers have been greatly concerned with word-of-mouth communication. Advertising for Seagram's V-O has stressed the theme "the reputation built by word-of-mouth." This theme implies that the beverage must be of very high quality in order to receive favorable comments among friends. This type of favorable communication is considered important because it is (allegedly) unbiased by the distiller.

TABLE 9-3.
Classification Scheme for Interpersonal Communication

Receiver's Input Channels	Source's Output Stimuli During Communication			
	Permanently Unchangeable and Uncontrollable Stimuli	Temporarily Unchangeable and Uncontrollable Stimuli	Stimuli Which Change Relatively Little	Stimuli Which Change Quite a Bit
1. Visual	a. Physical Features (race, sex, age, etc.)	a. Clothing (style, neatness)	a. Posture	a. Body Movement
		b. Physical Features (hair style, beard)	b. Distance Between Speakers	b. Facial Expression
				c. Gesture
				d. Head Orientation
2. Auditory	a. Basic Speech Patterns	a. Accent	a. Accent	a. Laughing, Crying
			b. Voice Pitch	b. Hesitation ("uh . . .")
			c. Articulation	
3. Tactile and Olfactory		a. Personal Odor		
		b. Touching Behavior		

Source: Adapted from James Hulbert and Noel Capon, "Interpersonal Communication in Marketing: An Overview," *Journal of Marketing Research*, Volume 9, February 1972, p. 29.

A number of propositions concerning word-of-mouth communication have been tested in a well-designed study.[14] This study involved homemakers who were interviewed using the telephone and a mail questionnaire. The interviews covered homemaking, nutrition, and eating habits. Of special concern was the response of homemakers to a new food product. Three of the propositions are particularly relevant here. One proposition supported by the data and which is somewhat contrary to other studies is Proposition 9-13 in Exhibit 9-3. The greater a consumer's confidence in his or her ability to evaluate a product, the greater the likelihood of that consumer participating in word-of-mouth communication. Such consumers may feel there is little risk that they will give friends and associates poor or inaccurate information. Thus, they probably feel free to tell others about a product.

Another proposition supported by this work is Proposition 9-14, which states that the more consumers are exposed to other sources of information about a product (such as advertising or actual use of the product), the more likely they are to discuss the product. The larger the number of sources of information, the more confident consumers will be in their judgments about the product (see Proposition 9-13), particularly if their information is derived from personal use of the product.

A third proposition, Proposition 9-15, posits that people who recall (unaided) the brand name are more likely to talk about the product than people who do not recall it. Unaided recall implies a greater interest in or involvement with the product, and people are more likely to talk about things in which they are interested or with which they are involved.

The researcher in this study did not suggest that these three propositions are related. However, it is probable that they are. Possible relationships are shown in Figure 9-13. The more information consumers have, the more confident they are about their judgments concerning the product (see Chapter 12 on information processing). Another plausible proposition is that greater nonword-of-mouth communication makes the brand name more obvious (due to repetition) and more easily recalled.

There are several action implications which can be derived from the last three interrelated propositions. It is important to use nonword-of-mouth communication, such as distributing mail samples of a product which can "communicate" information about the product directly to the consumer. This may stimulate word-of-mouth communication directly—"I have just received a sample of fabric softener, have you?"—and indirectly—"I've used it and

---

[14]Shlomo I. Lampert, "Word-of-Mouth Activity During the Introduction of A New Food Product," in John V. Farley, John A. Howard, and L. Winston Ring, *Consumer Behavior: Theory and Application,* Boston: Allyn and Bacon, 1974, pp. 67–88.

EXHIBIT 9-3.
Propositions About
Word-of-Mouth
Communication

PROPOSITION 9-13.
The greater a consumer's confidence in his or her ability to evaluate a product, the greater the likelihood of that consumer participating in word-of-mouth communication.

PROPOSITION 9-14.
The more consumers are exposed to other sources of information about a product (such as advertising or actual product use), the more likely they are to discuss the product.

PROPOSITION 9-15.
People who recall (unaided) the brand name are more likely to talk about the product than people who do not recall it.

found it to be..." The samples enhance consumers' abilities to judge and to recall the brand, and, hence, their willingness and ability to talk about it. Messages attached to the sample might urge users to speak with other people about the product. Information should be given in unambiguous and direct ways to enhance consumers' feelings about the soundness of the information they have and about their abilities to judge the product. Catchy brand names may also stimulate word-of-mouth communication.

Receiver and Destination

Many personal characteristics such as self-esteem or dogmatism have been related to persuasibility. This relationship frequently has an inverted "U" shape. This means that people with very low or very high levels of self-esteem might be less easily persuaded than those with moderate levels of self-esteem. Chapter 15 focuses on the various personality traits which may be related to persuasibility. Here we shall cite some basic ideas about personality-persuasibility relationships.[15] Personality factors appear to be important considerations in all steps of the persuasive communication process: Presentation-Attention-Comprehension-Yielding-Retention-Overt Behavior. A personality trait which facilitates one step, however, may make another step

[15]McGuire, *op. cit.,* pp. 239 ff.

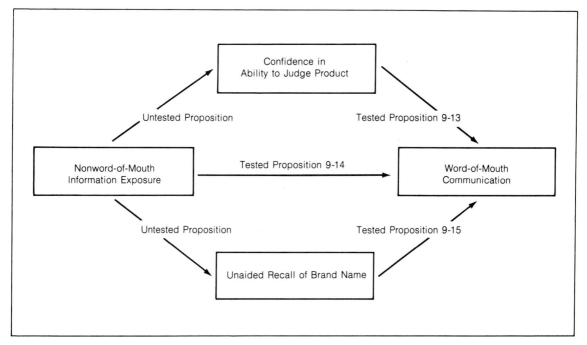

FIGURE 9-13.
*Factors Affecting
Word-of-Mouth
Communication*

difficult. An insecure person may yield readily and change an attitude relatively quickly. But the same insecure person might be very hesitant to change his or her overt behavior. Different steps in the persuasive communication process are differentially relevant. Sometimes comprehension is especially important. This is likely when the communication is complex and difficult to understand. Thus, personality and other traits associated with comprehension tend to be more important than traits associated with less important steps.

Destination issues concern what happens after a persuasive communication has entered the mind of the receiver. If there is a change in attitude, how long will the change last? How does a communicator make the audience less likely to be influenced by a competing communicator? There are several approaches to this last question, one of which is to get the consumer to make a commitment to the product prior to being exposed to a competing communication. This is especially effective when the commitment is done in public. Another approach is to link one attitude to another attitude which is firmly held and difficult to change.

COMMUNICATION AND THE ORGANIZATION

Thus far the discussion of communication has been primarily in terms of individual consumers. But communication is an essential aspect of organizational life and of central importance to understanding organizations as consumers.[16] Communication is what binds organizations internally and is the way in which organizations relate to their environments.

Communication with the External Environment

External environments are very important and may be defined as "those relevant physical and social factors *outside* the boundaries of the organization or specific decision unit that are taken directly into consideration in the decision-making behavior of individuals in that system."[17] Physical factors include the depletion of raw material resources or adverse weather conditions affecting a crop. Social factors include employee strikes, government regulations, or changes in the number of competitors.

Organizations buy from their external environment. They also depend to a great degree on information from their environment to guide their purchase decisions. Purchase-related information may come from any of several components of the external environment, such as those shown in Table 9-4. The identification of the most appropriate component(s) in the environment for a particular purchase decision is important for both buyer and seller. Certainly not all the components in Table 9-4 can or should be considered in any purchase-related decision. For example, should the purchasing behavior of competitors be studied? One researcher found in a study of industrial firms which use paper as a major product component that seeking and getting information from persons in competing firms was an important part of the purchase decision process.[18] Discussions with competitors may be direct via telephone or take place at conferences and trade shows. Trade shows have been labeled as the most neglected selling tool available to marketers. Apparently, organizations are placing more and more emphasis on this component of the environment.

---

[16]Daniel Katz and Robert L. Kahn, *The Social Psychology of Organizations,* NY: John Wiley & Sons, Inc., 1966; Richard H. Hall, *Organizations: Structure and Process,* Englewood Cliffs, NJ: Prentice-Hall, 1972; and Everett M. Rogers and Rekha Agarwala-Rogers, *Communication in Organizations,* NY: The Free Press, 1976.

[17]Gerald Zaltman and Robert Duncan, *Strategies for Planned Change,* NY: Wiley Interscience, 1977, p. 250.

[18]John A. Martilla, "Word-of-Mouth Communication in the Industrial Adoption Process," *Journal of Marketing Research,* Vol. 8, May, 1971, pp. 173–178.

TABLE 9-4.
Factors Comprising the Organization's External Environment

EXTERNAL ENVIRONMENT

Customer Component
A. Distributors of product or service
B. Actual users of product or service

Suppliers Component
A. New materials suppliers
B. Equipment suppliers
C. Product parts suppliers
D. Labor supply

Competitor Component
A. Competitors for suppliers
B. Competitors for customers

Socio-political Component
A. Government regulatory control over the industry
B. Public political attitude toward industry and its particular product
C. Relationship with trade unions with jurisdiction in the organization

Technological Component
A. Meeting new technological requirements of own industry and related industries in production of product or service
B. Improving and developing new products by implementing new technological advances in the industry

Source: Zaltman and Duncan, *op. cit.,* p. 251.

An important finding in the general literature on organizational environment is that the more "open" or willing an organization is to accept and even seek new ideas from its external environment, the more innovative it is.[19] This is Proposition 9-16 in Exhibit 9-4. This innovativeness expresses itself in organizational buying decisions in at least two ways. Organizations may purchase innovative products and services to improve their present production process. Additionally, by being innovative, the organization may undertake entirely new activities, such as entering a particular market for the first time.

[19]Michael Tushman, "Special Boundary Roles in the Innovation Process," *Administrative Science Quarterly,* Vol. 22, No. 4, December, 1977, pp. 587–605; John A. Czepiel, "Communications Networks and Innovation in Industrial Communities," paper presented at the *International Symposium on Industrial Innovation,* University of Strathclyde, Glasgow, Scotland, September 5–9, 1977; and Gerald Zaltman, Robert Duncan and Jonny Holbek, *Innovations and Organizations,* NY: Wiley-Interscience, 1973; also Zaltman and Duncan, *op. cit.,* Chapter 11.

EXHIBIT 9-4.
*Propositions About
External Environment
and Organizational
Innovativeness*

PROPOSITION 9-16.
The more open an organization is to its external environment, the more innovative it is likely to be.

PROPOSITION 9-17.
The more rapidly its relevant environment changes, the more innovative an organization is likely to be.

This new activity may require that they begin purchasing particular products and services for the first time.

Proposition 9-16 can be augmented by Proposition 9-17. Proposition 9-17 states that the more rapidly its relevant environment changes, the more innovative an organization is likely to be.[20]

These two propositions can be diagrammed as shown in Figure 9-14. A rapidly changing environment creates a greater need to change as old markets become less profitable and competition increases. Thus, even organizations that are relatively "closed", i.e., not amenable to new ideas and activities, may be forced to innovate. Even if an organization could get along without changing, a changing environment may create new opportunities. So, it is possible that a rapidly changing environment may cause some organizations to become more open to their environments.

Changing environments create uncertainty for organizations. Closed organizations try to ignore information about these changes for as long as possible, while open organizations attempt to reduce this uncertainty by opening communication channels with the environment to learn about such changes. For some organizations, a changing environment results in more openness to the environment. Some organizations even try to control their environment instead of merely adjusting to it. Such organizations are believed to be more innovative.[21] Thus, organizational innovativeness can produce environmental change.

The action implications of Propositions 9-16 and 9-17 are numerous. Firms that are open to their environments are usually good prospects for adopting new products and services in areas of importance to them. By virtue

[20]Zaltman, *et al., op. cit.,* 1973, p. 110.
[21]Rogers and Agarwala-Rogers, *op. cit.*

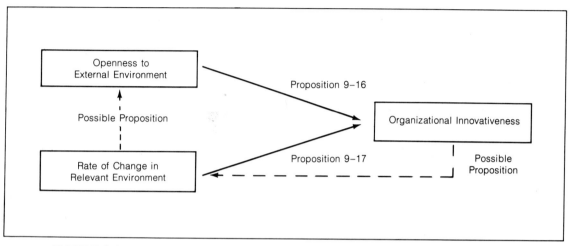

FIGURE 9-14.
External Environment and Organizational Innovativeness

of their openness, such firms find it easy to obtain information about the new products from customer-dominated channels. Therefore, a vendor or salesperson should be careful to present both the advantages and disadvantages of the product since this information (especially about the disadvantages) is likely to be obtained anyway. The open firm is also likely to be exposed to many marketer-dominated channels. This means that the salesperson's own competitors also have a chance to convey the disadvantages of the salesperson's products. By presenting unfavorable aspects of products as well as the favorable, the salesperson may be able to immunize prospects against competitors' statements.

The organization which is relatively closed to its environment is a late adopter of innovations, responding only when circumstances make it difficult not to change. Such firms use fewer sources of information and rely heavily on what actions they notice their more successful competitors are taking. It is important for a salesperson to be able to point to successful, satisfied customers who can serve as demonstrators or opinion leaders for these more conservative firms. Although the evidence for this next implication is not rooted in the conventional research, it appears that the quality of the personal relationships a salesperson has with "closed" firms is an important factor in their purchase decisions. This factor is relatively less important with more open firms.

The salesperson should realize that he or she can be an important component of the open firm's environment. This is true not just in conventional industrial settings, but in other institutional areas such as medicine and education as well.[22] In high technology areas, a salesperson is often expected to serve in an expert advisory capacity, able and willing on occasion to recommend competing products and services. A firm in a rapidly changing environment, particularly a somewhat closed firm, faces considerable uncertainty. This may create a need for clarity. Consultants are sometimes used to satisfy this need. A salesperson may also play an important role in assisting firms to cope with a changing environment. Sales personnel are more valued, then, the better equipped they are to help a firm understand and adjust to a changing environment. This requires that sales personnel know more than just their own present product. They should also be knowledgeable about a present or potential customer's own market and the problems it is experiencing with competitors, other suppliers, changing industry regulations, and changing technology.

Communication Within the Internal Environment

"The *internal environment* consists of those relevant physical and social factors *within* the boundaries of the organization [which] are taken directly into consideration in the decision-making behavior of individuals in that system."[23] Table 9-5 contains the components of an organization's internal environment.

Formal and Informal Environments. There are, in fact, two overlapping internal environments. One is the formal internal environment, and the other is the informal internal environment. The formal internal environment involves such things as job descriptions, administrative procedures, and the organization chart. The informal aspect involves informal work groups, short cuts in procedures, and the "grapevine." The informal environment can be very important in purchase decisions. Although purchasing agents' job descriptions may limit their tasks to soliciting bids or identifying suppliers, they can informally exert much more influence on the actual purchase decision. Their advice may be solicited and greatly valued by those persons whose formal responsibility it is to make a final decision. Alternatively, a purchasing

[22]James S. Coleman, Elihu Katz, and Herbert Menzel, *Medical Innovation: A Diffusion Study,* Chicago: Bobbs Merrill Co., Inc., 1966; Henrik L. Blum, *Planning For Health: Development and Application of Social Change Theory,* NY: Human Sciences Press, 1974; Gerald Zaltman, David Florio, and Linda Sikorski, *Dynamic Educational Change: Models, Strategies, Tactics and Management,* NY: The Free Press, 1977.

[23]Zaltman and Duncan, *op. cit.*

TABLE 9-5.
Factors Comprising the Organization's Internal Environment

Internal Environment

Organizational Personnel Component

A. Educational and technological background and skills
B. Previous technological and managerial skill
C. Individual member's involvement and commitment to attaining system's goals
D. Interpersonal behavior styles
E. Availability of manpower for utilization within the system

Organizational Functional and Staff Units Component

A. Technological charactertistics of organizational units
B. Interdependence of organizational units in carrying out their objectives
C. Intraunit conflict among organizational functional and staff units
D. Interunit conflict among organizational functional and staff units

Organizational Level Component

A. Organizational objectives and goals
B. Integrative process integrating individuals and groups into contributing maximally to attaining organizational goals
C. Nature of the organization's product or service

Source: Zaltman and Duncan, *op. cit.,* p. 251.

agent with considerable formal responsibility may in fact informally delegate this responsibility to others. A discrepancy between formal and informal responsibility and influence occurs almost inevitably and may be very healthy for the organization. It is important for a marketer in an industrial setting to know about deviations from the formal system and to know what the informal system is for making purchases. This knowledge helps the salesperson decide on whom to call. It also helps the researcher know which persons to use as respondents in industrial marketing research.

The problems of learning the informal structure are indeed difficult, as was discussed in Chapter 7 in the section on the stages of role acquisition. Perhaps the best way to learn about the informal structure is through informal communications with different members of the client organization. For instance, a salesperson might ask a low level member in the organization who should be contacted for a certain type of information. Rather than relying on job titles, the insider will rely on his or her knowledge of the informal environment.

Organizational Structure and Communication. Organizational structure refers to the way components of an organization are arranged. The organization chart usually describes the formal organizational structure. The way an organization is structured influences the flow of communication and vice versa. Regarding the impact of organizational structure on communication, there are two basic considerations: vertical communication flows and horizontal communication flows. Vertical communication is between subordinates and their superiors and occurs less frequently than horizontal communication between peers. Also, more communication flows downward than upward. Information which flows upward is much less likely to contain negative information than is information which flows downward. One of the most important types of information flowing downward are purchase decision instructions.[24] This is especially common when reciprocity is involved. Reciprocity refers to the act of a firm's buying from a supplier because that supplier also buys from the firm.[25] This is another example of the informal system working. Reciprocity, because of the legal issues involved, must be handled very subtly. It is usually conveyed downward to the purchasing agent when it is to be practiced.

Some organizations are "tall" while others are "flat." Tall organizations have many levels while flat organizations have few. In flat organizations communication which flows upward moves more quickly than in tall organizations. There tends to be more communication downward in flat organizations, but the information comes more slowly when in response to a request for information.

Communication Problems. There are basically three types of communication problems in organizations. As communications move upward, intentional and unintentional filtering may occur. Aspects of messages are left out. This problem of *omission* occurs in a tall more often than in a flat organization. One reason for an industrial salesperson to call upon persons in all levels of an organization involved in a purchase decision is to make certain that essential information is not omitted and to provide it when it is omitted. It is also important to call upon upper management to correct any *distortion* in information which is passed upward to them. Distortion is the altering of the meaning of a message as it moves through an organization. The larger the number of people involved in the transmission of a message, the greater the likelihood of distortion and omission.[26] Another problem, one especially possible in flat organizations, is information *overload*. Overload occurs when information comes in faster than a manager can process it while also attending

---

[24]Katz and Kahn, *op. cit.*

[25]Thomas V. Bonoma, Gerald Zaltman, and Wesley Johnston, *Industrial Buying Behavior: Findings and Research Issues,* Boston: Marketing Science Institute, 1977.

[26]J. Eugene Haas and Thomas E. Prabek, *Complex Organizations: A Sociological Perspective,* NY: Macmillan Publishing Co., 1973.

to other normal duties. Overload may lead to omission and distortion. In the process of making communications to supervisors as brief and concise as possible, important information may be left out or presented inaccurately.

Communication Roles. Earlier in this chapter, as well as in previous chapters (see Chapter 7 on roles), we identified roles such as opinion leaders and gatekeepers that are especially important in the communication process. These roles are as important within organizations as they are in individual consumer markets. As Rogers and Agarwala-Rogers note: "Certain individuals keep the organization's gate on message flows; they are gatekeepers. Others are located in a crucial position so as to connect the canvas of cliques; they are liaisons. Some are dominantly influential in an informal way; they are opinion leaders. 'Boundary spanners' or cosmopolites are the organization's 'windows to the world,' in that they relate the system to its environment."[27] These four roles have important functions, as is shown in Table 9-6. These important roles are described graphically in Figure 9-15.

A secretary may be a *gatekeeper* in determining whether a salesperson or telephone call reaches the boss. A purchasing agent may be a gatekeeper by deciding which potential suppliers are identified for the buying committee or the vice-president for purchasing and what information about potential suppliers reaches key decision makers. A gatekeeper may be very important in reducing information overload for other persons in the organization. The gatekeeper also has considerable potential for distortion or omission of information.

The *liaison* role has been described as the glue which holds together the various parts of an organization. The liaison is the "individual who interpersonally connects two or more cliques within a system, without himself belonging to any clique."[28] The liaison exerts a strong influence on how quickly information flows between groups. The liaison then is a potential bottleneck as well as a potential facilitator of communication. It is important that information be sent to the liaison directly if rapid and efficient information dissemination is desired. As in Figure 9-16a, the salesperson may make the initial call to only one group. This information must flow from the first group to the liaison (step 1) and from the liaison to another relevant group (step 2). The two steps involved after the initial contact by the salesperson represent opportunities for both distortion and omission to occur. In Figure 9-16b the salesperson must make two separate calls to create awareness within each relevant group. This

---

[27]Rogers and Agarwala-Rogers, *op. cit.*, pp. 132–133.
[28]*Ibid.*, p. 135.

TABLE 9-6.
Communication Roles

Communication Role	Function in the Network
1. Gatekeeper	Prevents information overload by filtering and receiving messages.
2. Liaison	Integrates and interconnects the parts (cliques) of the network.
3. Opinion Leader	Facilitates informal decision making in the network.
4. Cosmopolite (Boundary Spanner)	Relates the system to its environment by providing openness.

FIGURE 9-15.
Individual Communication Roles in Organizations

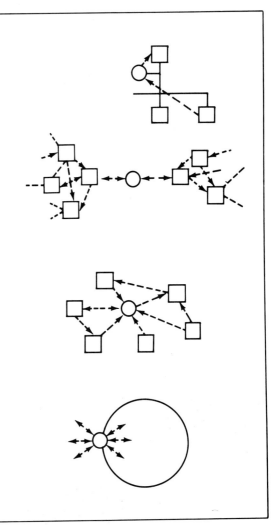

Gatekeeper
—an individual who is located in a communication structure so as to control the messages flowing through a communication channel

Liaison
—an individual who interpersonally connects two or more cliques within a system, without himself belonging to any clique

Opinion Leadership
—an individual able to informally influence other individuals' attitudes or overt behavior with relative frequency

Cosmopolite
—an individual who has a relatively high degree of communication with the system's environment

Source: Rogers and Agarwala-Rogers, 1976, *op. cit.*, p. 133.

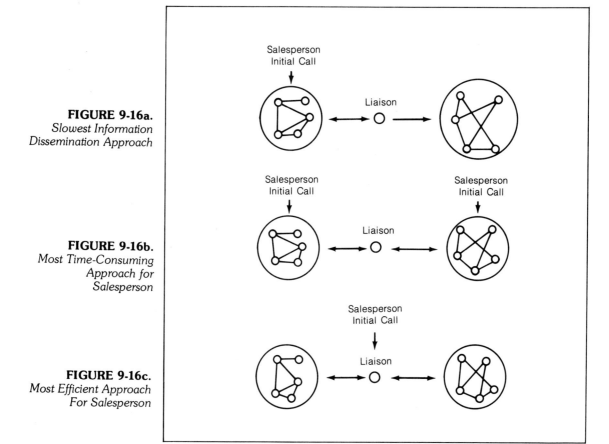

FIGURE 9-16a.
Slowest Information Dissemination Approach

FIGURE 9-16b.
Most Time-Consuming Approach for Salesperson

FIGURE 9-16c.
Most Efficient Approach For Salesperson

minimizes the potential for omission and distortion but requires twice the effort on the part of the salesperson just to create awareness. In Figure 9-16c the salesperson makes just one call to the liaison. Only one step is involved in getting information from the liaison to each relevant group. Figure 9-16c is probably the best way to create initial awareness in an organization of a product or service. This requires that a salesperson be able to identify the liaison in each organization. A frequent liaison is the purchasing agent.

Little study has been devoted to *opinion leadership* in the context of formal organizations such as business firms. Opinion leaders are informal leaders and may be found at almost any level of the organization. They, typically, are well informed in their area of expertise and are relatively accessible to followers. One researcher, in a study of paper converters (e.g., greeting card manufacturers and envelope manufacturers), found opinion leadership to be very important, especially at the consideration or evaluation stage in the adoption process.[29] Opinion leaders were also found to be important in reducing post-purchase uncertainty among key decision makers. That is, after the purchase, they helped decision makers see that they had made a good decision. Opinion leaders were found to be exposed to more impersonal sources of communication than other key participants involved in the purchase decision (Proposition 9-18 in Exhibit 9-5). Opinion leaders were also found to have greater depth of exposure to the information they encountered (Proposition 9-19). Depth of exposure is the degree of care with which a document is read or examined. The greater the number of exposures to impersonal sources of information and the more information gleaned per exposure, the more likely a person is to have expertise in the topic matter of concern. This is illustrated by Figure 9-17. Once their expertise is observed by others, they will usually solicit opinions and advice when faced with uncertainty in their topic area.

Cosmopolites are the persons linking the organization with its external environment. Rogers and Agarwala-Rogers suggest that cosmopolites are concentrated at the top and bottom of an organization.[30] Executives who travel widely and maintain many contacts with other organizations are cosmopolites, as are the salespeople who deal with customers and the purchasing agents who deal with many different suppliers. Cosmopolites may also be liaison persons, opinion leaders and gatekeepers. Cosmopolites are important as experts on future directions taking place in the external environment. They are instrumental in helping the organization cope with its external environment. The more rapidly the external environment changes, the more important the role played by cosmopolites.

EXHIBIT 9-5.
Propositions Concerning Industrial Opinion Leaders

PROPOSITION 9-18.
In industrial settings, exposure to impersonal sources of information will be greater for opinion leaders than for nonleaders.

PROPOSITION 9-19.
In industrial settings, opinion leaders have greater depth of exposure to impersonal sources than do nonleaders.

[29]Martilla, *op. cit.*
[30]Rogers and Agarwala-Rogers, *op. cit.*

FIGURE 9-17.
*Communication
Exposure and
Opinion Leadership*

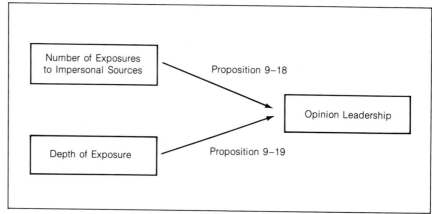

SUMMARY   In order for a communication to be persuasive, the source of the communication must be credible. Though consumers sometimes rely on their own experiences as a guide for making judgments, they are generally influenced by sources that are perceived to be trustworthy, attractive, and objective.

Fear or humor appeals are effective message techniques. Persuasion increases as fear about physical harm increases, unless the level of the fear appeal is so extreme that consumers react against the message, refusing to admit their own vulnerability. Though humorous messages may detrimentally affect comprehension, on the whole they attract attention, enhance source credibility, create a positive mood about the product, and hence, contribute to persuasion. It is also sometimes effective in messages to present both a product's advantages and disadvantages, so as to inoculate consumers against counteradvertising.

When both the mass media and the interpersonal channels of communication are used creatively together, they are very powerful in changing attitudes, increasing awareness, and changing behavior. Word-of-mouth communication is often considered by marketers to be the most important and persuasive.

Persuasibility is also contingent upon the personality of the consumer or receiver. For instance, people with low or high self-esteem might be less easily persuaded than those with moderate levels of self-esteem.

Communication binds organizations internally and relates them to their environments. Organizations depend to a great degree on information about the relevant physical and social factors outside the organization's boundaries, for a rapidly changing environment creates the need for innovation as old markets become less profitable and competition increases. Organizations must also take into account the internal environment when making decisions. An organization's structure, the communication problems of omission, distortion, and overload, and the communication roles within an organization comprise an internal environment that is important both for those within and outside the organizational boundaries.

KEY CONCEPTS
Channel
Commitment actualization
Communication
Communication participation
Comparison advertising
Cosmopolite
Counterargumentation
Cross pressure
Decision period
Destination
Distortion
Feedback
Gatekeeper
Liaison
Message
Omission
Opinion leader
Overload
Receiver
Reciprocity
Source

PSYCHOLOGICAL PERSPECTIVES

PART

3

LEARNING AND CONSUMER BEHAVIOR

10

CHAPTER GOALS   The objective of this chapter is to help the reader understand:
1. **the basic processes involved in human learning;**
2. **how these processes occur in everyday consumer situations.**

INTRODUCTION   Along with the social system and small group processes discussed in the previous chapters, consumer behavior researchers also examine processes which occur primarily within the individual. One of these processes is learning, the understanding of which is integral to a complete understanding of consumer behavior. Learning can be defined as the "more or less permanent acquisition of tendencies to behave in particular ways in response to particular situations or stimuli."[1] The vast amount of research into learning processes is generally reported in the psychological literature. Research into learning processes is concerned with:

1. How much can a person learn? What differences in learning capacity exist between people? Does this capacity change with increasing age? How and when are limits to learning set?

2. Do all types of learning improve with repetition? Does improvement vary directly with the amount of repetition? Is it possible to interfere with learning by too much repetition, or with repetition occurring in too brief a time period? Is one type of practice more effective than other types in producing learning?

[1]Michael L. Ray, "Psychological Theories and Interpretations of Learning," in Scott Ward and Thomas S. Robertson (eds.), *Consumer Behavior: Theoretical Sources*, Englewood Cliffs, N.J.: Prentice-Hall, 1973, p. 47.

3. Will the promise of a reward produce learning at a more rapid rate than the threat of punishment? Under what circumstances will an external impetus to learning be more influential than an internal impetus? Does having a goal or objective affect the learning rate?

4. What things do we learn spontaneously and why? What things require *studious* effort and why?

5. How much transfer of training takes place? Under what conditions does it take place? What is the nature of this transfer?

6. Why do we remember some things and not others? How much control do we have over the process?[2]

Obviously, this research is relevant to the study of consumer behavior, for learning essentially involves the linking of *stimuli,* such as a package or advertisement, with *responses,* such as remembering, understanding, and purchasing. The explicit application of learning research to consumer behavior, however, falls well below its potential. Perhaps one reason for this is that much of the research on learning has involved nonhumans or, where humans are involved, the context is a highly artificial laboratory setting which often focuses on simple verbal behavior. Thus, it is very difficult to generalize with confidence from these learning research findings to complicated humans in complicated social environments. This difficulty is reflected in the treatment of learning theory in consumer behavior textbooks. Only a small proportion of the discussion of learning theory and research in these texts is directly or explicitly related to consumer behavior. Given the problems in applying learning research to consumer behavior, however, the efforts made to discuss its application are commendable.

There are many different theories and approaches to the study of learning. Perhaps the best discussion of these theories and the best model for applying learning research and concepts to the study of consumer behavior is to be found in Michael L. Ray's synthesis of the literature.[3] Ray uses an eclectic framework which borrows from all basic learning theories. So, rather than becoming bogged down in a review of each of the different theories, we shall discuss Ray's synthesis and avoid the "pseudo-conflicts between various theories when all must be used for a thorough analysis of behavior."[4] The basic framework involves the concepts of response (R), stimulus (S), drive (D), incentive motivation (K), and habit (H), where:

$$R = f(S, D, K, H)$$

[2]Ernest R. Hilgard and Gordon H. Bower, *Theories of Learning,* NY: Appleton-Century-Crofts, 1966.
[3]*Ibid.,* pp. 45–117.
[4]*Ibid.,* p. 70.

CAUSAL VARIABLES We shall first consider the four basic causal variables which are stimulus (S), drive (D), incentive motivation (K), and habit (H), and then discuss their joint effect on response.

Stimulus A stimulus is a cue which determines the characteristic response and when and where it occurs. Usually, the stronger the stimulus, the more likely a consumer is to respond. For instance, the higher the quality of a product, the more likely it is to be purchased. Of course, reversal effects (e.g., a decrease in attention or remembering) are possible. A large amount of a stimulus often produces the reverse effect of what was produced by a lesser amount of the same stimulus. For example, if an excessive level of fear is used in an advertisement, people may forget the ad, whereas a lesser level of fear appeal may attract attention and lead to a longer retention of the message.[5] The level at which reversal occurs is determined in part by the magnitude of other stimuli or the past use of the stimulus, rather than by the absolute level of the stimulus. So, consumers not accustomed to high fear appeals may display the reversal effect at lower levels than consumers who are accustomed to high fear appeals.

An interesting finding established in early learning research is that a new stimulus elicits the response of the stimulus to which it is most similar (Proposition 10-1 in Exhibit 10-1). A new brand which is a "me too" product will probably elicit much of the same response as the brand it is imitating. Likewise, a new product which has only a modest resemblance to existing products will elicit only a modest amount of the responses that the existing products yield. This phenomenon is known as *generalization:* what is learned in one situation may be transferred to other similar situations. Generalization is the tendency to respond to a stimulus in proportion to the degree of its similarity to previous situations in which a response was rewarded or punished. *Discrimination,* another important concept, is established by rewarding consumers when they respond to one set of stimuli and not rewarding them when they respond to another set.

The concepts of generalization and discrimination have important implications for the marketing manager. The *generalization principle* suggests that products which are quite similar in appearance to successful competing items should be made readily available and given intensive distribution. It also suggests that these products should be distributed by outlets located in an area already populated by competing distributors. For example, Ford Motor

---

[5]K. L. Higbee, "Fifteen Years of Fear Arousal: Research on Threat Appeals," *Psychological Bulletin,* Vol. 72, 1969, pp. 426–444.

Company has advertised its Granada by comparing it to a Mercedes. The intent is that consumers will begin to think of and respond to the two cars in a similar fashion. On the other hand, the *discrimination principle* suggests that products that are distinctive and have a demonstrable relative advantage may be profitably distributed on a selective or exclusive basis.

EXHIBIT 10-1.
Proposition About
Stimuli

PROPOSITION 10-1.
The greater the similarity between two stimuli, the greater the extent to which the consumer will generalize his or her responses from the original stimulus to situations in which the more recent stimulus is present.

The generalization principle applies mostly to *convenience goods,* such as staples or impulse items. Here, the product stimuli of competing brands are essentially the same to consumers. One product may easily be substituted for another without loss of satisfaction (reward) to the consumer. *Shopping goods,* on the other hand, are relatively expensive, nonstandardized items that, in the eyes of consumers, merit careful price and quality comparison. Consumers are more apt to search out and discriminate among alternative products in this category. Therefore, a policy of market segmentation would be easy to maintain.

Specialty goods provide an excellent example of how a distribution policy may become part of the product mix. The policies of product differentiation and market segmentation are used to create this type of product. Specialty goods are items that possess a high degree of discrimination for consumers. They are products that a sizable groups of buyers insist upon having and will make special efforts to obtain. As a consequence, these products may have a limited availability, and selective or exclusive distribution may be used to support relatively high prices.

The principles of generalization and discrimination suggest why buyers prefer particular outlets. Once the response of frequenting an outlet has been satisfactorily rewarded, the generalization process increases the probability that the individual will shop at the same type of outlet again. For example, the restaurants of the Howard Johnson's chain have uniform buildings that are designed to serve as stimuli relating a goal object (food) to a drive (hunger). The intent is to induce patrons whose hunger was pleasantly satisfied previously at a Howard Johnson's restaurant to postpone satisfying their hunger until they again encounter the "Howard Johnson's pattern." Thus, the physical characteristics of distribution channels may also function as cues that will support product characteristics.

Relevant here is a special kind of stimulus referred to as a *secondary reinforcer,* which is a stimulus that has become a reinforcing agent through previous association with another reinforcing stimulus. Before a stimulus can become a secondary reinforcer, it must first become a discriminative stimulus. This means that the new stimulus (secondary reinforcer) must be present on many of the occasions when the response is reinforced and it must be absent when the response is not reinforced.

The secondary reinforcer concept has important implications for the marketing manager. If the product is considered the primary stimulus, a retail outlet will become a secondary reinforcer. This will happen if the store is patronized when a shopping trip (response) produces the desired product or brand with a minimum "cost" (reward or reinforcement). In addition, the outlet must *not* be the store that is patronized when a shopping trip is not rewarded. Both producer and retailer must cooperate in order to establish a particular outlet as a secondary reinforcer. It is the retailer's job to make sure that a customer knows that he or she may purchase a given product there, and it is the manufacturer's job to be sure that the retailer always has an adequate supply of the product on hand by making punctual deliveries. The degree of brand loyalty among customers determines whether the manufacturer or the retailer will suffer most from such shortages. Controlling stock-outs also helps prevent buyer frustration which might keep the retail outlet from becoming a secondary reinforcer. Frustration also results when there is unnecessary effort or cost in locating an item within a store or choosing from a wide variety of products. By carrying only the necessary variety of items, the retailer can lessen these costs. In exceeding the necessary variety and when inventory space is limited, the danger of stock-outs and customer frustration is increased. Customers may grow suspicious if an advertised product cannot be found on retailers' shelves and they may take this as evidence that the product was not so good after all.

A final concept relating to stimuli is the *contrast* or *differential threshold.* Marketing experts are interested in learning how consumers become aware of the differences between a stimulus and one of its previous forms, or other similar stimuli. The term differential threshold refers to the minimum difference that can be perceived between two stimuli. The stronger the initial stimulus, the more different subsequent stimuli must be in order for the consumer to be able to see the contrast (this is Proposition 10-2 in Exhibit 10-2). In other words, the important factor is not the absolute characteristics of the stimuli but rather the relation between them.

The notion of a differential threshold is important when introducing a new product or a modified version of an existing product. Will the new product or product modification be perceived as differing from other alternatives or from its earlier form? How much of a change is necessary to reach the differential threshold? What change(s) should be made, if any? There are many ways in which a product may be perceived as "new." Consumers will look upon newness as a positive, negative, or neutral quality, depending upon their frame of reference in evaluating the new product. Thus, it is essential that extensive consumer research be done before modifying an existing product. Reliance upon management's judgment alone may actually result in innovations which have less appeal and less relative advantage for consumers than existing products.

EXHIBIT 10-2.
Proposition About Stimuli

PROPOSITION 10-2.
The stronger the initial stimulus, the greater must be the difference between the initial stimulus and a subsequent stimulus for this difference to exceed a consumer's contrast threshold.

A new product or a slight modification in package design (a change in stimuli) will usually be compared by consumers with the stimuli of other packaged products of the same type. A unique item designed to meet a certain need will usually be evaluated in terms of the comparative expense and convenience of using a combination of goods that may presently be required to meet that same need. Thus, the marketing manager must know what existing products or customer costs will be used as criteria for judging an innovation. What will be the consumer reaction, for example, if foods normally packaged in metal containers are packaged in glass jars? These factors are particularly important when considering consumer reactions to price changes. Clearly, a five-cent increase in an item originally priced at ten cents will be more noticed and unfavorably received than a two dollar increase in the price of an item previously costing sixty dollars.

Modifications or changes in existing products may be made in the hope that consumers will not be able to discriminate between the previous and the present version. For example, the manufacturer may try to use a less expensive ingredient and then determine through tests whether the change is above or below consumers' contrast thresholds. Similarly, the actual weight or size of the product may be reduced (as has been happening over the years with candy bars) while packaging and price remain the same. The market researcher's task is to see if this change is above or below consumers' contrast thresholds. On the other hand, consumer educators try to develop in consumers a keener and more finely discriminating contrast threshold.

Drive   A drive is a motivating force which is either innate (such as hunger) or learned (such as a desire to excel in a vocation). Chapters 14 and 15 concerning needs and motivation are basically extended discussions of drives, and for this reason the concept of drive will not be developed further here.

Incentive   What incentives and what expectations of reward or punishment motivate
Motivation   consumers? There are many answers to this question. For example, observing others' experiences with a product may be a sufficient incentive to try (or not try) the same product. Research on the adoption of new products suggests that relying on other consumers' experiences serves as a very important incentive motivation for consumers who are among the last people to try a new product. Simply being informed by a reliable source of information that the purchase of a new product will be satisfying might also constitute an adequate incentive. Or, the results of one's own previous experiences with a similar product may be an incentive to try (or to avoid) the new product.

One of the most prevalent tools in marketing is the use of incentives such as cents-off coupons and contests. Advertisers distributed a record 45.8 billion cents-off coupons in 1976. This is more than double the 20.3 billion coupons distributed in 1971.[6] Unfortunately, little reliable research has been conducted which helps us understand the role of such incentives in the consumer learning process;[7] and, there is little in the learning research literature which is very helpful due to its use of nonhumans as subjects or the artificial contexts in which human subjects are studied. Fortunately, the use of incentives with consumers in noncommercial marketing contexts has been studied and is suggestive of how incentives affect consumers in traditional marketing settings.[8]

Incentives can be classified in many ways. A specific classification includes: (1) free samples; (2) money-saving coupons; (3) temporary price reductions; (4) attachment of a free product to the one being promoted; and (5) free gifts with proof of purchase. Perhaps the best way to classify incentives is more general. First, there are *individual and group incentives*. The incentive may be given directly to the individual consumer. An example is the offering of a cents-off coupon to be cut out from a newspaper advertisement. Discounts on airline tickets and theatre tickets for groups of ten or more

---

[6]*Advertising Age,* February 21, 1977, p. 22.

[7]See Howard M. Turner, Jr., *The People Motivators,* NY: McGraw-Hill, 1973.

[8]For example, Everett M. Rogers, *Communication Strategies for Family Planning,* NY: The Free Press, 1973, especially Chapter 5; Selma J. Mushkin (ed.), *Consumer Incentives for Health Care,* NY: Prodist, 1974; Gerald Zaltman and Robert Duncan, *Strategies for Planned Change,* NY: Wiley-Interscience, 1977; and Gerald Zaltman, *et al., Dynamic Educational Change,* NY: The Free Press, 1977.

people are examples of group incentives. Secondly, there are *positive and negative incentives.* A positive incentive would be a price discount if a bill is paid within ten days of its receipt (this is common with utilities). A negative incentive is the interest charge added to a bill if it is not paid within a certain period of time (companies issuing credit cards often use this technique). Thirdly, there are *monetary and nonmonetary incentives.* Giving a fifty-cent rebate if a package label is mailed to the manufacturer is an example of monetary incentive. A nonmonetary incentive would be the giving of dishware with the purchase of a full tank of gasoline. A fourth type of incentive distinction is *immediate and delayed.* Placing a face cloth or small towel in a box of detergent is an immediate incentive because the consumer receives it simultaneously with the purchase. Trading stamps illustrate a type of deferred or delayed incentive. They are valuable only after enough purchases have been made to qualify for the gifts offered. There are also *graduated and nongraduated incentives.* A nongraduated incentive is one which involves giving with each purchase one book of a multibook encyclopedia or one item in a multipiece table setting regardless of the size of the purchase. A graduated incentive involves giving extra items in the table setting as the size of the purchase increases, but in a disproportionate way. For example, a consumer with a thirty dollar grocery bill receives one item, a consumer with a forty-five dollar grocery bill receives two items, and a consumer with a fifty-five dollar grocery bill receives three items.

What do we know about the effect of incentives on consumers? Available evidence from traditional as well as social marketing contexts suggests the following observations:

1. Incentives motivate many consumers who would not ordinarily buy a product to try it or who would not ordinarily shop in a given store to shift patronage to that store.
2. Incentives motivate consumers to try products earlier than might otherwise be the case.
3. Incentives motivate consumers in all major market segments, such as different income, education, and sex segments.
4. Incentives are effective for a broad array of products and services.
5. Incentives themselves do not significantly influence how consumers perceive a product either before or after the first purchase.
6. Incentives usually do not cause consumers to try a product about which they have strong negative expectations, or to continue using a product which has performed unsatisfactorily.

Other observations are that:

1. Group incentives usually have a greater impact than individual incentives.
2. Positive incentives are usually more effective in the long run than negative incentives.

3. Delayed incentives are more effective in establishing habitual purchases or brand loyalty than are immediate incentives.
4. Immediate incentives are more effective than are delayed incentives in obtaining early use of a product.
5. Graduated incentives are more effective than nongraduated incentives in securing high volume use of a product or service.
6. Nonmonetary incentives are more effective than monetary incentives in securing early use of an existing product.

Habit Strength   Habit refers to the automatic connection of a stimulus with a response. It appears that as stimuli such as advertising are presented at a fast rate, habituation is more rapid. Similarly, the more frequently consumers perform an act, the higher their rate of habituation. Proposition 10-3 in Exhibit 10-3 expresses this idea. The major implication of this proposition is that high frequency advertising may lead to the desired behavior more rapidly than low frequency advertising. More importantly, an advertising message repeated twice as often may lead to the desired behavior with more than twice the speed than if the message were repeated half as often. When a stimulus is stopped after habit is established, consumers tend to return to earlier states. Thus, once an advertisement achieves its purpose, it still may be necessary to continue the ads, particularly if there is substantial advertising by competitors.

EXHIBIT 10-3.
Propositions About Habit

PROPOSITION 10-3.
The faster the rate of stimulation, the faster the rate of habituation.

PROPOSITION 10-4.
Habituation is faster for weak stimuli, provided that discrimination is not required.

The more important a purchase is, the slower habits are to develop concerning the purchase. More formally, habit is established more quickly for weak stimuli, providing that consumers do not have to make discriminations (Proposition 10-4 expresses this idea). Thus, consumers develop habits about a product more rapidly the less important the product is to them. If the consequences of a wrong decision are important for social reasons, however, consumers will be slower to develop a habit such as brand loyalty.

An interesting phenomenon exists when a consumer has developed a pattern of frequent purchase of a given brand of, for instance, a dairy product as a result of an intensive promotion effort. If for some reason the intensive promotional program ceases, there is a good possibility that the consumer's brand loyalty may lessen. A competitor may then undertake an intensive promotional program of its own. Will brand loyalty develop for the competitor's product? Interestingly, evidence from learning research suggests that the new stimulus—the competitor's advertising—may rekindle the response to the original stimulus—the original firm's advertising.[9] This means the competitor's advertising could bring back a consumer's original brand loyalty to another product. So, for such consumers, the competitor's advertising will have an effect opposite of what was intended.

If a habit is strong, the response to the stimulus will also be strong. This suggests Proposition 10-5: The more familiar consumers are with a buying situation and the more satisfied they are with their previous responses in that situation, the more likely they are to respond again in the same way. Thus, brand loyalty will be greater among satisfied customers who have had more experiences with the product category than among satisfied customers who are new to that product category. Brand managers should be especially concerned with securing repeat purchases among those persons who are new to a product category. First-time parents, for example, have less brand loyalty to particular baby food brands than parents with more than one child. There is even some possibility that heavy promotional efforts directed to consumers who are loyal to the promoted brand may backfire; that is, there may be an "overlearning reversal effect."

EXHIBIT 10-4.
Propositions About Habit

PROPOSITION 10-5.
The more familiar consumers are with a buying situation and the more satisfied they are with their previous responses in that situation, the more likely they are to respond again in the same way.

PROPOSITION 10-6.
As repetition increases, inattention and reactance cause a lack of persistence in recall.

The overlearning reversal effect is comparable to the phenomenon referred to in advertising as wearout. Wearout is the decrease in the ability to recall

[9]Mackworth, 1970.

a message as exposure to the message increases. Worth noting here is a recent study which attempted to determine the wearout effects of high levels of repetition in print ads on brand name recall.[10] This study reports that when the level of repetition was three times the level necessary to learn brand names, subjects showed significantly poorer recall than when the repetition was just twice the level needed for learning. Thus, it is postulated that as repetition increases, inattention and reactance cause a lack of persistence in recall (this is Proposition 10-6). The marketing implications of this are clear. An optimal level of repetition exists. Increasing repetition facilitates learning up to a point but excessive levels of repetition may cause cognitive responses that inhibit consumer learning. Also, habit may lead to boredom or a desire to vary one's experiences in a product category by trying different brands.

EFFECTS OF THE CAUSAL VARIABLES

Response *tendency* is the inclination or disposition to respond to a stimulus. Thus, the "R" in the equation presented earlier is not necessarily an overt, easily recognizable response. There are multiple measures of response tendencies. In the consumer behavior literature this is reflected in the various decision-making stages through which consumers presumably pass when considering the purchase of a new product.[11] The reader may have encountered this idea elsewhere in the term "hierarchy of effects." For example, a first response tendency—one at the bottom of a hierarchy—is to become aware of a new product, a second response tendency—which is higher up in the hierarchy of possible responses—is to develop specific attitudes toward the product, while a third and still higher level of response is to develop intentions to buy or not buy. Chapter 16 discusses attitudes, intentions, and behavior in detail and contains an extended discussion of what learning researchers and theorists call response tendency.

Ray summarizes several basic ideas about response tendencies. These are formulated as Propositions 10-7 through 10-10 in Exhibit 10-5. Proposition 10-7 posits that the more strongly inclined consumers are to respond, the larger is the number of products and services which serve as stimuli to elicit the response. As the desire to own an automobile increases, so does the

[10]C. Samual Craig, Brian Sternthal, and Clark Leavitt, "Advertising Wearout: An Experimental Analysis," *Journal of Marketing Research,* November, 1976, pp. 365–372.
[11]See Chapter 18; see also, Thomas S. Robertson, *Innovative Behavior and Communication,* NY: Holt, Rinehart & Winston, 1971.

number of different automobile makes and models which could trigger an actual automobile purchase. Proposition 10-8 suggests that the more strongly inclined consumers are to make a purchase, the larger is the number of different ways in which they will express this inclination or response tendency. For example, the more interested consumers are in buying an automobile, the more activities in which they will engage that express this interest. Not only will consumers read advertisements, but they will also talk with friends and colleagues about automobiles. As consumers' response tendencies increase still further, they may consult *Consumer Reports* and begin visiting automobile showrooms. Proposition 10-9 simply states that the stronger the intention to buy an automobile, the more likely it is to be expressed when the consumer encounters a stimulus relating to automobiles. The inclination to buy an auto is likely to be expressed by increased attention paid to auto advertisements (the stimulus) in magazines. Finally, Proposition 10-10 suggests that while considering an automobile purchase, consumers are likely to notice advertisements about other vehicles such as motorcycles and campers more than they did prior to being concerned with an auto purchase.

EXHIBIT 10-5.
Propositions About Response Tendencies (Dispositions to Respond). Adapted from Ray, op. cit., pp. 82–83.

PROPOSITION 10-7.
The stronger the disposition to respond, the more stimuli there are that will elicit a response.

PROPOSITION 10-8.
The stronger the disposition to respond, the greater the number of measures it will be manifested in.

PROPOSITION 10-9.
The stronger the disposition to respond, the more likely it will be elicited.

PROPOSITION 10-10.
The stronger the disposition to respond, the more dissimilar to the original stimulus a stimulus can be and still elicit the observable response.

In understanding response tendencies, it is necessary to realize there may be conflicting response tendencies which prevent any one response from occurring. Too many advertisements for different brands, each claiming to be superior, may cause confusion and prevent any brand from being purchased.

There is an interrelationship among the fundamental learning factors. Stimuli are the distinctive characteristics of a product or innovation, and if the value of these stimuli is high, the amount of reward perceived is correspondingly high. In other words, the customer perceives the stimuli as a means of reducing the drive. This stimulus-response connection is the essence of learning. Stimuli may take the form of a brand name, a package design, a product category or a price-size relationship, a certain quality, or any other product attribute. For example, a desire for a particular type of food may be aroused by an advertisement or by observing others eating that food. A stimulus, in the form of a low price or a well-known brand name, may encourage a favorable shopping response. If consumers are rewarded to their satisfaction, they will continue to respond favorably to the same stimuli or goal-objects because of this gratifying experience. The satisfaction serves as an incentive motivation for reducing a drive by purchasing the same bundle of stimuli, i.e., the same product or brand, which produced the satisfaction. The buyer has learned that this stimulus is a means of satisfying a drive. The buyer may also learn that a competing brand does not satisfy the same need as economically or as quickly. This may result in a permanent change in behavior—the consumer may habitually avoid the competing product. Thus, a continually rewarded response results in *discrimination* among products. *Comparative shopping is an important part of the process whereby a consumer learns that the purchase of one product or brand is more rewarding than the purchase of another.* A habit of buying the preferred brand is established.

Again, when learning has occurred there will usually be a hierarchy of responses. For example, suppose that a shopper has in mind certain price-quality-size relationships that must be met before his or her drive can be satisfied. Past results have established that some brands just meet these requirements, some go beyond, and some brands fall short. A relatively consistent preference for brand A over brands B, C, and D is evidence that learning has occurred. Learning is also characterized by the consistent buying of brand B (rather than C or D) when A is absent, if B is known by the consumer to fulfill the minimum price-quality-size requirements of the drive. This can have a negative effect on brand A, of course. The greater the perceived similarity between A and B, the greater the chances that the consumer will substitute B for A. If A and B are brands of aspirin with the same ingredients and the same price, they are equally attractive goal-objects. This would cause a high degree of *generalization*. Generalization, in this instance, occurs when the consumer responds favorably to products that are similar to the one he or she preferred originally. The minimum differences between A and B that are perceivable to the consumer are known as the *differential threshold*.

A Learning Scenario Perhaps the dynamics of learning can best be conveyed by means of a short scenario. Helen Overman, the central figure in this scenario, is a fifty-two year old office worker who has recently been widowed. She also recently entered the workforce. Her only child, a married daughter, lives two miles away. Mrs. Overman and her daughter have a very close relationship and visit each other often. Mrs. Overman frequently (and with enjoyment) baby-sits with her two grandchildren. The Overmans lived in a small apartment building located near the center of the city and within a short walking distance of her late husband's place of employment. For this reason, the Overmans did not own an automobile. The neighborhood is a rather stable one, with a strong ethnic character. Most tenants in the apartment building know each other and socialize frequently. In fact, the neighborhood is a very friendly and cohesive community.

Although her husband left a small estate, it became very evident to Mrs. Overman that she would have to find employment to maintain her standard of living (an incentive motivation). Through a series of social contacts involving her in-laws, Mrs. Overman found an unusually well-paying job in an office located in a suburb ten miles away. Unfortunately, no convenient public transportation to this suburb was available. This job was particularly attractive to Mrs. Overman not only because of its salary, but because she was having trouble finding a job nearer her home which she would consider socially acceptable. The attractiveness of the job, together with its inconvenient location, created a tension or drive to be reduced, leading to the consideration of buying an automobile. This consideration triggered by the drive is a response tendency, although a somewhat low level one. Her role transition to widowhood (a sociological phenomenon), could be considered as a drive or motivating force causing her to join the workforce (a response tendency), which in turn serves as a drive leading to her thinking about an auto purchase. The high compensation plus the greater social acceptability of the job in the suburb are stimuli for selecting this particular place of employment (a high level response tendency). The desire to stay near her daughter, grandchildren, and longtime neighborhood friends is an additional social incentive motivating Mrs. Overman to keep from moving nearer to her place of work, further establishing her need for her own transportation. Mrs. Overman's fondness for and familiarity with her neighbors and her frequent interaction with her daughter and her family constitute social habits which further contributed to her inclinations (or response tendency) to purchase an auto. This contemplated auto purchase may be viewed as solving the problem created by her desire to choose a particularly attractive job, while at the same time remaining in her present neighborhood and continuing her habitual social patterns.

Mrs. Overman then had to face the dilemma of whether to buy a used car (or as one neighbor later called it, a "pre-owned" car) or a new car.

Having no previous experience with automobiles, no established habits to guide her, and no comfortable sense of the general purchase situation, Mrs. Overman felt very uncertain and ill at ease. This created a strong drive to seek assistance, and the first person to whom she turned was her son-in-law. He urged her to consider a new car, pointing out that she would probably receive a cash rebate (an incentive motivation) depending on what make she bought. He presented several stimuli for her to consider such as lower maintenance costs, less worry, and longer and broader warranty coverage. Lately she had begun relying on her daughter and son-in-law for advice or assistance in a variety of matters. Usually she followed their advice.

Mrs. Overman mentioned to a neighbor that she was planning to purchase a new, economy-size car and that her daughter and son-in-law were planning to help out with the downpayment (a possible incentive). Two days later, Mrs. Overman received a letter from Mr. Charles Cappaco, a cousin of the neighbor, indicating that he was in the "pre-owned" automobile business. He described a few special bargains and indicated he would telephone her. That evening Mrs. Overman received the promised call. After asking for Mrs. Overman, the salesman began referring to her on a first name basis. He described several automobiles (stimuli for visiting his business place) which he felt would be just right for her needs. Moreover, Mr. Cappaco offered two special incentives. First, he offered to drive over in one of the cars and transport her to his place of business and return her home, "without, of course, any obligation on your part." Secondly, he also offered to pay for her first four driving lessons if she did purchase a car from him. Her response to this was one of great appreciation which she expressed by agreeing to visit his dealership. Cappaco promptly set up an appointment for the next morning.

Upon hearing of this from his wife, Mrs. Overman's son-in-law became furious and openly expressed his anger about Mrs. Overman's intentions to visit Cappaco's dealership the next day. This anger functioned as a disincentive for Mrs. Overman and created a conflicting response, i.e., a tendency or inclination to cancel her visit. Mrs. Overman did, however, visit the dealership, partly because she wanted to avoid the embarrassment of having to explain to Cappaco why she was cancelling the visit. Besides, she reasoned that Cappaco was a cousin of a friend (a stimulus) and certainly didn't sound like a person who could be as dishonest as her son-in-law maintained used car dealers were. He actually sounded quite nice (still another stimulus).

Mrs. Overman had never visited an auto dealer before. She had very little habitual behavior which could function in this setting and serve as a basis for structuring the situation. She was totally overwhelmed with the assortment of cars and the multitude of facts and figures Cappaco presented to her with obvious expectations of her being impressed. The fact was she just couldn't handle the information. This was not the case when she talked with her son-in-law, nor when Cappaco introduced her to the first couple of cars. The situation became worse when Mrs. Overman returned from the display lot and Mr. Cappaco began discussing price, cash, and credit terms for the cars he particularly recommended. Mrs. Overman, suffering from information overload, listened in confusion and finally told Cappaco that she wanted her son-in-law to choose one of the cars for her. When Cappaco asked which cars she liked, Mrs. Overman momentarily "drew a blank" (she suffered an acute case of the overlearning reversal effect). With very little conviction, she described one of the cars as being especially nice and again said she would have her son-in-law come look, knowing he never would. A very uncomfortable Mrs. Overman then asked to have a taxi called, but Mr. Cappaco insisted on driving her home. During the trip back, Mr. Cappaco deliberately refrained from discussing cars, which Mrs. Overman silently appreciated very much.

SUMMARY The response of consumers to advertising involves a learning process. Stimulating advertising provides incentives which motivate the consumer to purchase the product. Discrimination, or reinforcement, is used to reward people when they respond to one set of stimuli and not reward them when they respond to other stimuli. Given such a reinforcement, consumers will most likely buy the product, or, if the product lacks distinctiveness, consumers might generalize and buy a similar product. Because of the tendency to generalize, it is necessary for marketers to learn how and at what point consumers differentiate between stimuli or products.

Through providing satisfying incentives, an advertising stimulus—if presented at the proper rate—can create a habitual response on the part of the consumer. The more satisfied consumers are with their previous responses to a stimuli, the more likely they are to habitually respond in a positive way to that same, or similar, stimuli. Consumers learn that the purchase of one product or brand is more rewarding than the purchase of another, and thereby form a habit of buying the preferred brand.

KEY CONCEPTS Differential threshold

Discrimination

Generalization

Habit

Learning

Response tendency

Reversal effects

Secondary reinforcer

Stimulus

Wearout

LEARNING IN ACTION: CONSUMER SOCIALIZATION, PERCEPTION, AND BRAND LOYALTY

CHAPTER GOALS

The objective of this chapter is to help the reader understand:
1. how children learn to be consumers and develop consumption-related skills and preferences;
2. consumers' perceptions of products based on the prices of these products;
3. when consumers will have perceptions of risk associated with products and how these perceptions of risk affect their behavior toward these products;
4. how self-perceptions and product perceptions are related;
5. the relationship between distributors' and consumers' perceptions;
6. organizational differences in perceptions of the environment;
7. how brand loyalty develops and how it should be conceptualized and measured.

INTRODUCTION

In this chapter we examine learning-related research in three selected areas. First, we discuss the learning of consumer behavior by children. Next, we examine the concept of perception which relates to receiving and interpreting stimuli. Finally, the issue of brand loyalty is discussed as a special case of habit formation. These three topics are of considerable importance for understanding consumer behavior and are not addressed explicitly in other chapters of this book. Children's consumer behavior learning is a topic of growing interest to consumer behavior researchers, public policy makers, and marketers, although the literature on this topic is just beginning to grow. Consumer perception research generally focuses on the interpretation of stimuli rather than on the mechanics of perception. The topics and papers cited here are representative of the general treatment of perception in the consumer behavior literature.

A very large body of research exists concerning brand loyalty. Therefore, the discussion of this topic covers only the most central and current findings.

CONSUMER LEARNING AMONG CHILDREN

It is interesting to think of children as people who are constantly in the process of acquiring the roles of an adult (see the section on role acquisition in Chapter 7). Part of this process involves learning how to be a consumer. Possibly the most thorough study of this process is contained in the research on children's learning conducted by three researchers.[1] These researchers describe the process whereby children learn to buy. Learning to buy is referred to as consumer socialization or the acquisition of marketplace skills.

Of course, the family influences a child's consumer learning, and does so in at least three ways: (1) children learn by observing their parents' behavior, (2) by interacting with their parents in a consumption situation, and (3) by engaging in consumption under parental direction. Interestingly, the research findings indicate that parents do not engage in any substantial overt teaching of consumer skills:

> The most striking impression to emerge from these data is that consumer behavior is not an area in which parents consciously set about training their children to any great extent. The mothers in our sample generally had only a few rather general goals, and typically they said they used only one method to teach their child. The consumer training that does occur in the home is more likely to arise through parents' modeling behaviors for the child or in situations where parents are harassed by children for products, or when parents check on what children do with their allowances.... There seem to be few attempts to plan direct methods of training children to be 'good' consumers. (pp. 142–143)

The imitation of parents' behavior is one way that children learn, but they also learn by direct interaction with their parents. Parents may initiate a discussion of the costs of products, where they can be purchased, the child's preference for things being purchased for him or her, and whether or not the child may purchase a certain product. Overall, the researchers found that 36 percent (n = 607) of the mothers in their survey discussed one or more of these issues with a high frequency, while 38 percent did so with medium frequency, and 26 percent with low frequency. Such discussions were not affected very significantly by the age of the child (e.g., kindergarten, third grade, or sixth grade) nor by the family's socioeconomic status.

[1]This work was originally presented in Scott Ward, Daniel Wackman, and Ellen Wartella, *Children Learning to Buy: The Development of Consumer Information Processing Skills,* Cambridge, MA: The Marketing Science Institute, November, 1975, Report No. 75-120.

Most mothers discuss advertisements with their children, although kindergarteners' mothers do so somewhat less frequently than the mothers of third and sixth graders. Also, mothers from higher socioeconomic groups tend to discuss advertisements somewhat more frequently than middle- and lower-status mothers. Mothers are more likely to make general rather than specific comments about advertisements, and the great majority of general comments are negative in nature. Thus, it appears that in mother-initiated learning events, items of information tend to be general and negative.

Parental teaching opportunities occur most frequently when the child initiates the interaction by requesting the parent to make a purchase. In such instances of child-initiated purchase requests, the parent has four options: (1) to make the purchase requested by the child, (2) to discuss the purchase and negotiate a mutually acceptable decision with the child, (3) to refuse the child's request and explain why it was refused, or (4) to refuse the child's request without giving an explanation. The amount of learning that occurs differs depending on which option the parent chooses. If the parent makes the purchase or refuses to make the purchase and does not explain the decision to the child, little learning, if any, will occur. A better learning situation occurs when the parent discusses the decision regardless of whether the decision is to make the purchase or to refuse the child's request.

The research examined how frequently each of these options was chosen by mothers with children in three age groups—kindergarten, third grade, and sixth grade—and by mothers in low, middle, and high socioeconomic groups. There were no differences connected with the child's age or family socioeconomic status in whether mothers made or refused the purchase without discussion. That is, mothers in all groups chose these options with approximately equal frequency. Mothers with older children and with a higher socioeconomic status are more likely to discuss and negotiate a specific purchase request. These findings are represented by Propositions 11-1 and 11-2 in Exhibit 11-1. Of course, older children can do more things which can be negotiated (such as chores around the house) than can younger children. Also, the older child may have better developed persuasive skills which can be used in negotiations about purchase requests.

The research also indicated that as children get older, mothers are less likely to use the refuse-but-explain strategy (see Proposition 11-3 in Exhibit 11-1), probably because the older child is more apt to engage in the negotiation strategy. It was also found that the use of a refuse-but-explain strategy varies with mothers' socioeconomic status. As the socioeconomic status of mothers increases, so does the use of refuse-but-explain strategies (Proposition 11-4).

The researchers also present data showing that children are provided with considerable opportunities to learn about buying by accompanying their mothers on shopping trips (presumably the same is also true about shopping

EXHIBIT 11-1.
Propositions Concerning
the Consumer Learning
of Children of Sixth
Grade Age and Younger

PROPOSITION 11-1.
The older the child, the more likely negotiation is to take place between mother and child. (Note: This must be restricted to situations where the child's age ranges between kindergarten and sixth grade age levels.)

PROPOSITION 11-2.
The higher the mother's socioeconomic status, the more likely negotiation is to take place between mother and child.*

PROPOSITION 11-3.
Use of a refuse-but-explain strategy decreases with the child's age.*

PROPOSITION 11-4.
Use of a refuse-but-explain strategy increases with mothers' socioeconomic status.*
*See note for Proposition 11-1.

trips with fathers, but the researchers only interviewed mothers). Learning is likely to be especially high if the child is able to make a purchase during these trips. The data suggest that the older the child, the more likely a purchase is to be made and the more independent the child is in making the purchase. Socioeconomic status is particularly relevant in this case. Interestingly, as older children have more opportunities to learn about consumption through their own purchases, parental instruction lessens. Of course, if instructions are given when the child is young, less instructions may be necessary later, but we can only speculate on this.

Another analysis suggests that, for kindergarten children, mother-child interaction is more important than mothers' own consumer behavior, mothers' attitudes, and children's independent contributions to their own learning of consumer skills. This does not, however, pertain as clearly to older children. In fact, it appears that mothers' shopping behaviors are the most consistently important variable in third and sixth graders' learning, while the effects of the other variables are more mixed. Thus, the consumer socialization or learning process changes as children grow older.

Therefore, all four major family context variables—mother-child interaction, mother's own behavior, mother's goals/attitudes, and children's opportunities—have an influence on children's learning as consumers. But, the relative importance of these categories, the consistency of their importance, and how they are important differs by the children's ages as reflected by school grade. A significant difference among age groups exists between kindergarten age on the one hand, and third and sixth grade age on the other hand.

As we have already mentioned, the data from this research only cover children up to grade six. Thus, additional work is needed for a more complete picture of consumer socialization processes. Two other researchers have reported some interesting findings on the consumer learning of adolescents.[2] Their study was based upon 157 male and 155 female students ranging from sixth through the twelfth grade in a rural community in Wisconsin. Four indices of consumer learning skills were used: knowledge of prices, advertising slogan recall, ability to correctly specify brand names, and attitude toward advertising. Price accuracy and brand specification are believed to represent more complex learning skills. The researchers found that older students were more accurate in their specification of price and could specify more brands more readily than younger students. This supported one of their contentions which is presented as Proposition 11-5. No significant differences associated with age were found for slogan recall, which is a simple consumer learning skill. With regard to attitude toward advertising, it was found that the attitudes became more negative as age increased (Proposition 11-6). The data give some tentative support to the idea that cognitive learning skills, at least as measured in this study, are well integrated and may even be learned together.[3] Most tentatively, this is true more for older rather than younger adolescents (Proposition 11-7).

Several action implications can be derived from these propositions about children's consumer learning. Given the explanations by parents of why they decided to accept or refuse a child's purchase request, consumer educators can design consumer education programs for parents rather than for children if resources are limited to the development of one program. The education program for parents would offer suggestions on how to improve their purchase processes as well as how to pass these considerations on to their children. For example, the consumer educator might encourage parents to explain to their children why they decide to purchase or not purchase products suggested by the children. The consumer educator may also offer parents suggestions on how to deal with children as they become older. For example, the consumer educator may suggest that decisions be explained to younger children, whereas more decisions should be negotiated with children as they

[2]Roy L. Moore and Lownder F. Stephens, "Some Communication and Demographic Determinants of Adolescent Consumer Learning," *Journal of Consumer Research*, Vol. 2, June, 1976, pp. 80–92.
[3]*Ibid.*, p. 86.

EXHIBIT 11-2.
*Propositions Concerning
Older Children's
Consumer Learning*

PROPOSITION 11-5.
"Older adolescents have acquired complex (brand specification and price accuracy) consumer learning skills to a significantly greater degree than younger adolescents."

PROPOSITION 11-6.
"Older adolescents hold significantly more negative general attitudes toward advertising than younger adolescents."

PROPOSITION 11-7.
"Consumer learning skills are well integrated (i.e., moderately correlated and at fairly high levels of proficiency) among older adolescents but not among younger adolescents."

Source: Moore and Stephens, *op. cit.,* p. 82.

become older. Finally, as children become even older they should be allowed to make more purchases on their own while on shopping trips with parents.

The propositions concerning socioeconomic status also have implications for the consumer educator. The fact that refuse-but-explain strategies are used less frequently by mothers of low rather than high socioeconomic status implies that the mothers from lower status families are more in need of consumer education as described above.

There are implications which can also be drawn for marketers of some products. If the product is one about which the parents will make explanations to their children or one which will involve parent-child negotiation, the product ideally should be designed to offer benefits to both the parent and the child. For example, Ovaltine, a nutritional milk additive, was designed at a time when it was rare for parents to permit children to negotiate with them concerning which products would be consumed. Thus, although the product was nutritional, it was not considered by children to be as tasty as other chocolate-flavored powders which were added to milk. The other powders offered flavor, but no added nutritional benefits. As times changed, parents encouraged parent-child negotiations about products, and more and more chose a strategy of making the recommended purchases. In such a situation, Ovaltine sales began to decline. Recently, however, the company changed the process of manufacturing Ovaltine so that it offers the same nutritional benefits as the previous version, but with tastier chocolate and malt flavors. Thus, the product was redesigned and now offers benefits to both parents and children (i.e., nutrition and good tasting flavors). The company expects that the product will sell better in situations where parents and children discuss and negotiate which products will be purchased.[4]

Marketers can also make use of the way children learn how to be consumers by modeling their parents' behaviors. For example, for years many banks have encouraged parents who are customers to open savings accounts for their children into which the children can add money from their allowances or from odd jobs. Some banking institutions give the child a special bank in which to put the saved money. This little bank can often be opened only by tellers at that banking institution. The purpose of this type of program is to encourage children to learn how to save money and to get the children to think of that banking institution as their own.

PERCEPTION   The process of giving meaning to stimuli is referred to as perception. One text on consumer behavior defines perception as "a process through which we make sense out of the world."[5] Another more traditional definition is that "perception is a complex process by which people select, organize, and interpret sensory stimulation into a meaningful picture of the world."[6] A large body of literature on perception discusses how people's perceptions are influenced by their moods or frames of mind, their physical abilities to experience sensation, their personalities and motivations, the social and physical context in which they are perceiving things, the social and physical context of the stimuli being perceived, and the physical composition of the stimuli. In fact, there are few variables which do not influence whether we choose to notice things and how we interpret what we do perceive.

Thus, it is hardly surprising that consumers' perceptions of products and advertisements are a function of many factors such as the consumers' states of mind, their social context, and the physical attributes of the product or ad.[7] Factors such as product size, color, and shape may greatly affect perception.[8]

[4]Kevin V. Brown, "How to Make a New Product from an Old Product," *Product Management,* December, 1976, pp. 27–31; "New Flavored Ovaltine Comes Out of the Closet," *Product Management,* September, 1976, p. 66.

[5]Kenneth E. Runyon, *Consumer Behavior and the Practice of Marketing,* Columbus, OH: Charles E. Merrill Publishing Co., 1977, p. 298.

[6]Rom J. Markin, Jr., *Consumer Behavior: A Cognitive Orientation,* NY: Macmillan Publishing Co., 1974, p. 198.

[7]Irwin A. Horowitz and Russell S. Kaye, "Perception and Advertising," *Journal of Advertising Research,* Vol. 15, No. 3, June, 1975, pp. 15–21.

[8]Donald W. Hendon, "How Mechanical Factors Affect Ad Perception," *Journal of Advertising Research,* Vol. 13, No. 4, August, 1973, pp. 39–44; Lyman E. Ostlund, "Perceived Innovation Attributes as Predictors of Innovativeness," *Journal of Consumer Research,* Vol. 1, September, 1974, pp. 23–29.

The size of an advertisement, the amount of illustration, the location on a page, and the size and number of words in a headline are a few of the factors which affect perception of advertisements. Since there is strong competition for consumers' attention, it is especially important for marketers to take notice of those factors which affect advertisement perception.

Advertising Age reports, for example, that the average adult male in the United States is exposed daily to an average of 285 advertising messages in television, radio, magazines, newspapers, and outdoor media. Adult females are exposed to an average of 305 advertisements in these same media.[9] Only about 26 percent of these ads, however, are noticed by consumers. It is not known how many of those noticed ads are recalled or remembered for more than an hour. Probably very few are retained for more than a day.[10] This problem of getting consumers to notice one's ads or products is why ads are sometimes done in fluorescent colors and in-store product displays are often constructed to have moving parts.

Perceptions may vary in their stability over time, although relatively little is known about this beyond the finding that perceptions of frequently purchased products are more stable than perceptions of infrequently purchased products.[11] Having an unstable perception means that the consumer perceives the product differently from time to time. The issue of perceptual stability is important for product positioning and market segmentation strategies. It is more difficult to position a product for which consumers have an unstable perception than it is to position a product for which consumers have stable perceptions. Similarly, it is expensive to resegment a market on the basis of consumer perceptions if those perceptions change often or in unpredictable ways.[12]

Very little published research exists in the consumer behavior literature about the many different aspects of perception. For example, little or no consumer research directly addresses the impact of mood on consumer perception or how and why some consumers accentuate ("sharpen") some aspects of an advertisement, while other consumers reduce ("level") the distinctiveness of the very same aspects of the advertisement. Similar claims can be made with regard to most of the basic concepts of perception. The traditional treatment of perception in most consumer behavior texts is to

[9]"A Mere 305 Ads Hit Mom Every Day, Not 1500, BBDO Reports," *Advertising Age,* October 19, 1970, pp. 1ff.

[10]Hendon, *op. cit.*

[11]Chem L. Narayana, "The Stability of Perceptions," *Journal of Advertising Research,* Vol. 16, No. 2, April, 1976, pp. 45–49.

[12]Lyman C. Ostlund, "Identifying Early Buyers," *Journal of Advertising Research,* Vol. 12, No. 2, April, 1972, pp. 25–30.

merely describe these basic concepts and suggest that they are important for understanding behavior. So, discussions of perception in consumer behavior texts vary little from that given in introductory psychology books. In this chapter we shall deliberately forego an extended discussion of those concepts of perception which have not been researched in consumer settings. We do recommend, though, that the interested reader consult one or more of the superior discussions of these concepts.[13] The emphasis in this chapter will be on findings from studies of perception involving people in consumer settings. The issue of perception is implicit, however, in many of the chapters throughout this book.

Perceptions of Price

An issue of concern to many marketers involves consumer perceptions of price. For instance, does a relationship exist between a product's price and its perceived quality? Also, are product prices ending with an odd number perceived differently than prices ending in an even number? One writer has reviewed extensively the literature on consumers' subjective perceptions of price.[14] We shall present a number of the findings discussed in this excellent survey of price perception research.[15]

---

[13]See Ronald H. Forgus, *Perception: The Basic Process in Cognitive Development,* NY: McGraw-Hill, 1966; George S. Klein, *Perception, Motives and Personality,* NY: Alfred A. Knopf, 1970; Ernest R. Hilgard and Richard C. Atkinson, *Introduction to Psychology,* (fifth ed.), NY: Harcourt, Brace & Jovanovich, 1976; Joe Kent Kerby, *Consumer Behavior: Conceptual Foundations,* NY: Dun-Donnelley Publishing Corp., 1975; Runyon, *op. cit.;* and Markin, *op. cit.*

[14]Kent B. Monroe, "Buyers' Subjective Perceptions of Price," *Journal of Marketing Research,* Vol. 10, February, 1973, pp. 70–80.

[15]The reader interested in pursuing some of the more important studies on price perception should read the following research papers:

Alexis, Marcus, George Haines, Jr., and Leonard Simon. "A Study of the Validity of Experimental Approaches to the Collection of Price and Product Preference Data," paper presented at 17th International Meeting of the Institute of Management Sciences, 1970.

Emery, Fred. "Some Psychological Aspects of Price," in Bernard Taylor and Gordon Wills, (eds.), *Pricing Strategy,* Princeton, NJ; Brandon/Systems Press, 1970, pp. 98–111.

Gabor, Andre and Clive Granger. "The Attitude of the Consumer to Price," in Bernard Taylor and Gordon Wills, (eds.), *Pricing Strategy,* Princeton, NJ: Brandon/Systems Press, 1970, pp. 132–151.

Gabor, Andre and Clive Granger, and Anthony Sowter. "Comments on Psychophysics of Prices," *Journal of Marketing Research,* 8, May 1971, pp. 251–252.

Jacoby, Jacob, Jerry Olson, and Rafael Haddock. "Price, Brand Name, and Product Composition Characteristics as Determinants of Perceived Quality," *Journal of Applied Psychology,* 55, December 1971, pp. 470–479.

Monroe, Kent, "Measuring Price Thresholds by Psychophysics and Latitudes of Acceptance," *Journal of Marketing Research,* 8, November 1971, pp. 460–464.

1. There is no clear or consistent set of findings about price-consciousness. It is not evident what kind of consumers are price-conscious or for what set of products price-consciousness is most likely to develop.

2. Although research findings are not yet conclusive, there appears to be a positive relationship between price and perceptions of product quality at least within some price ranges and for some product categories. Consumers seem to rely more on price in situations involving high risk, when they have low self-confidence, and when other indicators of product quality are absent. When a clear-cut brand image is present, it is more important than price as an indicator of quality. Generally, the larger the number of stimuli available about a product, the less price is used as an indicator of product quality.

3. It appears that consumers maintain absolute thresholds, that is, they have an upper and lower limit on prices they are willing to pay. Consumers, therefore, shop for a product whose price is within the upper and lower limits.

4. Monroe raises an important, but largely unaddressed question: "When and under what circumstances are differentially priced but similar products perceived as different offers?" (p. 75). This involves the concept of differential threshold, which concerns the amount of change which has to occur to be noticeable to consumers. It may be that for some products consumers perceive an upward change in price more readily than they would perceive an equally large but downward change in price.

5. There are good reasons for believing that consumers' price perceptions depend on the relationship between the actual price and the price consumers use as a reference point.[16] Consumers may develop a set of standard prices for different product categories and quality levels which serves as a frame of reference. The standard price may be derived in a number of ways, such as by averaging prices, or by referring to the price of the leading brand. Consumers use this standard price when evaluating the price of a particular brand or product.

Overall, the researcher concludes that despite a large literature "we know very little about how price affects a buyer's perceptions of alternative

Monroe, Kent. "Psychophysics of Prices: A Reappraisal," *Journal of Marketing Research,* 8, May 1971, pp. 248–250.

Newman, Diane and James Becknell. "The Price-Quality Relationship as a Tool in Consumer Research," *Proceedings,* 78th Annual Conference, American Psychological Association, 1970, pp. 729–730.

Shapiro, Benson. "Price as a Communicator of Quality: An Experiment," unpublished doctoral dissertation, Harvard University, 1970.

[16]Harry Helson, *Adaptation-Level Theory,* NY: Harper & Row, 1964.

purchase offers, and how these perceptions affect his response" (p. 78). Along with the price itself, the context in which the price is perceived is a very important variable to consider.

Recent research on price-quality relationships suggests that it may be fruitful to direct future attention to: (1) price-quality perceptions under postpurchase conditions, and (2) considering quality in terms of its component parts, such as performance quality and durability.[17]

Social Norms and Perception

Social norms and the degree to which consumers participate in them have an important impact on perception. An example is the ecological norm that consumers should not purchase products which endanger the environment. Consumers subscribe to this norm in varying degrees. Those who strongly participate in this norm are likely to be sensitive to a product's environmental impact. One research report found that consumers' perceptions of laundry products varied according to the degree of their ecological concern.[18] "The higher a buyer's ecological concern the more salient is the ecological dimension in perception, and the greater the perceived similarity of brands that are ecologically nondestructive."[19] This suggests two general propositions. First, the stronger the consumer's participation in or support of a social norm, the more important that norm will be in influencing the consumer's perception of alternative brands. Secondly, the stronger the consumer's participation in a norm, the more similar will be his or her perception of alternative brands which are seen as compatible with that norm. These ideas are expressed as Propositions 11-8 and 11-9.

If Proposition 11-8 is true, it is necessary for the marketing manager to determine: (1) what norms will affect perceptions of the class of products sold by the firm, and (2) how strongly these norms are held by the major market segments for those products. The larger the number of consumers strongly affected by a norm, the more that norm has to be considered in the design and promotion of the product(s) relating to the norm. For instance, if many consumers feel strongly about ecology, then laundry detergent manufacturers may want a low sudsing level and may want to advertise this fact. If Proposition 11-9 is true, then the marketing manager needs to be especially concerned with distinguishing his or her brand from other brands also compatible

---

[17]George W. H. Scherf and George F. Karvash, "Husband/Wife Comparisons of Price-Quality Relationships in the Post-Purchase Situation," *The Journal of Social Psychology,* October, 1976, pp. 99–106.

[18]Thomas C. Kinnear and James R. Taylor, "The Effect of Ecological Concern on Brand Perceptions," *Journal of Marketing Research,* Vol. 10, May, 1973, pp. 191–197.

[19]*Ibid.,* p. 196.

EXHIBIT 11-3.
Propositions
Concerning
Social Norms and
Perception

PROPOSITION 11-8.
The stronger a consumer's participation in a norm, the greater will be the impact of that norm on the perception of alternative brands related to that norm.

PROPOSITION 11-9.
The stronger a consumer's participation in a norm, the more similar will be the perception of alternative brands of a product which are compatible with that norm.

---

with the relevant norm(s), since consumers tend to perceive norm compatible brands similarly. This makes the creation of brand loyalty more difficult.

Norms may also be relevant for distinguishing market segments. For instance, the majority of consumers may not subscribe to the ecological norm and it therefore may not affect their product perceptions. There may be a sizable minority, however, whose perceptions are primarily guided by ecological concerns. In this case, there is a market segment whose perceptual processes differ from the rest of the population in the dimensions or criteria used for evaluating products. Communications aimed at this segment would therefore have to be based on these perceptual differences.

Perceptions of Risk

Consumer perceptions of risk are important determinants of consumer behavior. There are at least two different types of perceived risk, inherent risk and handled risk.[20] Consumers perceive inherent risk when thinking about a product class, such as vacuum cleaners, without taking into account particular brands of vacuum cleaners. Just how risky are vacuum cleaners generally?— this is the question consumers pose when no information about specific brands is assumed. Handled risk is the degree of risk involved once the consumer has information about at least one brand. A consumer may feel vacuum cleaners are generally risky products to buy. For example, they may be perceived as breaking down fairly often. Thus, perceived inherent risk is high. But, after trial use of a particular brand or talking with several owners of a particular brand, the consumer may learn that the inherent risk does not apply to this particular brand. In this case, perceived handled risk is low. The

---

[20]James R. Bettman, ''Perceived Risk and Its Components: A Model and Empirical Test,'' *Journal of Marketing Research,* Vol. 10, May, 1973, pp. 184–190.

purchase of the brand in question is perceived to be less risky with regard to breakdowns than would be a random selection of a vacuum cleaner.

When consumers perceive significant quality variations among products in a given category, inherent risk is high. Accordingly, Proposition 11-10 posits that consumers may be particularly brand conscious when considering a purchase in a product class with high inherent risk. As a result, special promotional efforts stressing quality and reliability become an important marketing strategy. It follows from Proposition 11-10 that the larger the perceived number of quality brands, the lower the inherent risk. Moreover, as the average quality of all brands increases, inherent risk will decrease. Propositions 11-11 and 11-12 express these ideas. Trade associations might undertake promotional campaigns to lower perceived risk by stressing the overall high quality of brands in their product class. Possibly, comparative advertising may cause consumers to lower their perceptions of overall product quality in a product class, thus leading to an increase in perceived inherent risk.

As stated in Proposition 11-13, if the inherent risk is high, consumers will experience some concern for a particular brand no matter how risk-free it promises to be. The preferred brand will experience "guilt by association" by being in a product class which is perceived as having high inherent risk. As the amount of useful information about a product class increases, however, so does consumer psychological comfort with particular brands. The more certain consumers are about the information they have, the lower the level of handled risk. Propositions 11-14 and 11-15 express these ideas. When perceived handled risk is high, it is important for the marketing manager to provide enough relevant information to the consumers, and special efforts should be made to increase consumer confidence in this information. This may be done by using testimonials from highly credible people and choosing media channels which have high credibility.

Several observations which are worth noting have been made by one writer on perceived risk and consumer behavior.[21]

1. Engaging in word-of-mouth communication about a product is an important way of reducing risk (see Chapter 9 on communication).

2. Consumers who perceive a product category as risky (high perceived inherent risk) are likely to be the last group to adopt (if at all) a new product in that category (see Chapter 18 on the adoption of innovations).

---

[21]Ivan Ross, "Perceived Risk and Consumer Behavior: A Critical Review," *Proceedings of the Association for Consumer Research, Advances in Consumer Research,* Vol. 2, 1975, pp. 1–19.

EXHIBIT 11-4.
Propositions Concerning
Perceived Risk

PROPOSITION 11-10.
The higher the degree of variation in perceived product quality, the higher the perceived inherent risk for a product class.

PROPOSITION 11-11.
The larger the number of acceptable brands in a product class, the lower the perceived inherent risk.

PROPOSITION 11-12.
The higher the perceived average quality of brands in a product class, the lower the perceived inherent risk.

PROPOSITION 11-13.
The higher the perceived inherent risk for a product class, the higher the perceived handled risk.

PROPOSITION 11-14.
The higher the level of useful information about a product class, the lower the level of perceived handled risk.

PROPOSITION 11-15.
The greater the degree of confidence consumers have in their information about a product class, the lower the level of perceived handled risk.

Note: These propositions are derived from Bettman, *op. cit.*

3. Brand loyalty and store loyalty are greatest among persons who perceive considerable risk in product selection and in-store selection, but who have found a satisfactory brand and a satisfactory outlet.
4. There is little reliable data, if any, about the relative degrees of perceived risk among different retail outlets, e.g., mail order, regular in-store, telephone orders, and door-to-door selling.

Self-Perceptions   Consumers' self-perceptions appear to influence their selection of brands and retail stores. There is a substantial body of research relating self-perception with the perception of brands and products. This research yields the following observations:

1. Differences in self-perception exist between users and nonusers of a product category.[22]
2. Differences in self-perception exist between users of one brand and users of other brands within a product category.[23]
3. Consumers perceive preferred brands and products to be much more similar to their own self-perceptions than nonpreferred brands and products.[24]
4. Consumers express their self-perceptions through the purchase of brands and products which are perceived as similar to themselves.[25]
5. Consumers of a particular brand perceive it differently than nonusers of the same brand.[26]
6. Consumers' perceptions of their preferred brands are quite different from their perceptions of competing nonpreferred brands.[27]
7. Consumers perceive the characteristics of a nonpreferred brand to differ from their self-perceptions.[28]

The implications of these statements are important. Consumers' self-perceptions should be considered in the design of products and the development of promotional material. With the consumers segmented on the basis of their self-perceptions, the marketer can select the appropriate market segment and design the product and promotional efforts to fit the self-perceptions of that market segment.

Thus, we have Proposition 11-16: The more congruent consumers' self-perceptions are with their perceptions of a particular brand or product, the more likely they are to purchase the particular brand or product.

[22]Edward L. Grubb, "Consumer Perception of 'Self-Concept' and Its Relationship to Brand Choice of Selected Product Types," doctoral dissertation, University of Washington, 1965.

[23]Edward L. Grubb and Gregg Hupp, "Perception of Self, Generalized Stereotypes, and Brand Selection," *Journal of Marketing Research,* Vol. 5, February, 1968, pp. 58–63; and Edward L. Grubb and Bruce L. Stern, "Self-Concept and Significant Others," *Journal of Marketing Research,* Vol. 8, August, 1971, pp. 382–385.

[24]Ira J. Dolich, "Congruence Relationships Between Self-Images and Product Brands," *Journal of Marketing Research,* Vol. 6, February, 1969, pp. 80–84.

[25]Wayne Delozier and Rollie Tillman, "Self-Image Concepts—Can They Be Used to Design Marketing Programs?" *Southern Journal of Business,* Vol. 7, November, 1972, pp. 9–15.

[26]Al Birdwell, "A Study of the Influence of Image Congruence on Consumer Choice," *Journal of Business,* Vol. 41, January, 1968, pp. 76–88.

[27]Rudolph P. Lamone, "The Use of the Semantic Differential in a Study of Self-Image, Product Image, and the Prediction of Consumer Choice," doctoral dissertation, University of North Carolina at Chapel Hill, 1966.

[28]Grubb and Stern, 1971, *op.cit.*

A related idea has been put forth by several researchers.[29] This research found that consumers select retail outlets which they perceive as having attributes congruent with their own self-perceptions (this is Proposition 11-17). They also found that consumers perceive stores they do not patronize to be significantly different in "character" from their perceptions of themselves. From a marketing standpoint, the implications are clear: "In order successfully to attract a desired market segment to one's store, the decor, merchandise, and policies of the store need to be engineered so that they closely parallel the characteristics of the customer. In addition, to discourage customer store switching, the store image should be dissimilar to those of competing stores so that the matching process between the self- and store image is simplified for the consumer."[30]

EXHIBIT 11-5.
Propositions About Self-Perception and the Perceptions of Retail Firms

> PROPOSITION 11-16.
> The more congruent consumers' self-perceptions are with their perceptions of a particular brand or product, the more likely they are to purchase the particular brand or product.
>
> PROPOSITION 11-17.
> "Consumers patronize stores whose characteristics are congruent with their perceptions of themselves." (Stern, *op. cit.,* p. 64)

Distribution Perceptions

An important task for a marketing manager is to determine whether consumers and distributors have common perceptions concerning what product attributes are most important. If there are discrepancies between the perceptions of the two parties, the distributor (e.g., the salesperson, retailer, or wholesaler) may stress the wrong attributes or fail to educate consumers about which product attributes are actually most important. Also, a producer may rely on retailers' perceptions of what consumers believe to be important. If the retailers' perceptions are wrong, marketing strategies become faulty. Two researchers have examined this problem in the context of the marketing of retail

---

[29]Bruce L. Stern, Ronald F. Bush, and Joseph F. Hair, Jr., "The Self-Image/Store Image Matching Process," *Journal of Business,* Vol. 50, No. 1, January, 1977, pp. 63–69.
[30]*Ibid.,* pp. 68–69.

appliances.[31] They report significant discrepancies between retailers and consumers, particularly concerning which attributes consumers feel are important and in the way competitive brands are rated. Their main findings are:

1. Retailers consistently underestimate the strengths with which consumers view the importance of service and warranty, ease of use, and style in the appliance purchase decision. (Retailers are most accurate in their portrayal of consumers' views on automatic clothes washers and least accurate on ranges.)
2. Price is the special concern of appliance retailers who own their stores as contrasted with buyers or managers of larger stores.
3. Retailers tend to view attributes of competitive brands differently from consumers. These images are either over-sensitive or under-sensitive to specific attributes and seem to reflect historic stereotypes rather than current consumer brand images.[32]

Perceptions by Organizations

The way in which an organization perceives its environment will be a major factor influencing organizational buying behavior. "Perceived variations in environmental influences may result in different ways of organizing the purchasing activities, besides influencing purchase goals and decision strategies employed."[33] One researcher distinguishes between two types of organizations. One type, product-dependent organizations, includes those firms which depend heavily on the marketplace for survival.[34] A for-profit business organization in a very competitive setting would be an example. The second type, product-independent organizations, includes those organizations which are dependent upon regulatory agencies or others whom they do not service directly. An example would be a utility company which is heavily dependent on a regulatory agency's decision about rates to charge consumers. A total of twenty product-dependent organizations and twenty-eight product-independent organizations were studied.

Moreover, the researcher studied two kinds of purchases: first-time purchase and rebuy. Organizational differences were found concerning competition and budgetary matters. Product-dependent organizations were more sensitive to competition and perceived fewer budgetary restrictions. These ideas are expressed as Propositions 11-18 and 11-19. Also, product-

---

[31]Peter J. McClure and John K. Ryans, Jr., "Differences Between Retailers' and Consumers' Perceptions," *Journal of Marketing Research,* Vol. 5, February, 1968, pp. 35–40.
[32]*Ibid.,* p. 40.
[33]Kjell Grønhaug, "Exploring Environmental Influences in Organizational Buying," *Journal of Marketing Research,* Vol. 13, August, 1976, p. 225.
[34]Grønhaug, *ibid.*

dependent organizations are more apt than product-independent organizations to have purchasing centers or formal purchasing agents. A consequence of this is that organizations with formal purchasing agents or departments will have more accurate perceptions of their environments. Thus, product-dependent organizations may have more accurate perceptions of their environments than do product-independent organizations.

EXHIBIT 11-6.
Propositions About Perceptions by Organizations

PROPOSITION 11-18.
Product-dependent organizations perceive competition more often than do product-independent organizations.

PROPOSITION 11-19.
Product-dependent organizations perceive fewer budgetary restrictions placed on them than do product-independent organizations.

PROPOSITION 11-20.
Product-dependent organizations more than product-independent organizations tend to perceive formal information sources as more appropriate for the buying task.

Product-dependent organizations more than product-independent organizations tend to perceive formal sources of information as more appropriate before making a purchase (Proposition 11-20). For example, product-dependent firms did more soliciting of bids and more analyses of promotional materials while also doing less contacting of suppliers and organizations who had experience with the product being studied. It was also found that both types of organizations did less information searching for repurchase than for first-time purchases. This finding is evidence of the presence of organizational learning processes.[35]

This research suggests that the presence of a formal purchasing agent or purchase department in product-dependent firms makes it easier for salespersons to identify and approach influential people in these firms. It appears, too,

---

[35]See also J. G. March and J. P. Olsen, "The Uncertainty of the Past: Organizational Learning Under Ambiguity," *European Journal of Political Research,* Vol. 3, 1975, pp. 145–171.

that formal promotional materials are more important for product-dependent firms. The marketer should foster the contacting of other product users by product-independent firms, and should place relatively more emphasis on the use of sales personnel rather than relying on formal printed promotional materials.

BRAND LOYALTY

Most marketing efforts are aimed at developing a group of people who will repeatedly purchase and even search for a particular brand. Advertising and product development costs are too high to warrant aiming only for one-shot use by consumers. Many gimmicks and even hoaxes can be used to persuade consumers to purchase something once. As has been discussed in this and the previous chapter, however, consumers learn from their purchase experiences and will not purchase unsatisfactory products again if there are alternatives which would provide satisfaction. Therefore, most marketing efforts must try to develop repeat purchasers. In addition, marketers must understand who their brand loyal consumers are and why they are brand loyal, so that any changes in the firm's marketing program will not cause erosion in the loyalty of this group.

Brand loyalty is one type of repeat purchase. In this section, we will discuss brand loyalty as a special case of habit formation. First, the process leading to brand loyalty will be highlighted and a model reflecting this process will be discussed. Next, the conditions which are necessary for brand loyalty to occur will be discussed. Finally, various measures of brand loyalty will be discussed.

The Emergence of Brand Loyalty

Brand loyalty is just what the name implies—loyalty to a particular brand demonstrated by purchases of that brand. A person who always buys and uses a certain brand of toothpaste and who would go to a different store if one store was out of that brand is highly brand loyal. A person who prefers a particular brand of wine and who makes trips to a different state in order to obtain it is extremely high in brand loyalty. A person who prefers and usually buys one brand of apple juice, but will occasionally purchase another brand when the preferred brand is not in stock, is somewhat brand loyal. Thus, consumers differ in their degree of brand loyalty for any particular product.

How do consumers become brand loyal? Some consumers go through a period of time trying different brands. They may try a different brand with each purchase. Then, based on their experiences with each brand and the information they have from package labels and ads, they decide which brand they prefer. From that time on, these consumers purchase the preferred brand. This group, however, may be very likely to try new products when they are first introduced. In such a case, they would try the new brand and compare it to their present preference. Thus, they are brand loyal, but may change their loyalty.

Other consumers rely less on their own evaluation of alternatives, and instead accept someone else's evaluation. For instance, some consumers continually choose the brand which was preferred and purchased by their parents. Other consumers rely on the evaluations reported in consumer guides such as *Consumer Reports.*

Another group may try one brand and then evaluate it. If it is not satisfactory, they continue trying other brands. If it is satisfactory, they consistently purchase that brand.

Other people go through periods of different brand loyalties. For instance, a consumer might buy one brand of shampoo for five months and then decide that he or she is getting tired of purchasing that brand. Then another brand might be selected and purchased regularly for a time period.

All four of these are ways of developing brand loyalty. What they have in common is the underlying learning process. A consumer learns about a brand and may then develop a commitment toward purchasing it whenever an item from that product class is needed. Thus, purchasing the brand becomes a habit.

A Model of Brand Loyalty
Several models of brand loyalty have been developed.[36] It is not necessary to review all of them here since they fall more in the domain of marketing management than consumer behavior. One of these models, however, will be briefly reviewed here because of its derivation from learning theory. This model is Kuehn's linear learning model.[37] In this model, the probability of purchasing a brand in the present time period depends on the probability of purchasing it in the last period and whether or not it was actually purchased. Thus, the probabilities of purchase change over time.

Take the example of a person buying a particular brand of toothpaste. If the person had a 50 percent probability of buying the toothpaste at time *t,* and the person purchased it, then he or she would have a 70 percent probability of buying this brand in the next time period. This brand loyalty is shown in Figure 11-1. If he or she did not buy the brand, however, then the probability of a purchase of this brand in time *t* + 1 would drop to 35 percent. But,

---

[36]For a review of these, see Philip Kotler, *Marketing Decision Making: A Model Building Approach,* NY: Holt, Rinehart and Winston, 1971, Chapter 16: "Brand Share Sales Models," pp. 488–518; Jacob Jacoby and Robert W. Chestnut, *Brand Loyalty: Measurement and Management,* NY: John Wiley and Sons, 1978.

[37]Alfred A. Kuehn, "Consumer Brand Choice as a Learning Process," *Journal of Advertising Research,* Vol. 2, December, 1962, pp. 10–17.

FIGURE 11-1.   *Kuehn's Linear Learning Model*

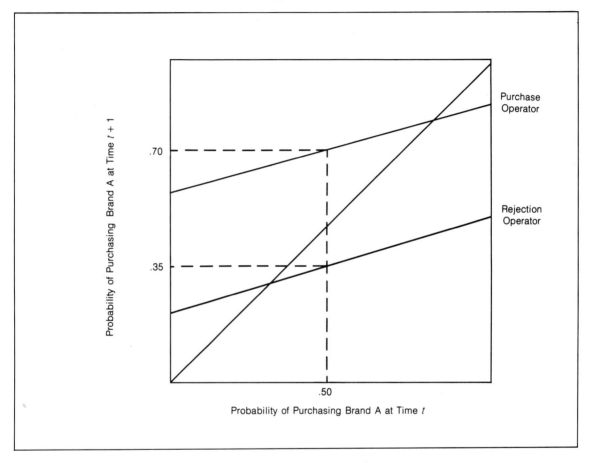

even if a person has always bought the brand, there is always the possibility that brand switching could occur in the future. Therefore, the probability of purchase never reaches 1 and never falls to 0. This indicates that habits, once formed, are not unchangeable. Their degree of permeability is reflected in the slopes and intercepts of the two operators.

This is a learning model because each purchase is dependent on prior circumstances. The probability of purchase increases after each prior purchase and decreases after each alternative choice.

There is a major problem, however, with this formulation of the linear learning model. Two researchers have pointed out that contrary to the linear learning model, a consumer's probability of purchasing a brand may decrease after purchasing that brand if the experience with the product is unsatisfactory.[38] Thus, we might revise the meaning of the rejection operator. It may apply not only when an alternative choice is made, but also when the consumer was dissatisfied with his or her previous purchase of the brand. The effect of dissatisfactions on future probabilities of purchase of the brand will be discussed in greater detail in Chapter 17 on attributions.

Necessary Conditions for Brand Loyalty

Because brand loyalty has been studied from so many different bases, some researchers in the area decided to attempt a conceptual description of what constitutes brand loyalty.[39] They were particularly concerned about the frequent misunderstanding of the differences between brand loyalty and repeat purchasing behavior. Coming from a psychological orientation which includes the concept of commitment as well as an interest in learning theories, they were dismayed by the focus on behavior (that is, repeated purchases of a brand) to the exclusion of the underlying psychological processes.

Their definition of brand loyalty is therefore designed to include these psychological processes.

> The definition is expressed by a set of six necessary and collectively sufficient conditions. These are that brand loyalty is (1) the biased (nonrandom), (2) behavioral response (i.e., purchase), (3) expressed over time, (4) by some decision-making unit, (5) with respect to one or more alternative brands out of a set of such brands, and (6) is a function of psychological (decision-making, evaluative) processes.[40]

Thus, brand loyalty is a particular kind of repeat purchasing behavior which includes a commitment or preference which is the cause of the pattern of repeated purchases of the brand.

Measures of Brand Loyalty

Given the six conditions for the occurrence of brand loyalty, not much more is required to translate these into criteria for measuring the extent of a person's brand loyalty. This is not to say that developing such criteria has been a simple or uncontroversial process. In this discussion we will focus only on some of those measures which at least meet the necessary conditions as specified above.

It has been suggested that operational measures include an attitudinal as well as a behavioral component.[41] That is, researchers should determine

---

[38]V. Srinivasan and R. Kesavan, "An Alternate Interpretation of the Linear Learning Model of Brand Choice," *Journal of Consumer Research,* Vol. 3, September, 1976, pp. 76–83.

[39]Jacob Jacoby and David B. Kryner, "Brand Loyalty vs. Repeat Purchasing Behavior," *Journal of Marketing Research,* Vol. 10, February, 1973, pp. 1–9.

[40]*Ibid.,* p. 2.

[41]George S. Day, "A Two-Dimensional Concept of Brand Loyalty," *Journal of Advertising Research,* Vol. 9, September, 1969, pp. 29–35.

which brands a consumer prefers as well as which brands the consumer buys. A consumer who prefers a brand and consistently buys it is brand loyal. A person who buys one brand not because it is preferred, but because it is the only brand in stock is not highly brand loyal. If a researcher were to focus only on the behavioral component of brand loyalty, this consumer might be wrongly classified as brand loyal to the unpreferred brand. In some empirical work, one researcher found that a bit more than 20 percent of the respondents would have been misclassified in this way.[42] These different types of consumers are shown in Table 11-1. This misclassification of consumers as brand loyal is detrimental because it misleads marketers into thinking that consumers are responding more favorably to the product than they really are.

TABLE 11-1.
Categorization of Respondents Using Two-Dimensional Concept of Brand Loyalty

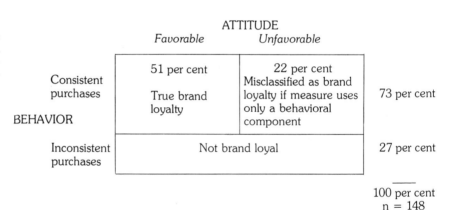

| | | ATTITUDE | | |
		Favorable	*Unfavorable*	
BEHAVIOR	Consistent purchases	51 per cent True brand loyalty	22 per cent Misclassified as brand loyalty if measure uses only a behavioral component	73 per cent
	Inconsistent purchases	Not brand loyal		27 per cent

100 per cent
n = 148

Two other researchers have underscored the recommendation that both attitudinal and behavioral components of brand loyalty be included.[43] In fact, they found that attitudinal loyalty data correlated more strongly with several marketing variables than did behavioral loyalty data. It is from this work that we derive Propositions 11-21 and 11-22 relating brand loyalty to less price sensitivity and less willingness to try new brands when they are introduced.

In keeping with these studies, other researchers have explored the use of a Bayesian analysis to determine the relative weights of the attitude and

---

[42]*Ibid.*

[43]Lance P. Jarvis and James B. Wilcox, "Repeat Purchasing Behavior and Attitudinal Brand Loyalty: Additional Evidence," in Kenneth Bernhardt (ed.), *Proceedings of the 1976 Fall Conference of the American Marketing Association,* pp. 151–152.

EXHIBIT 11-7.
*Propositions About
Brand Loyalty*

PROPOSITION 11-21.
The greater a consumer's brand loyalty, the less sensitive he or she will be to price changes of the preferred brand relative to alternatives.

PROPOSITION 11-22.
The greater a consumer's brand loyalty, the less frequently he or she will try new brands when they are introduced.

behavioral components.[44] They relied on panel diaries which included attitudinal and behavioral reports, and suggest that such analysis can provide a clearer understanding of brand loyalty in a diversity of contexts. The implication of the work of all these researchers is that organizations should try to determine the level of brand loyalty for their products using only good, reliable measures which include both an attitudinal and a behavioral component.

SUMMARY
One way of describing consumer learning is in terms of socialization or acquisition of buying skills. Children's learning of these buying or consumer skills is influenced by the family context. Children learn by modeling their parents' behavior, interacting with the parents in the purchase situation, and buying under parental direction.

The process of perception gives meaning to stimuli. Although perception is important in understanding consumer behavior, very little research has been devoted to the topic. Of concern to marketers are such issues as consumer perceptions of price, the impact of social norms on perception, the handling of perceived risk, and the influence of self-perception on the selection of brands and stores. In the organizational setting, perceptions of the environment influence organizational buying behavior, and are affected by the type of organization (e.g., product-dependent and product-independent) and the kind of purchase (first time versus rebuy).

---

[44]Richard J. Lutz and Paul R. Winn, "Developing a Bayesian Measure of Brand Loyalty: A Preliminary Report," in Ronald C. Curhan (ed.), *Proceedings of the 1974 Fall Conference of the American Marketing Association,* pp. 104–108.

Brand loyalty is a special case of habit formation. The consumer learns about a brand and may develop a commitment toward purchasing it. Because consumers sometimes buy products that are not preferred, perhaps because nothing else is in stock, such purchases should not be considered the result of brand loyalty. So, there are both attitudinal and behavioral components to brand loyalty, both of which should be taken into account by marketers.

KEY CONCEPTS   Brand loyalty

Consumer socialization

Perception

Product-dependent organizations

Product-independent organizations

CONSUMER INFORMATION PROCESSING*

12

CHAPTER GOALS
The objective of this chapter is to help the reader understand:
1. **factors affecting how consumers acquire, integrate and evaluate information;**
2. **how to relate information processing issues to public policy concerns.**

INTRODUCTION
Consumers respond to product-related stimuli such as the color of a sweater, the design of a package, and the price and ingredients of a jar of peanut butter. Whether consumers respond at all to a stimulus and what that response is depends upon how they process the content, amount, form, and complexity of the information presented by those stimuli. Knowing how consumers understand or process information relevant to the purchase and use of products and services is central to understanding consumer choices in the marketplace.

For example, in Chapter 9 we discussed persuasive communications. By studying how consumers process information we can better understand what happens when the consumer receives the message. Similarly, when a person reads information on a product label in a store, the person, to some greater or lesser extent, processes the information. In an industrial context, purchasing agents are often given printed material which gives a large amount of information about the product being considered. What will be remembered, how the

---

*The first draft of this chapter was written by Lakshmanan Krishnamurthy, currently a doctoral student in marketing at the Graduate School of Business, Stanford University.

bits of information are combined, and what the consumer will decide to do based on this information are all topics studied by people interested in information processing.

Considerable attention is being devoted now to the study of how individuals, groups, and organizations process information. The study of the information processing of individuals became very important when it became necessary for humans to program computers to process information.[1] The importance of this area of study has also been heightened by the increasing amounts of product-related information which is given to consumers, especially as a result of legislation, e.g., nutrition information on food products, interest rate information on loans, and warranty information on appliances.

An individual can be viewed as an information processing system. Such a system can receive information, manipulate symbolic information in elementary ways, store symbols in memory, and give out information.[2] Thus, both computers and people can be viewed as information processing systems. This is not to say, however, that people are simply computers. Rather, in their ability to function as information processing systems, people are similar to computers.

In this chapter, information processing is divided into three phases—acquisition, integration, and evaluation leading to choice. Each phase is discussed separately, relevant research findings are cited, and key propositions are elaborated. There is much concern today about the public policy issues related to consumer information processing. Research is now being directed at the quality and quantity of information which should be made available to consumers, and the manner in which such information should be presented. The research issues relevant to these issues are discussed in the final section of the chapter.

INFORMATION ACQUISITION

Although there is a tendency to consider information processing as occurring in an orderly sequence, this is not always the case. For a new product, for example, such sequential processing would very likely occur (this is shown in Figure 12-1). However, for a frequently purchased item, all stages and substages in this sequence may not occur.

---

[1]Three classic works on the information processing of humans are Allen Newell, J. C. Shaw and Herbert A. Simon, "Elements of a Theory of Human Problem Solving," *Psychological Review,* Vol. 65, May, 1958, pp. 151–166; Allen Newell and Herbert A. Simon, *Human Problem Solving,* Englewood Cliffs, NJ: Prentice-Hall, 1972; and Harold M. Schroder, M. J. Driver, and Seigfried Streufert, *Human Information Processing,* NY: Holt, Rinehart and Winston, 1967.

[2]Newell and Simon, *op. cit.,* Chapter 2.

FIGURE 12-1.
*Information Processing
Phases for a Completely
New Product*

1. *Acquisition* of Information (includes attention, perception, and search)
2. *Integration* of Information (includes memory)
3. *Evaluation* of Information

What is more difficult to decide is which substages to include in each of the three phases. Attention, perception, and search may properly be classified as part of the acquisition process. The memory component, however, is a link between information acquisition and integration. That is, a person first conducts an internal search by looking at information stored in memory. It is only when this internal search proves unsatisfactory that the person will begin an external search for information.

Information acquisition includes the processes a person goes through in acquiring or getting information, such as attention, perception, and search. Each of these three substages will be discussed.

Attention

Attention to some stimulus is the allocation of processing capacity to that stimulus.[3] To attend to a stimulus means that the person directs physical senses to the stimulus. This can occur without the person translating the information into meaningful symbolic structures and without storing the information in memory. For instance, in reading a magazine a woman might focus her eyes for a brief moment on an advertisement for a line of fashionable clothing. She may notice one dress that is attractive, but may turn the page and immediately forget about the dress as she turns her attention to the article on the following page.

For this reason, researchers cannot measure attention by asking people if they remember a particular advertisement, because memory is something apart from mere attention. Therefore, rather than relying on verbal reports, attention is often measured by relying on physiological measurements. A researcher might present a consumer with a magazine and then observe (by using special equipment) the path that the person's eyes take as they move over a page, when the person's pupils dilate, when the person's palms begin to perspire (measured by Galvanic Skin Response), and when and if the person begins to salivate. The idea behind these techniques is that a person's physiological reactions to different stimuli (particularly ads) indicate when that person is aroused by the stimulus.

Some researchers, however, have expressed doubts about the use of such techniques. For example, a person's pupils are supposed to enlarge for pleasant stimuli and constrict for unpleasant stimuli. Yet, this type of mea-

---

[3]Daniel Kahneman, *Attention and Effort*, Englewood Cliffs, NJ: Prentice-Hall, 1973.

surement provided contradictory findings in one study.[4] In addition, the meanings of some of the other measurements are questionable. For example, a person's eyes may linger on advertisements to which the person is very attracted as well as those with which the person strongly disagrees. Similarly, people's palms may perspire when they see a pleasant advertisement as well as when they are angered by an advertisement. Thus, the problem with these measures of arousal is that the participants are often unable to tell the researchers if they are pleasantly or unpleasantly aroused by the advertisement.

Often we hear someone say about an ad, "It may seem dumb, but it gets your attention, doesn't it?" Those stimuli, however, which draw attention to an advertisement by making people dislike the advertisement or the company are unlikely to be successful in encouraging people to try or use a product or service. Therefore, although it is important to draw consumers' attention to an advertisement, this is not the sole objective of the communication effort. The marketer tries to draw attention to a message for a product in order to *facilitate* (rather than inhibit) further information processing and product evaluation on the part of the consumer.

Given that the marketer wants to draw attention to an advertisement for a product or service and also wants to facilitate further information processing, what can be done? That is, what kinds of stimuli have been found to increase the number of people who attend to the stimuli? There are three important aspects that aid in eliciting attention: (1) distinctiveness, (2) media differences in acquiring attention, and (3) advertisement structures.

One writer distinguishes between voluntary and involuntary attention.[5] Involuntary attention occurs when a distinctive or interesting idea is presented without warning. For example, a person, while watching television at night, may get up during a commercial break to fix a snack, but the person's attention may be diverted back to the television if the advertisement is presenting something distinctive. A distinctive advertisement is one which is different from other ads or which is very interesting or relevant to the person. People selectively attend to distinctive stimuli (see Figure 12-2). For example, if there is a sudden change in an advertisement, such as introducing sound in a previously silent advertisement, the person will be more likely to direct his or her attention to the stimulus.[6] Other examples of distinctiveness would be a totally silent television advertisement, a magazine advertisement with words only in one small section of the page and white space in the rest of the page, or a package which has a very different shape than that of competitors' products.

[4]Roger D. Blackwell, James S. Hensel, and Brian Sternthal, "Pupil Dilation: What Does It Measure?" *Journal of Advertising Research,* Vol. 10, August, 1970, pp. 15–18.

[5]Kahneman, *op. cit.*

[6]Xavier Kohan, "A Physiological Measure of Advertising Effectiveness," *Journal of Advertising Research,* Vol. 8, December, 1968 pp. 41–48.

FIGURE 12-2. *Selective Attention*

Source: *Detroit Free Press,* Sunday, July 3, 1977.

The amount of structure of an advertisement as well as its distinctiveness can draw attention. Advertisements which are properly structured can draw people in and encourage them to become more active in processing information about the advertised product or service. One researcher studied the effect of the amount of advertisement structure on thinking, looking, and feeling.[7] Thinking was defined as the thoughts which came to mind spontaneously while an ad was being viewed. Looking was measured by eye movements, and feeling was defined in terms of the intensity of the response. Three ads of high, medium, and low product-specificity and structure were shown to respondents. A highly structured ad would contain a high amount of product-specific facts and bits of information. For example, a very structured automobile ad might give price, a list of features, type of tires, engine size, type of brakes, type of suspension system, and many other facts about the automobile.

Krugman found that the ad with the least structure generated the most thoughts per respondent, the widest variety of responses, and the most thoughts expressing desire for the product. The opposite was true for the highly structured ad. This result indicates that the ad structure may have as much, or more of, an effect as the content of the ad. A highly structured or product-specific advertisement, while it may be most communicative or informative, may be least motivating or persuasive. Thus, by having less structure or specific relation to the product, an ad may produce more involvement. (See Proposition 12-1.)

EXHIBIT 12-1.
A Proposition Concerning Amount of Advertisement Structure

PROPOSITION 12-1.
The less structured and product-specific an advertisement is, the more thinking, looking, and feeling it will elicit from the consumer.

According to research, media differ with regard to how they affect attention.[8] Print and broadcast media can have very different effects, depending on the level of involvement of the consumer. In print media, the information rate is adjusted by consumers, in that they can take as long or as little time as they want reading the information. This can be important when dealing with

---

[7]Herbert E. Krugman, "Processes Underlying Exposure to Advertising," *American Psychologist*, Vol. 23, April, 1968, pp. 245–253.

[8]Peter L. Wright, "Analyzing Media Effects on Advertising Responses," *Public Opinion Quarterly*, Vol. 38, 1974, pp. 192–205.

groups such as the elderly whose information processing speed declines with age. Thus, information processing is easier when it is self-paced, as with print media.[9] Similarly, children who do not yet know how to read, or who are not yet proficient readers, will be more likely to pay attention to messages contained in broadcast media. Therefore, some people may be more likely to focus their attention on a stimulus if it is presented in certain media.

Perception   Following attention is perception (discussed in depth in the previous chapter), which is "a complex process by which people select, organize, and interpret sensory stimulation into a meaningful picture of the world."[10] Different people may perceive the same stimuli very differently. Their responses are influenced by individual biases, and by the tendency to look for and see only what they expect. People often develop prior expectations of what will be seen based on familiarity with ads or upon what is stored in memory. An environmentalist could react to an ad for aerosol deodorant sprays as a threat to the ozone layer of the atmosphere. A person concerned about perspiration might simply respond to the convenience and effectiveness of such sprays.

Perception is like a gatekeeper. If the stimuli which produce attention are of little or no interest to the person, the stimuli may not be perceived at all. Generally, in such cases, storage in memory does not occur.

Search   Once a stimulus has been attended to and perceived, the next question to ask is whether it has been perceived previously. If it has, then at least a portion of the information about the stimulus may be stored in the person's memory. If it has never been perceived before, or if the person did not store any information in memory after previously perceiving the stimulus, then the stimulus represents new information. If the new information is of value to the consumer or if the consumer wants to add more information to what is already stored in memory, then the consumer may decide to find out more about the stimulus. This is what consumer behavior researchers refer to as the *search* for additional information. Also, there can be either an internal or external search for information. *Internal search* involves searching the person's own memory for information related to the stimulus. *External search* involves deliberately searching for information from sources other than one's own memory. Most research on consumer behavior has focused on external search for information rather than internal search. This is probably because the marketer can

[9]Lynn Phillips and Brian Sternthal, "Age Differences in Information Processing: A Perspective on the Aged Consumer," *Journal of Marketing Research,* Vol. 14, November, 1977, pp. 444–457.

[10]Rom J. Markin, Jr., *Consumer Behavior: A Cognitive Orientation,* NY: Macmillan Publishing Co., 1974, p. 198.

play an important role in the external search process through salespeople, advertising, product demonstrations, and printed information. The following scenario will illustrate various aspects of the search process.

An Illustration.   A consumer goes to a store to purchase toothpaste and is in and out of the store in minutes; he or she has simply purchased a favorite brand (see the section in the previous chapter on brand loyalty). This consumer has built up a memory base about the brand—its clean, minty taste and its whitening power—and considers this internal memory sufficient for performing the decision task. Consider the same consumer contemplating the purchase of a microwave oven which was advertised frequently on television. This person is unwilling to spend three hundred dollars on a microwave oven only on the basis of the meager data provided by the television ad, and therefore engages in a search for external information. This may result in a visit to a store where the person can look at the available brands and talk to salespeople. The consumer could also ask friends what brands of microwave ovens they purchased or could read *Consumer Reports*. The consumer in this case actively seeks information before deciding which brand to purchase.

Evaluating the Costs and Benefits of External Search.   In facing a decision about whether to search for additional information about a product or service, it would seem that the consumer would consider the costs and benefits of that search. This would apply particularly in the case of external search. Costs of search include the amount of time, effort, and money which must be expended in gathering the information. Benefits include the possibility of making a better choice after gathering additional information as well as the personal satisfaction of feeling that a thorough job of comparing alternatives preceded the choice. As such, the person will engage in external search when the benefits exceed the costs (Proposition 12-2).

For example, in considering the purchase of a new automobile, the person is confronted with an extremely large number of possible information sources. The person could ask friends for their opinions about various automobiles, visit a showroom and talk to a salesperson, test drive several makes, read booklets which are available in the showroom, call the Better Business Bureau to see if any complaints have been registered about any of the dealers being considered, pay close attention to all automobile advertisements encountered, and read articles in *Consumer Reports* and *Road and Track* which evaluate various new cars. If the person wanted additional information, he or she could write to the manufacturers, take a tour through several assembly plants to see whether the workers all appear to be doing a good job, or the person could even take a job in an assembly plant so he or she would know how well particular cars are assembled. Obviously, few, if any, individuals use all of these sources of information. Somehow, by compar-

EXHIBIT 12-2.
*Propositions Concerning
External Search*

PROPOSITION 12-2.
The more the anticipated benefits derived from external search exceed the anticipated costs of seeking the information, the greater will be the extent of external search.

PROPOSITION 12-3.
The higher the costs of external search, the higher will be the incidence of repeat purchases of the same brand.

PROPOSITION 12-4.
The greater the amount of perceived risk, the greater the amount of external search for information.

ing costs and benefits individuals decide which types of information are worth enough to them that they will engage in the external search.

Research has shown that shoppers visit more stores (a form of external search) if travelling costs are low.[11] Also, if consumers have no attractive alternative task other than search behavior, they involve themselves in more external search.[12] A third study was conducted to see whether people would engage in less external search if a cost of search was imposed.[13] This experiment was also designed to measure whether expectations and brand loyalty were related to search costs. Using students as respondents, the researcher found that search was lower when costs were imposed. This is empirical support for Proposition 12-2. Also, people engaged in less search when their past experience with the product exceeded their expectations for it. In this case they engaged in repeat purchases of the same brand rather than incur the costs of search for information about other brands. In general, repeat purchases of a brand occurred more often when search costs were present. This finding is summarized in Proposition 12-3.

Several implications can be drawn from Propositions 12-3 and 12-4. If a marketer is dealing with a new product or a product about which not many

[11]Louis P. Bucklin, ''Testing Propensities to Shop,'' *Journal of Marketing,* Vol. 30, January, 1966, pp. 22–27.

[12]Frederick M. Winter, ''Laboratory Measurement of Response to Consumer Information,'' *Journal of Marketing Research,* Vol. 12, November, 1975, pp. 390–401.

[13]John E. Swan, ''Search Behavior Related to Expectations Concerning Forward Performance,'' *Journal of Applied Psychology,* Vol. 56, 1972, pp. 332–335.

consumers know, then it is necessary to get consumers to search for and be receptive to new information. This can be done by emphasizing the benefits of search ("You'll never know what you're missing unless you listen to what we have to say about our product"). Alternatively, the marketer can attempt to reduce the costs of information search by making information easier to obtain, perhaps by advertising in channels which the consumer may reach easily. Public service messages which ask listeners to send for more information by sending a dollar plus a stamped, self-addressed envelope to an address which is flashed very rapidly on the television screen impose too many costs on the information search process. Coupons for requesting additional information are easier for consumers to use if they are perforated and can be easily removed from the page rather than if they must be cut out with scissors. Also, consumer educators should encourage consumers to consult several reliable sources of information before making any major purchase.

Risk and External Search. Several researchers have been interested in how a person's perception of the risks associated with a purchase will affect the extent to which a person engages in external search. It appears that a consumer will engage in more external search if there is a distinct risk of making an unsatisfactory purchase.[14] So, marketers of products which are high in perceived risk must be particularly attentive to their potential consumers' needs for information. This probably accounts for the large expenditures by automobile manufacturers on advertising and other sources of consumer information such as booklets, salespeople, and test drive policies.

Two researchers measured the relationship between the amount of social risk and performance risk in a product and type of search.[15] The categorization of sources of information which was used is as follows:

1. Impersonal Advocate, e.g., mass media advertising;
2. Impersonal Independent, e.g., *Consumer Reports*;
3. Personal Advocate, e.g., sales clerks;
4. Personal Independent, e.g., friends' opinions or word-of-mouth;
5. Direct Observation/Experience.[16]

---

[14]Jagdish N. Sheth and M. Venkatesan, "Risk-Reduction Process in Repetitive Consumer Behavior," *Journal of Marketing Research,* Vol. 3, August, 1968, pp. 307–310; and Richard J. Lutz and Patrick J. Reilly, "An Explanation of the Effects of Perceived Social and Performance Risk on Consumer Information Acquisition," in Scott Ward and Peter Wright (eds.), *Advances in Consumer Research,* Vol. 1, Chicago: Association for Consumer Research, 1974, pp. 393–405.

[15]Lutz and Reilly, *op. cit.*

[16]A. R. Andreasen, "Attitudes and Customer Behavior: A Decision Model," in H. H. Kassarjian and T. S. Robertson (eds.), *Perspectives in Consumer Behavior,* Glenview, IL: Scott, Foresman and Co., 1968, pp. 498–510.

For products which had low-to-moderate social and performance risk, such as a box of facial tissues, consumers would rather try the product than seek information from external sources. On the other hand, for products high in social risk and/or performance risk, consumers would not make purchases without further information. In such cases, consumers predominantly go by their past experiences with products if they have had experiences with the product category. Additional sources of information for this type of product are impersonal independent sources such as *Consumer Reports* and personal independent sources such as word-of-mouth.

This implies that the market for low perceived risk products will be somewhat unstable because consumers will be willing to try new products without searching for information about them. Thus, there may be a considerable amount of brand switching in low perceived risk product categories.

Measuring External Search Behavior. Because consumers tend to overstate the amount of information they search for and use in making product choices, survey techniques are not well-suited for studying external search behavior. Following people around and observing what product-related information they gather is too time consuming and expensive to be used in studying external search behavior. Therefore, using an information display board, a technique for studying external search behavior in the laboratory has been developed.[17]

In studies involving display boards, consumers are presented with a matrix of product information. An illustration of such a matrix is shown in Figure 12-3. The brands (i.e., purchase alternatives) are listed across the top of the matrix, while the types of information available (i.e., information dimensions such as price, net weight, ingredients) are listed down the side of the matrix. Each row of information in the matrix represents a dimension of information (e.g., price) across all the brands presented. Each cell in the matrix contains a pocket of ten cards. The blank sides of the cards face the respondent. On each card is information about the brand on that dimension. For example, in the cell marked with an asterisk in Figure 12-3 would be ten cards. On the back side of each card would be printed the net weight of the tube, such as "6.4 ounces." Similarly, all of the cards in the other cells would have product information on them.

In the study referred to above, real brand names were used (sometimes only letters are used to identify the purchase alternatives). Respondents were

[17]Jacob Jacoby, Robert W. Chestnut, Karl C. Weigel, and William Fisher, "Pre-Purchase Information Acquisition: Description of a Process Methodology, Research Paradigm, and Pilot Investigation," *Advances in Consumer Research,* Vol. 3, 1976, pp. 306–14.

FIGURE 12-3.
Information Matrix for Toothpaste

Dimensions	Brands			
	Colgate	Crest	Gleem	Pepsodent
Ingredients				
Price				
Net Weight	*			
Flavor				
ADA approval				
Cavity-prevention capability				
Whitening capability				

asked to act as if they were shopping for one brand among the set of brands provided. They were told they could seek as much or as little information as they wanted. They could take as much or as little time as they desired, gather information from the cells in any order, and choose the product simply by brand name if that was their usual procedure.

The researcher therefore had a record of the information which was selected by the respondents and the order in which it was selected. The respondent chose a cell, looked at the information on a card from that pocket, and then placed the card face down in a collection tray. The pile of cards in the collection tray was the record of the information chosen and the order in which it was chosen. There were initially ten cards in each pocket in order to give the respondent an opportunity to obtain the same information from a previously chosen cell. This gives the researcher the opportunity to know how often and when the consumer had access to an information card, but did not store the information in long-term memory and then later chose to use that piece of information once again.

Though memory will be discussed more fully in the next section, it is important here to point out that there is a component of memory which cannot be studied using the information display board. The use of the board cannot tell the researcher when the respondent relies on information stored in memory before the beginning of the study. For example, in the toothpaste situation shown in Figure 12-3, many consumers could make a purchase choice using only the brand names. This does not mean that people do not use information when making choices. Instead, it indicates that for that product category, sufficient information is stored in memory about the various brands so that a choice can be made using only brand name information. Obviously, this probably would not be the case for a new category of products.

In the study described above,[18] there were 560 available information values (sixteen brands of ready-to-eat breakfast cereal × thirty-five dimensions). Half of the sample of sixty respondents acquired less than 2 percent of the information (i.e., less than eleven information cells). The median number of cells used was seven. Twelve respondents made a purchase decision using only the brand names (i.e., they chose to use none of the information cards).

These results point out two characteristics of human information processing. First, in free choice situations individuals seem to choose only that information which they see as most relevant rather than evaluating the product based on all available information. This is not to say that the amount of information given to consumers should be limited or that they should be given only that information which most people see as relevant. Rather, individuals differ from each other in what pieces of information they consider relevant. Therefore, information must be provided in a quantity and quality that satisfies the varied needs of individuals for information.

The second issue raised by the study is the fact that people not only selectively acquire information, but they also organize it for storage in memory. This has been termed "chunking." In a classic article, one researcher formulated the hypothesis of a limited size for short-term memory.[19] Basically, Miller said that people are only able to hold seven chunks of information (plus or minus two) in short-term memory at a time. A chunk of information is an organized and meaningful information structure. For example, in copying words from one page to another, a person can remember only about seven words at a time. If the size of each chunk is increased, however, then the amount of stored information can be increased. For example, if the organizing principle is a meaningful phrase rather than a word, the amount of stored information can be increased.

A brand name can serve as the organizing principle for a chunk. Obviously, this was the case with the twelve respondents who made their purchase choices using the brand names of the products. It is easier to absorb information in meaningful wholes rather than as individual bits which must then be integrated. Thus, if advertisers and product manufacturers can help consumers form chunks of information, it will be possible for consumers to acquire more information which they can subsequently process. One way of accomplishing this with nutrient information on packaged food products would be to provide quality indices for *overall* protein content, vitamin content, and mineral content. Often there are numerous vitamins and minerals which are

[18]Jacoby, *et al., op. cit.*

[19]George A. Miller, "The Magical Number Seven, Plus or Minus Two: Some Limits on Our Capacity for Processing Information," *Psychological Review,* Vol. 63, 1956, pp. 81–97.

each listed separately. This information system could be changed to one which forms the separate bits of information into chunks. Though the change would thus reduce the number of information dimensions available, each dimension would be a chunk rather than a single bit of information. This change would thus reduce the number of separate protein, vitamin, and mineral dimensions a consumer must process.

INFORMATION INTEGRATION   Integration involves the combining of different items of information obtained during the acquisition process. A vital link in this combination is memory. Several consumer decision-making rules may be used in combining newly acquired information with information previously stored in memory. This section discusses memory and the rules used for making decisions.

Memory   Memory is utilized during all three major stages of information processing but is a particularly important component of information integration.

It is useful to think of memory as having a two-part structure. Short-term memory (STM) is the part of memory which is used for active processing, while long-term memory (LTM) is the part of memory which is used for permanent storage. The sequence of processing new information is from STM to LTM. The sequence of processing for reconsidering information previously stored in memory is LTM to STM and then possibly back into LTM. Information is put into STM for only the short period of time during which it is actively processed. It can be held there for only a brief time because STM has a limited capacity. The LTM, however, has an unlimited capacity. In LTM, information can be permanently stored but can only be transferred to LTM after it has been sufficiently processed in STM.

Retrieval from long-term memory is an important control process. In some cases retrieval can be instantaneous, and in other cases it may be impossible. In the latter case, it is possible that the basis used for coding the information prior to storage has been forgotten. For example, if a person uses a special clue to store complex information, he or she may find it impossible to retrieve the information if the special clue is forgotten.

Repetition is a strategy often used by marketers to increase the probability that information will be processed in STM and then transferred to LTM. There is strong evidence to indicate that repetition significantly aids recall.[20] In

[20]Michael L. Ray and Allan G. Sawyer, "Repetition in Media Models: A Laboratory Technique," *Journal of Marketing Research,* Vol. 8, February, 1971, pp. 20–29; and Alan G. Sawyer, "The Effects of Repetition: Conclusions and Suggestions About Experimental Laboratory Research," in G. David Hughes and Michael L. Ray (eds.), *Buyer/Consumer Information Processing,* Chapel Hill, NC: University of North Carolina Press, 1974, pp. 190–219.

other words, the more an advertisement is repeated, the more likely it is that consumers will be able to remember the message of the advertisement. Similarly, the more often a person is exposed to a product, the more likely it is that the person will remember what the product is (these ideas are derived from Proposition 12-5).

PROPOSITION 12-5.
The greater the number of times a person is exposed to a stimulus (i.e., the greater the repetition of stimulus exposure), the greater the probability that the person will recall the stimulus at a later point in time.

We must be careful, however, in interpreting this proposition. Repetition affects purchase behavior less than it affects cognitive elements such as learning, brand evaluation, and intention to purchase. Repetition will help a consumer remember an advertisement but will not necessarily result in a purchase of the advertised product or service. In fact, if a message is repeated too often, the consumer may begin to develop a negative image of the brand.[21] Therefore, it is important to insure not only that consumers remember a message or a product but that they also store in their LTMs a positive evaluation of the message, product, and company.

Differences in presentation format, as well as in repetition, have an effect on memory. Research shows that respondents' recognition capabilities increased significantly if pictures were used, because information could be mentally coded in visual patterns.[22] In particular, children tend to mentally code information using pictures.[23] This implies that manufacturers of children's products should facilitate the children's information processing and information storage in LTM by using pictures in advertisements and on packages to organize the product-related information. For instance, product characters (e.g., the Trix rabbit) may be remembered by the children better than brand names. Brand names are also necessary, however, because they are used by parents for chunking information.

---

[21]"Value of Repetition," *Media/Scope,* Vol. 7, August, 1973, p. 19.

[22]Roger N. Shepard, "Recognition Memory for Words, Sentences, and Pictures," *Journal of Verbal Learning and Verbal Behavior,* Vol. 6, 1967, pp. 156–163.

[23]John R. Rossiter, "Visual and Verbal Memory in Children's Product Information Utilization," in B. B. Anderson (ed.), *Advances in Consumer Research,* Vol. 3, Chicago: Association for Consumer Research, 1976, pp. 523–527

Decision Rules   There are several ways a consumer can go about combining the various bits of information gathered about a product in deciding whether to purchase the product. Marketers are very interested in learning what decision rules are adopted by consumers under which conditions. This enables marketers to design effective marketing programs. One researcher suggests several avenues open to the marketer: "Marketing activity can (1) accept the choice strategy as a given and adjust to accommodate it, (2) try directly persuading the consumer to use another strategy more favorable to ultimate selection of the advocated product, or (3) try to help the consumer restructure [the] decision problem (e.g., reduce it to a simpler task) which in turn induces [the consumer] into using a different choice rule."[24]

In experimental and field situations consumers make choices *as if* they used the rules described below. Of course, when formulas are involved, consumers do not pull out a pad of paper and a pencil and begin applying a particular rule. To repeat, consumers make choices *as if* these were the decision rules used; it is not yet clear whether they do in fact directly apply the rules.

In highlighting six basic types of decision rules, we will discuss their application in the context of the purchase of a house.[25]

Affect-Referral Rule.   A consumer using this rule relies on a previously formed global attitude or feeling toward each purchase alternative (in this case, toward each house). The information integration and evaluation is based on a single overall impression and the alternative which leaves the consumer with the best overall impression is chosen. For example, a person might choose to buy one of four houses because it seems like the perfect house. In the case of housing, it is likely that this rule would be applied to a set of houses, all of which have already met certain other criteria (e.g., size, cost, and area of the city).

Linear Compensatory Rule.   A consumer using this rule would evaluate each house on several dimensions and would create a mental matrix. Each dimension is given a weight based on the dimension's importance to the consumer. The weights are used to determine the contribution of each dimension to the overall evaluation. Then, the weighted evaluations of the

---

[24]Peter L. Wright, "Consumer Choice Strategies: Simplifying vs. Optimizing," *Journal of Marketing Research*, Vol. 12, February, 1975, pp. 60–67.
[25]The rules discussed are those stated by Wright, *op. cit.*

house on each dimension are combined to get an overall rating of each house, and the house with the highest rating is chosen. Expressed as a formula, this rule or choice strategy is:

$$E = \Sigma W_i V_i$$

where E = evaluation index,
W_i = weight assigned to attribute i,
V_i = value of attribute i.

For example, consider a person looking for a house. The person is concerned with size (the bigger the better), cost (the lower the better), and distance from place of employment (the closer the better). These are the three dimensions. Their importance to this consumer is reflected in the following weights:

Size	.4
Cost	.4
Distance from Office	.2

Notice that the weights must sum to 1. The person has evaluated two houses on each dimension.

	House A	House B
Size	3	2
Cost	1	2
Distance	2	3

where rating 1 = poor
2 = moderate
3 = excellent

In this case, the overall ratings of each of the houses are

House A = .4(3) + .4(1) + .2(2) = 2.0
House B = .4(2) + .4(2) + .2(3) = 1.8

Therefore, the consumer using the linear compensatory rule will choose House A, which has the higher overall evaluation. The model is called compensatory because high values on one dimension can compensate for low values on another. For example, House A's excellent size compensates for its high cost.

Conjunctive Rule.   Using the conjunctive rule, a consumer also uses the mental matrix, but in a different way. The consumer has prespecified cutoff points for each dimension. Any house which does not meet all of the cutoff points will be eliminated. For example, the consumer may eliminate from consideration any house with fewer than three bedrooms and which does not have at least two bathrooms. The house which exceeds the minimum cutoff values specified by the consumer on *all* attributes is chosen. This is noncompensatory: high values on one attribute cannot compensate for a substandard value on another attribute. A house with five bedrooms but only one bathroom will not be chosen. More than one house can be selected by this rule. If this is so, then another rule will be used to select from those houses.

Disjunctive Rule.   This rule also uses cutoff points, but in a different way. If an alternative passes the minimum standard established on *any* attribute, it is included in the set of acceptable alternatives. For example, if the standards are three bedrooms and two bathrooms, any house which meets or exceeds *at least one* of these standards is included in the set of acceptable houses. Therefore, the house with five bedrooms but only one bathroom would be considered if the consumer is using a disjunctive rule but not if he or she is using a conjunctive rule. The disjunctive rule is also noncompensatory and allows more than one alternative.

Lexicographic Rule.   Dimensions are ranked in order of importance and the alternatives are compared on the most important attribute. If one alternative is preferred over all others on this attribute, it is chosen. If there is a tie, the tied houses are compared on the next most important attribute and so on. For example, distance from work, number of bedrooms, and cost may be the rank order of dimensions in decreasing order of importance. First, the houses would be compared on their distance from work. The house which is closest to work would be chosen. This rule is noncompensatory also. In this example, no amount of cost difference can overcome differences in distance from work.

There is a variant of this rule which is referred to as the lexicographic semiorder rule. This rule is similar to the lexicographic rule, except that a second attribute is considered in cases where the differences in first attribute values are not significant. For example, if distance from work is the most important attribute to a consumer, and all houses are within one block of each other, then the second most important attribute, number of bedrooms, will be used in making the choice.

Hybrid Rules.   A combination of several rules can be used in stages. For example, a conjunctive rule which selects more than one house in the first stage can be combined with a linear compensatory rule in the second stage. So a conjunctive rule might be used to select houses within a certain area with at least three bedrooms and two bathrooms. Then a linear compensatory rule might be used to evaluate these houses on their overall size (in square feet), cost, and distance from work.

Processing Patterns   When integrating and evaluating a set of information about several brands, most consumers use one of two strategies. The consumer goes through a mental matrix such as the one in Figure 12-2 either row-by-row (which is called attribute processing) or column-by-column (which is called brand processing).[26] (A small number of people combine the two strategies.) Attribute processing involves evaluating all brands on one attribute, and then going on to process all of the brands on another attribute. Brand processing involves evaluating each brand separately, based on its attributes.

In general, research indicates a preference for attribute processing.[27] The supermarket environment, however, facilitates brand processing rather than attribute processing. Package information is given by brands and to carry out attribute processing, a consumer would have to gather together the brands in question and go from one package to another making the comparisons. One researcher suggests an in-store display which would present for an entire product class a listing of all brands and sizes with summary nutrient information.[28] This matrix-type format would facilitate both brand and attribute processing. Similar to this suggestion, another group of researchers suggest that a simple list of all brands and sizes and their unit prices be provided as an effective arrangement of unit-price information.[29] An experimental setup using this idea helped consumers choose the cheapest brand. This, once again, is based on the processing by attribute principle.

INFORMATION EVALUATION   Most information integration and each decision rule involve evaluation. Brand processing involves evaluating a brand over all dimensions and obtaining a rating score, and attribute processing involves evaluating all brands one dimension at a time. Most often, though, consumers resort to the use of simple heuristics or rules of thumb in buying contexts. Examples include restricting

[26]James R. Bettman and Jacob Jacoby, "Patterns of Processing in Consumer Information Acquisition," in B. B. Anderson (ed.), *Advances in Consumer Research,* Vol. 3, Chicago: Association of Consumer Research, 1976, pp. 315–318.

[27]Amos Tversky, "Intransitivity of Preferences," *Psychological Review,* Vol. 76, January, 1968, pp. 31–48; Edward J. Russo and Larry D. Rosen, "An Eye-Fixation Analysis of Multi-Alternative Choice," *Memory and Cognition,* Vol. 3, May, 1975, pp. 267–276; John W. Payne, "Task Complexity and Contingent Processing in Decision Making: An Information Search and Protocol Analysis," *Organizational Behavior and Human Performance,* Vol. 16, August, 1976, pp. 366–387; and Bettman and Jacoby, 1976, *op. cit.*

[28]James R. Bettman, "Issues in Designing Consumer Information Environments," *Journal of Consumer Research,* Vol. 2, December, 1975, pp. 169–177.

[29]J. Edward Russo, Gene Kreiser, and Sally Miyashita, "An Effective Display of Unit Price Information," *Journal of Marketing,* Vol. 39, April, 1975, pp. 11–19.

the number of brands under consideration to four, eliminating brands which cost more than a certain price, and ignoring large-size models because of space restrictions at home. It is quite possible that a careful evaluation of all attributes and brands might lead to a different brand choice. Usually, however, the consumer has neither the time nor the ability to undertake the detailed processing which this evaluation process entails. Consumers very often *satisfice* rather than *optimize*.[30] That is, consumers choose a satisfactory brand from those which are immediately available rather than wait and make a detailed search of all stores in the neighborhood in order to choose the "best" brand.

CONSUMER INFORMATION AND PUBLIC POLICY

The consumer in the supermarket, or elsewhere, faces a mass of detailed information. Some policy makers have argued that it does not matter whether the consumer actually uses the information, for its availability to the consumer is an ethical and legal right. As one writer has stated: "Congress has passed the Truth-in-Lending law on the issue of the right to know rather than on any evidence of whether or not the consumer uses the information...Congress was correct. The use the consumer makes of information is peripheral to the main issue of right to know."[31]

The behavioral sciences provide an alternative perspective. Based upon considerable research in the area of human information processing, consumer researchers and behavioral scientists argue that there are finite limits to the ability of human beings to assimilate and process information during any given unit of time.[32] Once these limits are surpassed, behavior tends to be confused and dysfunctional.

One group of researchers concluded from their experiments on information overload that as the total amount of information available increased, consumers felt more certain, more satisfied, less confused, and desired less additional information.[33] Consumers, however, made poorer purchase deci-

---

[30]Herbert A. Simon, *Models of Man,* NY: John Wiley and Sons, Inc., 1957.

[31]Green Bymers, "Seller-Buyer Communication: Point of View of a Family Economist," *Journal of Home Economics,* Vol. 64, February, 1972, pp. 59–63.

[32]Miller, 1956, *op. cit.;* and James Hulbert, "Information Processing Capacity and Attitude Measurement," *Journal of Marketing Research,* Vol 12, February, 1975, pp. 104–106; and Wright, *op. cit.*

[33]Jacob Jacoby, Donald E. Speller and Carol A. Kohn Berning, "Brand Choice Behavior as a Function of Information Load," *Journal of Marketing Research,* Vol. 11, February, 1974, pp. 63–69, and "Brand Choice Behavior as a Function of Information Load: Replication and Extension," *Journal of Consumer Research,* Vol. 1, June, 1974, pp. 63–69.

sions. Information overload may create greater perceived certainty about the choice made, but less than optimal choices.

What implications does the information overload concept have for public policy? Policy makers have no real control over the number of brands in various product classes in the market. The government can, however, create legislation concerning the number and order of attribute presentation. One general conclusion from the research is that consumers perform better when given more attributes rather than more brands.[34] So, action to reduce the amount of information about attributes would not be the sensible thing to do. Rather, policy makers should focus on determining which attributes are most relevant for consumers and how information can be presented in order to facilitate chunking.

There is evidence indicating that lower-income consumers are more vulnerable to abuses by the distribution system partially because they usually have little understanding of their rights.[35] Caplovitz states that low-income consumers should be treated differently from the rest of society because they are no match for the sophisticated marketer.[36] More research is needed on the information handling capability of poor vs. wealthy consumers and highly educated vs. poorly educated consumers. If significant differences are found, the disadvantaged groups must be protected in the marketplace.

SUMMARY
There are three phases of information processing: the acquisition of information, which includes attention, perception, and search; the integration of information, which includes memory; and the evaluation of the information.

Attention is the direction of the senses to the stimulus, and can occur without storing the information in memory. Those advertising stimuli which gain attention are based on the structure of the advertisement, the use of the media, and the distinctiveness of the advertisement. If one's attention is stimulated by an advertisement so that one perceives its appeal, a consumer may begin a search either in memory or in the external environment (other ads, or friends, family, and salespeople) for further information about the product. Ultimately, consumers "chunk" information, organizing it into a meaningful structure.

---

[34]*Ibid.*

[35]David Caplovitz, *The Poor Pay More,* Toronto: The Free Press, 1963, pp. 170–178; Frederick D. Sturdivant, "Better Deal for Ghetto Shoppers," *Harvard Business Review,* Vol. 46, March-April, 1968, pp. 130–139; and Alan Andreasen, *The Disadvantaged Consumer,* NY: The Free Press, 1975.

[36]Caplovitz, *op. cit.,* p. 190.

Memory is a vital link in the process of information integration. It is important not only that consumers remember a message or product, but that they also store in their memories a positive evaluation of the message or product.

Marketers are interested in how consumers combine information when deciding whether to purchase a product, and try to furnish the customer with information that will facilitate product evaluation and acceptance. It is important both for marketers and policy makers to determine which product attributes are most relevant so as to satisfy, rather than confuse, the consumer in his or her information gathering.

KEY CONCEPTS

Attention

Chunk

Long-term memory (LTM)

Memory

Search

Short-term memory (STM)

CONSUMER NEEDS*

13

CHAPTER GOALS The objective of this chapter is to help the reader understand:
1. **what needs are;**
2. **two typologies of needs which are related to consumer behavior;**
3. **how people resolve need conflicts in consumption settings;**
4. **how organizations meet needs which arise from stress and strain.**

INTRODUCTION No matter where we begin the study of consumer behavior as a part of marketing, we must eventually deal with the topic of needs, because the marketing concept is built upon the determination of needs and how to serve and satisfy them.[1] Peter H. Engel, the president of Helena Rubenstein, Inc., claims that any firm's success is heavily dependent on a determination of consumer needs: "You must always identify consumer need and provide products to fill it...I had to learn what consumers wanted, and the [significant] differences in such things as lipstick shades."[2] This noted marketer also cautions about confusing one's own personal bias for a product with what consumers actually want or need. The tendency for a manager to confuse his or her own product needs with those of consumers is one of the major reasons for having a formal research program for assessing consumer needs.

*We would like to acknowledge the assistance of Professor Wesley Johnston, Ohio State University, in the preparation of this chapter.

[1]Philip Kotler, *Marketing Management: Analysis, Planning, and Control,* Englewood Cliffs, NJ: Prentice-Hall, 1972, p. 18.

[2]*Product Marketing,* February, 1977, p. 36.

This chapter addresses first the elusiveness of a generally accepted definition of needs. Maslow's hierarchy of needs and McClelland's learning needs theory are discussed next. The concepts of conflict among needs and complementarity of needs are also explored. This chapter also discusses needs experienced by organizations and concludes with a discussion of the scant research on consumer needs.

A DEFINITION OF NEED

A problem in studying needs as they affect behavior lies in finding a generally acceptable definition of needs. Different researchers and writers use various definitions of need, while others use altogether different terms, such as drive, want, or goal, interchangeably with need.[3] A review of these definitions and alternate terms would add needless confusion.

A need is best defined as *the gap or discrepancy experienced between an actual and desired state of being.* This experience may be biological or social in nature. A consumer may feel out-of-fashion by virtue of having only older clothes which are not in style (an actual state) and at the same time preferring to be fashionable (a desired state). The greater the felt discrepancy between the style of the consumer's present wardrobe and the style of the desired wardrobe, the greater the consumer's need for a new wardrobe. Similarly, the greater the felt discrepancy between the performance of current equipment and the potential performance of new equipment, the greater the firm's need to purchase new equipment.

When thinking about needs as a central concept in consumer behavior, it is also useful to think of preferences. Consumers may prefer to satisfy one need more than, or rather than, another. Consumers may also prefer to satisfy a need in one particular way, rather than in another way. Thus, both consumer preferences and needs are critical factors to be considered. In fact, the marketer and consumer advocate are actually more concerned with affecting preferences than affecting needs. Though most marketing scholars and consumer behavior researchers do not believe needs are capable of being manipulated in the short run, it is nevertheless important to understand needs. The marketer benefits from this understanding by being better able to provide products and services which will satisfy consumers, and hence are more likely to be purchased. The consumer benefits by having products available which

---

[3]For a sample of definitions, see Funk and Wagnalls Standard Dictionary of the English Language International Edition, Vol. 2, NY: Funk and Wagnalls, 1970, p. 848; James C. Coleman, *Abnormal Psychology and Modern Life,* 3rd ed., Glenview, IL: Scott, Foresman Co., 1964, p. 666; Irving L. Janis, George F. Mahl, Jerome Kagan and Robert R. Holt, *Personality: Dynamics, Development and Assessment,* NY: Harcourt, Brace and World, Inc., 1969, p. 494; and John Howard and Jagdish Sheth, *The Theory of Buyer Behavior,* NY: John Wiley and Sons, Inc., 1969, p. 99.

yield more satisfaction than might otherwise occur. This position is expressed by Richard L. Lesher, the president of the United States Chamber of Commerce: "I don't think advertising creates new cravings in us—at least not in any basic way. It can, and does, play on *existing* needs and emotions. But then so does entertainment, or art, or music. In this sense, advertising can make us aware of a greater variety of ways to satisfy our differing tastes."[4]

This raises the issue of whether marketing responds to inherent needs or in fact creates needs so people will consume products. Because few needs arise in a social vacuum, that is, in the absence of contact with other people, it is difficult to determine which needs are genuine and which might be superimposed on consumers by marketers. The position taken here is that all needs are genuine, and that marketing strategies attempt to channel or give direction to the actions that consumers take in response to these needs.

FIGURE 13-1.
Example of a Product Which Does Not Meet a Perceived Need

THE WALL STREET JOURNAL

"Until this moment, I never realized we needed a food chopper with a built-in transistor radio."

Other writers have avoided the definition issue by simply listing various needs. A partial list is presented here to give the reader a feeling for these typologies[5]:

the need for affiliation
the need for dreaming
the need for identity
the need for power

---

[4]*Advertising Age,* January 2, 1978, p. 19.
[5]C. N. Cofer and M. H. Appley, *Motivation: Theory and Research,* NY: John Wiley and Sons, Inc., 1964.

the need for rest
the need for satisfaction
the need for security
the need for sex
the need for sleep
the need for stimulation

Another crucial issue in attempting to define need is the issue of consciousness or awareness. Some writers believe that a basic need may or may not be known by an individual; that is, a need may be conscious or unconscious. When the person does recognize a need, however, it then becomes a motivator, and the person desires or wants to satisfy the need. This conceptualization is shown diagrammatically below.

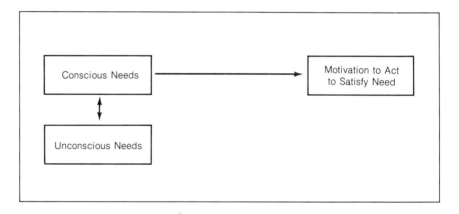

Others have argued that a need is not a deficiency, but that the existence of a deficiency can cause one to become aware of a need. For example, few people are aware of the need for water until they are forced to go without it for a long time. Then, like the person in the desert, all their efforts may go toward satisfying the need for water, which they have become acutely aware of because of the deficiency.

In summary, needs are fundamental and underlie all human behavior. It is not possible to explain consumer behavior without understanding the needs operating within the consumer. Consumer needs contain elements of biological or physiological drive (necessary for survival) as well as psychological and social feelings of desires and deficiencies.

TYPOLOGIES OF NEEDS

There have been many attempts to categorize the needs that affect individuals. Each categorization adds something to the understanding of the concept of needs, but lacks the ability to bring together the many different views on the subject. In this section, we examine the two most widely known categorizations of needs, those of Abraham Maslow and David McClelland.

Maslow's Hierarchy of Needs   The theory of motivation proposed by Maslow is in the form of a ranking or hierarchy of the individual's needs.[6] This is probably the most widely known theory of motivation and needs. The basic idea of Maslow's theory is that needs are arranged in a hierarchy. The lowest level needs are the physiological needs, sometimes referred to as drives, and the highest level needs are the self-actualization needs. Maslow's hierarchy of needs consists of:

1. physiological needs;
2. safety needs;
3. the need for belongingness;
4. the need for esteem;
5. the need for self-actualization.

Physiological needs refer to the need for food, drink, physical protection or shelter, and the relief from pain. *Safety needs* include both the actual need for physical safety and the need to feel secure from threatening events and/or surroundings. Physiological and safety needs are personal needs. Once the individual can maintain a reasonably satisfactory level of providing for these needs, he or she is capable of relating to other people. The *need for belongingness* is the need to be part of a social group, to interact with and be accepted by others in friendship, affiliation, interaction, and love. The *need for esteem* is the need to be valued both by the social group (peer recognition) and by one's self (self-esteem). The highest level of need is the *need for self-actualization,* which is the need to fulfill one's self by maximizing the use of abilities, skills, and potential. The emergence of the need for self-actualization depends upon reaching a satisfactory level on the lower needs of the hierarchy. The hierarchy of needs is usually depicted as a pyramid with the broad base being the physiological needs and the top being the need for self-actualization. This is shown in Figure 13-2. Maslow later modified this list of needs by adding the need to know and understand plus esthetic needs to the hierarchy.[7]

Maslow argued that, over time, an individual strives to achieve each of these needs in order. Except in the case of the need for self-actualization, a satisfied need ceases to motivate the person. In other words, the motivating force of the first four needs decreases when deficiency conditions (e.g., hunger, thirst, loneliness) are met. Self-actualization needs, however, are

---

[6]Abraham H. Maslow, "A Theory of Human Motivation," *Psychological Review,* Vol. 50, 1943, pp. 370–396.

[7]Abraham H. Maslow, *Motivation and Personality,* NY: Harper & Row, 2nd edition, 1970.

FIGURE 13-2.
Maslow's Hierarchy of Needs

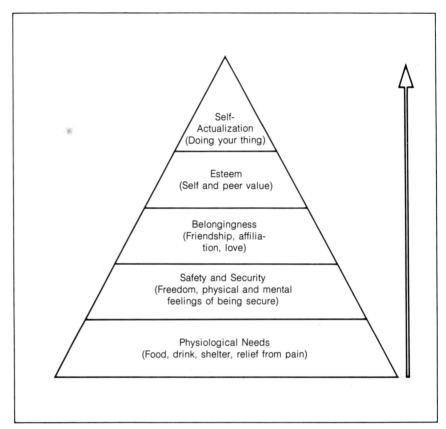

heightened by previous self-expression.[8] Since people have a need to grow and develop, as they satisfy their lower level needs they move on to attempting to satisfy the next level of need in the hierarchy. Maslow proposed that the typical adult has satisfied about 85 percent of the physical need, 70 percent of the safety and security need, 50 percent of the need to belong and to love, 40 percent of the need for esteem, and only 10 percent of the self-actualization need. An interesting way of picturing this appears in Figure 13-3. The level of satisfaction of needs varies across individuals within a society as well as across societies. (This was touched upon in the discussion of the differentiation of social structures in Chapter 4.)

Needs themselves become more abstract and difficult to satisfy the higher one moves in the hierarchy. When a person is hungry or thirsty (realiz-

---

[8]Abraham H. Maslow, *Toward a Psychology of Being,* 2nd ed., NY: Van Nostrand, 1968.

FIGURE 13-3.
*Proportion of Needs
Satisfied*

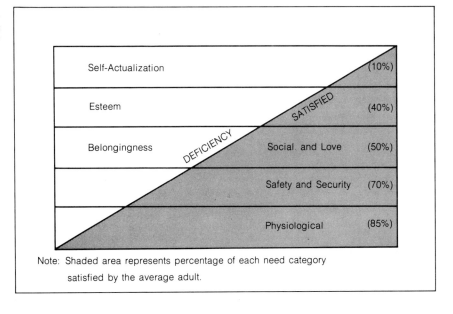

Note: Shaded area represents percentage of each need category

    satisfied by the average adult.

Source: From a presentation in James L. Gibson, John M. Ivancevich and James H. Donnelly, Jr., *Organizations Behavior, Structure, Processes,* Dallas, Texas, Business Publications, Inc., 1976.

ing physiological needs), it is fairly simple to satisfy these needs. At a higher level, let us say belongingness and love, people often recognize the need, but are less certain about how to satisfy it. The top of the hierarchy, the need for self-actualization, is often obscure and difficult to understand, let alone accomplish.

EXHIBIT 13-1.
*Propositions About
Maslow's Need
Hierarchy*

PROPOSITION 13-1.
The higher the need in an overall hierarchy of needs, the more uncertain the person will be about the specific ways in which it can be satisfied.

PROPOSITION 13-2.
The higher a need is in a hierarchy of needs, the less likely it is to be fulfilled.

One implication of this proposition is that when a product is intended to satisfy needs at the higher levels of the hierarchy, the connection between the product and the need may not be totally clear to the consumer. It is easier for consumers to make the connection between products and their physiological needs. The marketer must recognize this and take the necessary steps to ensure that the consumer knows what needs the product can satisfy and how. In effect, the marketer must say, "If you have this need, then this is a product which will satisfy it." Such statements must, of course, be credible. Perhaps this explains the dubious credibility of many promotional claims which promise love if one uses a particular cologne, admiration from one's friends if one uses a particular toilet bowl cleaner, or fulfillment if one flies on a particular airline.

It is important to understand that there is not a one-to-one relationship between products and services and the needs they can be used to satisfy. Steak can simply be eaten (physiological need), or it can be served to company in an attempt to gain friendship (belongingness or esteem needs). Cooking can be done in a distinct, creative way to satisfy self-actualizing needs, as well as routinely to meet biological needs. A house can provide shelter and safety, while also serving as the center of social activity, thus fostering love and belongingness. Decorating or designing the house may satisfy self-actualization needs. Thus, marketers must understand that different segments of the market can be formed for the same products based upon different needs. Various appeals to different needs may be more efficient than a one level appeal to any specific need.

Research shows that there is a positive correlation between the position of the need in the hierarchy and the degree of product differentiation: The higher the level of the need, the greater the opportunity for product differentiation (this is implied in Proposition 13-1). The marketer with products aimed at the higher levels of needs should consider differentiating that product more than one aimed at lower-level needs.

Moving back for a moment to Figure 13-3, we can see that needs at the top of the hierarchy tend to be less fully satisfied. Two qualifications are necessary when considering this proposition. First, a need higher in a hierarchy may be fulfilled to a lesser extent because lower-order needs are being fulfilled inadequately or with difficulty. So, these basic needs, which must be attended to first, consume resources at the expense of higher level needs. When lower-order needs are easily satisfied, however, more attention can be given to higher-order needs and hence the likelihood of their being satisfied may increase substantially. Secondly, needs at any level can be satisfied either elaborately or simply. Physiological needs can be satisfied by gourmet dining or by consuming canned pet food (a practice not uncommon in some low income areas). Self-actualization needs may be satisfied by whittling a stick or pursuing a doctoral degree. Thus, it is necessary at all levels to take into account how simply the consumer is trying to satisfy needs. The less simple the strategy used by the consumer, the less likely total fulfillment is to occur.

McClelland's Learned Needs Theory

Maslow believed that the individual was born with a basic set of needs, though society played an important role in defining how some of these needs were satisfied. A different perspective was offered by David McClelland, who proposed a theory of learned needs.[9] This theory of needs is closely associated with the concepts of learning and personality, and stresses the acquisition of needs from culture (see Chapters 4, 10, 11, and 15).

The need most thoroughly examined by McClelland and his colleagues was the need for achievement, or the achievement motive. Other needs studied included the needs for affiliation and for power. The *need for achievement* reflects the desire to take responsibility for solving problems. People who have a high need for achievement tend to set moderate goals and are willing to take risks of a known nature. Such people also desire feedback on their performance. For example, a purchasing agent with a high need for achievement may expend a lot of time and energy trying to get unusually low prices on purchases of materials. A person in the same job with a lower need for achievement may accept the standard prices for these items. The *need for affiliation* reflects a desire to interact with people on a social basis. A person with a high need for affiliation is concerned about the quality of important personal relationships, and social relationships usually take precedence over task accomplishments for such people. The *need for power* reflects a desire to obtain and exercise power and authority. A person with a high need for power is concerned with influencing others and winning discussions. McClelland found power to have two possible directions: (a) negative, emphasizing dominance and submission; or (b) positive, emphasizing persuasion and inspirational behavior.

The main hypothesis of McClelland's theory is that these needs are learned through childhood socialization processes. Behavior which is rewarded is found to reoccur more than behavior which is either not rewarded or punished. Therefore, learned needs can be attributed to past behavior—either achievement, affiliation, or power displays—which was rewarded. Because each individual has a different record of past experiences, behaviors, and rewards, each individual also has a unique set of needs that will motivate future behavior.

Given that many needs are learned and take on the character or flavor of the social context in which they were learned, it becomes necessary to con-

[9]David C. McClelland, *Personality,* NY: Holt, Rinehart & Winston, 1951.

sider both the social context in which a need was learned and the social context in which it is being satisfied. (See diagram below.) The closer in time the two social contexts are, the more important it is to consider the social context in which a need was learned. The recency of the situation will make this need more prominent in the consumer's mind. For example, assume that a need for power was learned in a context of strong sibling rivalry. This family context might be especially appropriate when promoting products to these children. When these same children become adults, references to sibling rivalry will have less impact, and current contextual factors will be more important. This is true even though the basic power needs which were learned in childhood will still be present. The more similar the two contexts are to one another, the less relevant the time lag between the two contexts.

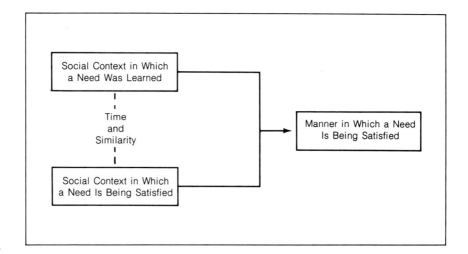

NEED CONFLICT AND RESOLUTION

Need conflict results when a person is prompted simultaneously by incompatible tendencies to satisfy one or more operating needs. There are four basic types of conflict situation.[10]

Approach-Approach Conflict

Sometimes individuals are compelled simultaneously and to an equal degree by two desirable but mutually exclusive action alternatives. The consumer

---

[10]Kurt Lewin, *Environmental Forces in Child Behavior and Development,* in C. Murchison (ed.). *A Handbook of Child Psychology,* Worcestor, Mass.; Clark University Press, 1931, and N. E. Miller, *Experimental Studies of Conflict,* in J. McV. Hunt (ed.), *Personality and the Behavior Disorders,* NY: Ronald Press, 1944.

trying to decide between two equally attractive brands of the same product class is in an approach-approach conflict situation. The consumer has equal positive preferences for each brand, though, often, one of the brands becomes more preferred than the other. This preference may be only slight, but it will be enough to break the conflict. The greater the perceived similarity of competing brands, the greater the likelihood of this type of conflict. Proposition 13-3 expresses this idea. This indicates the importance to the manager of developing strategies to make the promoted brand seem different from competing products.

EXHIBIT 13-2.
Propositions About Need
Conflict and
Complementarity

PROPOSITION 13-3.
The greater the perceived similarity of brands addressing the same need, the greater the likelihood of the consumer experiencing conflict in attempting to satisfy that need.

PROPOSITION 13-4.
The greater the complementarity of needs and resources between the buyer and seller, the greater the likelihood that a transaction will occur.

Approach-Avoidance
Conflict

Individuals are often prompted simultaneously to both do and not do something. The introduction of avoidance tendencies changes the nature of the conflict drastically. No external force or barrier is needed to keep the individual from just leaving or forgetting the situation, since the individual is trapped there by a desire to attain the goal and satisfy the relevant need. At the same time, the person is kept from the objective by fear or some other negative incentive associated with the goal. The individual usually vacillates to some extent, both approaching and retreating from the goal. A consumer who is considering the purchase of a product because of its need-satisfying potential, yet is concerned about spending the money, is in an approach-avoidance conflict situation. Final resolution may not necessarily occur; the consumer may continuously want the product, yet never purchase it.

Marketers should attempt to identify both the desirable and undesirable qualities of their products. This will enable them to either modify the product or accent the positive attributes and lessen the negative ones in promotional campaigns, credit policies, or service contracts.

Avoidance-
Avoidance Conflict

When a person is prompted to avoid two goals or courses of action, an avoidance-avoidance conflict exists. The individual who dreads going to the dentist, yet fears cavities, is in an avoidance-avoidance conflict situation. Since there is no way to avoid making a decision, the individual may vacillate back and forth until he or she is forced, perhaps by a toothache, into resolving the conflict. This is a case where, as the saying goes, not to decide is to decide.

Double Approach-Avoidance Conflict

In some conflict situations, each of two goals or lines of action invokes an approach-avoidance conflict. What often appear to be simply approach-approach or avoidance-avoidance conflicts are actually double approach-avoidance conflict situations. Consider the example of the individual who is afraid to visit the dentist. This can be described as a double approach-avoidance conflict if we view the trip to the dentist as providing the benefits of good health care for the individual's teeth at the cost of possibly being painful and expensive. On the other hand, we have the alternative of avoiding the dentist and thereby any pain or expense (a positive outcome if avoided) at the expense of the health of the teeth. A two-goal situation can be a double approach-avoidance situation when the two goals are mutually exclusive and exhaustive and both elicit avoidance as well as approach tendencies.

Figure 13-4 diagrams the four types of basic conflict situations which are likely to be encountered by consumers trying to satisfy their needs.

Need Complementarity

Group interaction may either facilitate or interfere with the satisfaction of an individual's needs and those of other members of the group. When the needs of two or more persons can be mutually satisfied through interpersonal activities, their needs are considered compatible or complementary. When their needs cannot be satisfied through interaction, they are incompatible.

The greater the complementarity of the needs and resources of the buyer and seller, the more likely it is that a transaction will occur between them (as represented by Proposition 13-4). In consumer and industrial buying behavior, the buyer is searching for the seller whose product or service best matches the desired requirements. The seller is searching for the segment of the market for whom the available product will offer the greatest benefits. Thus, the product offering of the seller must complement the needs of the buyer in order for their relationship to be mutually satisfactory.

The main implication of Proposition 13-4 concerns market segmentation. The marketer cannot be all things to all people, but must seek and identify that portion of the total potential market for which the product or service provides the greatest benefit or satisfaction. Again, market research for the purpose of identifying the needs and resources of the consumer is essential. Assessment of the strengths and weaknesses inherent in the marketing organization is also required. A careful matching of the strength of the marketing organization and the needs of the consumer results in the best relationship between buyer and seller.

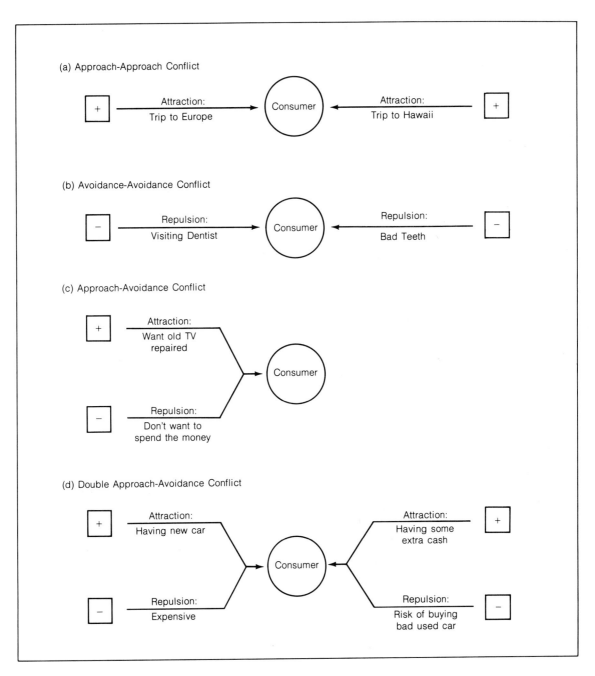

FIGURE 13-4   Adapted from Cofer and Appley, *Motivation: Theory and Research,* p. 434; and Janis, *et*
Need Conflict   *al., Personality Dynamics Development and Assessment,* pp. 221–22.

NEEDS IN ORGANIZATIONS

Organizations as well as individuals have needs. These needs are rooted in the stress and strain that organizations experience. *Organizational strain is the inconsistency existing between or among different parts of the organization.* [11] Strain may exist in a purchase decision when the production department prefers an expensive version of a machine, while the financial department urges a less expensive version. The importance of initial price and maintenance costs to a director of purchasing and/or to a buying committee may be very salient if this strain is very strong. *Organizational stress is reflected by the difference between what is demanded of the organization and what it is capable of providing.* Demand for an organization's output might exceed what its production facilities are able to provide. This condition may create the perceived need for new production machinery or equipment. This stress may produce strain in the organization's decision process concerning what machine to buy. Strain and stress are related because each may influence the other.

Stress and strain are present in all organizations. The causes, location, and level of stress and strain typically fluctuate over time within any organization. An important determinant of an organization's behavior as a consumer is how the organization manages stress and strain. Does the production department usually get its way in purchase decisions? Does the organization usually respond quickly to unanticipated changes in demand by expanding or contracting its capacity? Unfortunately, there appear to be no published studies in the marketing or organizational behavior literature which discuss the impact of stress and strain on the consumer behavior of organizations. There is, however, a very substantial literature on organizational stress and strain in general. Some of this material lends itself to translations to organizational buying behavior. Since the discussion to follow is in need of empirical verification, no formal propositions will be suggested.

Organizational Strain

Strain may arise from inconsistent norms. A purchasing agent may be charged with the responsibility of identifying the best suppliers (quality norms) and minimizing the cost of goods purchased (economic norms). But, the suppliers whose delivery time and product quality are best may also submit the highest bids. Or, the purchasing agent may want to favor one firm over another for reasons unrelated to product quality or bid price (e.g., norm of reciprocity).

---

[11]Peter Abell, (ed.), *Organizations as Bargaining and Influence Systems*, NY: Halsted Press, 1975.

Strain may also occur between people because of *disagreement over norms* which relate to their positions. The purchasing agent may believe that part of that position involves participating in the selection of the actual supplier, in addition to the task of identifying good potential suppliers. Other members of the buying committee may disagree with this interpretation of the purchasing agent role. One reason for their disagreement might be that the purchasing agent would be too influential if he or she were involved in identifying potential suppliers as well as soliciting and evaluating those bids.[12] Thus, strain may develop between the purchasing agent and others in the company. (This was partially discussed in the section on role strain in Chapter 7.)

Situations occur in which too many demands are made of a person. This, too, creates strain when, for example, the purchasing agent must establish priorities about whose needs in the organization will be attended to first. Those persons or groups assigned a low priority will protest and the conflict will produce strain.

Strain may also result when norms are very clear and perceived to be equitable, but where department heads may be *personally incompatible*. This will often surface in such situations as buying committee meetings and can result in drawn out purchase decision processes.

Another type of strain results from *inadequate and incompatible resources*. For example, the competition for funds within an organization may produce strain among different parts of the organization. This competition may heighten or produce interpersonal unpleasantries.

Thus, three basic and interrelated factors contribute to organizational strain. These are shown in Figure 13-5.

Organizational Stress   There are various organizational stresses which constitute needs to be satisfied. Stress may arise from changes in one or both of two factors: changes in demands upon the organization, and changes in organizational capacity.

Changes in demands include quantitative changes, changes in priorities, and qualitative changes. Quantitative changes in the demand for an organization's products or services precipitate stress when: (1) contingency plans do not exist to cover the demand change; (2) the change is sudden; and (3) the change is unanticipated. The change in demand may be upward or downward. Stress will be manifest when disagreement exists about whether a response is necessary, as well as what the response to the change should be. The organization, in effect, shops for a solution to the problem. The solution

---

[12]Gerald Zaltman and Thomas V. Bonoma (eds.), *Organizational Buying Behavior*, Chicago: American Marketing Association, 1978.

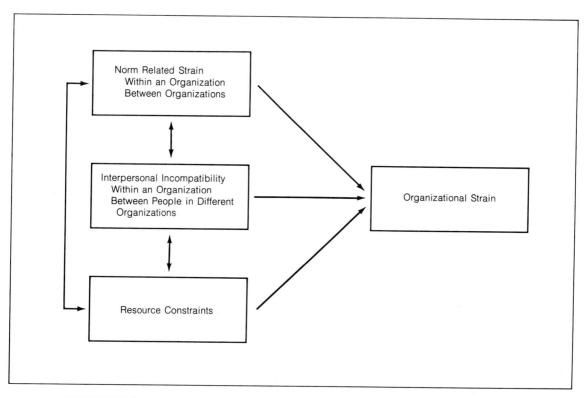

FIGURE 13-5.
Factors Contributing to
Organizational Strain

might be one which affects buying behavior, such as the acquisition of additional equipment and supplies in the case of an increase in demand.

There may also be changes in the priorities assigned to various activities of the firm. If allocations to promotion are based on a percentage of sales, a decrease in demand may result in a cutback on advertising and other promotional activity which would create problems for the marketing division. Obviously, this also affects the selling of media time and space by representatives of the mass media. Also affected will be future sales since promotional activity was decreased. This may create additional stress in the future. Environmental protection legislation and rulings may require a firm to place greater emphasis upon pollution control, which in turn may affect the allocation of resources within a firm and make it a better potential customer of pollution control devices and technology.

Qualitative changes are important, too. These are changes which constitute a type of demand not previously experienced or perhaps demands for an improvement in the way a firm is meeting current demands. A decision to enter a new market because of the profit potential of demand in that market could produce stress as the firm makes errors in becoming familiar with the market. Stress may also occur when customers demand more reliable products, but where existing technology is not adequate enough to permit the desired improvements.

Changes in organizational capacity are the second major source of stress. Whenever an organization loses critical resources, such as personnel, or experiences shortages in materials needed for production, stress will increase. Thus, even the absence of product or market information at the time a purchase decision or market entry decision must be made may constitute a change in organizational capacity.

When strain due to interpersonal conflict becomes too excessive, the organization may experience a loss of capacity, and thus undergo stress. As mentioned earlier, interpersonal conflict within a buying committee may result in a longer decision process and perhaps a lower quality decision. The head of the buying committee may prefer a compromise solution rather than a solution which is optimal from the standpoint of a given purchase need.

As shown below, changes in demand and capacity influence each other, as well as the level of stress.

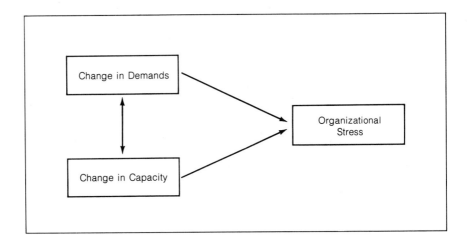

Organizational strain and stress are fluctuating, but permanent, features of nearly all organizations, and have important impacts on organizational buying behavior. Organizational stress and strain influence what purchases are made, as well as how purchase decisions are made. States of organizational strain and stress dictate the needs to be satisfied.

RESEARCH RELATED TO THE NEED CONCEPT IN MARKETING

The concept of needs is central to the discipline of marketing because the marketing concept essentially involves the identification and satisfaction of consumer needs. At this point, we examine some of the research marketers have done on consumer needs. Some of the research has been of a general nature concerning the total idea of needs, while other research has concentrated on specific needs and their effects on consumer behavior.

Distinguishing Between Needs, Wants, and Demands

One writer proposed a conceptual distinction between needs, wants, and demands on the basis of their level of specificity.[13] *Needs* were seen as broad, fundamental requirements which propel behavior, but which are less likely to give any specific direction to that behavior. Needs, then, represented requirements which could accept a wide variety of satisfactory solutions. Thus, needs correspond to the product group. *Wants* were seen as more specific and as relating to the product level class, while *demand* belongs at the brand or variant level. For example, a need for protection and safety can be met in many different ways. One way might be through the use of personal cleanliness and personal care products (a product group). A consumer might want to have clean-smelling breath as well as protection from germs, and so this consumer might use mouthwash (a product class). Furthermore, the consumer might have a preference for (demand) a particular brand which meets those wants and needs.

Need for Achievement

More specific research has been conducted on the need for achievement and its effect on consumer preferences and behavior.[14] One study used a measure of the need for achievement to study differences in product perceptions between consumers with high and low need for achievement.[15] The results indicated that consumers differ in their perceptions of products in relation to their self and ideal self-images.

---

[13]Johan Arndt, "How Broad Should the Marketing Concept Be?" *Journal of Marketing,* Vol. 42, January, 1978, pp. 101–103.

[14]F. B. Evans, "Psychological and Objective Prediction of Brand Choice," *Journal of Business,* 1959, Vol. 32, pp. 340–369; A. Koponen, "Personality Characteristics of Purchases," *Journal of Advertising Research,* Vol. 1, 1960, pp. 6–12; T. S. Robertson and J. H. Myers, "Personality Correlates of Opinion Leadership and Innovative Buyer Behavior," *Journal of Marketing Research,* Vol. 6, 1969, pp. 164–168; E. L. Landon, Jr., "A Sex-Role Explanation of Purchase Intention Differences of Consumers Who are High and Low in Need for Achievement," *ACR Proceedings,* 1972, pp. 1–8; and David M. Gardner, "An Exploratory Investigation of Achievement Motivation Effects on Consumer Behavior," *ACR Proceedings,* 1972, pp. 20–23.

[15]Landon, *op. cit.*

In a second study, the same researcher presented additional findings on the relationship between the need for achievement and intentions to buy products and the timing of those intentions.[16] The results of this study showed that males with a high need for achievement plan to buy more of some kinds of products than do males with low needs for achievement. Females with a high need for achievement plan to buy some products sooner and some products later than do low need for achievement females. Figure 13-6 illustrates some of these differences.

FIGURE 13-6.
Some Differences in Intentions to Buy Various Products and the Need for Achievement (n Ach)

	Male	*Female*
High n Ach	Boating equipment Straight razor Skis Manual (push) lawn mower	Mouthwash Aluminum foil Headache remedy
Low n Ach	Automatic dishwasher Headache remedy Mouthwash Electric toothbrush Deodorant	Color telephone Luggage Fabric softener Electric toothbrush

Gardner also examined the effects of achievement motivation on consumer behavior.[17] In his study, he examined various relationships between consumers' purchases and preferences and their need for achievement.

This study had several interesting findings:

1. Male consumers with a high need for achievement had a preference for purchasing suits and sport coats from specialty clothing stores.
2. Consumers with a high need for achievement tend to buy more products classified in the outdoor sports category and less clothing of the mod
3. design. This may be because of risk avoidance.
   More difficult to explain is the low ranking given to luxury cars by con-
4. sumers with a high need for achievement.
   A very high percentage of the consumers with a moderately high need for achievement are cigarette smokers. This is consistent with earlier research.

---

[16]E. L. Landon, Jr., "Role of Need for Achievement in the Perception of Products," *APA Proceedings,* 1972.

[17]Gardner, *op. cit.,* p. 23.

(5) There was little evidence to support the suggestion that brand names are more important to consumers with high need for achievement.

The researcher believed that brand names do not influence the amount of perceived risk and/or are not subject to reference group influence.

As a result of the findings of these two studies, we arrive at Proposition 13-5 in Exhibit 13-3.

EXHIBIT 13-3.
Propositions About the Needs for Achievement and Stimulation

PROPOSITION 13-5.
With respect to male consumers, the higher the need for achievement, the more likely the consumer is to shop in specialty and department stores.

PROPOSITION 13-6.
The higher the consumers' need for stimulation, the more likely they are to use innovative shopping facilities.

The implication of this proposition for the marketer is that male consumers tend to shop for certain products and services and in certain stores based upon their need for achievement. By identifying the relationship between the need for achievement and consumer behavior, marketers can place the products in stores that have the appropriate image.

Need for Stimulation   A group of researchers studied consumer need for stimulation as it related to innovative shopping behavior.[18] In their research, the recent phenomenon of recycling urban facilities, such as an old warehouse, into shopping complexes was linked with innovation types and an individual's optimal level of stimulation. The researchers hypothesized that the attractiveness of recycled urban facilities used as retail shopping centers varied according to the customers' needs for stimulation. More specifically, the proportion of customers seeking a high level of stimulation who:[19]

1. are aware of the retail innovation,

---

[18]S. L. Grossbart, R. A. Mittelstaedt, and S. P. DeVere, "Customer Stimulation Needs and Innovative Shopping Behavior: The Case of Recycled Urban Places," *ACR Proceedings,* Vol. 3, 1976, pp. 30–35.

[19]*Ibid.,* p. 32.

2. consider shopping at the retail innovation,

3. symbolically accept the idea of the retail innovation,

4. actually shop at the retail innovation, and

5. confirm the decision to continue shopping at the retail innovation,

will exceed the proportion of low stimulus seeking customers exhibiting the same behavior.

The research supported all the formulated hypotheses and led to Proposition 13-6: The higher consumers' needs for stimulation, the more likely it is that they will accept and use innovative shopping facilities. This implies that, when introducing a new shopping facility, and perhaps even a new type of product, those consumers with a high need for stimulation should be the initial target market for the service or product. A major problem lies in differentiating between high and low stimulus seeking consumers on the basis of easily used market segmentation variables. Difficulties may arise when measuring the need for stimulation and finding ways to reach consumers who are high in this need. Do high (compared to low) stimulus seeking consumers read different magazines, watch different television programs, or patronize different types of stores? If the answers to such questions are in the affirmative, then the need for stimulation may be a useful concept.

SUMMARY Though the concept of needs is an important part of the marketing concept, its study has received less than the deserved emphasis. There has been no attempt by marketers to define clearly what is implied when they use the term "need." Each theory of needs borrowed from psychology defines need in a particular context from which it cannot be removed or used very readily to define consumer needs.

There is little or no integrated theory of the several typologies and theories of needs (e.g., Maslow and McClelland) which marketers have used in examining consumer behavior.

Far too little empirical research has been conducted and with very little success. Several attempts (not reported here) have failed to validate Maslow's hierarchy of needs. Achievement motivation has received more attention than the other types of needs in research concerned with buyer behavior. One can only speculate about the results of an integrated attempt also concerned with power and affiliation needs, as well as achievement, and the many other needs which can be listed.

For the concept of needs to become meaningful in the understanding of consumer behavior, marketers must define need on a level useful to the field of marketing; operationalize the concept so that meaningful hypotheses can be tested; develop an integrated theory of how needs affect consumer behavior; and empirically test and validate the theory.

KEY CONCEPTS   Approach-approach conflict
Approach-avoidance conflict
Avoidance-avoidance conflict
Need
Need for achievement
Need for affiliation
Organizational strain
Organizational stress
Self-actualization

CONSUMER MOTIVATION*

14

CHAPTER GOALS

The objective of this chapter is to help readers understand:
1. **several psychological theories of motivation;**
2. **a taxonomy of motives and how these motives are reflected in consumer behavior;**
3. **the contributions and limitations of motivation research;**
4. **the similarity between ultimate consumers and industrial buyers in their motivations as consumers.**

INTRODUCTION

Prior to our choosing one product rather than another, what motivates us to buy in the first place? The answer to this question may or may not seem obvious, but any study of consumer behavior is incomplete unless one addresses the problem of consumer motivation—an area of behavior that underscores the link between individual and group (or social) psychology.[1]

What kinds of motivations are there? When we are caught in heavy rain without anything to protect us, our desire to keep dry will most likely motivate us to buy an umbrella in a nearby store, or to have a cup of coffee in a cafe while we wait for the storm to pass. Our desire for entertainment might, on another occasion, lead us to a film, a concert, or a restaurant. A different type of motivation would result from our ambition for rapid promotions within a company, an ambition that might compel us to do (or purchase) anything necessary to achieve our goal.

---

*Professor Wesley Johnston, Ohio State University, is co-author of this chapter.

[1]See Don Hellriegel and John W. Slocum, Jr., *Organizational Behavior: Contingency Views*, St. Paul: West Publishing Company, 1976.

So, when marketing managers ponder "What motivates consumer behavior?" they are trying to determine which one, or set, of the following types of motivations is important in a given situation:

(1) an environmental determinant which precipitated the behavior in question—the application of some irresistible force which of necessity led to this action;

(2) the internal urge, wish, feeling, emotion, drive, instinct, want, desire, demand, purpose, interest, aspiration, plan, need, or motive which gave rise to the action;

(3) the incentive, goal, or object value which attracted or repelled the (customer).[2]

A problem confronting marketers in the area of consumer motivation is the difficulty of integrating the many theories and models that have been proposed. In this chapter we will first review several theories and models of motivation. Then, a very recent and quite comprehensive taxonomy of motivations will be presented. This will enable the reader to obtain an overall understanding of the motivation concept. Finally, several attempts to employ motivations as explanatory variables in trying to understand consumer behavior will be discussed.

Most of us have an intuitive definition of motivation. For instance, we commonly hear such statements as "I must get motivated and start getting things done," or "He's hard to motivate," or "I don't know what motivated me to do that." Coming to an explicit definition, however, has been a problem for many people.[3] As we will see in discussing different theories of motivation, each theorist has a slightly different approach to the concept. For our purposes, motivation is a force which leads a person to act in a particular way in response to a need. This force can be physiological, social, internal, or external to the consumer, conscious or unconscious, and instinctual or learned. Thus, needs are more basic than motives. Needs are channeled and fulfilled in a particular way by motives.

THEORIES OF MOTIVATION

A comprehensive review of all the theories of motivation is not possible here. (The interested reader should see Cofer and Appley, or Weiner.)[4] What will be

[2]C. N. Cofer and M. H. Appley, *Motivation: Theory and Research,* NY: John Wiley & Sons, Inc., 1964, p. 5.

[3]C. Glen Walters, *Consumer Behavior, Theory and Practice,* Homewood, IL: Irwin, 1974, p. 120; P. T. Young, *Motivation and Emotion: A Survey of the Determinants of Human and Animal Activity,* NY: Wiley, 1961, p. 24; and Thomas S. Robertson, *Consumer Behavior,* Glenview, IL: Scott, Foresman and Company, 1970, p. 32.

[4]C. N. Cofer and M. H. Appley, 1964, *op. cit.;* Bernard Weiner, *Theories of Motivation: From Mechanism to Cognition,* Chicago: Markham Publishing Co., 1972.

presented is a brief development of the major movements and theories of motivation, including the instinct theories of Sigmund Freud and William McDougall, the drive theory of C. L. Hull, field theory as conceptualized by Kurt Lewin, Murray's social motives, and McClelland's extension of Murray's work.

Instinct Theories

Scientific theories of motivation appear to have originated with Charles Darwin's theory of evolution.[5] Until Darwin, people had been viewed by psychologists as essentially rational beings responsible for their actions. Darwin thought, however, that certain "intelligent" actions (called "reflexes" and "instincts") were inherited, and therefore not all behavior was preplanned and controlled by thought.

Following Darwin's lead, William James, Sigmund Freud, and William McDougall developed instinct theories, making instinct an important explanatory concept in psychology. The concept of irrational people, lacking control over their own behavior, was central to the development of Freud's psychoanalytic theory. Freud's theory placed the motivational emphasis on sexual and aggressive instincts (see Chapter 15 on personality). McDougall compiled the following list of instincts which he felt accounted for most or all of behavior: flight, repulsion, curiosity, pugnacity, self-abasement, self-assertion, parenting, reproduction, hunger, gregariousness, acquisitiveness, and constructiveness.[6]

The instinct theories dominated the psychological view of motivation for the first twenty-five years of this century. The major problem encountered toward the end of this period was the growth of the list of instincts by which behavior could be explained: "Each author added a few more until by the nineteen-twenties the list totaled nearly 6,000 instincts, including an 'instinct to avoid eating apples in one's own orchard'."[7] The instinct theories were then replaced by the concept of drive.

Drive Theories

The concept of drive remained perhaps the most prominent concept in the field of motivation until recently. In 1918, Woodworth used this concept to describe the "energy" that impels an organism to action, as opposed to the view that habits steer behavior in one direction or another.[8] The term "drive"

---

[5]Charles Darwin, *The Decent of Man and Selection in Relation to Sex,* NY: Appleton, 1896.

[6]W. McDougall, *An Introduction to Social Psychology,* NY: Barnes and Noble, 1960 (original 1908).

[7]Edward J. Murray, *Motivation and Emotion,* Englewood Cliffs, NJ: Prentice-Hall, Inc., 1964, p. 6.

[8]*Ibid.,* p. 6.

describes the motivational aspect of bodily disequilibrium, such as would come from lack of food, resulting in a striving for satisfaction of needs and a return to equilibrium. Motivation was defined as the drives arising out of an imbalance or tension.

The drive concept has had its greatest influence on the field of learning (see Chapter 10). Clark L. Hull's primary interest was in the formation of habits and the activation of those associations.[9] He believed that learning occurs as a consequence of reinforcement. He also assumed that all rewards are ultimately based on the reduction of primary, homeostatic drives. The heart of Hull's theory is the mathematical formulation of the relationship between drive and habit strength:

$$\text{strength of motivation} = \text{a function of (drive} \times \text{habit)}$$

Habit strength is a result of previous factors of reinforcement, and drive is the total sum of the physiological imbalances caused by the deprivation of the commodities necessary for survival. Though today, most consumers in developed countries are not deprived of the commodities necessary for survival, Hull's theory can provide us, nevertheless, with some useful marketing ideas.

If, through advertising or use, a product or service can be associated with the reduction of a drive, the product or service will come to be a secondary reinforcer. That is, because of the positive association, seeing or remembering the product will elicit a drive to obtain the product. This is based on the assumption that a product or service, although itself not a primary reinforcer or drive-reducer, can acquire the properties of a reinforcer if it occurs repeatedly and consistently in close connection with a reinforcing stimulus or state of affairs. For instance, ice cream may be associated with fun family outings when one is a child, and these associations will reinforce a consumer's belief that ice cream is fun to eat.

The more a specific action associated with a product or service has been rewarded in the past, the stronger will be the desire to repeat the action when the drive arises again (this idea is Proposition 14-1). This implies that marketers must make certain that consumers receive and are aware of receiving rewards for purchasing and using particular products.

Many psychologists, however, have found drive theory to be unsatisfactory, their primary criticism being that drive theory is too simplistic to explain the complicated and deep aspects of human behavior. Drive theory says humans are identical to animals which are moved by external stimuli and respond in the only way possible given previous experiences. More recent approaches demonstrate that human cognition or thought should be taken into account in any theory attempting to explain motivation.

---

[9]Clark L. Hull, *Principles of Behavior*, NY: Appleton-Century-Crofts, 1943.

EXHIBIT 14-1.
*Propositions
Concerning Drive*

> PROPOSITION 14-1.
> The more a specific action associated with a product or service has been rewarded in the past, the stronger will be the desire to repeat the action when the drive arises again.
>
> PROPOSITION 14-2.
> The longer a state of tension exists because a goal has not been reached, the stronger the motivation toward that goal will be.

Field Theory

Field theory, as conceptualized by Kurt Lewin, offers a more cognitive approach to the study of behavior and motivation.[10] This theory focuses more on the actual thoughts of the person, rather than on instincts or habits. Field theory states that behavior is a function of the field at a moment in time—the whole situation must be considered. This position originated with the Gestalt psychologists. Lewin believed with the Gestaltists that behavior is a function of the person and the environment; that the person and the environment comprise the life space representing psychological reality. This life space depicts the totality of factions which determine behavior at a moment in time. The life space is represented as a finitely structured space, as in Figure 14-1, which depicts the environment of an individual who wants to go to a football game. The regions represent the instrumental activities required and the path through which the individual must pass to reach the goal or desired object.

A need creates a state of tension in a system, and each tense state is associated with a particular class of goal objects (such as products). The disequilibrium of tense states initiates either a push or pull force on the individual to move toward or away from the goal. The attainment of a goal usually reduces the level of tension within the individual. Goal attainment, however, need not involve the actual consumption of the desired object. The level of tension may be reduced by just thinking about some object or event, or, in our example, by going to an actual game. This is an important contrast to the drive theory of Hull, for in Hull's conception it is difficult to condition goal responses if the goal is not consumed.

An interesting idea of Lewin's is that motivation may increase if tension is maintained very long. This is reflected in Proposition 14-2 of Exhibit 14-1,

---

[10]Kurt Lewin, *The Conceptual Representation and the Measurement of Psychological Forces,* Durham, NC: Duke University Press, 1938.

FIGURE 14-1.
Life Space

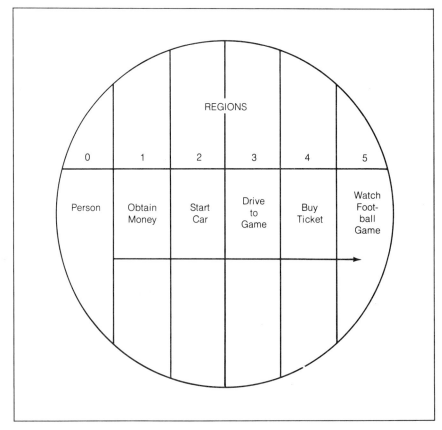

REGIONS

| 0 | 1 | 2 | 3 | 4 | 5 |

| Person | Obtain Money | Start Car | Drive to Game | Buy Ticket | Watch Football Game |

Adapted from Weiner, op. cit., p. 112.

which states that motives grow in strength to the extent that frequent preoccupation with a set of goals is not accompanied by gratification of the motive. Advertising, then, may demonstrate that a product satisfying a goal for another person can do the same for the audience. To the extent that the audience recognizes the goal object portrayed, and the number of exposures to the product increases, their motivation toward buying the product should increase.

Achievement Theory and Other Social Motives

Edward J. Murray introduced the idea that behavior was not only a cognitive process, but also a function of the social environment. Murray formed a list of "psychogenic needs" or, as they are sometimes called, "social motives."[11]

---

[11]Edward J. Murray, *op. cit.*, p. 97.

Murray's list of social motives is presented in Table 14-1. It is useful to go through Table 14-1 and try to think of products or purchase strategies which would reflect each of the motives listed. For example, a person may purchase

TABLE 14-1.
*List of Murray's Social Motives**

Social Motive	Brief Description
Abasement	To submit passively to external force. To accept injury, blame, criticism, punishment.
Achievement	To accomplish something difficult. To master, manipulate, or organize physical objects, human beings, or ideas.
Affiliation	To draw near and enjoyably cooperate or reciprocate with an allied other (an other who resembles the subject or who likes the subject).
Aggression	To overcome opposition forcefully. To fight.
Autonomy	To get free, shake off restraint, break out of confinement. To be independent and free to act according to impulse.
Counteraction	To master or make up for a failure by restriving. To obliterate a humiliation by resumed action. To overcome weaknesses, to repress fear.
Defendance	To defend the self against assault, criticism, and blame.
Dominance	To control one's human environment. To influence or direct the behavior of others by suggestion, seduction, persuasion, or command.
Exhibition	To make an impression. To be seen and heard.
Harm avoidance	To avoid pain, physical injury, illness, and death. To take precautionary measures.
Infavoidance	To avoid humiliation. To quit embarrassing situations or to avoid conditions which may lead to belittlement, the scorn, derision, or indifference of others.
Nurturance	To give sympathy and gratify the needs of a helpless object.
Order	To achieve cleanliness, arrangement, organization, balance, neatness, tidiness, and precision.
Play	To act for "fun" without further purpose. To like to laugh and make jokes.
Rejection	To exclude, abandon, expel, or remain indifferent to an inferior object. To snub or jilt an object.
Sentinence	To seek and enjoy sensuous impressions.
Sex	To form and further an erotic relationship. To have sexual intercourse.
Succorance	To have one's needs gratified by the sympathetic aid of an allied object. To always have a supporter.
Understanding	To ask or answer general questions. To be interested in theory.

*From C. S. Hall and G. Lindzey, *Theories of Personality,* NY: Wiley, 1957.

deodorant because of motives of infavoidance and order. Murray did not contend that behavior could be explained given only a knowledge of the motives or personality makeup of the individual, but believed, like Lewin, that behavior is a function of the characteristics of the environment, as well as the properties of the person. Murray developed the Thematic Apperception Test (TAT) which was used by his followers who delved deeper into the area of achievement motivation. These followers included John Atkinson and David McClelland, who were discussed in Chapter 13 on needs. For example, the needs McClelland primarily examined (the need for achievement, for affiliation, and for power) were derived from Murray's list.

A CLASSIFICATION OF MOTIVATIONS

It is very difficult to collect and form the many theories into an overall classification. There has been, however, a recent attempt to integrate the many theories of motivation.[12] This classification of motives capsulizes most of the theories of motivation which are supported by psychologists and others concerned with human motivation. Figure 14-2 portrays this graphic classification of motives. Each of these types of motivation is potentially relevant to consumer behavior. They are not mutually exclusive. In fact, different theories seem to explain different behaviors.

The major division among the motives discussed in the chart is between those that are cognitive and those that are affective in nature. This distinction might be clarified by viewing cognitive motives as those forces that *orient the individual's thinking.* Affective motives can be viewed as stressing the aspects of motivation that *energize a person's feelings.* "The cognitive motives stress the person's information processing and attainment of ideational states, while the affective motives stress the person's feelings and attainment of certain emotional states."[13] The other dimensions along which the table of motives is divided are initiation by the individual (active or passive); the orientation of the motive to the individual (internal or external); and the stability of the individual with respect to the motive (growth or preservation). These distinctions will become clearer as each of the cells is discussed.

Cognitive Motives

1. Consistency. As was discussed in Chapter 12 on information processing, consumers may be viewed as processing units for the conflicting forces and pieces of information that come to their attention. The motive to organize

---

[12]William J. McGuire, "Psychological Motives and Communication Gratification," in J. G. Blumier and Elihu Katz (eds.), *The Uses of Mass Communications: Current Perspectives on Gratifications Research,* Vol. 3, Beverly Hills, CA: Sage Publications, Inc., 1974, p. 172.

[13]*Ibid.,* p. 173.

FIGURE 14-2.
A Structuring of Sixteen
General Paradigms of
Human Motivation

INITIATION Mode \ Orienta-tion and Stability		ACTIVE		PASSIVE	
		Internal	External	Internal	External
Cognitive	Preservation	1. Consistency	2. Attribution	3. Categorization	4. Objectification
	Growth	5. Autonomy	6. Stimulation	7. Teleological	8. Utilitarian
Affective	Preservation	9. Tension-reduction	10. Expressive	11. Ego-Defensive	12. Reinforcement
	Growth	13. Assertion	14. Affiliation	15. Identification	16. Modeling

Source: McGuire, 1974, p. 172.

all of these diverse data into a coherent picture of the world can be called the consistency motive. Maintaining an inner balance, one that is consistent and coherent, is the basic motivation.

A consumer's tendency to perceive positive relationships between price and quality, or between store prestige and both product quality and quality of assistance provided by the store's sales personnel, may be a result of the consistency motive. If quality is uncertain and price is high, the consumer may reason that price is high because of the added expense of producing a well-made product. Thus, perceptions of product quality become consistent with price perceptions. The consumer may similarly reason that a prestigious store would not stock poor quality merchandise or employ inept sales personnel. One is motivated to seek or perceive consistency in order to lessen the discomfort of having information which is uncertain or incompatible with other information.

2. Attribution. The focus here is on the consumer's orientation toward external happenings in the environment. The desire to explain why something occurred, to know the cause of a particular event and thereby to understand one's world, is characteristic of the motive of attribution. Chapter 17 focuses extensively on attributions, so we shall not elaborate upon this subject here.

3. Categorization. Consumers confront an overly complex world, and therefore, some have the desire to simplify their experiences and the actions required of them by sorting their experiences into a set of categories. It is as if consumers were motivated to set up mental file folders for categorizing their experiences; but, the mental filing system helps them order their experiences and retrieve them from memory. The motive of categorization is more passive than others.

In some industrial settings, purchasing agents have begun using computers to help process information about alternative suppliers. Without computers it is extremely difficult to assess past supplier information along with detailed and often complex product information, pricing arrangements, and delivery schedules. Computer systems are one technique for handling information without losing any because of memory failure or selective perception. The computer programs usually sort different suppliers into categories which represent groups of varying desirability.

The individual consumer has a few facilitating mechanisms for categorizing information. Unit pricing is an attempt to provide consumers with information which allows them to make direct comparisons between products on a price-per-unit-of-weight basis. This allows them to bypass the various mental tasks of calculating this themselves or remembering the unit prices of products. Introducing a new product under a family brand name, such as Heinz or General Mills, is a strategy which draws upon the tendency to "lump" products of the same brand name together. In effect, the company hopes the consumer will file the new product information in the same category as information on other products with the same family brand name. The new product is conveniently assigned by the consumer the positive and negative attributes of the family brand name, and the consumer avoids having to determine in an explicit way what the actual positive and negative attributes are.

4. Objectification. Many consumers are unable to understand themselves by self-reflection alone, so they often gain insights into their motives by observing their behaviors and inferring what the reason(s) for acting a certain way must have been. This is similar to watching the behavior of others in order to understand the motive behind the other person's behavior. When consumers are required to develop a viewpoint on a subject, they first review their behavior, and then, based upon their previous actions, decide upon an attitude toward the subject. For instance, when required to give an opinion on football, consumers review their behavior toward football in the past, and finding that they have never gone to a game and rarely watch it on television, decide they do not like football very much (see the section on self-attributions in Chapter 17).

5. Autonomy. This is the epitome of the humanistic approach toward what motivates people, characterizing some consumers as seeking self-realization through forming an integrated, autonomous identity. Maslow's hierarchy of needs (self-actualization theory) examined in Chapter 13 on consumer needs is an example of this concept. This theory of motivation stresses the individual's growth needs. Thus, some consumption choices would be based on a motive to grow and feel more fulfilled.

6. Stimulation. Some consumers have a need or desire for stimulation. The consumer is naturally curious and seeks novelty. The stimulation motive leads people to try different activities and products.

The stimulation motive is believed to be responsible for much innovative behavior among consumers. Consumers with a high stimulation motivation may be "low loyals." That is, what caused them to try a new product or brand may prevent them from continuing to use it for very long, especially if competitive items become available to them. Thus, brand loyalty might be difficult to achieve among consumers with high motives for stimulation.

7. Teleological. Teleologically motivated consumers constantly compare their ideal or desired situation with their perceptions of the present situation, trying to make the real situation become as close as possible to the ideal. Various activities, such as product or service selection and use, are constantly monitored by consumers to determine whether the gap between the desired and perceived present situation is increasing or decreasing. If a new product's performance is closer to the ideal than a previously used brand, the new product will be adopted. Comparison shopping behavior may be stimulated by teleological motivations. When a consumer is inspecting merchandise in a store and finds the products to be of lower quality than desired, the consumer is likely to visit another store to see whether product quality is better and therefore closer to the desired situation.

8. Utilitarian. Utilitarian consumers are motived by external opportunities to solve problems, and thereby desire to gain useful information or new skills to be used in coping with life's challenges. The consumer assumes a positive attitude toward the problems that life presents and views these problems as a valuable source of helpful and relevant information. Lewin's field theory of motivation views such a person as moving through the regions of the life space, constantly gaining new skills and abilities for coping. For example, shopping decisions are perceived to be challenges which can best be met by first gathering as much product information as possible through both marketer- and consumer-dominated channels of information.[14]

Legislators and other public policy formulators often behave as if all consumers were accurately described by the utilitarian model of consumer motivations. This assumption would account for the frequent use of informa-

---

[14]Joseph W. Newman and Bradley D. Lockman, "Informational and Normative Social Influence in Buyer Behavior," *Journal of Consumer Research,* Vol. 2, No. 3, December, 1975, pp. 216–222.

tion disclosure regulations to help consumers make better consumption choices. This will be elaborated upon in Chapter 20 on consumer benefit programs.

Affective Motives   **9. Tension-reduction.**   This approach to motivation views the consumer as a system seeking homeostasis or equilibrium. Any reduction of arousal or drive is gratifying and any increase is unpleasant. Hull's drive theory, discussed earlier in this chapter, would be an example of a theory incorporating this type of motivation. Consumers are motivated to reduce the tension caused by their drives until they reach the point of zero arousal. The problem with this perspective, however, is that some drives are for positive stimulation and are self-reinforcing. Drug addiction is an example. In other words, some consumers are motivated to reduce tension, while others are motivated to seek stimulation.

10. Expression.   Consumers are sometimes motivated by desires for self-expression. Acting out one's feelings and beliefs is seen as rewarding. Expression motives lead a consumer to desire to be remembered by others such as through an achievement or by changing the world through one's own powers. These actions would be rewarding in themselves, with a value totally independent of the utilitarian return that they might create. Dressing in unique ways may reflect an expression motivation. The classic clothing sales line, "That suit (dress) is definitely you!" reflects the presence and importance of this motivation.

11. Ego-Defense.   The essential idea underlying the concept of ego-defense motivations is that people desire to protect their own self-images. They are comfortable with these images, and because they enable persons to cope with themselves and with life, persons are motivated to defend these self-images.

12. Reinforcement.   The consumer guided by strong reinforcement motivations behaves in ways which have been rewarded or reinforced in the past. Experiences that were associated with rewards in the past also acquire positive motivational force or secondary reward value. Brand loyalty is established in part by the presence of reinforcement motivation (see Chapter 10 on learning and the section in Chapter 11 on brand loyalty). The stimulus-response theories of Watson, Pavlov, and Skinner would come under the reinforcement concept of motivation.

13. Assertion.   The assertion view of motivation stresses the idea that consumers are competitors interested in achievement and success, admiration, and power. Striving to do better and to develop one's potential is a way to enhance both self-esteem and admiration from one's peers. The needs for achievement and power are motives of an assertional type (see the discussion of these needs in Chapter 13). Thus, some products and services are acquired because they symbolize the successful satisfaction of assertion motives: "I made it." Figure 14-3 is an advertisement for a brand of scotch and reflects the attempt to demonstrate the association between this scotch and the successful achievement of financial security.

14. Affiliation. Consumers motivated by affiliation are basically concerned with the welfare of others, and are gregarious in nature. Their motivational force is the need or desire to establish positive interpersonal relationships. Such a motivation may account in part for the preference of some consumers for shopping in small specialty stores where salesperson-customer interaction is high and very personal.

15. Identification. Some consumers find satisfaction, self-acceptance, and pleasure through acquiring roles to play or by increasing the importance of those roles that are already a part of their self-concept. Consumers are seen basically as role-players or identity-adopters who are motivated by their own perceived importance.

16. Modeling. Finally, some people are motivated to act in ways similar to the people they observe and to empathize with and imitate others' actions. Interpersonal similarity, or being just like "the other guy," is a source of pleasure to the consumer. Presumably, late adopters of new products and services model earlier adopters (this is discussed in greater detail in Chapter 18 on adoption and resistance to innovations). Children's purchase patterns may reflect parents' purchase patterns (see the section in Chapter 11 on childhood socialization).

Thus, consumers differ with regard to their primary motivations. In addition, any particular consumer may be motivated differently in different situations. For example, a person may have been motivated to model the behavior of others as a child. Later in life the same person may be motivated to achieve on the job, but may be motivated by affiliation and stimulation needs at home and in informal gatherings.

MOTIVATION RESEARCH AS MARKETING RESEARCH

In the late fifties, marketers began to make formal attempts to understand consumer motivations and how they affected the way consumers viewed the products they purchased. Marketers believed that if motivation research could determine what motivational forces were influencing the consumer while purchasing a product, then the question of why people choose one product or brand over another could be answered. The leading proponents of motivation research tended to be of the psychoanalytic or Freudian school of psy-

"Do you own any stocks, bonds or Chivas Regal?"

Time, July 26, 1976

chology. Perhaps the most important implication of this approach was that buyers are viewed as being motivated by symbolic, as well as economic and functional, product characteristics. Brand image and attitudes toward a product were viewed as being equally important with price in determining whether a brand is purchased.

Motivation research produced many interesting, sometimes bizarre, and often nonoperational hypotheses concerning what may be in the consumer's mind with respect to various products. For instance:

Men prefer odoriferous cigars as a sign of masculinity.

A convertible can serve its owner as a substitute mistress.

Men who wear suspenders are reacting to an unresolved castration complex.

A woman is symbolically giving birth when she bakes a cake, and therefore this is a very serious act not to be overly simplified.

Prunes are disliked because they are a symbol of parental authority.

Motivation research encountered many difficulties. Depth interviews and projective techniques were often used. These are intensive techniques in which an interview with only one person often required several hours to complete. This meant either very large research budgets or very small sample sizes.

The approach was Freudian, more often than not, and required a trained psychoanalyst to conduct and interpret the results, for marketers were often unable to interpret the results themselves.

Motivation researchers often found disparate and conflicting results when studying the same products. For instance, two prominent motivation researchers, Ernest Dichter and James Vicary, were employed by two different and independent groups from the prune industry in an attempt to determine why so many people disliked prunes. Dichter's findings indicated that prunes aroused feelings of old age and insecurity in people. Vicary's findings indicated that people had an emotional block about prunes' laxative qualities.

The primary contribution of motivation research to the study of consumer behavior was an expansion of the inventory of research techniques. The techniques developed by the motivation researchers (depth interviews, focus groups, and projective techniques) are still used today in marketing research. In addition, until the introduction of motivation research, marketers used primarily demographic variables (see Chapter 3) to explain consumer behavior. Motivation research, however, was a whole new approach to studying and explaining consumer behavior, such as needs, motivations, perceptions, life styles, and the effects of social class and group memberships. This was the point at which the study of consumer behavior moved from traditional economics toward psychology, social psychology, and sociology.

CONCEPTS OF MOTIVATION IN INDUSTRIAL BUYER BEHAVIOR

Early works on the motives operating in industrial buying behavior viewed these motives as being different from those of individual consumers. Researchers commonly stated that industrial buyers were motivated by economic considerations (often referred to as "rational" motives). It was believed that industrial buying motives were therefore different from the complex of economic, psychological, and social motives (which were, by default, "irrational") of individual consumers.

After a time, however, consumer behavior researchers realized that there was an inherent fallacy in this line of reasoning. One can't seriously believe that the same consumer who buys a certain brand of toothpaste because it offers "sex appeal" can experience a complete change in motives since it is now 9:00 a.m. and he or she is a purchasing agent considering the purchase of office equipment. Humans, in any situation, can only be humans. They do not become economic machines simply because they are in an industrial setting.

Besides, because a motivation is economic does not make it "rational." Similarly, psychological and social motives are not necessarily "irrational." We can only define as rational those motives which make sense for the overall satisfaction of that individual. Thus, rationality is not a definition we can impose on other consumers, or confine exclusively or inherently to industrial buying situations. The labeling of a motive as rational must take into account the perspective of the individual. In both ultimate consumer and industrial consumer situations, the behavior of consumers is based on economic, psychological, and social motives.

SUMMARY

The instinct theories of Freud, McDougall, and Hull were too narrow an account of the complexity and variety of human motivations and behavior, and were replaced by the more adequate concept expressed in Hull's drive theory, that humans are motivated primarily by the desire to reduce bodily disequilibrium and tension. In terms of consumer behavior, people buy, and continue to buy, those products that are associated with the satisfaction of needs. The shortcoming of the drive theory, however, is that humans are viewed as determined solely by these needs, external stimuli, and rewards; and therefore, drive theory gave way to field theory, which considers human behavior in the context of the surrounding physical and social environment. As developed by Lewin, field theory focuses on the thoughts of persons, rather than on instincts or habitual drives. The achievement theory of Murray centers around the social motives for behavior, such as the desires for affiliation, autonomy, play, and the avoidance of pain.

In attempting to synthesize these theories, the result is a classification divided between those motives that are cognitive in nature, such as the desires for consistency or categorization, and those that are affective, such as the needs for tension-reduction and reinforcement. Such a survey of theories leads us to the conclusion that people are, of course, motivated in many ways, that these motives cause them to buy products for many different reasons, that industrial consumers are motivated by the same desires and perceptions as private consumers, and that the task of the marketer is to harmonize the product's image with the appropriate desires and needs of the consumer.

KEY CONCEPTS   Assertion

Autonomy

Categorization

Cognitive psychology

Consistency

Drive

Ego-defense

Field theory

Motivation

Objectification

Reinforcement

Teleological motivation

Utilitarian

FIVE SELECTED APPROACHES TO THE HUMAN PERSONALITY*

15

LEARNING GOALS   The objective of this chapter is to help readers understand:
1. what is meant by personality and how it is measured;
2. why researchers as yet have been unable to find a consistent correlation between personality and actual consumer behavior;
3. the basic concepts and ideas of five personality theories and the implications they have for marketing and consumer behavior.

INTRODUCTION   "Only a student with an outgoing personality would buy a loud print shirt like that." "The very fact that he bought a small sports car tells you a lot about his personality." "She only buys from the most expensive stores because she's a snob."

None of these statements seems unusual or inappropriate because people generally believe that there is a strong relationship between a person's personality and how that individual acts as a consumer. Researchers in consumer behavior have also held this implicit assumption. Those who have systematically studied this relationship, however, have run into a number of problems. Although many studies have been conducted in this area, it is still not clear what relationship (if any) exists between personality and consumer behavior.

Because research in this area is so inconclusive, this chapter is organized differently from other chapters in this text. We begin with a discussion of the major issues and problems involved in the general study of personality, and then discuss briefly the ways in which consumer researchers have studied

---

*Professors Valerie Valle and Ronald S. Valle, on the University of Pittsburgh, are coauthors of this chapter.

personality and its relationship to consumption. Five selected approaches for studying personality and the implications of these approaches for understanding consumer behavior are presented.[1] However, no attempt is made to determine which of these approaches is the "best" or most "true"; rather, each approach is treated as a possible source of insight into consumer behavior. The reader must determine in what ways each of these approaches is personally useful. Since no attempt is made to cover every significant approach to personality, the approaches we chose to discuss are those which (a) have generated research in consumer behavior, or (b) have potential importance for understanding consumers, yet have not been previously discussed in that context.

Definition and Measurement of Personality

There are probably as many different definitions of personality as there are personality theorists. Each particular definition is a direct outgrowth of that theorist's conception of human nature, and each theorist defines as the basic constituents of personality those variables which he or she views as most important. There are similarities, however, between the technical and everyday conceptualizations of personality. First, the concept of personality would be useless if it referred to ways in which everyone is exactly the same; rather, it necessarily reflects *individual differences* in behavior and in the way a person thinks and feels. Secondly, personality does not vary from minute to minute, but represents a dispositional *consistency* in the individual. Finally, a behavioral component must be included in the definition. Behavior always occurs in a context where each individual's personality is reflected in his or her reactions to the environment (i.e., the person's behavior is *situated*). Definitions or concepts of personality are aimed at organizing or categorizing the consistencies in a person's individual reactions to situations encountered in the environment.

As there are many definitions of personality, there are also different ways of measuring it. These measurements fall into two basic categories: (a) those which are qualitative or subjective in nature, and (b) those which are quantitative or objective.

The *projective test*—where the person spontaneously projects his or her underlying needs, thoughts, and feelings into stories which are written in response to ambiguous stimuli—is perhaps the most common qualitative

---

[1]For a more detailed description of these and other approaches to personality, see Calvin S. Hall and Gardner Lindzey, *Theories of Personality* (3rd ed.), NY: John Wiley, 1978. Included in this classic book on personality are sections on the theories of Gordon Allport, Kurt Lewin, B. F. Skinner, and Carl Rogers, all of whom have relevance for the study of consumer behavior. Several of the approaches discussed in this chapter are also discussed in Hall and Lindzey.

approach to measuring personality. Any ambiguous stimulus can be used, such as an ink blot (see the Rorschach in Figure 15-1), a photograph or drawing (in the Thematic Apperception Test in Figure 15-2), or a verbal statement. The responses are then examined for revelations of personality characteristics. For example, McClelland has developed his method for determining "need for achievement" to such a degree that his scoring is now considered to be quite "objective" (see Figure 15-2).[2]

FIGURE 15-1.
Rorschach Inkblot Test

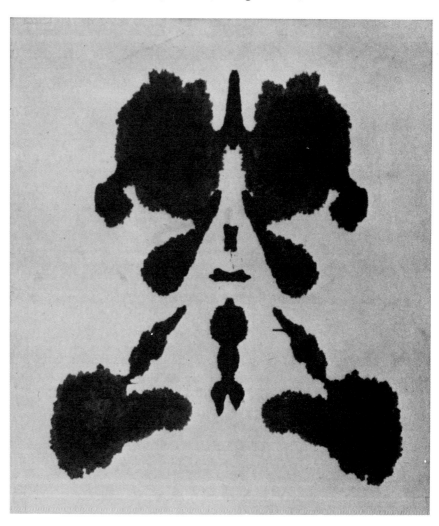

Source: *The Psychology Primer,* Linda Wood (ed.), Publisher's Inc., 1975, p. 200.

FIGURE 15-2. *Picture Used by McClelland to Elicit Stories by People for Scoring on "Need for Achievement"*

Just look at the picture briefly (10-15 seconds), turn the page and write out the story it suggests.

Source: David Kolb, Irwin M. Rubin, and James M. McIntyre, *Organizational Psychology: An Experimental Approach,* Prentice-Hall, 1971, p. 59.

In the second approach to measuring personality, the researcher presents the individual with a series of specific questions which are usually about the individual's behavior or attitudes. These objective tests take two general forms. The first consists of a series of questions revolving around the same personality trait. They seem plausible because anyone reading the questions

[2]D. C. McClelland, J. W. Atkinson, R. A. Clark, and E. L. Lowell, *The Achievement Motive,* NY: Appleton-Century, 1953.

can see that they are related to the trait being measured. For instance, the introversion-extroversion scale (developed by Eysenck) is made up of questions which obviously reflect the degree to which an individual enjoys being with other people. The test includes questions such as "Are you inclined to keep in the background on social occasions?" and "Would you be very unhappy if you were prevented from making numerous social contacts?"[3]

The second type of objective test consists of a series of questions which on the surface appear to have no relationship to the trait being measured. The MMPI (Minnesota Multiphasic Personality Inventory) is probably the best example of this type of test. In order to determine which particular questions should make up each scale of the test, a large battery of questions were given initially to people who were judged to be high on each trait. For example, in order to determine which questions would be used to measure schizophrenia, a large number of questions were first given to people who had been clinically diagnosed as schizophrenic. Those items which were consistently answered one way by schizophrenics and another way by "normal" people was used to construct a scale designed to measure schizophrenic tendencies. An important point to remember about this kind of test is that it does not matter what the particular question is, only that people who fulfill some criteria answer that question in a different way than those who do not fulfill the criteria.

Personality and Behavior

The biggest problem for personality research has been its failure to find strong correlations between measures of personality and a person's actual behavior. For personality to be a useful concept, it must be possible to make behavioral predictions based on a person's personality (we do this implicitly in our everyday life). Personality tests, however, have rarely been able to account for very much of a person's behavior.

The correlation between a personality test and the trait that the test is designed to measure is usually not very high. Researchers in consumer behavior use tests which are designed to measure specific traits (such as "need for achievement") in order to predict some specific consumer behavior rather than the trait itself. How can these researchers expect a test of this kind to predict behavior in an unrelated area? Predictability and validity are common problems in the conventional use of such a test, and these problems are greatly magnified when applying the test to a new area.

There is an obvious discrepancy between the belief that it is possible to predict an individual's behavior based on personality traits and the fact that researchers are consistently unable to find correlations between personality

[3]H. J. Eysenck, *Dimensions of Personality*, London: Routledge and Kegan Paul, 1947.

and behavior. There have been many attempts to deal with or explain this inconsistency. Bem and Allen suggest that in our everyday life we approach the problem of determining a person's personality in quite a different manner than the way it is approached by personality researchers.[4] After we have observed a person in a number of different situations and have noted the consistencies and inconsistencies in his or her actions, we attempt to describe the individual with one or more personality traits. For example, we use the term "generous" to describe an individual who is often willing to give time and money to various people in numerous situations. On the other hand, we may use the term "extrovert" to describe an individual who enjoys being with other people, likes to give parties, and is very talkative. We feel no need to think of the first individual in terms of how extroverted he or she is, and we also feel no need to think of the second person in terms of his or her generosity. We use whichever trait is most appropriate for describing a given individual's behavior in different situations. Traditional personality research, however, has attempted to describe all people using the same set of traits. That is, each individual studied is given a score on both generosity and on extroversion.[5] Bem and Allen assert that if it were possible to systematically study an individual's personality looking only at those traits which are appropriate for an individual, it should be possible to predict behavior from these given traits.[6] This, however, is quite difficult. Each individual must be studied separately, and the traits which are used to describe one individual will be different from those used to describe others.

Research on Consumer Behavior

The idea that measures of personality can be used to predict consumer behavior has a great deal of intuitive and theoretical appeal (see Figure 15-3 for an advertisement which reflects this belief without seriously implying that the listed traits have actually been found to be associated with the described product choice). There would certainly be advantages for the marketing practitioner if it were possible to know something about the personality of actual and potential consumers of a product. For these reasons, a large number of studies have investigated the relationship between personality and various

---

[4]Daryl J. Bem and Andrea Allen, "On Predicting Some of the People Some of the Time: The Search for Cross-situational Consistencies in Behavior," *Psychological Review,* Vol. 81, 1974, pp. 506–520.

[5]The first approach of selecting only the relevant traits is called the *idiographic approach.* The second approach of using the same traits to describe all people is called the *nomothetical approach.*

[6]Bem and Allen, *op. cit.*

FIGURE 15-3.
*An Advertisement
Reflecting the General
Belief that Personality is
Related to Consumer
Behavior*

WHAT KIND OF NUT ARE YOU?

| SMOKEHOUSE® | ROASTED SALTED | ONION GARLIC |
| Popular, humorous | Rugged, positive | Assertive, aggressive |

| BLANCHED SALTED | CHEESE FLAVORED | BARBECUE |
| Sophisticated, witty | Mild-mannered, agreeable | Extroverted, generous |

WHOLE NATURAL
Unaffected, self-determined

A simple psychological test based on the perception that people prefer the Blue Diamond Snack Almond that fits their personality type. Find the traits most like your own, and you will quickly discover which of our seven fantastic snack almonds you should buy.*

*Can't find your personality? Do you embrace more than one category? Feel free to nibble all.

ONE NIBBLE IS NEVER ENOUGH

Crisp, crunchy almonds from California.

the **Almond People**®

California Almond Growers Exchange
P.O. Box 1768
Sacramento, CA 95808

aspects of consumer behavior, but the results from these studies have been at best "equivocal."[7]

The difficulty in finding consistent relationships between consumer behavior and personality is the result of two key problems. First, most of the personality measures used in consumer research have been developed by psychologists to be used in clinical practice. Personality dimensions, such as extroversion or dominance, are very important for clinicians who are trying to understand the way in which their patients interact with the world. They are not, however, the most relevant traits for understanding a consumer's purchasing behavior. Also, scales developed in psychology have been validated using specific populations which may not be similar to the populations used in consumer research.

The second major problem with this research is that it lacks a theoretical basis. A short discussion of the nature of personality theories is necessary in order to understand this particular problem. The major theories of personality are *integrated* theories, which are each based on a particular philosophy of human nature. Each of these theories attempts to explain (not just predict) human actions by explaining consistencies in behavior. Comparisons of these theories have revealed that each contains discussions of seven different areas:

1. The basic nature of humans.
2. What constitutes an explanation of behavior.
3. What motivates people.
4. The function of the unconscious.
5. The self and the self-concept.
6. The effects of socialization and childhood training.
7. What constitutes psychological health.

Though the different theories place varying degrees of emphasis on each of these areas, they are called *integrated* theories because they bring together discussions of all seven areas. Basically, each theory asserts that certain basic variables are necessary to explain behavior. For example, Freud (who will be discussed later in this chapter) believed that the relevant personality variables are related to oral, anal, phallic, or genital fixations. The important point is that the variables used to explain behavior are derived from and are dependent upon a theoretical explanation about why those particular variables lead to the behavior in question.

---

[7]H. H. Kassarjian, "Personality and Consumer Behavior: A Review," *Journal of Marketing Research,* Vol. 5, 1968, pp. 155–164; H. H. Kassarjian and Mary Jane Sheffet, "Personality and Consumer Behavior: One More Time," in Edward M. Mazze (ed.), *1975 Combined Proceedings of the Spring and Fall Conferences of the American Marketing Association,* pp. 197–200.

Unfortunately, much of the research relating personality to consumer behavior has not had a firm theoretical basis. Often these researchers merely chose a convenient, easy-to-administer scale and correlated it with some behavior without any real consideration of what such a correlation might mean. This has been described as the "shotgun" approach. If one gives enough scales, the odds are that at least one of them will correlate with a behavior. Unfortunately, this approach does not have a theoretical base to support the choice of scales or to explain why the scores might be related to certain kinds of purchases. Because the correlations are thereby difficult to interpret, their usefulness is quite limited. This research, like any other scientific research, should begin with a theory which leads to specific hypotheses that can either be supported or disproved. Personality scales, and the behaviors which they are meant to predict, should be chosen with some theoretical model in mind. The results would then be interpretable within the context of the chosen theory.

As was mentioned earlier, many consumer researchers take a personality scale developed in another context and attempt to relate it to purchasing behavior. The studies by Evans of the differences between Ford and Chevrolet buyers are typical.[8] In these two studies (the second is merely a replication of the first study at a later point in time) buyers of two types of automobiles were compared. The personality instrument used was the EPPS (Edwards Personal Preference Schedule), which is based on Murray's typology of psychological needs (see Chapter 13 on needs). Evans concluded that there was not a large enough difference between the two groups to make predictions about the purchases of different individuals, and this is not surprising, given the absence of a theoretical basis for the research.

Other studies have found correlations between various scales and purchasing behaviors, but invariably the relationship has been weak. Researchers have investigated personality differences between those who purchase filter and nonfilter cigarettes,[9] and between customers of banks and of savings and loan associations.[10] Others have studied the personalities of those who buy headache remedies, vitamins, mouthwash, alcoholic drinks, automobiles,

[8]Franklin B. Evans, "Psychological and Objective Factors in the Prediction of Brand Choice," *Journal of Business,* Vol. 32, October, 1959, pp. 340–369; Franklin B. Evans, "Ford Versus Chevrolet: Park Forest Revisited," *Journal of Business,* Vol. 41, October, 1968, pp. 445–459.

[9]Arthur Koponen, "Personality Characteristics of Purchasers," *Journal of Advertising Research,* Vol. 1, September, 1960, pp. 6–12.

[10]Henry J. Claycamp, "Characteristics of Owners of Thrift Deposits in Commercial Banks and Savings and Loans Associations," *Journal of Marketing Research,* Vol. 2, May, 1965, pp. 163–170.

chewing gum, new fashions;[11] and coffee, tea, and beer.[12] There has been no theoretical work done in the area of personality by anyone with a particular interest in its application to consumer-related questions, and, without this theoretical basis, the results continue to be weak.

Though there are some researchers who are beginning to construct a personality measure based on consumer behavior, it is necessary at present to use approaches that were developed in psychology. In discussing Freud's psychoanalytic theory, Jung's analytic psychology, Kelly's theory of personal constructs, the factor-analytic trait approach, and the existential-phenomenological approach, we develop propositions with regard to how these theories might apply to the understanding of consumer behavior. Since there is very little data which demonstrate that personality traits are good predictors of behavior, these propositions must remain tentative. Despite these restrictions and the fact that one will not be able to accurately predict *all* behavior, it is nevertheless worthwhile to think about how various approaches to the study of personality relate to consumer behavior. If these approaches can aid the marketer in detecting the important variables, then they are useful.

FREUD'S PSYCHOANALYTIC THEORY

The theory of personality that has been most influential both within psychology and in our everyday life is the psychoanalytic theory developed by Sigmund Freud. Many of the ideas and concepts that were revolutionary in Freud's time have now become part of our everyday thinking. For example, we all accept or "know" that there is an unconscious part of the mind, that is, that there are motivations of which we are not aware. Freud was also the first person to discuss the prevalence of sexuality in all aspects of our lives.

The Structure of the Personality

Freud believed that in every person there is a given amount of psychic energy which is distributed among the different facets of the personality. The *id,* which includes all the instincts and psychic energies which exist at birth, aims for immediate gratification of all of the individual's needs. If the person is hungry, for instance, the id presents (or tempts) the person with a mental picture of food (this mental image does not, of course, satisfy the actual physical need).

---

[11]William T. Tucker and John Painter, "Personality and Product Use," *Journal of Applied Psychology,* Vol. 45, October, 1961, pp. 325–329.

[12]William F. Massey , Ronald E. Frank, and Thomas M. Lodahl, *Purchasing Behavior and Personal Attributes,* Philadelphia: University of Pennsylvania Press, 1968.

Since the id is unable to gratify physical needs, the *ego* (the second system of personality) develops from the id. In attempting to satisfy his or her needs, the individual must learn how to relate to the world. The ego's primary role is to mediate between the instinctual requirements of the organism and the conditions of the surrounding environment.

The third structure that develops is the *superego,* which represents the traditional values and ideas of the society in which the child develops. These values or morals are a direct outgrowth of identification with the parents. The main functions of the superego are to inhibit the impulses of the id, to persuade the ego to substitute moral goals for instinctual ones, and to strive for perfection. These goals tend to cause the superego to be in conflict with both the id and the ego, and the conflicts among the three structures are the source, Freud believed, of most of the problems in psychological development.

It must be remembered that these are merely names for psychological processes. They do not have an existence of their own, and they have no corresponding physical structures within the brain. In a person with a healthy personality, the three function together as a team under the leadership of the ego. Freud said that there is always some conflict between these three aspects of the personality, so that the relatively healthy person is the one who manages to resolve most of these conflicts.

Developmental Stages

Freud also believed that each individual passes through a number of stages during his or her first few years of life which are decisive in the formation of the adult personality. At each stage, the child expresses sexual pleasure through a different zone of the body. In addition, at each stage of development there is a crisis which must be resolved. If a person is unable to satisfactorily resolve one of these crises, he or she becomes "fixated" at that stage of development. By fixation, Freud meant that the person continues to react to the world in the same manner as during that particular stage of development. These stages are the oral, the anal, the phallic, and the genital.

During the oral stage of development (from birth to about eighteen months), the primary source of pleasure is the mouth. The infant incorporates the world through passive sucking and later by biting and active chewing. The primary crisis during this stage is weaning, for at some point the child must give up the pleasure derived by sucking on the breast or bottle. If this crisis is not satisfactorily resolved, the child may become fixated at the oral stage. A person who is fixated at the passive "incorporative" phase is willing to "swallow almost anything"; pleasure is derived from taking things in. A person fixated at the active "aggressive" phase of the oral stage enjoys eating, chewing, and "biting" sarcasm.

The next stage of development is the anal period (from eighteen months to three years). At this stage the child's primary pleasure comes from relieving anal tensions through elimination. The primary crisis to be resolved at this stage is toilet training. The child must learn to postpone the pleasure in relieving himself or herself in order to please the parents. If the parents are very strict during toilet training, the child may hold back the feces and become constipated. This personality type is called "anal retentive." On the other hand, the child may vent rage by expelling feces at the most inappropriate time. This type is called "anal expulsive." A person who has not fully resolved the conflicts of toilet training may still have certain anal characteristics as an adult. Someone who is obstinate, stingy, and excessively neat is said to be anal retentive. The person who is messy, disorderly, and destructive is called anal expulsive.

During the third or phallic stage of development (ages three to four and one-half), sexual pleasure begins to be associated with the genital area. The crisis of this stage centers around the Oedipal Complex. The name comes from the classic Greek character, Oedipus, who inadvertently killed his father and married his mother. During this stage the child develops sexual desires for the parent of the opposite sex and hostile feelings toward the same-sexed parent. In the male child, the desire for the mother leads to a fear that the father will retaliate by castration. This castration anxiety is the source of the child's identification with his father. This identification is a source for both the child's sexual identity and for his moral code through the development of the superego. The female child undergoes a similar type of process, called the Electra Complex. Her desire for her father leads to hostility towards her mother.

The phallic stage is followed by several years in which sexual motivation is less important (the latency period). This period lasts until the onset of puberty. Finally, with adolescence the healthy individual learns to derive pleasure from relationships with the opposite sex and is able to begin to love and care for other people. This mature sexuality becomes evident during what is referred to as the genital stage. The crisis of this last stage is the conflict we face all of our lives: we are constantly attempting to balance our selfish desire to satisfy our pleasures with our altruistic motives and concern for others.

Defense Mechanisms

Conflicts within the personality or between the person and the environment often create an anxiety which is too great for the ego to handle. When anxiety reaches this level, the ego deals with it through unconscious processes called defense mechanisms.

One of the most powerful defense mechanisms is *repression*. In order to eliminate the anxiety caused by unacceptable desires or feelings, the person is motivated to forget them and represses these feelings into the unconscious. When a feeling has been repressed, it is impossible for the person to willfully bring that feeling back to conscious awareness. Repression interferes with normal functioning because a person is distorting his or her reactions to the world.

Through the defense mechanism of *sublimation,* the individual finds socially acceptable expressions for unacceptable motives. For example, a person with sadistic desires may become a soldier or surgeon in order to safely express the desires to kill or cut up other people.

Through the defense mechanism of *reaction formation,* a person expresses unacceptable feelings by behaving in exactly the opposite manner. For instance, a mother who hates or resents her child may smother the child with love.

Another common defense mechanism is that of *projection.* People who have trouble accepting their own feelings or motivations project these feelings and see them in others, but not in themselves. So, an individual who is filled with what to him or her are unacceptable sexual desires may perceive that the rest of the world is obsessed with sexuality.

Implications for Marketing

From this brief description of Freud's theory of personality, it can be seen that there are many implications for understanding consumer behavior. Freud's most important contribution is the idea that people are motivated by both conscious and unconscious forces. Obviously, people's decisions to purchase products are based, at least to some extent, on unconscious motivations (see Proposition 15-1 in Exhibit 15-1). Therefore, when analyzing the appeal of a product, the marketer should consider not just the conscious, rational aspects of the product but also the consumer's unconscious motives. A product is much more than simply its physical attributes, and it represents many things to the consumer, depending upon its shape, color, texture, packaging, and promotional campaign.

Freud based much of his theory on the idea that sexuality pervades all of our thoughts and actions (see Proposition 15-2 in Exhibit 15-1). If this is true, it is important to include implicit sexual content in appeals. There are many potential ways of appealing to sexuality. For example, the shape of a container can have sexual implications, and the use of sexually attractive people in advertisements has become commonplace. Such advertising, however, should remain at the symbolic level and not be so blatant as to be offensive or ridiculous. Some advertisements are so obvious in their appeal to sexual motives that the symbolic appeal is lost. What is supposed to symbolize sex begins to look or seem less and less like a symbol (see Figure 15-4). In fact, Freud would probably judge this as violating the Principle of Complication, which states that the more hidden the true motive (and in our example the motive is *not* well hidden!), the better the work of art, and the more easily and comfortably people will respond to it.

Many people in our society are, to some extent, fixated at one of the various stages of development, and these different fixations imply different needs and desires. Proposition 15-3 suggests that market segmentation could be based on the stage of development at which a person is fixated. Although

EXHIBIT 15-1.
Propositions from
Freud's Psychoanalytic
Theory

PROPOSITION 15-1.
People's purchase decisions are determined by unconscious as well as conscious motivations.

PROPOSITION 15-2.
The more a product appeals to unconscious sexual desires, the greater will be the consumer's interest in the product.

PROPOSITION 15-3.
The more complete the segmentation of markets into groups of similarly fixated people, the more likely it is that appeals can be developed which utilize Freudian notions of behavioral orientation.

PROPOSITION 15-4.
The more aware a marketer is of the unconscious symbolic meaning of products, packages, logos, and advertisements, the more likely these symbolic meanings will be used to make the product more attractive.

PROPOSITION 15-5.
The less a purchase creates conflict within the personality, the more likely it is that the purchase will occur.

some people may be more responsive to certain products or appeals because of their fixations at certain stages, there is no way as yet to determine who these people are, how many of them exist, or how to reach them.

Since individuals who are fixated at the oral stage of development get most of their pleasure from stimulation of the mouth, there should be a large market for various items which the person can suck or chew. A quick look at successful products in our society indicates the pervasiveness of products which stimulate the mouth but are not nutritional (e.g., candy mints, cigarettes, and chewing gum). Promotional materials which stress the potential oral pleasures of a product should appeal to persons fixated at the oral stage. For example, there was recently a television advertisement in which a snack chip, which is large and supposedly tasty, also makes a very loud crunch when one bites into it. The advertisement's action centers on people crunching at each other, a clear example of oral aggression.

It is also possible to think of products which would specifically appeal to people fixated at the anal stage. People who are anal retentive should be

FIGURE 15-4.
Appeal to
Sexual Motives

Source: *The New York Times Magazine,* October 17, 1976

interested in buying those things which help them to be neat and orderly, such as tool boxes with separate compartments. People who are anal expulsive will be more interested in products and services that provide them with opportunities to be disorderly and messy in a socially acceptable manner (e.g., house painting, cosmetic mud packs, and cooking and baking). Such products are quite prevalent among children's toys. Finger painting may be the ultimate way to express an anal expulsive personality.

Individuals fixated at the phallic stage are particularly sensitive to phallic symbolizations. Producers wishing to appeal to such individuals should, therefore, choose containers, logos, and names for their symbolic value.

Symbolism.   Freud's approach to psychotherapy stresses the importance of dreams for understanding an individual's unconscious motivation. Freud's study of dreams caused him to see the unconscious implications or symbolic nature of much of our environment. Here are some of the most common dream symbols and their psychoanalytic interpretation: (a) a king and queen represent parents; (b) little crawling creatures (e.g., mice) represent siblings; (c) elongated objects, such as sticks, tree trunks, or umbrellas, represent the penis; (d) boxes, cases, and chests represent the uterus; (e) steps, ladders, and staircases represent sexual intercourse; (f) playing with a small child represents masturbation; (g) water or bathing represents birth; (h) decapitation, losing teeth, or having a haircut represents castration; and (i) rooms represent women (it is interesting to note whether the room is locked or open). Obviously, it is important for marketers to be aware of the symbolic nature of their products and packaging (see Proposition 15-4 in Exhibit 15-1). Though one naturally wants to avoid unintended symbolic messages, if used correctly symbolism can enhance product appeal. For example, several brands of cosmetics for young women are packaged in cylindrical containers which are obviously phallic symbols. The usefulness, however, of such packaging for increasing sales has not yet been demonstrated.

Conflicts.   Freud's discussion of the problems created by conflicts between the three structures of the personality also has implications for marketing (see Proposition 15-5). Since the id, ego, and superego represent different needs and functions within the personality, there are times when the purchase of a product leads to conflicts between these structures. A promotional strategy designed to appeal to that aspect of the personality least likely to desire the product should help to ease the conflict and increase the probability of a sale.

Imagine a person who is considering the purchase of a luxury car. The person is attracted to this purchase because of the comforts involved. The basic need of the id would be satisfied by such a purchase, so the id wants it. The superego, however, may not be interested in such a car because the purchase is seen as wasteful, extravagant, and, given the energy situation today, unethical. There is much conflict within this individual's personality. A marketer, however, may be able to present a promotional campaign which would counter the superego's arguments against buying the car and substantiate the id's claims.

It is also possible to have conflicts between the ego and superego. A good example of this would be the purchase of birth control devices. The ego perceives that it is best to prevent pregnancy when a child is not desired. The superego, however, may object to birth control or the satisfaction of impulsive sexual desires. Therefore, it is important to package and distribute the birth control devices in a way which will help the ego win out over the superego. One should remember that the id, ego, and superego (although treated as if they were independent of one another) represent different processes going on within *one* individual.

Defense Mechanisms. An understanding of the various defense mechanisms—such as sublimation and reaction formation—suggests ways in which one might go about marketing different products. There are products which, for some people, allow the expression of unacceptable motives in a socially acceptable manner (sublimation). A product which helps a person sublimate his or her desires should contain many of the components of the unacceptable motives, but should not explicitly express these motives. For example, hunters may buy rifles in order to sublimate their desire to destroy and kill. A promotional campaign for rifles, then, should not appeal to those unacceptable motives, but rather should appeal to socially acceptable reasons for hunting. An anti-gun campaign should stress the actual sublimated desire to kill which is one motivation for gun purchases.

People who are using the defense mechanism of reaction formation are motivated to "do good" because they have an unconscious desire to do the opposite. A product which is promoted as the correct or appropriate way to express love and caring will appeal to such people. For example, the child who has unconscious negative feelings toward his or her mother will be motivated to overexpress the opposite feeling of love. This child may, therefore, be strongly motivated to purchase flowers or cards on Mother's Day as an expression of "love."

Motivation Research. Motivation research, developed by Ernest Dichter, was an early attempt to use Freud's personality theory for understanding consumer behavior.[13] (See Chapter 14 for a fuller discussion of consumer motivations and motivation research.) The primary research tool is the in-

---

[13]Ernest Dichter, *The Strategy of Desire,* NY: Doubleday, 1960.

depth interview, which is an extended, probing, unstructured interview with a consumer that attempts to discern that particular individual's conscious and unconscious thoughts and feelings about a product. From this data, the researcher determines the "real" reasons why an individual engages in a certain type of consumer behavior. For example, it has been suggested that a man buys a convertible as a substitute for a mistress, and likes corn flakes because eating them is reminiscent of crunching an enemy's bones. Although this research methodology delivers intriguing and interesting explanations for consumer behavior, its validity has not as yet been demonstrated. A major problem is that the conclusions are based on interviews with just a few individuals. Although this kind of research can be very useful in the clinical setting, it is not at all clear that the reactions of one individual are representative of the reactions of all consumers.

JUNG'S ANALYTIC PSYCHOLOGY

Carl Gustav Jung was a close associate and friend of Sigmund Freud who later broke with Freud because of personal and intellectual differences. His theory of personality, although sharing many similarities with Freud's, contains major modifications and additions. One of the major disagreements between Jung and Freud was on the importance of sexual motivation. In Jung's theory, sexual motivation plays a much less important role, while the "mystical" side of human nature is examined extensively. The two major contributions of Jung's theory are the idea of the collective unconscious and his description of the major personality dimensions.

The Collective Unconscious

Jung believed that there exists a collective unconscious in addition to the conscious ego and the personal unconscious described by Freud. The collective unconscious is common to all people and contains inherited memories from the entirety of human history. These memories are not like memories of personal experiences because we cannot actively bring them to our conscious awareness. Rather, they manifest themselves in consciousness as symbols and the potential for reacting in a given way.

A diagram is useful at this point to illustrate the relationship between the various structures of the personality (see Figure 15-5). Imagine each individual as an island in an ocean. Each island has three levels. That which is totally above the high water line is freely accessible and corresponds to the *conscious mind.* That part of the island that lies just below water level is usually inaccessible, but, when the water line is low, can be reached. This corresponds to the *personal unconscious* of which we are dimly aware and are occasionally able to bring into consciousness. An observer approaching a group of islands would see them as totally separate, just as each individual's consciousness

FIGURE 15-5.
Various Structures of the Personality

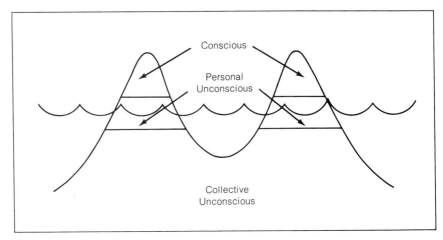

appears to be completely separate from that of others. Under the surface of the water, however, islands are merely parts of a common mountain range. Similarly, each individual's consciousness is based on a common *collective unconscious.*

The collective unconscious is structured around archetypes, or universal thought-forms. These archetypes do not have an existence in and of themselves, but rather predispose the individual to organize experience in a particular way. The nature of the archetype can be explained by an example. All people of all times have experienced a "mother," that is, a female who took care of them when they were very small. Jung says that all people have an inherited tendency to develop an archetype of the mother. Though the specific form of this archetype depends somewhat upon the individual's relationship to the mother, everyone will have a great deal of energy invested in this mother image. The tendency to form an archetype is innate, but the specific content involved will depend upon the person's culture and his or her experiences. These collective unconscious archetypes have a powerful effect on the way an individual relates to the world both emotionally and behaviorally. A few of the more important archetypes are discussed below.

Jung believed that all people have both a masculine and a feminine side to their natures. For males, the masculine side is more fully and consciously developed, while the feminine side remains unconscious. For females, the opposite is true—the feminine is well developed, and the masculine is unconscious. The feminine side of a man's personality and the masculine side of a woman's personality each form an archetype. The feminine archetype in a man is called the *anima,* whereas the masculine archetype in a woman is called the *animus.* A man's anima takes the form of his idealized woman, while the animus forms the woman's idealized man. There are commonalities across these idealized images even though each person's anima or animus is a result of his or her own particular past experiences. Some people try to find their anima or animus in a real person, but they are doomed to disappointment since no living person can live up to such an ideal. Instant infatuations, however, or "love at first sight" can be attributed to seeing one's anima or animus in another.

Another important and powerful archetype is that of the *shadow.* The shadow represents the animal side of human nature, including all the unpleasant and asocial thoughts, feelings, and actions which we do not allow into our consciousness. The passion of those animal instincts that are represented in the shadow, however, are necessary for a healthy, full-bodied personality. The shadow must form a whole with the good side of the personality just as the two sides of the Yin/Yang symbol complement each other and form a whole (see Figure 15-6).

FIGURE 15-6.
Yin/Yang: "Though its principles are in tension, they are not flatly opposed. They complement and counterbalance each other. Each invades the other's hemisphere and establishes itself in the very center of its opposite's territory. In the end both are resolved in an all-embracing circle, symbol of the final unity."

Source: Huston Smith, *The Religions of Man,* NY: Harper and Row, 1958, p. 211.

Still another important archetype is that of the *persona*. The persona is the mask which people adopt in order to fulfill social convention. This public image is contrasted with the private personality which exists behind the social facade. If a person identifies completely with the persona, however, he or she becomes no more than a person playing a part and will eventually become alienated from his or her own feelings. A persona of some type is necessary, however, for adequate functioning in the social world.

There are many other archetypes which Jung discusses, such as the wise old man, the hero, the sun, the moon, the trees, and mother nature. Each of these archetypal images occurs and reoccurs in ancient myths, religions, dreams, modern art, and children's fantasies. It is the recurrence of these images and symbols in many different contexts and cultures that led Jung to the concept of a collective unconscious.

Dimensions of Personality

Jung described four major ways in which a person may interact with the world: thinking, feeling, sensing, and intuiting. Thinking is a cognitive, intellectual attitude which is concerned with comprehending the nature of the world by weighing information and coming to a conclusion. Feeling is evaluative, based on the individual's subjective pleasure or pain. Sensing is concerned with the perception of concrete facts, seeing things the way they are. Intuition goes beyond facts, searching for a global conception of the essence of reality.

An individual can react to a situation using any one or several of these functions. Consider this example. Imagine a group of students who go to a symphony concert and listen to Beethoven's Ninth Symphony. Each of the students can react in a number of ways. One may *think* about this symphony as the perfection of the symphonic form or about Beethoven's place in musical history. Another student may *feel* the beauty of the music, and be brought to ecstasy by the richness of the final movement. A third student might experience the symphony using primarily the *sensing* function, listening to each note and how it is played, but not experiencing more than the purity of the music. Finally, the fourth student, using the *intuiting* function, may experience the mystical nature of the final movement as revealing the basic nature of the universe and the hope for humanity.

Although all people have the potential for using all four of these functions, they are rarely equally developed. People who usually approach the world from a thinking perspective tend to keep their feeling functions unconscious. People who react to the world through sensation are often unconscious of their intuiting side (see Figure 15-7). Thus, there are usually trade-offs between thinking and feeling, as well as between sensation and intuition. The person with a completely balanced personality (a rare occurrence) is at the center of this circle and is able to use whichever function is most appropriate for a given situation.

FIGURE 15-7.
Jungian Cognitive Dimensions

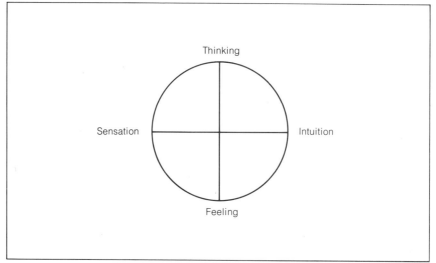

Where a persons fits in with these dimensions has been shown to correlate with many behaviors. For instance, strong correlations have been found
between personality type and occupational choice. The relationships are as
follows:

sensing-thinking: accounting, economics, law
sensing-feeling: sales, nursing, social work
intuiting-thinking: counseling, teaching, psychology
intuiting-feeling: inventors, writers, humanistic philosophers

Jung was also concerned with describing the growth and development of
the individual. The goal toward which psychic development moves is termed
the "self," the archetype which represents the person's striving for unity and
balance. Jung described the personality in terms of the relative strengths of
opposites, such as thinking vs. feeling, masculinity vs. femininity, and consciousness vs. unconsciousness. Rather than emphasizing one or the other of
the opposites in each pairing, Jung believed that in each case the self strove
for balance between the two. The ultimate goal of the process of self-
realization is to fully develop all sides of the personality in order to achieve a
healthy, functioning balance (such as that typified by the classic Yin/Yang
drawing in Figure 15-6). This perfect balance is rarely, if ever, achieved;
rather, the individual (symbolized as the "self") moves progressively toward
that goal.

Implications for Marketing

Unlike Freud's theory, Jung's analytic psychology has not been applied to the
consumer behavior area. There are two reasons for this. First, Jung's theory
was not widely known or respected until quite recently. Few people outside of

psychology were familiar with his ideas, while Freud's theories have become part of the popular culture. Secondly, Jung's philosophy of the nature of human beings is less deterministic than Freud's. That is, Freud believed that a person's reactions were determined by his or her past, implying that it was possible to predict and potentially control that person's behavior (consumption, for example). Jung, on the other hand, felt that the bases of a person's reactions were much more complex. An individual's behavior is not only affected by his or her personal experiences, but also by the collective unconscious and that individual's projected future. The importance of the perceived future in understanding the present personality was an important aspect of Jung's approach. He believed that in order to fully understand a person it is necessary to know not only where the person has been but also where the person thinks he or she is going.

The concept of the archetype should be seriously considered by marketing practitioners (see Proposition 15-6 in Exhibit 15-2). Since each archetype acts as a reservoir of unconscious energy, anything which taps into an archetype has the potential for producing strong reactions in the individual. Marketers should, therefore, be aware of the symbolic nature of their products, packaging, and advertising. Although each individual's archetypes are unique to some extent, there are also commonalities. One should remember that any attempt to appeal to a specific archetype will not necessarily assure a specific reaction in the consumer. Although the archetype of "mother" will probably create very positive reactions in most consumers, the triggering of this archetype could cause a negative response to a product for those who have negative feelings about their maternal parent.

EXHIBIT 15-2.
Propositions From Jung's Analytic Theory

PROPOSITION 15-6.
The more a product, package, or advertisement activates an archetypal image within a consumer, the more powerful will be the effects the product has on the consumer.

PROPOSITION 15-7.
The more a promotional campaign appeals to the mode of relating to the world which is most commonly used by the target population, the more effective it will be in communicating information or feelings.

PROPOSITION 15-8.
Consumption is a function of a person's perceived future as well as his or her past experiences.

The anima and animus, as idealized images of the opposite sex, can and have been used, either explicitly or implicitly, in advertising. The mysterious, attractive woman (or man) who does not really express her or his own uniqueness, but rather lets others project what they want to see, can be very appealing. In advertisements, a woman presented as a mysterious, unknown entity causes a great deal of interest in the male audience. There has been much discussion of the prevalence of sex in advertising recently, with the ads becoming more and more explicit. To appeal to a man's anima, however, one should not be overly explicit because too much knowledge decreases the opportunity for the individual to project his own anima. Rather, one should emphasize mystery and possibility. See, for example, Figure 15-8 which depicts two advertisements which include the anima or animus (p. 380−381).

Although Jung was not personally concerned with categorizing people in terms of the personality dimensions discussed above, personality scales have been developed to measure each of these dimensions.[14] Using these scales, it is possible to determine whether an individual is (a) more thinking or more feeling, and (b) more sensing or more intuiting. Different types of promotions can be developed to appeal to each of the four different types of individuals (see Proposition 15-7 in Exhibit 15-2). In order to appeal to a sensing-thinking individual, a promotional campaign should be oriented toward facts and concrete, objective information (see the two ads in Figure 15-9a and b. On the other hand, in order to appeal to an intuiting-feeling person, the promotional campaign should be centered on global, general ideas which can be responded to in an intuitive manner (see Figure 15-9c). For market segments composed of sensing-feeling people, a promotional campaign should focus on emotional attachments to specific others and the feelings one has toward them (see the two ads in Figure 15-10). Finally, an intuiting-thinking person would be attracted to promotions stressing the analytical achievement of possibilities, especially those concerned with scientific inquiry (see Figure 15-11). Also, ads can be designed to appeal to more than one type of person.

Finally, a marketer should consider the idea that consumers' reactions in the present are not only related to where they have been, but also to where they think they are going (see Proposition 15-8 in Exhibit 15-2). Jung describes life as an ongoing process of growth toward self-realization. A marketer should not only think of helping to satisfy the current needs of consumers, but also try to develop ways of aiding the personal growth process. There is, undoubtedly, a market for products and services that can help the individual achieve a more fully-developed self. The rapid increase in the sales of services

[14]Isabel B. Myers, *The Myers-Briggs Type Indicator,* Princeton: Educational Testing Service, 1962.

FIGURE 15-8a. *Woman with her Animus, Which Also Brings Out Elements of the Shadow Archetype*

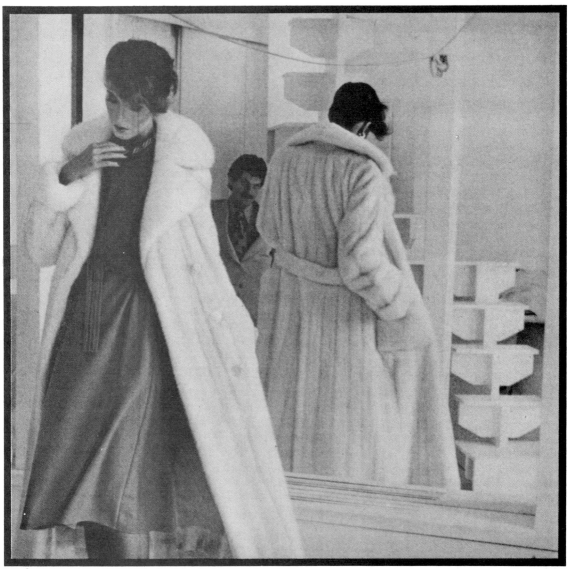

Mink. There is nothing else remotely like it.

Source: *New York,* November 15, 1976.

FIGURE 15-8b. *Man with his Anima*

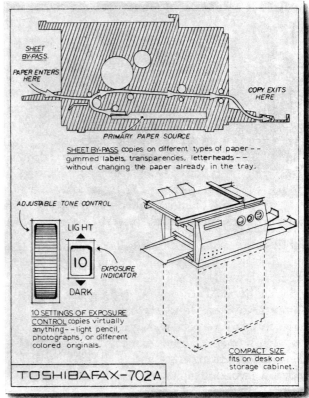
Source: *Business Week,* September 20, 1976.

FIGURE 15-9b.
Ad Appealing to the Sensing-Thinking Individual

Source: *Time,* November 15, 1976, p. 39.

FIGURE 15-9c.
*Ad Appealing to the
Intuiting-Feeling Person*

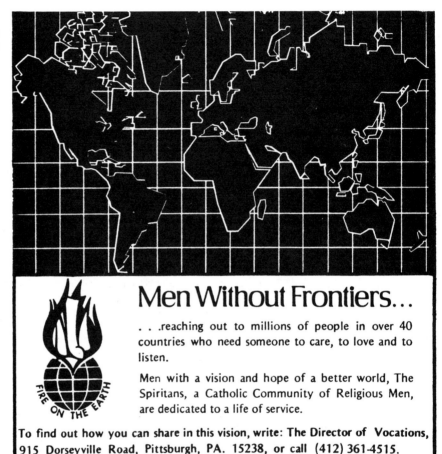

Men Without Frontiers...

. . .reaching out to millions of people in over 40 countries who need someone to care, to love and to listen.

Men with a vision and hope of a better world, The Spiritans, a Catholic Community of Religious Men, are dedicated to a life of service.

To find out how you can share in this vision, write: **The Director of Vocations,** 915 Dorseyville Road, Pittsburgh, PA. 15238, or call (412) 361-4515.

Source: *Psychology Today,* March, 1977, p. 78.

such as sensitivity training, instruction in meditation, and other programs designed for individual growth are testimony to the importance of satisfying these needs.

KELLY'S THEORY OF PERSONAL CONSTRUCTS In contrast to the theorists discussed above, George Kelly was concerned with the rational, thinking aspects of the human personality.[15] He saw people as scientists who actively attempt to make sense of their environment. The indi-

---

[15]George A. Kelly, *The Psychology of Personal Constructs,* NY: Norton, 1955.

FIGURE 15-10a. *Ad Appealing to a Sensing-Feeling Individual*

When you're doing all you can to build something for those you love, you want help to keep it growing. A living trust is just one way Mellon Bank can offer you that kind of help.

Through a living trust, constant, careful attention is paid to your financial goals. The plan can be changed as your needs change. The amount of control you retain is up to you.

Your money in a living trust at Mellon Bank will be managed to provide for you and your family according to your wishes.

Whatever your financial objectives, our professional money managers can shape a plan to help you meet them. Call William Latimer at (412) 232-5465. You'll find that trusts need not be a complex subject.

For our brochure on living trust, or for any information on starting a trust, write to Mellon Bank, Trust Department, Mellon Square, Pittsburgh, Pennsylvania 15230. And let's begin.

Trust. It's the beginning of something.

Mellon Bank

Source: *Business Week,* September 20, 1976.

FIGURE 15-10b. *Ad Appealing to a Sensing-Feeling Individual*

Introducing Belle de Jōvan Perfume.
Open. Apply. Experience. Savor. Whisper.
Touch. Caress. Stroke. Kiss...

Legend tells us that a wealthy prince once challenged the master perfumers of Jōvan to create the world's most beautiful perfume. For his cherished princess.

"Use only the most precious flowers," he advised, "for she must experience the greatness of my gift."

Belle de Jōvan is that very fragrance. A sensual, long-lasting blend of French Jasmine, Bulgarian Roses, Italian Orange Blossoms, East Indian Sandalwood, Florentine Iris and other precious flowers.

A fragrance treasure to be given by every man who has ever cherished a woman. And to be worn by every woman who desires to be cherished.

Available in perfume and cologne spray mist. Ask for it. At cosmetic counters of fine stores everywhere.

PERFUME

Belle de Jōvan

1/3 FL OZ. 10 CC.ml

Wear it for him.
Before someone else does.

Jovan, Inc., 875 North Michigan Avenue, Chicago, Illinois 60611.   ©1976, Jovan, Inc.

Source: *New York,* November 15, 1976.

FIGURE 15-11. *Ad Appealing to the Intuiting-Thinking Individual*

A great astronomer surveys the ideas, principles and processes of his discipline

Myth-shattering reality: the behavior you didn't expect

Trace the original Americans for 30,000 years

Everything you want to know about every plant and creature

Come! All the worlds of man and nature await you in the
Natural Science Book Club

34210. THE ARCHAEOLOGY OF NORTH AMERICA. *Dean Snow. Photographs by Werner Forman.* With nearly 200 photographs, maps and charts, resurrects the world of the North American Indian, from the first crossings onto this continent 30,000 years ago to the discovery of the last stone-age man who died in the 20th century. **$18.95**

36395. BLACK HOLES, QUASARS AND THE UNIVERSE. *Henry L. Shipman.* An absorbing exploration of the frontiers of astronomy. **$12.95**

56720. ISLAND OF ISIS. *William MacQuitty.* A beautifully written introduction to the culture, religion, history and geography of ancient Egypt. Illustrated. **$14.95**

61710. THE MEDIEVAL MACHINE. *Jean Gempel.* An enlightening look at the times, the men, the conditions and the remarkable inventions of the Middle Ages. Many illustrations. **$12.95**

69311. PLAGUES AND PEOPLES. *William H. McNeill.* A fresh, groundbreaking study of the history of infectious disease and its effect on civilizations, past and present. **$9.95**

34670. ASTRONOMY AND COSMOLOGY. *Fred Hoyle.* Over 700 pages, with 617 illustrations, provides a solid understanding of the physical processes and relationships at the core of astronomical phenomena. **$16.50**

50610. THE GREAT INTERNATIONAL DISASTER BOOK. *James Cornell.* Fascinating survey of every major disaster from the eruption of Vesuvius in A.D. 79 to the Guatemala earthquake of 1976. **$12.50**

36645. THE BOOK OF SHARKS. *Written and illustrated by Richard Ellis.* Covers all major types, with explanations of their biology and behavior, plus vignettes of the divers, photographers, filmmakers and fishermen who know them best. Illustrated. *Counts as 2 of your 3 books.* **$25.00**

50415. GOLD, GALLEONS AND ARCHAEOLOGY. *Robert F. Burgess and Carl J. Clausen.* Superbly researched account of the membership of the 1715 Spanish Plate Fleet sunk in a hurricane off the coast of Florida . . . and the Great Florida "gold rush" to salvage the treasure. **$12.95**

41981. THE DESERT. *Russell D. Butcher.* A beautiful, guided tour of America's six desert regions, how they were formed, the persistence of their life-forms in intensely fragile ecologies. **$17.50**

87195. WILD CATS OF THE WORLD. *C. A. W. Guggisberg.* One of the world's leading authorities on wild cats offers definitive natural histories of eachsof the 37 species of wild cats. **$15.95**

55190. THE INCREDIBLE DR. MATRIX. *Martin Gardner.* The delightful, incredibly brilliant Dr. Matrix returns with more amazing feats and adventures in number theory, sleight of word, numerological analysis and puzzles. **$8.95**

Take any 3 books (values to $56.40) for only 99¢ each
if you will join now for a trial period and agree to take 3 more books—at handsome discounts—over the next 12 months

(Publishers' Prices shown)

85090. THE UNIVERSE. *Lloyd Motz.* Absorbing account of modern cosmological theory examines the origin, evolution, and future of the universe. **$15.00**

85820. VENOMOUS ANIMALS OF THE WORLD. *Roger Caras.* Explores the entire scope of this remarkable group of animals—from the common honeybee and ant to more deadly creatures. *Counts as 2 of your 3 books.* **$25.00**

77620. THE SECRET LIFE OF ANIMALS. *Lorus and Margery Milne and Franklin Russell.* Lavishly illustrated account of the dramatic discoveries recently made about the behavior of animals. Over 300 full-color photographs. *Counts as 2 of your 3 books.* **$29.95**

48705. FORECASTS AND FAMINES AND FREEZES. *John Gribbin.* Explores some fascinating questions about the earth's future, the greenhouse effect, a new ice age and shifting magnetic poles. **$8.95**

73337. THE RAPE OF THE NILE. *Brian Fagan.* The plundering of ancient Egypt's treasures and the rise of Egyptology. Illustrated. **$14.95**

MEMBERSHIP BENEFITS ● In addition to getting three books for 99¢ each when you join, you keep saving substantially on the books you buy. ● If you continue your membership past the trial period, you will be eligible for our Bonus Book Plan—an important way to save even more, at least 70% off publishers' prices. ● Your Book Club News, describing the coming Main Selection and Alternate Selections, will be sent to you 15 times a year at three to four week intervals. ● If you wish to purchase the Main Selection, do nothing and it will be sent to you automatically. ● If you prefer one of the Alternates or no book at all, simply indicate your decision on the reply form always enclosed with the News and mail it so we receive it by the date specified. ● The News is mailed in time to allow you at least 10 days to decide if you want the coming Main Selection. If because of late mail delivery of the News, you should ever receive a Main Selection without having had the 10 day consideration period, that Selection may be returned at Club expense.

36512. THE BOG PEOPLE/THE MOUND PEOPLE. *P. V. Glob.* Perfectly preserved 2,000-year-old bodies buried in peat bogs, all murdered . . . 6-ft-long oak coffins hidden within mounds of earth . . . two ancient mysteries solved by an eminent archaeologist. *The set counts as 2 of your 3 books.* **$25.00**

65220. ODDITIES OF THE MINERAL WORLD. *William B. Sanborn.* Handsomely illustrated, knowledgeable guide that spotlights some of the more peculiar and unusual mineral formations. **$9.95**

55000. THE ILLUSTRATED ENCYCLOPEDIA OF ASTRONOMY AND SPACE. *Ian Roxburgh.* Covers the full range of astronomical knowledge and space exploration, from ancient times to now. **$16.95**

48470. FIELDBOOK OF NATURAL HISTORY. *E. Laurence Palmer and H. Seymour Fowler.* The most authoritative and comprehensive guide to natural history available. With the aid of over 2,000 illustrations, it explores all major plant and animal species as well as rocks and minerals, the earth, moon, sun, and planets, and space exploration. **$19.95**

73240. QUASARS, PULSARS, AND BLACK HOLES. *Frederic Golden.* A thorough review of the spectacular discoveries in astronomy, as told by the science editor of *Time* magazine. Illustrated with twelve drawings and twenty-four color photographs. **$7.95**

Natural Science Book Club   4-5AK
Riverside, New Jersey 08075

Please accept my application for membership and send me the three volumes indicated, billing me only 99¢ each. I agree to purchase at least three additional Selections or Alternates during the first 12 months I am a member, under the club plan described in this ad. Savings range up to 30% and occasionally even more. My membership is cancelable any time after I buy these three books. A shipping and handling charge is added to all shipments.

3 books for 99¢ each.
Indicate by number the 3 books you want.

A few expensive books (noted in book descriptions) count as 2 choices.

Name _____

Address _____

City _____ State _____ Zip _____
(Offer good in Continental U.S. and Canada only. Prices slightly higher in Canada.)

vidual first experiences different events, perceives similarities and differences between them, formulates concepts or *constructs* to order these phenomena, and then uses these constructs to anticipate future events. In other words, Kelly believed that people are capable of actively engaging and anticipating the environment, rather than merely responding to it.

The Construct   According to Kelly, people use *constructs* to describe and organize the similarities and differences that they perceive in the world. This idea is best illustrated with an example. Consider the construct "tall-short." If all people were the same height, there would be no need to employ terms for describing relative height differences. Of course, we know of people who are somewhat "higher" or "larger" than others, and so we find "tall" and "short" a useful way of categorizing individuals. Kelly claims that at least three elements are necessary to make up any given construct. Two of the elements are perceived as similar and a third is perceived as different on some dimension. In order for the construct "tall-short" to be useful, one would have to know at least two tall people and one short person or one tall person and two short people. If the individual only knew one tall and one short person, he would then use other constructs (ones which would provide useful information) to describe these two individuals (e.g., name, race, sex).

A construct can also be described by its *range of convenience,* which spans all of those situations where the construct is considered useful. For example, we can easily talk about a tall or short child, a tall or short professor, or even a tall or short animal, but it is meaningless to talk about a tall or short lecture. In other words, children, professors, and animals lie within the range of convenience for the construct "tall-short," while lectures are outside the range of convenience for that construct.

In addition, constructs also vary on their *focus of convenience,* those particular events for which the construct is most useful. For the construct "tall-short," human individuals constitute the primary focus of convenience.

Individual (personality) differences are manifested in the constructs that a person uses. People differ in the constructs which they use, where they place items on that construct, the items they include within the construct (range of convenience), and the types of situations for which they find each construct most useful (focus of convenience). For example, a man who was very conscious of the fact that he was short might find "tall-short" to be the most useful construct for describing other people, while someone who was not concerned about height might find this dimension very unimportant in dealing with others. In addition, the 5'1" person might consider everyone over 5'6" as tall, while the 6'6" person would consider everyone under 5'8" as short.

Implications for Marketing   Although Kelly's theory has obvious implications for marketing, very few people have previously discussed this theory within the context of consumer behavior.[16] The personality theories which have received the most attention from marketers are those which center on the irrational, emotional, and unconscious aspects of an individual's personality. Kelly's theory provides a much-needed balance by centering on the logical, rational aspect of the personality.

An important implication of Kelly's theory for marketing is that the perception of a product depends upon the nature of the constructs that a consumer uses when evaluating that product (see Proposition 15-9 in Exhibit 15-3). When making a purchase decision, a consumer evaluates the various options using the constructs that he or she has found to be useful for such decisions. For example, let us consider the purchase of a new automobile. Consumers vary markedly in which constructs they choose as well as in the number of constructs they can coordinate when evaluating a particular product. Some of the constructs which are usually employed in evaluating an automobile include: "Economical-uneconomical," "safe-unsafe," "comfortable-uncomfortable," and "high status-low status." A man who is insecure about his own status and feels that one of the important functions of an automobile is to express the social position of the owner will give the "high status-low status" construct a great deal of weight in determining his choice. He will be aware of the position of the car on the other dimensions, but will not see those as particularly important. In evaluating a number of automobiles, two people could use the same set of constructs and rate each automobile in the same manner (e.g., both might perceive the same car as equally "economical"), yet still purchase different automobiles because they weigh the constructs differently. On the other hand, the purchase decisions of two individuals may not coincide because, although they are using the same construct, they do not rank the automobiles in the same order on that dimension. For instance, both consumers may consider status to be important. The Cadillac buyer perceives the Cadillac as a high status car, while the Mercedes-Benz owner perceives the Cadillac to be of low status.

EXHIBIT 15-3.
A Proposition from Kelly's Theory of Personal Constructs

PROPOSITION 15-9.
A person's perception of a product is a function of the constructs which that person believes to be useful for evaluating that type of product.

[16]For an exception, see G. David Hughes, "The Measurement of Beliefs and Attitudes," in Robert Ferber (ed.), *Handbook for Marketing Research,* NY: McGraw-Hill, 1974, pp. 3–16 to 3–43, where Hughes discusses a way of studying consumer perceptions of brand attributes.

From the above discussion, it follows that a marketer would want to emphasize certain constructs when promoting a product. A promotional campaign should stress constructs which differentiate a given brand from others in a positive manner. For example, for a compact car with good gas mileage, one would want the potential customer to think of cars in terms of their economy. The marketer would also want the product to be within the range of convenience of constructs which the consumer thinks are important. For example, the producers of high-priced stereo equipment realize that their potential customers are a subset of people with a reasonably high family income. If it is determined that these people find the construct "fashionable-unfashionable" to be important in determining their stereo purchases, then the stereo manufacturer would emphasize that buying the latest equipment is necessary to be fashionable.

Sometimes, however, there are no significant differences between the different brands of a given product. For example, research has indicated that consumers have difficulty differentiating brands of beer. One manufacturer, in an implicit response to this, invented a new construct to describe beer—"gusto-no gusto." It is never clear in the advertisements exactly what "gusto" is, but it is clear that its beer has it and other beers do not. The obvious hope is that beer drinkers will incorporate this construct into their beer buying decisions.

An understanding of the differences in the way customers use constructs is quite important for the salesperson. Once the constructs which are important to the consumer have been discerned, the salesperson can then emphasize those aspects of the product. If a car salesperson realizes that a potential customer is particularly concerned with comfort, he or she can emphasize the luxury aspects of the automobile and avoid references to fuel consumption or pollution. The salesperson must remember, though, that fuel consumption may be the most important construct for another customer. In addition, the salesperson or the consumer educator must make sure that the information given to the prospective buyer satisfies the relevant constructs without overloading the person with information on irrelevant constructs.

PERSONALITY TRAITS: THE FACTOR-ANALYTIC APPROACH

Underlying much of the research which has attempted to measure personality with the purpose of predicting behavior is the assumption that some set of "traits" can adequately describe the human personality. "Trait" has been defined in a number of ways, but generally refers to underlying dispositions. These dispositions are inferred from the consistencies which one perceives in the behavior of the individual in question. The term trait also implies a dimension on which people can be rated; and, in fact, various personality scales have been developed to measure the degree to which an individual displays a given trait.

Most of those who have studied the human personality have used insight and "clinical experience" (rather than systematic research) to determine which traits are important. Some psychologists, however, have become displeased with this approach. In response, they have applied a mathematical technique called factor analysis in order to quantitatively determine which of the underlying traits are most relevant.

Let us begin the description of factor analysis with a discussion of the concept of causality. If two things vary systematically with one another (i.e., when one is present, the other is present and when one is absent, the other is absent), they are said to be *correlated*. For example, the aching in a person's joints may be correlated with the onset of rain, or people who fly airplanes may also be those who buy sports cars. A simple correlation, however, does not indicate what, if any, causal relationship exists between the two events. For example, rain may cause one's joints to ache, aching joints may cause the rain (although this is highly unlikely), or both may be caused by a drop in air pressure. Similarly, flying an airplane may create a desire for a sports car, owning a sports car may cause a person to want to learn to fly, or both flying and owning a sports car may be the result of an underlying tendency to take risks.

Factor theory assumes that if certain responses repeatedly occur together (for a large number of people), then those responses reflect some underlying trait. For example, if (in a large sample) all individuals who bought sports cars also flew airplanes and responded on questionnaires that they enjoyed taking risks, a factor theorist would conclude that risk-taking was an important trait underlying these behaviors.

In practice, the factor theorist uses a large number of measures (e.g., questions about attitudes, preferences and interests, observations of behavior, tests of ability, and ratings from others) to gather data on various individuals. In order to maximize the chance that all of the important underlying factors will be uncovered, it is necessary that these measures tap many different aspects of behavior. Statistical techniques are then used to determine which of these measures correlate with one another. Measures which consistently intercorrelate (but which do not correlate with other measures) are grouped into factors. The process of determining factors is not completely objective, however, since the researcher must decide how many factors to include and exactly which of several possible statistical techniques should be used.

Once the factors have been determined, the researcher must provide a description of each one. Sometimes the measures which make up a factor have obvious commonalities, while at other times they are quite diverse. In any case, describing factors is not a straightforward process, for the researcher's subjective preconceptions concerning personality influence his or her labeling process. It should be remembered, therefore, that even though factor analysis presents a quantitative method for determining the underlying traits of personality, it is not completely objective, as it relies heavily on the researcher's insight.

To maximize the validity of a factor analytic study, it is necessary to use a wide variety of measures. If these measures do not sample an important aspect of the human personality, that aspect will not be reflected in the factors which emerge. Raymond Cattell has done extensive factor analysis in order to determine those traits which underlie personality (see Table 15-1).[17] These factors have emerged from extensive studies of both life data (i.e., existing records of an individual's behavior and others' ratings of that person) and self-rating questionnaires (which record each individual's own statements).

TABLE 15-1.
Major Personality Factors Found in Factor Analytic Work by Cattell

Letter Symbol	Technical Title	Popular Label
A	Affectothymia-Sizothymia	Outgoing-reserved
B	Intelligence	More intelligent-less intelligent
C	Ego strength	Stable-emotional
E	Dominance-Submissiveness	Assertive-humble
F	Surgency-Desurgency	Happy-go-lucky—sober
G	Super-ego Strength	Conscientious-expedient
H	Parmia-Threctia	Venturesome-shy
I	Premsia-Harria	Tender-minded—tough-minded
L	Protension-Alaxia	Suspicious-trusting
M	Autia-Praxernia	Imaginative-practical
N	Shrewdness-Artlessness	Shrewd-forthright
O	Guilt proneness-Assurance	Apprehensive-placid

If one were able to determine all of the factors which influence personality, and to know where a given person fell on each of these factors, one would have a complete description of that individual's personality. From this, it would be possible to predict the individual's behavior. Cattell suggests, that by using these traits, equations can be developed that would predict a person's behavior in a given situation.

With these equations, it is possible to use personality traits to predict specific responses, but *no one trait* will accurately predict a given behavior. Only a combination of *all* the relevant traits can make an accurate prediction. Unfortunately, most research applying personality to the understanding of consumer behavior has attempted to predict specific behaviors using only one or, at best, a limited group of traits (without knowing which traits would

[17]R. B. Cattell, *The Scientific Analysis of Personality,* Chicago: Aldine, 1966.

actually be the ones most relevant for that behavior). Cattell's theory implies that in order to determine the relationship between personality and consumer behavior, one must study not only the consumer's personality, but also the specific situation.

It was stated earlier that one of the biggest problems of research on personality and consumer behavior was a lack of theory. Factor analysis suggests a way in which one can approach this problem. The traits which Cattell emphasized were ones that emerged from a large number of items that he and his colleagues believed were relevant to personality, but these items were chosen without an explicit concern for how they would relate to consumer behavior. In order to determine those traits or factors that are relevant to their particular concerns, marketing researchers should factor analyze a variety of measures which are related to consumption (e.g., purchasing behavior, income, brand loyalty, life-style, current interests, and, of course, personality inventories). It should be noted that factor analysis has been employed in one attempt to relate personality to consumer behavior— psychographic research. This research, however, has not led to a comprehensive theory.[18]

In order to use the factor analytic method to develop a general theory of consumer behavior, it will be necessary to do extended research into a multitude of variables across a wide array of products. Such research is expensive and time consuming. In the long run, however, such an effort should lead to a more systematic understanding of the relationship between personality and consumer behavior.

THE EXISTENTIAL-PHENOMENO-LOGICAL APPROACH

We now turn to a theoretical approach, existential-phenomenology, whose application to psychology, in general, and to personality and its assessment, in particular, has only recently been presented in a systematic fashion.[19] To date, there have been no attempts to discuss its implications for marketing. From its very name, existential-phenomenological psychology is quite obviously the result of a blending of two interrelated disciplines: *existentialism,* a name given to a number of similar philosophies, and *phenomenology,* a name given to a number of similar methodologies. Although it is quite impossible to review each of these in the present context, let us take a brief look at both to see what makes this approach somewhat unique.

---

[18]W. D. Wells and D. J. Tigert, "Activities, Interests, and Opinions," *Journal of Advertising Research,* August, 1971, pp. 27–35.

[19]R. S. Valle and M. King (eds.), *Existential-Phenomenological Alternatives for Psychology,* NY: Oxford University Press, 1978.

Existentialism, as a formal philosophical school, seeks to understand the human condition as it manifests itself in our concrete, *lived* situations. Its concern for these situations includes not only the physical characteristics (such as the people and places involved), but also all of our moments of joy, absurdity, and indifference, as well as the range of freedom we believe we have in our responses to these various moments. The natural scientific approach which underlies behavioristic psychology as it is currently practiced investigates only the observable, physical, measurable aspects. It is quite oblivious to the *lived* quality of psychological situations we all face on a day-to-day basis.

Consider the following example: Suppose a man and woman have been happily married for many years, living together and sharing their life experiences for perhaps five decades. Suddenly and without warning, the wife is stricken with an illness and is dead within three days. After attending her wake and funeral, the man returns to his home in which he has lived with her for fifty years. One would be hard pressed to argue that this home is the same home he lived in the day before his wife was stricken ill. Yes, physically the house is identical—the rooms are the same size and color, the furniture is identically placed and of the same physical dimensions, the hallways are the same length, and the house smells as it did before the woman's death. But, this home *as lived* in by the man is completely different. In addition to his intense feelings and emotions, think of the perceptual changes he might have experienced. His home would be transformed, given the realization of his wife's death. Think of how the rooms and hallways he previously took for granted suddenly became the focus of his attention, every chair, every corner "speaking" to the overwhelming absence of his wife; or consider how his body, which once moved so quickly and so efficiently through his everyday tasks, now moves hesitantly and with great heaviness. If one ignored these lived dimensions in looking at the psychology of this particular individual, and examined only the measurable behaviors involved (physical or verbal), a true understanding of the man and his situation could never be accurately realized. It is the current *meaning* of his house to him that must be understood.

The major and, perhaps, the most critical issue for the phenomenologist is that people are not just objects in nature. Rather, the existential-phenomenological psychologist speaks of the total, indissoluble unity or interrelationship of the individual and his or her world. The existential man or woman is more than simply natural man or natural woman. In the truest sense the person is viewed as having no existence apart from the world, and the world as having no existence apart from persons. Each individual and his or her world are said to *co-constitute* one another, as opposed to traditional psychology where people and their environment are seen, in effect, as two separate and distinct things or poles.

This notion of *co-constitutionality* can be a difficult one to grasp. Let's begin with a simple perceptual example. Figure 15-12 shows the popular "vase and faces" drawing. In this picture one can either treat the center portion as "figure" and the outer area as "ground" (in which case one sees the vase), or one can treat the center as "ground" and the outer area as "figure" (in which case one sees two facial profiles facing one another). In this drawing, then, it is quite clear that the vase and faces cannot exist without one another. Remove one and the notion of the other has *no meaning. So it is with people and their world;* if one is discarded, any talk of the other is meaningless. The human individual is "contextualized," for it is impossible to conceive of a person

FIGURE 15-12
Vase and Faces Drawing

Source: Linda Wood (ed.), *The Psychology Primer,* Publisher's Inc., 1975, p. 116.

without the familiar surrounding world (houses in which that person lives, trees among which that person walks, sky upon which that person gazes, and others to whom that person talks). It is via the world that the very *meaning* of the person's existence emerges both for the person and for others. The converse is equally true. It is each individual's existence that gives his or her world meaning. Without a person to reveal its sense and meaning, the world would not exist as it does. Each is, therefore, totally dependent on the other for existence. This is why in existential-phenomenological thought, existence *always* implies that being is actually "being-in-the-world."

Again, *meaning* emerges as the critical issue to be understood. The phenomenologist sees meaning as the temporary, situational expression of a psychological phenomenon's *structure.* In other words, it is through the perception of meaning that one perceives the very nature or structure of the particular phenomenon being considered. Psychological phenomena, as they are present to us, reveal themselves in different ways depending on how we look at them or "take them up" in our many, varied perspectives and life situations. Regardless of which of the phenomenon's particular variations is revealed at any given time, the phenomenon is seen as having the same essential meaning when it is perceived over time in many different situations. The perceived phenomenon is analogous to a mineral crystal which appears to have many different sizes and shapes depending on the intensity, angle, and color of the light which strikes its surfaces. Only after seeing these different reflections and varied appearances on repeated occasions does the constant, unchanging crystalline *structure* become known to us.

Consider an example from the psychological realm: "Being anxious" is an experience which has meaning for all of us. "Being anxious," however, never arises in exactly the same way; we may be anxious before taking an examination for which we have not studied, when anticipating the ending to a horror movie, before going to the dentist, or, very often, for no apparent reason at all. These are all different manifestations which constitute the meaningful experience which we label as "being anxious." This form, recognized despite its many variations, is evident in *each one* of these different instances. This unchanging commonality among instances is the *structure* of the particular phenomenon.

The existential-phenomenological approach is concerned with understanding phenomena through description rather than with predicting and controlling human behavior. Therefore, rather than suggesting specific ways in which products can be marketed, it poses questions which can be asked or topics which should be considered by marketers. A better understanding of the phenomena related to consumption will be an aid to the marketer or policy maker when making decisions.

An individual does not merely use the products he or she purchases. Rather, these products have a *lived* quality which is expressed and thereby revealed in the individual's everyday experience (see Proposition 15-10 in Exhibit 15-4). The marketer should not merely ask how a product will be used or what needs it satisfies, but should also be concerned with how the product is lived. For example, one could ask the question: "How does a specific individual experience life differently after purchasing a new car?" One might find that the consumer has a different perception of himself or herself when riding in the car and that he or she feels higher in status, more important, and generally, a better person. In other words, the marketer would be asking about the meaning that a new product has for an individual. This is quite different from merely knowing a person's attitude toward a product (whether it be positive or negative, for example). Phenomenological understanding is concerned with the manner in which the product affects how the individual lives his or her life.

EXHIBIT 15-4.
Propositions from Existential-Phenomenological Psychology

PROPOSITION 15-10.
Products are not just things that an individual uses; they have a lived quality.

PROPOSITION 15-11.
A product and the individual user or consumer cannot be completely understood separately since they co-constitute one another.

The concept of co-constitutionality also has important implications for the way marketers can approach the study of consumers (see Proposition 15-11 in Exhibit 15-4). For example, one cannot think of a product as separate in some way from the person who is buying or using it. The product has no meaning when thought of apart from the context provided by the particular consumer, and supposedly identical products are therefore different when they are used by different people. It is incorrect for a company to say that it has sold a thousand identical dresses, when the essence of *each* dress is co-determined by the woman wearing it. The woman and the dress *co-constitute* one another. It is a different dress, with a different meaning, for each woman. Similarly, the woman is different depending upon what clothes she wears. A salesperson should be aware of this, and realize that each sale is different. Each sale is uniquely co-constituted by the product and the consumer.

Needless to say, the methodology used to descriptively examine the meaning of a product for the consumer is different from the methodology which is used to study the demographic variables that correlate with the purchase of a particular product. Although this is not the place to describe phenomenological methodologies,[20] researchers studying the phenomena of consumption should consider the possibility and importance of investigating the structure of the experience "being desirous of," a phenomenon which clearly underlies all of consumer behavior.

SUMMARY Psychological approaches to the study of personality have implications that are useful for the study of consumer behavior. Of specific importance are Freud's psychoanalytic theory, Jung's analytic psychology, Kelly's theory of personal constructs, the factor-analytic trait approach, and the existential-phenomenological approach.

For Freud, the different facets of the personality—the id, ego, and superego—struggle for control as the person passes through various developmental stages. During this process, anxiety-causing conflicts result in the activation of defense mechanisms such as repression, sublimation, reaction formation, and projection. Since persons are motivated by both conscious and unconscious forces, consumer behavior is also based, to some extent, on these forces.

In addition to the conscious mind and the personal unconscious, Jung believed that there is a collective unconscious which is structured around universal thought-forms, or archetypes. Such archetypes as the anima (a man's idealized woman), animus (a woman's idealized man), shadow (the animal side of human nature), and persona (the public self) have an integral influence on one's consumer and other behavior. Jung's cognitive dimensions of thinking, feeling, sensing, and intuiting are the ways in which he believed people relate to the world. One implication for marketing is that promotional campaigns should appeal to the mode of relating to the world which is most commonly used by the target population of the campaign.

According to Kelly, people are capable of actively dealing with and anticipating life, rather than merely responding to it. Through personal constructs, people order life's phenomena and anticipate future events. Rather than focusing on the irrational, emotional, or unconscious aspects of personality, Kelly's theory focuses on the logical, rational facets of the person. Since the perception of a product is contingent upon the constructs with which the individual consumer evaluates the product, an advertising campaign should emphasize constructs which differentiate the product from others in a positive way.

---

[20]See P. F. Colaizzi, "Psychological Research as the Phenomenologist Views It," in R. S. Valle and M. King (eds.), *op. cit.*

Factor-analytic theory assumes that, if particular responses continually occur together for a large number of people, then those responses indicate an underlying trait. So, if one knew all of the traits that influenced a person, one would have a complete description of that person's personality, and from that it would be possible to predict behavior.

Within the existential-phenomenological approach, individual perceptions and personalities are inextricably bound with their lived situations or environment. With such an interrelationship between the individual and his or her world, where the person and the world co-constitute each other, the marketer must keep in mind that a consumer and a product cannot be understood separately. Since the same products become different when used by different people, marketers must focus on how products affect the lives of individuals.

Though more study is required concerning the relationship between personality and consumer behavior, especially in the area of theory, each of the five approaches mentioned has important implications for marketers and is applicable in relevant consumer situations.

KEY CONCEPTS

Anima, animus

Archetypes

Collective unconscious

Construct

Ego

Electra complex

Existentialism

Focus of convenience

Id

Idiographic approach

Nomothetic approach

Oedipal complex

Personality

Projective test

Range of convenience

Superego

ATTITUDES AND ATTITUDE CHANGE AND MEASUREMENT

16

CHAPTER GOALS   The objective of this chapter is to help the reader understand:
1. **a widely used model of attitudes;**
2. **those variables which mediate the relationship between attitudes and behavior, such as the certainty of the attitude, personal factors, and situational factors;**
3. **how attitudes can be measured;**
4. **a model of the ways attitudes change.**

INTRODUCTION   The concept of attitude is perhaps the most thoroughly studied area in the current consumer behavior literature. Attitudes are indeed important because they reflect what consumers think, feel, and are inclined to do about a product or service. Knowing what consumer attitudes are and whether they may be altered is extremely valuable information for a marketer, and large sums of money are expended to uncover and influence consumer attitudes. For this reason, it is important for the reader to be familiar with the key issues and findings in attitude research as it relates to consumer behavior.

There are many definitions of attitudes in the social psychology and marketing literatures. Perhaps the best definition is provided by Martin Fishbein and Icek Ajzen *"[an] attitude can be described as a learned predisposition to respond in a consistently favorable or unfavorable manner with respect to a given object."*[1] The important dimensions of this definition are: (1) that an

---

[1]Martin Fishbein and Icek Ajzen, *Belief, Attitude Intention and Behavior,* Reading, MA: Addison-Wesley Publishing Company, 1975, p. 6.

attitude is learned, (2) that an attitude involves a predisposition or tendency to behave in a certain way, and (3) that the relevant aspects of the behavioral response are its favorability (either favorable or unfavorable) and its consistency. Not all persons studying attitudes agree on what these three dimensions mean or how they should be measured. Though a review of all of the different theories about attitudes would be too large an undertaking for this book, there are a number of sources the reader may consult for a review of attitude theories.[2]

In this chapter we give a basic overview of the relationship between attitudes and consumer behavior. In the first section we discuss the Fishbein model of attitudes. This model is not the only model of attitudes which has been suggested, nor is it without its faults; however, the Fishbein model adequately serves as a structure for the discussion in this chapter. In the next section we explore the consistency between attitudes and behavior, and the several factors which may account for differences between attitudes and behavior. Following this, we turn to an explanation of several methods used by researchers for measuring attitudes. Finally, the process through which marketers attempt to change consumers' attitudes is described.

THE FISHBEIN MODEL OF ATTITUDES

In this chapter, attitudes are viewed as having two basic components—beliefs and values. (Some researchers identify a third component, intention to act. This is also treated in this chapter.) "Values are determined by what society considers good or bad. A belief is a state of knowledge, called a *cognition* by psychologists. Operationally, a belief is measured as the probability that something exists. Awareness and unawareness represent the extremes of belief. The mathematical product of a belief times a value yields an attitude. For example, if a consumer values tooth decay prevention highly [as an attribute] and if he or she believes that there is a high probability that brand A has this

---

[2]Fishbein and Ajzen, *ibid;* G. David Hughes, *Attitude Measurement for Marketing Strategies,* Glenview, IL: Scott, Foresman and Co., 1971; Gary Cronkhite, *Persuasion: Speech and Behavioral Change,* Indianapolis, Bobbs-Merrill, 1969; George S. Day, "Theories of Attitude Structure and Change," in Scott Ward and Thomas S. Robertson (eds.), *Consumer Behavior: Theoretical Sources,* Englewood Cliffs, NJ: Prentice-Hall, 1973, pp. 353–383; Charles A. Kiesler, Barry E. Collins, and Norman Miller, *Attitude Change: A Critical Analysis of Theoretical Approaches,* NY: John Wiley & Sons, Inc., 1969; Nan Lin, *The Study of Human Communication,* Indianapolis: Bobbs-Merrill, 1973; and Joe Kent Kerby, *Consumer Behavior: Conceptual Foundations,* NY: Dun-Donnelley Publishing Corp., 1975.

attribute, the consumer will have a favorable attitude toward this brand."[3] A product or service has many features or attributes, and the consumer will have an attitude toward each of these attributes. The *sum* of all these attitudes, favorable and unfavorable, represents the consumer's overall attitude toward the product. In other words, the overall attitude results from the consumer's assessment or evaluation of the satisfaction a product is likely to provide. Attitudes may be favorable or unfavorable, strong or weak, and important or unimportant.

The most widely discussed attitude theory in marketing is the so-called Fishbein model. (There are several good papers which discuss and elaborate this model in marketing contexts.[4]) Fishbein's first basic formulation of an attitude was:

$$A_o = \sum_{i=1}^{n} B_i a_i$$

Where:

A_o is the attitude toward an object,

B_i represents the strength of the belief that attribute "i" is related to the object (e.g. that the toothpaste has a decay fighting ingredient), and

a_i is the value of this attribute to the consumer.

Thus, an attitude toward a brand of toothpaste can be described verbally as follows:

Attitude Toward a Brand = (the believed likelihood it has an effective decay fighting chemical *times* the "goodness" of this attribute) *plus* (the believed likelihood it has an effective tooth brightener *times* the goodness of this attribute) *plus*... and so on for all attributes.

---

[3]Hughes, *op. cit.*, p. 9.

[4]Olli T. Ahtola, "The Vector Model of Preferences: An Alternative to the Fishbein Model," *Journal of Marketing Research,* Vol. 12, February, 1975, pp. 52–54; Neil E. Beckwith and Donald R. Lehmann, "The Importance of Halo Effects in Multi-Attribute Attitude Models," *Journal of Marketing Research,* Vol. 12, August, 1975, pp. 265–275; Joel B. Cohen, Martin Fishbein and Olli T. Ahtola, "The Nature and Uses of Expectancy-Value Models in Consumer Attitude Research," *Journal of Marketing Research,* Vol. 9, November, 1972, pp. 456–460; William L. Wilkie and Edgar A. Pessemier, "Issues in Marketing's Use of Multi-Attribute Attitude Models," *Journal of Marketing Research,* Vol. 10, November, 1973, pp. 428–441; Michael J. Ryan and E. H. Bonfield, "The Fishbein Extended Model and Consumer Behavior," *Journal of Consumer Research,* Vol. 2, No. 2, September, 1975, pp. 118–136; Peter D. Bennett and Gilbert D. Harrell, "The Role of Confidence in Understanding and Predicting Buyers' Attitudes and Purchase Intentions," *Journal of Consumer Research,* Vol. 2, No. 7, September, 1975, pp. 110–117; and Jagdish N. Sheth, "A Field Study of Attitude Structure and the Attitude-Behavior Relationship," in Jagdish N. Sheth (ed.), *Models of Buyer Behavior: Conceptual, Quantitive, and Empirical,* NY: Harper & Row, 1974, pp. 242–268.

This basic idea, as put forth by Fishbein, has been extended in recent years. One extension was developed by Fishbein himself and is commonly referred to as the Extended Fishbein Model. This revised model incorporates attitudinal and social influences in attempting to explain the emergence of *intentions* to behave.[5] We will use it as a basis for discussing attitudes. But first we must examine the components of the Extended Fishbein Model.

This extended model describes behavioral intentions ("I plan to buy…") which result from a person's attitudes toward performing the behavior in question and the person's subjective perception of the norm concerning that behavior. The subjective perception of a norm is the person's perception of how others will look upon that behavior (see Chapter 5 on groups and norms). Thus:

Intention to Behave = (Attitude toward performing a behavior *times* some weight) *plus* (the subjective norm concerning the behavior *times* some weight).

Each of the two components of Intention to Behave can be further specified. The attitudes toward the performance of the behavior depend upon what the person believes will happen if he or she performs the behavior. This also takes into account the individual's evaluation of the consequence. Thus:

Attitude Toward Performing a Behavior = the belief that the behavior leads to a specified consequence *times* the individual's evaluation of that consequence.

For example, if a consumer believes that using a particular kind of toothpaste will lead to brighter teeth and the consumer evaluates bright teeth highly, the consumer will have a favorable attitude toward using that toothpaste. There may, of course, be many consequences of a specific behavior which are being considered at the same time.

The subjective norm is based on the normative belief of some reference person or group concerning whether or not the behavior should be performed. Subjective norms also take into account how motivated a person is to comply with that reference group's norms. Thus:

The Subjective Norm Concerning the Behavior = the normative beliefs about a behavior *times* the individual's motivation to comply with those norms.

There are likely to be many reference groups and/or persons who have normative beliefs about performing a given behavior.

---

[5]Fishbein and Ajzen, *op. cit.*

Thus, a consumer's intention to buy or not to buy a product is basically a result of the consumer's attitude toward the very act of going out and buying the product, and all the activities and experiences involved in that purchase process, plus what the consumer thinks about the social desirability of buying the product.

Consider, for example, the intention of purchasing a large automobile. Some consumers like comparison shopping and interacting with sales personnel, and others dislike these activities. The first group of consumers has favorable attitudes toward the buying process involving automobiles. They may believe that these activities result in much better decisions, and they may place greater importance on making the best decision. The second group has unfavorable attitudes. On the basis of this information, we may begin to make a prediction about whether each group is likely to express an intention to actually buy a large automobile within a given period of time. But we also have to consider some other factors besides how much the experiences of going about buying a car are liked or disliked. In this case we have specified a large car. Let's assume "large" carries with it the attribute or characteristic of poor gas mileage. To the extent that this is true and that social norms exist which are unfavorable to the purchase of energy wasting products ("small is better"), consumers in either group might be reluctant to purchase a large automobile. They only *might* be, however. How influential this norm is depends on how motivated the consumer is to comply with the norm. If we know how motivated consumers are to comply with norms relevant to the purchase situation, we can make a prediction about whether they are likely to express an intention to actually buy a large car.

The discussion thus far might be summarized in the following way:

		ATTITUDE TOWARD THE ACT OF BUYING A (LARGE) CAR	
		Favorable	Unfavorable
MOTIVATION TO COMPLY WITH RELEVANT NORMS WHICH ARE OPPOSED TO THE PURCHASE OF LARGE CARS	High	Cell 1	Cell 2
	Low	Cell 3	Cell 4

Consumers in cell 2 would probably express little or no intention to buy a large car. Not only is the buying process unattractive, but social norms with which they wish to comply are against it, too. On the other hand, consumers in cell 3 will probably express a serious intention to buy a large car. Presumably, consumers in cells 1 and 4 fall between consumers in cells 2 and 3 in their intention to buy a large car.

Will consumers in cell 1, who like the buying act but are highly influenced by a norm against buying, express a stronger intention to buy than consumers in cell 4 who are relatively unaffected by the norm but don't like the idea of buying a large car? This question points out an important omission thus far. What is the importance of attitude toward the purchase and the importance of subjective norms? These two components of intention to behave are not necessarily equal in influence. Therefore, it is necessary to assign a weight to each of them. The discussion of reactance in Chapter 5 on norms and groups suggests that consumers may be strongly motivated not to comply with norms, and may therefore make purchases even when attitudes toward the act of buying may not be particularly favorable. Thus, to know whether consumers in cell 1 are more or less likely than consumers in cell 4 to express an intention to buy a large car, we would need to know the relative weights they assign to their attitudes and subjective norms. Thus, the verbal formula for an intention to behave involves multiplying the two basic components of that formula by some weights.

Before going on, let us consider one more example. Using the two components of an intention to behave, we will examine a plant manager's recent plans to purchase the services of a marketing research consultant for assistance in developing and introducing a new product into the market. This particular manager had a very positive attitude toward the purchase, and believed that the consultant could provide useful information about the potential consumers. He also believed that it was very probable that purchasing the services would bring favor from top management for his objectivity in relying upon experts. But, though both of these attributes were important to him, there was, within his plant, a subjective norm against relying on outsiders. Workers within the plant liked to view themselves as self-sufficient and free from the need for outside consultants. Since top management's favor and useful market information were more important to the plant manager than his motivation to comply with the self-reliance norm at the plant, he planned to purchase the services of the marketing research consultant.

Before continuing with the discussion of attitudes, however, it is very important to address one particular issue, namely the relationship between attitudes and behavior. One of the major reasons why marketers have been interested in attitudes is that they are believed to be the basis for actual behavior—if a consumer has a favorable attitude toward a brand or store, it is usually assumed that the consumer will purchase that brand or patronize that store. This assumption is discussed below.

ATTITUDE-BEHAVIOR CONSISTENCY

A major concern in social psychology and in the study of consumer behavior is the apparent weak relationship between attitudes and behavior.[6] The problem is that certain attitudes and behaviors are not related to each other, although intuitively at least, it seems as if they should be.[7] Allan W. Wicker, in his review of empirical studies, anticipated the conclusions of the most recent researchers' writings about attitude-behavior consistency: "Taken as a whole, these studies suggest that it is considerably more likely that attitudes will be unrelated or only slightly related to overt behaviors than that attitudes will be closely related to actions. Product-moment *correlation coefficients* relating the two kinds of responses are rarely above .30, and *often are near zero.*"[8] In other words, people very often do not do what they have said they will do. For instance, consumers may tell a survey researcher they would be extremely pleased if a new shopping center opened within two miles of their home. Yet, because of other factors, they may never visit such a shopping center if it opens.

Why don't attitudes predict behavior? As yet there are no clear answers. The most basic reason, perhaps, is that we are expecting too much when we think that attitudes, *taken alone,* should be able to predict behavior. Obviously, there are many other factors that determine how humans behave. In fact, there are two major classes of factors affecting the relationship between attitudes and behavior: those that are personal and those that are situational. Both types will be discussed shortly. Another reason for the weak predictive relationships, which will not be examined in detail here, concerns the methodologies involved in the study of attitudes and their relationships to

[6]For several recent discussions of this issue see: Steven J. Gross and C. Michael Niman, "Attitude-Behavior Consistency: A Review," *Public Opinion Quarterly,* Fall, 1975, Vol. 39, No. 3, pp. 358–368; I. Deutscher, *What We Say/What We Do: Sentiments and Acts,* Glenview, IL: Scott, Foresman & Co.; Howard J. Ehrlich, "Attitudes, Behaviors, and the Intervening Variables," *American Sociologist,* Vol. 4, February, 1969, pp. 29–34; Allan E. Liska, "Emergent Issues in the Attitude-Behavior Consistency Controversy," *American Sociological Review,* Vol. 39, No. 2, April, 1974, pp. 261–272; John Sample and Rex Warland, "Attitude and Prediction of Behavior," *Social Forces,* Vol. 51, March, 1973, pp. 292–304; and William A. McGuire, "The Concepts of Attitudes and Their Relations to Behaviors," in H. W. Sinarko and L. A. Broedling (eds.), *Perspectives on Attitude Assessment: Surveys and Their Alternatives,* Washington, D.C.: Smithsonian Institute, 1975, pp. 16–40. An advanced but excellent treatment of this issue can be found in Martin Fishbein and Icek Ajzen, *Belief, Attitude, Intention and Behavior: An Introduction to Theory and Research,* Reading, MA: Addison-Wesley Publishing Co., 1975, esp. Chapters 7 and 8.

[7]C. A. Kiesler, D. C. Collins and W. Miller, *Attitude Change,* NY: John Wiley, 1969. At best the concept of attitude accounts for very little in predicting behavior (Gross and Niman, *op. cit.,* pp. 362–363).

[8]Allan W. Wicker, "Attitudes versus Actions: The Relationship of Verbal and Overt Behavioral Responses to Attitude Objects," *Journal of Social Issues,* Vol. 25, No. 4, Autumn, 1969, p. 65, italics added.

behavior.[9] This explanation for attitude-behavior inconsistency is derived from the poor measures often used in research on attitudes and behavior, for often, researchers do not measure these two variables very carefully. Measurement problems, however, do not account for all of the failures to predict behavior from attitudes.

Certainty of the Attitude

It appears that the more certain a person is about an attitude, the more that attitude will be an accurate predictor of some behavior. The less certain a person is about an attitude, the less it will predict behavior and the more important will be personal variables, such as abilities, and situational variables, such as the ease of buying a product.[10] Propositions 16-1 and 16-2 in Exhibit 16-1 express these very important ideas. People's attitudes about a particular behavior become more certain as the time at which the behavior will occur approaches. Thus, consumers are much more certain of their attitudes toward purchasing a particular grocery item (e.g., bread or canned corn) this week than they are of their attitudes toward purchasing the same item two years from now.

EXHIBIT 16-1.
Propositions Concerning Attitude Certainty and Behavior

PROPOSITION 16-1.
The more certain a consumer is about an attitude, the more accurate that attitude will be in predicting the consumer's behavior.

PROPOSITION 16-2.
The less certain a consumer is about an attitude, the more important will be personal and situational variables in predicting the consumer's behavior.

Two researchers studied the role of buyers' confidence in the formation of attitudes and intentions to purchase.[11] Physicians were tested in regard to

---

[9]For a good example of the methodological issues involved, see Russell H. Weigel and Lee S. Newman, "Increasing Attitude-Behavior Correspondence by Broadening the Scope of the Behavioral Measure," *Journal of Personality and Social Psychology,* Vol. 33, No. 6, 1976. pp. 793–802.

[10]Sample and Warland, *op. cit.*

[11]Peter D. Bennett and Gilbert D. Harrell, "The Role of Confidence in Understanding and Predicting Buyers' Attitudes and Purchase Intentions," *Journal of Consumer Research,* Vol. 2, September, 1975, pp. 110–117.

the brands of drugs they prescribed for treating a form of diabetes. This study led the researchers to conclude that the level of confidence in one's beliefs about a brand, whether the confidence is favorable or unfavorable, is related to intention to behave toward the brand. So, marketing researchers should not just measure consumers' attitudes, but should also determine how developed these attitudes are. If consumers are uncertain concerning an attitude, the marketer interested in predicting consumer behavior should look for other variables on which to base prediction. We turn now to some of these other variables.

Personal Factors

Personal factors are those characteristics of an individual which moderate the relationship between that person's attitudes and behavior. These factors are discussed below.

Other Attitudes. For any individual, some attitudes are stronger than others. It is reasonable to expect that a strong attitude may override a weaker, incompatible one. For example, a consumer may feel a certain fabric, such as silk, is especially attractive in an article of clothing, thus suggesting that this consumer would purchase silk clothes. But another attitude, perhaps a feeling that it is improper to be extravagant about clothing quality, may lead the consumer to avoid the purchase of silk clothing. Thus, a marketer must try to determine what array of attitudes are related to a purchase, and determine which of these attitudes are strongest.

Abilities. A consumer may lack the abilities necessary for translating an attitude into action. For example, a person might not understand how to order a product through a mail-order catalogue or may not be able to remember a telephone number stated unexpectedly in an advertisement. Also, consumers may not be able to articulate a particular attitude very well, with the result that a market researcher may obtain an inaccurate picture of what the attitude really is. In an industrial setting, a purchasing agent may express a genuinely favorable attitude toward a product, but not recommend its purchase because it is not compatible with the other equipment or supplies with which it would have to be used. The firm may lack the ability to integrate the product into its current productive capacities.

Activity Levels. Some people are more active consumers than others, even taking into account financial and other factors affecting the ability to consume. This does not mean that their attitudes toward a particular brand or product category are necessarily stronger than those of less active consumers. Rather, the active consumer simply has a greater opportunity to reflect attitudes through purchases. Thus, it is important when predicting the response of a market segment to a new product to take into account the consumption level of that market segment. The higher the level of consumption, the more likely an attitude is to accurately predict behavior concerning the relevant product.

Situational Factors Situational factors are characteristics of the social environment of a consumer which may affect the relationship between that consumer's attitudes and behavior. A desired product may be out of stock, or the store distributing a particular product may be located too far away from where the consumer lives or works. In addition, the attitude toward a particular type of clothing (e.g., blue jeans) may depend upon the intended context of use (e.g., to wear to class at a university or to wear to a job interview).

For example, two researchers found that by combining measures of situational variables with measures of attitudes toward various soft drinks they were able to significantly increase their understanding of behavioral intentions.[12] This indicates that situational variables are necessary for explaining the link between attitudes and behavior.

One writer has listed five types of situational characteristics.[13] These are:
1. Physical Surroundings
2. Social Surroundings
3. Temporal Perspective
4. Task Definition
5. Antecedent States

Physical surroundings include the building or outdoor setting in which the behavior occurs. Social surroundings include the other people present in the situation. Temporal perspective includes such things as time of day, season, and the amount of time since the last meal. Task definition is the way the person perceives the task at hand (e.g., the purchase of a pair of shoes for hiking or the purchase of a pair of shoes for a dance class). Antecedent states are temporary circumstances such as the consumer's moods or cash on hand. Several examples of the effects of these situational variables on consumer attitudes and behavior will be discussed.

Norms and Presence of Other People. The presence of nonsales persons at the time of purchase is a social surroundings situation variable and one of the

---

[12]William O. Bearden and Arch G. Woodside, "Interactions of Consumption Situations and Brand Attitudes," *Journal of Applied Psychology,* Vol. 61, December, 1976, pp. 764–769.
[13]Russell W. Belk, "Situational Variables and Consumer Behavior," *Journal of Consumer Research,* Vol. 2, December, 1975, pp. 157–164.

less frequently studied aspects of consumer behavior. A consumer may actually like an inexpensive brand of soup but, if shopping with a friend, may feel some social pressure to buy a more expensive (presumably better) brand. The same buyer's statements in a telephone interview concerning the inexpensive brand would be inconsistent with actual in-store behavior. Similarly, a husband's attitudes toward a new fashion in men's clothing may be neutralized by a stronger, contrary attitude expressed by his wife when helping him shop for clothes. In other words, in different buying situations a consumer's attitude is altered because of forces which change either the person's beliefs or the person's evaluation of a brand on a particular attribute.

The presence of other people at the time an attitude is solicited can also affect what attitude is expressed. Respondents may tell an interviewer what they think an interviewer wants to hear. Or, if other people are present during the interview, the attitude expressed may reflect the respondent's need for approval from these other people rather than a "true" attitude. Thus, social norms can influence what attitude is expressed, as well as what behavior occurs when the people supporting or advocating those norms are present. Social norms influence attitudes even if members of the relevant reference group are not present. This is so because each person has internalized norms which operate even in the absence of those who might enforce the norm.

External Barriers. Even though favorable attitudes toward a product exist, there are many obstacles which can prevent those attitudes from being expressed in actual behavior. Some of these barriers may be elements of the physical surroundings. A stock-out due to poor inventory management may occur in one of the chains carrying a product. The manufacturer will not necessarily know that distribution was inadequate, and may conclude that the wrong type of premiums were used. Or, perhaps the manufacturer would attribute the lack of consumer response to a heavily promoted "special" or to the communication campaign used.

Specificity of Attitude Objects. Often an attitude is measured in a general way, while the behavior which is being associated with the attitude is highly specific. For example, attitudes toward fabric softeners in general may be very favorable among some clearly defined consumer group. This does not necessarily mean that this group will respond favorably to a particular brand. The general idea of the softener may be attractive, but a specific brand is more than a general idea. It is a specific idea with a specific color, texture, fragrance, and size. Any of these specific attributes may elicit very unfavorable feelings among consumers. These unfavorable feelings toward a specific brand may outweigh the favorable attitude toward the product class. This difference between the attitude and the behavior might therefore stem from differences in the task definition.

In a summary of the literature on personal and situational factors, two writers suggest two findings.[14] One finding is that situational factors are better predictors of behavior than personal factors. The other finding is that the more the situation in which an attitude is measured is similar to the situation in which the overt behavior is measured, the more consistent the two measurements will be (Propositions 16-3 and 16-4).

EXHIBIT 16-2.
Propositions About Personal and Situational Factors and Behavior

PROPOSITION 16-3.
Situational factors are better predictors of consumer behavior than are personal factors.

PROPOSITION 16-4.
The more the situation in which an attitude is measured is similar to the situation in which behavior is measured, the more accurate attitudes will be in predicting behavior.

General Comments on Attitude-Behavior Consistency

Considering Propositions 16-1 to 16-4 together, we can conclude that attitudes held with great certainty are likely to be accurate predictors of consumer behavior. This is especially likely when the situations in which the attitudes and the behavior are observed are similar. When attitude certainty is low, however, the marketers should focus especially on situational factors as well as on personal factors.

Research suggests that attitudes, especially attitudes toward doing what a product implies, should be considered primarily in connection with *intentions* to behave, rather than overt behavior. Intentions to behave, then, should be connected with behavior after taking into account factors intervening between intentions and overt behavior. For example, Fishbein and Ajzen suggest the paradigm shown in Figure 16-1.[15] This paradigm says simply that consumers take into account what could happen if a fabric softener (stimulus) is used in doing laundry, and what their feelings are about those consequences. This will influence the consumers' feelings toward *using* a fabric softener (which may differ from feelings about fabric softeners in general). Consumers also take into account their own personal standards about using fabric softeners, as well as what they perceive significant other people think about what should

[14]Gross and Niman, *op. cit.*
[15]Adapted from Fishbein and Ajzen, *op. cit.*, p. 334 and p. 16.

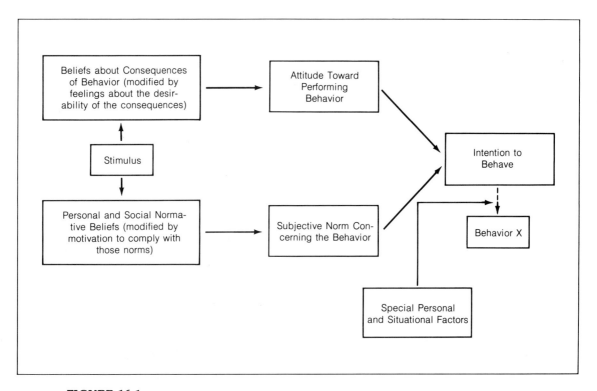

FIGURE 16-1.
A Stimulus-Intention-Behavior Paradigm.

be done with regard to fabric softeners. There may or may not be strong motivation to comply with these personal and social norms. These norms and the level of motivation to comply with them yield a general subjective norm concerning the use of a fabric softener, So, the attitude toward the act of using a fabric softener together with the subjective norms determine whether intentions to purchase and use a fabric softener are high, low, or somewhere in between. If these intentions are high, for example, we would expect the consumer to use the product. This expectation, however, would be warranted only if the important personal and situational barriers discussed earlier are not operating. For instance, the consumer may be in a situation where his or her laundry is done by someone else. Hence, favorable attitudes toward certain laundry products will not directly lead to action such as purchasing and using these products. Personal and situational factors may also be operating at the initial stimulus point.

The research literature cited earlier permits a few general propositions concerning attitude-behavior consistency, which are contained in Exhibit 16-3. First, it is not always clear to consumers how to express a particular

EXHIBIT 16-3.
*Propositions About
Attitude-Behavior
Consistency*

PROPOSITION 16-5.
The less clear a consumer is about how to express an attitude through overt behavior, the lower will be the degree of attitude-behavior consistency.

PROPOSITION 16-6.
The less easily disclosed an attitude is, the less likely it is that particular behaviors can be labelled as either consistent or inconsistent with an attitude.

PROPOSITION 16-7.
The smaller the degree to which a marketer (observer) and consumer share a common interpretation of a consumer's behavior, the greater the likelihood the marketer will see the consumer as being inconsistent in attitude and behavior when, in fact, the consumer is being consistent.

attitude in terms of behavior. They may therefore express it by acting in a way different from that expected by the researcher. Incomplete learning can cause this to happen and consumers may indicate that they would indeed like more product information or information about, for instance, credit terms. But, they may not possess or may not have learned the necessary skills to interpret the data about nutrients, tire life, or insurance policy actuarial data. When presented with this information, they may, in effect, behave indifferently and not use it. Related to ability is the issue of accessibility. In the examples above, consumers may not know where to obtain information, or they may not be provided with the opportunity to obtain it. Under these circumstances, behavior could not be expected to be consistent with attitudes.

People vary in the degrees to which they are willing to disclose their attitudes. Thus, while certain attitudes might be inferred from behavior, it may be difficult to obtain verbal or written expressions of attitudes concerning the product in question. Manufacturers of colored condoms have been vexed in their efforts to determine what experiences and attitudes concerning sex are associated with the marked preference for gaily-colored condoms over the traditional neutral color.

Finally, a consumer may express a very favorable attitude toward a cereal product, but may only infrequently repeat the purchase. This could be interpreted in many ways. For instance, it might be the result of a dislike of the product by others in the family. The consumer may maintain a favorable attitude toward the cereal, but purchase it infrequently because of a desire to vary the cereals consumed. This behavior is not inconsistent with the expressed attitudes, although the marketer, if unaware of consumers' needs for variation in their diets, will probably conclude that their behavior is inconsistent.

The Effect of Behavior on Attitudes

In discussing the subject of attitude-behavior consistency, we have focused on attitudes as determinants of a behavior. Yet it also appears that one's behavior affects one's attitudes. The process of translating past behaviors into attitudes is known as self-attribution. Basically, self-attribution theory states that we come to know our attitudes by examining our behavior and the context in which it occurs. Because of the importance of attribution processes for the study of consumer behavior, they are explored in a separate chapter (see Chapter 17). However, the key point here is that attitudes affect behavior, and behavior affects attitudes.

ATTITUDE MEASUREMENT

Five general categories of attitude measurement can be distinguished:
1. Measures in which inferences are drawn from self-reports of beliefs, behaviors, etc.
2. Measures in which inferences are drawn from the observation of ongoing behavior in a natural setting.
3. Measures in which inferences are drawn from the individual's reaction to or interpretation of partially structured stimuli.
4. Measures in which inferences are drawn from the performance of "objective" tasks.
5. Measures in which inferences are drawn from physiological reactions to the attitudinal object or representations of it.[16]

Self-Report Measures

Most consumer behavior studies use a self-report approach involving paper and pencil tests. Several types of scales used in such paper and pencil tests are discussed below.

Thurstone's Equal-Appearing Interval Scale. Thurstone's approach involves having "judges" scale attitude statements along an attitude continuum:

The pool of items collected by the investigator is given to a sample of judges representative of the population of subjects whose attitudes are to be

---

[16]Kiesler, et al., op. cit.

assessed. . . . The judges are required to indicate the amount of favorableness or unfavorableness toward the attitude object implied by agreement with a given item. More specifically, the judges sort each item into one of eleven categories that they are to consider equal intervals along the evaluative dimension, ranging from "unfavorable" through "neutral" to "favorable" toward the attitude object.[17]

The consumer is then presented with a list of statements which do not have any numerical indication of their degree of favorableness or unfavorableness toward the attitude object. The consumer merely indicates agreement or disagreement with each statement. Then, those statements which were agreed with are categorized by the researchers according to the degree of favorableness toward the attitude object which expert judges believe the statements reflected. Extremely favorable statements are categorized as an eleven; extremely unfavorable statements are coded as a one. Intermediate categories express intermediate degrees of favorableness or unfavorableness. There should be the same degree of difference in favorableness, for example, between category eleven and category ten as there is between category ten and category nine. The use of judges and the problems of ensuring their expertise prevents widespread use of this scaling technique in much consumer research.

Hence, in a study of consumer reactions to fabric softeners which are used in the dryer, a panel of judges might be given the following three statements about the product:

a. I would postpone doing my laundry if I were out of a dryer-type fabric softener. (11)
b. I like the way my clothes feel after using a dryer-type fabric softener. (9)
c. It doesn't matter to me what kind of fabric softener I use or whether I even use a fabric softener. (3)

The numbers following the statements are the Thurstone scale categories to which these statements might be assigned by the judges.

These statements would then be presented to consumers (without the numerical categories attached). Each consumer would state whether he or she agrees or disagrees with each statement. Using the previously assigned scale values, the researchers can then determine how favorably a particular respondent feels toward the product. The respondent's attitude is scored as the median of the numerical categories of the items with which he or she agrees. This scoring system is valid only if each respondent agrees with only one item or with items that are adjacent to each other in their numerical categories. When a researcher finds that a large number of respondents are

---

[17]Fishbein and Ajzen, *op. cit.*, p. 69.

agreeing with a very diversified set of statements, the usefulness and validity of the obtained data should be questioned.

Likert's Method of Summated Ratings.   With the Likert method, which is very popular in consumer research, the consumer respondent is asked to indicate the degree of approval or agreement with a statement. The consumer is given five response categories: Strongly Agree, Agree, Uncertain, Disagree, and Strongly Disagree. Each of these categories is assigned a numerical value, e.g. Strongly Agree = 5, Agree = 4. Each consumer "has a score for every item in the test ranging from one to five. His scale score is then simply the sum of the scores he received on each item."[18] Items used in the test are analyzed carefully to determine whether they tap the same attitude as the other items which were used in the test. If an item seems to tap a different attitude it is eliminated. An example of a Likert scale is given below.
1.   A and P Stores are clean.
    Strongly Agree   Agree   Uncertain   Disagree   Strongly Disagree
2.   A and P Stores are friendly places.
    Strongly Agree   Agree   Uncertain   Disagree   Strongly Disagree
Consumers would be asked to underline or circle the category which best expresses their feelings. If the consumer underlined "Strongly Agree" in statement 1, he or she would receive a value of 5 on that item. If the consumer indicated "Uncertain" in item 2, he or she would receive a value of 3. So, 8 would be the total score in this oversimplified two-item test. This score would be compared to those obtained by other respondents. The higher the score, the more favorable the attitude. It is important to go beyond merely the total score since a score of 8 could be arrived at in many ways—such as by underlining two "Agree" statements.

Guttman's Scaleogram Analysis.   With the Guttman scale, statements are scaled in a hierarchical order such that if a person agrees with a strong statement, he or she would also be expected to agree with weaker statements. The classic example of this is the social distance scale, in which respondents are asked to indicate whether they would be willing to admit a member of a minority group to one or more of the following group situations:
1.   close kinship by marriage;
2.   a private club;
3.   residency in the neighborhood;
4.   employment in one's occupation;
5.   citizenship in one's country.

[18]Kiesler, *et al., op. cit.,* p. 13.

The more items checked, the more favorable the attitude toward a member of a minority group. Also, if people indicated they would not mind a minority group member living in their neighborhood, then presumably the respondents also wouldn't mind the minority group member working in the same occupation or having the same citizenship. If the respondent would deny minorities membership in a private club, then probably the respondent would not like a minority group member as a part of his or her family.

Osgood's Semantic Differential Technique.   The semantic differential scale is widely used in consumer behavior studies. Bipolar scales, e.g. good vs. bad, friendly vs. unfriendly, and strong vs. weak, are used in a variety of ways, for example:

A and P Stores

Friendly _ _ _ _ _ _ _ Unfriendly

A consumer would place a mark on the line which best represents his or her feelings about the A and P chain. This format varies considerably. For example:

Instructions: Please evaluate the performance of Federated Airlines by circling the number that represents your evaluation.

	Very Good		Fair		Very Poor	
Airport counter service	6	5	4	3	2	1
Convenient flight connections	6	5	4	3	2	1
Prompt baggage delivery	6	5	4	3	2	1

Source: Hughes, op. cit., p. 93.

There are many variations of the semantic differential technique and many issues to consider in their use.[19]

Observation of Overt Behavior   Attitudes can sometimes be inferred from behaviors. Attitudes toward stores may be inferred from consumers' patronage of a store. Does a consumer shop in a store at all? How much shopping? Does he or she bypass more conveniently located substitute stores to shop at the store in question? Attitudes toward products may also be inferred by observing the behavior of

[19]See Hughes, op. cit., for a good discussion of the various issues.

people at the point of purchase. Extended comparisons of alternatives may indicate that the consumer is not very certain about his or her attitudes.

Other Measures

Reactions to or Interpretation of Partially Structured Stimuli. This approach involves having a person interpret the behavior or situation represented in a picture. The kind of feelings expressed in this interpretation are believed to represent attitudes toward the people, objects, or situations represented in the picture.

Performance on "Objective" Tasks. How a person performs a task may sometimes be used to estimate attitudes toward the task. Is the person interested? Enthusiastic? Conscientious? The basic assumption is that task "performance may be influenced by attitude and that systematic bias in performance reflects the influence of attitude."[20]

Physiological Reactions. Involuntary physiological reactions, such as galvanic skin response, pupil dilation, and voice pitch, are believed by some researchers to reflect attitudes.[21] There is considerable disagreement on this issue, however, and physiological reactions are not commonly used to measure attitudes in consumer research.

ATTITUDE CHANGE

The issue of attitude change is very important in understanding consumer behavior, as is shown by our interest in attitude change throughout this book. Keeping in mind that attitudes are composed of beliefs and values, there are several ways attitudes can be changed. For instance, attitudes may be changed by altering beliefs that consumers have about a product, or by altering consumers' evaluations about the attributes of a product. A marketer may also attempt to change both beliefs and evaluations of a product. Let us look first at changes in beliefs.

Changing Beliefs

Consider a consumer who is thinking about purchasing a new car. The consumer may see an advertisement for a compact car which asserts that this particular car has more interior space than any other compact car. Prior to viewing this advertisement, the consumer probably believed that it was un-

---

[20]Kiesler, et al., *op. cit.,* p. 19.

[21]For a discussion of voice pitch analysis, see "Voice Pitch Analysis," *Marketing News,* January 28, 1977, p. 21.

likely that he or she would be able to find a compact car which was roomy. The target of this advertisement, then, is the consumer's belief about the interior space of compact cars. The marketer hopes that by changing the consumer's belief the consumer's attitude toward the product will be more favorable, and therefore the consumer will have a higher probability of purchasing the product.

The belief about the roominess of a car is a target belief. It may be, however, that while this belief helps determine an attitude, it cannot be changed easily. The marketer might then focus on a different belief, such as a belief about gas mileage, and not the belief about roominess. One of the most important tasks of marketing research is to determine which beliefs directly determine attitudes; that is, which beliefs are primary beliefs and which of these the firm should try to change. The changeable beliefs are the target beliefs.

Changing Evaluations

It is one thing to change a consumer's belief that a car is or is not likely to be roomy, and it is another thing to change a consumer's evaluation of roominess. Is roominess good? Is it bad? Does it really matter? If roominess doesn't matter, then converting people from a position where they do not believe the car in question is roomy to a position where they are highly certain it is, will have little effect on the consumer's attitude. Efforts must be made to increase the salience or importance of this attribute; otherwise, it is necessary to select another more salient attribute on which to focus promotional efforts. It is possible, too, that one attribute may increase in salience, while another attribute may have an offsetting decrease in salience. The same is true for beliefs. Changes in two or more beliefs about a product may offset each other.

The Overall Change Process

Fishbein and Ajzen present several basic guidelines for attitude change.[22] First, a somewhat modified version of their conceptualization of the overall change process is presented in Figure 16-2. In order to persuade customers to visit an automobile showroom (cell 1), it is necessary to change the intentions of consumers to visit the showroom (cell 2). (We are assuming that initially the consumers are not inclined to visit the showroom.) In order to change that intention, it is necessary to alter consumers' attitudes or norms about visiting the showroom (cell 3). The attitude toward visiting the showroom may be influenced by changing beliefs about what will be learned by a visit (cell 4) and/or by influencing the evaluation of what might be learned by a visit (cell 5).

---

[22]Fishbein and Ajzen, *op. cit.,* pp. 406ff.

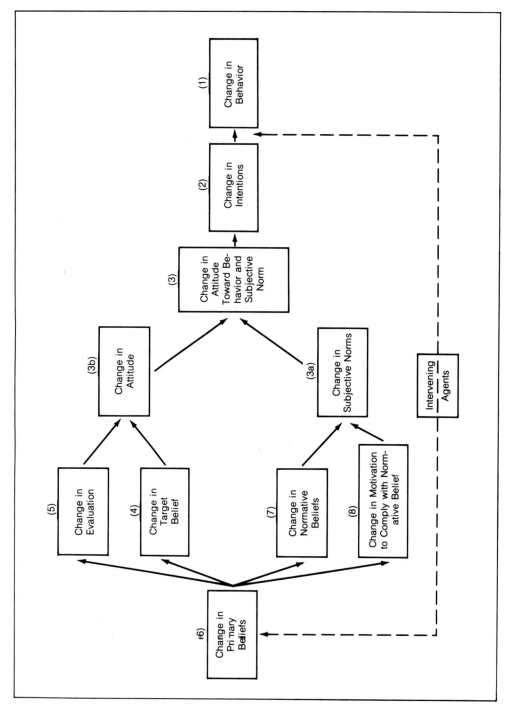

FIGURE 16-2. *The Overall Change Process* (Adapted from Fishbein and Ajzen, op. cit., p. 407).

These changes could result from a change in primary beliefs about attributes attached to an automobile showroom visit. The change in subjective norms (cell 3a) could result from a change in the consumers' feelings about visiting showrooms at a given point in the prepurchase decision process (cell 7). A norm might be that printed advertising should be examined first, or that unless you are serious about a car, you shouldn't take up a salesperson's time or use the demonstration vehicle. The motivation to comply with this norm becomes an important factor. Any change in this norm (cell 8) could alter all subsequent factors in Figure 16-2 (e.g., cells 1 to 3). Changes in primary beliefs (cell 6) would account for changes in normative beliefs and the motivation to comply.

Referring to an earlier illustration we can also use the Fishbein and Ajzen conceptualization of attitude change (as presented in Figure 16-2) to examine ways that the people within the consumer products plant (particularly those in the market research department) can change the plant manager's planned purchase of the services of an outside marketing research consultant. The market research department manager may realize that the main purpose is to change the plant manager's behavior (from purchase to not purchase). Therefore, a successful change attempt should focus on elements closest to the desired change. Since the desired change is in cell 1, we will work backwards through the figure to determine what the strategies might be. Thus, a change in the anticipated behavior must be preceded by a change in intentions (cell 2). Yet, the market research manager must look further back in the change process to see how the plant manager's intentions can be changed. The norms (cell 7) already favor the change, but the problem is that the plant manager's motivation to comply with the norms (cell 8) is not high. So, one strategy might be for the market research department to attempt to formalize adherence to the norm by writing it into a contract with the plant manager. The negative sanctions imposed if the plant manager broke the contract would hopefully provide sufficient motivation to comply such that the plant manager would not purchase the services of the consultant. Alternatively, the market research department might informally increase the plant manager's motivation to comply with the norm by threatening to refuse to cooperate with any outside consultants. Such an action might also change the plant manager's belief that hiring an outside consultant would provide useful information as well as top management favor. The plant manager may now believe that hiring the consultant will produce disruptive conflict within the plant as well as top management disapproval. This would constitute a change in target beliefs (cell 4). The important point for the marketer (the consultant in this case) is to remember that there are many other influences affecting a prospective client's attitudes and intentions. In planning marketing strategies, it is important to understand these influences as well as those brought about by one's own efforts.

Additional Attitude Change Strategies The marketing literature contains many other guidelines for efforts to change attitudes. Persuasive communication is one general strategy. (Persuasive communication was discussed in Chapter 9.) Another is to involve consumers in a product experience. This is the main objective of trial offers and free product samples. These strategies make use of the effect of behavior (trial) on attitudes. (This will be more thoroughly discussed in Chapter 17 on attribution processes.) Another type of participation is *interpersonal contact,* which is especially important in service situations. Contact with sales personnel may alter the image a consumer has of a store, a manufacturer, and even the products or services being provided. If the salesperson appears to be honest, the consumer is more likely to believe that a product has a particular attribute when the salesperson makes this claim, as compared to the consumer's image prior to the sales call or store visit. Interpersonal contact with sales personnel and users of the product can create new beliefs or alter the way a particular product attribute is evaluated.

Role playing is another way of inducing attitude change. For example, in a study of attitudes toward credit managers in banks, finance companies, and department stores and toward the use of credit, it was found that persons who assumed the role of a credit agent in the simulation developed more favorable attitudes toward these agents after the role-playing experience.[23] Persons playing this role also developed more favorable attitudes toward the use of credit in making purchases. A similar technique has been used in attempts to change people's attitudes toward smoking and smoking behavior. Playing the role of either a patient being told he or she has lung cancer due to smoking or the role of the doctor informing the patient led to changes in attitudes and intentions (intentions to reduce smoking). However, playing the role of a debater arguing against smoking did not have significant effects. Thus, role playing is only effective when it involves embedding oneself in the feelings of the situation. Playing a more detached role (that of a debater) does not seem to produce changes.[24] In some ways, the trial use of a product creates a role playing situation. The consumer is able to undertake on a limited basis the behavior of an actual user without making all the commitments a "real" user would make.

[23]Gerald Zaltman, "Consumer Attitude Change In a Simulation Game," Working Paper, The Department of Social Relations, The Johns Hopkins University, 1967.

[24]Robert Foss, "Personality, Social Influence, and Cigarette Smoking," *Journal of Health and Social Behavior,* Vol. 14, September, 1973, pp. 279–286; Leon Mann, "The Effects of Emotional Role Playing on Desire to Modify Smoking Habits," *Journal of Experimental Social Psychology,* Vol. 3, October, 1967, pp. 334–348; Leon Mann and Irving L. Janis, "A Follow-up Study on the Long-Term Effects of Emotional Role Playing," *Journal of Personality and Social Psychology,* Vol. 8, April, 1968, pp. 339–342.

Counterattitudinal behavior involves getting consumers to adopt a product or service which is not preferred or even disliked. This often happens when a product is needed, and only a disliked brand is available. For instance, counterattitudinal behavior may occur when only a scented version of a fabric softener is produced when consumers actually prefer an unscented version. During the period in which a disliked or nonpreferred product is being used, the consumer may alter his or her evaluations and beliefs as a direct result of the experience. This may also occur after sales personnel or advertising have had a chance to reinforce the behavior of choosing or using the previously nonpreferred product or brand.

Counterattitudinal behavior raises the issue of whether attitude change necessarily precedes behavioral change. This question has often been raised in consumer behavior contexts. The critical issue is not which comes first, but rather, "under what conditions does attitude change precede behavior change."[25] Several conditions appear to be relevant to this issue. First, when a product or service is not reversible, that is, if it cannot be discontinued or returned, attitude change is likely to precede behavior change (see Proposition 16-8 in Exhibit 16-4). Examples of products which fall into this category are refrigerators, food products (after they have been consumed), and carpeting. Consumers are much more likely to develop a favorable attitude before making those purchases, rather than purchasing them and then deciding whether or not they like the product. This does not mean unexpected disappointment or enjoyment cannot result from the actual purchase and use of the product. In such a case, attitudes would probably be altered. Second, consumer innovativeness is relevant to the question of whether behavioral change can precede attitude change. The more innovative a consumer is in a particular context, the more likely he or she is to try a new product before attitudes are well developed. The person will be trying the new product as a means of acquiring information on which to base an attitude (see Proposition 16-9). Late adopters often utilize the product experiences of early adopters or innovators as a foundation for forming their attitudes prior to the decision to adopt or not adopt the product. Third, incentives, such as cents-off coupons and free dishware, are likely to precipitate behavior change prior to attitude change. Fourth, group pressure may precipitate purchases prior to attitude change. There are many other factors which may cause consumers to change a behavior, such as purchasing a nonpreferred product, before they change their attitude toward that behavior or toward the product.

---

[25]Christian Pinson and Eduardo L. Roberto, "Do Attitude Changes Precede Behavior Change?" *Journal of Advertising Research,* Vol. 13, No. 4, 1973, pp. 33–38.

EXHIBIT 16-4.
Propositions About the
Attitude-Behavior
Sequence

PROPOSITION 16-8.
The less reversible a purchase decision is, the more likely attitude change is to precede behavioral change.

PROPOSITION 16-9.
Innovators are more likely to adopt an innovation prior to the firm development of attitudes than are later adopters.

One very important factor the reader should keep in mind is that changes in attitudes may arise from the availability of alternative choices, as well as from changes in any of the components of a given attitude toward a product or service. A consumer may evaluate an attribute of a lawn mower very favorably partly because no other lawn mower performs as well with regard to that attribute. Once the consumer, however, becomes aware of a better alternative mower—relative to the attribute in question—his or her frame of reference is altered, and the first mower may become less attractive. Thus, to fully understand attitudes toward any given brand or store, it is helpful to know attitudes toward alternatives. Just as attitudes toward a given product change over the prepurchase-purchase-postpurchase sequence, so do attitudes toward alternatives.

SUMMARY Attitudes consist of two basic components—beliefs and values. Fishbein and Ajzen attempted to explain behavioral intentions through a model which includes the person's attitudes toward performing a particular behavior and the person's perception of how others will regard the behavior (the subjective norm). These two components must be multiplied by various weights according to how much they influence the intention to behave.

Those who study consumer behavior are concerned about the apparent weak relationship between attitudes and behavior. Among the reasons for the inability of attitudes to predict behavior are the following:

1. Poor methodology has often been used to measure attitudes and behavior;
2. Researchers have concentrated on one isolated variable, attitude, and have ignored other factors that interact with attitudes to explain behavior.

Some of these other factors are the certainty of the attitude, personal factors (including the existence of other attitudes that may be incompatible with the one being studied, the consumer's abilities to translate the attitude into actual behavior, and activity levels), and situational factors. Researchers have found situational factors to be more important in predicting behavior than personal factors.

Self-report measures, involving several kinds of scales, have been used extensively to measure attitudes. Among other measurement techniques are observations of overt behavior and task performance.

Persuasive communication and involving consumers in a product experience are two strategies the marketer can use in his or her attempts to change attitudes. In some cases, such as when a product or service is not reversible, attitude change is likely to precede behavioral change. The opposite may occur, however, in situations in which the consumer is innovative, has received an incentive, or is subjected to group pressure.

KEY CONCEPTS   Attitude

Belief

Cognition

Intentions (to behave)

Subjective norms

Target beliefs

Value

CONSUMER ATTRIBUTIONS*

17

CHAPTER GOALS   The objective of this chapter is to help the reader understand:
1. **the processes through which people determine the causes of events;**
2. **how a person infers something about another person based on the other person's behavior;**
3. **how people determine the causes of their own behavior;**
4. **what types of attributions about successes and failures are made in certain kinds of situations.**

INTRODUCTION   From the three-year old who drives her parents crazy with the constant question "Why?" to the nuclear physicist concerned with the source of the sun's energy, people spend much of their time attempting to determine the causes of events. The area of psychology called attribution theory is concerned with how people perceive the causes of events in their everyday lives. For example, an attribution theorist might try to determine what factors affect whether a person will attribute a poor test score to a failure to study or to unfairness on the part of the instructor. The concern is not with the "real" cause of something, but with the *perceived* cause.

The systematic study of perceived causality began with Fritz Heider,[1] who believed that it was important to study what he called "naive" or "com-

---

*Dr. Valerie Valle, Univeristy of Pittsburgh, is a co-author of this chapter.
[1]F. Heider, *The Psychology of Interpersonal Relations,* NY: John Wiley, 1958.

monsense" psychology as expressed in our everyday language and experience. There are two basic reasons why the study of "commonsense" psychology is important for both the psychologist and the marketing practitioner. First, people's assumptions about human behavior guide their interactions with other people. Therefore, one must understand an individual's implicit psychological assumptions in order to predict how that person will behave. Second, this "commonsense" psychology has sprung from people's attempts to adequately understand their world and, hence, contains insights which are useful in the generation of hypotheses and the development of psychological theory.

Although this area of research is called attribution theory, it may be more appropriately labeled "attribution theories" because a number of different approaches to the problem of perceived causality have sprung from Heider's original formulation. There are many different types of situations in which people attribute causality, and a body of theory and research has developed around each type of situation. It is, therefore, impossible to present one coherent theory in this chapter. Rather, each of the major approaches and its implications for marketing is presented separately.

Harold E. Kelley's general theory, in which he defines the information necessary for a person to be confident that something is the cause of a given effect, is presented first.[2] The second theory, initially proposed by E. E. Jones and K. E. Davis, deals with situations where people infer that an individual's behavior represents the underlying characteristics or attitudes of that person.[3] How people make attributions concerning their own behavior is then considered.[4] Finally, the research concerning how people perceive the causes of success or failure is presented.[5]

[2]Harold E. Kelley, "Attribution Theory in Social Psychology," in D. Levine (ed.), *Nebraska Symposium on Motivation,* University of Nebraska Press, 1967; Harold E. Kelley, "Causal Schemata and the Attribution Process," in Edward E. Jones, D. E. Kanouse, H. H. Kelley, R. E. Nisbett, S. Valins, B. Weiner (eds.), *Attribution: Perceiving the Causes of Behavior,* Morristown, NJ: General Learning Press, 1971, pp. 151–174.

[3]E. E. Jones and K. E. Davis, "From Acts to Dispositions: The Attribution Process in Person Perception," in L. Berkowitz (ed.), *Advances in Experimental Social Psychology,* Vol. 2, NY: Academic Press, 1965, pp. 219–266.

[4]D. J. Bem, "Self-Perception Theory," in L. Berkowitz (eds.), *Advances in Experimental Social Psychology,* Vol. 6, NY: Academic Press, 1972, pp. 1–62.

[5]B. Weiner, I. Frieze, A. Kukla, L. Reed, S. Rest, and R. Rosenbaum, "Perceiving the Causes of Success and Failure," in E. E. Jones, D. E. Kanouse, H. H. Kelley, R. E. Nisbett, S. Valins, B. Weiner (eds.), *Attribution: Perceiving the Causes of Behavior,* Morristown, NJ: General Learning Press, 1971, pp. 95–120.

DETERMINING THE CAUSES OF EVENTS

Scientists have developed systematic methods for determining the causes of events, so, before discussing how the average person determines causality, let us consider a scientific example. A scientist is searching for the cause of cancerous tumors in rats. He or she believes that certain chemicals in the food of animals lead to cancer. In order to check this hypothesis, he or she systematically varies the diet of the experimental rats. If he or she finds that the development of cancer *covaries* with the presence of a certain chemical in the diet (i.e., cancer is present when the chemical is present and absent when the chemical is absent), then the chemical may be considered a cause of cancer in rats.

A scientist, however, is never satisfied with one experiment when making a causal judgment. It is possible that the relationship between the chemical and cancer was just due to chance. Therefore, replications are required. That is, the same covariance of cause and effect must appear consistently over time. Our scientist would probably put several groups of rats through the same procedures, and only if he or she consistently achieved the same results would he or she conclude that the chemical caused cancer. It is possible, however, that this particular scientist's methods and perceptions are inaccurate. Therefore, for the scientific community to be convinced that the chemical does indeed cause cancer in rats, other scientists doing similar research would have to demonstrate the same results. In summary, for a scientist to be certain that an effect is due to a specific cause, the effect must occur uniquely and consistently in the presence of that cause.

Kelley's Basic Theory

Kelley sees people as naive scientists who base attributions of causality on the covariance of cause and effect.[6] In other words, he believes that in our everyday lives we use a process similar to that used by a scientist to determine the cause of events. For a person to be certain that his or her reaction to something is due to the thing itself, the reaction must be unique (i.e., different from reactions to other things) and consistent over: (a) persons, (b) time, and (c) modality.

For example, suppose you have just come from a movie which you did not enjoy. You might feel that your disappointment was due to the quality of the film itself, or you could attribute your lack of enjoyment to something else, such as a bad mood before the movie began, unpleasant companions, or a broken projector. In order to be certain that your reaction is due to the film, you must first determine whether this reaction is unique. If you are the type of person who never enjoys films, you cannot say that this particular movie is

---

[6]Harold E. Kelley, 1967, *op. cit.*

either good or bad. There is no *distinctiveness* in your reaction, and, therefore, you have no reason to believe that the film was the cause of your reaction.

Other information is also necessary to be certain that your reaction is due to the film itself. You would want to know how others reacted to the film *(consistency over persons)*. If you discover that all your friends liked the film, you would be inclined to think that it was something about you, not the film, that caused your negative reaction. If, however, all the people who attended the film with you agreed with your negative evaluation, you would feel more confident that it was indeed a poor film.

You might also want to know whether your reaction to the film was *consistent over time*. If you returned to the theatre and enjoyed the movie, you would perhaps feel that your initial evaluation was due to your mood. On the other hand, if you reacted in the same manner following several viewings, you would be even more certain of your negative evaluation.

Finally, you may wonder if your reaction would vary over the *modality*. If, upon viewing the film on television or at a theatre where the projector was working properly, you enjoyed it, you would be inclined to doubt your initial perceptions. But, if you still disliked the film when it was shown with a better projector, you would be even more certain that it was an inferior film.

Of course, few people, except an overzealous film critic, would go to that much trouble to determine why they disliked a film. Attributions are usually made with much less than perfect information. We often tell others a film is bad even though we have seen it only once, and the people with whom we have discussed the film disagree on their evaluation. It can be stated, however, that the more information an individual has that a reaction is consistent over persons, time, and modality, the more certain he or she will be about the true cause of that reaction. Also, if the reaction varies along one of these dimensions, there will be a tendency to see that dimension as a cause of the reaction.

Perceptions of a Product

After a person has used a product, he or she has either a favorable, unfavorable, or neutral reaction to that product. The person also makes some kind of attribution concerning the cause of that reaction. Kelley's theory suggests the variables that are important in determining the type of attributions people make about product performance.

Distinctiveness.   The first proposition is that the greater the distinctiveness of a consumer's reaction to a product (i.e., the reaction occurs with that product, but not with other products), the more certain that consumer will be that his or her satisfaction or dissatisfaction is due to the product itself (see Proposition 17-1 in Exhibit 17-1). Therefore, a firm should try to make posi-

EXHIBIT 17-1.

Propositions Concerning Perceptions of a Product

PROPOSITION 17-1.
The greater the distinctiveness of a consumer's reaction to a product (i.e., the reaction occurs with that product, but not with other products), the more certain the consumer will be that his or her satisfaction or dissatisfaction is due to the product itself.

PROPOSITION 17-2.
The more consistent a consumer's experience with a product at different times, the more certain the consumer will be that his or her satisfaction or dissatisfaction is due to the product itself.

PROPOSITION 17-3.
The more similar a consumer's experience with a product is to the reported experiences of others, the more certain that consumer will be that his or her satisfaction or dissatisfaction is due to the product itself.

PROPOSITION 17-4.
The more consistent a consumer's experience with a product in different situations, the more certain the consumer will be that his or her satisfaction or dissatisfaction is due to the product itself.

tive aspects of the product appear unique to their company, while suggesting that any weak points in the product are inherent to all products in that product category. Positive reactions might then be attributed to the product, while negative reactions are attributed elsewhere.

In addition, it is important that a brand be promoted as having some unique characteristics which differentiate it from other brands. If there is nothing unique about a brand, a person's satisfaction will be attributed to the product class rather than to the particular brand. Unless the satisfaction is attributed to the brand itself, purchasing decisions will be based on factors other than brand loyalty.

It is also important for the company to discourage attributions to the brand when a customer is dissatisfied. This is probably best accomplished at the time of a complaint by suggesting that the problem is inherent in this type of product. (Other ways of discouraging product attributions of dissatisfaction are discussed later in this chapter.)

Consistency Over Time. The more consistent a consumer's experience with a product is at different times, the more certain the consumer will be that his or her satisfaction or dissatisfaction is due to the product itself (see Proposition 17-2). This proposition emphasizes the importance of quality control, especially when introducing a new product. In order to develop a good reputation and brand loyalty, it is extremely important that the product be of consistently high quality. Once loyalty has been established, that is, once consumers attribute their satisfaction to a particular brand, an occasional problem will probably be attributed to something other than the product, regardless of the real cause of the dissatisfaction.

Consistency Over Persons. One of the most important determinants of a consumer's reaction to a product is what Kelley calls consistency over persons. Knowing how others have reacted to a product is extremely important to consumers when determining whether their reactions are due to the product or due to something unusual about themselves (see Proposition 17-3). Information about social consensus is a very powerful tool in promotional strategy. If a satisfied consumer discovers that many other people are satisfied with a product, he or she will be confident that this satisfaction is due to the product itself. If a dissatisfied consumer learns that others are satisfied, the tendency will be to attribute the dissatisfaction to something other than the product, such as the way the product was used.

 This proposition also suggests the importance of communication within the consumer movement. If individual consumers believe they are the only ones who are dissatisfied with a product, they will usually attribute the problem to themselves rather than to the product. When consumers learn, however, that many others are also dissatisfied, they are more likely to blame their dissatisfaction on the product and take some form of action. Therefore, one of the important jobs of a consumer activist is to establish awareness among dissatisfied consumers that they are having a common experience.

Consistency Over Modality. In determining whether their reactions are due to the product itself, consumers look to see if the reaction occurs consistently over different modalities. That is, if they react similarly to the product in different situations, then they will be more certain that the reaction is due to the product itself (see Proposition 17-4). For example, a child may be persuaded to try hot lima beans one evening at dinner. Euphemistically, we can refer to the reaction as product dissatisfaction. At another time, parents may try to persuade the child that lima beans in cold bean salad or lima beans in vegetable soup are different from hot lima beans at dinner. But, after trying lima beans again in the salad or the soup, the child may have the same dissatisfied reaction. In such a case, the child's reaction is consistent over different situations or modalities and is attributed to the product (lima beans).

Communication Effectiveness

Kelley is also concerned with how one individual can influence the attributions of another. The confidence a person has in an attribution is a function of the amount of consistent information available. If a person does not have enough information to make a confident attribution, he or she will be susceptible to influence. There are basically two ways in which one person can influence the attributions of another. The first is to provide the individual with data related to the consistency of an effect over time or modality. For example, the influencer can suggest new ways of looking at a problem (different modalities) or present an "objective" statement concerning the performance of a product at various times. The perceiver's feelings about the source of the information are not particularly important in this type of communication.

The second type of influence attempt involves presenting one's own opinion as consensus information. In this case, the effectiveness of the communication is dependent upon the perceiver's evaluation of the sender. Obviously, another's opinion affects the perceiver's perception of consistency over persons only when the perceiver attributes the opinion to the communicator's true experience. This, therefore, presents the perceiver with another attributional problem. The perceiver must determine whether the statement is due to the object of discussion or to the person presenting the consensus information. The same criteria are relevant for this attributional problem as are relevant for attributing the cause of one's own reaction (i.e., distinctiveness and consistency).

This second type of influence is extremely important in promotional campaigns. Unless consumers believe that statements made about products in advertisements or by the sales force represent the speakers' true feelings about the product, they are unlikely to change their opinion of the product. Kelley's theory leads to a number of suggestions for making promotional campaigns more effective.

The most important criterion for making a confident attribution is that the effect is somehow distinctive. If a communicator describes all products in the same way, others will be more likely to attribute the description to something about the communicator rather than to something about the product (see Proposition 17-5 in Exhibit 17-2). So, those who give testimonials for a company's product should be chosen with care to make certain that their descriptions of the product differ from their descriptions of other products. If a famous celebrity produces advertisements for a number of different products and speaks highly of all of them, the viewer will question whether this praise is due to the good qualities of the product or just to the nature of the celebrity. Sales representatives should also be aware of this problem. If a customer is presented with uniform praise of all the products represented, the customer

EXHIBIT 17-2.
*Propositions Concerning
Attributions About
Communications*

PROPOSITION 17-5.
The greater the distinctiveness of the communicator's description of a product, the more likely the perceiver will attribute that characteristic to the product.

PROPOSITION 17-6.
The greater the consistency of a communication over time and situation, the more likely the perceiver will attribute the information to the product.

will be unable to use this information to make attributions about the products. If there is no distinctiveness, there is no usable information.

Settle and Golden tested a similar idea based on Kelley's theory.[7] They hypothesized that a promotional message which contained some negative information about a product, in addition to all the positive aspects of the product, would lead to more confident attributions. Consumers were presented with hypothetical advertisements, some of which contained all good points about the product, and some which contained one negative bit of information (such as a short cord on an appliance). The negative information was never a highly important aspect of the product. They found that this negative information did not decrease the consumer's liking for the product. Unfortunately, they did not directly measure attributions. This research suggests that it may be possible to increase the credibility of a promotional campaign by including some insignificant negative information.

In addition to distinctiveness, there must be consistency in the communication so that the perceiver attributes the information to the product itself (see Proposition 17-6). If a communication varies from time to time or from situation to situation, the message must be attributed to the time or situation, rather than to the product. Hence, it is essential for a salesperson to be consistent over time. If a sales representative tells one individual in a corporation one thing and tells another person something else, when these two individuals communicate they will attribute the information to the salesperson's desire to please, rather than to the nature of the product.

---

[7]R. B. Settle and Linda Golden, "Attribution Theory and Advertiser Credibility," *Journal of Marketing Research,* Vol. 9, 1974, pp. 181–185.

ATTRIBUTIONS ABOUT OTHER PEOPLE

Kelley's theory is concerned with how a person determines when a reaction or statement can be accurately attributed to something in the environment. Jones and Davis, on the other hand, developed a theory concerned with how a person determines when an action accurately represents the underlying disposition (i.e., the character or attitudes) of the actor.[8]

Jones and Davis' Basic Theory

For Jones and Davis, the significance of an action is derived from a consideration of the alternatives available to the actor. That is, a perceiver understands the dispositions underlying an action by comparing the effects of that action to the effects of other possible actions. The researchers introduced the term *correspondence,* which represents the degree to which a person perceives the actions of another to accurately reflect (or correspond to) the true feelings or dispositions of that person. An example is the best way to introduce the major concepts of this theory.

Consider the case of Mr. Smith, who has just donated several valuable paintings to a local art museum. One's first reaction would be to attribute this act to Mr. Smith's obvious generosity. If one then discovered that Mr. Smith was in a high tax bracket, needed a tax deduction, and had the paintings appraised as being worth much more than he originally paid for them, his generosity might be questioned. In addition, one learns that Mr. Smith has been trying to gain acceptance into a highly selective social club whose members hold contributions to the arts in very high regard. It is now much more difficult to be certain of the accuracy of an attribution about Mr. Smith's contributions. He had several alternatives: keep the paintings, give them to the museum, sell them at a profit, or give them to a friend as a gift. His choice of giving the paintings produced a number of *effects* which were different from, or *not common* to, the effects produced by his other alternatives. These are: (a) helping the museum; (b) reducing his taxes; and (c) increasing his social status. An observer is not sure how important each of these effects was in determining Mr. Smith's actions, and, therefore, does not know why Mr. Smith made the contribution.

Now consider another individual who gives a gift to the museum anonymously, and does not use it as a tax deduction. Of the two alternative explanations (generosity and personal desire for a tax deduction), there is only one effect which differentiates them, which is the helping of the museum without personal gain. One would have much more confidence that the latter donation was an act of pure generosity. This demonstrates that the less the number

---

[8]E. Jones and K. Davis, *op. cit.*

of unique, noncommon effects of a person's actions, the more confidence one has when making an attribution about that person's underlying dispositions. Using Jones and Davis' terminology, the *correspondence* of an attribution is an inverse function of the number of unique or *noncommon effects* following the action (see Proposition 17-7 in Exhibit 17-3).

So far in this example, only the positive outcomes which followed from contributing to the museum have been cited. No longer having the paintings in the home or having less wealth were not considered as possible causes for these individuals' actions, even though these effects did follow their actions. Similarly, we assume a person goes into debt in order to have the pleasure of owning a car, not that a person takes on the burden of owning a car in order to be in debt. Indeed, if there are negative consequences of an act, we are more certain that the person really wanted to achieve the positive effects.

People tend to attribute an action to effects which are considered *socially desirable*. A socially desirable or expected action, however, gives a perceiver much less information on which to base an attribution than a less socially desirable action. When people act exactly as expected, one does not know whether they are basing their actions on their own internal beliefs or are trying to do the appropriate thing (see Proposition 17-8).

A study by Jones, *et al.* demonstrated that behavior which conforms to clearly defined role requirements gives less information about the individual's

EXHIBIT 17-3.
Propositions Concerning Attributions About Other People

PROPOSITION 17-7.
The correspondence of an attribution is an inverse function of the number of noncommon effects which follow the action.

PROPOSITION 17-8.
The more socially desirable the effects of an action are, the less information one has concerning the actor's true disposition.

PROPOSITION 17-9.
The more an individual believes that an action was intended to either help or hurt him or her, the more correspondent an attribution concerning that action will be.

PROPOSITION 17-10.
People tend to attribute characteristics to a consumer based on the products that the consumer buys.

personal characteristics than out-of-role behavior.[9] Students listened to one of four tape-recorded hypothetical job interviews in which those interviewed were applying to be either a submariner or an astronaut. The ideal submariner was described as a person who can get along easily and enjoys being with others, while the ideal astronaut was described as a person who enjoys being alone.

On half of the recordings the interviewees' responses were consistent with the job requirements (the astronaut was inner-directed, the submariner was other-directed). On the other half of the recordings, the responses were not consistent with the job requirements (the astronaut was other-directed, the submariner was inner-directed).

After listening to these tapes, the students were asked what they thought the interviewee was "really" like. The ratings for the in-role recordings tended to be moderate (slightly inner- or other-directed) and lacking in confidence. The ratings for the out-of-role recordings tended to be extreme (in the direction of the person's statements) and showed a great deal of confidence.

If an action has *hedonic relevance* (i.e., there is a direct positive or negative effect) for a person, he or she usually makes a correspondent inference. This becomes particularly important when the person believes that his or her presence was a primary motivation for the action (see Proposition 17-9). In other words, people tend to be much more certain that an action accurately reflects another's underlying characteristics when they believe that the action was directly aimed at helping or hurting them.

Attributions About a Communicator

Jones and Davis' theory of attributions about other people is particularly relevant to the understanding of marketing communications. The effectiveness of a communication regarding a product is dependent upon the attributions which are made about the communicator. Two major sources of information about a product are advertising and sales personnel. The implications of Jones and Davis' theory for each type of communication are now presented.

Advertising. Statements made about a product are only believed if ulterior motives for that statement are not perceived. This presents a problem for advertisers. When a celebrity states that a given brand is his or her favorite beer, car, bed, or coffee, most viewers are sophisticated enough to realize that the celebrity is being paid. In other words, there are at least two noncommon

[9]E. E. Jones, K. E. Davis, and K. J. Gergen, "Role Playing Variations and Their Informational Value for Person Perception," *Journal of Abnormal and Social Psychology,* Vol. 63, 1961, pp. 302–310.

effects produced by the celebrity's participation in the advertisement: (a) he or she has had the opportunity to say something good about the product; and (b) he or she has been paid. The viewer does not know which of the two was the primary reason for the statement, and is, therefore, unable to make a correspondent inference. This can be contrasted with a situation in which a celebrity mentions the good qualities of a product in an environment where ulterior motives are not perceived, such as a television talk show. Since there appears to be only one noncommon effect, people viewing the show are more likely to attribute the statement to the true beliefs of the individual.

Advertisers have dealt with the problem of perceived ulterior motives by using hidden cameras or unsolicited testimonials. These techniques are only effective, of course, if people perceive only one noncommon effect following these statements, and, therefore, make a correspondent inference concerning the individual's true feelings toward the product. (This issue was discussed in the section on source credibility in Chapter 9 on communication.)

The importance of research to determine the types of attributions people make about advertising cannot be overstressed. An important study by Robertson and Rossiter investigated the development of children's perceptions of the intent of advertising.[10] They found that the older the child, the more likely he or she was to perceive that the purpose of advertising is to persuade the viewer to purchase a product. They also found that children who perceived persuasive intent were less likely to trust commercials or desire the advertised products.

Sales Personnel. The effectiveness of sales personnel is also dependent upon the type of attribution a customer makes. The consumer is aware of the fact that the sales representative has a number of motives for his or her actions. Therefore, the consumer is unlikely to make a correspondent inference when the representative praises the product being sold. Jones and Davis' theory suggests several ways in which a sales representative can encourage correspondent attributions.

As stated above, when a person acts in ways which are completely consistent with his or her role, an observer does not know whether the person is acting on the basis of true beliefs or in order to obtain social approval. So, a person is unlikely to believe a car salesperson who perfectly fits the stereotyped role of the "used car salesperson." All of the salesperson's statements will be seen as merely part of that role. If salespeople, however, occa-

---

[10]Thomas S. Robertson and John R. Rossiter, "Children and Commercial Persuasion: An Attribution Theory Analysis," *The Journal of Consumer Research*, Vol. 1, 1974, pp. 13–20.

sionally say something slightly disparaging about their company, do not always smile, or do not dress like typical salespeople, they will be perceived as basing their actions on true beliefs, rather than role requirements. This would lead to more credibility. For example, a car salesperson who points out one or two minor problems with a car (an out-of-role behavior) is much more likely to be believed.

A sales representative can also do other things to encourage more correspondent inferences on the part of the customer. People tend to be more certain of the cause of another's actions when they perceive that the actions are directed specifically at them. A sales representative, therefore, may develop credibility by making the customer feel that he or she is reacting to the customer personally. This can be done by remembering the interests of the customers, or by making special deals that appeal to their specific needs. Credibility may be greatly damaged, though, if a customer discovers that what he or she had thought was a special personal deal is actually given to every customer.

Attributions About an Individual Who Purchases a Product

There are many sources of information which can be used to attribute characteristics to a person. One of these sources is the products a person purchases (see Proposition 17-10). Calder and Burnkrant found that women based attributions about a consumer's personality on the products they purchased.[11] Variables such as brand image, available options, and private versus public use of a product were important for determining the type of attribution made. The effect of these variables, however, depended upon the type of product.

It is important for a marketing manager to be aware of the types of attributions made about people who purchase a particular product. A classic study by Mason Haire, in which housewives described the purchasers of lists of food products, showed that the user of instant coffee was perceived as being lazy.[12] This information helped the coffee industry develop promotional campaigns to deal with these perceptions. Although these results are probably no longer valid descriptions of people's perceptions of instant coffee, they demonstrate that people make attributions about people based on others' consumption.

---

[11]Bobby J. Calder and Robert E. Burnkrant, "Interpersonal Influence on Consumer Behavior; An Attribution Theory Approach," *Journal of Consumer Research,* Vol. 4, June, 1977, pp. 29–38.

[12]Mason Haire, "Projective Techniques in Marketing Research," *Journal of Marketing,* Vol. 14, 1950, pp. 649–656.

SELF-ATTRIBUTIONS The theories described above have examined the process by which people make causal attributions about the behavior of others. People also make attributions about the causes of their own behavior, including the causes of their purchasing behavior. It is generally believed that our behavior is based on our attitudes, and, therefore, that the process of attributing the cause of our own behavior is very simple and straightforward. For example, a person could say that the reason he or she bought a Ford is that he or she has always had the attitude that Fords are the best brand of automobile. One researcher, however, states that just the opposite is true; that is, that we infer our attitudes from our behavior.[13] In other words, we determine the cause of our own behavior in the same way as we determine the causes of other people's behavior. In the example above, it may be more accurate to say that the consumer likes Fords because he or she has bought one. Since this approach was developed as an alternative to dissonance theory, a brief review of dissonance theory and research is necessary before discussing the self-attribution approach.

Dissonance Theory Cognitive dissonance is described as a state of psychological discomfort due to a disequilibrium or dissonance between two cognitive elements. Cognitive elements have been defined as "any knowledge, opinion, or belief about the environment, about oneself, or about one's behavior."[14] Cognitive dissonance occurs when one cognitive element implies the negation of the other (e.g., "I hate pizza, but I freely ordered and am eating pizza!"). When a state of cognitive dissonance exists, the individual is motivated to achieve consonance, that is, to make the cognitive elements imply each other (e.g., "I freely ordered and am eating pizza; therefore, I must like pizza!").

The most interesting applications of dissonance theory are to situations where people perform actions which are inconsistent with their beliefs. In these situations, dissonance theory predicts that, since the action cannot be changed, people will change their beliefs in order to be consistent with their actions. It also predicts that the greater the inducement to perform the action, the less the dissonance, and, therefore, the less the attitude change.

The classic dissonance experiment was conducted by Festinger and Carlsmith.[15] After subjects had worked on a boring task, they were offered

---

[13]D. J. Bem, *op. cit.*

[14]L. Festinger, *A Theory of Cognitive Dissonance,* NY: Row, Peterson, 1957, p. 3.

[15]L. Festinger and J. M. Carlsmith, "Cognitive Consequences of Forced Compliance," *Journal of Abnormal and Social Psychology,* Vol. 58, 1958, pp. 203–210.

either one dollar or twenty dollars to tell another subject that the task had been interesting. It was predicted that subjects would feel dissonance because they were lying to the other subject, and that those who were paid one dollar would experience more dissonance and attitude change than those paid twenty dollars. Those who had been paid one dollar reported that the experience was more interesting than those who were paid twenty dollars. This study, and many others, has shown that people change their attitudes to be consistent with their public behavior when there is insufficient justification for that behavior.[16]

Bem's Self-Perception Theory

Bem believed that there is no need to postulate a drive or motive to reduce dissonance in order to account for these results. Rather, he posited that people determine their own beliefs in the same manner that they learn about others' beliefs, by observing actions. According to Bem, the subjects did not perceive that they were changing their attitude; they merely observed how they acted, and, from that information, determined what their attitudes must be. An observer who knew that a subject told another subject that the experiment was interesting and who knew how much he or she was paid would be fairly certain that the individual who was paid one dollar actually thought that the experiment was interesting (because there was no other reason for that action). On the other hand, the person who was paid twenty dollars has sufficient justification to lie (there is more than one noncommon effect). In this case, therefore, the observer could not be certain whether or not the subject liked the experiment.

This means that one of the ways that people determine their attitudes toward a product is by observing their own behavior (see Proposition 17-11 in Exhibit 17-4). So, if a consumer takes a positive action toward a product (such as purchasing or using it), he or she will tend to have a positive attitude toward that product. This means that a producer should make a special effort to persuade consumers to buy a product, since they will have a more positive attitude toward the product after investing time and money in it.

The use of incentives, such as cents-off coupons and free samples, is an accepted marketing technique. But, the effective use of incentives is a complicated matter (see Proposition 17-12). If an incentive is too large, the shopper will attribute the purchase to the incentive, not to his or her own attitude. Therefore, the consumer will be less likely to develop a positive attitude

---

[16]See also Leon Festinger, Henry W. Riecken, and Stanley Schachter, *When Prophecy Fails,* NY: Harper and Row, 1964, for an interesting description of a field study on cognitive dissonance.

EXHIBIT 17-4.
Propositions Concerning
Self-Attributions

PROPOSITION 17-11.
One of the ways that consumers determine their attitudes toward a product is by observing their behavior in relation to that product.

PROPOSITION 17-12.
The greater the incentive to buy a product, the less likely it is that the consumer will attribute that purchase to his or her attitude toward that product.

toward the product. An incentive should be as small and inconspicuous as possible in order to encourage self-attributions which lead to a positive attitude toward the product. On the other hand, the incentive must be large enough to encourage consumers to buy the product.

ATTRIBUTIONS IN ACHIEVEMENT SITUATIONS

A body of research has developed concerning the types of attributions people make concerning a person's success or failure. This research has implications for understanding consumer satisfaction or dissatisfaction with a product, especially when one realizes that, at least to some extent, the purchasing of a product is an achievement situation. An achievement situation occurs when an individual's actions lead to an outcome which can be perceived as either a success or failure. Americans define a great number of situations in terms of achievement. For example, a happy marriage is often described as a "success," while a divorce is called a "failure." Children quickly learn to see their school experiences in terms of success or failure. Even interpersonal relations are often perceived in achievement terms—a person can feel he or she was a "success" or "failure" at a party.

There are many indications that the purchasing of a product also has the potential to be perceived as an achievement situation. Since money and possessions are often perceived as symbols of achievement, people try to maximize their material possessions as an indication of achievement. One way that traditional homemakers believe they can add to the standard of living of their families is through intelligent purchasing decisions. This suggests that consumption behavior is one of the few outlets for the traditional homemaker's achievement strivings.

Weiner's Basic Model

Weiner and his associates developed a two-dimensional schema for representing the possible causes of an achievement behavior (see Figure 17-1).[17] A success or failure can be attributed either to something about the actor (internally), or to something about the environment or situation (externally). In addition, the performance can be attributed to something which does not vary over time (stable), or to something which varies over time (unstable). Ability is an example of something that is internal and relatively stable. Effort and mood are examples of internal, unstable attributions. The difficulty of the task is external and relatively stable. Finally, luck is external and unstable.

Attributions concerning satisfaction or dissatisfaction with a product also fit into this model. To believe that a good purchase was a result of one's ability to bargain is a stable, internal attribution. The perception that a poor purchase was made because one was tired and in a hurry is an unstable, internal attribution. Blaming the manufacturer for producing a poor product is a stable, external attribution. Finally, perceiving that a product is a "lemon" or a "peach" (i.e., an unusual example of a poor or a good product) is an unstable, external attribution.

It has been found that an observer of a performance often makes attributions which are different from those made by the performer.[18] Observers tend to attribute the performance to something internal to the actor, while the actor is more likely to attribute the performance to something about the situation. This means that consumers are less likely than some outside observer to see themselves as a possible cause of their dissatisfaction with a product (see Proposition 17-13 in Exhibit 17-5). A consumer is more likely to be aware of the surrounding situation than of his or her own actions. Therefore, the consumer is more likely to attribute dissatisfaction with a product to something external, such as the product or the retailer. On the other hand, an observer is sensitized to the consumer's actions. This leads the observer to be more likely than the actor to attribute the consumer's dissatisfaction to something about the consumer, such as incorrect use of the product.

Some of the difficulties encountered by complaint departments may be due to differences in attributions between the consumer and the representative of the store or corporation. The consumer is unlikely to attribute the problem to his or her behavior, whereas the company representative often sees the consumer as partly responsible. This difference in attributional perspective can lead to bad feelings on the part of the customer, for the

---

[17]Weiner, *et al., op. cit.*

[18]E. E. Jones and R. E. Nisbett, "The Actor and the Observer: Divergent Perceptions of the Causes of Behavior," in E. E. Jones, D. E. Kanouse, H. H. Kelley, R. E. Nisbett, I. Valins, and B. Weiner (eds.), *Attribution: Perceiving the Causes of Behavior,* Morristown, NJ: General Learning Press, 1971, pp. 79–94.

FIGURE 17-1.
*Weiner's Two
Dimensional Schema*

LOCUS OF CONTROL

Internal   *External*

STABILITY

	Internal	*External*
Stable	Ability	Task Difficulty
Unstable	Effort	Luck

consumer may believe that he or she has been unreasonably blamed for something which is not his or her fault. If company representatives who deal with complaints are made aware of these differences in perspective, they might be more able to adequately deal with consumers.

The Relationship Between Attributions and Expectations

The perceiver's expectations have been found to be very important in determining how people react to a performance. A number of studies have shown that the more similar a performance is to the perceiver's expectations, the greater the probability that a stable attribution will be made about the cause of that performance.[19] From this follows Proposition 17-14: The closer a product's performance is to the consumer's expectations of that performance, the greater the probability that the consumer will make a stable attribution. The

EXHIBIT 17-5.
*Propositions Concerning
Attributions in
Achievement Situations*

PROPOSITION 17-13.
The consumer is less likely to see himself or herself as the cause of dissatisfaction with a product than is some outside observer.

PROPOSITION 17-14.
The closer a product's performance is to the consumer's expectations of that performance, the greater the probability that the consumer will make a stable attribution.

PROPOSITION 17-15.
The attributional process helps to reinforce existing expectations; therefore, it is very difficult to change expectations.

[19]N. J. Feather and J. G. Simon, "Attribution of Responsibility and Valence of Outcome in Relation to Initial Confidence and Success and Failure of Self and Other," *Journal of Personality and Social Psychology,* Vol. 18, 1971, pp. 173–188.

predicted attributions following a satisfactory or unsatisfactory performance of a product are summarized in Figure 17-2.

From the seller's point of view, the optimal attribution is for the consumer to be satisfied with a product and to attribute that satisfaction to stable characteristics of the product (e.g., all samples of that product will perform well). From Figure 17-2 it can be seen that this is the attribution made when a product expected to perform well actually does perform well. The attribution made about a product expected to perform well, but which does not live up to expectations, is also reasonably favorable toward the product, because it assumes that this is a rare case. On the other hand, the attributions made about a product expected to do poorly are both rather negative. If the product performs well, an unstable attribution is made, implying that this is a rare instance of a good performance by that product. If the product performs poorly, it is seen as due to the nature of the product. This model stresses the importance of developing an image of excellence about a product so that consumers will have high expectations.

FIGURE 17-2.
Predicted Attribution Following Product Performance

PERFORMANCE	EXPECTATION	
	High	Low
Good	Stable (e.g., excellent product)	Unstable (e.g., luck; rare, good performance)
Bad	Unstable (e.g., unlucky, "lemon")	Stable (e.g., poor product)

In addition, it has been found that, within achievement situations, attributions affect expectations for the future.[20] Results which have been attributed to stable aspects of the situation have more influence in determining future expectations than do results attributed to unstable aspects. This means that the attribution process reinforces existing expectations, making it very difficult to change expectations (see Proposition 17-15). Expected performances are attributed to stable characteristics which give them importance when determining expectations in the future. Unexpected performances are attributed to

[20]V. A. Valle and I. H. Frieze, "The Stability of Causal Attributions as a Mediator in Changing Expectations for Success," *Journal of Personality and Social Psychology,* Vol. 33, 1976, pp. 579–587.

unstable characteristics which give them less importance when determining expectations in the future.

This model stresses the importance of first impressions. A corporation should be certain when first introducing a product that it is of a consistently high quality. When a product is new and the firm's reputation is not salient, consumers may be unsure of their expectations; therefore, their early experience with the product is crucial for developing expectations. Once consumers have had a good or bad experience with a product, expectations are developed concerning that product; once the expectations are established, the attribution process makes it difficult to change them. This reinforces the importance of maintaining a quality image. Such an image can be important in determining expectations, which are important for a person's reaction to a product.

Proposition 17-15 may also explain brand loyalties which on the surface appear irrational. If a consumer has been satisfied with a particular brand in the past, he or she naturally expects it to perform well in the future. If the consumer is occasionally disappointed with the brand's performance, he or she will attribute the performance to something unstable and will continue to have high expectations for that brand. It is not that the consumer is irrational when staying with his or her favorite brand. Rather, he or she has explained the disappointment in a way that lets him or her retain the previous image of the brand.

SUMMARY Attribution theory is concerned with the study of "commonsense" psychology, which is important to the marketing practitioner as well as to the psychologist. Kelley views people as naive scientists who base attributions of causality on covariance of cause and effect. In order for a person to be certain that his or her reaction is because of the thing itself, the reaction must be unique and consistent over person, time, and modality. One person can influence the attributions of another by either providing the individual with data related to the consistency of an effect over time or modality, or by presenting one's own opinion as consensus information. This latter point has implications for promotional strategy.

Jones and Davis' theory, on the other hand, specifies how a person determines when an action accurately represents the underlying disposition of the actor through comparing the effects of that action to the effects of alternatives. Consumers will therefore believe advertisers' statements only to the extent that ulterior motives for the statements are not perceived.

People also make attributions about the causes of their own behavior. Bem has shown that attitudes are inferred from behavior. Therefore, if a consumer takes a positive action toward a product (purchases or uses it), he or she will tend to have a positive attitude toward the product. Marketers should then make a special effort to induce consumers to buy their products, since the purchaser tends to have a more positive attitude toward the product after investing time and money in it.

Weiner and his associates developed a model depicting achievement behavior which can be used when examining attributions concerning satisfaction or dissatisfaction with a product. A success or failure can be attributed either to the actor (internally), or to the environment (externally). Also, the performance can be attributed to something which does not vary over time (stable) or to something that does vary over time (unstable). The consumer is more likely to attribute dissatisfaction with the product to something external (the product or channel), while the observer is more likely to attribute the consumer's dissatisfaction to something about the consumer (e.g., misuse of the product).

KEY CONCEPTS
Achievement situation

Attribution theory

Cognitive dissonance

Cognitive elements

Correspondence

Hedonic relevance

SPECIAL TOPICS

PART

4

INDIVIDUAL ADOPTION AND RESISTANCE BEHAVIOR

18

CHAPTER GOALS The objective of this chapter is to help the reader understand:
1. how innovations diffuse through the population;
2. **the stages through which individuals go in deciding whether to adopt an innovation;**
3. **the sources of consumer resistance at each stage;**
4. **a specific method which marketers can use to identify those consumers who are the best prospects for a new product or service;**
5. **how the attributes of innovations affect the probability that consumers will move through the stages of the adoption process.**

INTRODUCTION Each year hundreds of products and services which are perceived by consumers to be new and different are introduced into the market. Very substantial—even huge—resources are expended by businesses in order to develop and market these new offerings. Yet, it appears that most new products and services become market failures.[1] Hence, understanding how and why consumers purchase or do not purchase a product or service which they perceive as new to them is of considerable importance to the marketer and of great interest and challenge to the academic researcher.

Because of the importance of adoption and resistance, two chapters are needed. This chapter is concerned with how individual consumers adopt and resist new products. In the next chapter we consider the adoption of innova-

---

[1]C. Merle Crawford, "New Product Failure Rate," *Journal of Marketing,* April, 1977, p. 51.

tions by organizations. By splitting individual and organizational adoption and resistance into two chapters we are not saying that the two processes are completely different. On the contrary, they are very similar. In this chapter we first discuss the diffusion of innovations. Then we turn to individuals to examine the stages which they go through in the adoption process. This will include discussing psychological sources of resistance at each stage. In the next section we briefly discuss three other sources of resistance which come from the individual's environment and interaction with others. Following this discussion of individuals, we examine a method which marketers can use for identifying those consumers who are the best prospects for the new product or service. Finally, we discuss the attributes of innovations and how they can be modified in order to fit the needs of the consumers. In all, this chapter is a discussion of consumer learning about new products.

DIFFUSION OF INNOVATIONS

Innovations are ideas, practices, or objects which people see as new and different. There are two processes connected with innovations: the *adoption* process and the *diffusion* process. Adoption is the process in which an individual becomes committed to continued use of an innovation. Resistance is incomplete adoption resulting from rejection. Diffusion is the process by which adoption spreads through the population. One way of thinking of this is that the knowledge or use of new products spreads through a group of people much like a contagious disease, or news of an important world event. Thus, adoption and resistance are individual phenomena, and diffusion is a group or aggregate phenomenon. Though most of this chapter is concerned with adoption and resistance processes, the diffusion process must be explained first along with the ways in which diffusion researchers have classified people into adopter groups.

People differ in terms of when they adopt an innovation (relative to the time when the innovation is introduced). Some adopt soon after the introduction of the product, while others adopt a long time after introduction or perhaps not at all. Based on these differences, people can be clustered into groups of consumers who adopt at roughly the same time. This segmentation approach has been empirically verified in a number of contexts.[2] Figure 18-1 shows this classification. Diffusion follows a normal distribution over time, with few adopters either very early or very late in the diffusion process. Most

---

[2]Everett M. Rogers and Floyd Shoemaker, *The Communication of Innovations: A Cross Cultural Approach,* NY: The Free Press, 1971.

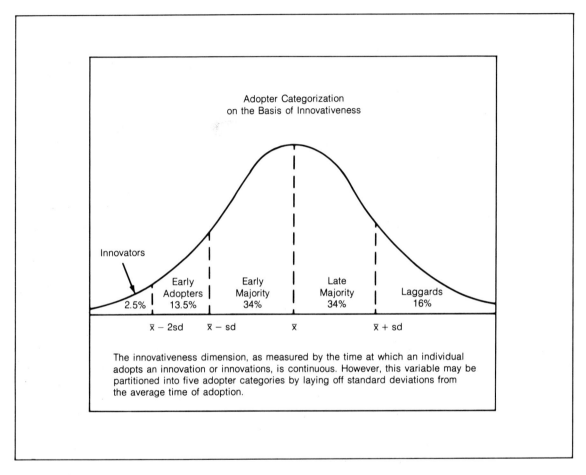

Adopter Categorization
on the Basis of Innovativeness

Innovators

Innovators	Early Adopters	Early Majority	Late Majority	Laggards
2.5%	13.5%	34%	34%	16%

$\bar{x} - 2sd$ $\bar{x} - sd$ $\bar{x}$ $\bar{x} + sd$

The innovativeness dimension, as measured by the time at which an individual adopts an innovation or innovations, is continuous. However, this variable may be partitioned into five adopter categories by laying off standard deviations from the average time of adoption.

FIGURE 18-1.
Adopter Categorization

Source: E. M. Rogers and F. F. Shoemaker, *The Communication of Innovations: A Cross Cultural Approach,* NY: Free Press, 1971, p. 23.

people lie somewhere in the middle. The people within each group of adopters are similar, not only in the time at which they adopt, but also in their values, attitudes, and behavior (especially with regard to communication). These similarities are listed below:

Innovators: venturesome
Early Adopters: respected by others; opinion leaders
Early Majority: followers; will try after someone else has "gone first"
Late Majority: skeptical
Laggards: traditional; adopt when it is no longer an innovation

The primary importance of examining the diffusion process is that it takes into account interpersonal communications which are very significant in decisions of whether to adopt a new product or service. In particular, it is the early adopters who are important in convincing others to adopt an innovation. That is, early adopters are likely to be opinion leaders (see Chapter 9 on communications for a discussion of opinion leadership). Thus, diffusion research examines the social networks of individuals and their communication patterns.

Product managers need to know how to reach early adopters, since these persons are often very influential among other consumers. Promotional themes should appeal to these consumers. As time passes, promotional themes might be altered to be more appealing to the early and late majority groups.

One of the major oversights of diffusion research is that it does not examine "non-diffusion." (The fact that there is not even a word to describe the phenomenon is evidence of the magnitude of this neglect.) Thus, in this chapter we examine both adoption (which in aggregate form over time is diffusion) and resistance to change (the individual level counterpart to "non-diffusion").

A SYNTHESIS MODEL OF THE INDIVIDUAL ADOPTION PROCESS

Many researchers find it useful to develop flow charts of the processes whereby individuals and groups adopt products and services. Adoption is considered to be the repeated or continued use of an innovation. A model or flow chart is presented in Figure 18-2 which represents a synthesis of various other models. A special model is needed for adoptions of innovations because there is a distinction between decisions involving innovations and decisions involving other established products and services. Evidence exists indicating that "the decision making process preceding the purchase of an innovation differs from that process preceding the purchase of an established alternative...."[3] One difference is that in the case of an innovation, information from friends and salespersons is acquired later in the decision process than with an established product.[4]

In Figure 18-2 the basic adoption process stages are in boxes and run from left to right (perception to adoption). Above each box is the source of

---

[3]Carol A. Kohn Berning and Jacob Jacoby, "Patterns of Information Acquisition in New Product Purchases," *Journal of Consumer Research,* Vol. 1, September, 1974, p. 21.
[4]*Ibid.,* p. 21.

FIGURE 18-2.
Adoption Model

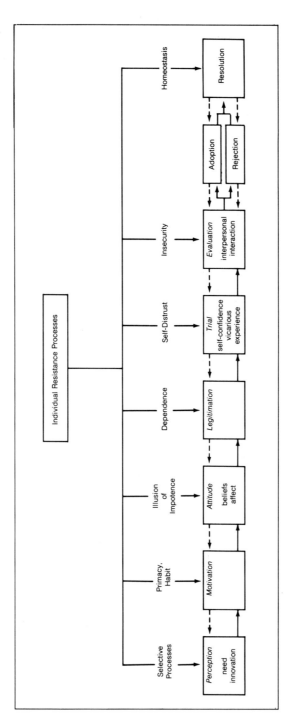

resistance usually associated with that stage. We discuss consumer resistance in the next section of this chapter. First, let us examine the basic adoption stages.

Perception The internal process of adoption begins with perception. (This general topic was treated in Chapter 11 in the section on perception.) Both the innovation and the need for the innovation must be perceived by the individual in order for eventual adoption to occur.

Consumers' perceptions of an innovation often change as the consumers move through the various stages of adoption. What is perceived as new or different in the early stages may eventually be perceived as commonplace in the later stages. Changes in perception such as these would have important effects on consumer behavior. Thus, perception should be traced through the entire process for possible changes. Do innovators change their perceptions more rapidly than others? Or, do they adopt because of the newness involved, while others require more familiarity with the product? Conceivably, too, some people may be early adopters because they see the item as familiar.

The important factors affecting the consumer at this stage are selective attention and selective retention. Both of these are perceptual processes which help one screen out some messages (for a variety of reasons) and pay attention to others. Selective attention is the process which occurs when a person listens to or watches some messages and ignores others. Selective retention occurs when a person remembers some messages and forgets others. More than just a result of currently held attitudes, these selective processes may originate as a result of the cultural, social, or communicative climate.[5]

Motivation A necessary step in overcoming resistance to change is motivation. (This was discussed at length in Chapter 14.) Behaviors which are comfortable, such as the habit of buying the same brand, are normally resistant to change. Consumer perceptions of an existing need and a new product must be very positive in order to provide the impetus or motivation for further action.

Attitude The next stage of the adoption process is attitude formation. (This was examined in Chapter 16.) Attitudes contain two components: affect and cognition or beliefs. As consumers move through the attitude stage, they develop beliefs or cognitions about the new product based on information from other people, advertisements, and reports on the product published in various

---

[5]Jack R. Gibb, "Defensive Communication," *Journal of Communication*, Vol. 11, September, 1961, pp. 141–148.

consumer magazines. The affective or "feeling" component is probably not strong at this stage, and may be limited to liking or disliking the product or idea. The strength or intensity of this emotional component supplies the impetus for the behavior which follows. Greater intensity may mean a more rapid progression through the remaining stages of the process. Research on this component could reveal the actions of such factors as acceptance or repression of emotion in the behavior of innovators and laggards, as well as the effects of the strength of this emotional component on the rapidity of adoption or rejection.

An important type of resistance at the attitude stage is consumers' feelings of impotence or inadequacy. These feelings may cause them to think they cannot satisfy their needs because they lack the abilities to use the innovation.

Legitimation   In the legitimation stage, consumers seek reinforcement for the purchase they are contemplating. The appropriateness of the purchase is of prime importance. This may be determined by observing whether other important people have made similar purchases, or by seeking approval from peers or relatives. Increases in interpersonal contacts might be an important criterion for recognizing the onset of the legitimation stage.[6]

Dependence on other people for approval may be a source of resistance to the adoption of an innovation, for these other people may be opposed to the innovation and may support the status quo. Also, time may be required to find the appropriate people to ask for guidance about a purchase.

Trial   During the trial stage, the consumer puts the innovation to a personal test prior to complete acceptance. Two researchers have found, for example, that during the trial purchase of a completely new brand, an individual household tends to purchase a smaller quantity than it normally would in its purchase of established brands.[7] Occasionally, the nature of the innovation or the situation can make personal testing impossible and the individual might "try" the new product by psychologically sharing vicariously in the experience of another consumer who is actually using the product. Also, consumers who lack self-confidence in their own abilities to use a product may be reluctant to try the product themselves first, and prefer to wait until others have demonstrated it is easy to use.

---

[6]Udai Pareek and Y. P. Singh, "Communication Nets in the Sequential Adoption Process," *Indian Journal of Psychology,* Vol. 44, 1969, pp. 33–35.

[7]Robert W. Shoemaker and F. Robert Shoaf, "Behavioral Changes in the Trial of New Products," *Journal of Consumer Research,* Vol. 2, September, 1975, p. 105.

Evaluation   Evaluation is the stage between the trial and adoption stages. Following trial, the consumer reviews the pros and cons of continued or increased use. The existence of this stage was uncovered in the Pareek and Singh study. They found that much of the interpersonal discussion about a product occurred following the trial stage (where interaction was almost nonexistent). While it is quite probable that informal or brief evaluation follows each stage in the adoption process, a major evaluation is probably necessary before a formal commitment is made. Therefore, evaluation precedes adoption in the model.

If consumers feel insecure about their abilities to evaluate a product, they may be hesitant to go ahead and adopt it, even though the trial experience was satisfactory. Consumers may feel they have overlooked some important information or may believe themselves inadequate judges of a product's merits. Such insecurity is a source of resistance at the evaluation stage.

Adoption/Rejection   The adoption stage represents the final movement toward commitment to repeated or continued usage. This stage, like the attitude stage, has cognitive and affective components, but also has a behavioral component. There is quite a difference between this stage and the attitude stage, however. The cognitive component at the adoption stage contains beliefs based upon personal experience from the trial stage. These beliefs are more strongly held than the beliefs of the attitude stage. In fact, the beliefs formed in the adoption stage may supplement or supplant the beliefs formed in the attitude stage.

The affective or emotional component is also likely to be stronger here than in the attitude stage. It is only logical that it takes a greater incentive to actually commit oneself to continuous use of a product or service than to merely continue thinking about using it.

The alternative to adoption, at this point, is rejection. Unsatisfactory outcomes in the process prior to this stage may result in negative feelings and beliefs. The components of rejection are the same as those of adoption and achieve similar intensity.

Resolution   The final stage is that of resolution.[8] This concept includes dissonance reduction, but is more inclusive. Dissonance is a cognitive stage which one experiences when two beliefs are in conflict. Post-decision dissonance results when a person has made a decision but has some doubts about the wisdom of that decision. Or, dissonance can result when one must choose between two or more attractive alternatives. But, many new products may be far superior to anything previously known, or may be the only known alternative available to

---

[8]Rex R. Campbell, "A Suggested Paradigm of the Individual Adoption Process," *Rural Sociology,* Vol. 31, December, 1966, pp. 458–466.

solve a problem. In such cases, dissonance is not the inevitable result of adoption. Since some innovations are adopted without regret, even enthusiastically, the resolution stage can include reactions other than dissonance. The broader perspective suggested by resolution could lead to fruitful investigative results. Resolution includes all of the adjustments (some positive and some negative) made as a result of the decision to adopt (or not adopt) an innovation.

An Example   To show how a consumer passes through these eight stages in the process of considering an innovation, we will use the following hypothetical example. Although it is hypothetical, it is based upon the actual experiences of consumers.

Several years ago, microwave ovens were introduced in the ultimate consumer market. Let us imagine a family at that point in time. First, some family member became aware that microwave ovens existed and that they were different from other ovens. Thus, the innovation was perceived. This initial perception may have come about in any of a number of ways: an advertisement on television or in a magazine, a friend's description of the product, or an in-store cooking demonstration. Also, someone in the family perceived a need for this type of oven. This need may have resulted either from a breakdown in the present oven, or, more likely, from the problems inherent in the family's present situation. For instance, both adults in the family may be employed and are therefore interested in anything which will help them prepare dinners quickly.

If microwave ovens are not seen as relevant to their lives, the family members are less likely to continue through the adoption process. That is, they will not be motivated to learn more about microwave ovens.

Next, the family members begin to form an attitude toward microwave ovens. This may begin almost immediately after perception or may not occur for some time. For example, upon seeing a television advertisement, the husband may ask the wife, "What do you think about that?" Or, upon receiving a Christmas bonus check, the wife may say to the husband, "Remember those microwave ovens? Let's look into the possibility of buying one." During this stage they will begin to consider the cost, cooking time saved, safety, and size of microwave ovens. Then, attitudes are formed toward different brands and models of microwave ovens. Legitimation for these attitudes may be sought from friends, from salespeople, or from reports on microwave ovens in consumer magazines.

Actual trial of such a large item is difficult because it cannot be broken down into small packages, such as repeat purchase items like a new tooth cleanser. This does not mean, however, that the family members cannot try a microwave oven before becoming committed to it. They may do any of the following: dine at the house of a friend who has a microwave oven, eat food prepared by a salesperson in the store, get a one week at-home trial period after which they can return the oven to the store if they are not satisfied, or talk to someone who owns and uses a microwave oven and thereby vicariously experience a trial of the product.

After the trial the oven is evaluated. If the trial period is satisfactory, the family will adopt the product. If it is unsatisfactory (e.g., a dislike of food which is cooked but not browned, or realizing that much of the time spent in the kitchen is used preparing food before it goes into the oven), the family may reject the innovation. If these dissatisfactions occur after the purchase, the family will have a microwave oven, but will not be frequent users of it. Finally, they will resolve post-purchase consequences and somehow fit the product into their lives.

SOME ADDITIONAL OBSERVATIONS ON RESISTANCE

Resistance to change is a major consumer response to new ideas, practices, and products. In fact, a very substantial number (close to 65 percent) of new products fail within their first six months, and still many more fail within the next six months because of consumer resistance. In this section of the chapter, we explore various ideas about consumer resistance to new products and services. First, two observations are in order. First, resistance to change is often considered a bad thing. This is the pro-innovation bias which exists in marketing.[9] The literature in marketing and other areas refers to resisters as "laggards." This is a decidedly negative term. Seemingly, laggards have something wrong with them; *they* are to blame if a new product doesn't gain widespread adoption. This focus is not only inappropriate, but can create blindspots for marketers who do not focus on their own role in the consumer resistance process.

A second observation is that resistance may be healthy. Not all new products are in some objective sense "good" or represent significant improvements over earlier products. So, some products should be resisted. In addition, the marketer may want to diffuse resistance to other competing products. Thus, one can picture marketing strategies designed to keep or expand present consumers by inducing resistance to alternatives. Consumer activists may also want to diffuse resistance to purchasing certain types or makes of products.

Thus, when thinking about resistance, one should think positively, for resistance is not necessarily bad. The potential threat of resistance may cause

---

[9]Everett M. Rogers, "New Product Adoption and Diffusion," *Journal of Consumer Research*, Vol. 2, March, 1976, pp. 290–301.

marketers to be more careful in designing and introducing new products and services. Resistance may also result in the avoidance of harmful products. When consumers display resistance, they are telling the marketer something which was either not known earlier by the marketer or was ignored. In this instance, the nature of resistance is an important element of the information necessary for developing the marketing mix.

Resistance to change may be defined as any conduct that serves to maintain the status quo in the face of pressure to alter the status quo. Though resistance to change is not widely discussed in the marketing literature or other related literature, it is the normal response of consumers in the marketplace since there are fewer people who change than who resist change. There are many sources of resistance in any setting. Three not mentioned in Figure 18-2 are: cultural barriers, social barriers, and barriers brought about by the marketer.

Cultural Barriers   At a general cultural level, resistance can be found in basic belief and value systems. The greater the incompatibility of a product with a deeply held belief, the less likely it is that the product will be adopted by persons holding that belief (Proposition 18-1 in Exhibit 18-1). A common barrier to purchasing preventive medicines, such as vitamins or enriched foods, is the belief that a person has little control over what happens to him or her, that such matters are in the hands of God, or are otherwise uncontrollable.

A related barrier concerns cultural values. The greater the incompatibility of a product with a basic value, the less likely it is that the product will be adopted by persons having that value (see Proposition 18-2). Such values may be general (such as being home-centered, resulting in one's not listening to new information from strangers) or specific to the innovation (such as cultural taboos).[10] The do-it-yourself phenomenon popular in the United States has not caught on among middle- and upper-class consumers in certain Latin American countries because it supposedly violates the value that these groups hold for not working with their hands.

Proposition 18-1 and 18-2 imply that business firms and their representatives should be sensitive to the issue of cultural pride and should localize the marketing mix as much as possible. This is not to say that products are not highly regarded if they come from another country. Rather, a foreign version of some product may be particularly attractive as a prestige item. The important point is to avoid conveying the message that the product is coming from

---

[10]Bernard Dubois, ''A Cultural Approach to the Study of Diffusion and Adoption of Innovations,'' in M. Venkatesan (ed.), *Proceedings of the Third Annual Conference of the Association for Consumer Research,* 1972, pp. 840–850.

EXHIBIT 18-1.
Propositions About
Cultural Barriers to
Change

PROPOSITION 18-1.
The greater the incompatibility of a product with a deeply held belief, the less likely it is that the product will be adopted by persons holding that belief.

PROPOSITION 18-2.
The greater the incompatibility of a product with a basic value, the less likely it is that the product will be adopted by persons having that value.

the outside and implying that the adopter's culture is inferior in some way related to the product.

Social Barriers   There are several social barriers to change. Some of these are presented as propositions in Exhibit 18-2. Since earlier chapters have already discussed groups and social norms (particularly Chapters 5 and 6 on small-scale structures), we will not elaborate on these propositions or their action implications.

Barriers Brought   Resistance may result from marketer actions as well as consumer actions. One
About by the   source of difficulty, particularly at the perception stage, is a failure of the
Marketer   marketer to comprehend the consumer's situation. In general, the less the marketer understands the consumer situation, the less able the marketer is to help consumers perceive a problem or identify a potential solution to a problem. The marketer should be especially aware of consumer defense mechanisms which may prevent consumers from seeing a problem, and which may also cause them to feel satisfied with the status quo.

At the motivation stage, the marketer could fail to communicate clearly what the product or service is about. The less clear communications are about the advantages of an innovation, the less likely it is that consumers will be motivated to seek further information (Proposition 18-9 in Exhibit 18-3). An action implication of this proposition is that the marketer must be very explicit in communications with consumers in order to prevent faulty and incomplete consumer information processing.

The marketer may also fail to present information in a convincing way. Thus, Proposition 18-10 is especially relevant at the attitude stage. The less convincing the information is, the less likely consumers are to develop: (a) favorable predispositions toward the product, and (b) strongly held predispositions. One action implication of this proposition is that the marketer

EXHIBIT 18-2.
*Propositions About
Social Barriers to
Change*

PROPOSITION 18-3.
The greater the solidarity of intergroup ties, the greater the resistance to innovations stressing individualism.

PROPOSITION 18-4.
The greater the solidarity of a group, the more likely it is that group
members will reject an outsider and the new product that the outsider is trying to introduce.

PROPOSITION 18-5.
The stronger the conformity to norms, the greater the resistance to a
new product which is not consistent with those norms.

PROPOSITION 18-6.
The less aware a group is of its inadequacies, the less responsive it
will be to products which promise to remedy the inadequacies.

PROPOSITION 18-7.
If a new product or innovation is perceived by one group within a
firm to enhance the power of another group in the firm, the former
group will resist the change.

PROPOSITION 18-8.
The greater the opposition to change among group leaders, the less
likely it is that a new product will be adopted.

must be sensitive to consumer complacency and suspended judgment. The
marketer should design communications to create an initial favorable predisposition toward the product and encourage the belief that the product would
indeed solve a problem.

At the legitimation stage, the marketer can fail to provide confirming
evidence that the favorable attitude is warranted and that the consumer
should proceed in his or her decision-making process. In general, the less
credible the source of a communication, the less likely legitimation is to take
place in the minds of consumers (see Proposition 18-11). The marketer
should be careful to select media and/or persons with high credibility to
disseminate information. This is especially important if consumers are under
social pressure not to adopt a new product.

EXHIBIT 18-3.
Propositions About
Marketer-Induced
Resistance

PROPOSITION 18-9.
The less clear communications are about the advantages of an innovation, the less likely it is that consumers will be motivated to seek further information.

PROPOSITION 18-10.
The less convincing information is, the less likely consumers are to develop: (a) favorable predispositions toward the product, and (b) strongly held predispositions.

PROPOSITION 18-11.
The less credible the source of a communication, the less likely legitimation is to take place in the minds of consumers.

PROPOSITION 18-12.
The less clear marketers are about how consumers may go about trying a product on an experimental basis, the less likely trial is to: (a) occur at all, or (b) occur properly.

PROPOSITION 18-13.
The less clear marketers are about the advantages of their product relative to alternatives, the less favorably impressed consumers will be with the advocated product.

In the trial stage, consumers use the product on a limited basis or seriously think what it would be like to adopt the product on a full and permanent basis. Thus, the less clear marketers are about how consumers may go about trying a product on an experimental basis, the less likely trial is to: (a) occur at all, or (b) occur properly (Proposition 18-12). There are at least three implications of this last proposition. First, marketers must provide ways for the potential adopter to try the innovation on a small scale (either through small packages of innovations, such as food products, or prototypes of products, such as air conditioners). Secondly, the marketer should overcome any inadequacies consumers may feel about their abilities to try a product. Thirdly, marketers must correct consumer misperceptions that if consumers use the product on a trial basis and decide not to adopt it, they will experience some cost and no benefits. The benefits of trial, as well as those of adoption, must be stressed.

As the consumer enters the final evaluation stage, the marketer must provide conclusive evidence which demonstrates the superiority of the new product over alternatives. The less clear marketers are about the advantages of their product relative to alternatives, the less favorably impressed consumers will be with the advocated product (see Proposition 18-13).

After adoption occurs a consumer might discontinue use of the product. Discontinuance increases as the involvement of the marketer with past and current adopters decreases. This may occur because the marketer does not alter the product to meet the changing needs and circumstances of previous adopters or does not offer assistance in implementing or adjusting to the change. This is particularly true in the case of organizational buyers. Care must also be exercised by the marketer not to allow unrealistic expectations to develop.

Also, after adoption consumers must receive assistance in modifying the product to meet their individualized needs. This process has been termed reinvention, that is, changing the innovation during the implementation process in order to make it fit one's own needs.[11] Often, however, the reinvention process is a waste of resources, which makes no significant improvements in the innovation. Reinvention can occur in various degrees: complete reinvention, adaptation, or modification. Marketers must decide whether or not they believe adopters could reinvent the innovation during the implementation process, and if so, to what degree. Then, innovations should be designed in order to facilitate or inhibit this process. One example of facilitating reinvention (in the modification sense) is the present trend toward modular furniture where the purchaser decides how many units of furniture will be needed and in what positions they will be placed. An example of inhibiting reinvention is warning consumers of unsafe (and seemingly unlikely) ways of using (or discontinued use of) the product, such as using a hairdryer while bathing, using a lawnmower for trimming hedges, or disconnecting the wiring for seat belt buzzers.

A THEORY OF THE BEST POTENTIAL CUSTOMER

Consumers proceed through their adoption decision processes at different times and even at different speeds. This leads us to several propositions derived from the summarizing works of Rogers and Shoemaker[12] and Robertson.[13] These propositions are presented in Exhibit 18-4.

---

[11]Rekha Agarwala-Rogers, "Re-invention: Limits on a Growth of Innovation," draft of discussion ideas for the Industrial Buying Behavior Workshop, held at the University of Pittsburgh, Graduate School of Business, April 23–24, 1976.

[12]Everett M. Rogers and Floyd Shoemaker, *The Communication of Innovations: A Cross Cultural Approach,* NY: The Free Press, 1971.

[13]Thomas S. Robertson, *Innovative Behavior and Communication,* NY: Holt, Rinehart and Winston, 1971.

EXHIBIT 18-4.
Propositions Concerning Differential Consumer Response to Innovations

PROPOSITION 18-14.
Different consumers in the same social system become aware of innovations at different times.

PROPOSITION 18-15.
Consumers vary in the length of time required to proceed from the perception stage to the resolution stage.

PROPOSITION 18-16.
A given consumer tends to become aware of innovations in a particular product category at a similar time in the life cycles of these innovations.

The three propositions in Exhibit 18-4 have substantial research support in a wide variety of contexts. They have the following action implication: marketers should identify those consumers who learn about a particular innovation soon after its introduction and who also move through the adoption decision process rapidly. Because of the great importance of this action implication, we devote the next few pages to a discussion of how this action implication can be developed through consumer research.

An important category of consumers is referred to as early adopters.[14] These consumers are important because they are the market which provides the first returns on investment. Even more importantly, they are sometimes very influential in the adoption or rejection decisions of many other consumers. A general proposition which is supported in industrial, as well as ultimate consumer settings, is Proposition 18-17: Opinion leadership is greater among early adopters than among later adopters.[15] Baumgarten found that opinion

---

[14]John O. Summers, "Media Exposure Patterns of Consumer Innovators," *Journal of Marketing,* Vol. 36, January, 1972, pp. 43–49; Rogers and Shoemaker, *op. cit.;* Thomas S. Robertson, *op. cit.*

[15]John A. Czepiel, "Word-of-Mouth Process in the Diffusion of a Major Technological Innovation," *Journal of Marketing Research,* Vol. 11, May, 1974, pp. 172–180; Jacob Jacoby, "Opinion Leadership and Innovativeness: Overlap and Validity," in M. Venkatesan (ed.), *Proceedings of the Third Annual Conference of the Association for Consumer Research,* 1972, pp. 632–649; Steven Baumgarten, "The Innovative Communicator in the Diffusion Process," *Journal of Marketing Research,* Vol. 12, February, 1975, pp. 12–18.

EXHIBIT 18-5.
A Proposition About
Opinion Leadership

PROPOSITION 18-17.
Opinion leadership is greater among early adopters than among later adopters.

leaders (influential people) and early adopters overlapped significantly, at least in the context of clothing fashion. This study found that people who are both opinion leaders and early adopters of new fashions are distinctly different from others who are only opinion leaders, or only early adopters, or neither. This general pattern has been established by others in both industrial and consumer settings.[16] Table 18-1 presents a summary of information about opinion leader traits.

TABLE 18-1.
Summary Profile of
Opinion Leader Traits

Characteristic	Findings
Age	Varies by product category
Social Status	Generally same as person who receives advice
Gregariousness	High
Cosmopolitanism	Limited evidence that it is higher than that of the people receiving advice
Knowledge	Generally greater for area of influence
Personality	No major distinguishing traits
Norm Adherence	Generally greater than people receiving advice
Innovativeness	Higher than people receiving advice

Source: Robertson, *op. cit.,* p. 179.

Identifying the Best Once a decision has been made to launch a new product, the critical question
Prospect becomes: *How can a company identify and effectively reach the best poten-*
tial early adopters for a specific new product that is ready to be launched? Not
all potential early adopters are influential with other consumers (as indicated
above). There are many other important factors to consider in selecting the

---

[16]James H. Donnelly, Jr. and John M. Ivancevich, "A Methodology for Identifying Innovation Characteristics of New Brand Purchases," *Journal of Marketing Research,* Vol. 6, August, 1974, pp. 331–334; Michael J. Baker, *Marketing New Industrial Products,* NY: Holmes & Meier Publishers, Inc., 1975, especially Chapter 6, pp. 109–152.

market segment to which initial appeals should be targeted. Two writers have developed an approach which helps identify the best prospective customers.[17] Their model can be summarized in the following way:

> The Net Value of Potential Adopters = Adoption Propensity (Volume Propensity + Influence Propensity) − Cost of Effective Exposure

Thus, before launching a new product, the task is to define the value of different prospects for a new product. Let us assume that a new product could be advertised through a direct mail campaign. Assume that thousands of names of potential users of the product are available, and that we cannot advertise to all of them. The mailing list supplier is able to answer only four questions about the names on the mailing list. What four questions would a marketer want to ask?:

1. What is the probability that the prospect would be an early purchaser of the product upon exposure? (Call this probability A = *early adoption propensity.*)
2. How much is the prospect likely to buy per year if he or she tries the new product? (Call this amount Q = *heavy volume propensity.*)
3. How much additional purchasing per year is this prospect likely to stimulate in others through interpersonal influence? (Call this amount I = *influence propensity.*)
4. What is the cost of an effective communication exposure to this person? (Call this cost C = *cost of an effective communication exposure.*)

We can combine the four factors into the following formula to find the value (V) of a prospect:

$$V = A (Q + I) - C \qquad (1)$$

To illustrate this formula, assume that the first prospect on the list has a likelihood of only .05 of being an early buyer of this product upon exposure; if this person buys, he or she will probably like the product and buy $5 worth a year. This person is likely to stimulate another $6 of purchases a year in others; and it will cost $0.20 to communicate an effective message to him or her. According to the formula, this prospect would be worth:

$$V = .05 (\$5 + \$6) - \$.20 = \$.35$$

Now consider a second prospect for whom the likelihood is .1 of being an early buyer of this product exposure. If this person buys, he or she will probably like it and buy $3 worth a year. This person is likely to stimulate $1 of purchases a year in others; and it will cost $0.20 to communicate an

---

[17]Philip Kotler and Gerald Zaltman, "Targeting Prospects for a New Product," *Journal of Advertising Research*, Vol. 16, No. 1, February, 1976, pp. 7–20.

effective message to him or her. According to the formula, this prospect would be worth:

$$V = .1 (\$3 + \$1) - \$.20 = \$.20$$

Here we see that although the second prospect is twice as likely to be an early adopter of the new product as the first prospect, he or she is a less valuable prospect because he or she will personally consume less and influence fewer people than the first prospect. Thus, being an *early adopter* is not automatically equivalent to being the *best early prospect*. Suppose it could be shown, for example, that early adopters buy less of a given brand than later adopters because early adopters are always trying out new brands and dropping the ones they just started using. That is, they are low in loyalty because of their need for variety. In this case, it can be questioned whether early adopters are the best targets for new product launchings.

Given that the value of a prospect is defined by the factors in formula (1), what subfactors underlie each of the major factors?

Early Adoption Propensity.   Early adoption propensity is defined as the probability that a person will be an early purchaser of the product as the result of an *effective communication exposure*. Early adoption propensity is a function of the following subfactors:

1.   The extent to which the product has strong need-fulfillment potential for the person. (Call this F = *need-fulfillment potential.*)
2.   The extent to which the person has a new product orientation. (Call this N = *innovative disposition.*) This is determined by cultural values and by individual personality.[18]
3.   The extent to which the product is highly accessible to the individual. (Call this D = *accessibility.*)
4.   The extent to which his or her income makes the price less important. (Call this Y = *income sufficiency.*)

Each of these factors is important in determining whether or not a person has a high propensity to adopt a particular new product. Let us assume that each factor can be scaled from zero to one. These factors would combine in a *multiplicative* way to affect the early adoption propensity:

$$A = F \times N \times D \times Y \qquad (2)$$

For example, the highest early adoption propensity would be found in a person who has a strong need for the new product, tends to search out new products, can easily acquire it without much effort, and can afford the price.

---

[18]Dubois, *op. cit.*

The formula is multiplicative because if any factor is weak, the early adoption propensity drops considerably. It is not the case that the propensity would be high simply because two or three factors are very high.

Heavy Volume Propensity.   Heavy volume propensity is the amount of the new product that the person is likely to buy per period if he or she tries it. This propensity depends upon the following factors:

1.   The probability that this type of person will be sufficiently satisfied with the new product upon trial to buy it again. (Call this $T = $ *trial satisfaction probability.*)
2.   The number of times per year that the person makes a purchase in this product class. (Call this $R = $ *product class repurchase frequency.*)
3.   The average amount purchased by this person per purchase occasion. (Call this $K = $ *average amount purchased per purchase occasion.*)
4.   The probable share that the new product will enjoy of this person's purchases within the product class. (Call this $S = $ *new product's share of the total purchases in the product class.*)

These factors probably combine in a multiplicative way to determine the person's heavy volume propensity:

$$Q = T \ (R \times K \times S) \tag{3}$$

For example, suppose the person makes a purchase from this product class three times a year; he or she buys $2 worth of items in the product class each time and buys the brand half of the time. This would yield a new product purchase volume per year of:

$$R \times K \times S = 3 \times \$2 \times \tfrac{1}{2} = \$3$$

But will the individual be sufficiently satisfied as a result of trial to adopt the new product? Let us assume that this probability is .75. Then:

$$Q = .75(\$3) = \$2.25$$

That is, the probability of sufficient trial satisfaction is used to scale down the value of his or her purchases, if satisfied.

Influence Propensity.   Influence propensity is the amount of additional purchasing per year that the prospect is likely to stimulate in others through interpersonal influence.[19] This propensity depends upon the following factors:

1.   The number of persons this person interacts with on a conversational basis. (Call this $M = $ *the number of acquaintances.*)

---

[19]The reader is reminded here of the discussion of role accumulation in Chapter 7.

2. The percentage of persons he or she influences during the year to try the product who would not have tried it otherwise. (Call this L = *influence ratio.*)

3. The average volume an influenced person buys per year of the new brand. (Call this W = *the influenced person's volume.*)

These factors also probably work in a multiplicative way:

$$I = M \times L \times W \qquad (4)$$

The prospect's influence potential depends on the number of people he or she knows, the proportion of them he or she influences, and the average volume an influenced person buys. We leave aside the fact that the influenced person will, in turn, influence other persons to try the product during the year.

As a further refinement, the proportion of persons that the prospect influences (I) depends upon three factors:

1. The person's *new product conversational propensity.*

2. *The percentage of his or her acquaintances who are potential purchasers* of this product.

3. The degree to which other persons look upon this person as a *new product legitimator.*

So, the prospect shows a higher influence propensity the more he or she talks about new products he or she has tried, the more he or she talks to others who are interested in the product class, and the more he or she is seen as a legitimator of new product ideas.

For example, suppose a particular person knows only a few people (M = 10), but influences many of them (L = .8). And suppose that each of the influenced people would purchase a fairly large volume of the product ($100 per year). This might be the case with an instructor at a tennis camp for country club tennis pros. Each of the pros is likely to purchase a large number of tennis balls or other tennis equipment in a year. Since all of the influenced people are potential purchasers and they all may see the instructor as a new product legitimator, the instructor's influence propensity is high. Then, in numerical terms:

$$I = M \times L \times W = 10 \times .8 \times \$100 = \$800$$

This is very high influence propensity.

Prospect Communication Cost. Prospect communication cost is the cost of delivering an effective message with a given media vehicle to a given prospect. This cost is defined as a function of the following factors:

E_1 = probability that the person will be exposed to the message with the media

E_2 = probability that the person will see the message

E_3 = probability that the person will comprehend the message

E_4 = probability that the person will be favorably impressed by the message

O = actual cost of getting the given message exposed to the given individual with the given media

The function will not be specified except to note that the real cost of communication (C) is higher than the actual cost (O) to the extent that the message-media combination is less than perfectly effective in exposing, informing, and motivating the prospect.

In summary, these four values (adoption propensity, volume propensity, influence propensity, and cost of effective exposure) combine to give an estimate of the net value to the firm of a particular potential adopter. Since in the individual consumer context it is impossible to develop strategies based on what each will do, this calculation is done for segments of the market. This helps the marketer determine which segments are most profitable to pursue. In the industrial consumer context (discussed in the next chapter), the calculations can be done for individual consumers if the market is characterized by a few large consumers, or for segments if a larger number of buyers exists.

PERCEIVED ATTRIBUTES OF INNOVATIONS

In this section we take into account how ultimate consumers perceive a new product or service. Remember that innovations are defined in terms of perceived newness, and exactly what is perceived becomes very important in influencing whether the innovation or new product is purchased. In fact, consumers' perceptions of the nature of the innovation may be more important than the personal characteristics of consumers and their social situations in determining whether the innovation is adopted.[20]

Attributes of Innovations

Innovations can be characterized using a schema of attributes. The following are important attributes to consider when evaluating the possibility that a particular innovation will be a market success.

1. Relative advantages: what the new product does that alternatives do not do or do not do as well.
2. Complexity: (a) how difficult it is to use the new product; and (b) how difficult it is to understand how the product works.
3. Compatibility: (a) how well the new product fits in with the customer's thinking; (b) how well the new product fits in with the customer's social

---

[20]Lyman E. Ostlund, "Perceived Innovation Attributes as Predictors of Innovativeness," *Journal of Consumer Research*, Vol. I, September, 1974, pp. 23–29.

situation; and (c) how well the new product fits in with other related or connected products.

4. Trialability: how easily the new product may be tried without full commitment.

5. Divisibility: how easily the new product can be tried in a mini form.

6. Reversibility: how easily the new product can be discontinued without adverse effect.

7. Communicability: how easy it is to receive and send information about the new product.

8. Adaptability: how easy it is to modify the new product to the unique circumstances of the user.

9. Cost: the magnitude of the financial and nonfinancial resources required.

10. Realization: how soon the benefits of having a new product are experienced.

11. Risk: the magnitude of the dysfunctional consequences of the new product and the likelihood of their being experienced.

To the extent that an innovation has the ratings on these attributes given in Table 18-2, consumers will find the innovation easier to adopt (this is also Proposition 18-18 in Exhibit 18-6). Not all of these attributes will be important or equally important for a given innovation. Thus, in assessing the innovation, differential attention should be given to different attributes.

TABLE 18-2.
Desirable Characteristics of Innovations

High	Low
Relative advantages	Complexity
Compatibility	Cost
Trialability	Risk
Divisibility	
Reversibility	
Communicability	
Adaptability	
Realization (soon)	

Unfortunately, no sound information is available about the relative importance of different attributes under varying circumstances, such as industrial versus ultimate consumer settings or appliances versus furniture. Some information exists, however, about the relative importance (when holding other things constant) of various attributes at different stages in the adoption process. Relative advantages and complexity are especially important attributes at the perception and motivation stages. Compatibility, communicability, and risk are particularly salient at the attitude stage. Compatibility is again important at the legitimation stage. At the trial stage, trialability, divisibility, and reversibility become important. During the evaluation stage, the attributes of cost, realization, and adaptability are especially important. All attributes are

EXHIBIT 18-6.
Propositions About Innovation Characteristics

PROPOSITION 18-18.
The greater the relative advantages, compatibility, trialability, divisibility, reversibility, communicability, and adaptability, the sooner the realization, and the lower the complexity, cost, and risk associated with an innovation, the more likely a consumer is to adopt the innovation.

PROPOSITION 18-19.
"The rate of adoption among consumers of single innovations with incremental effects will be faster than the rate of adoption of single innovations with preventive effects."[21]

PROPOSITION 18-20.
The rate of adoption among consumers of a combination innovation is faster than the rate of adoption of a single (incremental or preventive) innovation.

important at the adoption/rejection decision stage. While many attributes again become important at the resolution stage, the attribute of adaptability usually stands out. The important consideration for the reader is simply that at different decision-making stages different attributes are of special concern to customers. The marketer must be sensitive to this especially in face-to-face selling situations, where it may be easier relative to mass marketing situations to determine what stage of thinking a potential customer is in.

A Classification Scheme

An interesting approach to classifying innovations has been suggested recently.[22] This is an approach which would be useful in studying innovations in marketing settings and is based on the *effects of innovations* rather than consumer perceptions of innovation attributes as discussed in the preceding section.

---

[21]Virginia Lansdon Koontz, *Determinants of Individual's Level of Knowledge and Attitude Towards and Decisions Regarding a Health Innovation in Maine,* unpublished Ph.D. thesis, Ann Arbor: University of Michigan, 1976, Chapter 5.
[22]*Ibid.*

Incremental Innovations. These are ideas, practices, or products which the consumer perceives as new, but which increase the amount of some desired event. A farmer's purchase of fertilizer increases the amount of important chemicals in the land needed to also increase production. A highly automated home kitchen oven increases the amount of time a person can devote to noncooking activities.

Two basic types of incremental innovations can be identified. There is the "true" incremental innovation which provides an increase not previously attained. The purchase of radial tires means the consumer may travel a greater distance before having to replace the tires. The second type of innovation is referred to as a reinstatement innovation. This, too, is intended to increase something the consumer values. In this case, however, the intent is to reestablish a previously experienced level of the value. An ill person uses a particular type of medication to reestablish an earlier level of well-being. New capital equipment is purchased to replace worn out or otherwise malfunctioning manufacturing equipment.

Preventive Innovations. These are adopted to avoid some unpleasant event. Seat belts may be used to prevent injuries, and insurance may be purchased to minimize the financial effects of fire and theft.

There are three basic types of preventive innovations. The first type is a "true" prevention innovation which directly affects whether or not an undesired event happens. Immunizations against childhood diseases, changing auto oil filters as prescribed by the auto care booklet, rust proofing, and comparison shopping are intended to reduce the likelihood that damage will occur. A second class of preventive innovations are detection-oriented. These are innovations which help determine whether something has happened or whether it is likely to happen. Termite and pest control inspections fall into this category, as do certain types of medical examinations, dental checkups, and state required auto inspections. Alleviation innovations are the third type of preventive innovations. This type of innovation lessens the severity of an event's consequences. It is often purchased or used prior to the actual event. Seat belts and hay fever injections are examples. As mentioned in the preceding paragraph, wearing a seat belt may lessen the severity or occurrence of an injury, but does not lessen the likelihood of an accident occurring.

Combination Innovations. These are innovations that lead to both incremental and preventive effects. A consumer's decision to join a health maintenance organization may result in better health and also help prevent illnesses. These benefits are derived from the way health maintenance organizations are designed and operated.

Propositions 18-19 and 18-20 are derived from this classification scheme. Proposition 18-19: "The rate of adoption among consumers of single innovations with incremental effects will be faster than the rate of adoption of single innovations with preventive effects.''[23] Proposition 18-20 is also appropriate: The rate of adoption among consumers of a combination innovation is faster than the rate of adoption of a single (incremental or preventive) innovation. The first proposition is warranted because the effects of an incremental innovation are more obvious to other people, and hence are more easily communicated. The second proposition is warranted because a wider range of benefits is more likely with combination rather than with single innovations. Thus, the innovation will have a greater appeal.

The action implications of these two propositions include the following ideas. First, it may be necessary to plan more promotional activity when introducing a preventive innovation as compared to an incremental innovation. Special efforts might be necessary to communicate and demonstrate the advantages of a preventive innovation. Second, where possible, marketers should stress both the incremental and preventive nature of a product or service. For example, recent retirement savings plans are being promoted by banks and other financial institutions on the basis of their higher interest rates and, consequently, the larger amount of savings at the time of retirement. Banks and other institutions are also stressing the importance of planning and saving now to prevent financial hardships at retirement.

SUMMARY New product introduction, involving both high risks and potentially large profits, is one of the most important areas in marketing. Research into the diffusion of innovations examines the social networks of individuals and their communication patterns.

The adoption process includes the stages of perception of the product, motivation, attitude, legitimation (where consumers seek reinforcement for the purchase they are contemplating), trial, evaluation, and the final stages of adoption/rejection and resolution. The marketer should also be aware of the nature of resistance to adoption or change. If a product is incompatible with the consumer's basic belief and value systems, or with the norms or perceptions of the groups to which he or she belongs, resistance will be high. Also, if the marketer does not understand the consumer's situation, and fails to provide information in a convincing way, the consumer is less likely to consider an innovation. It is important to give consumers assistance in modifying products to meet their individual needs, and to redesign products in order to minimize attribute gaps. Of primary importance to the marketer is the identifi-

---

[23]*Ibid.,* pp. 135–136.

cation of the best prospective customers, for not all potential early adopters buy in large quantities, or influence others to buy.

In addition to examining consumer perceptions of innovation attributes, it is useful to look at the effects of innovations. Innovations may increase the amount of a desired event, they may avoid an unpleasant event, or they may do both. Since the rate of adoption differs according to the type of effect, the marketer must develop a mix which takes the effect into account and uses promotional strategy accordingly.

KEY CONCEPTS
Adoption

Combination innovations

Diffusion

Early adopters

Early adoption propensity

Early majority

Evaluation

Heavy volume propensity

Incremental innovations

Influence propensity

Innovation

Innovative communicators

Innovators

Laggards

Late majority

Legitimation stage

Preventive innovations

Prospect communication cost

Reinvention

Resistance

Resolution

Selective attention

Selective retention

Trial stage

ORGANIZATIONAL ADOPTION AND RESISTANCE

19

CHAPTER GOALS   The objective of this chapter is to help the reader understand:
   1. **the stages through which an organization goes in deciding whether to adopt an innovation;**
   2. **how the structure of the organization affects the ease with which the organization is able to move through the stages in the adoption process;**
   3. **which attributes of innovations are particularly relevant to certain organizational structures during the adoption of an innovation.**

INTRODUCTION   A recent study of the food processing industry examined the adoption of the five most significant food processing innovations in the past thirty years.[1] The study determined, among other things, how long it took for the first 50 percent of all organizations in this industry to adopt these five innovations. The average time for the first 50 percent of the industry to adopt any one of these innovations was fourteen years. For one particular innovation a minimum of eight years was required. Two other innovations each required nineteen years. The obvious conclusion was that firms in this industry were slow to adopt significant innovations. A major reason advanced for this slowness was that the process whereby organizations decide to adopt or reject significant innovations is often subtle and complex. Many interrelated factors

---

[1]G. Haywood and J. Masterson, *Study of the Characteristics of Innovation in the Capital Equipment Field,* Social Science Research Council Report No. HR2269/2, 1977.

are involved in such decision making which do not make such decisions easy or automatic. Numerous other studies support this same conclusion about organizations in nearly all industries.[2] This chapter identifies the more important factors which influence whether an organization adopts an innovation, and how quickly—or slowly—the innovation can be expected to be adopted.

Two sets of factors which, working together, affect organizational innovative behavior are described first. These two sets of factors are the decision-making stages and the organizational structures in the innovation adoption decision process. We examine the effect of different organizational structures on the potential for innovation at different stages of the innovation adoption decision process. Following this we look at some of the ways the attributes of an innovation may interact with organizational structure in determining whether the decision-making process will continue.

A SYNTHESIS MODEL OF THE ORGANIZATION ADOPTION PROCESS

In this section the stages of the organizational decision process are described (see Figure 19-1). As with the individual model of adoption presented in the preceding chapter, sources of resistance at each stage are examined.

FIGURE 19-1.
Organizational Adoption/Resistance Model

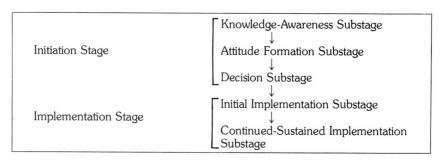

Initiation Stage	⌈ Knowledge-Awareness Substage
	↓
	Attitude Formation Substage
	↓
	⌊ Decision Substage
	↓
Implementation Stage	⌈ Initial Implementation Substage
	↓
	Continued-Sustained Implementation Substage ⌋

[2]See, for example, Joseph P. Guiltinan, "Factors Influencing Buyer Behavior and Acquisition Management in R&D Organizations," in Thomas V. Bonoma and Gerald Zaltman (eds.), *Organizational Buying Behavior,* Chicago: American Marketing Association, 1978; Richard R. Nelson and Douglas Yates, *Innovation and Implementation in Public Organizations,* Lexington, MA: Lexington Books, 1978; and Patrick Kelly, Melvin Kranzberg, *et al., Technological Innovation: A Critical Review of Current Knowledge,* Atlanta: Georgia Tech, 1975.

Initiation Stage   The *initiation stage* is the stage in which the organization learns about alternatives, evaluates them, and comes to a decision. The initiation stage has three substages. The *knowledge-awareness substage* focuses on how the organization becomes aware of an innovation which may produce change. Integral to this awareness substage are performance gaps. Performance gaps occur when a discrepancy exists between what the organization is doing and what its decision makers believe it ought to be doing.[3] The performance gap then increases the search for alternative courses of action; hence, the performance gap is a stimulus to change.

Knowledge-awareness of an innovation which could cause change can occur in two ways, depending on how the performance gap is identified. The organization might recognize the *need to change,* which increases the search for alternative ways of dealing with specific problems. This increased search then brings the organization into contact with a new practice. For example, an organization might realize that its information gathering capabilities are not what they should be (i.e., a performance gap exists), and thus searches for alternative ways to improve this situation. Then the organization might discover a new management information system that it might try.

A second way in which knowledge-awareness can occur is if the organization initially *becomes aware* of an innovation. Once aware of this innovation, the organization may decide that it could be performing better. In this case, a performance gap indicating a need is produced after awareness. For example, an organization may initially have no particular need to try something new. But, as its managers travel to conventions, they might become aware of a new, more sophisticated, or more efficient information system. Aware of this new system, managers realize that their organization could be much more effective in gathering and processing information. This awareness causes them to increase their performance expectations such that they now experience a need to change their practices by implementing the new information system. Thus knowledge-awareness can occur in two ways: (1) a need to change exists, which creates search, which then leads to awareness; or (2) awareness of a better alternative leads to dissatisfaction with existing practice which then creates a need to change.

One source of resistance at this stage is the need for stability. The adoption of a new product or a new supplier may disrupt the equilibrium of a firm. Hence, information about better alternative products and suppliers is blocked by the persons who would be adversely affected by the new product. Local pride may also be an obstacle. The idea that the organization is unique and that standard products are not relevant causes resistance to information.

---

[3]Anthony Downs, *Inside Bureaucracy,* Boston: Little, Brown & Co., 1967.

The *attitude formation substage* of the initiation stage focuses on organizational members forming attitudes toward an innovation. Attitudes which form the climate for change play an important role in whether the organization decides to implement or reject the innovation.

Attitudes toward innovations in general are important because they create the setting in which the change takes place. For example, in a study of innovation in health systems, it was found that the values supporting change among executive directors and those who participate in strategic decisions are a more important predictor of the implementation of change than such variables as organizational complexity, decentralization, or formalization.[4] A study of health departments in the United States and Canada also indicates the importance of top level support for innovation.[5] This study found that the executive's attitude toward innovations was important in the actual implementation of change. It may be that executives who are key elites in an organization have more potential and impact in creating change since they are not seen as "deviants" to traditional norms when they do support change. Since they have more formal power to implement these supportive attitudes to change, they may be seen by the rest of the organization as communicating a new direction of ideology for the organization. Apparently, these attitudes communicate commitment to a change process which, in turn, motivates others in the organization to accept change.

There is an action implication here for the salesperson. The more the salesperson can use the favorable attitudes toward change of executives and key elites in an organization, the more successful the attempt at change will be.

The *decision substage* focuses on the choice of whether to implement the change. During the decision substage, the information gathering and processing needs become great as organizational decision makers decide whether to implement a change.

There are many sources of resistance at the attitude formation and decision substages. If there are many layers in an organization, it is difficult to send information about a product from the bottom of the organization to the top. Also, if there are many roles in an organization which are sharply and narrowly defined, many different attitudes are likely to develop that make consensus difficult. This, in turn, makes decision making more difficult and more drawn out over time.

---

[4]J. Hage and R. Dewar, "Elite Values vs. Organizational Structure in Predicting Innovation," *Administrative Science Quarterly*, Vol. 18, 1974, pp. 279–290.

[5]Lawrence B. Mohr, "Determinants of Information in Organizations," *American Political Science Review*, Vol. 63, 1969, pp. 111–126; also see George W. Downs, Jr. and Lawrence B. Mohr, "Conceptual Issues in the Study of Innovations," *Administrative Science Quarterly*, Vol. 21, No. 4, December, 1976, pp. 700–714.

Implementation Stage

Implementation is the second major stage of the change process and consists of two subphases. The *initial implementation substage* occurs when the organization implements the change on a trial basis to determine if it is practical. This is done before a long-term commitment is made to utilize the change or innovation.

Resistance may occur at the initial implementation substage for many reasons. Disruption is greatest at this stage, since not all contingencies can be anticipated. Also, resistance may be passive as well as active. Passive resistance may be manifested by subordinates not following through on orders or not using the product or service fully or correctly. Members of an organization may also resist implementation if they have not been consulted about the change, and if they believe they are being manipulated.

The *continued-sustained implementation substage* occurs when, after a successful trial, the organization decides to formalize the implementation of the innovation on a long-term basis into the ongoing processes of the organization. For example, an organization might use in one of its divisions a new management information system on a trial basis. After a six-month trial, the organization may consider this innovation successful, and thus decide to implement it in the rest of the organization and make a long-term commitment to its use.

Resistance to a new product or service might develop at some point after its initial implementation if the innovation does not live up to its expectations, or if it creates conflict which the firm finds too disruptive. The new product or service, while performing as anticipated, may also have other unfortunate and unexpected consequences. In addition, products and suppliers may be discarded as a result of changes to new personnel who have preferences different from those of the persons preceding them.

In summary, the process of organizational change and innovation has two distinct stages. *Initiation* is concerned with how the organization becomes aware of change, forms attitudes toward it, and then makes a decision about implementation. *Implementation* is concerned with the process by which the organization integrates the change into its ongoing processes.

ORGAN-IZATIONAL STRUCTURE AND INNOVATION

Organizations have various characteristics which affect the likelihood of their purchasing a new product or service. For instance, different companies within the same industry differ in the likelihood of their adopting new management techniques or purchasing new types of machinery. A different probability of adoption is often due to differences in the way firms are organized or structured. So, the marketer of industrial products is very interested in understanding and learning how to work with firms having different structures.

Structural Variables

Organizations can be viewed as varying in their degree of complexity, formalization, and centralization—three variables which are important organizational structure variables. *Complexity* refers to such matters as the number of occupational specialties within the organization and how various jobs differ from one another. *Formalization* refers to the degree of emphasis placed on following specific rules and procedures. *Centralization* refers to the locus of authority and decision making, i.e., the level at which decisions are made and the number of organizational members who participate in the decision-making process.

Two propositions which relate the effects that the variables of organizational structure have on the two basic stages in the innovation adoption process are presented in Exhibit 19-1. The first proposition is that the initiation of new ideas, products, or services is facilitated by: (a) high complexity, (b) low formalilzation, and (c) low centralization.[6] Table 19-1 describes the particular elements of the types of social structures which lead to easier initiation of new products. Different aspects of Table 19-1 are discussed throughout this chapter.

EXHIBIT 19-1.
Propositions About Organizational Structure and Innovation Adoption and Implementation

PROPOSITION 19-1.
The initiation of new ideas, products, or services is facilitated by: (a) high complexity, (b) low formalization, and (c) low centralization.

PROPOSITION 19-2.
The implementation of new ideas, products, or services is facilitated by: (a) low complexity, (b) high formalization, and (c) high centralization.

A second proposition is that the implementation of new ideas, products, or services is facilitated by: (a) low complexity, (b) high formalization, and (c) high centralization.[7] Table 19-1 also describes how these social structures affect the implementation of new ideas, products, or services.

[6]Gerald Zaltman and Robert Duncan, *Strategies for Planned Change,* NY: Wiley-Interscience, 1977.
[7]*Ibid.*

These two very important propositions can be described below.

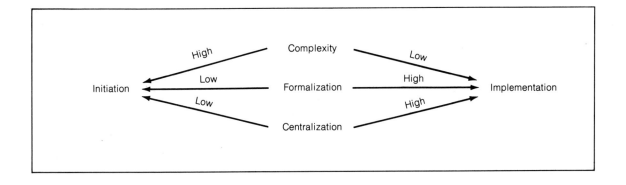

Structure \ Stage	Stage	
	Initiation	*Implementation*
Complexity	High complexity facilitates initiation. Contact with many sources of information facilitates awareness (professionals aware of new development in their fields) (See role accumulation section in Chapter 3).	High complexity hinders implementation. Difficult to gain consensus on proposals. Conflicting interest groups.
Formalization	High formalization hinders initiation. Limits the search for new sources of information. Not flexible to alternative courses of action.	High formalization facilitates implementation. Singleness of purpose provides easier implementation. Procedures to follow are specified; thus low role conflict or ambiguity. Better understanding of how to go about implementation.
Centralization	High centralization hinders initiation. Uncertainty by members not in decision making-group Communication channels don't provide information on negative aspects of present situation—thus performance gap recognition is limited.	High centralization facilitates implementation. Clear role prescriptions and authority to sanction role behavior facilitates compliance.

Research supports the contention that organizations with high complexity facilitate the initiation of innovation.[8] When decision making involves many different types of people as opposed to only one or a small number of similar persons, there is greater contact with suppliers, greater reading of advertisements and brochures, and a larger number of information sources used. This study also indicated that decisions involving many people are more frequent when a unique buying problem is involved, when the size of the purchase is large, and when the firm is large.

Providing Assistance

An organization's need for different structures to meet the various requirements of the two stages (initiation and implementation) in the innovation process increases in different situations. These situations exist when: (1) the organization's need for change is great, (2) uncertainty associated with the change is great, and (3) the change is radical (i.e., it differs considerably from existing alternatives).

What does all this mean? First, marketers of new industrial products should segment the organizations in their market on the basis of their complexity, formalization, and centralization. This will identify those organizations which may need help in the initiation stage and those which may need help in the implementation stage. Strategies for each can then be formulated.

Organizations which need help in the initiation stage might be reached by wide distribution of information about the availability of the new product and its superiority over present alternatives. Marketers of new products which are targeted toward organizations with such structures must be particularly careful in making certain that the information reaches those few people in the organization with decision-making power. This does not always mean that the information should be directed to top management. Rather, the marketer must discover who has decision-making power with respect to the adoption of such new products and direct the information to these people. Thus, this type of organization requires more of the salesperson's time in prospecting the potential purchasers.

Organizations which need help in the implementation stage might be aided by marketer-developed programs which give guidelines on how the organization should operate during this stage. Since the organization has already decided to purchase the new product or service, many marketers neglect to follow through and offer this type of assistance. However, it is necessary to engage in this activity for two reasons: (1) if the firm has difficulty

[8]Kjell Grønhaug, "Autonomous vs. Joint Decisions in Organizational Buying," *Industrial Marketing Management,* Vol. 4, 1975, pp. 265–271.

implementing the change, it is doubtful that it will make other purchases from the marketer in the future; and (2) if an early adopting firm has difficulty implementing the change, negative word-of-mouth communication is likely to occur. This may lead other organizations to avoid the new product, concept, or practice.

One reason why this type of assistance is not frequently given is that salespeople are usually rewarded on the basis of short-run criteria such as sales volume rather than the number of satisfied customers they produce. Also, they are rewarded for successful initiation rather than successful implementation. Perhaps there is an alternative strategy for the marketer. Just as the marketer employs a staff (specifically the sales force) which specializes in bringing customers to the decision to adopt, perhaps the marketer should also employ a staff which specializes in helping customers with the postpurchase implementation of the change. For lack of a better term, such persons would be called "implementation experts." Implementation experts would be more than technical persons who make sure, for instance, that the power lines of a plant can handle the addition of new machinery. Rather, implementation experts would help the firm implement a change, taking into account such things as specific personalities, interpersonal conflicts, and individual needs for recognition.

Improving Purchasing Activity

There is yet another implication. Organizations should be sensitive to the impact that organizational complexity, formalization, and centralization have on their effectiveness as consumers. For example, a major container manufacturer with plants at several locations throughout the United States underwent a major capital improvement program in a number of its plants. Each plant was responsible for making its own capital equipment purchases. The first plant involved in this program is located in the San Francisco area. The experience of this first plant was very unfortunate. Considerable time was used in reaching decisions and the quality of the decisions was not good. Two consultants were asked to diagnose what went wrong and why, and to suggest guidelines for other plants to follow so they could avoid the first plant's mistakes. It was determined that the poor decisions were caused to a significant degree by the fact that the organization had only one person assigned to gathering information about suppliers, and this person's expertise was rather narrow. This weakness was believed to be a direct result of the low degree of complexity in the organization.

A way of temporarily altering this aspect of the organization's structure was suggested in the hopes that other plants with low complexity would also make a temporary change. This was done in a Chicago plant by hiring, on a consultant basis, a production management specialist and an engineer to be members of the buying committee and by assigning someone from the finance department and from the marketing group to the buying committee as well. Ordinarily in the Chicago plant, the chief plant manager and the purchasing agent would have been the major participants in the decision-making process. Expanding the variety of people in the buying committee greatly enhanced the amount and variety of information used to reach a decision. Similarly, other temporary changes were suggested to offset the negative effect of each structural condition on either the initiation or implementation stage. For example, the suggestion for the highly complex organization (and buying committee) which tends to have trouble in implementing decisions was to assign implementation responsibility to one or two people only and remove the responsibility from a complex group of people. This does not mean that many people should not be consulted, particularly those affected by the implementation of a decision. Rather, implementation responsibility should be very centralized.

In most cases, the suggestions were used successfully. In these instances, initiation and implementation of capital improvement decisions were far more successful than in the instance of the San Francisco plant, despite structural similarities.

We turn now to a more complete discussion of the three main structural characteristics of organizations: complexity, formalization, and centralization.

ORGANIZATIONAL STRUCTURE AND NEW PRODUCT ATTRIBUTES

There appear to be no systematic attempts to link attributes of new products to organizational structure variables such as complexity, centralization, and formalization. Many of these product attributes were discussed in the previous chapter. The basic research question for this chapter is, which attributes, if any, are particularly relevant to a given organizational structure? The next questions would be, what is the nature of their relevance (positive? negative?), and why does a particular relationship hold?

Complexity

First, consider the structural factor of organizational complexity. Several ideas involving selected product attributes and organizational complexity are now presented. For the most part, these and the other ideas to follow are in need of empirical testing; they are, however, consistent with related research in the published literature.

Product Uncertainty. Risk and uncertainty about an innovation are less inhibitive in the adoption decision process if the potential adopting organization is relatively complex and if many of the departments or units in the organization are involved in the decision. Two reasons might account for this.

First, the more people involved in a decision to purchase a product, the easier it is to spread the blame for subsequent product failures. Secondly, inputs from different specialties make everyone more confident about the decision, since more expertise was brought to bear than if one party had been responsible for covering all areas of expertise.

One implication is that the industrial salesperson should obtain inputs from various experts in and out of the client firm. These endorsements will help the purchasing agent with the uncertainty inherent in a particular product or service. The more complex an organization is, the larger is the number of sources of internal legitimation needed relative to external sources.

Communicability.   The greater the complexity of an organization, the greater must be the effort expended by a marketer to communicate the real or potential value of successful product adoption. Because complex organizations have more internal boundaries (i.e., they have a larger number of specialized groups) and because boundaries tend to be barriers to communication, it is necessary to counteract these barriers by heightening the ease and effectiveness with which the results of the innovation can be communicated within the firm. This idea suggests that a salesperson should assume the role of communicator within a client firm if there are many groups or individuals who do not frequently communicate directly among themselves, but who either influence or are influenced by the purchase decision.

Alternatively, it may be necessary to broaden the scope of advertising. For example, for a given piece of medical equipment, it may be necessary to communicate through different media to the hospital purchasing agent, the medical technician who operates the equipment, and physican specialists for whom the equipment is operated. This is necessary because it is unlikely that the physician would interact about the nature of available equipment.

Product Impact.   Products having a potential impact on many aspects of an organization are less likely to be adopted by complex organizations. They also involve a longer decision process than products with less impact. This is particularly true when the organization tends more towards a collective decision-making process than an authoritarian process. In a complex organization, more groups stand to be affected, and so the probability of there being an adverse effect is higher. This in turn increases the number of sources of resistance within the firm or agency. The greater the number of changes or adjustments perceived necessary as a consequence of adopting a product, the greater the resistance to the adoption.

When dealing with complex organizations and potentially pervasive products or services, it is especially necessary for the marketer to consider altering the product to minimize the negative impact a purchase might have. If a product cannot be readily altered, then it becomes necessary to consider providing additional services or products which could help deal with any negative consequences of a purchase decision. For example, the marketers of an organizational development kit found it necessary to make available a limited amount of consulting time to help a school system deal with various problems the adopting schools encountered in their use of the kit.

Compatibility. Compatibility is another organizational attribute related to organizational complexity. The following idea is suggested: The greater the complexity of an organization, the greater the potential variation in values, experiences, and needs in the organization. Therefore, there is a greater probability of there being a poor fit between the innovation and some component of the organization. Thus, when a salesperson communicates with various subgroups within a client firm, it should be remembered that their different values and needs cause them to be concerned with different aspects of the innovation. Hence, the content and, perhaps, the format of a communication may need to vary according to the different groups.

Relative Advantage. Innovations with unique relative advantages for different subgroups within complex organizations are more likely to be adopted than innovations having a unique relative advantage for only one subgroup within an organization. This is particularly likely when many people are involved in the decision-making process. Ideally, then, a product or service should be designed which meets the most salient needs of all parties affected by the purchase decision. Since this is unlikely in most cases, it is necessary to identify the optimal mix of needs that a given product can be designed to satisfy. In the case of capital equipment, should the mix of needs be those of the production department or of the finance department? Each group has different concerns.

Divisibility. The more divisible a product is in terms of where it can be used in an organization, the more likely it is to be tried by a complex organization. Divisibility, in effect, renders organizational complexity neutral since one subgroup may try it without the need of cooperation with other subgroups.

It is desirable, then, for it to be possible for the innovation to be tried by one subgroup in a complex organization. For example, a sensitivity group session was suggested for the heads of all departments in a very complex organization in the printing industry. Initial resistance by most departments was strong. The head of the sales division felt it would be good for the people in that division and tried the sensitivity training within the sales division. The experience was successful and another division head tried it successfully soon afterwards. If one or two other subgroups in the firm try this, it is likely that the session will be tried by all division heads.

Susceptibility to Modification. Susceptibility to later modification is the capability of a product to be adopted by the organization and then adapted or changed slightly as the use context changes or as it differs from the needs which it is expected to meet. The greater the ease with which an innovation can be adapted to meet different needs or different circumstances, either over time for the same user(s) or at one point in time for different users in the same social system, the more likely it is to be adopted on a sustained basis. In general, the greater the complexity of an organization and the wider the impact of the innovation, the more susceptible to modification the product needs to be for an adoption to occur. For example, a complex organization is more likely to purchase an expensive duplicating machine if additional components for collating, folding, stuffing envelopes, and postage printing are available and can be added if the need arises.

Formalization The second organizational attribute is *formalization*. The greater the formalization of an organization, the more readily it will implement an innovation adoption decision, although the initiation of that decision-making process will be relatively difficult. As with complexity, the characteristics of an innovation may have a special interaction with formalization. The impact of various product attributes and formalization are presented below.

Radicalness. The less similar a product is to current alternatives, the more radical it is. When a radically different product is contemplated, organizational rules and procedures for responding to the product situation are likely to be unclear. The reverse is true in the case of routine products.

The more formalized an organizational structure is, the more likely it is to have a mechanism for dealing with products or innovations which are radical in nature. Individuals are "protected" if they are involved with an unsuccessful product which successfully makes it through the various rules and procedures of the firm; they, in effect, share responsibility for a wrong decision with the system of rules and procedures. A very important distinction must be made, however, between organizations which have rules and procedures that are highly developed for very specific and limited situations only and organizations which have rules and procedures for a broad array of situations. Thus, the more broadly structured rules and procedures are (i.e., the wider the conditions they cover), the more likely an organization is to initiate new product decision making with regard to radical products. The more detailed the rules are, the easier it is to implement a radical product.

Divisibility and Reversibility. A high degree of formalization within a firm may cause inflexibility or rigidity. Given this, it is particularly important for a new product to be easily reversed and divided. Divisibility enables the organization to keep most of its rules and procedures intact by limiting the innovation to only one subpart of the firm. Reversibility enables the organization to easily reinstitute or retrieve previous rules and procedures dropped or altered as a result of adopting a new product. Thus, when approaching a firm which has a highly formalized internal structure, the salesperson or supplier firm should make it easy for the buyer firm to try the innovation on a limited basis and without an immediate and major long-term commitment. Short-term contracts may be more attractive to buyer organizations when there is little doubt that adequate supplies exist at stable prices. If supply is a concern to buyers, renewal options within short-term contracts may be used.

Commitment. The greater the degree of commitment a product requires, and the more formalized an organization is, the longer the decision-making period and the less likely it is that full adoption will take place.[9] Formalization requires that an innovation meet a large number of standards. This takes time as changes are made in the innovation to conform to many standards, or simply as a large number of procedures are invoked and completed. This often requires a "product champion." A product champion is a highly partisan supporter of a new product or service. The product champion's commitment to the product sustains interest and attention within the firm with respect to the innovation as formal procedures and rules are satisfied.

Compatibility. The compatibility of an innovation with a highly formal organization has a direct positive impact on the adoption decision. The more compatible an innovation is with a firm's rules and procedures, the more likely it is to be adopted. Compatibility, of course, may be achieved by the committed product champion who sponsors an innovation which can be modified to fit the various rules and procedures. Thus, the lower the initial degree of commitment in the organization as a whole and the lower the initial compatibility of the product with the formalized aspect of the organization, the more important it is for the product to be modified to enhance the "fit" of the product with the structure of rules and procedures.

General Comments on Formalization. A large number of rules and procedures in a highly formalized structure suggests the presence of a large number of gatekeepers acting in succession. In other words, for each channel of information, there are successive gatekeepers, each of whom could prevent information from flowing in that channel simply by not passing on the information to the next gatekeeper. This is referred to as serial gatekeeping. Highly

---

[9]Zaltman and Duncan, 1977, *op. cit.*

formalized organizations are likely to have serial gatekeeping. In such cases, it is difficult to initiate and implement new product adoption decisions.

Under circumstances where there are many gatekeepers in a given channel, salespersons need to identify and prospect many people within a firm. The people prospected should be individuals who occupy key positions with respect to various decision-making procedures. For example, a sales representative for an industrial lubricant manufacturer described an effective approach toward potential customers. The salesperson first calls upon the purchasing agent to learn how the organization places orders. This frequently results in later prospecting of plant managers and the vice-president in charge of manufacturing or production. The salesperson generally tries to speak with plant overseers and equipment maintenance personnel as well. The exact nature of the decision-making process determines the sequence of the contacts and how often the salesperson revisits particular people.

In concluding this section on formalization and new product attributes, it should be indicated that having many rules and procedures does not automatically create barriers to the initiation of change nor does it necessarily facilitate implementation. The character of the rules themselves and the conditions under which they operate are crucial considerations.

Centralization Extreme centralization makes the initiation of innovations difficult, but facilitates their implementation. Several key product attributes interact with organizational structure in determining the processes and outcomes of the innovation process.

Commitment. Products requiring strong and widespread commitment in order to function effectively are more successful when decision making is decentralized. The increased participation implied by a decentralized decision-making structure enhances commitment among the organization members involved. Also, the more decentralized the decision, the larger the number of members who are able to participate and become committed. A decision-making structure at any level which has many participants may facilitate the adoption of a complex product. The larger the number of participants of diverse backgrounds, the greater the pool of different kinds of expertise which may be used to clarify the nature of a complex product. Diverse participants in a decision may also result in better initiation and implementation of products having a strong impact on interpersonal relationships. The diverse backgrounds represented in the purchase decision-making process help anticipate problems of an interpersonal nature caused by the product.

Divisibility and Reversibility. Highly centralized decision-making structures are more important and efficient the less divisible, the less reversible, and the broader the impact of the innovation. This is particularly true in a complex social structure where coordination among subsystems is weak. The assumption underlying this contention is that a department relatively low in the organizational hierarchy will be reluctant, by itself, to make a decision which affects other groups in the firm on a relatively permanent basis or where the firm as a whole may be disrupted when a change has been tried and discontinued. When this situation exists, salespeople should direct most of their activity toward senior-level managers and the group of managers immediately below them who often assemble and process the information that senior managers use to reach a decision. It may also be desirable to have the counterparts of these managers from the vendor company visit with the senior management and the group immediately below them. This reduces the status differential which exists between a salesperson and the vice-president or director of plant operations or manufacturing.

PROCESS AND PRODUCT INNOVATIONS IN ORGANIZATIONS

The preceding chapter (as well as this chapter) discussed various attributes of innovations which affect their adoption. The preceding chapter also discussed the possible perceived effects of innovation (preventive and incremental) which affect their adoption. There are many other ways in which innovations are classified. A particularly interesting distinction especially relevant to organizations is a distinction between *process innovations* (such as a new way of casting steel or administering a chemical treatment to clothing fabrics) and *product innovations* (such as a new food dye or a new scientific instrument for analyzing blood chemistry). What is interesting about this distinction is that factors relevant to the adoption of process innovations by business firms may not all be equally relevant to the adoption of product innovations.

Two researchers studied the adoption of forty-five technology innovations—both process and product—by commercial firms.[10] They found several factors to be related to process innovations. The compatibility of a firm's existing technology with an innovation influenced adoption success. The existence of a recognized need also influenced successful use of a process innovation, as did the quality of information from the marketer. The higher the quality of information received from the source of the process innovation, the more likely successful adoption is to occur. That is, not only is adoption

---

[10]Alok W. Chakrabarti and Albert H. Rubenstein, "Interorganizational Transfer of Technology: A Study of Adoption of NASA Innovations," *IEEE Transaction on Engineering Management,* Vol. EM-23, No. 1, February, 1976, pp. 20–34.

more likely to take place when high quality information is provided, but satisfaction with the use of the innovation is likely to be high as well. It was found, too, that the availability of personnel skilled in the implementation of the innovation is important. These ideas are expressed as propositions in Exhibit 19-2. These propositions apply primarily to process innovations and are less applicable to product innovations.

EXHIBIT 19-2.
Propositions About Successful Adoption of Process Innovations

PROPOSITION 19-3.
The greater the degree of compatibility between a firm's existing technology and a process innovation, the more likely successful adoption is to take place.

PROPOSITION 19-4.
The higher the quality of information from the source of a process innovation, the more likely successful adoption is to take place.

PROPOSITION 19-5.
The greater the availability of personnel to implement a process innovation, the more likely successful adoption is to take place.

The propositions in Exhibit 19-2 stress the importance of technical factors. A number of proposed relationships between organizational factors and degree of successful adoption were not supported. The researchers concluded that the adoption decision is made primarily by the technical person in charge of operations and his or her supervisor. Therefore, the organizational climate and buying center decision-making styles are of less importance than technical factors.

An organization is more likely to have a satisfactory experience putting a product innovation into effect when its members identify with the organization. Employees in an organization that encourages feelings of belonging are less likely to perceive an innovation as personally threatening. This decreases the possibility of disruption in implementing an innovation. Chakrabarti and Rubenstein also found that product innovations are more likely to be adopted without undue conflict and implemented effectively when there is strong support for the product innovation among top management.[11] Also, the

---

[11]*Ibid.*

greater the ease of obtaining funds to implement the innovation, the more successful the firm is in adopting the innovation. These ideas are expressed as propositions in Exhibit 19-3. These propositions apply primarily to product innovations and are not particularly applicable to process innovations.

EXHIBIT 19-3.
Propositions About Successful Adoption of Product Innovation

PROPOSITION 19-6.
The more the organizational climate stresses identity with one's organization, the more likely successful implementation of a product innovation is to take place.

PROPOSITION 19-7.
The greater the degree of top management's support for a product innovation, the more likely successful adoption is to take place.

PROPOSITION 19-8.
The greater the ease of obtaining financial resources for implementation, the more likely successful adoption of a product innovation is to take place.

It appears that a different set of factors is relevant in the case of product innovations. Support by top management is particularly important for product innovations. Also, organizational factors in general are more important for product innovations than for process innovations. These conclusions are shown as propositions in Exhibit 19-3. The action implication of this is clear: When selling process innovations, effort should focus on the operating technical person and his or her supervisor. When selling product innovations, many persons in the firm, including top management, should be prospected and attention should be given to the organization's overall climate. For product innovations, the salesperson should first try selling to organizations whose members identify closely with it and who are prone to risk taking. For process innovations, the salesperson should concentrate on the technical and economic feasibility of the technology. In this regard, the *maturity* of the innovation should be stressed. Mature processes are those which have been "tested and evaluated, where performance characteristics are well established and further research is not needed for adoption."[12]

---

[12]*Ibid.*

SUMMARY The adoption of innovations by organizations is a process which is very similar to the process which occurs when individuals consider innovations. The complexity of the process is increased, however, in the case of the organization because of the number of people involved. Organizations go through two main stages in their adoption or resistance of innovations: the initiation stage and the implementation stage. Each of these stages includes several substages. For the initiation stage there is the knowledge-awareness substage, in which the organization becomes aware of an innovation which might produce change; the attitude formation substage, in which the organizational members form attitudes toward an innovation; and the decision substage, which focuses on the choice of whether to implement the change. During the implementation stage there is the initial implementation substage, during which the organization implements the change on a trial basis to determine its practicality; and the continued-sustained implementation substage, when the implementation of the innovation is formalized on a long-term basis.

An organization's structure has a significant impact on whether the organization is able to move through these stages. The greater the complexity and the lower the degree of formalization and centralization, the easier the process is during the initiation stage. During the implementation stage, however, the process is easier if the organization has low complexity and high formalization and centralization.

Relevant to organizations is the distinction between process innovations and product innovations. Necessary for process innovations is technological compatibility, qualitative information, and the availability of personnel to implement the process innovation. For process innovations, the technological factors of implementation are of great importance. The requirements for satisfactory product innovation are identity within the organization, management support for the innovation, and financial resources for the innovation. The organizational climate and buying center decision-making styles are also very important.

KEY CONCEPTS Attitude formation stage

Centralization

Complexity

Continued-sustained implementation substage

Decision substage

Formalization

Initial implementation substage

Initiation stage
Implementation stage
Knowledge-awareness substage
Performance gap
Process innovation
Product champion
Product innovation
Serial gatekeeping

PERSPECTIVES FOR STUDYING AND IMPLEMENTING CONSUMER BENEFIT PROGRAMS*

CHAPTER GOALS   The object of this chapter is to help the reader understand:
1.   **how consumer behavior concepts can be applied in the context of consumer benefit programs;**
2.   **the basic principles about designing effective consumer benefit programs.**

INTRODUCTION   The various concepts and propositions discussed in this book have been developed largely in terms of their managerial implications. These concepts, however, are also important for their implications for persons and agencies concerned with helping people to be better consumers. Although an extensive literature on consumerism issues exists, there is relatively little information about the use of consumer behavior research findings to educate consumers. The first section of this chapter explores the possible use of consumer research for consumer education programs. The sample of consumer research selected here is drawn from earlier chapters. The second section of this chapter addresses various considerations a consumer advocate agency should take into account in developing and implementing a social change program based on consumer research findings. These considerations are the action implications for social marketing managers.

*The first section of this chapter is adapted from M. Wallendorf and G. Zaltman, "Perspectives for Studying and Implementing Consumer Education," in W. Perreault (ed.), *Advances in Consumer Research,* Vol. 4, 1977, pp. 376–379.

CONSUMER EDUCATION

Many advances have been made in the past few years in the area of consumer education. There now exists a variety of consumer education programs. These cover many subject areas, using many media and presentational forms, and are designed for all age and ethnic groups. Yet, consumer educators remain concerned about how to best study and implement consumer education. Perhaps the best way is to look to the field of consumer behavior for insights into the processes. Specifically, consumer educators can use consumer behavior findings to learn how buyers make choices, what influences those choices, how these influences operate, and the processes underlying post-purchase feelings of satisfaction and/or dissatisfaction. By understanding these behavioral processes and their explanations, consumer educators can design more appropriate and more effective programs. In addition, the process involved in the adoption of consumer educational materials by various organizations (whether schools, local public television stations, state governments, or private corporations) can be better understood by studying organizational innovation adoption and resistance.

Specifically, this section deals with five different topics in consumer behavior which have relevance for the consumer educator. Each topic provides a unique perspective for viewing consumers. These topics are also examined for their implications for consumer education. These perspectives are not exhaustive; they have been chosen because they are often overlooked, yet provide considerable explanatory power and richness. Others have written on the more traditional perspectives of attitude change and cognitive information processing as they relate to consumer benefit programs.[1] The five perspectives are:

1. The influence of large-scale social structures.
2. The influence of smaller-scale social structures.
3. Role behavior.
4. Individual adoption and resistance.
5. Communication processes.

All of these perspectives have implications for the design of consumer education materials and programs, as well as implications for the efforts made to persuade consumers to read/watch/listen to the materials. Thus, it is not only what reaches consumers, but also how they are reached, which is crucially important for effective change to take place. In each of the five sections, propositions about consumer behavior are translated into the consumer education context. Such translation naturally implies the need for empirical research to test whether the translation is reasonable. Toward this end, an

---

[1]James R. Bettman, "Issues in Designing Consumer Information Environments," *Journal of Consumer Research,* Vol. 2, December, 1975, pp. 169–177.

attempt is made to state the propositions in such a way as to facilitate the task of testing them. Nearly all of the propositions have been discussed in earlier chapters although not in the context of consumerism. Since most of them have appeared elsewhere in this book, we shall not isolate them in exhibits.

The Influences of Large-Scale Social Structures

Large-scale social structure is the organization of differences among people in a society. Various aspects of large-scale social structure include social class structures, group differences in communication patterns and channels, value sets, educational level variations, industry structures, and ethnic differences in behavior patterns (see Chapter 4). Large-scale social structure is perhaps the most pervasive influence on, rather than merely the backdrop for, consumer behavior and consumer education.[2] As has been shown in many research efforts, changes in the structure of interaction clearly produce changes in the behavior of individuals as well as in people's feelings about their behavior and interactions.[3]

The structure of communication (i.e., its content and channels) in a society influences what can be done to persuade consumers to engage in consumer education activities, as well as what content these activities can have. *The larger the number and variety of mass media channels in the society, the greater the communication exposure among its consumers and hence the more favorable the climate for change in that society.* Exposure to more information is likely to increase the perceived need to change and to increase knowledge about opportunities to satisfy that need. In addition, *to the extent that exposure to a variety of media makes individuals aware of more desirable alternatives for satisfying current needs, these communication media can create or enhance a perceived need for change.* Therefore, consumer educators can increase the number of communication channels, for instance, by introducing new magazines similar to *Consumer Reports,* or new television programs (e.g., "Consumer Survival Kit") to disseminate their messages.[4] Alternatively, they can increase the variety of communication channels (e.g., nutrition information on supermarket paper bags or fresh produce wrappers, nutrition booths in supermarkets or shopping centers, co-sponsorship of youth group work weeks that emphasize consumer education opportunities in the community).

---

[2]Everett M. Rogers, "Social Structure and Social Change," *American Behavioral Scientist,* 1971, pp. 767–782.

[3]For example, see Harold J. Leavitt, "Some Effects of Certain Communication Patterns on Group Performance," doctoral dissertation, MIT, 1949.

[4]See Hans B. Thorelli and Sarah V. Thorelli, *Consumer Information Systems,* Ballinger Publishing Co., 1977.

Large-scale social structure issues also focus, however, on the structure of differences in people's lives. These differences are often relevant for the consumer educator. For instance, *the greater the desire for excellence in order to accomplish personal goals, the more favorable is a society's climate for change.* Thus the high achievement motivation which is transmitted through social institutions to individuals in the United States creates a favorable climate for change.[5] Those individuals who are most affected by this motivation transmission process—those who have a high need for achievement—will be good prospects for consumer education. This may partially account for the repeated finding that consumer activists are better educated and have higher incomes and higher occupational status than the average consumer.[6] That is, the need for achievement may explain the efforts to become knowledgeable about consumer interests on the one hand, and the desire for high levels of education, income, and occupational status on the other. This also explains why it is difficult to reach consumers with lower levels of education and income when attempting to implement consumer benefit programs.

Closely related to this are two other propositions concerning individual differences. *The better the reading skills of consumers and the more accustomed they are to reading, the greater their flexibility in thinking, and thus the more readily they can accept new products. The greater consumers' reading abilities and the more materials they read, the more likely it is that they possess the knowledge or skills necessary to accept and use new products in an effective manner.* Therefore, if we consider consumer education as the new product referred to in the above propositions, another reason for the "upscale bias" becomes evident. The problem is larger than simply making certain that consumer materials and programs are readable for the general public. Even if the level of reading complexity of consumer education materials is reduced, educators are still faced with the problem of dealing with people who may not readily accept new programs and may not have the knowledge and skills necessary for such acceptance. This makes the challenge of reaching less educated consumers even greater. Perhaps materials which are used in reading training (especially for teenage youths and adults) can be

---

[5]David C. McClelland, *The Achieving Society,* Princeton, NJ: Van Nostrand, 1971.

[6]Jacques C. Bourgeois and James G. Barnes, "Consumer Activists: What Makes Them Different?", *Advances in Consumer Research,* Vol. 3, 1976, pp. 73–80; Monroe Peter Friedman, "The 1966 Consumer Protest as Seen by Its Leaders," *Journal of Consumer Affairs,* Vol. 5, Summer, 1971, pp. 1–23: Robert O. Herrmann, "The Consumer Movement in Historical Perspective," in David A. Aaker and George S. Day (eds.), *Consumerism: Search for the Consumer Interest,* 2nd ed., NY: The Free Press, 1974, pp. 10–18.

designed so that their content centers on consumer issues, while their main intent centers on increasing reading levels.

Another individual difference which varies by culture, as well as within cultures, is that of the locus of control. *The less consumers believe they are able to control their futures (that is, the more they have an external locus of control), the less likely it is that they recognize the importance of trying to respond to a problem.* For people with an external locus of control, frequent and recurring product dissatisfactions may not be enough to result in a consumer action such as registering complaints or seeking additional information about the product and/or choice strategies used. One function of consumer education, then, might be to assist consumers in seeing that it is possible, at least in some consumer situations, to partially control one's future by responding to a problem.

The social and communication networks of consumers are also elements of the social structure which influence the diffusion of programs such as consumer education. *The greater the number of public and private professional associations in a given context, the more readily a new product or service will be diffused in that context.* Initially, there were few organizations which had as a major interest the facilitation of consumer education programs. In the past few years, however, many more organizations have been formed, and some already-existing organizations (in particular, public high schools) have taken on consumer education as a goal. Consumer educators would be wise to make use of the pervasive existing organizations of the contemporary urban social structure. Since it now appears that the United States is characterized by many group memberships per person,[7] consumer educators should make use of these existing organizational ties by attempting to persuade various existing organizations to adopt consumer education as a goal. For instance, consumer educators could work with the Girl Scouts, Boy Scouts, and Campfire Girls in developing "Consumer Awareness" badges. Speakers' bureaus and programming aides could serve existing organizations. These strategies would extend the organizational range of consumer education. Recent research on the relationship between the involvement of elderly consumers in social groups and their awareness of unfair marketing practices supports this idea.[8] Thus, greater social involvement would create more opportunity to learn about unfair marketing practices.

---

[7]Peter Blau, "Presidential Address: Parameters of Social Structure," *American Sociological Review,* Vol. 39, October, 1974, pp. 615–635.

[8]Gerald Zaltman, Rajendra K. Srivastava, and Rohit Deshpande, "Perceptions of Unfair Marketing Practices: Consumerism Implications," in H. Keith Hunt (ed.), *Advances in Consumer Research,* Vol. 5, 1978, pp. 247–253.

The Influence of Small-Scale Social Structures

Small-scale social structures include small group patterns, norms, collective decision-making patterns, and the impact of small groups on individual behaviors and choices. Hence, these are the social structures which differentiate people in small-scale social systems such as families and informal social groups (see Chapters 5 and 6). The structure of interaction in these groups affects the likelihood that individuals within them will adopt an innovation. In this context, as in others, we can think of consumer education as an innovation in the perceptions of those consumers who have not yet participated in the programs or seen the materials.

One of the ways groups have an impact on their members is through norms. Norms are collective expectations about behavior which are enforced and which reflect the values of a group. One of the advantages of diffusing consumer education through existing groups is that the content of the educational effort may become a group norm. One research study found that "in a consumer decision-making situation where no objective standards are present, individuals who are exposed to a group norm will tend to conform to that group norm."[9] Thus, consumer education materials will be most effective in a group context when they relate to decision-making situations for which the members do not have specific standards for evaluation. This implies that educational efforts should be undertaken prior to the time a consumer begins to purchase a particular class of products. Therefore, *the less previous experience consumers have in purchasing a particular class of items, the more effective will be consumer education efforts aimed at setting norms about decision-making criteria.*

Attempts to get consumers who are in such a situation to adopt these decision-making criteria may backfire, however. This can happen if the educational attempts are perceived by the consumers as coercive. The same research study found that "in a consumer decision-making situation where no objective standards are present, individuals who are exposed to a group norm and are induced to comply, will show less tendency to conform to the group judgment."[10] This implies that consumer education efforts should be directed at existing groups and organizations. But, attendance at programs and understanding of the material should not be required or formally enforced. If the program planners attempt to enforce attendance or compliance, consumers may react and behave contrary to what is suggested. This raises serious questions concerning the recently enacted laws in several states which require that high school students satisfactorily complete a consumer education course or module.

---

[9]M. Venkatesan, "Consumer Behavior: Conformity and Independence," *Journal of Marketing Research,* Vol. 3, November, 1966, pp. 384–387.

[10]M. Venkatesan, *op. cit.*

With regard to the content of educational materials, it appears that, at least from the perspective of norms, generality is preferable to specificity. That is, *the more a norm applies to a wide array of situations, the more likely it is that consumers will conform to it in any given situation.* Thus, guidelines for making purchase decisions are more likely to be followed if they are stated generally. To the extent possible, price-quality relationships should be defined in terms of product classes, rather than in terms of specific items or specific stores. A few general guidelines may be much more effective than handbooks prescribing product-by-product choice criteria and decision strategies.

Educators must also be conscious of different kinds of norms which operate in groups. For instance, moral norms are ideal behaviors, or what members believe should be done. Behavioral norms are beliefs about what one's peers actually do. *The actual behavior of consumers is somewhere between the moral norm and the behavioral norm; it is closer, therefore, to the behavioral norm.*[11] This partially explains why consumer utilization of product information disclosures is so low. Although almost everyone would agree that making careful choices is the ideal behavior, they may think it too difficult to do and not worth the effort. This is especially so if they believe that their peers make choices in a casual way. This leads people to make their own purchase decisions somewhat carelessly. One strategy for consumer educators, then, would be to encourage stronger enforcement of the moral norm. This seems difficult, if not impossible. A more realistic strategy would be to increase the perception that others do, in fact, make careful choices based on available information.

Role Behavior A role is a structured set of norms, values, and interaction patterns which are expected of persons who occupy a certain position (e.g., mother, student, scientist). Although individuals do personalize the ways in which they carry out a certain role,[12] expected role behavior is essentially independent of the particular occupant of the position. In fact, *role acquisition is an evolving process of decreasing formalization and increasing personalization.* In other words, new occupants of a particular position are more likely to carry out the idealized role behaviors and have high consensus about what this ideal is. They adjust to fit the role. As time passes, however, role occupants rely more heavily on their own conception of what should be done. They adjust the role to fit themselves.

---

[11]M. D. Buffalo and Joseph W. Rodgers, "Behavioral Norms, Moral Norms, and Attachment: Problems of Deviance and Conformity," *Social Problems,* Vol. 19, Summer, 1971, pp. 101–113.

[12]Russell Thornton and Peter M. Nardi, "The Dynamics of Role Acquisition," *American Journal of Sociology,* Vol. 80, January, 1975, pp. 870–885.

The implication of this phenomenon becomes obvious when we view consumer education as the process of acquiring the role of an educated or informed consumer. Therefore, consumption guidelines must be stated in such a way that new occupants of a role can have a clear idea of what constitutes "ideal" consumption behavior and choice processes. These guidelines must also be stated in such a way that persons who have occupied the educated consumer role for a period of time can personalize or modify the guidelines to meet their own needs and situation. This implies that market segmentation is in order. Materials with very clear guidelines should be given to "new occupants"; other materials which assist in personalizing the role should be developed for others. It is with the latter group that consumer educators must be careful not to emphasize the rigidity of the distinction between judicious and injudicious choices.

The question arises as to how to insure that informed consumers will continue in that role. Here again, work in the consumer behavior field gives us insights. *The probability of continuing in a role is greater, (a) the greater the consistency between personal values and the role, (b) the greater the net balance of immediate rewards over costs, and (c) the greater the cost of acquiring and continuing alternative roles.* Additionally, these conditions are listed in order of decreasing importance to the role continuation decision. The most important condition (personal value consistency with consumer education) can most easily be met by designing the program or material to reflect and demonstrate value consistency with the audience. Perhaps one problem of consumer education programs (as with all self-improvement programs) is that they promise long-term rewards in return for immediate costs (such as time spent becoming informed). Thus, efforts should be addressed toward satisfying these conditions so that informed consumers will decide to continue in that role.[13]

Individual Adoption and Resistance   Adoption and resistance are relevant to consumer education in two ways. The first way relates to the decision by an entity (either a person, group, or organization) of whether to become involved in consumer education. The decision by an individual about involvement in consumer education is treated here. The second way in which adoption and resistance relate to consumer education is in the area of persuasion by a message. In this case, the actual content of the educational materials, not just the decision to become involved in it, is subject to adoption/resistance processes. This is treated in the next section which discusses communication processes in the consumer education context.

[13]See Hans B. Thorelli, Helmet Becker, and Jack Engledow, *The Information Seekers*, Ballinger Publishing Co., 1975.

One of the major prerequisites for adoption of an innovation is that the potential adopter must perceive the need for the change. *The less aware people are of their inadequacies, the less responsive they are to innovations which promise to remedy the inadequacies.* In other words, it is critical that consumer educators spend considerable energies creating an awareness on the part of consumers of the potential values of more informed choices. This, by implication, would develop a performance gap such that consumers would be receptive to available programs and materials.

There are also implications for the person who can successfully carry out consumer education programs. In this case, the educator is a marketer of consumer education. *The less a marketer understands the consumer situation, the less able the marketer is to help consumers perceive a problem or identify a potential solution.* Being able to make consumers aware of their own performance gaps can be done most successfully by a person who is adept at role-taking. Role-taking is the ability to view things (including oneself) the way another person views them.[14] Thus, role-taking is simply an extension of the marketing concept which stresses the starting of marketing planning with the study of consumer needs. So, role-taking provides a means of gaining insights into those needs.

The rate of adoption is also influenced by expectations about the effects derived from adoption. Two types of innovations exist: Those with incremental effects and those with preventive effects. Incremental innovations are those which increase the frequency of a desired event. If consumer education is perceived as a means of obtaining more dollar value in purchases, it would be considered an incremental innovation. Preventive innovations, on the other hand, are those which are adopted to avoid an unpleasant event. If consumer education is perceived as a means of avoiding fraud and deception, it would be considered a preventive innovation. Obviously, the two types are not mutually exclusive. One study has found that *incremental innovations are adopted at a faster rate than are preventive innovations. Innovations perceived as having both incremental and preventive effects are adopted, however, at a faster rate than either of the two kinds separately.*[15] Therefore, the optimum strategy is for consumer educators to stress both the incremental and the preventive effects. In situations where, due to resource limitations, educators can stress only one type of effect, they should emphasize incremen-

---

[14]Ralph H. Turner, "Role-Taking, Role Standpoint, and Reference Group Behavior," *American Journal of Sociology*, Vol. 61, 1965, pp. 316–327.

[15]Virginia Lansdon Koontz, "Determinants of Individual's Level of Knowledge and Attitude Towards and Decisions Regarding a Health Innovation in Maine," unpublished Ph.D. dissertation, Ann Arbor: University of Michigan, Chapter 5.

tal effects. If a situation occurs in which they must stress preventive effects, these effects must be made perceivable and communicable (which is difficult since the aim is to get the consumer to perceive the absence of something).

Finally, one must recognize that the adoption process does not end with a decision to use or purchase the innovation. Rejection can follow what was, at an earlier time, adoption. *Discontinuance of the use of an innovation increases as the involvement of the marketer with past and current adopters decreases.* This implies that consumer educators should continue to send follow-up reports, additional information, and descriptions of the value of informed choices to persons who have previously completed consumer education programs.

Communication Processes

Obviously, any educational effort involves communication processes because it transfers information or experiences from one person to another. This, then, is another way of viewing consumer education. This view highlights such phenomena as source credibility, message effects, and communication participation.

A source's credibility, and thus his or her persuasiveness, is reduced when the audience perceives that the source has something to gain from these persuasive attempts. This implies that consumer education should not come directly from a manufacturer or retailer. However laudable such efforts may be from the perspective of the social responsibility of business, it is probable that these efforts are not very effective in changing the behaviors of consumers. Thus, what appears to be socially responsible may be merely a demonstration of the desire to *appear* socially responsible. This proposition and implication are expected to hold, particularly when, at the end of the consumer eduation message, the sponsor (manufacturer or retailer) concludes that (or tries to lead consumers to conclude that) the sponsoring firm is better than competitors because of its sponsorship of such activities or materials. In such cases, resources might be better spent by contributing to independent consumer education organizations.

One way to avoid this destruction of source credibility and still have the manufacturer or retailer directly involved is to restructure the message. *The low credibility source can increase his or her influence by arguing for a position which is perceived to be against his or her own self-interest.* The message can still contain the same information bits, but the nature of the presentation can be changed to increase persuasiveness.

The discussion to this point has implied that consumer education communications are unidirectional: from a source to a consumer. But, *the greater the degree of participation of the intended audience in the communication process, the earlier the time at which members of the audience will decide to implement the recommended change.* Thus, the strategies used by some consumer education materials and programs of having on-the-spot quizzes

("Consumer Survival Kit") or forms for determining one's own purchase requirements (*Consumer Reports*) develop participation, and thus enhance the persuasion process.

MAJOR PITFALLS TO AVOID

Consumerism is a dominant feature of the consumer market today. Efforts by all parties concerned with improving consumer welfare have been largely unsuccessful, however, even where legislation has been enacted. At the very least, the conclusion is warranted that consumerist, government, and commercial organizations that have tried to enact beneficial change or consumer protection have not obtained good results. This assertion is a very serious one. The interested reader can find considerable supporting documentation relating to this issue.[16]

In this section we take what we believe is a constructive approach by first identifying common pitfalls which consumer advocacy groups, business, legislators, and other government agencies often encounter when attempting social change to benefit consumers. Secondly, we identify criteria which those in the consumerism field should consider when attempting to create social change. Specific principles are introduced as guidelines. Since these ideas are so well supported, they merit stronger or firmer status than propositions. Hence, they are presented here as principles rather than propositions. Also, the most effective way to formulate these ideas is not in the form of easily tested propositions. Although these principles may at times seem obvious, they are frequently ignored or forgotten in a wide variety of planned change programs.

Rationalistic Bias

Rationalistic bias is characterized by the belief that individuals are guided by reason and are rational according to conventional criteria. Therefore, the regulator or change agent assumes that all that is required to cause change is

---

[16]Frank, Angell, "Some Effects of Truth-in-Lending Legislation." *Journal of Business,* Vol. 44 (January, 1971), 79–84; *Annual Report to Congress on Truth-in-Lending for the Years 1969 and 1970,* Board of Governors of Federal Reserve System; George S. Day and William K. Brandt, "Consumer Research and the Evaluation of Information Disclosure Requirements: The Case of Truth-in-Lending." *Journal of Consumer Research,* Vol. 1 (June, 1974), 21–52; Robert M. Levy and Allan R. Brown, "Untoward Effects of Drug Education," *American Journal of Public Health,* Vol. 63 (December, 1973), 1071–1073; George Maisel, *et al.* "Analysis of Two Surveys Evaluating a Project to Reduce Accidental Poisoning Among Children," *Public Health Reports,* Vol. 82 (June, 1967), 555–560; Leon S. Robertson. "The Buzzer-Light Reminder System and Safety Belt Use," *American Journal of Public Health,* Vol. 64 (August, 1974), 814–815; Leon S. Robertson, *et al.,* "A Controlled Study of the Effect of Television Messages on Safety Belt Use." *American Journal of Public Health,* Vol. 64 (November, 1974), 171–180.

to present the information and knowledge regarding the change to the intended consumer. This ignores the fact that what a consumer considers rational for himself or herself is not necessarily what the change agent believes is rational for the consumer. Thus, a regulatory agency may inappropriately perceive its task as less complex than it actually is. This leads to Principle 1 in Exhibit 20-1 which stresses the importance of considering rationality from the consumer's viewpoint.

Poorly Defined Goals

Change attempts are often characterized by poorly defined goals. Goals or objectives are frequently stated only in diffuse and ambiguous ways. Is the intention of a bill, trade regulation, or consumer education program to change awareness? Knowledge? Attitudes? Behavior? All of these? In the short or long run? A consequence of poorly defined goals is that they are likely to create ambiguity, uncertainty, and anxiety for those who are supposed to benefit from the change. Worse still, poorly defined goals may produce the reverse of their intended effects.[17] Thus, Principle 2 in Exhibit 20-1 concerns the need for explicit goal statements.

Poorly Defined Problems

Problem definition is one of the most difficult tasks in science. Too often we are solving the wrong problem. Symptoms are mistaken for causes of problems, thus resulting in the misapplication of remedial efforts and the ineffective use of resources. Is nutrition poor among some groups of people because they lack information to make proper food selection? Or is it because they lack the ability to use information? Or perhaps it is because their life style puts nutritional considerations in a low priority in the pecking order of things to worry about from day to day? Different definitions of problems can lead to very different kinds of solutions. It is critical, then, to be certain about what the problem is before seeking a solution (this is expressed in Principle 3).

Overemphasis on Individuals

Another major difficulty in conducting successful social change programs is the common assumption that individuals behave in a vacuum and are not influenced by those around them. Change programs geared to altering the attitudes and/or behavior of the individual often forget that the individual's behavior is affected quite dramatically by the interpersonal environment. If a person, say a homemaker, is asked to change behavior not supported or reinforced by other household members, then behavioral change is unlikely to occur or to be maintained if it does occur. Thus, change strategies that

---

[17]Kenneth E. Warner, "The Effects of the Anti-Smoking Campaign on Cigarette Consumption," *The American Journal of Public Health,* Vol. 67, No. 7, July, 1977, pp. 645–650.

PRINCIPLE 1.
Rationality in a change program should be defined in terms of the consumer's frame of reference, not that of the change agent. The change should be designed to be compatible with the consumer's way of thinking.

PRINCIPLE 2.
The goals of a change program should be stated very explicitly to facilitate implementation efforts, evaluation efforts, and control activities.

PRINCIPLE 3.
The exact nature of a consumer problem must be fully described before explicit goals can be stated and appropriate remedial programs developed and launched.

PRINCIPLE 4.
Social change programs must recognize that individuals exist in an interpersonal environment and seldom think or act in the absence of considerable influence from some past, ongoing, or anticipated interpersonal event.

PRINCIPLE 5.
Implementation considerations are as important as the task of developing an innovation; indeed, implementation constraints and opportunities should be considered in the development of a social change program.

neglect the social and physical context of the situation in which change takes place are missing some of the important causes of behavior (see Principle 4 in Exhibit 20-1).

Technocratic Bias   Technocratic bias is the over emphasis on the *development* of a change program, without an accompanying plan for implementation. There are many examples of nutritional foods developed specifically for consumption by poor and uneducated people in less-developed countries which never gained acceptance because of inadequate marketing practices. While considerable research and development went into product development, very little thought was given to such factors as packaging, merchandising techniques, and distribution strategies. The results were low visibility of the product, unattractive packaging leading to poor impressions about product quality, and unavailability in places where the intended user shopped. Principle 5 summarizes the implications of these experiences.

OTHER CONSIDER-ATIONS FOR LAUNCHING A CONSUMERIST PROGRAM

Many criteria must be satisfied in order for a social change program to be effective. Zaltman and Duncan have isolated several criteria which they believe are important to most planned social change programs.[18] Their criteria seem highly applicable to social change programs intended to improve consumer welfare. A review of several studies of relatively unsuccessful consumer welfare improvement efforts indicated that many of these criteria were not followed.[19] Some of these important criteria are presented below. A principle expressing each criterion is suggested.

Perceived Need for Change

Making a service available does not guarantee its utilization. There must be a perceived need for the advocated change and, importantly, there must be a belief among the intended consumers that the need can be met without undue social, psychological or financial cost. The proposed change must be linked clearly and directly to a felt need for change among consumers. For example, many experts agree that the nutritional practices of many Americans must be drastically improved. It seems doubtful, however, that the general public has a strong felt need to change their nutritional practices (see Principle 6 in Exhibit 20-2).

Capacity to Change

The capacity of a consumer or social system of consumers to change is a function of many, often interrelated, factors, which have been discussed in earlier chapters. One such factor is the individual's knowledge base. Do consumers have the requisite information and skills to allow them to take advantage of nutrient labeling or credit disclosure terms? If not, legislation requiring that this information be disclosed will not have the intended effect. Another dimension of the capacity to change concerns society's general openness to change. (Chapter 4 identified several dimensions of this criterion.) Principle 7 summarizes the importance of the capacity to change.

---

[18]Zaltman and Duncan, *op. cit.*

[19]Gerald Zaltman, *An Assessment of Consumer Benefit Programs,* a report to the Consumer Research Institute, 1975.

PRINCIPLE 6.
An innovation should be presented to consumers as being in direct response to a strongly felt need which they believe can be satisfied without undue social, psychological, or financial cost.

PRINCIPLE 7.
An innovation should not be introduced unless consumers have or can very readily acquire the necessary capacity—cognitive, social, and psychological—to accept it.

PRINCIPLE 8.
The lower the degree of commitment to change among consumers, the more the innovation-inducing agency must make it easier for consumers to adopt it. Alternatively, the lower the degree of commitment among consumers, the greater the effort which must be made by the change agency to heighten commitment.

PRINCIPLE 9.
Planning phases should include efforts to determine what a consumer must know or be able to do in order to effectively use a proposed change. Then, ways must be designed to see that the target audience possesses the requisite knowledge and skills and is aware that these can be used in a particular way.

PRINCIPLE 10.
When designing an innovation and developing a program to gain its widespread adoption, it is highly desirable to determine whether the intended adopters can be segmented into meaningful groups which might benefit from a differentiated innovation and/or implementation plan.

PRINCIPLE 11.
Diagnosis of potential cultural, social, and psychological sources of resistance to change should be undertaken early in the process of planning for social change so that strategies can be developed for reducing resistance.

Degree of Commitment

Having a felt need is important in the change process. Equally important, however, is a commitment or strong intent to undertake remedial action. In general, the lower the consumer's motivation to solve a problem or satisfy a need, the easier it must be made for him or her to use a service not currently being used. Thus, programs which enhance commitment and motivation to change may often need to be part of the effort to introduce new regulations to help consumers help themselves (see Principle 8).

Consumer Awareness of a Change Program

It is one thing to establish a law or agency to help consumers and quite another matter to make consumers aware of the aid which has been made available. A serious problem often stems from a lack of awareness of how to use a consumer complaint bureau or when certain product information must be made available on consumer demand. Many consumers are not aware of the rights and options provided to them by local, state and federal regulations (see Principle 9).

Segmentation of Consumers

Consumers often differ in their needs and in the way their needs are best satisfied. Accordingly, it is frequently desirable to cluster consumers into meaningful groups and to differentiate marketing strategies for the different groups. Consumers may be segmented on any one of three bases: 1) on the basis of their ability to use product information which a regulation requires be made available; 2) on the basis of the severity of their felt need and/or need as judged by experts; or 3) on conventional criteria, such as stage of life cycle, income, or cultural attributes (see Chapter 3 on demographics). Thus, as indicated by Principle 10, consumers should not be considered as an undifferentiated group of potential beneficiaries.

Anticipated Sources and Levels of Resistance

Chapter 18 addressed the issue of resistance to change. It was noted that resistance is a very common phenomenon, even though it is infrequently studied. There are three interrelated sources of resistance to change. These take the form of cultural barriers, social barriers, and psychological barriers. Sources of resistance must be anticipated and an assessment made of their severity in each relevant context.

Individuals and groups such as nuclear families and friends are not naturally complacent but do seek a comfortable level of arousal and stimulation and tend to maintain that level or state. Many programs of social change involve a level of arousal and stimulation well above what is comfortable to the individual. An example would be a situation in which a purchaser of a new car is given several booklets of information about the car, accessories, warranties, and recommended service. In such instances, there is a natural tendency to avoid or resist such overstimulation. For most consumers, utilization of all displayed nutrient information would require a level of activity, increased motivation, and greater effort to understand how to effectively use nutrient data far beyond customary practices. This suggests that agency or government consumer protection activity (such as requiring substantial nutrient disclosures) may be a major cause of consumer resistance. This contention has received recent support from a study in the nutrition area.[20] Principle 11 expresses the need to consider resistance to change.

Time Requirements In many instances where groups or individuals are ready to implement change, an informational change strategy may produce change relatively quickly. Those consumers for whom nutrient content or true interest rate charges are already relevant or useful, but simply not readily available, could change their behavior quite rapidly when disclosure of such information becomes mandatory. Often, many consumers require considerable time to learn how to use such information. For these persons, changes in consumer practices are slow in coming. Care must be exercised by change agents or change agencies not to overestimate the speed with which change can occur, since this may lead to unrealistic expectations and subsequent disappointment (see Principle 12 in Exhibit 20-3).

Magnitude of the Change The larger or more significant the advocated change, the greater the inducement to change needs to be. The planning agency requires more power over the potential adopters or users and generally needs to undertake a variety of strategies in addition to information dissemination. It is useful to distinguish between the magnitude of the initial change and the magnitude of the continued change. Should efforts be concentrated on securing initial change? Should efforts be concentrated on continuing change? Do resources exist to maintain substantial efforts at both the initial and continuing stages? Perhaps one of the most common errors is underestimating the magnitude of the change being planned and hence underestimating the level of effort required to successfully create social change. Often, shortcuts may be necessary, such as special inducements or incentives unrelated to the intrinsic aspects of the change. An example is the offering of gifts or trading stamps as rewards for attending consumer education programs. Principle 13 in Exhibit 20-3 expresses this idea.

---

[20]John A. Quelch and Alden G. Clayton, "Nutrition and the American Consumer: A Survey of Interest Groups," Marketing Science Institute Report No. 77–116, November, 1977.

EXHIBIT 20-3.
Principles Concerning Change Programs

PRINCIPLE 12.
Careful projections must be made about the speed with which a change will occur among different consumer groups. This requires a careful coordination of activities over time.

PRINCIPLE 13.
The larger the magnitude of change required for the adoption of an innovation, the greater the need for inducement or incentives beyond so-called rational justifications.

PRINCIPLE 14.
The salient attributes of an innovation as perceived by consumers should be determined, and alterations in innovation design and communication plans should be made, if necessary, to minimize dysfunctional attributes and capitalize upon positive attributes.

PRINCIPLE 15.
Every effort should be made to identify potential undesirable consequences of a change program and to develop contingency plans for countering these consequences should they materialize.

PRINCIPLE 16.
Prior to the full-scale implementation of a program, a limited trial (test market or pilot program) should be undertaken.

PRINCIPLE 17.
An effective change program should have a built-in evaluation research component to permit constant evaluation of the program's impact, which in turn would lead to changes in the program over time to improve its functioning. Evaluation research should be begun with at least two benchmark surveys well in advance of the program's implementation.

Perceived Attributes of the Change

Too frequently, efforts are not made in the design of legislation and social programs to determine how consumers will perceive the advocated change. Is the telephone hot line at the Consumer Product Safety Commission perceived to be a service to remedy complaints or just a service to register complaints? Is it perceived to be a source of information prior to making purchases? Clearly, consumers' perceptions of what a social change effort is affects their use of it and their subsequent attitudes towards it. Many attributes of innovations were discussed in Chapter 18, and all of those attributes are relevant here. A consumer advocate should always consider these attributes in designing a proposed change. For example, is the relative advantage clear? Is the advocated change easy or complex to use? Is the change compatible with consumers' current attitudes and behaviors? The importance of this general concern is summarized in Principle 14.

Unintended/ Unanticipated/ Dysfunctional Consequences

Planned change may yield intended and unintended consequences. The unintended consequences may or may not have been anticipated and may or may not be useful or helpful from the consumer's standpoint. Many change programs fail or achieve less than full impact because unfortunate unintended effects occur which are not anticipated.[21] An example of such effects or consequences is confusion about the change which leads to selective filtering of information associated with it. This results in the mistaken assumption that the change is more protective than it actually is, and consequently, less critical judgment is exercised by consumers. Principle 15 is concerned with this problem.

One important way of detecting unfortunate or dysfunctional consequences is to undertake test marketing (see Principle 16). Another way is to conduct social change programs for consumers as major experiments with evaluation research built in (see Principle 17).[22]

SUMMARY

Consumer educators can use the findings of consumer behavior research to aid them in designing materials and programs that will be effective in persuading consumers to respond to their efforts. Five areas of inquiry in consumer behavior are particularly relevant to the consumer educator: (1) the influences of large-scale social structures; (2) the influences of smaller-scale structures; (3) role behavior; (4) individual adoption and resistance; and (5) communication processes.

---

[21]Warner, *op. cit.*; Day and Brandt, *op. cit.*

[22]A good example of evaluation research methodology in consumerism contexts may be found in Louis W. Stern, *et. al., The Evaluation of Consumer Protection Laws: The Case of the Fair Credit Reporting Act,* Boston, MA: Marketing Science Institute, 1977.

Attempts by consumerist groups to enact beneficial changes or consumer protection have been largely unsuccessful. Such programs have been plagued by a variety of problems, including poorly defined goals, an overemphasis on individuals, and technocratic bias. Criteria which have been found to be significant in planned social change programs can be applied to consumer welfare efforts to increase their effectiveness.

KEY CONCEPTS   Behavioral norms
Consumerism
Moral norms
Rationalistic bias
Technocratic bias

MODELS OF CONSUMER BEHAVIOR

21

CHAPTER GOALS The objective of this chapter is to help the reader understand:
1. what models are;
2. some of the existing models of consumer behavior;
3. consumer behavior as a holistic process rather than as the operation of a single phenomenon such as attitudes or roles.

INTRODUCTION One of the most challenging tasks facing consumer behavior researchers is that of integrating various research findings. It is all too easy to speak only of consumers' attitudes or their social roles. Yet, there is no single phenomenon, such as attitudes or roles or learning, which fully explains and predicts what consumers really do. The difficult task is to understand all of the separate components of consumer behavior *and* how they fit together. It may come as a surprise to discover that several comprehensive models of consumer behavior have been proposed to perform this difficult task. These models are simplified, explained, and then compared in this chapter. But first we must discuss what models are, what functions and dysfunctions they serve, and how to evaluate them.

MODELS AND THEORIES: DEFINITIONS AND FUNCTIONS A model is a representation of something (in our case, a process). Usually a model connects several components in such a way that there is a final whole which represents the "something." Thus, consumer behavior models are models in the same way that those small airplanes we constructed as children are models. Each represents in a simplified way something else. The plastic airplane is a model of the larger, more complicated machine. The consumer behavior model represents consumer decision processes. A model exhibits the structure of whatever is being modeled. Thus, a consumer behavior model shows the structure of the behavior of consumers. Usually the modeled behavior is the decision-making process. A model tells us something about the properties or activities of the phenomenon of consumer behavior. Thus, it is a framework, a schema, a representation of what is believed to actually occur when consumers make decisions about purchases.

There are many different kinds of models used in consumer behavior, some of which represent only one type of consumer behavior. Those which have already been discussed in this book are the basic attitude model (Chapter 16), the adoption model, and the diffusion model (both in Chapter 18). Since these have already been discussed, they will not be elaborated upon further. The models discussed in this chapter are those which are comprehensive, or, in other words, those which attempt to cover the full range of consumer behavior. We must be careful, however, to realize that even the comprehensive models are not all-inclusive. To model *each and every* aspect of an individual's behavior, including what affects it and what effects it has, is beyond our capabilities. Comprehensive models attempt to include all the elements which are crucially relevant to people's behaviors as consumers. So, even in trying to be comprehensive, we must limit and simplify our perspective to fit our goals of explaining and predicting consumer behavior.

This brings us to a second way of categorizing consumer behavior models—by their purpose. The models included in this chapter are concerned with what influences consumer decision processes and in what ways these influences operate. There are also models, however, which attempt to predict the outcomes of consumers' decisions. Usually these models are mathematical equations with the different influences on consumer behavior represented by numerical values.[1]

Before going on to discuss the functions and dysfunctions of using models, a few comments must be made on some things which are *not* models. A page full of boxes and arrows may or may not be a model. This can at first puzzle those who have flipped through the pages of this chapter and have seen so many boxes and circles all connected by arrows. Diagramming the major lines of influence in a model can be a shorthand way of representing the words which would otherwise be used to describe these lines of influence. Just as a picture of a skeleton is an easier way of representing "the-knee-bone-is-connected-to-the-thigh-bone...," so is a diagram of a model of con-

---

[1]W.F. Massey, D. B. Montgomery, and D. G. Morrison. *Stochastic Models of Buying Behavior,* Cambridge, Mass.: MIT Press, 1970.

sumer behavior an easier way of representing all of its components and their interrelationships. Though a model can be described verbally without a diagram, the diagram makes it easier to communicate. Even if there is a diagram, it may not be a model because the diagram may not represent the actual structure of something. Hence, not all models are diagrams, but diagrams can be useful ways of depicting models.

Functions and Dysfunctions of Models

Now that we have defined what a model is, we must ask what it does. Why does anybody bother to construct comprehensive consumer behavior models? What functions do they serve? What dysfunctions arise when they are used? Models provide a larger context within which research findings can be placed. Most research studies must focus on one small aspect of consumer behavior, but readers and users of that research must be able to see a broader picture within which the research fits. Models provide this broader picture. Second, models explicitly state relationships between their components. This explicit statement helps researchers organize data in such a way as to actually test the model, rather than merely to appear to test it. Third, since the study of consumer behavior is in essence a behavioral science, models provide a way for the behavioral scientists interested in consumer behavior to have a common ground of agreement. That is, models provide a common perspective. Those who do not agree with a particular model can, of course, propose, test, and attempt to substantiate alternative models. Therefore, models help the advancement of knowledge in the field. Finally, by examining what models leave out or what relationships are not yet firmly established by research, models inform us about what needs to be done in the field of consumer behavior. Thus, models identify findings, as well as gaps. (For more discussion of the role of models in scientific inquiry, see Kaplan[2] and Kuhn.[3])

Modeling consumer behavior has some dysfunctional consequences, however. As becomes evident later in this chapter, many of the models are greatly simplified and make the study of consumer behavior appear less complex than it truly is. Secondly, models draw artificial distinctions between concepts which in actuality are inseparable. For instance, where can one find an attitude without any connection to a personality? Each is included in humans. Attitudes and personalities, unlike hearts and stomachs, are not separate, distinguishable parts of humans; rather, attitudes and personalities are meshed together and comprise a whole that can only be artificially sepa-

---

[2]Abraham Kaplan, *The Conduct of Inquiry,* NY: Chandler, 1964.
[3]Thomas S. Kuhn, *The Structure of Scientific Revolutions,* 2nd ed., Chicago, The University of Chicago Press, 1970.

rated into parts. In studying consumer behavior, we are studying humans in all of their complexity and intricacy. We never *see* an attitude, but only the expression of an attitude by a person. Thus, it must be kept in mind that the models in this chapter represent the decision processes of humans.

Criteria for Evaluating Models

In examining these models, it would be useful to have criteria by which to evaluate them. But, this is more difficult to do than might be expected. A model is evaluated on different criteria, depending on who is doing the evaluation and what purposes and functions that person believes the model should perform.[4] For instance, the mathematician looks for quantitativeness and precision. A social scientist evaluates a model on the basis of its insight into human behavior and its explanatory power. A practitioner, such as a marketing manager or a public policy maker, looks for a model's applicability or utility in decision making.

General criteria for evaluating models can be derived, however, from existing work on the philosophy and methodology of science. Some desirable properties of a model are listed in Table 21-1.

Some actions can be predicted by mathematical equations, but the equations do not help explain why or how that action comes about. In other words, mathematical models which predict outputs (behaviors) which will occur given specific inputs are not the whole story. A model should also include the "throughputs" which explain how the inputs get transformed. Consumer behavior models should *explain and predict.* If there must be a choice between the two, predictive power should be sacrificed since later a good explanation can be reformulated to also predict. Consumer behavior

TABLE 21-1.
Desirable Properties of a Model

A model should be:
1. Capable of explanation as well as prediction
2. General
3. High in heuristic power
4. High in unifying power
5. Internally consistent
6. Original
7. Plausible (have face validity)
8. Simple
9. Supported by facts
10. Testable, verifiable

[4]Gerald Zaltman, Christian R. A. Pinson, and Reinhard Angelmar, *Metatheory and Consumer Research,* NY: Holt, Reinhart and Winston, 1973.

models should be sufficiently *general* so as to cover a wide range of buying situations. A model is more desirable if it has the *heuristic power* to pose new questions. Thus, the model should help one ask (as in Gertrude Stein's famous remark) not what the answer is, but rather, what is the question?

Unifying power is the model's capacity to bring together areas which have previously been viewed as unrelated. Thus, a good consumer behavior model considers the interrelationships among attitudes, personality, social roles, social structures, and learning processes. A model must be *internally consistent,* that is, free from logical incongruities (such as $A > B$, $B > C$, $A < C$), before it can be fruitfully employed in explaining consumer behavior.

Unless a model is *original,* it will not increase knowledge and therefore has few incremental benefits. A model that is *plausible* is one that, on the surface, seems to make sense (that is, it has face validity). Plausibility does not necessarily indicate that the model is conclusive in its representation, but that it at least makes sense. A model should also be *simple* enough that it can be understood. Any complexity which is not necessary for an explanation should be eliminated. At the time a model is constructed, it should be *based on existing facts.* That is, it should not deny the facts themselves although it may deny one particular explanation of the facts. Of course, after its initial construction, facts may come to light which disprove the model. In this case, the model must be reformulated to fit the new set of facts. Finally, a model must be *testable.* That is, it must be possible, at least in principle, to test the relationships postulated by the model. In other words, if a consumer behavior model states that awareness of a product precedes purchase of it, it must be possible to test whether this is the time sequencing which actually occurs.

There is not, nor is it possible that there could be, a model of consumer behavior which could satisfy all of these criteria. Thus, it is not necessarily a justifiable criticism to say that a particular model does not meet one of the criteria. In fact, it may be impossible to meet all the criteria since some of them imply trade-offs. For example, it may be difficult, although not impossible, to be original and still be firmly supported by known facts. Also, in order to be general, a model may have to forego some simplicity. This is preferable to its being overly simplistic, in which case it is doubtful that it will provide a thorough explanation as well as a sound prediction of behavior.

Thus, we believe the best manner in which to evaluate models is to give greater emphasis to certain criteria depending on the intended use or purpose of the model. Hence, this is the approach which is used in this chapter.

Now that it is clear what a model is supposed to be, our attention can turn to examining several actual consumer behavior models. One model, the Howard and Sheth model of buyer behavior, is explained in greater depth because of its wide acceptance and use. Several other models are outlined briefly. Then, in the final section of this chapter, an attempt is made to derive the essentials of all of the models and, therefore, of consumer behavior. This discussion describes the most basic consumer behavior variables and relationships between variables.

THE HOWARD AND SHETH MODEL OF BUYER BEHAVIOR

The Howard-Sheth model of buyer behavior is an elaboration of a model originally formulated by John Howard.[5] The Howard-Sheth model is a revision which includes more variables and is clearer in its linkages than was the original model. This model is perhaps the most widely used and discussed of all the different models of consumer behavior. It has even served as the foundation for other models, such as the Sheth model of industrial buyer behavior.[6] This model will be briefly discussed after a fuller explanation of the structure, strengths, and weaknesses of the Howard-Sheth model.

The Howard-Sheth model shows the processes and variables affecting an individual's behavior prior to and during a purchase. There is a heavy emphasis on three key variables: (1) perception, (2) learning, and (3) attitude formation. The model is meant to explain how consumers compare available products in order to choose one which fits their desires. Consumers learn by actively searching for information about products. This information is then used for comparing alternative brands according to various choice criteria. The basic structure is:

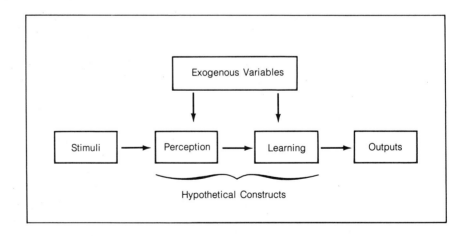

[5]John A. Howard and Jagdish N. Sheth, *The Theory of Buyer Behavior,* NY: John Wiley, 1969.

[6]Jagdish N. Sheth, ''A Model of Industrial Buyer Behavior,'' *Journal of Marketing,* Vol. 37, October, 1973, pp. 50–56.

Stimuli are perceived, learning occurs, and outputs (such as a purchase) result. The two middle stages are called hypothetical constructs because they are not observable, but they must exist for the outputs to occur. These stages are affected by exogenous variables, or variables outside the immediate system of the model, which are used in predicting perception and learning. The model, however, does not try to account for changes in these exogenous variables. They are given. All of the variables change over time as a result of new learning. This is why the model is dynamic—it can incorporate change.

Each of the components of the basic structure includes several different variables. For example, stimuli can come from either commercial or social sources. Stimuli include product quality, price, distinctiveness, service, and product availability, as well as information from one's family and reference groups. Exogenous variables include such socio-psychological buyer characteristics as the importance of the purchase to the person, the person's culture, social class, personality traits, the social and organizational setting, time pressure, and financial status. The Howard-Sheth model does not try to explain how these variables (e.g., a particular personality trait such as introversion) come about, but rather how they affect the perception and learning processes. Yet, throughout this book, it has been stated that one must take into account the sources of these particular variables. For instance, two people of the same social class (e.g., middle class) will behave quite differently if one was born and has remained in the middle class whereas the other was born of lower-class parents but has managed to attain a middle-class life-style, occupation, income, and level of education. Thus, the sources of change in exogenous variables are important for those interested in understanding consumer behavior.

Outputs   One of the distinctive elements of the Howard-Sheth model is the inclusion of five different, sequential output variables, rather than merely including purchase as an output. These five stages are shown on the following page. The solid lines are the direction of the behavior sequence; the dotted lines are feedback. This scheme means that in the process of buying a new pair of snow skis, a person first becomes aware of skis in a window or becomes aware of the need for skis for an upcoming trip. After this, the consumer finds out about different brands and forms an attitude toward those brands and toward skis in general. This attitude is the basis for intentions toward purchase and, later, for the actual purchase. The purchase and subsequent experience with the skis lead to revised attitudes which, in turn, lead to revised brand comprehension and attention. That is, a person who has purchased a particular brand may buy that brand in the future simply because he or she knows more about it than about other brands. Of course, any consumer may stop at any stage in the process. For instance, someone may get as far as having a

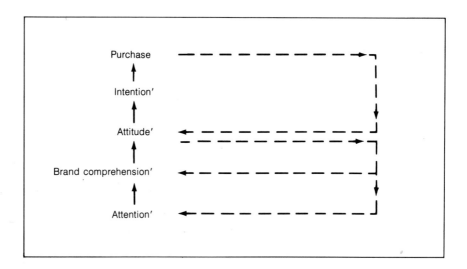

very positive attitude toward snow skis but never intend to purchase any because he or she lives in Miami, Florida.

A second feature of this output scheme is that the stages (e.g., Attitude') are the measurable counterparts of some of the hypothetical constructs. Since this is somewhat confusing even to those familiar with the model, explanation is needed. As was mentioned earlier, the hypothetical constructs are not observable. In other words, we can never observe an attitude toward a product or an intention to purchase. However, we can give a person an attitude scale to measure the attitude or ask the person about the likelihood that he or she will purchase a certain product. It is this measurement of an attitude and this response to a question about intentions which are included in the output sequence. These are called Attitude' and Intention', which are measurements of the real phenomena which are called Attitude and Intention.

An Example   Figure 21-1 is a simplified depiction of the Howard-Sheth model of buyer behavior. The original Howard-Sheth drawing is much more comprehensive and is in a different format. The figure has been redrawn here in order to simplify the model so its basic structure can be understood. In addition, this redrawn model facilitates comparisons of the different models discussed in this chapter.

In order to understand the model, it is necessary to follow an example through all of the boxes and arrows. Let us consider again a young man and the purchase of some snow skis. The part of the model being referred to is included in parentheses. Perhaps the young man is doing some shopping one day and notices a special sale on a pair of skis in a sporting goods store (this is

FIGURE 21-1.
*The Howard-Sheth
Model of Buyer
Behavior*

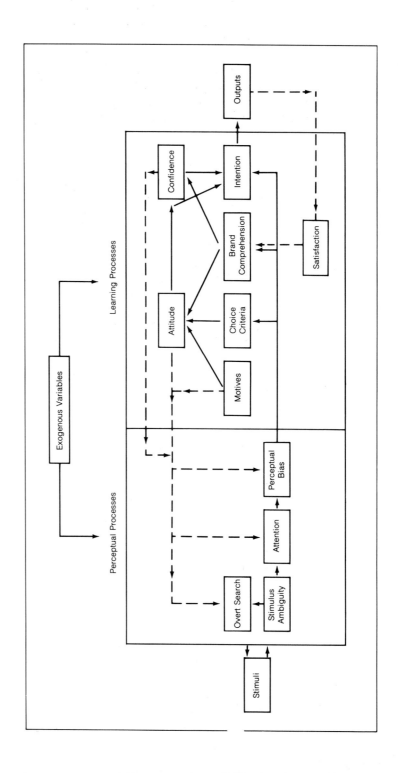

the stimulus). The young man does not know much about skis, however, and isn't sure what the skis will be like on the slopes (stimulus ambiguity). Thus, the young man goes into the store and asks the sales clerk several questions about the skis (overt search). Answers, as well as a descriptive booklet on different skis, are given to the young man by the salesclerk (more stimuli). The young man listens to the salesperson and glances over the information (attention). Of course, only certain parts of the information are remembered, and some bits of information are distorted in the process of sorting them in memory (perceptual bias). The young man may remember more information if the purchase is very important to him or if he is going to ask his parents to loan him the money for the purchase, which will involve answering their questions about skis (exogenous variables).

The next step is the formation of an attitude. This is done by combining choice criteria and brand comprehension. The young man may want skis so he can go to a ski resort and meet other people. Alternatively, he may want skis so he can enter some competitive races (motives). He may, therefore, just want skis which look nice and enhance his status at the resort. Or, he may want skis which are of the quality necessary for winning races (choice criteria). If he doesn't know which are the criteria he should use in his evaluation process, he will engage in extended problem solving. If he knows the criteria to use, but has not yet evaluated the available brands on these criteria, he will engage in limited problem solving to find out more about the brands. Of course, the extent of this behavior is dependent upon the young man's present knowledge of what the different lines of ski equipment have to offer (brand comprehension). The other type of problem-solving behavior exists when the consumer knows both the criteria to be used and how various brands rate on these criteria. This automatic or routinized response behavior is more typical in repeat purchases of convenience goods, such as toothpaste or laundry detergent.

The young man may then have a very strong positive attitude toward skis and skiing and may find one brand which fits his desire to meet people at the ski resort. Then, depending on how certain he is of his understanding of different brands (confidence), he will decide whether he plans to purchase the skis (intention). If he believes that he knows a fair amount about the status enhancement potential of various brands, he is more likely to plan to purchase the skis. But, if he is unsure as to whether this pair of skis will enhance or hurt his people-meeting potential at the resort (since people may be more likely to converse with a person having a certain brand of skis), he is less likely to make plans based on his present attitude. Once the plans are made, the young man might then go into the sporting goods store and buy the skis (output: purchase). During the time he is in the store a student doing a term project for a consumer behavior course could ask him whether he plans to buy the skis (output: intention').

Even if the young man plans to buy the skis, he may not actually buy them. He might not believe that he is enough of an extrovert to enjoy spending much time at a ski resort (exogenous variable: personality trait). Or, his parents may not be able to loan him the money to buy the skis (exogenous variable: financial status). If he does buy the skis and is pleased because they meet or exceed his expectations (satisfaction), he will remember this the next time he buys skis (brand comprehension).

Evaluation of the Model

Now that we have explored the basic structure of the model, it must be evaluated on the criteria discussed earlier in this chapter. The Howard-Sheth model has problems with explanation as well as prediction. For example, the model does not fully explain *when* certain phenomena are important. When is social class influential in determining purchase choices? Secondly, the model does not explain *how* certain variables influence the outcome. How does perceptual bias or confidence operate? The only answer provided is that the perceptual variables operate less strongly if the stimuli are from the social rather than the commercial environment. The explanation is particularly weak with respect to what are called the exogenous variables. No account is taken of the fact that the very act of considering, purchasing, and using a particular product may affect the consumer's personality (especially self-concept), financial status, time pressures, and social class. These variables are not as exogenous as they appear.

The Howard-Sheth model is also limited in its generality. It is most applicable to individual buyer behavior rather than collective decision making. If we consider that purchases made within a family as well as within an organization are instances of collective decision making, the limited applicability of the model becomes apparent. The model is also limited because it treats social influences in such a tangential way. Consumer behavior is essentially a social process. Therefore, the Howard-Sheth model covers only half of the buyer-seller dyad and avoids the truly interesting process of their interaction. More will be said about this later in the chapter. In addition, because of its attention to the evaluation of various brands, the model is most suited for explaining brand choice decisions (e.g., between two brands of toothpaste). It is less well suited for decisions between two different alternatives (e.g., having a child or buying a new automobile). Yet these decisions are just as important and common as brand decisions. It is equally important, if not more so, to ask, "Why do people buy toothpaste at all?" as to ask, "Why do people buy this brand rather than that brand?"

The Howard-Sheth model, through its heuristic power, has particularly benefited the study of consumer behavior. That is, the construction of the model and its evaluation by others has raised many new questions. For instance, much research has been conducted on attitude formation and information utilization to determine how people combine bits of information in forming an attitude toward a product (see Chapter 16 on attitudes and Chapter 12 on information processing).

The unifying power of the model, which is its ability to bring together several topical areas, is good. Other models, however, have also been able to unify the same theories of learning and perception. In addition, as was mentioned earlier, although many different variables are brought together, the linkages are sometimes not exactly specified. Thus, the effort to unify is not yet complete.

The model has some linkages which are original and others which had already been empirically demonstrated prior to its construction. It is original in its feedback link between satisfaction and confidence through brand comprehension,[7] but, for the most part, it combines variables which were commonly believed to be central determinants of consumer behavior. Yet, this is not a criticism of the model. In fact, the Howard-Sheth model made a large contribution in building a theory from proposed relationships between these variables. Prior to the formulation of the model, knowledge of consumer behavior had not been brought together and systematized, but existed only in unconnected fragments.

Although the model appears to be representative of actual consumer decision-making processes, empirical research has not confirmed all of the propositions included in the model. One of the strengths of the Howard-Sheth model, however, is that it has been empirically tested, whereas other models have not been tested and are therefore more tentative.

An empirical test of a model compares the predicted with the actual direction of relationships between variables. It asks: How much of the variation among individual consumers is explained by factors in the model? A test of the Howard-Sheth model has been conducted by Farley and Ring.[8] For this test, 693 households were sampled during the test marketing phase of the introduction of a new grocery product. The results from the sample were included in eleven equations derived from the model. The equations were of the following type:

Choice criteria = $f[\beta(\text{perceptual bias}), \gamma(\text{exogenous variables})]$

Equations take into account only the variables immediately preceding the variable to be explained. Thus, although attention does affect choice criteria, the linkage is not direct, and therefore it is not included in the equation. The second feature of the equation is the weights (e.g., β and γ). These weights

---

[7]Zaltman, *et al.*, 1973 *op. cit.*

[8]John U. Farley and L. Winston Ring, "An Empirical Test of the Howard-Sheth Model of Buyer Behavior," *Journal of Marketing Research*, Vol. 7, November, 1970, pp. 427–438.

are factors which are multiplied by the explanatory variables (e.g., perceptual bias and exogenous variables). The weights tell how important each of the variables is in explaining and predicting the relevant variable (e.g., choice criteria). For instance, on a six-point scale such as Warner's (see Chapter 4 in the section on social class), a consumer might be upper-middle class (an exogenous variable) and would therefore be scored as a four. If the weight of social class is three, then the contribution of social class would be twelve (3 × 4).

One problem with using this type of equation was that the model does not specify either the weights of the different variables or the way in which they combine (e.g., additively or multiplicatively) to produce the variable to be explained. The model only tells us what the direction of the relationships will be (e.g., the greater the stimulus ambiguity, the greater the likelihood that overt search will occur). So, a multiple equation regression system with eleven equations was constructed. The weights used were those which provided the best fit with actual values.

The test supported the general direction of most relationships. All of the relationships between endogenous variables (that is, all variables except the exogenous ones) were as hypothesized. Different exogenous variables were found to have a greater effect on certain other variables. For example, it appears that personality traits influence attitudes, and social class affects motives. In general, the Farley and Ring test supported the direction of the hypothesized relationships, although there may be other untested relationships which are equally or more important. Also, the test showed that certain parts of the model are in need of revision (particularly the link between attention and the inputs). More tests, including more variables, are needed.

The Howard-Sheth model, despite its flaws, was a significant contribution toward understanding consumer behavior. It unified many unrelated findings and provided the groundwork for future research. Also, it included many of the basic components of consumer behavior.

THE SHETH MODEL OF INDUSTRIAL BUYER BEHAVIOR From the original Howard-Sheth model of buyer behavior, another model was developed: the Sheth model of industrial buyer behavior.[9] Its generality is different than that of the original model as this model applies to group decision-making buying situations within an organization. Thus, it is more social in its nature; that is, it considers interactions between people and incorporates them into the model.

---

[9]Sheth, 1973, *op. cit.*

Figure 21-2 is a simplified drawing of the model. Once again, this figure has been redrawn from the original to facilitate comparisons. Note the similarities with the Howard-Sheth model: there are inputs or stimuli (the information sources), learning and perceptual processes (in the large box), exogenous variables (along the top row), and outputs (the supplier or brand choice). There has been one important addition, however. When the decision is a joint or group one, rather than an autonomous one, conflict resolution occurs. This is the negotiation which occurs when two or more people try to come to agreement on what choice is best for the firm as a whole. Therefore, in addition to individual perception and learning, the Sheth model includes interpersonal processes such as conflict resolution and negotiation.

Sheth also gives some attention to determining when a decision will be made jointly. Specifically, joint decisions are more likely when any of the following exist:
1. there is high perceived risk;
2. it is a capital expenditure rather than a routine purchase;
3. time pressure is low;
4. the organization is large; or
5. the organization is decentralized.

In these situations of joint decision making, conflict can be resolved in several different ways depending on the type of disagreement which exists. This is shown in Table 21-2. The first two ways of resolving conflict (problem solving and persuasion) are efficient in meeting the organization's goals, while the latter two are inefficient.

Clearly, this model includes many factors discussed earlier in this book. Expectations include needs and motivation. The use of information sources is a form of communication. The individual's background includes social class and roles. Company specific factors include the innovativeness of the firm. And conflict resolution is a social process, which in this case occurs within a group welfare system. Thus, it becomes obvious how models try to link up the basic components of consumer behavior.

TABLE 21-2.
Conflict Resolution Strategies

Conflict will be resolved by:	when there is:
Problem solving (seeking more information)	disagreement on expectations
Persuasion	disagreement on specific criteria for evaluation
Bargaining (reciprocity)	disagreement on fundamental buying goals
Politicking	disagreement on fundamental buying goals and on style of decision making

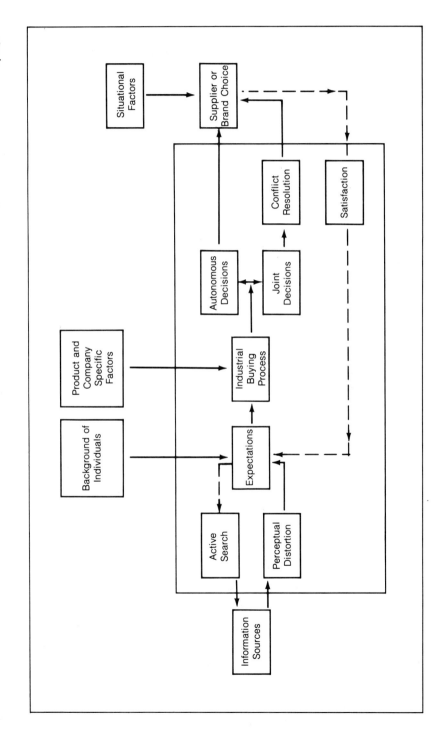

FIGURE 21-2.
Sheth Model of Industrial Buyer Behavior

The Sheth model has added a social negotiation process and has in this respect extended the original model. Nevertheless, many of the problems of the Howard-Sheth model remain. These include problems with insufficient explanation. For instance, it is not clear when causal relationships occur, how they operate, or what weights are associated with the variables. The Sheth model is unique in its contribution of a behavioral approach to industrial buyer behavior. This approach emphasizes the similarity between all forms of group decision making, including family purchases, purchases made by family-owned businesses, as well as purchases made by buying groups in multinational corporations.

THE ENGEL, KOLLAT, AND BLACKWELL MODEL OF CONSUMER BEHAVIOR

A model which is similar to the Howard-Sheth model in its scope and intent is that developed by Engel, Kollat, and Blackwell.[10] Like the Howard-Sheth model, the Engel, Kollat, and Blackwell (E-K-B) model is based on learning processes. Different types of search behavior occur, depending on how routine or unusual the purchase choice is. This is comparable to the extended, limited, and automatic problem-solving situations described by Howard and Sheth. The main point to be remembered is that the emphasis is on the information search process.

Figure 21-3 shows the E-K-B model redrawn in a way which facilitates comparisons between models. As with the Howard-Sheth model, the basic components are stimuli, processing of information, the decision process, and environmental influence. The stimuli encourage the consumer to become aware of information or a product. After filtering the information, the consumer evaluates it and forms an attitude. When a problem situation arises (e.g., when a person needs to find a birthday present for someone), the person searches through the information stored in memory and evaluates the alternatives (flowers, books, candy). If not enough information is stored, the person searches for additional information before coming to a decision. If the decision is routine, little or no external search or post-purchase evaluation takes place. Environmental influences affect whether the person continues through the output decision process. These influences include income, family, social class, and physical factors.

---

[10]James F. Engel, David T. Kollat and Roger D. Blackwell, *Consumer Behavior,* 2nd ed., NY: Holt, Rinehart and Winston, 1973, Chapter 4. The model has been revised in James F. Engel, Roger D. Blackwell, and David T. Kollat, *Consumer Behavior,* 3rd ed., Hinsdale, IL: Dryden Press, 1978. However, the basic core of the revised model and its strengths and weaknesses parallel the model from the 1973 edition which is presented here.

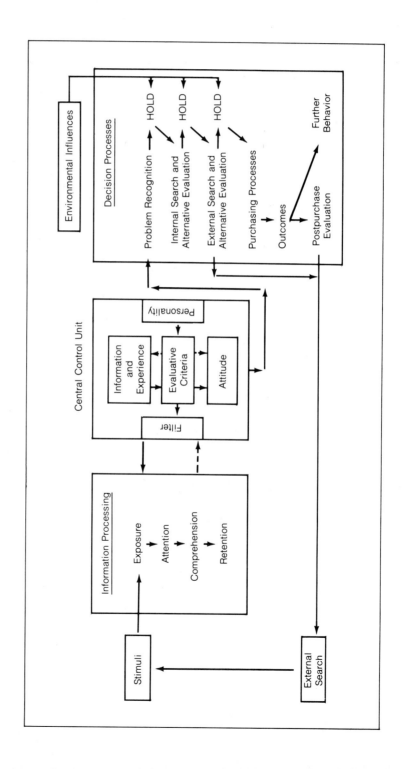

The Engel, Kollat, Blackwell model has many of the same problems with explanation which the Howard-Sheth model has. In other words, it does not explain when particular variables influence others (e.g., when personality affects evaluative criteria), how this influence occurs, or what the strength of the influence is. Ultimately, neither of these models is able to answer these questions because the answers are not yet known. Omitting this type of explanation is a problem in consumer behavior work as a whole, not just in these particular models.

Like the Howard-Sheth model, this model applies essentially to individual consumer purchasing situations. Although groups such as the family are included, they are not included in the search, evaluation, and decision processes. Negotiation and conflict resolution are not included in the model. Thus, this is a model of individual, rather than interpersonal choice behavior.

Also, like the Howard-Sheth model, this model is not high in originality. On the other hand, the model, as well as the text in which it appears, serve as frameworks for integrating and reporting findings of empirical research in consumer behavior. Thus, the strength and the major contribution of the model lie in its unification of concepts and propositions, rather than in the originality inherent in its linkages.

On the whole, the E-K-B model appears to have face validity. That is, most of the relationships and flows appear plausible. The only problem is that it is unclear why the central control unit is separate from parts of the decision processes, particularly internal search. The distinctions made between information processing, the central control unit, and output decision processing do not appear as clear in actual consumer behavior as they are described in the model.

The E-K-B model has never been tested, and it is not clear that it could be.[11] Several of the processes are not defined in such a way that they could be operationalized (i.e., put in measurable terms). It would be extremely difficult and highly speculative to develop mathematical equations for testing the model.

This model, then, is another way of conceptualizing consumer behavior. Many of its variables are comparable to others in the Howard-Sheth model. These comparable terms include:

Howard-Sheth Model	*E-K-B Model*
Exogenous variables	Environmental influences
Attitudes	Attitudes
Choice criteria	Evaluative criteria
Perceptual bias	Filter

---

[11]Zaltman, *et al., op. cit.*

The main difference between the two is that Engel, Kollat, and Blackwell place more emphasis upon processes between attitude formation and the development of an intention to purchase. This is the output decision process. This description of an active information seeking and evaluation process is the major contribution of the Engel, Kollat, and Blackwell model.

THE KERBY MODEL OF CONSUMER BEHAVIOR

A simple model of consumer behavior has been developed by Kerby.[12] The simplicity of this model is useful in deriving the essentials of models of consumer behavior. Also, the simplicity is in line with the objective of all modeling efforts—that is, to simplify the phenomena while still explaining them. Models, therefore, should include only those variables and linkages which are necessary and relevant.

Figure 21-4 shows that the basic pattern of the Kerby model is similar to the models already discussed. As with the previous model drawings in this chapter, this one has been redrawn from the original to facilitate comparisons. Stimuli produce a recognition of need by the consumer. If the situation is not routine, this triggers motivation toward action and the evaluation of alternatives which might satisfy the need. This, in turn, produces the major output, which is called purposive action. Humans are seen as being reflexive, and accordingly, the model provides for the evaluation of previous action. An action may become a habitual response if it is evaluated as being a response which is always satisfying and optimal, given the set of alternatives. The mediational center is the thought center through which the entire process works. The exogenous variables in the Howard-Sheth model are referred to here as the person factors and social factors. Person factors include perceptions, attitudes, learning, personality, attention, memory, and economic constraints. Social factors include emulation, social class, reference groups, and the cultural environment.

Kerby recognizes four main problems with the model. First, the person factors and the social factors are not connected. Yet, as was discussed in Chapter 4 in the section on social class, a person's attitudes and learning abilities are shaped in part by social class and reference groups. Second, there is no feedback to the person factors and social factors. That is, the model does not account for the fact that a person's attitudes, perceptions, personality, and cultural environment are affected by his or her purchase actions. Thirdly, the factors in the model are not given importance ratings. Therefore, it would be

---

[12]Joe Kent Kerby, *Consumer Behavior: Conceptual Foundations,* NY: Dun-Donnelley, 1975, Chapter 2.

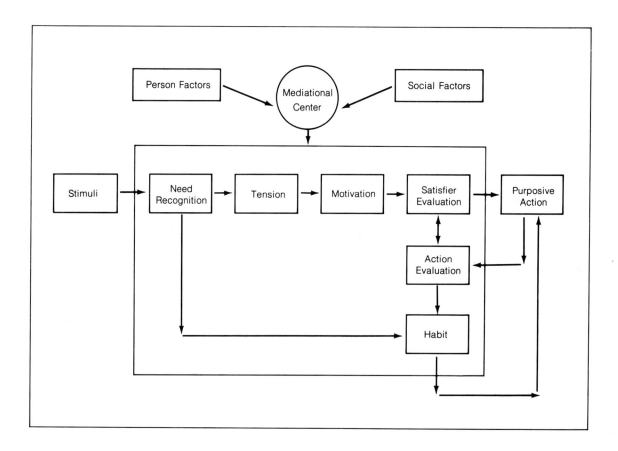

FIGURE 21-4.
*The Kerby Model of
Consumer Behavior*

difficult to translate the model into mathematical equations. Finally, the model is static. It does not allow for the continual change occurring in a human due to learning and experience. The model is derived from biological models of needs and drives as the basis of behavior. It is less firmly rooted in the tradition of viewing humans as active, inquisitive, learning beings.

The Kerby model is quite appropriate to examine, however, because it does simplify the processes underlying consumer behavior. It has included most of the basic variables, but has perhaps neglected some of the important linkages. This model, then, can serve as a guide in trying to uncover the basics of consumer behavior. Before discussing these basics, one additional approach to modeling consumer behavior must be examined.

THE DYADIC APPROACH: NICOSIA'S MODEL OF CONSUMER BEHAVIOR

One problem with many of the models of consumer behavior is that they consider an isolated individual who is affected by, but not interacting with, other individuals. Yet, since consumer behavior is essentially social in nature, as it involves interpersonal interaction (e.g., consumer—retailer, father—mother—child, purchasing agent—salesperson, clerk—client), a different approach is needed. This approach must explain not only the behavior of one of the parties or persons, but also the behavior of the other person, as well as the interaction of the two. Such an analysis is called the dyadic approach.[13]

The Basic Dyadic Model

A dyadic model of consumer behavior must include at least two interacting people. Most models treat only the behaviors of the buyer responding to a stimulus provided by the firm. A dyadic model, however, must go beyond this. Figure 21-5 shows the basic components of a dyadic model of consumer behavior. The seller is exposed to a stimulus (e.g., increased demand or a new market segment) which produces perception, learning, and an output behavior (e.g., a new product). Of course, this process is subject to exogenous variables, such as the personality (individual or collective), economic position, and family pressures of the manufacturer. The outputs of the seller become the stimuli for the buyer. Then another decision process is underway. The decision or output of the buyer becomes, in turn, a stimulus for the seller. Thus, there is a dyadic system in which each individual is affected by the behavior of the other as well as by his or her own behavior.

Nicosia's Model

There is only one consumer behavior model which explicitly includes the selling firm: Nicosia's model of consumer decision processes.[14] The emphasis is still on the consumer's half of the dyadic system, but the firm is included. The basic structure is shown on page 537. Thus, the firm affects the consumer, the consumer affects the firm, and the consumer's behavior affects his or her behavior in the future. There is no real beginning or end; the process can start anywhere.

Figure 21-6 shows the processes described by the model. These are divided into four fields. Field 1 includes all processes which take a message from the firm to the consumer. The firm and the consumer attributes referred

---

[13]Thomas V. Bonoma, Richard Bagozzi, and Gerald Zaltman. ''The Dyadic Paradigm with Specific Application toward Industrial Marketing.'' University of Pittsburgh working paper #138, 1975.

[14]Francesco Nicosia, *Consumer Decision Processes: Marketing and Advertising Implications.* Englewood Cliffs, N.J.: Prentice-Hall, 1967.

FIGURE 21-5.
*Basic Components of a
Dyadic Model of
Consumer Behavior*

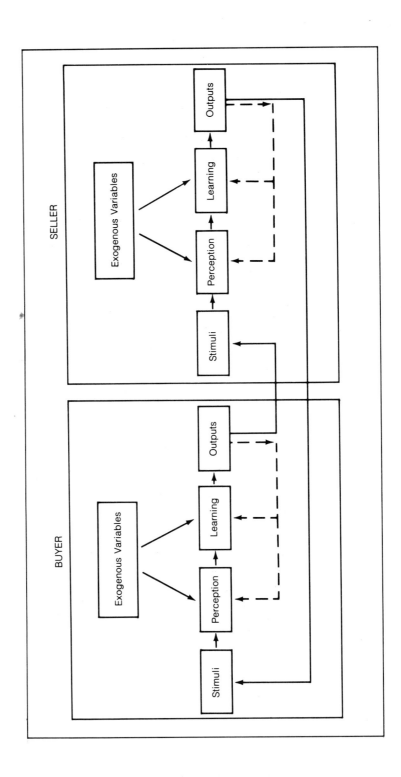

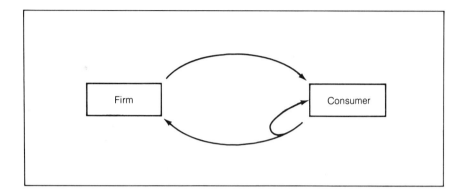

to are comparable to the two sets of exogenous variables in Figure 21-5. Field 2 includes immediate responses to the message. The consumer forms an attitude, evaluates alternatives, and then is ready to enter the action phase of the model. In Field 3, the consumer develops a motivation to act (also called intention to act in other models) and then acts. This action is the purchase of the product. Field 4 includes feedback linkages which take place after the purchase. For instance, the act of purchasing is fed back into the firm as a stimulus. Also, there is feedback within the consumer as the consumer goes through the processes of storing and using the product. This experience then alters the consumer's attributes (e.g., self-concept, learning processes, personality, role structure).

In addition to including the firm, the Nicosia model has various other strengths, several of which are connected to the explanation offered by the model. Primarily, the model recognizes the many steps which lie between attitude formation and actual behavior. Such a conceptualization helps us understand the problems that researchers have when they find that attitudes do not always predict behavior (see Chapter 16 on attitudes). The model, however, does present problems when used to make predictions. Propositions such as those given throughout this book are used for making predictions. They have the following form: The more A (e.g., how closely one's beliefs are upheld by the use of a product), the more likely it is that B will occur (e.g., the person will use that product). The Nicosia model is not presented in this form. The linkages show flows rather than causation.

The model is also strong in showing change in consumer attributes due to the experience of considering, choosing, purchasing, and using a product. There is intra-person feedback, i.e., consumers think to themselves and respond to their thoughts and acts. The model is not very explicit, however, in describing how and when the consumers' or firms' attributes function. To be truly explanatory, the model needs more elaboration on this point.

FIGURE 21-6.
*Nicosia Model of
Consumer Decision
Making*

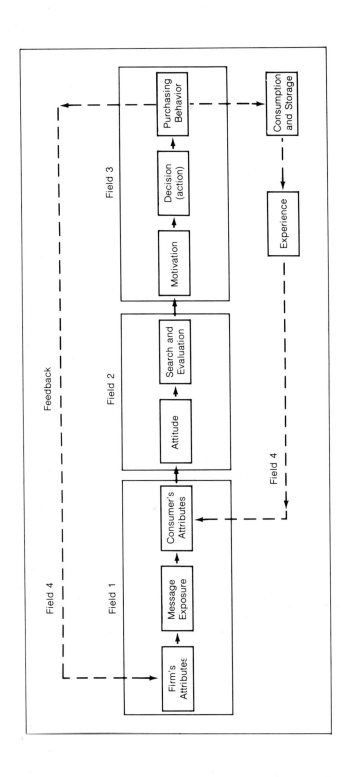

THE ESSENTIALS OF CONSUMER BEHAVIOR

If these models do in some ways represent consumer behavior, we should be able to infer from them what the essential elements of consumer behavior are. In other words, we should be able to answer two questions: What are the most fundamental variables affecting consumer behavior? What linkages between these variables must exist for the most rudimentary explanation of consumer behavior?

As we have mentioned several times in this chapter, the models in their original forms are much more complex and comprehensive than the versions presented in this chapter. The versions presented here have been simplified so as to make comparison easier. Now, in this concluding section, we make a further attempt to simplify. In diagram form we are moving toward the base of the funnel.

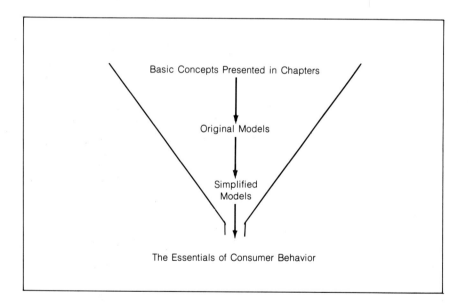

Thus, in this final section we draw from the simplified versions of the models the answers to the two questions above.

The basic variables and linkages of consumer behavior models are shown in Figure 21-7. External stimuli include a wide assortment such as advertisements, using the last bit of toothpaste from a tube, and what friends say and think. What is important in determining consumer choices, however, are internalized stimuli. These are what the person hears and remembers from the advertisement, what feelings and thoughts the person has upon using the last bit of toothpaste in the tube, what the person believes his or her friends

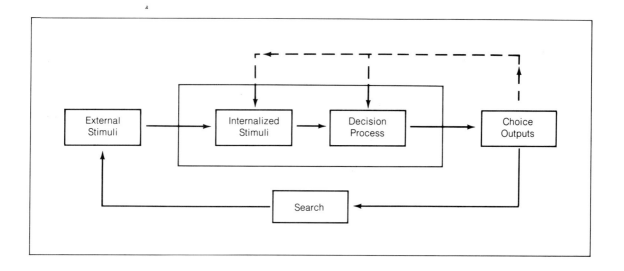

FIGURE 21-7.
*The Essentials of a
Consumer Behavior
Model*

think, and how the person interprets what the friends say. Internalized stimuli also include preferences due to the consumer's personality, how the person defines the roles he or she occupies, how the consumer responds to financial circumstances, and characteristic modes of problem conceptualization. Thus, there is a distinction made between external stimuli—stimuli as seen by someone else (the marketing manager, the advertising copywriter, a friend)—and internal stimuli—the set of meanings and interpretations generated by the person and used in the decision process. Even social interactions and environmental influences become internalized stimuli.

These internalized stimuli are used in reaching a decision. The decision process is assumed to be goal-directed (e.g., maximize gains and minimize losses as they are perceived, or satisfice a given set of alternatives). The output is a choice to buy, not buy, do nothing, or search for more information. The inclusion of search reflects a view of consumers as proactive. Learning is included by the feedback arrows from choice to internalized stimuli and decision process. This means that the outcomes of a particular choice affect future personality, information interpretation modes, role definitions, and ways of making a decision.

This is not meant to be interpreted as the optimal form of a consumer behavior model. Rather, it is a model which has been derived from existing models. It thus has many of their weaknesses (focus on individual rather than collective decision making, over-simplification, lack of predictive ability, and difficulty of empirical validation). This model, however, is meant to provide a very simplified way of conceptualizing the major categories of variables which affect consumer behavior. Providing a richer description and explanation is the purpose of the entire book. No model can include all of the details which are necessary for understanding such a complex, yet routine, process. For example, entire books and many journal articles have been written on what the decision process alone is like. Thus, this model shows the basic categories of variables which can be used for organizing an explanation of consumer behavior.

SUMMARY   Models serve as an abbreviated framework for representing the properties or activities of consumer behavior. In addition, a model must be able to direct and inspire new research. Ideally, a model should be capable of explanation as well as prediction, general in scope, high in both heuristic and unifying power, internally consistent, original, plausible, simple, supported by facts, testable and verifiable.

The Howard-Sheth model emphasizes the processes and variables which affect a person's behavior prior to and during a purchase. Within this schema, perception, learning, and attitude are the primary variables.

The Sheth model of industrial buyer behavior applies to group decision making within an organization. According to this model, joint decisions are more likely when there is a high perceived risk, when it is a capital expenditure, when time pressure is low, when the organization is large, or when the organization is decentralized.

The Engel, Kollat, and Blackwell model of consumer behavior is based on learning processes, with emphasis upon the information search process. The Kerby model is similar to the previous model, but is set apart by its simplicity. Stimuli produce a recognition of need, which motivates the evaluation of alternatives and purposive action. Nicosia's dyadic model emphasizes not only the behavior of the consumer, but also the behavior of the firm, as well as the interaction of the two.

KEY CONCEPTS   Consumer behavior model

Diagram

Dyadic approach

Empirical test
Explanation
Heuristic power
Internal consistency
Plausibility
Prediction
Unifying power

GLOSSARY

Achievement situation: one in which an individual's actions lead to an outcome which can be perceived as either a success or a failure.

Adoption: the process in which an individual becomes committed to continued use of an innovation.

Affectee: one who experiences the consequences of another person's use of a product but does not participate directly in the consumption of the product.

Affiliative group: reference groups to which a consumer belongs or is a member.

Anima, animus: the archetype of femininity in a male or masculinity in a female, respectively.

Approach-approach conflict: the situation in which individuals are prompted simultaneously and to an equal degree by two desirable, but mutually exclusive, alternatives.

Approach-avoidance conflict: the situation in which individuals are prompted simultaneously to both do and not do something.

Archetypes: in Jungian theory, universal forms of thought contained in the collective unconscious.

Aspirational overbuying: purchasing many material symbols of a role which are not absolutely necessary.

Aspiration group: reference groups to which a consumer would like to belong but does not.

Assertion: striving to gain achievement and success, admiration, and power; the development of one's potential as a means of enhancing self-esteem and admiration from peers.

Attention: the allocation of processing capacity to a stimulus.

Attitude: a learned predisposition to respond in a consistently favorable or unfavorable manner with respect to a given object.

Attitude formation substage: the substage of the initiation stage in which organizational members form attitudes toward an innovation.

Attribution theory: an area of psychology concerned with how people perceive the causes of events in their everyday lives.

Autonomic decision making: decision making in which approximately an equal number of decisions are made by each spouse, but these decisions are made separately.

Autonomy: the characteristic of a person who seeks self-realization through forming an integrated, self-sufficient, independent identity.

Avoidance-avoidance conflict: a situation in which a person is prompted to avoid two goals or courses of action.

Behavioral norms: the behavior one actually practices, or beliefs about what one's peers actually do.

Belief: the cognition relating to expectations about whether something exists or is true.

Boundary-spanning roles: social positions which overlap in two or more social systems.

Brand loyalty: the consistent preference and choice of a particular brand by a consumer.

Buying center: a group of persons within a firm that participates in a particular purchase decision process.

Career mobility: changes in a person's social class due to changes in career or life patterns.

Categorization: simplifying one's experiences and the behavior expected of one by sorting these into a set of categories.

Centralization: a variable which involves the locus of authority and decision making within an organizational structure and the number of organizational members who participate in the decision-making process.

Channel: the path or mode linking sender and receiver through which a communication is sent.

Chunk: an organized and meaningful information structure.

Cognition: a state of knowledge.

Cognitive dissonance: a state of psychological discomfort due to a disequilibrium between cognitive elements.

Cognitive elements: any knowledge, opinion, or belief about the environment, about oneself, or about one's behavior.

Cognitive psychology: a theory concerned with how individuals integrate and think about external stimulation.

Cohesiveness: the degree to which group members are attracted to each other.

Cohort: a group of persons who started a particular process (life, for example) at approximately the same time.

Collective unconscious: in Jungian theory, the inborn memories of human evolution that are shared by everyone on an unconscious level.

Combination innovations: innovations which lead to both incremental and preventive effects.

Commitment actualization: the time elapsed between a positive decision and the consumer's actual adoption.

Communication: the process of establishing a commonality of thought between two or more people.

Communication participation: the extent to which a consumer is active in giving, receiving, or passing on information or advice.

Comparison advertising: an advertising message in which direct statements are made comparing one's own product to one's competitor's (brand names are mentioned).

Competitive interdependence: the situation in which the gains available from some activity to person A result in often equal losses to person B.

Complexity: a variable of organizational structure which involves the number of occupational specialties within an organization and the degree to which the various jobs differ from one another.

Consistency: the motive to organize diverse data into a coherent picture of the world.

Construct: in Kelly's theory, the way in which people describe and organize the similarities and differences that they perceive in the world.

Consumer behavior: the acts, processes, and social relationships exhibited by individuals, groups, and organizations in the obtainment, use of, and consequent experience with products, services, and other resources.

Consumer behavior model: a framework, schema, or representation of what is believed to actually occur when consumers make decisions about products.

Consumerism: a movement intending to insure that market transactions are fair, safe, honest, and economical as regards the consumer.

Consumer socialization: the acquisition of skills applied in the marketplace.

Continued-sustained implementation substage: the substage that occurs when, after a successful trial, the organization decides to formalize the implementation of an innovation into the ongoing process of the organization on a long-term basis.

Cooperative interdependence: a situation in which the major problem confronting interacting people is how to work together effectively.

Correspondence: the degree to which a person perceives the actions of another to accurately reflect (or correspond to) the true feelings of that person.

Cosmopolite: an individual who has many communication contacts with persons outside the immediate environment (i.e., contacts in other organizations, cities, etc.).

Counterargumentation: the mental (not necessarily vocalized) rehearsal of arguments contrary to those presented in a communication message that occurs both during and after the presentation of the message (e.g., saying to oneself "I don't believe it," etc. during or after a television advertisement).

Cross pressure: pressure from conflicting sources to reach different decisions.

Decision maker: person who makes the often permanent commitment to purchase or not purchase a product.

Decision period: the time elapsed between initial awareness and a decision.

Decision substage: the substage of the initiation stage which focuses on the choice of whether to implement a change.

Demography: the study of population structure and processes.

Destination: the point at which a communication is received.

Deviance: the discrepancy between the behavior called for by a norm and the behavior that actually takes place.

Diagram: a useful way of representing all of the components of a model and their relationships.

Differential threshold: the minimum difference that can be perceived between two stimuli.

Diffusion: the process by which adoption spreads through the population.

Disassociation: the lessened participation of the person moving from one status to another in the norms, values, and pressures for conformity of either status level, resulting in insecurity.

Discrimination: the behavior which results from rewarding consumers for responding to one set of stimuli and not rewarding them when they respond to another set of stimuli.

Disparity system: a system characterized by the seller's being strong relative to the buyer(s) regarding resource possession and use.

Dissociative group: the reference group to which a consumer would not like to belong, although the consumer may in fact belong to that group.

Distortion: the altering of a message's meaning during its course from source to receiver.

Drive: the energy that impels an organism to action, as opposed to habits which steer behavior in a particular direction.

Dyadic approach: an analysis which explains not only the behavior of one party, but also the behavior of the other party, as well as the interaction of the two.

Early adopters: after innovators, the next group of persons to adopt innovations includes opinion leaders who tell others about an innovation.

Early adoption propensity: the probability that a prospect will be an early puchaser of a new product upon exposure.

Early majority: those persons who adopt an innovation after the opinion leaders have tried it successfully.

Ego: in Freudian theory, the rational aspect of the personality concerned with appropriately dealing with the world.

Ego-defense: the motivation to maintain one's self-image.

Electra complex: in Freudian theory, the desire of a female child to be with her father and reject her mother.

Emigration: the population movement out of a country. For instance, a person who leaves Norway for the United States is called an emigrant by those living in Norway.

Empirical test: a comparison of predictions with the actual direction of the relationships between variables in a model.

Evaluation: the stage between trial and adoption during which the consumer reviews the pros and cons of continued or increased use of an innovation.

Existentialism: a philosophical school which seeks to understand the human condition as it manifests itself in our concrete, lived situations.

Explanation: an answer to the question "Why P?" where P designates a proposition that is supposedly true and refers to a fact, event, or state of affairs.

Expressive norms: the behavior which reflects particular values or goals.

Family: a small social system that has a structure developed by its members within the prevailing cultural mores specifying the power, decision making, influence, responsibilities, activities, and role expectations of each member.

Feedback: a process whereby a receiver becomes a source who uncodes messages, and displays or dispatches them through a channel to the original source.

Field theory: a cognitive approach to the study of behavior and motivation which focuses more on the actual thoughts of the person, rather than on instincts.

Focus of convenience: in Kelly's theory, those events in which a given construct is considered most useful.

Formalization: a variable of organizational structure referring to the degree of emphasis placed on the conformity to specific rules and procedures.

Functional equivalence: a system in which neither party is so powerful that overt influence through force or manipulative punishments could be employed without the other party retaliating.

Gatekeeper: a person who filters information as it flows from the source to its ultimate destination.

Generalization: the tendency to respond to a stimulus in proportion to its degree of similarity to previous situations in which a response was rewarded or punished.

Group welfare system: a system in which the parties to consumption, because of affectional, organizational, or other bonds, consider themselves a functional unit and place the welfare of the unit above the satisfaction of any one member.

Habit: the virtually automatic connection of a stimulus with a response.

Hard modes: the subcategory of overt influence modes consisting of threats and promises.

Heavy volume propensity: the amount per year a prospect is likely to buy if he or she tries a new product.

Hedonic relevance: an action that has a direct positive or negative effect which results in a correspondent inference.

Heuristic power: a model's capacity to suggest and direct new research.

Id: in Freudian theory, the reservoir of psychic energy containing all the psychological processes present at birth, including instincts.

Idiographic approach: focusing only on those traits which are most appropriate for describing an individual's behavior.

Immigration: the population movement into a country. For instance, a Norwegian moving to the United States would be considered an immigrant by Americans.

Implementation stage: the stage in which an organization carries out its decision to adopt an innovation.

Implementor (buyer): one who carries out a decision and makes the actual purchase.

Incremental innovations: ideas, practices, or products which the consumer believes are new and which increase the amount of a desire event.

Influence propensity: the amount of additional purchasing per year the prospect is likely to stimulate in others through interpersonal influence.

Influencer: one who helps shape another's evaluation of, and ultimate decision about, a purchase or proper use of a product.

Initial implementation substage: when an organization implements a change on a trial basis to determine if a long-term commitment is practical.

Initiation stage: the stage of organizational adoption in which the organization learns about alternatives, evaluates them, and comes to a decision.

Innovation: ideas, practices, products, etc. which people see as new and different.

Innovative communicators: persons who are both opinion leaders and early adopters.

Innovativeness: the readiness to accept new ideas and products.

Innovators: the first persons to adopt an innovation.

Instrumental norms: behaviors which are appropriate as a means of achieving a goal.

Intentions (to behave): plans to act in a particular manner.

Interdependence: a situation in which the satisfactions received from any consumption-related activity are partially dependent upon the choices of others.

Intergenerational mobility: the social mobility which takes a person out of the social class of his or her parents.

Internal consistency: the degree to which there are no logical contradictions within a conceptual system.

Internal migration: when a population moves from place to place within a geographical or national area.

Interrole communication: an interaction between two persons who are not in a direct role relationship.

Knowledge-awareness substage: an organization's becoming aware during the initiation stage of an innovation which may produce change.

Laggards: those who, if they adopt the innovation at all, do so only after it has become a traditional product.

Late majority: that group of consumers who are skeptical about the new product or service, but who adopt it after the early majority.

Learning: the more or less permanent acquisition of tendencies to behave in particular ways in response to particular situations or stimuli.

Legitimation stage: the stage during the adoption process in which persons seek reinforcement for the purchase they are considering.

Liaison: a person who links two group (cliques) but is not a member of either group.

Long-term memory (LTM): that aspect of the memory that is utilized for the purpose of permanent storage.

Manipulative influence: a type of social influence in which the communicator rewards or punishes a person's behavior in order to increase (in the case of rewards) or decrease (in the case of punishment) the probability of that behavior occurring again.

Market segmentation: the process of dividing a market into segments of consumers who are similar, and toward whom an appeal utilizing one set of marketing strategies can be employed.

Media audience profiles: the descriptions of what types of people watch certain television programs or subscribe to particular magazines.

Memory: a component which can process information and store symbols.

Message: the thought symbol which is transmitted from source to receiver.

Mixed interdependency: a situation characterized by elements of both co-operation and competition.

Moral norms: ideal behaviors, or what group members believe should be done.

Motivation: a force which leads a person to act in a particular way in response to a need.

Need: a gap or discrepancy one experiences between an actual and a desired state of being.

Need for achievement: the desire to take responsibility for solving problems.

Need for affiliation: a desire to interact with people on a social basis.

Nomothetic approach: focuses on the same set of traits for everyone regardless of the appropriateness of each trait for describing the behavior of each individual.

Norm of reciprocity: the tacit agreement between two firms to buy each other's products.

Norms: the behaviors prescribed by society.

Objectification: observing the externalities of a situation and inferring one's reason for acting in a particular manner.

Oedipal complex: in Freudian theory, the desire of a male child to be with his mother and to avoid the threat of castration implied by his father.

Omission: leaving out certain aspects of a message as it is passed from source to receiver.

Opinion leader: an individual who informally influences the attitudes and/or behavior of others.

Organizational consumer: a formal organization, such as a business firm or hospital, which engages in consumer behavior.

Organizational strain: the inconsistency existing between or among different parts of the organization.

Organizational stress: the difference between what is demanded of the organization and what it is capable of providing.

Outshopping: the shopping which is done by consumers outside their local trade area.

Overload: a situation in which a person has received more information than he or she can process.

Overt influence: the use of a very explicit message from one person to another which offers or predicts rewards and/or punishments, depending upon how the recipient of the message behaves in the future.

Perception: a complex process by which people select, organize, and interpret sensory stimulation into a meaningful picture of the world.

Performance gap: the discrepancy between what an organization is doing and what its decision makers believe it ought to be doing.

Personality: a way of organizing and categorizing the consistencies of an individual's reactions to situations encountered in the environment.

Plausibility: the characteristic of a model that indicates that it makes sense (has face validity).

Prediction: (1) a deduction from known to unknown events within a conceptually static system; (2) an assertion about future outcomes which is based on the observation of regularities among sequences of events in the past.

Preventive innovations: those innovations which are adopted to avoid unpleasant events.

Primary group: a group in which there is face-to-face interaction (e.g. the family, work groups, etc.).

Process innovation: new ways of performing a function (e.g. a new process of casting steel or administering a chemical treatment to clothing).

Product champion: a highly partisan supporter of an innovation.

Product-dependent organizations: firms that are heavily dependent upon the marketplace for survival.

Product-independent organizations: firms that are dependent upon regulatory agencies or others whom they do not directly service.

Product innovation: new products (rather than processes).

Projective test: a way of measuring a person's personality by asking the person to invent a story about an ambiguous stimulus, such as an ink blot, picture, etc. Such responses are believed to be projections of the individual's personality.

Promises: a type of overt influence in which the source offers to directly and personally reward a person for performing the desired behavior.

Proposition: a statement which contains two related variables.

Prospect communication cost: the cost of delivering an effective message by means of a particular media vehicle to a given prospect.

Purchasing agent: a person in an organization whose major function is to make purchases for the organization.

Range of convenience: in Kelly's theory, those situations in which a given construct is considered useful.

Rationalistic bias: the belief that individuals are guided by reason and are rational according to conventional criteria.

Reactance: the negative responses to group pressure; the demonstration of freedom and individuality by acting contrary to the group.

Receiver: the person or organization to which a message is directed.

Reciprocity: the tacit agreement between two firms to buy each other's products.

Recommendations: a type of overt influence in which the source predicts favorable environmental or social consequences which he or she does not directly control.

Reference group: a group that a consumer considers when forming an attitude or behaving in a particular manner.

Reinforcement: a positive motivational force or secondary reward value resulting from experiences which have been associated with reward in the past.

Reinterpretation: a clinically derived technique in which the influencer attempts to feed back to the target in a slightly different form the same information the target has given the source.

Reinvention: to change an innovation during the implementation process in order to make it fit one's own need.

Relational analysis: an approach to studying consumer behavior in which relationships between two or more people are the main unit of study rather than the individual alone.

Resistance: any conduct that serves to maintain the status quo in the face of pressure to do otherwise.

Resolution: the final stage of the adoption process, including all of the adjustments made as a result of the decision to adopt (or not adopt) an innovation.

Response tendency: the inclination or disposition to respond to a stimulus.

Reversal effects: a situation in which a large amount of a stimulus produces the opposite effect of what was produced by a lesser amount of the same stimulus.

Role: a set of behaviors which are expected of individuals in interaction with other people.

Role accumulation: the process of acquiring additional roles as long as they provide net rewards.

Role acquisition: the process of assuming a new role during which one interacts with the role in a give-and-take manner.

Role salience: a factor affecting how quickly social change can alter various roles.

Role strain: the experience of stress due to the competing demands made by different roles.

Sanction: authoritative approval or endorsement.

Search: attempts to gather or retrieve additional information, either internally through memory, or externally from other outside sources.

Secondary group: a group in which interaction is not face-to-face. There is usually an organization which connects the members of such a group through impersonal channels of communication.

Secondary reinforcer: a stimulus that has become a reinforcing agent through previous association with another reinforcing stimulus.

Selective attention: the perceptual process which causes one to be more likely to listen to or watch some messages rather than others.

Selective retention: the perceptual process whereby persons remember some messages rather than others.

Self-actualization: the fulfillment of self through maximization of one's abilities, skills, and potential.

Self-disclosures: an influencer's statements of a personal and intimate nature, designed to draw reciprocal disclosures from the recipient.

Serial gatekeeping: a structure in which there are several successive gatekeepers, each of whom must pass information on to the next person in order for it to reach the ultimate receiver.

Short-term memory (STM): that aspect of the memory that is utilized for active processing of information.

Social class: a group of people with similar levels of prestige and esteem who also share a set of related beliefs, attitudes, and values which they express in their thinking and behavior.

Social conflict: a situation that arises when (a) two or more persons in a relationship each desire a resource which is in too short a supply to satisfy everyone, or (b) when the accomplishment of the preferences of one party to the interaction would prohibit the accomplishment of the other party's preferences.

Socialization process: the socially mobile consumer's behavioral changes that are viewed as incremental over an extended period of time.

Socially distant reference groups: groups with which the consumer does not regularly interact.

Social mobility: a movement from one level of social status to another.

Soft modes: the subcategory of overt influence consisting of warnings and recommendations.

Social status: a person's position within a social system as determined by variables such as education, occupation, income, family background, area of residence, etc.

Social structure: the patterns which result from differences within a social system which affect social interaction.

Social system: a group of individuals working together in pursuit of common goals.

Source: the person or organization who sends a communication message.

Status inconsistency: a condition in which a person's status on one dimension is not consistent with his or her status on another dimension (e.g., high income is inconsistent with low education).

Status of destination: the status position toward which the upwardly mobile consumer is moving.

Status persistence: a situation in which the characteristics of the class of origin remain with the socially mobile person.

Stimulus: a cue that determines which response will occur, as well as where and when it will occur.

Strategic probes: attempts by the seller to learn more about the buyer's preferences, in order to satisfy them more effectively.

Subjective norm: a person's perception of how others will respond (by rewarding or punishing) to a particular behavior.

Superego: in Freudian theory, the internalized representation of values and morals.

Target beliefs: those beliefs which a change agent attempts to change.

Technocratic bias: the overemphasis on development of a change program, without the accompanying plan for implementation.

Teleological motivation: the motivation of a person who constantly compares an ideal or desired situation with perceptions of the current actual situation.

Threats: a type of overt influence in which the source promises to personally provide the target of the communication with something unpleasant if the target behaves improperly from the communicator's standpoint.

Transaction process: the interactive and social nature of consumer behavior.

Trial stage: the adoption stage during which the consumer puts the innovation to a personal test prior to complete acceptance.

Ultimate consumer: a person or informal group which engages in consumer behavior.

Unifying power: a model's capacity to bring together previously unrelated areas.

User: a person who actually consumes the particular product or service.

Utilitarian Motivation: the motive to seek external opportunities to solve problems in order to gain useful information or new skills to be used in coping with life.

Value: an assessment held by a society about the ''goodness'' or ''badness'' of a particular action or goal.

Warnings: a type of overt influence in which the source of influence threatens the target with something unpleasant; the source predicts negative consequences which he or she does not have under his or her direct control.

Wearout: the decrease in the ability to recall a message as exposure to the message increases.

Word-of-mouth: usually face-to-face discussions devoid of the intent to sell something commercially.

INDEX

NOTE: Page numbers in *italics* indicate charts or tables.